Visual Bas
Programming with
the Windows API

by
Chris H. Pappas and William H. Murray

Prentice Hall PTR
Upper Saddle River, New Jersey 07458
www.phptr.com

ISBN 0-13-095082-3

90000

9 780130 950826

Library of Congress Cataloging-in-Publication Data

Pappas, Chris H.
   Visual Basic programming with the Windows API / by Chris H. Pappas
and William H. Murray.
      p.   cm.
   Includes index.
   ISBN 0-13-095082-3
   1. BASIC (Computer program language)   2. Microsoft Visual Basic
for Windows.   3. Microsoft Windows (Computer file)   I. Murray,
William H.   II.   Title.
QA76.73.B3P253   1998
005.26'8—DC21   98-9336
                                                             CIP

Editorial/Production Supervision: *Eileen Clark*
Compositor/Production Services: *Pine Tree Composition, Inc.*
Acquisitions Editor: *Jeffrey Pepper*
Marketing Manager: *Miles Williams*
Buyer: *Alexis R. Heydt*
Cover Design: *Design Source*
Cover Design Direction: *Jerry Votta*
Editorial Assistant: *Christy Schaack*

© 1998 Prentice Hall PTR
Prentice-Hall, Inc.
A Simon & Schuster Company
Upper Saddle River, NJ 07458

Prentice Hall books are widely used by corporations and government agencies for training, marketing, and resale. The publisher offers discounts on this book when ordered in bulk quantities.

For more information, contact
            Corporate Sales Department,
            Phone: 800-382-3419; FAX: 201-236-7141
            E-mail (Internet): corpsales@prenhall.com
Or write: Prentice Hall PTR
            Corp. Sales Department
            One Lake Street
            Upper Saddle River, NJ 07458

Printed in the United States of America

10   9   8   7   6   5   4   3   2   1

ISBN 0-13-095082-3

Prentice-Hall International (UK) Limited, *London*
Prentice-Hall of Australia Pty. Limited, *Sydney*
Prentice-Hall Canada Inc., *Toronto*
Prentice-Hall Hispanoamericana, S.A., *Mexico*
Prentice-Hall of India Private Limited, *New Delhi*
Prentice-Hall of Japan, Inc., *Tokyo*
Simon & Schuster Asia Pte. Ltd., *Singapore*
Editora Prentice-Hall do Brasil, Ltda., *Rio de Janeiro*

Table of Contents

Chapter 13
GDI Drawing Functions   145

Chapter 14

Chapter 15
Bitmaps, Cursors, and Icon Functions   187

Chapter 21

Printing: Devices, Documents, and Properties   285

Chapter 22

Printing: Forms, Jobs, Ports, and Printers   296

Chapter 23

File: Drive, Directory, and Time   312

Chapter 24

File: Registry Information   327

Chapter 25

File: File Operation Functions   341

Chapter 26

Character and String Functions   358

Chapter 27
Memory Allocation Functions   370

Chapter 28
Rectangle and Point Functions   380

Chapter 29
Cursor and Caret Functions   386

Appendix A
Win32 API Function and Subroutine Prototypes   393

Appendix B
Win32 API Structure Declarations   411

Appendix C
Win32 API Constant Declarations   482

Index   621

Chapter 1

Visual Basic
and Windows

Visual Basic is a language that was created for Windows application development. Think about it; almost all other major programming languages were initially developed for the command-line environment. Assembly Language, BASIC, Pascal, Ada, C, and C++ operated initially in a DOS environment and were eventually brought forth into a Windows environment. Many of us have made the trip with those languages and it has been anything but smooth. Were you there for the first versions of Pascal? Pascal is a wonderful language and is often used for the introduction of structured programming concepts. But something was initially missing from Pascal! The first versions of Pascal for the PC didn't allow a programmer to do any graphics on the screen—not even a dot. Desperate programmers resorted to assembly language patches in order to draw graphics primitives such as lines, boxes, and circles.

But life goes on—and languages mature. Borland fitted Pascal with nifty graphics commands for the DOS environment and all was well with the world. Heck, even with the introduction of Windows we could still run our DOS applications in a DOS compatibility window. Then it happened again! We eagerly awaited the initial release of OS/2 only to find that it was shipped as a command-line version without the Presentation Manager. What—no graphics? Nope, not even a dot.

1

But life goes on—and operating systems mature. Now, we can write fancy C and C++ applications for the Windows 95 and NT environments that would absolutely blow away DOS programmers. Multitasking, OLE (Object Linking and Embedding), Cut-and-Paste, dynamic linking, COM (Common Object Model)—it just goes on and on.

With the success of Windows 95 and Windows NT more and more demand has been placed on the programmer to design applications for these graphics environments. Microsoft designed Visual Basic with a graphical interface to make this type of Windows application development an easier process. Visual Basic now takes full advantage of the 32-bit Windows 95 and Windows NT environments. So, instead of the steep learning curve encountered by C and C++ programmers, Visual Basic offers a toolkit of development tools that allow the quick construction of very advanced applications. And all of this is done in a matter of hours, instead of weeks or months.

A Quick History

The way in which applications are designed has changed quite a bit over the last few years. This has occurred because of user demand for better applications and a result of dramatic hardware improvements.

The first challenge to operating systems developers was to be able to run more than one program at a time. The first solution for running multiple programs was the use of DOS enhancers. Products such as IBM's TopView, Quarterdeck's DESQVIEW, and early versions of Microsoft Windows permitted several applications to be initialized and swapped to and from the hard disk as needed. The problem with these layered environments was that they would lock up and frequently crash the whole system.

DOS enhancers were not the answer. The answer, however, would require both a hardware and software solution. The hardware solution came from Intel when they designed the 80386 chip. This chip was to be the forerunner of a new family of microprocessors designed specifically for multitasking environments. We've now seen several generations that include the faster and faster Pentium and Pentium II processors.

At the same time, Microsoft Windows seemed to be the solution to the software problem. At least that's what many think was the reason Microsoft pulled out of the OS/2 deal with IBM. They wanted a multitasking solution that was their design from the ground up. The advantage of Microsoft Windows over DOS was its common interface between applications. The user got a graphical point-and-click environment that was the same across all applications. Programmers got a predefined set of tools, called the Microsoft Windows Software Development Kit (SDK), that enabled them to create applications for this environment. Programmers were also freed from having to worry about unique hardware configurations. No longer did every application have to include video and printer drivers for hundreds of unique devices—Windows handled it all.

It was then that programmers recognized one tiny problem—the SDK had over 600 new functions to master. This turned out to be a quite a problem for traditional command-line programmers. Programmers were faced with the need to master the philosophy of event-driven programming, hundreds of new functions, and a new programming language! C was the language of choice for Windows program developers, but C was an emerging language at the time. More training.

Microsoft recognized that something had to be done to give the average programmer easy access to Windows. Visual Basic was their solution.

Visual Basic was designed to make developing a graphical Windows application as easy as possible. Visual Basic takes care of the more tedious tasks of creating an application's graphical look. This allows programmers more time to concentrate on an application's features rather than how to style it for Windows. All of this is accomplished by programming in the BASIC language.

Advantages of Visual Basic

As you probably already know, Visual Basic is probably the most addicting Windows application development environment you have ever worked in. Visual Basic's graphical tools and high-level language constructs make it easy and quick to go from a programming concept to a full-fledged running application.

Visual Basic is not only easy to use, but also fun to use. Visual Basic gives you the freedom to invent and experiment with new project designs.

There are three basic design steps to standard Visual Basic application design:

- Place the objects that make up the user interface on a form.
- Provide the methods and properties for each object in order to change their appearance and behavior, as needed.
- Write BASIC program code for each object.

Limitations of Visual Basic

Are there any limitations to what Visual Basic can do? Yes, but we'll get to that in just a paragraph.

A number of years ago, we told students that "if it could be done on a computer it could be done in assembly language." Actually, that statement is still true today. However, we wouldn't want to develop an Active-X control in assembly language! The point we were trying to make, at the time, is that all compilers suffer a common weakness—they are limited to the capabilities provided by the developers. Remember the story of the first Pascal compilers earlier in this chapter and their lack of graphical capabilities? C is the native language of Windows. It is sort of the de facto standard for Windows application development. We guess it can be said that "if it can be done in Windows, it can be written in C."

The same cannot be said for Visual Basic. While Visual Basic has grown and matured over the past few years, a number of programming options are still missing. For example, font and text manipulations are limited. Did you ever want to rotate a font for a vertical axis label? Did you ever try to rotate a rectangle or ellipse on the screen? These capabilities are not part of Visual Basic's innate capabilities. However, there is a solution. Visual Basic allows us to tap into the Win32 API (Application Program Interface) and harness the power of the same functions used by C programmers. And there are over 1,500 of them!

Programmers

This book was written for those programmers who have moved into the Windows 95 and NT environments. It is written exclusively for Win32 so older Win16 functions are not discussed.

This book was also written with three different categories of programmers in mind: Visual Basic programmers, C/C++ programmers, and programmers with experience in both languages.

Visual Basic programmers will need this book when they are ready to venture beyond Visual Basic's internal controls, methods, and properties. You'll want this book when you see something in a C/C++ application that you cannot duplicate with Visual Basic. You'll want this book when you discover that the Win32 API text file, provided with Visual Basic, is complete but without documentation and examples. You'll want this book when you want concise examples of how to use various Win32 API functions.

If you are a Visual C/C++ programmer, with experience in writing Windows applications, you are already familiar with the Windows API. All you need now is the bridge that will connect your C/C++ knowledge to Visual Basic. This book is for you. We have grouped, listed, and discussed the most popular Win32 functions as prototyped in the Win32api.txt file provided with your Visual Basic compiler. You'll learn how to call functions and pass parameters in Visual Basic just as you have done in C or C++. You'll also be amazed at the similarity of how this all takes place.

If you have programming experience in both Visual Basic and C/C++, you already know of the potential strength of combining the Windows API capabilities with Visual Basic. As you work through the book, you'll quickly learn which Windows API functions offer increased programming power and flexibility and which don't. For example, we recommend the traditional Visual Basic approach to designing dialog boxes and menus rather than using the Windows API. However, if your application uses a variety of fonts, you'll surely want to consider the functions provided by the Windows API.

About This Book

The goal of this book is to present as many of the most frequently used Windows API functions as possible while remaining concise and accurate.

Appendix A contains an alphabetical listing of all of the functions and subroutines contained in the Win32api.txt file provided with your Visual Basic compiler. We have covered a large number of these functions but not all of them. Hopefully, the knowledge you gain from studying the various chapters of this book will help you use any functions that were not specifically covered in a book chapter.

Chapter Groupings

Windows API functions are best discussed in groups—not alphabetically or as they appear in the Win32api.txt file. Some groups are natural, for example, functions dealing with fonts. Others functions can span several groups, such as character and string functions. When we divided the Windows API functions, we kept the groups of related functions as small as possible. This results in chapter sizes that are manageable. In some chapters, like those dealing with printer functions, we used two or three chapters rather than pack all of the functions into a single chapter.

Stand-Alone Chapters

In almost all cases, each chapter stands by itself. Many programmers will choose to use this book on a need-to-know basis, rather than studying it from chapter to chapter. If you are interested in printers, there is no need to study the chapter on fonts, too.

We designed a common format for the chapters. In each chapter dealing with Windows API functions there is a brief introduction, a table describing each function in the chapter, a listing of the function prototypes, a table describing function parameters and a listing of any Windows API structures and constants. Every chapter contains at least one sample application.

Concise Programs

We like to teach by example. All chapters end with at least one programming example highlighting several functions from the given chapter. The sample applications were kept as simple as possible to illustrate how to use the function rather than how to build a complicated application.

The programming examples will give you a concise, accurate programming example of the functions being illustrated.

Appendices

The Windows API text file that you will access for functions, structures, and constants is named Win32api.txt. This is an extremely large file. The problem with using this file is that it is not really organized in any particular fashion. Functions are not well grouped and structures and constants are scattered about the file. This makes it difficult for you to reference features as you develop applications. We took the time to fix some of this for you in Appendices A, B, and C.

Appendix A is an alphabetical listing of all of the files described in the Win32api.txt file. There are over 1,500 different functions. It was out of this group that we selected the most popular and frequently used functions discussed in the previous chapters of the book. You can find that group of functions by examining the index of this book.

Appendix B is an alphabetical listing of structures contained in the Win32api.txt file. If you are developing an application, this is where you'll want to look to quickly find a structure's declaration.

Appendix C is an alphabetical listing of constants used by the various functions described in the Win32api.txt file. There are hundreds of constants created specifically for the Windows API.

With Appendices A, B, and C in hand, you'll be able to locate functions, structures, and constants quickly. As you develop applications, you can load the Win32api.txt file into a word processor, such as Microsoft Word, and then cut and paste declarations directly into your Visual Basic projects. You learn how all of this is done in the next few chapters.

Chapter 2

Declaring
the Windows API

The Win32api.txt file, shipped with Visual Basic, is the gateway to interfacing Visual Basic with the Windows API functions. The Win32api.txt file is located off Visual Basic's main directory. For example, our setup uses the following path: C:\Vb\winapi\Win32api.txt. When you get to this location you are in for a big surprise—the Win32api.txt file is enormous. The file size approaches 700,000 bytes or the equivalent of approximately five floppy disks. Even with this enormous size, the Win32api.txt file contains little fluff. There are over 1,500 Windows API function declarations, more than 600 structure definitions, and over 6,000 unique constants. The Win32api.txt file can be viewed by loading it into a viewer named Apiload.exe. The viewer is found in the same subdirectory as the Win32api.txt file. The file can also be viewed in a word processor, such as Microsoft Word. We prefer the latter since Word provides familiar search and replace tools.

The creation of the Win32api.txt file must have been a major undertaking for Microsoft. They have done an excellent job throughout the file. The Win32api.txt file does suffer from some unavoidable shortcomings, the chief of which is organization.

Organization

How do you organize a file of this size? The file could be organized alphabetically or by groups or by popularity or by size, and so on. For example, if the Win32api.txt file were organized alphabetically, a user would have an easier time finding a function, but this organization would destroy groupings of related functions. Groups of related functions are very helpful in Windows programming because certain functions are frequently used together. Another question that arises is what do you do with structures and constants? Do you list them separately or with the functions? And since multiple functions use the same structures and constants, do you repeat the structure and constant for each function?

The Win32api.txt file is divided (sort of) by groups of related functions. Structures and constants are scattered throughout the file. Frequently used structures, such as RECT, are listed at the beginning of the file with others placed near the groups of functions that use them.

A viewer or word processor, such as Word, is an invaluable tool for searching and finding the desired function declaration and any structures and constants required for its use. You'll also want to make full use of Appendices A, B, and C in this book. Appendix A lists all 1,500 function declarations alphabetically. Appendix B lists approximately 400 alphabetized structure definitions used by these functions. Appendix C lists over 6,000 alphabetized constants also required by the Windows API functions. The appendices are as accurate as the Win32api.txt file from which they were derived.

A Quick Glimpse at the API

In this section we'll investigate what you will find as you search through the Win32api.txt file. The examples used will be representative of the functions, structures, and constants used in the remaining chapters of this book. We'll also follow these example functions through the next two chapters as you learn to develop applications with Visual Basic and the Windows API.

API Functions

There are two Windows API font functions that are used very frequently by Visual Basic programmers. The CreateFontIndirect() and CreateFont() functions will be used here to illustrate those features common to all functions contained in the Windows API.

The following listing shows the function declarations as they appear in the Win32api.txt file.

> **NOTE:** Throughout the book long function declarations are broken into several lines. Visual Basic does not allow line breaks in declarations such as these. If you do an actual cut-and-paste of a function declaration from the Win32api.txt file into your Visual Basic project, the function will be copied without line breaks.

```
Declare Function CreateFontIndirect Lib "gdi32" Alias
  "CreateFontIndirectA" (lpLogFont As LOGFONT) As Long


Declare Function CreateFont Lib "gdi32" Alias
  "CreateFontA" (ByVal H As Long, ByVal W As Long,
  ByVal E As Long, ByVal O As Long, ByVal W As Long,
  ByVal I As Long, ByVal u As Long, ByVal S As Long,
  ByVal C As Long, ByVal OP As Long, ByVal CP As Long,
  ByVal Q As Long, ByVal PAF As Long,
  ByVal F As String) As Long
```

All function and subroutine declarations in the Win32api.txt file begin with a **Declare** statement. (Now you know how we sorted the Win32api.txt file when we created Appendix A.) Declare statements are used at the module level of a standard module to declare a reference to an external procedure in a Dynamic Link Library (DLL). Declare statements can also be placed in class modules if the statements are Private.

Declarations will use either the keyword **Function** or **Sub** followed by the name used by the function or subroutine. In the previous listing, this is either **CreateFontIndirect** or **CreateFont**.

The **Lib** keyword followed by a name in quotes (for example, "gdi32") indicates a particular Microsoft Windows Dynamic Link Library or DLL. Table 2–1 describes a few of the most frequently encountered DLLs.

Table 2–1 Frequently Encountered DLL Libraries

DLL	Description
advapi32	Advanced API functions, such as SetServiceBit(), and so on.
comdlg32	Support for common dialog box functions and so on.
gdi32	Drawing, display, bitmaps, and metafiles functions.
kernel32	Low-level operating system functions.
netapi32	Network functions.
user32	Menu, dialog, message, and timer functions plus others.
winmm	Multimedia functions.

The **Alias** keyword, followed by text in quotes, is used in a declaration when a DLL procedure has the same name as a public variable, constant, or any other procedure in the same scope. Alias can also be used in situations where characters in the DLL name aren't permitted by the DLL naming convention.

Names placed between parentheses form the parameter list for the function. In the case of the CreateFontIndirect() function, the parameter list indicates the use of a LOGFONT structure.

```
(lpLogFont As LOGFONT)
```

In the case of the CreateFont() function, the parameter list is an extensive list of individual variables and their type.

```
(ByVal H As Long, ByVal W As Long,
ByVal E As Long, ByVal O As Long, ByVal W As Long,
ByVal I As Long, ByVal u As Long, ByVal S As Long,
ByVal C As Long, ByVal OP As Long, ByVal CP As Long,
ByVal Q As Long, ByVal PAF As Long,
ByVal F As String)
```

All Windows API functions end with the function return type. In our example functions, CreateFontIndirect() and CreateFont() use a **Long** as the return type.

API Structures

The data structures used by various Windows API functions are also located in the Win32api.txt file. The CreateFontIndirect() function uses the LOGFONT structure. Here is the LOGFONT structure found in the Win32api.txt file.

```
Type LOGFONT
  lfHeight As Long
  lfWidth As Long
  lfEscapement As Long
  lfOrientation As Long
  lfWeight As Long
  lfItalic As Byte
  lfUnderline As Byte
  lfStrikeOut As Byte
  lfCharSet As Byte
  lfOutPrecision As Byte
  lfClipPrecision As Byte
  lfQuality As Byte
  lfPitchAndFamily As Byte
  lfFaceName(LF_FACESIZE) As Byte
End Type
```

If you thought the LOGFONT structure would be located relatively close to the CreateFontIndirect() function, you would be wrong. It is, in terms of page count, found 16 pages ahead of the function declaration. Appendix B can help you locate structures quickly since they are listed in alphabetical order. Once you know the name and definition of a data structure you can use cut-and-paste techniques to transfer the information from the Win32api.txt file to your Visual Basic project.

> **NOTE:** There are several cases, in this book, where structure definitions include line breaks. Visual Basic does not allow line breaks in structure definitions. If you do an actual cut-and-paste of a structure from the Win32api.txt file into your Visual Basic project, the structure will be copied correctly without line breaks.

API Constants

If you study the LOGFONT structure discussed in the previous section, you will notice the use of a unique constant, LF_FACESIZE. If you use the Create-FontIndirect() function and LOGFONT structure, you will also have to include the definition of this constant. Constants are also located in the Win32api.txt file. If you know the constant's name, you can do a search for its location. Likewise, you can use Appendix C to quickly locate the value.

Here is the definition for the LF_FACESIZE constant as found in the Win32api.txt file:

```
'Logical Font
Public Const LF_FACESIZE = 32
Public Const LF_FULLFACESIZE = 64
```

> **NOTE:** There are a few cases, in this book, where constant definitions include a line break. Visual Basic does not allow line breaks in constant definitions. If you do an actual cut-and-paste of a constant definition from the Win32api.txt file into your Visual Basic project, the constant definition will be copied correctly without line breaks.

Where Does It Go?

If you are using Windows API functions in your Visual Basic projects, you now know that you are likely to need function declarations, structure definitions, and perhaps constants. Where does this information go in a Visual Basic project?

The answer is that it can go in several places. If the project is really simple, the information can be placed in any class module of the project. The preferred location for function declarations, however, is in a separate module. A separate module can be added to a Visual Basic project by using the Project | Add Module | Module menu selection. The default name for the first module is Module1.bas.

In this book, all Windows API function declarations, structures, and constants are always placed in a separate module file. This makes it especially easy to correctly declare functions, structures, and constants when cutting-and-pasting the information from the Win32api.txt file.

Show Me

You are now ready to see a complete working example of how a Visual Basic project can include Windows API functions. Chapter 3 will take you, step by step, through the actual project creation.

Coding with the Windows API

In the last chapter we discussed the location of the Win32api.txt file and what types of function declarations, structures, and constants could be found in that file. In this chapter we will illustrate programming techniques using the Windows API. Careful attention should be paid to the placement of Windows API function declarations, constants, and data structures.

Creating Simple Applications

In this section we'll examine the steps necessary to build simple Visual Basic applications that make use of the Windows API. The steps and techniques presented here are used throughout the remainder of the book.

Working with Fonts

In the first application, we'll work with the Windows API CreateFontIndirect() function and the associated data structure and constants. Visual Basic often provides internal functions that achieve results similar to the Windows API functions.

In Chapter 4 we will show you how to use both Visual Basic and the Windows API to manipulate fonts within the same application.

The Fancy Font Application

To build the font application, follow the next seven steps:

1. Open a new Visual Basic project and name it Test1.vbp.
2. Add a new module to the project using the Project|Add Module|Module menu option and name it Test1.bas.
3. Open a copy of the Windows API file, Win32api.txt, found in the Visual Basic subdirectory, C:\....Vb\Winapi\Win32api.txt.
4. Type or copy the following constants, structure, and function declarations from the Win32api.txt file into the Test1.bas file.

```
Public Const LF_FACESIZE = 32
Public Const LF_FULLFACESIZE = 64

Type LOGFONT
  lfHeight As Long
  lfWidth As Long
  lfEscapement As Long
  lfOrientation As Long
  lfWeight As Long
  lfItalic As Byte
  lfUnderline As Byte
  lfStrikeOut As Byte
  lfCharSet As Byte
  lfOutPrecision As Byte
  lfClipPrecision As Byte
  lfQuality As Byte
  lfPitchAndFamily As Byte
  lfFaceName(LF_FACESIZE) As Byte
End Type

Declare Function CreateFontIndirect Lib "gdi32" Alias
  "CreateFontIndirectA" (lpLogFont As LOGFONT) As Long

Declare Function SelectObject Lib "gdi32"
  (ByVal hdc As Long, ByVal hObject As Long) As Long

Declare Function TextOut Lib "gdi32" Alias "TextOutA"
  (ByVal hdc As Long, ByVal x As Long, ByVal y As Long,
  ByVal lpString As String, ByVal nCount As Long) As Long
```

5. Now, switch to Form1 and name this form Test1.frm.

6. Add the following code to Test1.frm:

```
Dim hnFont&, hoFont&
Dim lf As LOGFONT
Dim r&

Private Sub Form_Load()
  Form1.Show
End Sub

Private Sub Form_Paint()
  lf.lfHeight = 60
  For I = 20 To 100 Step 20
    lf.lfEscapement = 600
    hnFont = CreateFontIndirect(lf)
    hoFont = SelectObject(hdc, hnFont)
    r& = TextOut(hdc, I * 4, I * 4, "Radical", 7)
 Next I
End Sub
```

7. Use the Visual Basic Run|Run with Full Compile menu selection to test your code.

If your application is successful, you should see a screen similar to Figure 3–1.

As you view the code shown in the Test1.bas file, you'll notice that we selected a small number of functions, structures, and constants from the vast collection provided in the Windows API. How do you know, as a programmer, which functions, structures, and constants are necessary for a successful application? Ah! That is the purpose of the remainder of this book. The remaining chapters divide the most frequently used Windows API functions into groups of related functions, structures, and constants. Hopefully, as you study each chapter you learn how they interrelate. Chapter 17, for example, discusses font functions and describes in detail what is being achieved in this initial example.

Rotating a string of text is only one of many neat tricks you can achieve with the Windows API. If you are a Windows NT programmer, you'll also want to investigate your ability to manipulate the world transform as we do in the next example.

Rotating the Viewport under Windows NT

In this Windows NT application we'll show you how to rotate the viewport by manipulating the world transform. It can be made to appear that the objects are actually being rotated in a window by rotating the window's viewport. This, however, is only possible under Windows NT. Consider, for example, the Windows API Rectangle() function. Normally, under both Windows 95 and Windows NT the function draws rectangles only on the *X-Y* axis. That is why you cannot use the Rectangle() function to draw a rectangle at a 45 degree angle. Under Win-

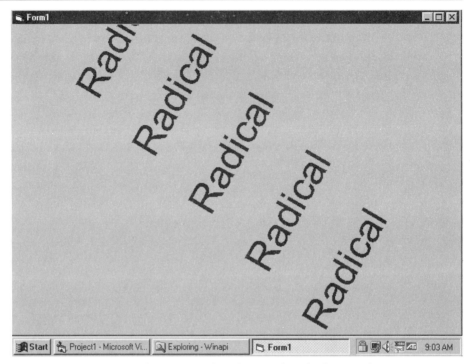

Figure 3–1   A string of text created and rotated with the Windows API Create-
FontIndirect() function.

dows NT, however, it is possible to draw the rectangle in the normal fashion and
then rotate the viewport. The overall effect is that it will appear as if the rectangle
were drawn at that angle! Now this is a feat that regular Visual Basic programmers
would find hard to duplicate.

The Viewport Rotate Application

Let's follow the same steps we used in the previous application to create the Windows NT viewport application. To build the viewport application, follow the next
seven steps:

1. Open a new Visual Basic project and name it Test2.vbp.
2. Add a new module to the project using the Project|Add Module|Module
   menu option and name it Test2.bas.
3. Open a copy of the Windows API file, Win32api.txt, found in the Visual
   Basic subdirectory, C:\....Vb\Winapi\Win32api.txt.

4. Type or copy the following constants, structure, and function declarations from the Win32api.txt file into the Test2.bas file.

```
'Graphics Modes
Public Const GM_COMPATIBLE = 1
Public Const GM_ADVANCED = 2
Public Const GM_LAST = 2

'Change all data declarations in XFORM structure
'from Double to Single for Win32.
Type XFORM
  eM11 As Single
  eM12 As Single
  eM21 As Single
  eM22 As Single
  eDx As Single
  eDy As Single
End Type

Declare Function SetGraphicsMode Lib "gdi32"
  (ByVal hdc As Long, ByVal iMode As Long) As Long
Declare Function SetWorldTransform Lib "gdi32"
  (ByVal hdc As Long, lpXform As XFORM) As Long
Declare Function Rectangle Lib "gdi32"
  (ByVal hdc As Long, ByVal X1 As Long,
  ByVal Y1 As Long, ByVal X2 As Long,
  ByVal Y2 As Long) As Long
Declare Function SetMapMode Lib "gdi32"
  (ByVal hdc As Long, ByVal nMapMode As Long) As Long
Declare Function SaveDC Lib "gdi32"
  (ByVal hdc As Long) As Long
Declare Function RestoreDC Lib "gdi32"
  (ByVal hdc As Long, ByVal nSavedDC As Long) As Long
```

5. Now, switch to Form1 and name this form Test2.frm.
6. Add the following code to Test2.frm:

```
Private Sub Form_Paint()
  Dim r&
  Dim newXForm As XFORM
  Dim orgDC&

  'Save original DC and set advanced graphics mode
  orgDC& = SaveDC(Me.hdc)
  r& = SetGraphicsMode(Me.hdc, GM_ADVANCED)

  'Draw a Rectangle at a 30 degree angle
  'Displace origin by x = 20 and y = 50
  newXForm.eM11 = Cos(30 * 3.14159 / 180)
```

```
newXForm.eM22 = Cos(30 * 3.14159 / 180)
newXForm.eM21 = Sin(30 * 3.14159 / 180)
newXForm.eM12 = -Sin(30 * 3.14159 / 180)
newXForm.eDx = 20
newXForm.eDy = 50

r& = SetWorldTransform(Me.hdc, newXForm)
r& = Rectangle(Me.hdc, 0, 0, 100, 50)

'Draw a Rectangle at a 45 degree angle
'Displace origin by x = 100 and y = 100
newXForm.eM11 = Cos(45 * 3.14159 / 180)
newXForm.eM22 = Cos(45 * 3.14159 / 180)
newXForm.eM21 = Sin(45 * 3.14159 / 180)
newXForm.eM12 = -Sin(45 * 3.14159 / 180)
newXForm.eDx = 100
newXForm.eDy = 100

r& = SetWorldTransform(Me.hdc, newXForm)
r& = Rectangle(Me.hdc, 0, 0, 120, 60)

'Draw a Rectangle at a 60 degree angle
'Displace origin by x = 180 and y = 150
newXForm.eM11 = Cos(60 * 3.14159 / 180)
newXForm.eM22 = Cos(60 * 3.14159 / 180)
newXForm.eM21 = Sin(60 * 3.14159 / 180)
newXForm.eM12 = -Sin(60 * 3.14159 / 180)
newXForm.eDx = 180
newXForm.eDy = 150

r& = SetWorldTransform(Me.hdc, newXForm)
r& = Rectangle(Me.hdc, 0, 0, 140, 70)

'Restore original DC and graphics mode
r& = RestoreDC(Me.hdc, orgDC&)
r& = SetGraphicsMode(Me.hdc, GM_COMPATIBLE)
End Sub
```

7. Use the Visual Basic Run|Run with the Full Compile menu selection to test
   your code.

If your application is successful, you should see a screen similar to Figure 3–2
when the application is executed under Windows NT.

Of course, we know you are just going to have to try running this application
under Windows 95 to see what happens! Well, the rectangles will be drawn, but
they will not be rotated or displaced from the origin. Figure 3–3 proves this result.

We know you'll want to study Chapter 11 where a complete discussion of the
use of the world transform exists.

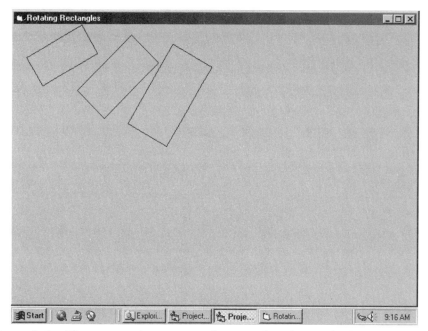

Figure 3–2 Three rectangles appear to be rotated as the window's viewport is rotated with the world transform under Windows NT.

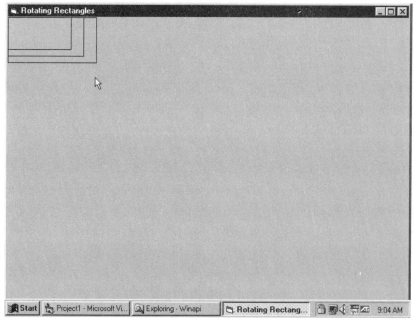

Figure 3–3 The rectangles are not rotated or displaced if the application is run under Windows 95 (or a later version).

19

Useful Techniques

The techniques for developing applications using the Windows API presented in this chapter will not change throughout the book. Every application will use a module file for the function, structure, and constant declarations copied from the Windows API file (Win32api.txt). Supporting code is then implemented on one or two Visual Basic forms. By using a consistent approach, you should find that experimenting with various Windows API functions becomes easier.

Once you learn how to incorporate Windows API functions, structures, and constants into a Visual Basic application, your job is reduced to learning how to use those functions correctly.

In the next chapter, we'll investigate how to achieve similar screen results directly from Visual Basic or with the use of the Windows API. The Windows API should never be viewed as a replacement for what Visual Basic can already do with built-in functions. Rather, it should be viewed as an extension to Visual Basic's powers that can be used when the need arises.

Chapter 4

Having It Both Ways

Many applications that you'll want to create under Visual Basic can be built with Visual Basic functions or Win32 API functions. We have a tendency to think that if you entered Windows programming using Visual Basic, you will shy away from the Win32 API. On the other hand, if you were a Pascal or C/C++ programmer you know the Win32 API fairly well and will probably shy away from standard Visual Basic functions.

In this chapter we'll take a look at two applications. The first project, Bar1.vbp, is designed to produce a simplified bar chart on the screen. It is written exclusively using Visual Basic functions. The second project, Bar2.vbp, is also designed to produce a bar chart on the screen. It is a modified version of the first project with portions of the original code replaced with Windows API function calls. The purpose of this little exercise is to show you that you can often have it both ways!

One note before continuing: No attempt was made to make both programs identical in terms of output. Also, there was no attempt to replace all of the Visual Basic function calls with Win32 API function calls in Bar2.vbp.

Bar1: Using Visual Basic Functions

This is a simple Visual Basic application that allows the user to enter the values for four bars in the range 0 to 250 and plots them on a bar chart. A title and vertical and horizontal axis labels are optional. The project uses two forms: one as a data entry form and the other for drawing the bar chart.

The first file, used by the Bar1.vbp, is a module file named Bar1.bas. Here is the code contained in this module:

```
DefInt A-Z
Global HBar1, HBar2, HBar3, HBar4, Temp
Global LabelWidth, LabelHeight, I, Length
Global Title$, XLabel$, YLabel$, Digit$
```

The second file is named Bar1A.frm. This is the data entry form for the project. Figure 4–1 shows the layout of this form.

The following code is used by Bar1A.frm for collecting data when either command button is pushed:

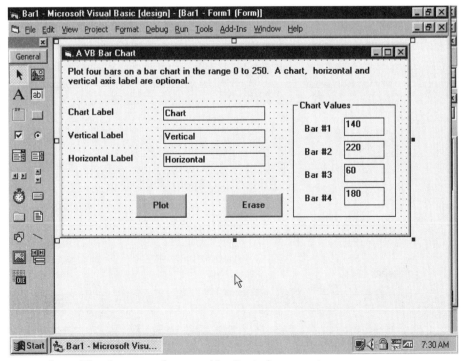

Figure 4–1   The data entry form used by Bar1.vbp.

```
Private Sub Command1_Click()
  Title$ = Text1.Text
  YLabel$ = Text2.Text
  XLabel$ = Text3.Text
  HBar1 = Val(Text4.Text)
  HBar2 = Val(Text5.Text)
  HBar3 = Val(Text6.Text)
  HBar4 = Val(Text7.Text)
  Form2.Show
  Call Form2.MyPlot
End Sub

Private Sub Command2_Click()
  Text1.Text = ""
  Text2.Text = ""
  Text3.Text = ""
  Text4.Text = ""
  Text5.Text = ""
  Text6.Text = ""
  Text7.Text = ""
End Sub
```

Notice that when the first command button is pushed, current data are returned to the application. If the second command button is pushed, the data are cleared on the entry form.

The third file used by the application is named Bar1B.frm. The form itself is initially blank. The following code listing is the code used by Bar1B.frm to support the drawing of the bar chart:

```
Private Sub Form_Load()
  Title$ = Form1.Text1.Text
  YLabel$ = Form1.Text2.Text
  XLabel$ = Form1.Text3.Text
  Call MyPlot
End Sub

Sub MyPlot()

  'set scale and clear form
  Cls
  ScaleWidth = 450
  ScaleHeight = 365

  'draw axis
  DrawWidth = 2
  Line (80, 330)-(400, 330)
  Line (80, 80)-(80, 330)

  'draw four bars in color
  DrawWidth = 1
  Line (81, 330 - HBar1)-(149, 328), QBColor(12), BF
  Line (151, 330 - HBar2)-(219, 328), QBColor(9), BF
```

```
Line (221, 330 - HBar3)-(289, 328), QBColor(14), BF
Line (291, 330 - HBar4)-(359, 328), QBColor(10), BF

'print horizontal axis label
FontSize = Height / 600
LabelWidth = TextWidth(XLabel$) / 2
LabelHeight = TextHeight(XLabel$) / 2
CurrentX = ScaleWidth / 2 - LabelWidth
CurrentY = (ScaleHeight * (61 / 64)) - LabelHeight
Print XLabel$

'string characters for vertical axis label
FontSize = Height / 600
LabelWidth = TextWidth(YLabel$) * 3 / 2
LabelHeight = TextHeight(YLabel$) / 2
CurrentX = ScaleWidth / 7 - LabelHeight
Temp = CurrentX
CurrentY = (ScaleHeight * (32 / 64)) - LabelWidth
Length = Len(YLabel$)
For I = 1 To Length
  Digit$ = Mid$(YLabel$, I, 1)
  Print Digit$
  CurrentX = Temp
Next I

'print title in color
ForeColor = QBColor(13)
FontSize = Height / 200
LabelWidth = TextWidth(Title$) / 2
LabelHeight = TextHeight(Title$) / 2
CurrentX = ScaleWidth / 2 - LabelWidth
CurrentY = (ScaleHeight * (5 / 64)) - LabelHeight
Print Title$
ForeColor = QBColor(0)
End Sub
```

If you enter and execute this project you'll see an initial bar chart similar to the bar chart shown in Figure 4–2.

In the next section, you'll see a similar bar chart application. However in this application key portions of the bar chart code have been implemented with the use of Win32 API functions.

Bar2: Using Win32 API Functions

This application also allows the user to enter the values for four bars, in the range 0 to 250, and plots them on a bar chart. A title and vertical and horizontal axis labels are optional. The project uses two forms, one as a data entry form and the other for drawing the bar chart.

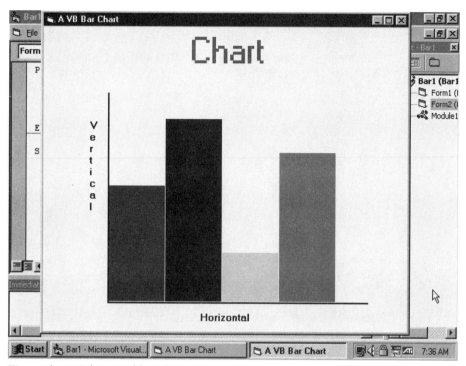

Figure 4–2   The initial bar chart produced by the Bar1.vbp project.

The first file, used by the Bar2.vbp, is a module file named Bar2.bas. This file, in addition to the global declarations used in the previous example, holds the constant, structure, and functions declarations used by the Win32 API functions. Here is the code contained in this module.

```
DefInt A-Z
Global HBar1, HBar2, HBar3, HBar4, Temp
Global LabelWidth, LabelHeight, I, Length
Global Title$, XLabel$, YLabel$, Digit$

Public hBrush

Type POINTAPI
  x As Long
  y As Long
End Type

Public Const LF_FACESIZE = 32
Public Const LF_FULLFACESIZE = 64

Type LOGFONT
  lfHeight As Long
  lfWidth As Long
  lfEscapement As Long
```

```
        lfOrientation As Long
        lfWeight As Long
        lfItalic As Byte
        lfUnderline As Byte
        lfStrikeOut As Byte
        lfCharSet As Byte
        lfOutPrecision As Byte
        lfClipPrecision As Byte
        lfQuality As Byte
        lfPitchAndFamily As Byte
        lfFaceName(LF_FACESIZE) As Byte
    End Type

    Declare Function CreateFontIndirect Lib "gdi32" Alias
        "CreateFontIndirectA" (lpLogFont As LOGFONT) As Long
    Declare Function CreateSolidBrush Lib "gdi32"
        (ByVal crColor As Long) As Long
    Declare Function LineTo Lib "gdi32"
        (ByVal hdc As Long, ByVal x As Long,
        ByVal y As Long) As Long
    Declare Function MoveToEx Lib "gdi32"
        (ByVal hdc As Long, ByVal x As Long,
        ByVal y As Long, lpPoint As POINTAPI) As Long
    Declare Function Rectangle Lib "gdi32"
        (ByVal hdc As Long, ByVal X1 As Long,
        ByVal Y1 As Long, ByVal X2 As Long,
        ByVal Y2 As Long) As Long
    Declare Function SelectObject Lib "gdi32"
        (ByVal hdc As Long, ByVal hObject As Long) As Long
    Declare Function TextOut Lib "gdi32" Alias "TextOutA"
        (ByVal hdc As Long, ByVal x As Long, ByVal y As Long,
        ByVal lpString As String, ByVal nCount As Long) As Long
```

> **NOTE:** Visual Basic requires all function declarations to be on a single line. Function declarations are broken, throughout the book, due to line length limitations.

Recall from the previous chapter that all constants, structures, and functions used by the Win32 API are found in the Win32api.txt file provided with your Visual Basic compiler. You can also find these various components listed alphabetically in Appendices A, B, and C of this book.

The second file is named Bar2A.frm. This is the data entry form for the project. Figure 4–3 shows the layout of this form. Notice that it is identical to the data entry form used by the Bar1.vbp.

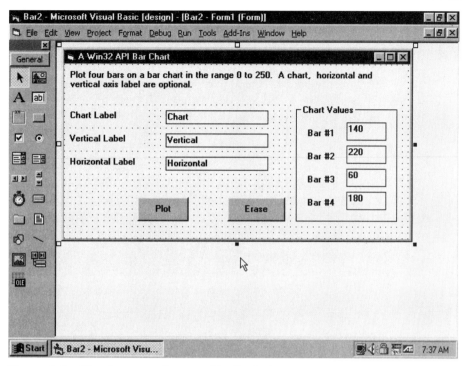

Figure 4–3   The data entry form used by Bar2.vbp.

The following code is used by Bar2A.frm for collecting data when either command button is pushed. This code is also identical to that used in the Bar1A.frm.

```
Private Sub Command1_Click()
  Title$ = Text1.Text
  YLabel$ = Text2.Text
  XLabel$ = Text3.Text
  HBar1 = Val(Text4.Text)
  HBar2 = Val(Text5.Text)
  HBar3 = Val(Text6.Text)
  HBar4 = Val(Text7.Text)
  Form2.Show
  Call Form2.MyPlot
End Sub

Private Sub Command2_Click()
  Text1.Text = ""
  Text2.Text = ""
  Text3.Text = ""
  Text4.Text = ""
```

```
    Text5.Text = ""
    Text6.Text = ""
    Text7.Text = ""
End Sub
```

The third file used by the application is named Bar2B.frm. The form itself is initially blank. The following code listing is the code used by Bar2B.frm to support the drawing of the bar chart:

```
Private Sub Form_Load()
  Title$ = Form1.Text1.Text
  YLabel$ = Form1.Text2.Text
  XLabel$ = Form1.Text3.Text
  Call MyPlot
End Sub

Sub MyPlot()
  Dim tempPoint As POINTAPI
  Dim r&
  Dim newbrush&
  Dim hnFont&, hoFont&
  Dim lf As LOGFONT

  'dummy values
  tempPoint.x = 0
  tempPoint.y = 0

  'clear form
  Cls

  'set line drawing width
  DrawWidth = 2
  'draw x axis
  r& = MoveToEx(hdc, 80, 330, tempPoint)
  r& = LineTo(hdc, 400, 330)
  'draw y axis
  r& = MoveToEx(hdc, 80, 80, tempPoint)
  r& = LineTo(hdc, 80, 330)

  'set line drawing width
  DrawWidth = 1
  'create a solid red brush
  hBrush = CreateSolidBrush(QBColor(12))
  newbrush = SelectObject(hdc, hBrush)
  r& = Rectangle(hdc, 81, 330 - HBar1, 150, 330)
  'create a solid blue brush
  hBrush = CreateSolidBrush(QBColor(9))
  newbrush = SelectObject(hdc, hBrush)
  r& = Rectangle(hdc, 151, 330 - HBar2, 220, 330)
  'create a solid yellow brush
```

```
hBrush = CreateSolidBrush(QBColor(14))
newbrush = SelectObject(hdc, hBrush)
r& = Rectangle(hdc, 221, 330 - HBar3, 290, 330)
'create a solid green brush
hBrush = CreateSolidBrush(QBColor(10))
newbrush = SelectObject(hdc, hBrush)
r& = Rectangle(hdc, 291, 330 - HBar4, 360, 330)

'print horizontal axis label
FontSize = 18
lf.lfHeight = FontSize
hnFont = CreateFontIndirect(lf)
hoFont = SelectObject(hdc, hnFont)
Length = Len(XLabel$)
r& = TextOut(hdc, 280 - (FontSize * Length * 3 / 8),
            340, XLabel$, Length)

'print vertical axis label
lf.lfHeight = FontSize
lf.lfEscapement = 900
hnFont = CreateFontIndirect(lf)
hoFont = SelectObject(hdc, hnFont)
Length = Len(YLabel$)
r& = TextOut(hdc, 60, 170 + (FontSize * Length * 3 / 8),
            YLabel$, Length)

'print title in color
ForeColor = QBColor(13)
FontSize = 80
lf.lfHeight = FontSize
lf.lfEscapement = 0
hnFont = CreateFontIndirect(lf)
hoFont = SelectObject(hdc, hnFont)
Length = Len(Title$)
r& = TextOut(hdc, 290 - (FontSize * Length * 3 / 8),
            0, Title$, Length)
ForeColor = QBColor(0)
End Sub
```

Examine this listing and compare it with the code in Bar1B.frm. Can you tell which parts of the first project have been replaced with Win32 API function calls?

If you enter and execute this project you'll see an initial bar chart similar to the bar chart shown in Figure 4–4.

In the next section, we'll compare portions of both projects and attempt to draw some simple conclusions concerning the use of the Win32 API in Visual Basic projects.

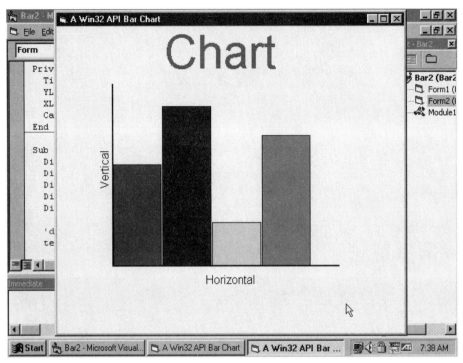

Figure 4–4   The initial bar chart produced by the Bar2.vbp project.

Comparing Code

In this section we'll examine portions of code in both the Bar1.vbp and Bar2.vbp projects. You'll see firsthand what must be done in order to produce similar results when replacing Visual Basic functions with Win32 API function calls.

Drawing Axes

The *X* and *Y* axes for the bar charts are drawn with simple line segments. The pen width is set to 2. The Visual Basic Line() function is used for this purpose.

```
'draw axis
DrawWidth = 2
Line (80, 330)-(400, 330)
Line (80, 80)-(80, 330)
```

To produce similar results with Win32 API function calls, two functions are required. The MoveToEx() and LineTo() functions are Win32 API functions used for drawing line segments. The pen width is 2.

```
'set line drawing width
DrawWidth = 2
'draw x axis
r& = MoveToEx(hdc, 80, 330, tempPoint)
r& = LineTo(hdc, 400, 330)
'draw y axis
r& = MoveToEx(hdc, 80, 80, tempPoint)
r& = LineTo(hdc, 80, 330)
```

As you can see, there is probably no real reason for using the Win32 API for drawing line segments. The functions add nothing to the application that cannot be achieved with the Visual Basic Line() function, except a couple of extra lines of code.

There is one subtle but interesting thing going on in the previous portion of code, however. Did you notice that the line drawing width for both portions of code was set with the Visual Basic DrawWidth() function? The drawing width can also be set with a call to the Win32 API CreatePen() function followed by a call to the SelectObject() function.

The point is simply this—you can intermix Visual Basic and Win32API functions in many situations, taking advantage of their unique abilities.

Drawing Bars

Under Visual Basic, the Line() function is versatile, allowing the programmer to create squares, rectangles, and so on. Thus, the Line() function is called four times to create each of the four bars used in the application.

```
'draw four bars in color
DrawWidth = 1
Line (81, 330 - HBar1)-(149, 328), QBColor(12), BF
Line (151, 330 - HBar2)-(219, 328), QBColor(9), BF
Line (221, 330 - HBar3)-(289, 328), QBColor(14), BF
Line (291, 330 - HBar4)-(359, 328), QBColor(10), BF
```

The Line() function is compact, allowing the drawing color and fill to be specified as the second and third parameters.

The Win32 API equivalent to the Visual Basic Line() function is not as compact. Examine this portion of code from the second project.

```
'set line drawing width
DrawWidth = 1
'create a solid red brush
hBrush = CreateSolidBrush(QBColor(12))
newbrush = SelectObject(hdc, hBrush)
r& = Rectangle(hdc, 81, 330 - HBar1, 150, 330)
'create a solid blue brush
hBrush = CreateSolidBrush(QBColor(9))
```

```
newbrush = SelectObject(hdc, hBrush)
r& = Rectangle(hdc, 151, 330 - HBar2, 220, 330)
'create a solid yellow brush
hBrush = CreateSolidBrush(QBColor(14))
newbrush = SelectObject(hdc, hBrush)
r& = Rectangle(hdc, 221, 330 - HBar3, 290, 330)
'create a solid green brush
hBrush = CreateSolidBrush(QBColor(10))
newbrush = SelectObject(hdc, hBrush)
r& = Rectangle(hdc, 291, 330 - HBar4, 360, 330)
```

The drawback here is that the fill brush for each bar requires a call to the CreateSolidBrush() and SelectObject() Win32 API functions. This is then followed by a call to the Rectangle() function. Ah, three functions calls must be used to replace the single call to the Visual Basic Line() function. Not a good trade!

Now it is true that Win32 API brushes can be much more involved than just a solid brush. For example, a variety of hatched, patterned, and indexed brushes are possible.

Drawing Text

There are three portions of code, in each application, used for drawing text to the screen. We'll look at just one to discover a real advantage of using Win32 API function calls.

Here is the portion of code used to draw the vertical axis label using Visual Basic functions. Since the string used for the label cannot be rotated, the string is parsed character by character and then printed in a vertical column. While the approach is not elegant, it is sufficient for a simple project.

```
'string characters for vertical axis label
FontSize = Height / 600
LabelWidth = TextWidth(YLabel$) * 3 / 2
LabelHeight = TextHeight(YLabel$) / 2
CurrentX = ScaleWidth / 7 - LabelHeight
Temp = CurrentX
CurrentY = (ScaleHeight * (32 / 64)) - LabelWidth
Length = Len(YLabel$)
For I = 1 To Length
  Digit$ = Mid$(YLabel$, I, 1)
  Print Digit$
  CurrentX = Temp
Next I
```

With the Win32 API it is possible to create and rotate the whole axis label. You saw similar code in the previous chapter. Now it is used to draw a vertical axis label on the bar chart—the way a vertical axis should be drawn!

```
'print vertical axis label
lf.lfHeight = FontSize
lf.lfEscapement = 900
hnFont = CreateFontIndirect(lf)
hoFont = SelectObject(hdc, hnFont)
Length = Len(YLabel$)
r& = TextOut(hdc, 60, 170 + (FontSize * Length * 3 / 8),
             YLabel$, Length)
```

Using the CreateFontIndirect() function and modifying the escapement parameter is a quick and easy way to draw text at any angle you desire.

The key to effectively using the Win32 API is not to replace every Visual Basic function with an equivalent Win32 API function, but to carefully select functions based on their strength, abilities, and ease of use.

Executable Program Size

If you are like us, we're sure the thought crossed your mind: "Well, how about the size of the executable file?" Well, we have a surprise for you!

When the Bar1.vbp project is compiled to executable format, the file size is 14,336 bytes. When the Bar2.vbp project is compiled to executable format the file size is 14,848 bytes. You'll have to admit that 512 bytes is a small price to pay for a good looking vertical axis label!

We, of course, concede that this is not a project requiring thousands of lines of code. However, isn't it interesting that the two executables are so close in size? In terms of file size, there is only a small penalty for using the Win32 API.

Let's Get Started

In the remaining chapters of this book we'll examine groups of related Win32 API functions that are frequently used by Windows programmers. In most cases, except for menus and dialog boxes, we'll let you reach your own conclusions as to whether to use Win32 API functions in a Visual Basic application.

Chapter 5

Keyboard Functions

The Windows API allows access to a number of functions related to using and controlling the system keyboard. With the Windows API keyboard functions you can query the keyboard for virtual key information, determine the layout and type, and even load and unload the layout. If you are developing applications that need to read or write to the keyboard, these functions are for you.

Character information is sent from the keyboard as a scan code. The scan code information is converted, once it arrives at the computer, into an ASCII value. For example, when the letter "D" is pushed, a virtual key code of VK_D is sent to the computer where it is converted to the ASCII value of 44h or 68d. A lowercase letter is simply the ASCII value of the uppercase letter with a 20h or 32d added to its value. The virtual key codes for other keys are shown in the listing of constants later in this chapter.

There are also a number of functions that are closely associated with keyboard functions, including OEM to ANSI conversion functions and code page functions. You'll want to study these functions along with the functions in this chapter for a complete understanding of how the keyboard interprets and processes character information.

API Keyboard Function Names and Descriptions

Table 5–1 shows 25 functions or subroutines and provides a brief description of their use.

One of the most interesting functions to work with in this group is the GetKeyState() function. With this function, your Visual Basic application can poll the keyboard and, for example, return the status of the NumLock, CapsLock, and ScrollLock keys.

In a similar manner, the SetKeyboardState() function can be used to set the state of the same virtual keys.

The example application provided in this chapter will illustrate the use of the GetKeyState() function.

Table 5–1   Keyboard Functions and Descriptions

Function	Description
ActivateKeyboardLayout	Activates a system keyboard layout.
GetACP	Gets the current code page.
GetAsyncKeyState	Gets virtual key information when the function is called.
GetCPInfo	Gets a valid code page.
GetKeyboardLayout	Gets the current keyboard layout.
GetKeyboardLayoutList	Gets a list of available keyboard layouts.
GetKeyboardLayoutName	Gets the name of a keyboard layout.
GetKeyboardState	Gets the state of all virtual keys.
GetKeyboardType	Gets the current keyboard type.
GetKeyNameText	Gets the name of a virtual key.
GetKeyState	Gets the state of a virtual key.
GetOEMCP	Gets code page for conversion.
IsValidCodePage	Finds if the code page is valid.
keybd_event	Produces a simulated key-press.
LoadKeyboardLayout	Loads a keyboard layout.
MapVirtualKey	Dies scan and character code conversions.
MapVirtualKeyEx	Same as MapVirtualKey() with extended capabilities.
OemKeyScan	Converts ASCII codes to OEM scan codes.
SetKeyboardState	Sets the state of all virtual keys.
ToAscii	Converts scan codes to an ASCII character.
ToAsciiEx	Same as ToAscii() with extended capabilities.
ToUnicode	Converts scan codes to a unicode character.
UnloadKeyboardLayout	Unloads a keyboard layout.
VkKeyScan	Converts ASCII codes to virtual key codes.
VkKeyScanEx	Same as VkKeyScan() with extended capabilities.

API Keyboard Function Declarations

The following listing contains the Windows API keyboard functions and subroutine declarations found in the Win32api.txt provided with Visual Basic.

```
Declare Function ActivateKeyboardLayout Lib "user32" Alias
  "ActivateKeyboardLayout" (ByVal HKL As Long,
  ByVal flags As Long) As Long

Declare Function GetACP Lib "kernel32" Alias
  "GetACP" () As Long

Declare Function GetAsyncKeyState Lib "user32" Alias
  "GetAsyncKeyState" (ByVal vKey As Long) As Integer

Declare Function GetCPInfo Lib "kernel32" Alias
  "GetCPInfo" (ByVal CodePage As Long,
  lpCPInfo As CPINFO) As Long

Declare Function GetKBCodePage Lib "user32" Alias
  "GetKBCodePage" () As Long

Declare Function GetKeyboardLayout Lib "user32" Alias
  "GetKeyboardLayout" (ByVal dwLayout As Long) As Long

Declare Function GetKeyboardLayoutList Lib "user32" Alias
  GetKeyboardLayoutList" (ByVal nBuff As Long,
  lpList As Long) As Long

Declare Function GetKeyboardLayoutName Lib "user32" Alias
  "GetKeyboardLayoutNameA" (ByVal pwszKLID As String) As Long

Declare Function GetKeyboardState Lib "user32" Alias
  "GetKeyboardState" (pbKeyState As Byte) As Long

Declare Function GetKeyboardType Lib "user32" Alias
  "GetKeyboardType" (ByVal nTypeFlag As Long) As Long

Declare Function GetKeyNameText Lib "user32" Alias
  "GetKeyNameTextA" (ByVal lParam As Long,
  ByVal lpBuffer As String, ByVal nSize As Long) As Long

Declare Function GetKeyState Lib "user32" Alias
  "GetKeyState" (ByVal nVirtKey As Long) As Integer

Declare Function GetOEMCP Lib "kernel32" Alias
  "GetOEMCP" () As Long

Declare Function IsValidCodePage Lib "kernel32" Alias
  "IsValidCodePage" (ByVal CodePage As Long) As Long
```

```
Declare Function LoadKeyboardLayout Lib "user32" Alias
  "LoadKeyboardLayoutA" (ByVal pwszKLID As String,
  ByVal flags As Long) As Long

Declare Function MapVirtualKey Lib "user32" Alias
  "MapVirtualKeyA" (ByVal wCode As Long,
  ByVal wMapType As Long) As Long

Declare Function MapVirtualKeyEx Lib "user32" Alias
  "MapVirtualKeyExA" (ByVal uCode As Long,
  ByVal uMapType As Long,
  ByVal dwhkl As Long) As Long

Declare Function OemKeyScan Lib "user32" Alias
  "OemKeyScan" (ByVal wOemChar As Long) As Long

Declare Function SetKeyboardState Lib "user32" Alias
  "SetKeyboardState" (lppbKeyState As Byte) As Long

Declare Function ToAscii Lib "user32" Alias
  "ToAscii" (ByVal uVirtKey As Long,
  ByVal uScanCode As Long, lpbKeyState As Byte,
  lpwTransKey As Long, ByVal fuState As Long) As Long

Declare Function ToAsciiEx Lib "user32" Alias
  "ToAsciiEx" (ByVal uVirtKey As Long,
  ByVal uScanCode As Long, lpKeyState As Byte,
  lpChar As Integer, ByVal uFlags As Long,
  ByVal dwhkl As Long) As Long

Declare Function ToUnicode Lib "user32" Alias
  "ToUnicode" (ByVal wVirtKey As Long,
  ByVal wScanCode As Long, lpKeyState As Byte,
  ByVal pwszBuff As String, ByVal cchBuff As Long,
  ByVal wFlags As Long) As Long

Declare Function UnloadKeyboardLayout Lib "user32" Alias
  "UnloadKeyboardLayout" (ByVal HKL As Long) As Long

Declare Function VkKeyScan Lib "user32" Alias
  "VkKeyScanA" (ByVal cChar As Byte) As Integer

Declare Function VkKeyScanEx Lib "user32" Alias
  "VkKeyScanExA" (ByVal ch As Byte,
  ByVal dwhkl As Long) As Integer

Declare Sub keybd_event Lib "user32" Alias
  "keybd_event" (ByVal bVk As Byte,
  ByVal bScan As Byte, ByVal dwFlags As Long,
  ByVal dwExtraInfo As Long)
```

Table 5–2 contains a brief description of the parameters used in the various keyboard functions and subroutine.

Table 5–2   Keyboard Function Parameters and Descriptions

Parameter	Description
bScan As Byte	Scan code for key.
bVk As Byte	Virtual key code.
bChar As Byte	Character's ASCII value.
bchBuff As Long	pwszBuff string buffer length.
bodePage As Long	Code page ID.
dwExtraInfo As Long	Not used.
dwFlags As Long	Zero or KEYEVENTF_ constant.
dwhkl As Long	Keyboard layout.
dwLayout As Long	Use zero for current keyboard; otherwise value is ID of thread.
flags As Long	Determines how the keyboard layout is activated. Uses KLF_ constant.
fuState As Long	0—menu inactive; 1—active.
HKL As Long	Handle for a keyboard layout or HKL_ constant.
lParam As Long	Bits 16 to 23 = scan code.
	Bit 24 = extended keyboard bit.
	Bit 25 = 0 to recognize difference between left and right shift keys.
lpCPInfo As CPINFO	Structure holds code page information.
lpbKeyState As Byte	Points to first value in an array holding keyboard states.
lpBuffer As String	String sized to hold key name.
lpKeyState As Byte	Points to first value in an array holding keyboard states.
lpList As Long	Points to location of first handle in a list of available keyboard layouts.
lppbKeyState As Byte	String contains state of each of 256 virtual keys.
lpwTransKey As Long	Holds translated character information.
nBuff As Long	Number of entries in the lpList array.
nSize As Long	Maximum length of lpBuffer string.
nTypeFlag As Long	0—keyboard type; 1—keyboard subtype; or 2—number of function keys.
nVirtKey As Long	Virtual key code.
pbKeyState As Byte	Points to the first element in an array holding 256 virtual key states.
pwszBuff As String	Buffer holds a string with unicode characters.
pwszKLID As String	A string KL_NAMELENGTH characters long.
ucode As Long	Scan code or character to convert.

Table 5–2 Keyboard Function Parameters and Descriptions *(Continued)*

Parameter	Description
umapType As Long	0—virtual key code; 1—scan code; 2—virtual key code (returns unshifted ASCII); 3—key code (with left and right shift info).
uScanCode As Long	Key's scan code.
uVirtKey As Long	Virtual key code using VK_ constants.
vKey As Long	Holds key code of the virtual key.
wCode As Long	Scan code or character to convert.
wFlags As Long	0—menu inactive; 1—active.
wmapType As Long	0—virtual key code; 1—scan code; 2—virtual key code (returns unshifted ASCII).
wOemChar As Long	Character's ASCII value.
wScanCode As Long	Key's scan code.
wVirtKey As Long	Key's virtual key code.

Many of the parameters described in Table 5–2 use constant values. The Win32api.txt file lists the following constants for keyboard functions:

```
'Keyboard Layout API
Public Const HKL_PREV = 0
Public Const HKL_NEXT = 1

Public Const KEYEVENTF_EXTENDEDKEY = &H1
Public Const KEYEVENTF_KEYUP = &H2

'Size of KeyboardLayoutName (number of characters),
'including nul terminator
Public Const KL_NAMELENGTH = 9

Public Const KLF_ACTIVATE = &H1
Public Const KLF_SUBSTITUTE_OK = &H2
Public Const KLF_UNLOADPREVIOUS = &H4
Public Const KLF_REORDER = &H8

'Virtual Keys, Standard Set
Public Const VK_LBUTTON = &H1
Public Const VK_RBUTTON = &H2
Public Const VK_CANCEL = &H3
Public Const VK_MBUTTON = &H4 'NOT contiguous with L RBUTTON
Public Const VK_BACK = &H8
Public Const VK_TAB = &H9
Public Const VK_CLEAR = &HC
Public Const VK_RETURN = &HD
Public Const VK_SHIFT = &H10
```

```
Public Const VK_CONTROL = &H11
Public Const VK_MENU = &H12
Public Const VK_PAUSE = &H13
Public Const VK_CAPITAL = &H14
Public Const VK_ESCAPE = &H1B
Public Const VK_SPACE = &H20
Public Const VK_PRIOR = &H21
Public Const VK_NEXT = &H22
Public Const VK_END = &H23
Public Const VK_HOME = &H24
Public Const VK_LEFT = &H25
Public Const VK_UP = &H26
Public Const VK_RIGHT = &H27
Public Const VK_DOWN = &H28
Public Const VK_SELECT = &H29
Public Const VK_PRINT = &H2A
Public Const VK_EXECUTE = &H2B
Public Const VK_SNAPSHOT = &H2C
Public Const VK_INSERT = &H2D
Public Const VK_DELETE = &H2E
Public Const VK_HELP = &H2F

'VK_A thru VK_Z are same as ASCII equivalents: 'A' thru 'Z'
'VK_0 thru VK_9 are same as ASCII equivalents: '0' thru '9'

Public Const VK_NUMPAD0 = &H60
Public Const VK_NUMPAD1 = &H61
Public Const VK_NUMPAD2 = &H62
Public Const VK_NUMPAD3 = &H63
Public Const VK_NUMPAD4 = &H64
Public Const VK_NUMPAD5 = &H65
Public Const VK_NUMPAD6 = &H66
Public Const VK_NUMPAD7 = &H67
Public Const VK_NUMPAD8 = &H68
Public Const VK_NUMPAD9 = &H69
Public Const VK_MULTIPLY = &H6A
Public Const VK_ADD = &H6B
Public Const VK_SEPARATOR = &H6C
Public Const VK_SUBTRACT = &H6D
Public Const VK_DECIMAL = &H6E
Public Const VK_DIVIDE = &H6F
Public Const VK_F1 = &H70
Public Const VK_F2 = &H71
Public Const VK_F3 = &H72
Public Const VK_F4 = &H73
Public Const VK_F5 = &H74
Public Const VK_F6 = &H75
Public Const VK_F7 = &H76
Public Const VK_F8 = &H77
```

```
Public Const VK_F9 = &H78
Public Const VK_F10 = &H79
Public Const VK_F11 = &H7A
Public Const VK_F12 = &H7B
Public Const VK_F13 = &H7C
Public Const VK_F14 = &H7D
Public Const VK_F15 = &H7E
Public Const VK_F16 = &H7F
Public Const VK_F17 = &H80
Public Const VK_F18 = &H81
Public Const VK_F19 = &H82
Public Const VK_F20 = &H83
Public Const VK_F21 = &H84
Public Const VK_F22 = &H85
Public Const VK_F23 = &H86
Public Const VK_F24 = &H87
Public Const VK_NUMLOCK = &H90
Public Const VK_SCROLL = &H91

'VK_L VK_R - left and right Alt, Ctrl and Shift
'virtual keys. Used only as parameters to
'GetAsyncKeyState() and GetKeyState(). No other
'API or message will distinguish left and right
'keys in this way.

Public Const VK_LSHIFT = &HA0
Public Const VK_RSHIFT = &HA1
Public Const VK_LCONTROL = &HA2
Public Const VK_RCONTROL = &HA3
Public Const VK_LMENU = &HA4
Public Const VK_RMENU = &HA5
Public Const VK_ATTN = &HF6
Public Const VK_CRSEL = &HF7
Public Const VK_EXSEL = &HF8
Public Const VK_EREOF = &HF9
Public Const VK_PLAY = &HFA
Public Const VK_ZOOM = &HFB
Public Const VK_NONAME = &HFC
Public Const VK_PA1 = &HFD
Public Const VK_OEM_CLEAR = &HFE
```

The GetCPInfo() function also makes use of the CPINFO structure which is also defined in the Win32api.txt file and is listed below.

```
Type CPINFO
  MaxCharSize As Long              'max length (Byte) of a char
  DefaultChar(MAX_DEFAULTCHAR) As Byte    'default character
  LeadByte(MAX_LEADBYTES) As Byte         'lead byte ranges
End Type
```

In the next section, we'll examine an application that makes use of the GeyKeyState() function.

Example Application

In this section we'll examine a very straightforward application named Key1.vbp. This project will read and report the status of the CapLock, NumLock, and ScrollLock keys using the GetKeyState() function.

The project contains a module file named Key1.bas that contains the constant and function declarations shown in the following listing:

```
Public Const VK_CAPITAL = &H14 '(CapLock)
Public Const VK_NUMLOCK = &H90 '(NumLock)
Public Const VK_SCROLL = &H91  '(ScrollLock)

Declare Function GetKeyState Lib "user32"
   (ByVal nVirtKey As Long) As Integer
```

The project's form contains six label controls. Three of the label controls serve as simple labels and the remaining three will have data on these keys returned as their label captions.

```
Private Sub Form_Load()
  Dim keylock As Long

  .'Report Caps Lock State
  keylock = GetKeyState(VK_CAPITAL)
  If keylock Then
    Label4.Caption = "On"
    Else
    Label4.Caption = "Off"
  End If

  'Report Num Lock State
  keylock = GetKeyState(VK_NUMLOCK)
  If keylock Then
    Label5.Caption = "On"
    Else
    Label5.Caption = "Off"
  End If

  'Report Scroll Lock State
  keylock = GetKeyState(VK_SCROLL)
  If keylock Then
    Label6.Caption = "On"
    Else
    Label6.Caption = "Off"
  End If
End Sub
```

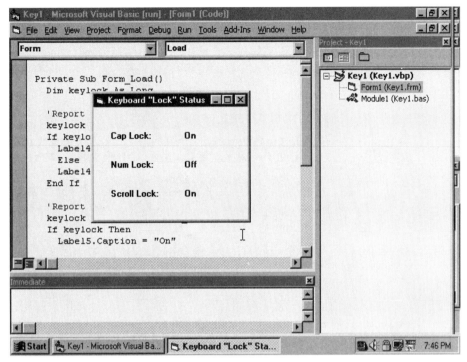

Figure 5–1   The key lock report for a sample test of the Key1.vbp application.

In this application a simple test is made to check the status of each virtual key used. If True is returned, then the lock is on. If False is returned, the lock is off. Figure 5–1 shows a screen output for an example run.

Chapter 6

Time and Timer Functions

The Windows API allows access to a large number of time and timer functions. In this chapter we'll examine functions that are not directly related to file functions. Time functions related to file I/O are discussed in Chapter 24.

The time and timer functions discussed in this chapter cover a wide range of system abilities. The get and set functions, for example, allow applications to access local, message, and system. Additionally, they include access to date/time format capabilities.

While Visual Basic includes its own set of powerful time and timer functions, look to the Windows API for complete control over this area.

API Time and Timer Function Names and Descriptions

Table 6–1 shows 27 popular Windows API time and timer functions and includes a brief description for their use.

Two simple applications at the end of this chapter will teach you how to build a simple timer and also how to read the computer's local date and time information.

Table 6–1   Time and Timer Functions and Descriptions

Function	Description
EnumCalendarInfo	Enumerates system's calendar information.
EnumDateFormats	Enumerates date formats.
EnumTimeFormats	Enumerates time formats
GetDateFormat	Gets date format.
GetDoubleClickTime	Gets double-click time for mouse.
GetLocalTime	Gets the local time.
GetMessageTime	Gets the time of the most recent message in milliseconds.
GetSystemTime	Gets the system's time.
GetSystemTimeAdjustment	Gets any time adjustment being applied by the system.
GetTickCount	Gets Window session time in milliseconds.
GetTimeFormat	Gets local's time format.
GetTimeZoneInformation	Gets time zone information.
KillTimer	Destroys the specified timer.
SetDoubleClickTime	Sets double-click time for mouse.
SetLocalTime	Sets the local time.
SetSystemTime	Sets the system's time.
SetSystemTimeAdjustment	Sets the time adjustment to be applied to the system.
SetTimer	Creates a timer with the given time-out value.
SetTimeZoneInformation	Sets time zone information.
SystemTimeToTzSpecificLocalTime	Converts system time to local time.
TimeBeginPeriod	Sets the minimum timer resolution for application or device driver.
TimeEndPeriod	Clears a previously set minimum timer resolution.
TimeGetDevCaps	Queries the timer device to find its resolution.
TimeGetSystemTime	Gets the system time in milliseconds. Data to MMTIME structure.
TimeGetTime	Gets the system time in milliseconds.
TimeKillEvent	Cancels a given timer event.
TimeSetEvent	Starts a given timer event.

API Time and Timer Function Declarations

The following listing contains the Windows API time and timer function declarations found in the Win32api.txt file provided with Visual Basic. As we mentioned earlier, there are additional time functions relating to file operations that are described in Chapter 24.

```
Declare Function EnumCalendarInfo Lib "kernel32" Alias
    "EnumCalendarInfoA" (ByVal lpCalInfoEnumProc As Long,
    ByVal Locale As Long, ByVal Calendar As Long,
    ByVal CalType As Long) As Long
```

```
Declare Function EnumDateFormats Lib "KERNEL32" Alias
   "EnumDateFormats" (ByVal lpDateFmtEnumProc As Long,
   ByVal Locale As Long, ByVal dwFlags As Long) As Long

Declare Function EnumTimeFormats Lib "KERNEL32" Alias
   "EnumTimeFormats" (ByVal lpTimeFmtEnumProc As Long,
   ByVal Locale As Long, ByVal dwFlags As Long) As Long

Declare Function GetDateFormat Lib "kernel32" Alias
   "GetDateFormatA" (ByVal Locale As Long,
   ByVal dwFlags As Long, lpDate As SYSTEMTIME,
   ByVal lpFormat As String,
   ByVal lpDateStr As String,
   ByVal cchDate As Long) As Long

Declare Function GetDoubleClickTime Lib "user32" Alias
   GetDoubleClickTime" () As Long

Declare Function GetMessageTime Lib "user32" Alias
   "GetMessageTime" () As Long

Declare Function GetSystemTimeAdjustment Lib "kernel32" Alias
   "GetSystemTimeAdjustment" (lpTimeAdjustment As Long,
   lpTimeIncrement As Long,
   lpTimeAdjustmentDisabled As Boolean) As Long

Declare Function GetTickCount Lib "kernel32" Alias
   "GetTickCount" () As Long

Declare Function GetTimeFormat Lib "kernel32" Alias
   "GetTimeFormatA" (ByVal Locale As Long,
   ByVal dwFlags As Long, lpTime As SYSTEMTIME,
   ByVal lpFormat As String,
   ByVal lpTimeStr As String,
   ByVal cchTime As Long) As Long

Declare Function GetTimeZoneInformation Lib "kernel32" Alias
   "GetTimeZoneInformation" (lpTimeZoneInformation As
   TIME_ZONE_INFORMATION) As Long

Declare Function KillTimer Lib "user32" Alias
   "KillTimer" (ByVal hwnd As Long,
   ByVal nIDEvent As Long) As Long

Declare Function SetDoubleClickTime Lib "user32" Alias
   "SetDoubleClickTime" (ByVal wCount As Long) As Long

Declare Function SetLocalTime Lib "kernel32" Alias
   "SetLocalTime" (lpSystemTime As SYSTEMTIME) As Long

Declare Function SetSystemTime Lib "kernel32" Alias
   "SetSystemTime" (lpSystemTime As SYSTEMTIME) As Long
```

```
Declare Function SetSystemTimeAdjustment Lib "kernel32" Alias
  "SetSystemTimeAdjustment" (ByVal dwTimeAdjustment As Long,
  ByVal bTimeAdjustmentDisabled As Boolean) As Long

Declare Function SetTimer Lib "user32" Alias
  "SetTimer" (ByVal hWnd As Long,
  ByVal nIDEvent As Long, ByVal uElapse As Long,
  ByVal lpTimerFunc As Long) As Long

Declare Function SetTimeZoneInformation Lib "kernel32" Alias
  "SetTimeZoneInformation" (lpTimeZoneInformation As
  TIME_ZONE_INFORMATION) As Long

Declare Function SystemTimeToTzSpecificLocalTime Lib
  "kernel32" Alias "SystemTimeToTzSpecificLocalTime"
  (lpTimeZoneInformation As TIME_ZONE_INFORMATION,
  lpUniversalTime As SYSTEMTIME,
  lpLocalTime As SYSTEMTIME) As Long

Declare Function timeBeginPeriod Lib "winmm.dll" Alias
  "timeBeginPeriod" (ByVal uPeriod As Long) As Long

Declare Function timeEndPeriod Lib "winmm.dll" Alias
  "timeEndPeriod" (ByVal uPeriod As Long) As Long

Declare Function timeGetDevCaps Lib "winmm.dll" Alias
  "timeGetDevCaps" (lpTimeCaps As TIMECAPS,
  ByVal uSize As Long) As Long

Declare Function timeGetSystemTime Lib "winmm.dll" Alias
  "timeGetSystemTime" (lpTime As MMTIME,
  ByVal uSize As Long) As Long

Declare Function timeGetTime Lib "winmm.dll" Alias
  "timeGetTime" () As Long

Declare Function timeKillEvent Lib "winmm.dll" Alias
  "timeKillEvent" (ByVal uID As Long) As Long

Declare Function timeSetEvent Lib "winmm.dll" Alias
  "timeSetEvent" (ByVal uDelay As Long,
  ByVal uResolution As Long, ByVal lpFunction As Long,
  ByVal dwUser As Long,
  ByVal uFlags As Long) As Long

Declare Sub GetLocalTime Lib "kernel32" Alias
  "GetLocalTime" (lpSystemTime As SYSTEMTIME)

Declare Sub GetSystemTime Lib "kernel32" Alias
  "GetSystemTime" (lpSystemTime As SYSTEMTIME)
```

Table 6–2 contains a brief description of the parameters used in the various time and timer functions.

Table 6–2   Time and Timer Parameters and Descriptions

Parameter	Description
btimeAdjustmentDisabled As Boolean	False—enable time adjustments; True—disable.
Calendar As Long	Used ENUM_ALL_CALENDARS. 1—Gregorian (localized); 2—Gregorian (English strings always); 3—Japanese era; 4—Year of the Republic of China; and 5—Tangun Era (Korea).
CalType As Long	Type of calendar information to obtain.
cchDate As Long	Gets the size, in bytes (ANSI version) or characters (Unicode version) of the lpDateStr buffer. If cchDate is zero, the function returns the number of bytes or characters required to hold the formatted date string, and the buffer pointed to by lpDateStr is not used.
cchTime As Long	Gets the size, in bytes (ANSI version) or characters (Unicode version) of the lpTimeStr buffer. If cchTime is zero, the function returns the number of bytes or characters required to hold the formatted time string, and the buffer pointed to by lpTimeStr is not used.
dwFlags As Long	Uses DATE_, LOCALE_ or TIME_ constants.
dwTimeAdjustment As Long	Incremental time added to system clock.
dwUser As Long	User-supplied callback data.
hwnd As Long	Handle to a window.
Locale As Long	Locale or ID used in finding calendars or formats to enumerate.
lpCalInfoEnumProc As Long	Points to function that is to be called for a given calendar.
lpDate As SYSTEMTIME	Structure holds system time.
lpDateFmtEnumProc As Long	Points to function that is to be called for each date format.
lpDateStr As String	Buffer holds formatted string with date information.
lpFormat As String	String holds time or date format. Can be a combination of h, hh, m, mm, s, ss format, for example. Use 0 for locale values.
	h—Hours with no leading zero for single-digit hours; 12-hour clock.
	hh—Hours with leading zero for single-digit hours; 12-hour clock.
	H—Hours with no leading zero for single-digit hours; 24-hour clock.
	HH—Hours with leading zero for single-digit hours; 24-hour clock.
	m—Minutes with no leading zero for single-digit minutes.
	mm—Minutes with leading zero for single-digit minutes.
	s—Seconds with no leading zero for single-digit seconds.
	ss—Seconds with leading zero for single-digit seconds.
	t—One character time marker string, such as A or P.
	tt—Multicharacter time marker string, such as AM or PM.
	d—Day of month as digits with no leading zero for single-digit days.
	dd—Day of month as digits with leading zero for single-digit days.
	ddd—Day of week as a three-letter abbreviation. The function uses the LOCALE_SABBREVDAYNAME value associated with the specified locale.

Table 6–2 Time and Timer Parameters and Descriptions *(Continued)*

Parameter	Description
	dddd—Day of week as its full name. The function uses the LOCALE_SDAYNAME value associated with the specified locale.
	M—Month as digits with no leading zero for single-digit months.
	MM—Month as digits with leading zero for single-digit months.
	MMM—Month as a three-letter abbreviation. The function uses the LOCALE_SABBREVMONTHNAME value associated with the specified locale.
	MMMM—Month as its full name. The function uses the LOCALE_SMONTHNAME value associated with the specified locale.
	y—Year as last two digits, but with no leading zero for years less than 10.
	yy—Year as last two digits, but with leading zero for years less than 10.
	yyyy—Year represented by full four digits.
	gg—Period/era string. The function uses the CAL_SERASTRING value associated with the specified locale. This element is ignored if the date to be formatted does not have an associated era or period string.
lpFunction As Long	Address of a callback function that is called upon expiration of an event.
lpLocalTime As SYSTEMTIME	Structure holds local time information.
lpSystemTime As SYSTEMTIME	Structure holds system time information.
lpTime As MMTIME	Address of an MMTIME structure.
lpTime As SYSTEMTIME	Structure holds system time information.
lpTimeAdjustment As Long	Time added to system clock.
lpTimeAdjustmentDisabled As Boolean	False—not disabled; True—disabled.
lpTimeCaps As TIMECAPS	Address of a TIMECAPS structure. This structure is filled with information about the resolution of the timer device.
lpTimeFmtEnumProc As Long	Points to function called for each time format.
lpTimeIncrement As Long	Clock's interrupt time.
lpTimerFunc As Long	Points to the function to be notified when the time-out value elapses.
lpTimeStr As String	String to hold time format information.
lpTimeZoneInformation As TIME_ZONE_INFORMATION	Structure holds time zone information.
lpUniversalTime As SYSTEMTIME	Structure holds system time.
nIDEvent As Long	Gives a nonzero timer identifier. If the hWnd parameter is NULL, this parameter is ignored.
uDelay As Long	Event delay (milliseconds). Function returns error if value is out of range (minimum and maximum event delays).
uElapse As Long	Gives the time-out value, in milliseconds.

(Continued)

Table 6–2   Time and Timer Parameters and Descriptions *(Continued)*

Parameter	Description
uFlags As Long	Timer event type. Uses TIME_ constant.
uID As Long	Identifier of the timer event to cancel.
uPeriod As Long	Timer period in milliseconds.
uResolution As Long	Resolution of the timer event (milliseconds).
uSize As Long	Size, in bytes, of an MMTIME or TIMECAPS structure.
wCount As Long	Mouse double-click time in milliseconds.

Many of the parameters described in Table 6–2 use constant values. The Win32api.txt file lists the following constants for time and timer parameters:

```
'Calendar Enumeration Value.
Public Const ENUM_ALL_CALENDARS = &HFFFF 'enumerate all

'Calendar ID Values.
Public Const CAL_GREGORIAN = 1 'Gregorian (localized)
Public Const CAL_GREGORIAN_US = 2 'Gregorian (U.S.)
Public Const CAL_JAPAN = 3    'Japanese Emperor Era
Public Const CAL_TAIWAN = 4   'Republic of China Era
Public Const CAL_KOREA = 5    'Korean Tangun Era

'Locale constants
Public Const LOCALE_SDATE = &H1D 'date separator
Public Const LOCALE_STIME = &H1E 'time separator
Public Const LOCALE_SSHORTDATE = &H1F 'short date format
Public Const LOCALE_SLONGDATE = &H20 'long date format
Public Const LOCALE_STIMEFORMAT = &H1003 'time format
Public Const LOCALE_IDATE = &H21 'short date format
Public Const LOCALE_ILDATE = &H22 'long date format
Public Const LOCALE_ITIME = &H23 'time format specifier
Public Const LOCALE_ICENTURY = &H24 'century format specifier
Public Const LOCALE_ITLZERO = &H25 'leading time field zeros
Public Const LOCALE_IDAYLZERO = &H26 'leading zeros in day
Public Const LOCALE_IMONLZERO = &H27 'leading zeros in month
Public Const LOCALE_S1159 = &H28   'AM designator
Public Const LOCALE_S2359 = &H29   'PM designator

Public Const LOCALE_SDAYNAME1 = &H2A 'long name for Monday
Public Const LOCALE_SDAYNAME2 = &H2B 'long name for Tuesday
Public Const LOCALE_SDAYNAME3 = &H2C 'long name for Wednesday
Public Const LOCALE_SDAYNAME4 = &II2D 'long name for Thursday
Public Const LOCALE_SDAYNAME5 = &H2E 'long name for Friday
Public Const LOCALE_SDAYNAME6 = &H2F 'long name for Saturday
Public Const LOCALE_SDAYNAME7 = &H30 'long name for Sunday
Public Const LOCALE_SABBREVDAYNAME1 = &H31 'abbr. Monday
```

```
Public Const LOCALE_SABBREVDAYNAME2 = &H32 'abbr. Tuesday
Public Const LOCALE_SABBREVDAYNAME3 = &H33 'abbr. Wednesday
Public Const LOCALE_SABBREVDAYNAME4 = &H34 'abbr. Thursday
Public Const LOCALE_SABBREVDAYNAME5 = &H35 'abbr. Friday
Public Const LOCALE_SABBREVDAYNAME6 = &H36 'abbr. Saturday
Public Const LOCALE_SABBREVDAYNAME7 = &H37 'abbr. Sunday
Public Const LOCALE_SMONTHNAME1 = &H38 'long name for Jan
Public Const LOCALE_SMONTHNAME2 = &H39 'long name for Feb
Public Const LOCALE_SMONTHNAME3 = &H3A 'long name for Mar
Public Const LOCALE_SMONTHNAME4 = &H3B 'long name for Apr
Public Const LOCALE_SMONTHNAME5 = &H3C 'long name for May
Public Const LOCALE_SMONTHNAME6 = &H3D 'long name for June
Public Const LOCALE_SMONTHNAME7 = &H3E 'long name for July
Public Const LOCALE_SMONTHNAME8 = &H3F 'long name for Aug
Public Const LOCALE_SMONTHNAME9 = &H40 'long name for Sep
Public Const LOCALE_SMONTHNAME10 = &H41 'long name for Oct
Public Const LOCALE_SMONTHNAME11 = &H42 'long name for Nov
Public Const LOCALE_SMONTHNAME12 = &H43 'long name for Dec
Public Const LOCALE_SABBREVMONTHNAME1 = &H44 'abbr. January
Public Const LOCALE_SABBREVMONTHNAME2 = &H45 'abbr. February
Public Const LOCALE_SABBREVMONTHNAME3 = &H46 'abbr. March
Public Const LOCALE_SABBREVMONTHNAME4 = &H47 'abbr. April
Public Const LOCALE_SABBREVMONTHNAME5 = &H48 'abbr. May
Public Const LOCALE_SABBREVMONTHNAME6 = &H49 'abbr. June
Public Const LOCALE_SABBREVMONTHNAME7 = &H4A 'abbr. July
Public Const LOCALE_SABBREVMONTHNAME8 = &H4B 'abbr. August
Public Const LOCALE_SABBREVMONTHNAME9 = &H4C 'abbr. September
Public Const LOCALE_SABBREVMONTHNAME10 = &H4D 'abbr. October
Public Const LOCALE_SABBREVMONTHNAME11 = &H4E 'abbr. November
Public Const LOCALE_SABBREVMONTHNAME12 = &H4F 'abbr. December

'Time Flags for GetTimeFormatW.
'do not use minutes or seconds:
Public Const TIME_NOMINUTESORSECONDS = &H1
Public Const TIME_NOSECONDS = &H2        'do not use seconds
'do not use time marker:
Public Const TIME_NOTIMEMARKER = &H4
'always use 24 hour format:
Public Const TIME_FORCE24HOURFORMAT = &H8

'Date Flags for GetDateFormatW.
Public Const DATE_SHORTDATE = &H1 'use short date picture
Public Const DATE_LONGDATE = &H2  'use long date picture

'timer error return values
Public Const TIMERR_NOERROR = (0) 'no error
'request not completed:
Public Const TIMERR_NOCANDO = (TIMERR_BASE + 1)
'time struct size:
Public Const TIMERR_STRUCT = (TIMERR_BASE + 33)
```

```
'flags for wFlags parameter of timeSetEvent() function
'program timer for single event:
Public Const TIME_ONESHOT = 0
'program for continuous periodic event:
Public Const TIME_PERIODIC = 1
```

There are several structures also used by these functions. The following listing contains those structures listed in the Win32api.txt file for the time and timer functions:

```
Type FILETIME
  dwLowDateTime As Long
  dwHighDateTime As Long
End Type

Type MMTIME
  wType As Long
  u As Long
End Type

Type SYSTEMTIME
  wYear As Integer
  wMonth As Integer
  wDayOfWeek As Integer
  wDay As Integer
  wHour As Integer
  wMinute As Integer
  wSecond As Integer
  wMilliseconds As Integer
End Type

Type TIMECAPS
  wPeriodMin As Long
  wPeriodMax As Long
End Type

Type TIME_ZONE_INFORMATION
  Bias As Long
  StandardName(32) As Integer
  StandardDate As SYSTEMTIME
  StandardBias As Long
  DaylightName(32) As Integer
  DaylightDate As SYSTEMTIME
  DaylightBias As Long
End Type
```

In the next section we'll examine two applications that illustrate the use of a simple timer and read date and time information from the system.

Example Applications

This section contains two programming examples that will serve to illustrate the use of time and timer functions. The first application uses the GetTickCount() function to pace the movement of an icon on the screen. The second application uses the GetLocalTime() subroutine to obtain local date and time information and return it to the user.

The Timer1 Project

In this application the GetTickCount() function will be used to count out a 100-millisecond (1/10 of a second) delay. With each cycle, a screen icon will be moved on the screen. The project is named Timer1.vbp and contains a module file and a form. The module file is named Timer1.bas and is listed next.

```
Global deltax1 As Integer

Declare Function GetTickCount Lib "kernel32" () As Long
```

The form file holds a picture box control. An icon from the Visual Basic graphics subdirectory is placed in the C directory for use by the application. The code actually responsible for the accurate time interval is shown in a bold font in the following listing.

```
Private Sub Form_Load()
  'Obtain icon from proper VB subdirectory
  Picture1.Picture = LoadPicture("c:\face05.ico")
  deltax1 = 110
End Sub

Private Sub Form_Paint()
  Dim timefirst&, timesecond&
  Cls

  'Implement a 1/10 second timer delay
  timefirst& = GetTickCount()
  While timefirst& + 100 > GetTickCount()
  Wend

  If Picture1.Left < ScaleLeft Then deltax1 = 110
  If Picture1.Left + Picture1.Width > ScaleWidth +
                                      ScaleLeft Then
    deltax1 = -110
  End If
  Picture1.Move Picture1.Left + deltax1

End Sub
```

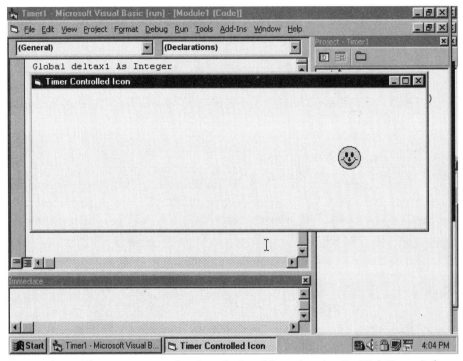

Figure 6–1   The movement of an icon is timed by using the GetTickCount() function.

When the application is run, a happy face is moved left and right across the screen. Figure 6–1 shows one temporary position for the happy face icon.

The Time1 Project

In this application the GetLocalTime() function will be used to return date and time information to a SYSTEMTIME structure. The project's name is Time1.vbp. This application uses a module file and a form. The module file is named Time1.bas and is listed below.

```
Type SYSTEMTIME
  wYear As Integer
  wMonth As Integer
  wDayOfWeek As Integer
  wDay As Integer
  wHour As Integer
  wMinute As Integer
```

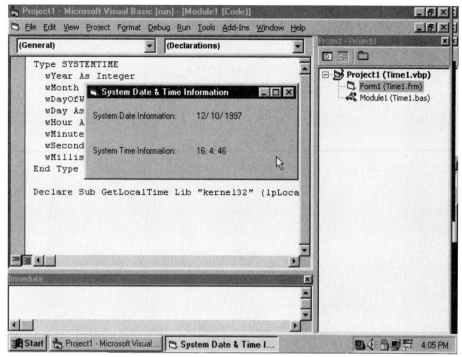

Figure 6-2 The GetLocalTime() subroutine is used to report the computer's date and time information.

```
   wSecond As Integer
   wMilliseconds As Integer
End Type

Declare Sub GetLocalTime Lib "kernel32"
   (lpLocalTime As SYSTEMTIME)
```

The Time1.frm uses several label controls. The caption properties of Label3 and Label4 will be used to report both date and time information to the screen. Remember when coding that GetLocalTime() is a subroutine.

```
Private Sub Form_Load()
   Dim loctime As SYSTEMTIME
   Dim totaldate$, totaltime$

   GetLocalTime loctime
   totaldate$ = Str$(loctime.wMonth) +
             "/" + Str$(loctime.wDay) +
             "/" + Str$(loctime.wYear)
```

```
      totaltime$ = Str$(loctime.wHour) +
               ":" + Str$(loctime.wMinute) +
               ":" + Str$(loctime.wSecond)
   Label3.Caption = totaldate$
   Label4.Caption = totaltime$
End Sub
```

When this application is run, the date and time of the local machine are reported to the user, as you can see in Figure 6–2.

Experiment a bit by substituting the GetSystemTime() subroutine in the previous application. Can you predict the results?

Chapter 7

Window Control Functions

The functions described in this chapter show how Windows establishes and controls the order of all windows in a system. Additionally, these functions allow control of such features as pop-up visibility, scrolling capabilities, and even tiling.

These functions are very closely related to the Windows functions described in Chapters 8 and 9. You'll want to study Chapters 8 and 9 in addition to this chapter to gain a complete understanding of how Windows manages a window's resources.

API Windows Control Function Names and Descriptions

Table 7–1 shows 44 Windows API Windows control functions and provides a brief description for their use.

Several functions in this group are used frequently. We'll use the GetNextWindow(), FlashWindow(), and DestroyWindow() functions to illustrate how these functions can be used in a simple application. This example is at the end of this chapter.

Table 7–1   Windows Control Functions and Descriptions

Function	Description
CascadeWindows	Cascades the windows or the child windows of the given parent window
CloseDesktop	Closes an open handle to a desktop object. A desktop is a secure object contained within a window station object and has a logical display surface and contains windows, menus, and hooks.
CloseWindow	Minimizes, but does not destroy, the given window.
CloseWindowStation	Closes an open window station handle.
CreateDesktop	Creates a new desktop on the window station associated with the calling process. The function returns a handle that can be used to access the new desktop. The desktop is a secure object contained within a window station object.
DestroyWindow	Destroys the window. If the window is a parent or owner window, the function also destroys the associated child or owned windows.
DrawAnimatedRects	Draws a wire-frame rectangle and animates it to show the opening of an icon or the minimizing or maximizing of a window.
EnableWindow	Enables or disables mouse and keyboard input to the given window or control. When disabled, the window does not receive input from mouse clicks and key presses.
EnumChildWindows	Enumerates the child windows that belong to the parent window by passing the handle of each child window, in turn, to an application-defined callback function.
EnumDesktops	Gets the handle of the window station associated with the calling process.
EnumDesktopWindows	Enumerates all windows in a desktop by passing the handle of each window to an application-defined callback function.
EnumProps	Enumerates all entries in the property list of a window by passing them to the callback function.
EnumPropsEx	Same as EnumProps() with extended capabilities.
EnumThreadWindows	Enumerates all nonchild windows associated with a thread by passing the handle of each window to an application-defined callback function.
EnumWindowStations	Enumerates all window stations in the system by passing the name of each window station to an application-defined callback function.
FindWindow	Finds the handle to the top-level window whose class name and window name match the given strings.
FindWindowEx	Same as FindWindow() with extended capabilities.
FlashWindow	Flashes the given window one time.
GetDesktopWindow	Gets the handle of the Windows desktop window. The desktop window covers the entire screen. The desktop window is the area on top of which all icons and other windows are painted.

Table 7–1 Windows Control Functions and Descriptions *(Continued)*

Function	Description
GetLastActivePopup	Gets the pop-up window owned by the given window that was most recently active.
GetNextWindow	Gets the handle of the next or previous window in the Z order. The next window is below the specified window; the previous window is above. If the specified window is a topmost window, the function retrieves the handle of the next (or previous) topmost window. If the specified window is a top-level window, the function retrieves the handle of the next (or previous) top-level window.
GetParent	Gets the handle of the given child window's parent window.
GetThreadDesktop	Gets a handle to the desktop associated with a given thread.
GetTopWindow	Looks at the Z order of the child windows associated with the given parent window and returns the handle of the child window at the top of the Z order.
GetUpdateRect	Gets the coordinates of the smallest rectangle that completely encloses the update region of the specified window. If the window was created with the CS_OWNDC style and the mapping mode is not MM_TEXT, the function gets the rectangle in logical coordinates. Otherwise, the rectangle is returned in client coordinates.
GetWindow	Gets the handle of a window that has the given relationship (Z order or owner) to the window.
GetWindowContextHelpId	Gets the help context identifier associated with the given window.
InvalidateRect	Adds a rectangle to the given window's update region. The region is a portion of the window's client area that will be redrawn.
LockWindowUpdate	Locks or unlocks drawing in the given window. Only one window can be locked at a time.
OpenDesktop	Gets a handle to an existing desktop. A desktop is a secure object contained within a window station object.
OpenInputDesktop	Gets a handle to the desktop that receives user input. The input desktop is a desktop on the window station associated with the logged-on user.
PaintDesktop	Fills the clipping region in the given device context with the desktop pattern or wallpaper.
RedrawWindow	Updates the given rectangle or region in a window's client area.
ScrollWindow	Use ScrollWindowEx().
ScrollWindowEx	Scrolls the content of the given window's client area.
SetParent	Changes the parent window of the given child window.
SetThreadDesktop	Assigns a desktop to the calling thread. All subsequent operations on the desktop use the access rights granted to hDesktop.

(Continued)

Table 7–1   Windows Control Functions and Descriptions *(Continued)*

Function	Description
SetWindowContextHelpId	Associates a help context identifier with the given window.
ShowOwnedPopups	Shows or hides all pop-up windows owned by the given window.
ShowWindow	Sets the given window's show state.
ShowWindowAsync	Sets the show state of a window created by a different thread.
SwitchDesktop	Makes a desktop visible and activates it. The desktop can then receive input from the user.
TileWindows	Tiles the given windows, or the child windows of the parent window.
ValidateRect	Validates the client area within a rectangle by removing the rectangle from the update region of the window.

API Windows Control Function Declarations

The following listing contains the Windows API Windows control function declarations found in the Win32api.txt file provided with Visual Basic. As we mentioned earlier, there are additional functions related to this group described in Chapters 8 and 9.

```
Declare Function CascadeWindows Lib "user32" Alias
   "CascadeWindows" (ByVal hwndParent As Long,
   ByVal wHow As Long, ByVal lpRect As RECT,
   ByVal cKids As Long, lpkids As Long) As Integer

Declare Function CloseDesktop Lib "user32" Alias
   "CloseDesktop" (ByVal hDesktop As Long) As Long

Declare Function CloseWindow Lib "user32" Alias
   "CloseWindow" (ByVal hwnd As Long) As Long

Declare Function CloseWindowStation Lib "user32" Alias
   "CloseWindowStation" (ByVal hWinSta As Long) As Long

Declare Function CreateDesktop Lib "user32" Alias
   "CreateDesktopA" (ByVal lpszDesktop As String,
   ByVal lpszDevice As String, pDevmode As DEVMODE,
   ByVal dwFlags As Long, ByVal dwDesiredAccess As Long,
   lpsa As SECURITY_ATTRIBUTES) As Long

Declare Function DestroyWindow Lib "user32" Alias
   "DestroyWindow" (ByVal hwnd As Long) As Long
```

```
Declare Function DrawAnimatedRects Lib "user32" Alias
  "DrawAnimatedRects" (ByVal hwnd As Long,
  ByVal idAni As Long, lprcFrom As Rect,
  lprcTo As Rect) As Long

Declare Function EnableWindow Lib "user32" Alias
  "EnableWindow" (ByVal hwnd As Long,
  ByVal fEnable As Long) As Long

Declare Function EnumChildWindows Lib "user32" Alias
  "EnumChildWindows" (ByVal hWndParent As Long,
  ByVal lpEnumFunc As Long, ByVal lParam As Long) As Long

Declare Function EnumDesktops Lib "user32" Alias
  "EnumDesktopsA" (ByVal hwinsta As Long,
  ByVal lpEnumFunc As Long, ByVal lParam As Long) As Long

Declare Function EnumDesktopWindows Lib "user32" Alias
  "EnumDesktopWindows" (ByVal hDesktop As Long,
  ByVal lpfn As Long, ByVal lParam As Long) As Long

Declare Function EnumProps Lib "user32" Alias
  "EnumPropsA" (ByVal hWnd As Long,
  ByVal lpEnumFunc As Long) As Long

Declare Function EnumPropsEx Lib "user32" Alias
  "EnumPropsExA" (ByVal hWnd As Long,
  ByVal lpEnumFunc As Long, ByVal lParam As Long) As Long

Declare Function EnumThreadWindows Lib "user32" Alias
  "EnumThreadWindows" (ByVal dwThreadId As Long,
  ByVal lpfn As Long, ByVal lParam As Long) As Long

Declare Function EnumWindowStations Lib "user32" Alias
  "EnumWindowStationsA" (ByVal lpEnumFunc As Long,
  ByVal lParam As Long) As Long

Declare Function FindWindow Lib "user32" Alias
  "FindWindowA" (ByVal lpClassName As String,
  ByVal lpWindowName As String) As Long

Declare Function FindWindowEx Lib "user32" Alias
  "FindWindowExA" (ByVal hWnd1 As Long,
  ByVal hWnd2 As Long, ByVal lpsz1 As String,
  ByVal lpsz2 As String) As Long

Declare Function FlashWindow Lib "user32" Alias
  "FlashWindow" (ByVal hwnd As Long,
  ByVal bInvert As Long) As Long

Declare Function GetDesktopWindow Lib "user32" Alias
  "GetDesktopWindow" () As Long
```

```
Declare Function GetLastActivePopup Lib "user32" Alias
  "GetLastActivePopup" (ByVal hwndOwnder As Long) As Long

Declare Function GetNextWindow Lib "user32" Alias
  "GetWindow" (ByVal hwnd As Long,
  ByVal wFlag As Long) As Long

Declare Function GetParent Lib "user32" Alias
  "GetParent" (ByVal hwnd As Long) As Long

Declare Function GetThreadDesktop Lib "user32" Alias
  "GetThreadDesktop" (ByVal dwThread As Long) As Long

Declare Function GetTopWindow Lib "user32" Alias
  "GetTopWindow" (ByVal hwnd As Long) As Long

Declare Function GetUpdateRect Lib "user32" Alias
  "GetUpdateRect" (ByVal hwnd As Long,
  lpRect As RECT, ByVal bErase As Long) As Long

Declare Function GetWindow Lib "user32" Alias
  "GetWindow" (ByVal hwnd As Long,
  ByVal wCmd As Long) As Long

Declare Function GetWindowContextHelpId Lib "user32" Alias
  "GetWindowContextHelpId" (ByVal hWnd As Long) As Long

Declare Function InvalidateRect Lib "user32" Alias
  "InvalidateRect" (ByVal hwnd As Long,
  lpRect As RECT, ByVal bErase As Long) As Long

Declare Function LockWindowUpdate Lib "user32" Alias
  "LockWindowUpdate" (ByVal hwndLock As Long) As Long

Declare Function OpenDesktop Lib "user32" Alias
  "OpenDesktopA" (ByVal lpszDesktop As String,
  ByVal dwFlags As Long, ByVal fInherit As Boolean,
  ByVal dwDesiredAccess As Long) As Long

Declare Function OpenInputDesktop Lib "user32" Alias
  "OpenInputDesktop" (ByVal dwFlags As Long,
  ByVal fInherit As Boolean,
  ByVal dwDesiredAccess As Long) As Long

Declare Function PaintDesktop Lib "user32" Alias
  "PaintDesktop" (ByVal hdc As Long) As Long

Declare Function RedrawWindow Lib "user32" Alias
  "RedrawWindow" (ByVal hwnd As Long,
  lprcUpdate As RECT, ByVal hrgnUpdate As Long,
  ByVal fuRedraw As Long) As Long
```

```
Declare Function ScrollWindow Lib "user32" Alias
   "ScrollWindow" (ByVal hWnd As Long,
   ByVal XAmount As Long, ByVal YAmount As Long,
   lpRect As RECT, lpClipRect As RECT) As Long

Declare Function ScrollWindowEx Lib "user32" Alias
   "ScrollWindowEx" (ByVal hwnd As Long,
   ByVal dx As Long, ByVal dy As Long,
   lprcScroll As RECT, lprcClip As RECT,
   ByVal hrgnUpdate As Long, lprcUpdate As RECT,
   ByVal fuScroll As Long) As Long

Declare Function SetParent Lib "user32" Alias
   "SetParent" (ByVal hWndChild As Long,
   ByVal hWndNewParent As Long) As Long

Declare Function SetThreadDesktop Lib "user32" Alias
   "SetThreadDesktop" (ByVal hDesktop As Long) As Long

Declare Function SetWindowContextHelpId Lib "user32" Alias
   "SetWindowContextHelpId" (ByVal hWnd As Long,
   ByVal dw As Long) As Long

Declare Function ShowOwnedPopups Lib "user32" Alias
   "ShowOwnedPopups" (ByVal hwnd As Long,
   ByVal fShow As Long) As Long

Declare Function ShowWindow Lib "user32" Alias
   "ShowWindow" (ByVal hwnd As Long,
   ByVal nCmdShow As Long) As Long

Declare Function ShowWindowAsync Lib "user32" Alias
   "ShowWindowAsync" (ByVal hWnd As Long,
   ByVal nCmdShow As Long) As Long

Declare Function SwitchDesktop Lib "user32" Alias
   "SwitchDesktop" (ByVal hDesktop As Long) As Long

Declare Function TileWindows Lib "user32" Alias
   "TileWindows" (ByVal hwndParent As Long,
   ByVal wHow As Long, lpRect As Rect,
   ByVal cKids As Long, lpKids As Long) As Integer

Declare Function ValidateRect Lib "user32" Alias
   "ValidateRect" (ByVal hwnd As Long,
   lpRect As RECT) As Long
```

Table 7–2 contains a brief description of the parameters used in the various
Windows control functions.

Table 7–2   Windows Control Function Parameters and Descriptions

Parameter	Description
bErase As Long	False—no erase; True—erase area.
bInvert As Long	False—return original state; True—switch window caption.
cKids As Long	Number of child windows in lpKids array.
dw As Long	Context help ID.
dwDesiredAccess As Long	Gives the type of access to the desktop using a DESKTOP_ constant.
dwFlags As Long	A bit flag parameter that controls how the calling application will cooperate with other applications on the desktop. Can be 0 or DF_ALLOWOTHERACCOUNTHOOK to allow processes in other accounts to set hooks in this process.
dwThread As Long	ID of the thread for which to return the desktop handle. Use GetCurrentThreadId() and CreateProcess() functions for obtaining thread IDs.
dwThreadId As Long	ID of thread.
dx As Long	Horizontal scroll distance.
dy As Long	Vertical scroll distance.
fEnable As Long	0—disables; nonzero enables.
fInherit As Boolean	States if the returned handle is inherited when a new process is created. False—will not inherit; True—will inherit.
fShow As Long	False—hides pop-up windows; True—shows pop-up windows.
fuRedraw As Long	Uses RDW_ constants.
fuScroll As Long	Uses SW_ constants.
hdc As Long	Handle to the device context (DC).
hDesktop As Long	Handle to desktop to close.
hrgnUpdate As Long	Handle of region for updating.
hWinSta As Long	Handle of window station to close. Handle is returned by CreateWindowStation() and OpenWindowStation() functions.
hwnd As Long	Windows handle.
hWnd1 As Long	ID of parent window whose child windows are to be searched.
hWnd2 As Long	ID of child window. Searches begin with the next child window in the Z order.
hWndChild As Long	Handle of child window.
hwndLock As Long	Handle of window to lock.
hWndNewParent As Long	Handle of new parent window.
hwndOwnder As Long	Parent window handle.
hwndParent As Long	Parent window handle.
idAni As Long	Use 0 value.

Table 7–2 Windows Control Function Parameters and Descriptions *(Continued)*

Parameter	Description
lParam As Long	User-defined value passed during function call.
lpClassName As String	Pointer to string containing a class name for the window. Use 0 for any class.
lpClipRect As RECT	Structure holds rectangular coordinates for clipping rectangle.
lpEnumFunc As Long	Points to a function to call for each child window.
lpfn As Long	Points to a function to call for each child window.
lpKids As Long	First entry in list of child windows.
lprcClip As RECT	Structure holds rectangular coordinates of clipping rectangle for scrolling.
lprcFrom As RECT	Originating rectangle.
lprcScroll As RECT	Structure holds rectangular coordinates of client area to scroll.
lprcTo As RECT	Destination rectangle.
lprcUpdate As RECT	Structure holds rectangular coordinates of area to update.
lpRect As RECT	Structure holds coordinates of rectangle.
lpsa As SECURITY_ATTRIBUTES	Structure holds information that determines if the returned handle can be inherited by child processes. NULL (0L) means the handle cannot be inherited.
lpsz1 As String	Pointer to a string giving the class name or is an atom that identifies the class-name string.
lpsz2 As String	Pointer to a string that gives the window name (the window's title). If this parameter is NULL (0L), all window names match.
lpszDesktop As String	Pointer to a string giving the name of the desktop to be created. Desktop names are case-insensitive and may not contain backslash characters (\).
lpszDevice As String	Reserved—set to NULL (0L). The desktop uses the default display driver loaded at boot time.
lpWindowName As String	Pointer to string containing window title or text. Use 0 for any title or text.
nCmdShow As Long	Uses SW_ constant.
pDevmode As DEVMODE	Reserved—set to NULL (0L).
wCmd As Long	Gives the relationship between the given window and the window whose handle is to be retrieved. Uses a GW_ constant.
wFlag As Long	States if the function returns the handle of the next window or of the previous window. Uses a GW_ constant.
wHow As Long	Uses MDITILE_ constant.
XAmount As Long	Horizontal scroll distance.
YAmount As Long	Vertical scroll distance.

Many of the parameters described in Table 7–2 use constant values. The Win32api.txt file lists the following constants for the Windows control functions just described:

```
'size of a device name string
Public Const CCHDEVICENAME = 32

'size of a form name string
Public Const CCHFORMNAME = 32

'Desktop-specific access flags
Public Const DESKTOP_READOBJECTS = &H1&
Public Const DESKTOP_CREATEWINDOW = &H2&
Public Const DESKTOP_CREATEMENU = &H4&
Public Const DESKTOP_HOOKCONTROL = &H8&
Public Const DESKTOP_JOURNALRECORD = &H10&
Public Const DESKTOP_JOURNALPLAYBACK = &H20&
Public Const DESKTOP_ENUMERATE = &H40&
Public Const DESKTOP_WRITEOBJECTS = &H80&

'GetWindow() Constants
Public Const GW_HWNDFIRST = 0
Public Const GW_HWNDLAST = 1
Public Const GW_HWNDNEXT = 2
Public Const GW_HWNDPREV = 3
Public Const GW_OWNER = 4
Public Const GW_CHILD = 5
Public Const GW_MAX = 5

'wParam values for WM_MDITILE and WM_MDICASCADE messages.
Public Const MDITILE_VERTICAL = &H0
Public Const MDITILE_HORIZONTAL = &H1
Public Const MDITILE_SKIPDISABLED = &H2

Public Const RDW_INVALIDATE = &H1
Public Const RDW_INTERNALPAINT = &H2
Public Const RDW_ERASE = &H4
Public Const RDW_VALIDATE = &H8
Public Const RDW_NOINTERNALPAINT = &H10
Public Const RDW_NOERASE = &H20
Public Const RDW_NOCHILDREN = &H40
Public Const RDW_ALLCHILDREN = &H80
Public Const RDW_UPDATENOW = &H100
Public Const RDW_ERASENOW = &H200
Public Const RDW_FRAME = &H400
Public Const RDW_NOFRAME = &H800

Public Const SW_SCROLLCHILDREN = &H1
Public Const SW_INVALIDATE = &H2
Public Const SW_ERASE = &H4
```

Several structures are also used by these functions. The structure declarations can also be found in the Win32api.txt file. The following listing contains the structures used by the Windows control functions:

```
Type RECT
  Left As Long
  Top As Long
  Right As Long
  Bottom As Long
End Type

Type SECURITY_ATTRIBUTES
  nLength As Long
  lpSecurityDescriptor As Long
  bInheritHandle As Long
End Type

Type DEVMODE
  dmDeviceName As String * CCHDEVICENAME
  dmSpecVersion As Integer
  dmDriverVersion As Integer
  dmSize As Integer
  dmDriverExtra As Integer
  dmFields As Long
  dmOrientation As Integer
  dmPaperSize As Integer
  dmPaperLength As Integer
  dmPaperWidth As Integer
  dmScale As Integer
  dmCopies As Integer
  dmDefaultSource As Integer
  dmPrintQuality As Integer
  dmColor As Integer
  dmDuplex As Integer
  dmYResolution As Integer
  dmTTOption As Integer
  dmCollate As Integer
  dmFormName As String * CCHFORMNAME
  dmUnusedPadding As Integer
  dmBitsPerPel As Integer
  dmPelsWidth As Long
  dmPelsHeight As Long
  dmDisplayFlags As Long
  dmDisplayFrequency As Long
End Type
```

In the next section we'll examine an application that makes use of several Windows control functions.

Example Application

This section contains a programming example that illustrates the use of the Windows control functions by using GetNextWindow(), FlashWindow(), and DestroyWindow().

The GetNextWindow() function will print the handle information for the next window in Windows Z order. The Z order of a window is the window's position in a stack of overlapping windows. The stack is aligned on an imaginary "z" axis that extends outward from the screen. The top Z order window overlaps all other windows.

Windows are added based on whether they are topmost, top-level, or child windows. A child window is ordered with its parent in Z order.

The FlashWindow() function will flash a given window once. The DestroyWindow() function destroys a window.

This application will print information concerning the type of Windows handles present, flash the window for five seconds, and permit the user to destroy the window.

The project is named Control1.vbp and contains a form (Control1.frm) with multiple labels and two command buttons. The project also contains a module file, Control1.bas that contains constant values and function declarations as shown in the next listing.

```
'GetWindow() Constants
Public Const GW_HWNDFIRST = 0
Public Const GW_HWNDLAST = 1
Public Const GW_HWNDNEXT = 2
Public Const GW_HWNDPREV = 3
Public Const GW_OWNER = 4
Public Const GW_CHILD = 5
Public Const GW_MAX = 5

Declare Function GetNextWindow Lib "user32" Alias
  "GetWindow" (ByVal hwnd As Long,
  ByVal wFlag As Long) As Long
Declare Function FlashWindow Lib "user32"
  (ByVal hwnd As Long,
  ByVal bInvert As Long) As Long
Declare Function DestroyWindow Lib "user32"
  (ByVal hwnd As Long) As Long
```

The code for this project is contained in the Command1 and Command2 subroutines, as shown in the next listing.

```
Private Sub Command1_Click()
  Dim r&
```

```
r& = GetNextWindow(hwnd&, GW_HWNDFIRST)
Label1.Caption = r&
r& = GetNextWindow(hwnd&, GW_HWNDLAST)
Label2.Caption = r&
r& = GetNextWindow(hwnd&, GW_HWNDNEXT)
Label3.Caption = r&
r& = GetNextWindow(hwnd&, GW_HWNDPREV)
Label4.Caption = r&
r& = GetNextWindow(hwnd&, GW_OWNER)
Label5.Caption = r&
r& = GetNextWindow(hwnd&, GW_CHILD)
Label6.Caption = r&
r& = GetNextWindow(hwnd&, GW_MAX)
Label7.Caption = r&

'Flash Window for 5 seconds
DelayTime = 5
Start = Timer 'Set start time.
Do While Timer < Start + DelayTime
  r& = FlashWindow(hwnd&, True)
Loop
```

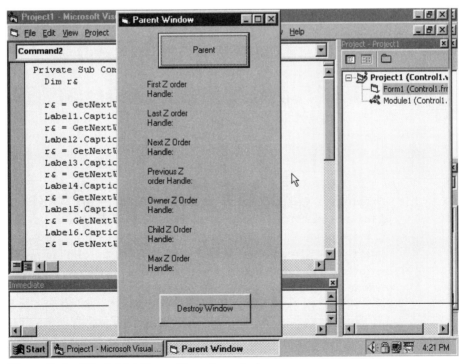

Figure 7–1   The initial Control1 project window.

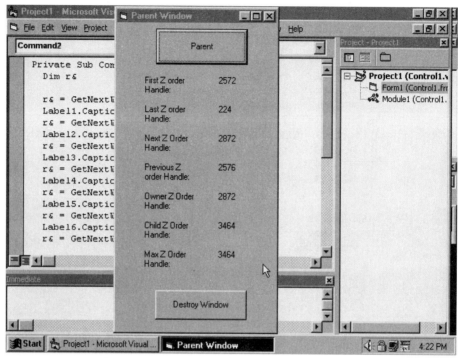

Figure 7–2   Z order window information is returned to the form.

```
   Finish = Timer 'Set end time.
End Sub

Private Sub Command2_Click()
   Dim r&

   r& = DestroyWindow(hwnd&)
End Sub
```

The project is executed and the window shown in Figure 7–1 is visible.

If the user clicks the "Parent" command button, the screen will flash for five seconds and produce information similar to that shown in Figure 7–2.

Finally, if the user clicks the "Destroy Window" command button, the window is destroyed. In the next chapter, you'll learn how to gain even more control over any window on the screen.

Chapter 8

Windows Manipulation Functions

In the previous chapter you learned about Windows API functions that allow you to create, open, and close desktops and windows. These functions, when combined with the Windows manipulation functions of this chapter, allow even further control of your system. The manipulation functions discussed in this chapter will allow you to bring a window to the top of the Z order, create a window, get and change the class information concerning a window, and so on. However, your study of Windows functions will also continue in Chapter 9 as you learn how to change various features in the windows and desktops you create.

API Windows Manipulation Function Names and Descriptions

Table 8–1 shows 67 Windows API Windows manipulation functions and provides a brief description for their use.

This grouping contains a number of frequently used functions. The IsChild(), IsIconic(), IsWindow(), IsWindowEnabled(), IsWindowUnicode(), IsWindow-Visible(), and IsZoomed() functions are useful for determining the state of a window or its child. Functions such as GetWindowRect(), GetWindowText(),

Table 8–1   Windows Manipulation Functions and Descriptions

Function	Description
AdjustWindowRect	Determines the required size of the window rectangle. Information can be passed to the CreateWindowEx() function to create a window with the determined client area.
AdjustWindowRectEx	Same as AdjustWindowRect() with extended capabilities.
ArrangeIconicWindows	Arranges the minimized (iconic) child windows of the parent window.
BeginDeferWindowPos	Assigns memory for a multiwindow position structure and then returns the obtained handle.
BringWindowToTop	Brings the window to the top of the Z order. Top-level windows are activated with this function. A child window's parent is activated with this function.
ChildWindowFromPoint	Finds the child windows belonging to a parent window that contains the given point.
ChildWindowFromPointEx	Same as ChildWindowFromPoint() with extended capabilities.
ClientToScreen	Converts the client coordinates of a given point to screen coordinates.
CreateWindowEx	Creates an overlapped, pop-up, or child window with an extended style.
DeferWindowPos	Updates the given multiwindow position structure for the window. The handle is then returned to the updated structure.
DefWindowProc	Calls the default window procedure. This procedure provides default processing for window messages not processed by the application.
EndDeferWindowPos	Updates the position and size of window(s) in a single screen-refreshing cycle.
ExitWindows	Logs the current user off.
ExitWindowsEx	Same as ExitWindows() with extended capabilities.
GetActiveWindow	Gets the window handle of the active window associated with the thread calling the function.
GetCapture	Gets the handle of the window that has captured the mouse.
GetClassInfo	Use of GetClassInfoEx() preferred.
GetClassInfoEx	Gets information on a window class and icon.
GetClassLong	Gets the 32-bit value from the WNDCLASS structure associated with the given window.
GetClassName	Gets the name of the class to which the window belongs.
GetClientRect	Gets the coordinates of a client area. The coordinates give the upper-left and lower-right corners of the client area.
GetFocus	Gets the handle of the window that has the keyboard focus.
GetForegroundWindow	Gets the handle of the foreground window.
GetMessageExtraInfo	Gets the extra message information for the current thread. This information can be an application or driver.
GetMessagePos	Gets a long value containing the cursor position in screen coordinates. The value represents the cursor position when the last message was retrieved.
GetMessageTime	Gets the last message's time (milliseconds) returned by the GetMessage() function. The time is determined from when the system is started until the message is created.
GetWindowLong	Gets information about the window. Function also obtains a 32-bit value at the offset into the extra window memory.

Table 8–1   Windows Manipulation Functions and Descriptions *(Continued)*

Function	Description
GetWindowPlacement	Gets the show state and the restored, minimized, and maximized positions of the window.
GetWindowRect	Gets the dimensions (in screen coordinates) of the bounding rectangle of the window.
GetWindowText	Gets the text in the window's title bar and places it in a buffer.
GetWindowTextLength	Gets the length (in characters) of the window's title bar text.
InSendMessage	Determines if the current window procedure is processing a message that was sent from another thread by a call to the SendMessage() function.
IsChild	Finds if a window is a child window or descendant window of a parent window.
IsIconic	Finds if the window is minimized or iconic.
IsWindow	Finds if the window handle identifies an existing window.
IsWindowEnabled	Finds if the window is enabled for mouse and keyboard input.
IsWindowUnicode	Finds if the window is a native unicode window.
IsWindowVisible	Gets the visibility state of the window.
IsZoomed	Finds if a window is maximized.
MapWindowPoints	Converts points from a coordinate space relative to one window to a coordinate space relative to another window.
MoveWindow	Moves the position and dimensions of the window. The position and dimensions of a top-level window are relative to the upper-left corner of the screen. Child windows are relative to the upper-left corner of the parent window's client area.
OpenIcon	Restores and activates a minimized window to its previous size and position.
PostMessage	Posts a message in the message queue associated with the thread that created the window and returns without waiting for the thread to process the message.
PostThreadMessage	Posts a message in the message queue of the thread and returns without waiting for the thread to process the message.
PostQuitMessage	Informs Windows that a thread requested termination.
RegisterWindowMessage	Creates a new and unique window message.
ReleaseCapture	Releases the mouse capture from a window in the current thread and restores normal mouse input processing.
ReplyMessage	Replies to a message sent through the SendMessage() function without returning control to the function that called SendMessage().
ScreenToClient	Converts the screen coordinates of a point on the screen to client coordinates.
SendMessage	Sends the message to a window or windows. SendMessage() calls the window procedure for the window and does not return until the window procedure has processed the message.
SendMessageCallback	Sends the message to a window or windows. The function calls the windows procedure for the window and returns immediately.

(Continued)

Table 8–1   Windows Manipulation Functions and Descriptions *(Continued)*

Function	Description
SendMessageTimeout	Sends the message to a window or windows. The function calls the window procedure for the window. If the window belongs to a different thread, it does not return until the window procedure has processed the message or the time-out period has elapsed. If the window belongs to the same queue as the thread, the window procedure is called directly.
SendNotifyMessage	Sends the message to a window. If the window was created by the calling thread, the function calls the window procedure for the window and does not return until the window procedure has processed the message. If the window was created by a different thread, the function passes the message to the window procedure and returns immediately.
SetActiveWindow	Activates a window.
SetCapture	Sets the mouse capture to the window belonging to the current thread.
SetClassLong	Sets the 32-bit value at the offset into the extra class memory or the WNDCLASS structure for the class to which the window belongs.
SetFocus	Sets the keyboard focus to the window.
SetForegroundWindow	Sets the thread that created the window into the foreground and activates the window.
SetMessageExtraInfo	Sets the extra message information for the current thread. This information can be an application or driver.
SetWindowLong	Sets an attribute of the window. The function also sets a 32-bit value at the offset into the extra window memory.
SetWindowPlacement	Sets the show state and the restored, minimized, and maximized positions of the window.
SetWindowPos	Sets the size, position, and Z order of a child, pop-up, or top-level window. Child, pop-up, and top-level windows are ordered according to their appearance on the screen. The topmost window receives the highest rank and is the first window in the Z order.
SetWindowsHookEx	Sets an application-defined hook procedure into a hook chain. A hook procedure can be used to monitor the system for certain types of events associated with a unique thread or with all threads.
SetWindowText	Sets the text of the window's title bar.
UpdateWindow	Updates the client area of the window by sending a WM_PAINT message to the window. The function sends a WM_PAINT message directly to the window procedure of the window, bypassing the application queue.
WaitMessage	Yields control to other threads when a thread has no other messages in its message queue. The function suspends the thread and does not return until a new message is placed in the thread's message queue.
WindowFromPoint	Gets the handle of the window that contains the point.

SetWindowText(), MoveWindow, and SetWindowPos() are useful for changing window title information along with window position and size. You'll see many of these functions illustrated in the two examples contained at the end of this chapter.

API Windows Manipulation Function Declarations

The following listing contains the Windows API Windows manipulation function declarations found in the Win32api.txt file provided with Visual Basic. As we mentioned earlier, there are additional functions related to this group described in Chapter 7 and Chapter 9.

```
Declare Function AdjustWindowRect Lib "user32" Alias
  "AdjustWindowRect" (lpRect As RECT,
  ByVal dwStyle As Long, ByVal bMenu As Long) As Long

Declare Function AdjustWindowRectEx Lib "user32" Alias
  "AdjustWindowRectEx" (lpRect As RECT,
  ByVal dsStyle As Long, ByVal bMenu As Long,
  ByVal dwEsStyle As Long) As Long

Declare Function ArrangeIconicWindows Lib "user32" Alias
  "ArrangeIconicWindows" (ByVal hwnd As Long) As Long

Declare Function BeginDeferWindowPos Lib "user32" Alias
  "BeginDeferWindowPos" (ByVal nNumWindows As Long) As Long

Declare Function BringWindowToTop Lib "user32" Alias
  "BringWindowToTop" (ByVal hwnd As Long) As Long

Declare Function ChildWindowFromPoint Lib "user32" Alias
  "ChildWindowFromPoint" (ByVal hWnd As Long,
  ByVal xPoint As Long, ByVal yPoint As Long) As Long

Declare Function ChildWindowFromPoint Lib "user32" Alias
  "ChildWindowFromPoint" (ByVal hWndParent As Long,
  ByVal pt As POINTAPI) As Long

Declare Function ChildWindowFromPointEx Lib "user32" Alias
  "ChildWindowFromPointEx" (ByVal hWnd As Long,
  ByVal pt As POINTAPI, ByVal un As Long) As Long

Declare Function ClientToScreen Lib "user32" Alias
  "ClientToScreen" (ByVal hwnd As Long,
  lpPoint As POINTAPI) As Long

Declare Function CreateWindowEx Lib "user32" Alias
  "CreateWindowExA" (ByVal dwExStyle As Long,
  ByVal lpClassName As String,
  ByVal lpWindowName As String,
  ByVal dwStyle As Long, ByVal x As Long,
```

```
            ByVal y As Long, ByVal nWidth As Long,
            ByVal nHeight As Long, ByVal hWndParent As Long,
            ByVal hMenu As Long, ByVal hInstance As Long,
            lpParam As Any) As Long

Declare Function DeferWindowPos Lib "user32" Alias
   "DeferWindowPos" (ByVal hWinPosInfo As Long,
   ByVal hwnd As Long,
   ByVal hWndInsertAfter As Long,
   ByVal x As Long, ByVal y As Long,
   ByVal cx As Long, ByVal cy As Long,
   ByVal wFlags As Long) As Long

Declare Function DefWindowProc Lib "user32" Alias
   "DefWindowProcA" (ByVal hwnd As Long,
   ByVal wMsg As Long, ByVal wParam As Long,
   ByVal lParam As Long) As Long

Declare Function EndDeferWindowPos Lib "user32" Alias
   "EndDeferWindowPos" (ByVal hWinPosInfo As Long) As Long

Declare Function ExitWindows Lib "user32" Alias
   "ExitWindows" (ByVal dwReserved As Long,
   ByVal uReturnCode As Long) As Long

Declare Function ExitWindowsEx Lib "user32" Alias
   "ExitWindowsEx" (ByVal uFlags As Long,
   ByVal dwReserved As Long) As Long

Declare Function GetActiveWindow Lib "user32" Alias
   "GetActiveWindow" () As Long

Declare Function GetCapture Lib "user32" Alias
   "GetCapture" () As Long

Declare Function GetClassInfo Lib "user32" Alias
   "GetClassInfoA" (ByVal hInstance As Long,
   ByVal lpClassName As String,
   lpWndClass As WNDCLASS) As Long
Declare Function GetClassInfoEx Lib "user32" Alias
   "GetClassInfoExA" (ByVal hInstance As Long,
   ByVal lpClassName As String,
   lpWndClassEx As WNDCLASSEX) As Long
Declare Function GetClassLong Lib "user32" Alias
   "GetClassLongA" (ByVal hwnd As Long,
   ByVal nIndex As Long) As Long

Declare Function GetClassName Lib "user32" Alias
   "GetClassNameA" (ByVal hwnd As Long,
   ByVal lpClassName As String,
   ByVal nMaxCount As Long) As Long
```

```
Declare Function GetClientRect Lib "user32" Alias
   "GetClientRect" (ByVal hwnd As Long,
   lpRect As RECT) As Long

Declare Function GetFocus Lib "user32" Alias
   "GetFocus" () As Long

Declare Function GetForegroundWindow Lib "user32" Alias
   "GetForegroundWindow" () As Long

Declare Function GetMessageExtraInfo Lib "user32" Alias
   "GetMessageExtraInfo" () As Long

Declare Function GetMessagePos Lib "user32" Alias
   "GetMessagePos" () As Long

Declare Function GetMessageTime Lib "user32" Alias
   "GetMessageTime" () As Long

Declare Function GetWindowLong Lib "user32" Alias
   "GetWindowLongA" (ByVal hwnd As Long,
   ByVal nIndex As Long) As Long

Declare Function GetWindowPlacement Lib "user32" Alias
   "GetWindowPlacement" (ByVal hwnd As Long,
   lpwndpl As WINDOWPLACEMENT) As Long

Declare Function GetWindowRect Lib "user32" Alias
   "GetWindowRect" (ByVal hwnd As Long,
   lpRect As RECT) As Long

Declare Function GetWindowText Lib "user32" Alias
   "GetWindowTextA" (ByVal hwnd As Long,
   ByVal lpString As String,
   ByVal cch As Long) As Long

Declare Function GetWindowTextLength Lib "user32" Alias
   "GetWindowTextLengthA" (ByVal hwnd As Long) As Long

Declare Function InSendMessage Lib "user32" Alias
   "InSendMessage" () As Long

Declare Function IsChild Lib "user32" Alias
   "IsChild" (ByVal hWndParent As Long,
   ByVal hwnd As Long) As Long

Declare Function IsIconic Lib "user32" Alias
   "IsIconic" (ByVal hwnd As Long) As Long

Declare Function IsWindow Lib "user32" Alias
   "IsWindow" (ByVal hwnd As Long) As Long

Declare Function IsWindowEnabled Lib "user32" Alias
   "IsWindowEnabled" (ByVal hwnd As Long) As Long
```

```
Declare Function IsWindowUnicode Lib "user32" Alias
    "IsWindowUnicode" (ByVal hwnd As Long) As Long

Declare Function IsWindowUnicode Lib "user32" Alias
    "IsWindowUnicode" (ByVal hwnd As Long) As Long

Declare Function IsWindowVisible Lib "user32" Alias
    "IsWindowVisible" (ByVal hwnd As Long) As Long

Declare Function IsZoomed Lib "user32" Alias
    "IsZoomed" (ByVal hwnd As Long) As Long

Declare Function MapWindowPoints Lib "user32" Alias
    MapWindowPoints" (ByVal hwndFrom As Long,
    ByVal hwndTo As Long, lppt As Any,
    ByVal cPoints As Long) As Long

Declare Function MoveWindow Lib "user32" Alias
    "MoveWindow" (ByVal hwnd As Long,
    ByVal x As Long, ByVal y As Long,
    ByVal nWidth As Long, ByVal nHeight As Long,
    ByVal bRepaint As Long) As Long

Declare Function OpenIcon Lib "user32" Alias
    "OpenIcon" (ByVal hwnd As Long) As Long

Declare Function PostMessage Lib "user32" Alias
    "PostMessageA" (ByVal hwnd As Long,
    ByVal wMsg As Long, ByVal wParam As Long,
    ByVal lParam As Long) As Long

Declare Function PostThreadMessage Lib "user32" Alias
    "PostThreadMessageA" (ByVal idThread As Long,
    ByVal msg As Long, ByVal wParam As Long,
    ByVal lParam As Long) As Long

Declare Sub PostQuitMessage Lib "user32" Alias
    "PostQuitMessage" (ByVal nExitCode As Long)

Declare Function RegisterWindowMessage Lib "user32" Alias
    "RegisterWindowMessageA" (ByVal lpString As String) As Long

Declare Function ReleaseCapture Lib "user32" Alias
    "ReleaseCapture" () As Long

Declare Function ReplyMessage Lib "user32" Alias
    "ReplyMessage" (ByVal lReply As Long) As Long

Declare Function ScreenToClient Lib "user32" Alias
    "ScreenToClient" (ByVal hwnd As Long,
    lpPoint As POINTAPI) As Long

Declare Function SendMessage Lib "user32" Alias
    "SendMessageA" (ByVal hwnd As Long,
```

```
     ByVal wMsg As Long, ByVal wParam As Long,
     lParam As Any) As Long

Declare Function SendMessageCallback Lib "user32" Alias
   "SendMessageCallbackA" (ByVal hwnd As Long,
   ByVal msg As Long, ByVal wParam As Long,
   ByVal lParam As Long, ByVal lpResultCallBack As Long,
   ByVal dwData As Long) As Long

Declare Function SendMessageTimeout Lib "user32" Alias
   "SendMessageTimeoutA" (ByVal hwnd As Long,
   ByVal msg As Long, ByVal wParam As Long,
   ByVal lParam As Long, ByVal fuFlags As Long,
   ByVal uTimeout As Long,
   lpdwResult As Long) As Long

Declare Function SendNotifyMessage Lib "user32" Alias
   "SendNotifyMessageA" (ByVal hwnd As Long,
   ByVal msg As Long, ByVal wParam As Long,
   ByVal lParam As Long) As Long

Declare Function SetActiveWindow Lib "user32" Alias
   "SetActiveWindow" (ByVal hwnd As Long) As Long

Declare Function SetCapture Lib "user32" Alias
   "SetCapture" (ByVal hwnd As Long) As Long

Declare Function SetClassLong Lib "user32" Alias
   "SetClassLongA" (ByVal hwnd As Long,
   ByVal nIndex As Long,
   ByVal dwNewLong As Long) As Long

Declare Function SetFocus Lib "user32" Alias
   "SetFocus" (ByVal hwnd As Long) As Long

Declare Function SetForegroundWindow Lib "user32" Alias
   "SetForegroundWindow" (ByVal hwnd As Long) As Long

Declare Function SetForegroundWindow Lib "user32" Alias
   "SetForegroundWindow" (ByVal hwnd As Long) As Long

Declare Function SetMessageExtraInfo Lib "user32" Alias
   "SetMessageExtraInfo" (ByVal lParam As Long) As Long

Declare Function SetWindowLong Lib "user32" Alias
   "SetWindowLongA" (ByVal hwnd As Long,
   ByVal nIndex As Long,
   ByVal dwNewLong As Long) As Long

Declare Function SetWindowPlacement Lib "user32" Alias
   "SetWindowPlacement" (ByVal hwnd As Long,
   lpwndpl As WINDOWPLACEMENT) As Long

Declare Function SetWindowPos Lib "user32" Alias
   "SetWindowPos" (ByVal hwnd As Long,
```

```
        ByVal hWndInsertAfter As Long,
        ByVal x As Long, ByVal y As Long,
        ByVal cx As Long, ByVal cy As Long,
        ByVal wFlags As Long) As Long

    Declare Function SetWindowsHookEx Lib "user32" Alias
        "SetWindowsHookExA" (ByVal idHook As Long,
        ByVal lpfn As Long, ByVal hmod As Long,
        ByVal dwThreadId As Long) As Long

    Declare Function SetWindowText Lib "user32" Alias
        "SetWindowTextA" (ByVal hwnd As Long,
        ByVal lpString As String) As Long

    Declare Function UpdateWindow Lib "user32" Alias
        "UpdateWindow" (ByVal hwnd As Long) As Long

    Declare Function WaitMessage Lib "user32" Alias
        "WaitMessage" () As Long

    Declare Function WindowFromPoint Lib "user32" Alias
        WindowFromPoint" (ByVal xPoint As Long,
        ByVal yPoint As Long) As Long
```

Table 8–2 contains a brief description of the parameters used in the various windows manipulation functions.

Table 8–2   Windows Manipulation Function Parameters and Descriptions

Parameter	Description
bMenu As Long	True—menu present; False—no menu present.
bRepaint As Long	False—explicit redraws only; True—will redraw window.
cch As Long	Length of string buffer (lpString).
cPoints As Long	Number of points to convert.
cx As Long	Width of a window.
cy As Long	Height of a window.
dsStyle As Long	Uses WS_ constants.
dwData As Long	Value to pass to callback function.
dwEsStyle As Long	Uses WS_EX_ Extended Windows Style constants.
dwNewLong As Long	Value of class information provided by nIndex parameter.
dwReserved As Long	Must be 0.
dwStyle As Long	Uses WS_ Windows Style constants.
dwThreadId As Long	Identity of thread to install hook for.
fuFlags As Long	How to send the message.
hInstance As Long	Handle of class instance.
hMenu As Long	Handle of menu.
hmod As Long	Handle of application instance.
hWinPosInfo As Long	Handle to structure returned by a call to BeginDeferWindowPos() or DeferWindowPos() functions.

Table 8–2   Windows Manipulation Function Parameters and Descriptions *(Continued)*

Parameter	Description
hwnd As Long	Handle to a window.
hwndFrom As Long	Handle to a window with source coordinates.
hwndInsertAfter As Long	Handle to a window. Can also be an HWND_ constant.
hWndParent As Long	Handle to a parent window.
hwndTo As Long	Handle to a window with destination coordinates.
idHook As Long	Uses WH_ constants.
lParam As Any	Holds additional message information.
lpClassName As String	Pointer to a class name.
lpdwResult As Long	Return value for synchronous call.
lpfn As Long	Address of hook procedure.
lpParam As Any	Pointer to window creation data.
lpPoint As POINTAPI	Initially holds point coordinates in one form and returns them after the function call in the opposite form.
lppt As Any	Holds first value in an array of point structures that will be converted.
lpRect As RECT	Structure holds bounding rectangle coordinates.
lpResultCallBack As Long	Function to receive message value.
lpString As String	String buffer holds window text plus one character.
lpWindowName As String	Pointer to a window name.
lpWndClass As WNDCLASS	Structure holds results of GetClassInfo() function call.
lpWndClassEx As WNDCLASSEX	Structure holds results of GetClassInfoEx() function call.
lpwndpl As WINDOWPLACEMENT	Structure holds location and state window information.
lReply As Long	Message-specific reply.
msg As Long	Holds the message.
nExitCode As Long	Exit code.
nHeight As Long	Height of window.
nIndex As Long	Uses GCL_ or GWL_ constants.
nMaxCount As Long	Length of lpClassName buffer.
nNumWindows As Long	Number of windows needing space allocation in structure.
nWidth As Long	Width of window.
pt As POINTAPI	Structure holds x and y point values (pixels).
uFlags As Long	Uses EWX_ constants.
un As Long	Skipping flags.
uReturnCode As Long	Must be 0.
uTimeout As Long	Time-out duration.
wFlags As Long	Uses SWP_ constants.
wMsg As Long	Message identifier.
wParam As Long	Additional message information.
x As Long	The x coordinate of the window.
xPoint As Long	The x value of a point (pixels).
y As Long	The y coordinate of the window.
yPoint As Long	The y value of a point (pixels).

Many of the parameters described in Table 8–2 use constant values. The Win32api.txt file lists the following constants for the Windows manipulation functions just described:

```
'EWX Flags
Public Const EWX_LOGOFF = 0
Public Const EWX_SHUTDOWN = 1
Public Const EWX_REBOOT = 2
Public Const EWX_FORCE = 4

'Class field offsets for GetClassLong() and GetClassWord()
Public Const GCL_MENUNAME = (-8)
Public Const GCL_HBRBACKGROUND = (-10)
Public Const GCL_HCURSOR = (-12)
Public Const GCL_HICON = (-14)
Public Const GCL_HMODULE = (-16)
Public Const GCL_CBWNDEXTRA = (-18)
Public Const GCL_CBCLSEXTRA = (-20)
Public Const GCL_WNDPROC = (-24)
Public Const GCL_STYLE = (-26)
Public Const GCW_ATOM = (-32)

'Window field offsets for GetWindowLong() and GetWindowWord()
Public Const GWL_WNDPROC = (-4)
Public Const GWL_HINSTANCE = (-6)
Public Const GWL_HWNDPARENT = (-8)
Public Const GWL_STYLE = (-16)
Public Const GWL_EXSTYLE = (-20)
Public Const GWL_USERDATA = (-21)
Public Const GWL_ID = (-12)

'SetWindowPos() hwndInsertAfter values
Public Const HWND_TOP = 0
Public Const HWND_BOTTOM = 1
Public Const HWND_TOPMOST = -1
Public Const HWND_NOTOPMOST = -2

'SetWindowPos Flags
Public Const SWP_NOSIZE = &H1
Public Const SWP_NOMOVE = &H2
Public Const SWP_NOZORDER = &H4
Public Const SWP_NOREDRAW = &H8
Public Const SWP_NOACTIVATE = &H10
'Frame changed - send WM_NCCALCSIZE:
Public Const SWP_FRAMECHANGED = &H20
Public Const SWP_SHOWWINDOW = &H40
Public Const SWP_HIDEWINDOW = &H80
Public Const SWP_NOCOPYBITS = &H100
'Don't do owner Z ordering:
Public Const SWP_NOOWNERZORDER = &H200
```

```
Public Const SWP_DRAWFRAME = SWP_FRAMECHANGED
Public Const SWP_NOREPOSITION = SWP_NOOWNERZORDER

'SetWindowsHook() codes
Public Const WH_MIN = (-1)
Public Const WH_MSGFILTER = (-1)
Public Const WH_JOURNALRECORD = 0
Public Const WH_JOURNALPLAYBACK = 1
Public Const WH_KEYBOARD = 2
Public Const WH_GETMESSAGE = 3
Public Const WH_CALLWNDPROC = 4
Public Const WH_CBT = 5
Public Const WH_SYSMSGFILTER = 6
Public Const WH_MOUSE = 7
Public Const WH_HARDWARE = 8
Public Const WH_DEBUG = 9
Public Const WH_SHELL = 10
Public Const WH_FOREGROUNDIDLE = 11
Public Const WH_MAX = 11

'Hook Codes
Public Const HC_ACTION = 0
Public Const HC_GETNEXT = 1
Public Const HC_SKIP = 2
Public Const HC_NOREMOVE = 3
Public Const HC_NOREM = HC_NOREMOVE
Public Const HC_SYSMODALON = 4
Public Const HC_SYSMODALOFF = 5

'CBT Hook Codes
Public Const HCBT_MOVESIZE = 0
Public Const HCBT_MINMAX = 1
Public Const HCBT_QS = 2
Public Const HCBT_CREATEWND = 3
Public Const HCBT_DESTROYWND = 4
Public Const HCBT_ACTIVATE = 5
Public Const HCBT_CLICKSKIPPED = 6
Public Const HCBT_KEYSKIPPED = 7
Public Const HCBT_SYSCOMMAND = 8
Public Const HCBT_SETFOCUS = 9

'Window Styles
Public Const WS_OVERLAPPED = &H0&
Public Const WS_POPUP = &H80000000
Public Const WS_CHILD = &H40000000
Public Const WS_MINIMIZE = &H20000000
Public Const WS_VISIBLE = &H10000000
Public Const WS_DISABLED = &H8000000
Public Const WS_CLIPSIBLINGS = &H4000000
Public Const WS_CLIPCHILDREN = &H2000000
```

```
Public Const WS_MAXIMIZE = &H1000000
Public Const WS_CAPTION = &HC00000 'WS_BORDER Or WS_DLGFRAME
Public Const WS_BORDER = &H800000
Public Const WS_DLGFRAME = &H400000
Public Const WS_VSCROLL = &H200000
Public Const WS_HSCROLL = &H100000
Public Const WS_SYSMENU = &H80000
Public Const WS_THICKFRAME = &H40000
Public Const WS_GROUP = &H20000
Public Const WS_TABSTOP = &H10000
Public Const WS_MINIMIZEBOX = &H20000
Public Const WS_MAXIMIZEBOX = &H10000
Public Const WS_TILED = WS_OVERLAPPED
Public Const WS_ICONIC = WS_MINIMIZE
Public Const WS_SIZEBOX = WS_THICKFRAME
Public Const WS_OVERLAPPEDWINDOW = (WS_OVERLAPPED Or
                                   WS_CAPTION Or
                                   WS_SYSMENU Or
                                   WS_THICKFRAME Or
                                   WS_MINIMIZEBOX Or
                                   WS_MAXIMIZEBOX)
Public Const WS_TILEDWINDOW = WS_OVERLAPPEDWINDOW

'Common Window Styles
Public Const WS_POPUPWINDOW = (WS_POPUP Or
                             WS_BORDER Or
                             WS_SYSMENU)
Public Const WS_CHILDWINDOW = (WS_CHILD)

'Extended Window Styles
Public Const WS_EX_DLGMODALFRAME = &H1&
Public Const WS_EX_NOPARENTNOTIFY = &H4&
Public Const WS_EX_TOPMOST = &H8&
Public Const WS_EX_ACCEPTFILES = &H10&
Public Const WS_EX_TRANSPARENT = &H20&
```

These functions also make use of several structures also defined in the Win32api.txt file. The following listing contains the structure declarations for the functions described in this chapter:

```
Type POINTAPI
  x As Long
  y As Long
End Type

Type RECT
  Left As Long
  Top As Long
  Right As Long
```

```
      Bottom As Long
   End Type

   Type WINDOWPLACEMENT
     Length As Long
     flags As Long
     showCmd As Long
     ptMinPosition As POINTAPI
     ptMaxPosition As POINTAPI
     rcNormalPosition As Rect
   End Type

   Type WNDCLASS
     style As Long
     lpfnwndproc As Long
     cbClsextra As Long
     cbWndExtra2 As Long
     hInstance As Long
     hIcon As Long
     hCursor As Long
     hbrBackground As Long
     lpszMenuName As String
     lpszClassName As String
   End Type

   Type WNDCLASSEX
     cbSize As Long
     style As Long
     lpfnWndProc As Long
     cbClsExtra As Long
     cbWndExtra As Long
     hInstance As Long
     hIcon As Long
     hCursor As Long
     hbrBackground As Long
     lpszMenuName As String
     lpszClassName As String
     hIconSm As Long
   End Type
```

In the next section we'll investigate two applications that make use of the Windows API manipulation functions described in this chapter.

Example Applications

The example applications contained in this section are divided into two catagories. The first example illustrates the use of the IsIconic(), IsWindow(), IsWindowEnabled(), IsWindowUnicode(), and IsZoomed() functions. The second example illustrates the use of the GetWindowRect(), GetWindowText(), SetWindowText(), and MoveWindow functions.

Application One

The first example project is named mani1.vbp. This project contains a module file named mani1.bas containing various function declarations. Those declarations are shown in the following listing:

```
Declare Function IsChild Lib "user32"
   (ByVal hWndParent As Long, ByVal hwnd As Long) As Long
Declare Function IsIconic Lib "user32"
   (ByVal hwnd As Long) As Long
Declare Function IsWindowVisible Lib "user32"
   (ByVal hwnd As Long) As Long
Declare Function IsWindowEnabled Lib "user32"
   (ByVal hwnd As Long) As Long
Declare Function IsWindowUnicode Lib "user32"
   (ByVal hwnd As Long) As Long
Declare Function IsWindow Lib "user32"
   (ByVal hwnd As Long) As Long
Declare Function IsZoomed Lib "user32"
   (ByVal hwnd As Long) As Long
```

The project's form, named mani1.frm, contains a number of label controls and a command button, as shown in Figure 8–1.

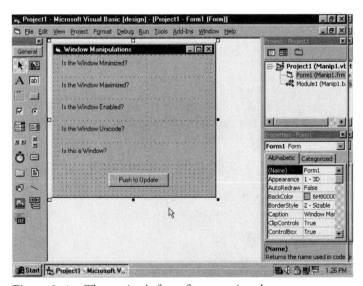

Figure 8–1   The project's form for reporting data.

In this simple project, information regarding the size of the window and so on is returned to a label caption when the command button is clicked. The code supporting this action is shown next.

```
Private Sub Command1_Click()
  Dim r&

  r& = IsIconic(hwnd)
  If r& <> 0 Then
    Label6.Caption = "Minimized"
  Else
    Label6.Caption = "Not Minimized"
  End If

  r& = IsZoomed(hwnd)
  If r& <> 0 Then
    Label7.Caption = "Maximized"
  Else
    Label7.Caption = "Not Maximized"
  End If

  r& = IsWindowEnabled(hwnd)
  If r& <> 0 Then
    Label8.Caption = "Enabled"
  Else
    Label8.Caption = "Not Enabled"
  End If

  r& = IsWindowUnicode(hwnd)
  If r& <> 0 Then
    Label9.Caption = "Unicode"
  Else
    Label9.Caption = "Not Unicode"
  End If

  r& = IsWindow(hwnd)
  If r& <> 0 Then
    Label10.Caption = "Window"
  Else
    Label10.Caption = "Not A Window"
  End If

End Sub
```

The window for which this information is being reported is, of course, Form1. Figure 8–2 shows the results for the initial window.

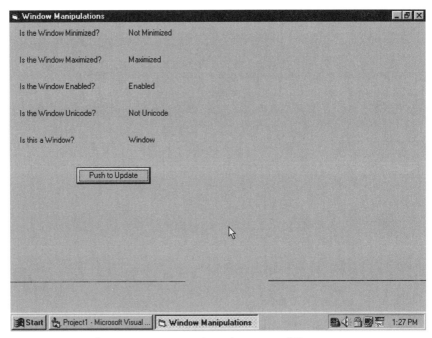

Figure 8–2 Information is returned on the status of Form1.

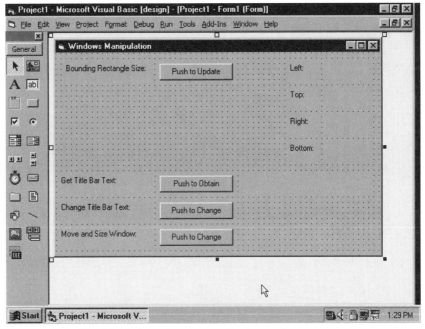

Figure 8–3 The initial form for the mani2.vbp project.

88

Application Two

The second example project is named mani2.vbp. This project contains a module file named mani2.bas containing a structure and several function declarations. Those declarations are shown in the following listing:

```
Type RECT
  Left As Long
  Top As Long
  Right As Long
  Bottom As Long
End Type

Declare Function GetWindowRect Lib "user32" (ByVal hwnd As Long,
lpRect As RECT) As Long
Declare Function GetWindowText Lib "user32" Alias "GetWindow-
TextA" (ByVal hwnd As Long, ByVal lpString As String, ByVal cch
As Long) As Long
Declare Function GetWindowTextLength Lib "user32" Alias
"GetWindowTextLengthA" (ByVal hwnd As Long) As Long
Declare Function SetWindowText Lib "user32" Alias "SetWindow-
TextA" (ByVal hwnd As Long, ByVal lpString As String) As Long
Declare Function MoveWindow Lib "user32" (ByVal hwnd As Long,
ByVal x As Long, ByVal y As Long, ByVal nWidth As Long, ByVal
nHeight As Long, ByVal bRepaint As Long) As Long
```

The project's form, named mani2.frm, contains a number of label controls and command buttons, as shown in Figure 8–3.

In this project, the size of the window (bounding rectangle) and title bar text can be returned to the screen. The project also allows you to force a text change for the title bar and then size and move the original window. The code supporting this action is shown next.

```
Private Sub Command1_Click()
  Dim r&
  Dim myrect As RECT

  r& = GetWindowRect(hwnd, myrect)
  Label5.Caption = myrect.Left
  Label6.Caption = myrect.Top
  Label7.Caption = myrect.Right
  Label8.Caption = myrect.Bottom
End Sub

Private Sub Command2_Click()
  Dim r&
  Dim mybuf$
```

```
    mybuf$ = String$(81, 0)
    r& = GetWindowText(hwnd, mybuf$, 80)
    Label9.Caption = mybuf$
End Sub

Private Sub Command3_Click()
  Dim r&

  'Force the window's title bar string to a new value
  r& = SetWindowText(hwnd, "This is the new title bar string")
End Sub

Private Sub Command4_Click()
  Dim r&

  'Force the Window to the new position and size.
  r& = MoveWindow(hwnd, 400, 200, 250, 250, True)
End Sub
```

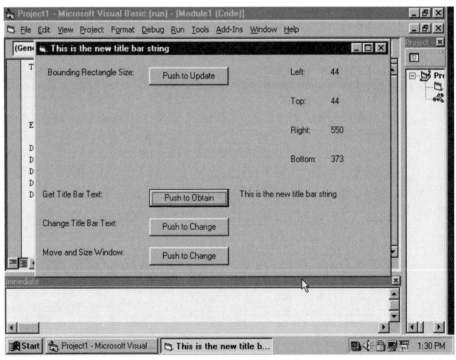

Figure 8–4   Reporting the results after several initial Windows values have been altered.

Figure 8–4 reports window information after several changes have been made to the window's original values.

Our work with Windows functions continues in Chapter 9 as we work with functions that allow us to change various Windows features.

Window Parameter and Information Functions

This is the third chapter, in a series of three, dealing specifically with Windows functions. We have grouped these chapters in order of control, manipulation, parameter, and information functions.

In this chapter, you will learn about functions that allow access to environment and system information, permit you to get and set system colors, and so on. In order to complete your study of the whole group, you'll also want to study the functions contained in Chapters 7 and 8.

API Parameter and Information Function Names and Descriptions

Table 9–1 shows 31 Windows API parameter and information functions and provides a brief description for their use.

The most popular functions in this group include the GetSystemInfo(), GlobalMemoryStatus(), GetVersionEx(), RegisterClass(), and RegisterClassEx() functions. Several of these functions will be included in the application at the end of this chapter.

Table 9–1   Parameter and Information Functions and Descriptions

Function	Description
AbortSystemShutdown	Aborts a system shutdown started by using the InitiateSystemShutdown() function.
AttachThreadInput	Attaches the input processing mechanism of one thread to the input processing mechanism of another thread.
Beep	Beeps simple tones on the speaker. This is a synchronous function and will not return control to its caller until the sound finishes.
EnumWindowStations	Enumerates the window stations in the system by passing each window station name to an application-defined callback function.
ExpandEnvironmentStrings	Expands environment variable strings and replaces them with their defined values.
FreeEnvironmentStrings	Frees a block of environment strings.
GetCommandLine	Gets a pointer to the command-line string for the current process.
GetComputerName	Gets the computer name established at system startup. This name is initialized from the system registry.
GetEnvironmentVariable	Gets the value of the variable from the environment block of the calling process. The value is a string of characters.
GetLastError	Gets the calling thread's last-error code value. This value is retained on a per thread basis. Thus, multiple threads do not overwrite each other's error codes.
GetSysColor	Gets the current color of the display element. These elements are the pieces of a window that appear on the system screen.
GetSystemInfo	Gets information for the current system.
GetSystemMetrics	Gets various system metrics and system configuration settings.
GetSystemPowerStatus	Gets the power status for the system. The status tells if the system is operating on line voltage or battery. If battery, also returns charging and battery life information.
GetUserName	Gets the user name for the current thread of the user currently logged onto the system.
GetVersion	Use GetVersionEx().
GetVersionEx	Gets extended information about the version of the operating system currently running.
GlobalMemoryStatus	Gets information on current available memory. Returns information on both physical and virtual memory.
InitiateSystemShutdown	Initiates a shutdown and optional restart of the computer.
MessageBeep	Beeps a waveform sound. The sound played is specified by an entry in the [sounds] section of the system registry.
RegisterClass	Same as RegisterClassEx() function but does not allow the use of the small icon.
RegisterClassEx	Registers a window class for subsequent use in calls to the CreateWindow() or CreateWindowEx() functions. Allows the use of the small icon.
SetComputerName	Sets the computer name to be used when the system is restarted.
SetEnvironmentVariable	Sets the value of an environment variable for the process.

(Continued)

Table 9–1   Parameter and Information Functions and Descriptions *(Continued)*

Function	Description
SetLastError or SetLastErrorEx	Sets the last-error code. In Windows 95 and NT, both functions are identical. The second parameter is not implemented.
SetSysColors	Sets the colors for various display elements. These elements make up the pieces of a window displayed on the system screen.
SetSystemPowerState	Suspends the system's operation. Operation can be suspended immediately or the system can poll for permission from all applications and device drivers.
Sleep	Suspends the execution of the current thread for the given interval.
SleepEx	Suspends the current thread's execution until (a) an I/O completion callback function is called, (b) an asynchronous procedure call (APC) is queued to the thread, or (c) the time-out interval elapses.
SystemParametersInfo	Queries or sets systemwide parameters.
UnregisterClass	Unregisters and removes a window class. Memory for the class is freed.

API Parameter and Information Function Declarations

The following listing contains the Windows API parameter and information function declarations found in the Win32api.txt file provided with Visual Basic. As we mentioned, there are additional functions related to this group of functions that are described in Chapters 7 and 8.

```
Declare Function AbortSystemShutdown Lib "advapi32.dll" Alias
  "AbortSystemShutdownA" (ByVal lpMachineName As String)
  As Long

Declare Function AttachThreadInput Lib "user32" Alias
  "AttachThreadInput" (ByVal idAttach As Long,
  ByVal idAttachTo As Long,
  ByVal fAttach As Long) As Long

Declare Function Beep Lib "kernel32" Alias
  "Beep" (ByVal dwFreq As Long,
  ByVal dwDuration As Long) As Long

Declare Function EnumWindowStations Lib "user32" Alias
  "EnumWindowStationsA" (ByVal lpEnumFunc As Long,
  ByVal lParam As Long) As Long

Declare Function ExpandEnvironmentStrings Lib "kernel32"
  Alias "ExpandEnvironmentStringsA" (ByVal lpSrc As String,
  ByVal lpDst As String, ByVal nSize As Long) As Long

Declare Function FreeEnvironmentStrings Lib "kernel32" Alias
  "FreeEnvironmentStringsA" (ByVal lpsz As String) As Long
```

```
Declare Function GetCommandLine Lib "kernel32" Alias
  "GetCommandLineA" () As String

Declare Function GetComputerName Lib "kernel32" Alias
  "GetComputerNameA" (ByVal lpBuffer As String,
  nSize As Long) As Long

Declare Function GetEnvironmentVariable Lib "kernel32" Alias
  "GetEnvironmentVariableA" (ByVal lpName As String,
  ByVal lpBuffer As String, ByVal nSize As Long) As Long

Declare Function GetLastError Lib "kernel32" Alias
  "GetLastError" () As Long

Declare Function GetSysColor Lib "user32" Alias
  "GetSysColor" (ByVal nIndex As Long) As Long

Declare Sub GetSystemInfo Lib "kernel32" Alias
  "GetSystemInfo" (lpSystemInfo As SYSTEM_INFO)

Declare Function GetSystemMetrics Lib "user32" Alias
  "GetSystemMetrics" (ByVal nIndex As Long) As Long

Declare Function GetSystemPowerStatus Lib "kernel32" Alias
  "GetSystemPowerStatus" (lpSystemPowerStatus As
  SYSTEM_POWER_STATUS) As Long

Declare Function GetUserName Lib "advapi32.dll" Alias
  "GetUserNameA" (ByVal lpBuffer As String,
  nSize As Long) As Long

Declare Function GetVersion Lib "kernel32" Alias
  "GetVersion" () As Long

Declare Function GetVersionEx Lib "kernel32" Alias
  "GetVersionExA" (ByVal lpVersionInformation As
  OSVERSIONINFO) As Long

Declare Sub GlobalMemoryStatus Lib "kernel32" Alias
  "GlobalMemoryStatus" (lpBuffer As MEMORYSTATUS)

Declare Function InitiateSystemShutdown Lib "advapi32.dll"
  Alias "InitiateSystemShutdownA" (ByVal lpMachineName As
  String, ByVal lpMessage As String,
  ByVal dwTimeout As Long,
  ByVal bForceAppsClosed As Long,
  ByVal bRebootAfterShutdown As Long) As Long

Declare Function MessageBeep Lib "user32" Alias
  "MessageBeep" (ByVal wType As Long) As Long

Declare Function RegisterClass Lib "user32" Alias
  "RegisterClass" (Class As WNDCLASS) As Long

Declare Function RegisterClassEx Lib "user32" Alias
  "RegisterClassExA" (pcWndClassEx As WNDCLASSEX) As Integer
```

```
Declare Function SetComputerName Lib "kernel32" Alias
  "SetComputerNameA" (ByVal lpComputerName As String) As Long

Declare Function SetEnvironmentVariable Lib "kernel32" Alias
  "SetEnvironmentVariableA" (ByVal lpName As String,
  ByVal lpValue As String) As Long

Declare Sub SetLastError Lib "kernel32" Alias
  "SetLastError" (ByVal dwErrCode As Long)

Declare Sub SetLastErrorEx Lib "user32" Alias
  "SetLastErrorEx" (ByVal dwErrCode As Long,
  ByVal dwType As Long)

Declare Function SetSysColors Lib "user32" Alias
  "SetSysColors" (ByVal nChanges As Long,
  lpSysColor As Long,
  lpColorValues As Long) As Long

Declare Function SetSystemPowerState Lib "kernel32" Alias
  "SetSystemPowerState" (ByVal fSuspend As Long,
  ByVal fForce As Long) As Long

Declare Sub Sleep Lib "kernel32" Alias
  "Sleep" (ByVal dwMilliseconds As Long)

Declare Function SleepEx Lib "kernel32" Alias
  "SleepEx" (ByVal dwMilliseconds As Long,
  ByVal bAlertable As Long) As Long

Declare Function SystemParametersInfo Lib "user32" Alias
  "SystemParametersInfoA" (ByVal uAction As Long,
  ByVal uParam As Long, ByVal lpvParam As Any,
  ByVal fuWinIni As Long) As Long

Declare Function UnregisterClass Lib "user32" Alias
  "UnregisterClassA" (ByVal lpClassName As String,
  ByVal hInstance As Long) As Long
```

Table 9–2 contains a brief description of the parameters used in the various parameter and information functions.

Table 9–2   Parameter and Information Function Parameters and Descriptions

Parameter	Description
balertable As Long	States if the function can terminate early because of an I/O completion callback function or an APC. If set to FALSE, the function does not return until the time-out period has elapsed.
bforceAppsClosed As Long	States if applications with unsaved changes are to be forcibly closed. TRUE—applications are closed; FALSE—a dialog box is displayed prompting the user to close the applications.

Table 9–2 Parameter and Information Function Parameters and Descriptions *(Continued)*

Parameter	Description
bRebootAfterShutdown As Long	Determines if the computer is to restart immediately after shutting down. TRUE—the computer will restart; FALSE—the system flushes all caches to disk, clears the screen, and indicates with a message that it is safe to power down.
Class As WNDCLASS	Structure must be filled with the appropriate class attributes before passing it to the function.
dwDuration As Long	NT only (95 ignores). Gives the duration of the sound in milliseconds.
dwErrCode As Long	Gives the last-error code for the thread.
dwFreq As Long	NT only (95 ignores). Gives the frequency, in hertz, of the sound. Value must be between 37 and 32,767.
dwMilliseconds As Long	Gives the time for the suspension in milliseconds. Use zero to force the thread to give up the remainder of its time slice to a thread of equal priority that is ready to run. A value of INFINITE causes an infinite delay.
dwTimeout As Long	Gives the time that the dialog box will be displayed, in seconds. As long as the dialog box is visible, the shutdown can be stopped with an AbortSystemShutdown() function call.
dwType	Gives the error type. Uses SLE_ constants.
fAttach As Long	Decides if to attach or detach the threads. TRUE—the threads are attached; FALSE—the threads are detached.
fForce As Long	Forced suspension. TRUE—the function sends a PBT_APMSUSPEND message to each application and driver, then suspends operation; FALSE—the function sends a PBT_APMQUERYSUSPEND message to each application to request permission to suspend operation.
fSuspend As Long	Suspension technique. TRUE—the system suspends using RAM-alive technique; FALSE—suspends using hibernate technique.
fuWinIni As Long	When a system parameter is being set, tells if the user profile is to be updated. This parameter can be zero or an SPIF_ constant.
hInstance As Long	ID of the instance of the module that created the class.
idAttach As Long	Gives the ID of the thread to be attached to another thread.
idAttachTo As Long	Gives the ID of the thread to be attached to.
lParam As Long	Gives a 32-bit application defined value to be passed to the callback function.
lpBuffer As MEMORYSTATUS	Structure holds information on current memory availability.
lpBuffer As String	Points to a buffer that receives the character string holding the computer's name, the value of the environment variable, or the user's logon name. The buffer must be large enough to hold the entire string.
lpClassName As String	Points to a string or is an integer atom. If a string, it gives the window class name.

(Continued)

Table 9–2   Parameter and Information Function Parameters and Descriptions *(Continued)*

Parameter	Description
lpColorValues As Long	Points to an array of unsigned long integers that holds the Red, Green, Blue (RGB) color value for each display element in the storage array.
lpDst As String	Points to a buffer that receives a copy of the source buffer. This takes place when all environment-variable name substitutions have been made.
lpEnumFunc As Long	Points to an application-defined EnumWindowStationProc() callback function.
lpMachineName As String	Pointer to the string that gives the network name of the computer where the shutdown is to be stopped. If lpMachineName is NULL or points to an empty string, the function stops the shutdown on the local computer.
lpMessage As String	Points to a string that gives a message to display in the shutdown dialog box.
lpName As String	Points to a string that gives the environment variable.
lpSrc As String	Points to a null-terminated string that can contain references to environment variable strings. The form is %variableName%
lpSysColor As Long	Points to an array of integers that shows which display elements will be changed.
lpSystemInfo As SYSTEM_INFO	Structure holds information returned by the function.
lpSystemPowerStatus As SYSTEM_POWER_STATUS	Structure holds information regarding system status information.
lpsz As String	Pointer to a block of environment strings. The pointer must be determined by calling the GetEnvironmentStrings() function.
lpValue As String	Points to a string containing the new value of the environment variable. A NULL value deleted it from the current process's environment.
lpVersionInformation As OSVERSIONINFO	Structure holds data on the operating system version. Set the dwOSVersionInfoSize member of the OSVERSIONINFO data structure to sizeof(OSVERSIONINFO) before calling this function.
lpvParam As Any	Depends on the system parameter being queried or set.
nChanges As Long	Gives the number of display elements in the array pointed to by the lpSysColor parameter.
nIndex As Long	Gives the display element whose color is to be retrieved using COLOR_ constants. (or) Gives the system metric or configuration setting to retrieve. Uses SM_ constants where all SM_CX* values are widths and SM_CY* values are heights.
nSize As Long	Gives the maximum number of characters that can be stored in the buffer. The count should include a terminating null character.

Table 9–2 Parameter and Information Function Parameters and Descriptions *(Continued)*

Parameter	Description
pcWndClassEx As WNDCLASSEX	Structure must be filled with the appropriate class attributes before passing it to the function.
uAction As Long	Gives the systemwide parameter to query or set using an SPI_ constant.
uParam As Long	Dependent on the system parameter being queried or set.
wType As Long	Gives the sound type using an MB_ constant.

Many of the parameters described in Table 9–2 use constant values. The Win21api.txt file lists the following constants for parameter and information functions:

```
'Win API COLOR_ Constants
Public Const COLOR_ACTIVEBORDER = 10
Public Const COLOR_ACTIVECAPTION = 2
Public Const COLOR_APPWORKSPACE = 12
Public Const COLOR_BACKGROUND = 1
Public Const COLOR_BTNFACE = 15
Public Const COLOR_BTNHIGHLIGHT = 20
Public Const COLOR_BTNSHADOW = 16
Public Const COLOR_BTNTEXT = 18
Public Const COLOR_CAPTIONTEXT = 9
Public Const COLOR_GRAYTEXT = 17
Public Const COLOR_HIGHLIGHT = 13
Public Const COLOR_HIGHLIGHTTEXT = 14
Public Const COLOR_INACTIVEBORDER = 11
Public Const COLOR_INACTIVECAPTION = 3
Public Const COLOR_INACTIVECAPTIONTEXT = 19
Public Const COLOR_MENU = 4
Public Const COLOR_MENUTEXT = 7
Public Const COLOR_SCROLLBAR = 0
Public Const COLOR_WINDOW = 5
Public Const COLOR_WINDOWFRAME = 6
Public Const COLOR_WINDOWTEXT = 8

'MessageBox() Flags
Public Const MB_ABORTRETRYIGNORE = &H2&
Public Const MB_APPLMODAL = &H0&
Public Const MB_COMPOSITE = &H2            ' use composite chars
Public Const MB_DEFAULT_DESKTOP_ONLY = &H20000
Public Const MB_DEFBUTTON1 = &H0&
Public Const MB_DEFBUTTON2 = &H100&
Public Const MB_DEFBUTTON3 = &H200&
Public Const MB_DEFMASK = &HF00&
```

```
Public Const MB_ICONASTERISK = &H40&
Public Const MB_ICONEXCLAMATION = &H30&
Public Const MB_ICONHAND = &H10&
Public Const MB_ICONINFORMATION = MB_ICONASTERISK
Public Const MB_ICONMASK = &HF0&
Public Const MB_ICONQUESTION = &H20&
Public Const MB_ICONSTOP = MB_ICONHAND
Public Const MB_MISCMASK = &HC000&
Public Const MB_MODEMASK = &H3000&
Public Const MB_NOFOCUS = &H8000&
Public Const MB_OK = &H0&
Public Const MB_OKCANCEL = &H1&
Public Const MB_PRECOMPOSED = &H1    'use precomposed chars
Public Const MB_RETRYCANCEL = &H5&
Public Const MB_SETFOREGROUND = &H10000
Public Const MB_SYSTEMMODAL = &H1000&
Public Const MB_TASKMODAL = &H2000&
Public Const MB_TYPEMASK = &HF&
Public Const MB_USEGLYPHCHARS = &H4    'use glyph chars
Public Const MB_YESNO = &H4&
Public Const MB_YESNOCANCEL = &H3&

'SLE_ Constants
Public Const SLE_ERROR = &H1
Public Const SLE_MINORERROR = &H2
Public Const SLE_WARNING = &H3

'GetSystemMetrics() codes
Public Const SM_CMETRICS = 44
Public Const SM_CMOUSEBUTTONS = 43
Public Const SM_CXBORDER = 5
Public Const SM_CXCURSOR = 13
Public Const SM_CXDLGFRAME = 7
Public Const SM_CXDOUBLECLK = 36
Public Const SM_CXFIXEDFRAME = SM_CXDLGFRAME
Public Const SM_CXFRAME = 32
Public Const SM_CXFULLSCREEN = 16
Public Const SM_CXHSCROLL = 21
Public Const SM_CXHTHUMB = 10
Public Const SM_CXICON = 11
Public Const SM_CXICONSPACING = 38
Public Const SM_CXMIN = 28
Public Const SM_CXMINTRACK = 34
Public Const SM_CXSCREEN = 0
Public Const SM_CXSIZE = 30
Public Const SM_CXSIZEFRAME = SM_CXFRAME
Public Const SM_CXVSCROLL = 2
Public Const SM_CYBORDER = 6
Public Const SM_CYCAPTION = 4
```

```
Public Const SM_CYCURSOR = 14
Public Const SM_CYDLGFRAME = 8
Public Const SM_CYDOUBLECLK = 37
Public Const SM_CYFIXEDFRAME = SM_CYDLGFRAME
Public Const SM_CYFRAME = 33
Public Const SM_CYFULLSCREEN = 17
Public Const SM_CYHSCROLL = 3
Public Const SM_CYICON = 12
Public Const SM_CYICONSPACING = 39
Public Const SM_CYKANJIWINDOW = 18
Public Const SM_CYMENU = 15
Public Const SM_CYMIN = 29
Public Const SM_CYMINTRACK = 35
Public Const SM_CYSCREEN = 1
Public Const SM_CYSIZE = 31
Public Const SM_CYSIZEFRAME = SM_CYFRAME
Public Const SM_CYVSCROLL = 20
Public Const SM_CYVTHUMB = 9
Public Const SM_DBCSENABLED = 42
Public Const SM_DEBUG = 22
Public Const SM_MENUDROPALIGNMENT = 40
Public Const SM_MOUSEPRESENT = 19
Public Const SM_PENWINDOWS = 41
Public Const SM_RESERVED1 = 24
Public Const SM_RESERVED2 = 25
Public Const SM_RESERVED3 = 26
Public Const SM_RESERVED4 = 27
Public Const SM_SWAPBUTTON = 23

'Parameter values for SystemParametersInfo()
Public Const SPI_GETACCESSTIMEOUT = 60
Public Const SPI_GETANIMATION = 72
Public Const SPI_GETBEEP = 1
Public Const SPI_GETBORDER = 5
Public Const SPI_GETDEFAULTINPUTLANG = 89
Public Const SPI_GETDRAGFULLWINDOWS = 38
Public Const SPI_GETFASTTASKSWITCH = 35
Public Const SPI_GETFILTERKEYS = 50
Public Const SPI_GETFONTSMOOTHING = 74
Public Const SPI_GETGRIDGRANULARITY = 18
Public Const SPI_GETHIGHCONTRAST = 66
Public Const SPI_GETICONMETRICS = 45
Public Const SPI_GETICONTITLELOGFONT = 31
Public Const SPI_GETICONTITLEWRAP = 25
Public Const SPI_GETKEYBOARDDELAY = 22
Public Const SPI_GETKEYBOARDPREF = 68
Public Const SPI_GETKEYBOARDSPEED = 10
Public Const SPI_GETLOWPOWERACTIVE = 83
Public Const SPI_GETLOWPOWERTIMEOUT = 79
```

```
Public Const SPI_GETMENUDROPALIGNMENT = 27
Public Const SPI_GETMINIMIZEDMETRICS = 43
Public Const SPI_GETMOUSE = 3
Public Const SPI_GETMOUSEKEYS = 54
Public Const SPI_GETMOUSETRAILS = 94
Public Const SPI_GETNONCLIENTMETRICS = 41
Public Const SPI_GETPOWEROFFACTIVE = 84
Public Const SPI_GETPOWEROFFTIMEOUT = 80
Public Const SPI_GETSCREENREADER = 70
Public Const SPI_GETSCREENSAVEACTIVE = 16
Public Const SPI_GETSCREENSAVETIMEOUT = 14
Public Const SPI_GETSERIALKEYS = 62
Public Const SPI_GETSHOWSOUNDS = 56
Public Const SPI_GETSOUNDSENTRY = 64
Public Const SPI_GETSTICKYKEYS = 58
Public Const SPI_GETTOGGLEKEYS = 52
Public Const SPI_GETWINDOWSEXTENSION = 92
Public Const SPI_GETWORKAREA = 48
Public Const SPI_ICONHORIZONTALSPACING = 13
Public Const SPI_ICONVERTICALSPACING = 24
Public Const SPI_LANGDRIVER = 12
Public Const SPI_SCREENSAVERRUNNING = 97
Public Const SPI_SETACCESSTIMEOUT = 61
Public Const SPI_SETANIMATION = 73
Public Const SPI_SETBEEP = 2
Public Const SPI_SETBORDER = 6
Public Const SPI_SETCURSORS = 87
Public Const SPI_SETDEFAULTINPUTLANG = 90
Public Const SPI_SETDESKPATTERN = 21
Public Const SPI_SETDESKWALLPAPER = 20
Public Const SPI_SETDOUBLECLICKTIME = 32
Public Const SPI_SETDOUBLECLKHEIGHT = 30
Public Const SPI_SETDOUBLECLKWIDTH = 29
Public Const SPI_SETDRAGFULLWINDOWS = 37
Public Const SPI_SETDRAGHEIGHT = 77
Public Const SPI_SETDRAGWIDTH = 76
Public Const SPI_SETFASTTASKSWITCH = 36
Public Const SPI_SETFILTERKEYS = 51
Public Const SPI_SETFONTSMOOTHING = 75
Public Const SPI_SETGRIDGRANULARITY = 19
Public Const SPI_SETHANDHELD = 78
Public Const SPI_SETHIGHCONTRAST = 67
Public Const SPI_SETICONMETRICS = 46
Public Const SPI_SETICONS = 88
Public Const SPI_SETICONTITLELOGFONT = 34
Public Const SPI_SETICONTITLEWRAP = 26
Public Const SPI_SETKEYBOARDDELAY = 23
Public Const SPI_SETKEYBOARDPREF = 69
```

```
Public Const SPI_SETKEYBOARDSPEED = 11
Public Const SPI_SETLANGTOGGLE = 91
Public Const SPI_SETLOWPOWERACTIVE = 85
Public Const SPI_SETLOWPOWERTIMEOUT = 81
Public Const SPI_SETMENUDROPALIGNMENT = 28
Public Const SPI_SETMINIMIZEDMETRICS = 44
Public Const SPI_SETMOUSE = 4
Public Const SPI_SETMOUSEBUTTONSWAP = 33
Public Const SPI_SETMOUSEKEYS = 55
Public Const SPI_SETMOUSETRAILS = 93
Public Const SPI_SETNONCLIENTMETRICS = 42
Public Const SPI_SETPENWINDOWS = 49
Public Const SPI_SETPOWEROFFACTIVE = 86
Public Const SPI_SETPOWEROFFTIMEOUT = 82
Public Const SPI_SETSCREENREADER = 71
Public Const SPI_SETSCREENSAVEACTIVE = 17
Public Const SPI_SETSCREENSAVETIMEOUT = 15
Public Const SPI_SETSERIALKEYS = 63
Public Const SPI_SETSHOWSOUNDS = 57
Public Const SPI_SETSOUNDSENTRY = 65
Public Const SPI_SETSTICKYKEYS = 59
Public Const SPI_SETTOGGLEKEYS = 53
Public Const SPI_SETWORKAREA = 47

'SystemParametersInfo flags
Public Const SPIF_SENDWININICHANGE = &H2
Public Const SPIF_UPDATEINIFILE = &H1
```

In addition to the constants listed in the Win32api.txt file, all of the structures used by these functions can be found there too. The following listing contains the structure declarations used by the functions included in this chapter:

```
Public Type MEMORYSTATUS
   dwLength As Long
   dwMemoryLoad As Long
   dwTotalPhys As Long
   dwAvailPhys As Long
   dwTotalPageFile As Long
   dwAvailPageFile As Long
   dwTotalVirtual As Long
   dwAvailVirtual As Long
End Type

Type OSVERSIONINFO
   dwOSVersionInfoSize As Long
   dwMajorVersion As Long
   dwMinorVersion As Long
   dwBuildNumber As Long
   dwPlatformId As Long
```

```
   szCSDVersion As String * 128 'Maintenance string
End Type

Type SYSTEM_INFO
  dwOemID As Long
  dwPageSize As Long
  lpMinimumApplicationAddress As Long
  lpMaximumApplicationAddress As Long
  dwActiveProcessorMask As Long
  dwNumberOrfProcessors As Long
  dwProcessorType As Long
  dwAllocationGranularity As Long
  dwReserved As Long
End Type

Type SYSTEM_POWER_STATUS
  ACLineStatus As Integer
  BatteryFlag As Integer
  BatteryLifePercent As Integer
  Reserved1
  BatteryLifeTime As Long
  BatteryFullLifeTime As Long
End Type

Type WNDCLASS
 style As Long
 lpfnwndproc As Long
 cbClsextra As Long
 cbWndExtra2 As Long
 hInstance As Long
 hIcon As Long
 hCursor As Long
 hbrBackground As Long
 lpszMenuName As String
 lpszClassName As String
End Type

Type WNDCLASSEX
  cbSize As Long
  style As Long
  lpfnWndProc As Long
  cbClsExtra As Long
  cbWndExtra As Long
  hInstance As Long
  hIcon As Long
  hCursor As Long
  hbrBackground As Long
  lpszMenuName As String
  lpszClassName As String
  hIconSm As Long
End Type
```

In the next section, we'll examine an application that make use of the GetSystemInfo(), GlobalMemoryStatus(), and GetVersionEx() functions.

Example Applications

This section contains a programming example that serves to illustrate the use of the functions contained in this chapter. Three very important functions are used in this application: GetSystemInfo(), GlobalMemoryStatus(), and GetVersionEx(). They allow us to retrieve information on the system, system memory, and Windows version numbers.

This Visual Basic project is named sys1.vbp and contains a form for drawing text on and a module file for structure and function declarations. The following listing shows the contents of the sys1.bas module file for this project. All of this information is provided within the Win32api.txt file.

```
Public Type SYSTEM_INFO
   dwOemId As Long
   dwPageSize As Long
   lpMinimumApplicationAddress As Long
   lpMaximumApplicationAddress As Long
   dwActiveProcessorMask As Long
   dwNumberOfProcessors As Long
   dwProcessorType As Long
   dwAllocationGranularity As Long
   dwReserved As Long
End Type

Public Type MEMORYSTATUS
   dwLength As Long
   dwMemoryLoad As Long
   dwTotalPhys As Long
   dwAvailPhys As Long
   dwTotalPageFile As Long
   dwAvailPageFile As Long
   dwTotalVirtual As Long
   dwAvailVirtual As Long
End Type

Type OSVERSIONINFO
   dwOSVersionInfoSize As Long
   dwMajorVersion As Long
   dwMinorVersion As Long
   dwBuildNumber As Long
   dwPlatformId As Long
   szCSDVersion As String * 128
End Type
```

```
Declare Sub GetSystemInfo Lib "kernel32"
  (lpSystemInfo As SYSTEM_INFO)
Declare Sub GlobalMemoryStatus Lib "kernel32"
  (lpBuffer As MEMORYSTATUS)
Declare Function GetVersionEx Lib "kernel32"
  Alias "GetVersionExA"
  (lpVersionInformation As OSVERSIONINFO) As Long
```

The project's form contains a Form_Load() subroutine. Here is the code that supports the information we wish to obtain.

```
Private Sub Form_Load()
  Dim r&
  Dim ThisSystem As SYSTEM_INFO
  Dim ThisMemory As MEMORYSTATUS
  Dim OS As OSVERSIONINFO
  Dim osvi As Integer
  GetSystemInfo ThisSystem
  GlobalMemoryStatus ThisMemory

  'Find Intel Processor Type
  If ThisSystem.dwProcessorType = 586 Then
    Text1.Text = "Intel Pentium Processor or clone"
    ElseIf ThisSystem.dwProcessorType = 486 Then
      Text1.Text = "Intel 80486 Processor or clone"
        ElseIf ThisSystem.dwProcessorType = 386 Then
          Text1.Text = "Intel 80386 Processor or clone"
            Else
              Text1.Text = "Unknown Processor Type"
  End If

  'Find Number of Intel Processors
  Text2.Text = ThisSystem.dwNumberOfProcessors

  'Set Structure Size
  OS.dwOSVersionInfoSize = 148
  'Get Windows Version Information
  r& = GetVersionEx(OS)
  Text3.Text = Str$(OS.dwMajorVersion) + "." +
               LTrim$(OS.dwMinorVersion) + "." +
               LTrim$(OS.dwBuildNumber)

  'Find memory information
  Text4.Text = ThisMemory.dwTotalPhys \ 1024
End Sub
```

The GetSystemInfo() function is capable of returning processor information on processors other than Intel's line. However, to demonstrate this function, the application only checks for Intel processors (or clones) from the Pentium down to the 80386.

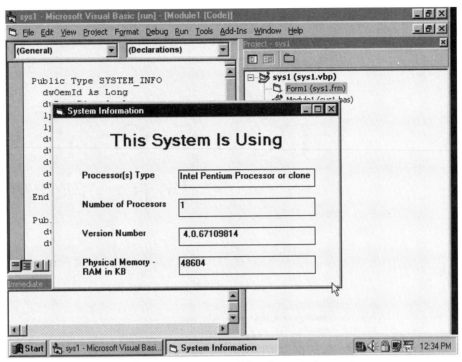

Figure 9–1   System information is returned by the sys1.vbp project.

The complete Windows version information is obtained with a call to the GetVersionEx() function. The version number is built from three pieces of information: *dwMajorVersion*, *dwMinorVersion*, and *dwBuildNumber*.

When the application is executed on our system, the information shown in Figure 9–1 is returned to the window.

Chapter 10

Device Context Functions

A *Device Context* (DC) is the gateway under Windows for sending all drawing and text to a device such as the screen or printer. Drawing and text output is never sent directly to the device. Drawing and text can also be sent to memory via a device context. When the DC is associated with memory rather than a physical device, it is often referred to as a *memory device context*. Most device contexts use a coordinate system (Chapter 11) and may also use clipping regions (Chapter 12).

A handle is used to provide communications to a specific device context. For example, you'll often see a generic *hdc* used in drawing and text functions. Likewise, the handle to a memory device context often uses the *hmdc* handle.

Device contexts fit into three broad categories: cached, user, and private. A cached device context is provided by Windows for all internal devices such as the screen, memory, and so on. Caching is used to conserve resources. User device contexts are created by the user when the need arises by using functions such as CreateDC(). Private device contexts exists for certain windows classes. The device context for private device contexts can be obtained with a call to a function such as GetDC().

In this chapter we'll examine the GetDeviceCaps() function as it relates to a device context. Throughout the book, you will gain experience with other device context functions.

Table 10–1   Device Context Functions and Descriptions

Parameter	Description
CreateCompatibleDC	Creates a memory DC compatible with the specific device DC.
CreateDC	Creates a DC for the specific device.
CreateIC	Creates an Information Context (IC) for the specific device.
DeleteDC	Deletes a DC or IC for the specific device.
GetDC	Gets a DC for the specific window.
GetDCEx	Same as GetDC(), with additional options.
GetDCOrgEx	Gets the origin, in screen coordinates, for the specific DC.
GetDeviceCaps	Gets information on the specific device's capabilities for the given DC.
GetWindowDC	Gets the DC for the whole window.
ReleaseDC	Releases the DC.
RestoreDC	Restores a saved DC from the DC stack.
SaveDC	Saves a DC on the DC stack.
ScrollDC	Scrolls a rectangle within a window specified by a DC.
WindowFromDC	Gets the handle for a window associated with a DC.

API Device Context Function Names and Descriptions

Table 10–1 shows 14 functions that are directly or closely related to the device context. Table 10–1 lists the functions and gives brief descriptions for their use.

The two functions we've used the most when creating applications using the Windows API when working with device contexts are CreateDC() and DeleteDC(). However, it is the GetDeviceCaps() function that returns the important information regarding any device context. The example application in this chapter will show you how to retrieve specific device context information with the use of this function.

API Device Context Function Declarations

The following listing contains the Windows API device context function declarations found in the Win32api.txt file provided with Visual Basic. As we mentioned earlier, there are additional functions related to device contexts that are described in Chapters 11 and 12.

```
Declare Function CreateCompatibleDC Lib "gdi32" Alias
  "CreateCompatibleDC" (ByVal hdc As Long) As Long

Declare Function CreateDC Lib "gdi32" Alias "CreateDCA"
  (ByVal lpDriverName As String,
  ByVal lpDeviceName As String, ByVal lpOutput As String,
  lpInitData As DEVMODE) As Long
```

```
Declare Function CreateIC Lib "gdi32" Alias "CreateICA"
  (ByVal lpDriverName As String,
  ByVal lpDeviceName As String,
  ByVal lpOutput As String, lpInitData As DEVMODE) As Long

Declare Function DeleteDC Lib "gdi32" Alias "DeleteDC"
  (ByVal hdc As Long) As Long

Declare Function GetDC Lib "user32" Alias "GetDC"
  (ByVal hwnd As Long) As Long

Declare Function GetDCEx Lib "user32" Alias "GetDCEx"
  (ByVal hwnd As Long, ByVal hrgnclip As Long,
  ByVal fdwOptions As Long) As Long

Declare Function GetDCOrgEx Lib "gdi32" Alias "GetDCOrgEx"
  (ByVal hdc As Long, lpPoint As POINTAPI) As Long

Declare Function GetDeviceCaps Lib "gdi32" Alias
  GetDeviceCaps" (ByVal hdc As Long,
  ByVal nIndex As Long) As Long

Declare Function GetWindowDC Lib "user32" Alias
  "GetWindowDC" (ByVal hwnd As Long) As Long

Declare Function ReleaseDC Lib "user32" Alias
  "ReleaseDC" (ByVal hwnd As Long,
  ByVal hdc As Long) As Long

Declare Function RestoreDC Lib "gdi32" Alias "RestoreDC"
  (ByVal hdc As Long, ByVal nSavedDC As Long) As Long

Declare Function SaveDC Lib "gdi32" Alias "SaveDC"
  (ByVal hdc As Long) As Long

Declare Function ScrollDC Lib "user32" Alias "ScrollDC"
  (ByVal hdc As Long, ByVal dx As Long, ByVal dy As Long,
  lprcScroll As RECT, lprcClip As RECT,
  ByVal hrgnUpdate As Long, lprcUpdate As RECT) As Long

Declare Function WindowFromDC Lib "user32" Alias
  "WindowFromDC" (ByVal hdc As Long) As Long
```

Table 10–2 contains a brief list and description of the parameters used in the various device context functions.

Many of the parameters described in Table 10–2 use constant values, also included in the Win32api.txt file. The following listings are the constants used by the device context functions.

The first listing gives the parameter information returned by *nIndex* for the GetDeviceCaps() function.

Table 10–2 Device Context Function Parameters and Descriptions

Parameter	Description
dx As Long	Units to scroll in horizontal direction.
dy As Long	Units to scroll in vertical direction.
fdwOptions As Long	DCX_ values that can be combined.
hdc As Long	Handle to the Device Context (DC).
hrgnclip As Long	Clipping region used with the window.
hrgnUpdate As Long	Region set to the area uncovered by scrolling.
hwnd As Long	Handle of window where DC is retrieved.
lpDeviceName As String	Name of device to use.
lpDriverName As String	vbNullString—passes a null.
	DISPLAY—get DC for screen.
	WINSPOOL—access to printer driver.
lpInitData As DEVMODE	Structure holds values for initialization.
lpOutput As String	vbNullString—passes a null.
lpPoint As POINTAPI	POINTAPI structure holds the origin for the screen coordinates of the DC.
lprcClip As RECT	RECT structure holds the clipping region where scrolling takes place.
lprcScroll As RECT	RECT structure holds rectangle to scroll.
lprcUpdate As RECT	RECT structure holds rectangular area uncovered by scrolling.
nIndex As Long	An index into the GetDeviceCaps index table.
nSavedDC As Long	ID of the Device Context to restore. A (-1) returns the most recently saved DC.

```
'Device Parameters for GetDeviceCaps()
Public Const DRIVERVERSION = 0      'Device driver version
Public Const TECHNOLOGY = 2         'Device classification
Public Const HORZSIZE = 4           'Horizontal size in
                                    'millimeters

Public Const VERTSIZE = 6           'Vertical size in
                                    'millimeters

Public Const HORZRES = 8            'Horizontal width in
                                    'pixels

Public Const VERTRES = 10           'Vertical width in
                                    'pixels

Public Const BITSPIXEL = 12         'Number of bits per pixel
Public Const PLANES = 14            'Number of planes
Public Const NUMBRUSHES = 16        'Number of brushes the
                                    'device has

Public Const NUMPENS = 18           'Number of pens the
                                    'device has
```

```
Public Const NUMMARKERS = 20        'Number of markers the
                                    'device has

Public Const NUMFONTS = 22          'Number of fonts the
                                    'device has

Public Const NUMCOLORS = 24         'Number of colors the
                                    'device supports

Public Const PDEVICESIZE = 26       'Size required for
                                    'device descriptor

Public Const CURVECAPS = 28         'Curve capabilities
Public Const LINECAPS = 30          'Line capabilities
Public Const POLYGONALCAPS = 32     'Polygonal capabilities
Public Const TEXTCAPS = 34          'Text capabilities
Public Const CLIPCAPS = 36          'Clipping capabilities
Public Const RASTERCAPS = 38        'Bitblt capabilities
Public Const ASPECTX = 40           'Length of the X leg
Public Const ASPECTY = 42           'Length of the Y leg
Public Const ASPECTXY = 44          'Length of the hypotenuse

Public Const LOGPIXELSX = 88        'Logical pixels/inch in X
Public Const LOGPIXELSY = 90        'Logical pixels/inch in Y

Public Const SIZEPALETTE = 104      'Number of entries in
                                       physical palette
Public Const NUMRESERVED = 106      'Number of reserved
                                    'entries in palette
Public Const COLORRES = 108         'Actual color resolution
```

The following listing gives the parameter information returned by *fdwOptions* for the GetDCEx() function.

```
Public Const DCX_WINDOW = &H1&          'DC obtained from
                                        'window.
Public Const DCX_CACHE = &H2&           'DC obtained from
                                        'cache.
Public Const DCX_NORESETATTRS = &H4&    'DC is not reset
                                        'to default attributes.
Public Const DCX_CLIPCHILDREN = &H8&    'Child windows not
                                        'affected by clip.
Public Const DCX_CLIPSIBLINGS = &H10&   'Sibling windows
                                        'above hWnd not
                                        'affected.
Public Const DCX_PARENTCLIP = &H20&     'Replaces class
                                        'styles.
Public Const DCX_EXCLUDERGN = &H40&     'Excludes hrgnClip
                                        'region.
Public Const DCX_INTERSECTRGN = &H80&   'Intersects hrgnClip
                                        'region.
```

```
Public Const DCX_EXCLUDEUPDATE = &H100& 'Excludes updates
                                        'region.
Public Const DCX_INTERSECTUPDATE = &H200& 'Intersects region
                                          'given by update.

Public Const DCX_LOCKWINDOWUPDATE = &H400& 'Permits drawing to
                                           'a locked window.

Public Const DCX_NORECOMPUTE = &H100000 'Does not recompute
                                        'the DC.
Public Const DCX_VALIDATE = &H200000     'Validates the DC
```

The following listing gives the parameter information used by functions employing the DEVMODE structure.

```
'current version of specification
Public Const DM_SPECVERSION = &H320

'field selection bits
Public Const DM_ORIENTATION = &H1&
Public Const DM_PAPERSIZE = &H2&
Public Const DM_PAPERLENGTH = &H4&
Public Const DM_PAPERWIDTH = &H8&
Public Const DM_SCALE = &H10&
Public Const DM_COPIES = &H100&
Public Const DM_DEFAULTSOURCE = &H200&
Public Const DM_PRINTQUALITY = &H400&
Public Const DM_COLOR = &H800&
Public Const DM_DUPLEX = &H1000&
Public Const DM_YRESOLUTION = &H2000&
Public Const DM_TTOPTION = &H4000&
Public Const DM_COLLATE As Long = &H8000
Public Const DM_FORMNAME As Long = &H10000

'orientation selections
Public Const DMORIENT_PORTRAIT = 1
Public Const DMORIENT_LANDSCAPE = 2

'paper selections
Public Const DMPAPER_LETTER = 1
'Letter 8 1/2 x 11 in
Public Const DMPAPER_FIRST = DMPAPER_LETTER
'Letter Small 8 1/2 x 11 in
Public Const DMPAPER_LETTERSMALL = 2
'Tabloid 11 x 17 in
Public Const DMPAPER_TABLOID = 3
'Ledger 17 x 11 in
Public Const DMPAPER_LEDGER = 4
'Legal 8 1/2 x 14 in
Public Const DMPAPER_LEGAL = 5
'Statement 5 1/2 x 8 1/2 in
```

```
Public Const DMPAPER_STATEMENT = 6
'Executive 7 1/4 x 10 1/2 in
Public Const DMPAPER_EXECUTIVE = 7
'A3 297 x 420 mm
Public Const DMPAPER_A3 = 8
'A4 210 x 297 mm
Public Const DMPAPER_A4 = 9
'A4 Small 210 x 297 mm
Public Const DMPAPER_A4SMALL = 10
'A5 148 x 210 mm
Public Const DMPAPER_A5 = 11
'B4 250 x 354
Public Const DMPAPER_B4 = 12
'B5 182 x 257 mm
Public Const DMPAPER_B5 = 13
'Folio 8 1/2 x 13 in
Public Const DMPAPER_FOLIO = 14
'Quarto 215 x 275 mm
Public Const DMPAPER_QUARTO = 15
'10x14 in
Public Const DMPAPER_10X14 = 16
'11x17 in
Public Const DMPAPER_11X17 = 17
'Note 8 1/2 x 11 in
Public Const DMPAPER_NOTE = 18
'Envelope #9 3 7/8 x 8 7/8
Public Const DMPAPER_ENV_9 = 19
'Envelope #10 4 1/8 x 9 1/2
Public Const DMPAPER_ENV_10 = 20
'Envelope #11 4 1/2 x 10 3/8
Public Const DMPAPER_ENV_11 = 21
'Envelope #12 4 \276 x 11
Public Const DMPAPER_ENV_12 = 22
'Envelope #14 5 x 11 1/2
Public Const DMPAPER_ENV_14 = 23
'C size sheet
Public Const DMPAPER_CSHEET = 24
'D size sheet
Public Const DMPAPER_DSHEET = 25
'E size sheet
Public Const DMPAPER_ESHEET = 26
'Envelope DL 110 x 220mm
Public Const DMPAPER_ENV_DL = 27
'Envelope C5 162 x 229 mm
Public Const DMPAPER_ENV_C5 = 28
'Envelope C3 324 x 458 mm
Public Const DMPAPER_ENV_C3 = 29
'Envelope C4 229 x 324 mm
```

```
Public Const DMPAPER_ENV_C4 = 30
'Envelope C6 114 x 162 mm
Public Const DMPAPER_ENV_C6 = 31
'Envelope C65 114 x 229 mm
Public Const DMPAPER_ENV_C65 = 32
'Envelope B4 250 x 353 mm
Public Const DMPAPER_ENV_B4 = 33
'Envelope B5 176 x 250 mm
Public Const DMPAPER_ENV_B5 = 34
'Envelope B6 176 x 125 mm
Public Const DMPAPER_ENV_B6 = 35
'Envelope 110 x 230 mm
Public Const DMPAPER_ENV_ITALY = 36
'Envelope Monarch 3.875 x 7.5 in
Public Const DMPAPER_ENV_MONARCH = 37
'6 3/4 Envelope 3 5/8 x 6 1/2 in
Public Const DMPAPER_ENV_PERSONAL = 38
'US Std Fanfold 14 7/8 x 11 in
Public Const DMPAPER_FANFOLD_US = 39
'German Std Fanfold 8 1/2 x 12 in
Public Const DMPAPER_FANFOLD_STD_GERMAN = 40
'German Legal Fanfold 8 1/2 x 13 in
Public Const DMPAPER_FANFOLD_LGL_GERMAN = 41
Public Const DMPAPER_LAST = DMPAPER_FANFOLD_LGL_GERMAN
Public Const DMPAPER_USER = 256

'bin selections
Public Const DMBIN_UPPER = 1
Public Const DMBIN_FIRST = DMBIN_UPPER
Public Const DMBIN_ONLYONE = 1
Public Const DMBIN_LOWER = 2
Public Const DMBIN_MIDDLE = 3
Public Const DMBIN_MANUAL = 4
Public Const DMBIN_ENVELOPE = 5
Public Const DMBIN_ENVMANUAL = 6
Public Const DMBIN_AUTO = 7
Public Const DMBIN_TRACTOR = 8
Public Const DMBIN_SMALLFMT = 9
Public Const DMBIN_LARGEFMT = 10
Public Const DMBIN_LARGECAPACITY = 11
Public Const DMBIN_CASSETTE = 14
Public Const DMBIN_LAST = DMBIN_CASSETTE

'device specific bins start
Public Const DMBIN_USER = 256 here

'print qualities
Public Const DMRES_DRAFT = (-1)
Public Const DMRES_LOW = (-2)
```

```
Public Const DMRES_MEDIUM = (-3)
Public Const DMRES_HIGH = (-4)

'color enable/disable for color printers
Public Const DMCOLOR_MONOCHROME = 1
Public Const DMCOLOR_COLOR = 2

'duplex enable
Public Const DMDUP_SIMPLEX = 1
Public Const DMDUP_VERTICAL = 2
Public Const DMDUP_HORIZONTAL = 3

'TrueType options
'print TT fonts as graphics
Public Const DMTT_BITMAP = 1
'download TT fonts as soft fonts
Public Const DMTT_DOWNLOAD = 2
'substitute device fonts for TT
Public Const DMTT_SUBDEV = 3 fonts

'Collation selections
Public Const DMCOLLATE_FALSE = 0
Public Const DMCOLLATE_TRUE = 1

'DEVMODE dmDisplayFlags flags
Public Const DM_GRAYSCALE = &H1
Public Const DM_INTERLACED = &H2
```

The function parameters often make additional use of unique structures. Here is a listing of the structures used by these functions. Structure types can also be found in the Win32api.txt file.

```
Type DEVMODE
  dmDeviceName As String * CCHDEVICENAME
  dmSpecVersion As Integer
  dmDriverVersion As Integer
  dmSize As Integer
  dmDriverExtra As Integer
  dmFields As Long
  dmOrientation As Integer
  dmPaperSize As Integer
  dmPaperLength As Integer
  dmPaperWidth As Integer
  dmScale As Integer
  dmCopies As Integer
  dmDefaultSource As Integer
  dmPrintQuality As Integer
  dmColor As Integer
  dmDuplex As Integer
  dmYResolution As Integer
  dmTTOption As Integer
```

```
            dmCollate As Integer
            dmFormName As String * CCHFORMNAME
            dmUnusedPadding As Integer
            dmBitsPerPel As Integer
            dmPelsWidth As Long
            dmPelsHeight As Long
            dmDisplayFlags As Long
            dmDisplayFrequency As Long
        End Type

        Type POINTAPI
          x As Long
          y As Long
        End Type

        Type RECT
          Left As Long
          Top As Long
          Right As Long
          Bottom As Long
        End Type
```

Example Application

The programming example in this section illustrates how information on a device context can be returned with the use of the GetDeviceCaps() function. This is an important function that returns information on display resolutions, brush and pen resources, aspect ratios, and so on.

The GetDeviceCaps() function is easy to use. The project is named Device1.vbp. In the next listing, Device1.bas, contains the declaration for the function. As you know, this declaration can be copied directly from the Win32api.txt file.

```
Dim hDC As Long

Declare Function GetDeviceCaps Lib "Gdi32" (ByVal hDC As Long,
ByVal nIndex As Long) As Long
```

This project's form, Device1.frm, contains a Form_Load() subroutine. Here is the code for accessing device data with the GetDeviceCaps() function.

```
Private Sub Form_Load()
  Dim devicedata As Long

  'horizontal size of display in mm
  devicedata = GetDeviceCaps(hDC, 4)
  Label16.Caption = Str$(devicedata)
```

```
'vertical size of display in mm
devicedata = GetDeviceCaps(hDC, 6)
Label17.Caption = Str$(devicedata)

'horizontal width in pixels
devicedata = GetDeviceCaps(hDC, 8)
Label18.Caption = Str$(devicedata)

'vertical height in pixels
devicedata = GetDeviceCaps(hDC, 10)
Label19.Caption = Str$(devicedata)

'number of bits per pixel
devicedata = GetDeviceCaps(hDC, 12)
Label20.Caption = Str$(devicedata)

'number of color planes
devicedata = GetDeviceCaps(hDC, 14)
Label21.Caption = Str$(devicedata)

'number of brushes
devicedata = GetDeviceCaps(hDC, 16)
Label22.Caption = Str$(devicedata)

'number of pens
devicedata = GetDeviceCaps(hDC, 18)
Label23.Caption = Str$(devicedata)

'number of markers
devicedata = GetDeviceCaps(hDC, 20)
Label24.Caption = Str$(devicedata)

'number of fonts
devicedata = GetDeviceCaps(hDC, 22)
Label25.Caption = Str$(devicedata)

'number of supported colors
devicedata = GetDeviceCaps(hDC, 24)
Label26.Caption = Str$(devicedata)

'aspect for x
devicedata = GetDeviceCaps(hDC, 40)
Label27.Caption = Str$(devicedata)

'aspect for y
devicedata = GetDeviceCaps(hDC, 42)
Label28.Caption = Str$(devicedata)

'aspect for xy
devicedata = GetDeviceCaps(hDC, 44)
Label29.Caption = Str$(devicedata)

'logical horizontal pixels/inch
devicedata = GetDeviceCaps(hDC, 88)
Label30.Caption = Str$(devicedata)
```

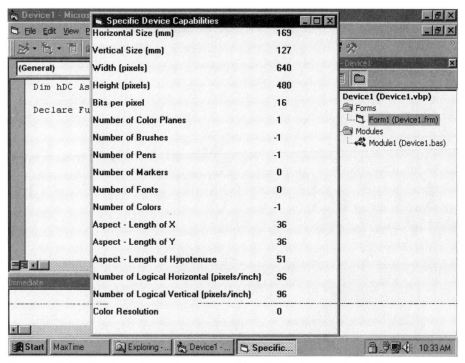

Figure 10–1   Device information returned by the GetDeviceCaps() function.

```
'logical vertical pixels/inch
devicedata = GetDeviceCaps(hDC, 90)
Label32.Caption = Str$(devicedata)

'logical horizontal pixels/inch
devicedata = GetDeviceCaps(hDC, 108)
Label35.Caption = Str$(devicedata)

End Sub
```

In this example, device information is returned on the display device and printed to the form. The information for our Toshiba Tecra 730CDT computer is shown in Figure 10–1.

Your computer will probably return different information. In Chapter 15 you'll learn how to create a memory device context. You might want to modify this application to return information about that device by passing the handle *hmdc* to the GetDeviceCaps() function.

This application was kept intentionally short. You might have noticed that we cheated just a bit. Instead of bringing the GetDeviceCaps() constants forward to this application, we just used the numerical equivalents for the constant values. These constants and numeric equivalents were shown in an earlier listing.

Chapter 11

Scaling and
Coordinate Functions

The Windows API allows programmers access to a variety of mapping modes, scaling, and coordinate functions when drawing to a window. These functions allow you to set the drawing surface size, coordinates, extents, origins, and so on. They allow more control over the DC device's drawing surface than the default MM_TEXT drawing mode and coordinates. The first programming example in this chapter will illustrate the use of many of these functions.

Windows NT programmers can also take advantage of World Transform functions, such as SetWorldTransform(). These powerful functions, in conjunction with the XFORM structure, allow the viewport to be rotated, sheared, and so on. A second programming example will illustrate how this function is used.

Many of the functions discussed in this chapter are closely associated with the device context (DC) functions described in Chapter 10 and the Clipping and Region functions described in Chapter 12. You might want to consider the examples in these chapters in order to expand your understanding of scaling and coordinate functions presented in this chapter.

Mapping Modes

The Windows Graphic Device Interface (GDI) operates, by default, in a pixel co-ordinate mode. It obtains information about the device driver and adjusts its graphics output to produce a figure in the correct aspect ratio and in the correct resolution for the hardware device. Seven other mapping modes arc available for drawing in metric, English, and user-defined units. The default mapping mode is MM_TEXT. If you are drawing to a VGA sized window, the extent will be set to 0 to 639 pixels horizontally and 0 to 479 pixels vertically.

Many applications use other drawing modes, such as MM_ISOTROPIC. This drawing mode will be highlighted in the first application in this chapter.

Information regarding the installed hardware that the GDI must contend with can be obtained by using the GetDeviceCaps() function. This function, discussed in Chapter 10, returns information on numerous hardware device attributes.

All the GDI graphics functions are dependent on the selected mapping mode. As mentioned earlier, the default mapping mode is MM_TEXT which measures point values in pixels. Table 11–1 lists all of the mapping modes available to the programmer.

Table 11–1   Windows Mapping Modes

Mode	Meaning
MM_ANISOTROPIC	Arbitrary units with arbitrarily scaled axes.
MM_HIENGLISH	Logical unit mapped to 0.001 inch.
	Positive x is to the right.
	Positive y is up.
MM_HIMETRIC	Logical unit mapped to 0.01 millimeter.
	Positive x is to the right.
	Positive y is up.
MM_ISOTROPIC	Arbitrary units with equally scaled axes.
MM_LOMETRIC	Logical unit mapped to 0.1 millimeter.
	Positive x is to the right.
	Positive y is up.
MM_LOENGLISH	Logical unit mapped to 0.01 inch.
	Positive x is to the right.
	Positive y is up.
MM_TEXT	Logical unit mapped to device pixel.
	Positive x is to the right.
	Positive y is down.
MM_TWIPS	Logical unit mapped to 1/20 of printer's point.
	Positive x is to the right.
	Positive y is up.

The mapping mode can be changed with a simple call to the SetMapMode() function. Regardless of the mapping mode selected, it is Windows' responsibility to map the given logical coordinates to device coordinates.

Coordinate Systems and Scaling Modes

Windows coordinate and scaling functions free the programmer from drawing to actual physical screen coordinates. Windows uses a logical coordinate system that maps to the physical screen (or device) coordinates. The advantage to this technique is that Windows handles all of the transformations for you. Under this system, it is possible to set the origin (0, 0) for a chart at the physical coordinates of (100, 100) in the window. Then instead of using (100, 100) as you would have been required to do under DOS, for example, you send (0, 0) and Windows automatically handles the transformation. In another case, you may require the y-axis value to increase upward from the bottom of the window. Under DOS, you must write the transformation. Under Windows, it is automatically handled by the selected coordinate system (see the first programming application).

Logical coordinates also allow you to scale the coordinate system to fit your needs. Windows then adjusts those coordinates to fit screens, such as VGA or SVGA, automatically.

For special manipulations, two functions allow conversions between logical and physical coordinate systems: DPtoLP() and LPtoDP().

Windows NT—World Coordinates

Windows 95 and NT applications take advantage of mapping logical coordinates to physical device coordinates. Windows NT also has the advantage of being able to perform world coordinate transformations.

Under Windows 95, the coordinate system is fixed on the x-y plane. The y-axis points up and down and the x-axis points left and right. The world coordinate system gives Windows NT applications the ability to rotate or shear the x-y plane. So, while Windows 95 rectangles, drawn with the Rectangle() function, could only exist on a standard x-y plane, Windows NT allows those same rectangles to be drawn at any angle by rotating the coordinate system. In addition, the coordinate system can then be sheared to create dramatic graphics effects.

The XFORM structure is associated with the world-space transform. This structure is unique in that its members are of type double. By using appropriate values in XFORM, the world coordinates for a window or viewport can be rotated. Angles values are given in radians. You can convert from degrees to radians by using the conversion 2 * pi = 360 degrees.

Table 11–2   XFORM Parameters

Function Member	When Used For
eM11	scaling: horizontal component.
	rotation: cosine of angle.
	reflection: horizontal component.
eM12	shear: horizontal proportionality constant.
	rotation: sine of angle.
eM21	shear: vertical proportionality constant.
	rotation: negative sine of angle.
eM22	scaling: vertical component.
	rotation: cosine of angle.
	reflection: vertical component.
eDx	Horizontal translation component (offset).
eDy	Vertical translation component (offset).

The XFORM structure can specify world-space to page-space transformations as shown in Table 11–2.

The offset values for *eDx* and *eDy* set the point of rotation for the center of a figure drawn to the window. The SetWorldTransform() function must be called each time the structure's member values are changed. The second application in this chapter highlights this function.

API Scaling and Coordinate Function Names and Descriptions

Table 11–3 shows 22 popular Windows API scaling and coordinate functions and provides a brief description for their use.

The functions that are most frequently used in this group are the SetMap-Mode() function and those that set the origins and extents for the window and viewport. The first application in this chapter illustrates the use of these functions. The second application manipulates the world coordinate system. This is for Windows NT programmers only.

API Scaling and Coordinate Function Declarations

The following listing contains the Windows API scaling and coordinate function declarations found in the Win32api.txt file provided with Visual Basic. As we mentioned earlier, there are additional functions related to those in this chapter found in Chapter 10 and 12.

Table 11–3   Scaling and Coordinate Functions and Descriptions

Function	Description
CombineTransform	Combines two transforms in sequence.
DPtoLP	Array of device coordinate points to logical points.
GetGraphicsMode	Win NT—gets graphics mode.
GetMapMode	Gets the current map mode.
GetViewportExtEx	Gets the DC viewport extents.
GetViewportOrgEx	Gets the DC origin in the viewport.
GetWindowExtEx	Gets the extent for the window in the DC.
GetWindowOrgEx	Gets the origin for the window in the DC.
GetWorldTransform	Win NT—Gets the current World Transform.
LPtoDP	Array of logical points to device coordinate points.
ModifyWorldTransform	Win NT—Changes world transform to given mode.
OffsetViewportOrgEx	Offsets the origin of the DC viewport.
OffsetWindowOrgEx	Offsets the window origin for the DC.
ScaleViewportExtEx	Scales the DC viewport's extents.
ScaleWindowExtEx	Scales the window's for the DC.
SetGraphicsMode	Win NT—sets graphics mode.
SetMapMode	Sets one of eight mapping modes.
SetViewportExtEx	Sets the DC viewport extents.
SetViewportOrgEx	Sets the DC origin of the viewport.
SetWindowExtEx	Sets the extent for the window in the DC.
SetWindowOrgEx	Sets the origin for the window in the DC.
SetWorldTransform	Win NT—Sets the current World Transform.

```
Declare Function CombineTransform Lib "gdi32" Alias
   "CombineTransform" (lpxformResult As xform,
   lpxform1 As xform, lpxform2 As xform) As Long

Declare Function DPtoLP Lib "gdi32" Alias "DPtoLP"
   (ByVal hdc As Long, lpPoint As POINTAPI,
   ByVal nCount As Long) As Long

Declare Function GetGraphicsMode Lib "gdi32" Alias
   "GetGraphicsMode" (ByVal hdc As Long) As Long

Declare Function GetMapMode Lib "gdi32" Alias "GetMapMode"
   (ByVal hdc As Long) As Long

Declare Function GetViewportExtEx Lib "gdi32" Alias
   "GetViewportExtEx" (ByVal hdc As Long,
   lpSize As SIZE) As Long

Declare Function GetViewportOrgEx Lib "gdi32" Alias
   "GetViewportOrgEx" (ByVal hdc As Long,
   lpPoint As POINTAPI) As Long
```

```
Declare Function GetWindowExtEx Lib "gdi32" Alias
   "GetWindowExtEx" (ByVal hdc As Long,
   lpSize As SIZE) As Long

Declare Function GetWindowOrgEx Lib "gdi32" Alias
   "GetWindowOrgEx" (ByVal hdc As Long,
   lpPoint As POINTAPI) As Long

Declare Function GetWorldTransform Lib "gdi32" Alias
   "GetWorldTransform" (ByVal hdc As Long,
   lpXform As xform) As Long

Declare Function LPtoDP Lib "gdi32" Alias "LPtoDP"
   (ByVal hdc As Long, lpPoint As POINTAPI,
   ByVal nCount As Long) As Long

Declare Function ModifyWorldTransform Lib "gdi32" Alias
   "ModifyWorldTransform" (ByVal hdc As Long,
   lpXform As xform, ByVal iMode As Long) As Long

Declare Function OffsetViewportOrgEx Lib "gdi32" Alias
   "OffsetViewportOrgEx" (ByVal hdc As Long,
   ByVal nX As Long, ByVal nY As Long,
   lpPoint As POINTAPI) As Long

Declare Function OffsetWindowOrgEx Lib "gdi32" Alias
   "OffsetWindowOrgEx" (ByVal hdc As Long,
   ByVal nX As Long, ByVal nY As Long,
   lpPoint As POINTAPI) As Long

Declare Function ScaleViewportExtEx Lib "gdi32" Alias
   "ScaleViewportExtEx" (ByVal hdc As Long,
   ByVal nXnum As Long, ByVal nXdenom As Long,
   ByVal nYnum As Long, ByVal nYdenom As Long,
   lpSize As SIZE) As Long

Declare Function ScaleWindowExtEx Lib "gdi32" Alias
   "ScaleWindowExtEx" (ByVal hdc As Long,
   ByVal nXnum As Long, ByVal nXdenom As Long,
   ByVal nYnum As Long, ByVal nYdenom As Long,
   lpSize As SIZE) As Long

Declare Function SetGraphicsMode Lib "gdi32" Alias
   "SetGraphicsMode" (ByVal hdc As Long,
   ByVal iMode As Long) As Long

Declare Function SetMapMode Lib "gdi32" Alias "SetMapMode"
   (ByVal hdc As Long, ByVal nMapMode As Long) As Long

Declare Function SetViewportExtEx Lib "gdi32" Alias
   "SetViewportExtEx" (ByVal hdc As Long, ByVal nX As Long,
   ByVal nY As Long, lpSize As SIZE) As Long
```

```
Declare Function SetViewportOrgEx Lib "gdi32" Alias
  "SetViewportOrgEx" (ByVal hdc As Long,
  ByVal nX As Long, ByVal nY As Long,
  lpPoint As POINTAPI) As Long

Declare Function SetWindowExtEx Lib "gdi32" Alias
  "SetWindowExtEx" (ByVal hdc As Long, ByVal nX As Long,
  ByVal nY As Long, lpSize As SIZE) As Long

Declare Function SetWindowOrgEx Lib "gdi32" Alias
  "SetWindowOrgEx" (ByVal hdc As Long, ByVal nX As Long,
  ByVal nY As Long, lpPoint As POINTAPI) As Long

Declare Function SetWorldTransform Lib "gdi32" Alias
  "SetWorldTransform" (ByVal hdc As Long,
  lpXform As xform) As Long
```

Table 11–4 contains a brief description of the parameters used in the various scaling and coordinate functions.

Several of the parameters described in Table 11–4 require constant values. These constant values are defined in the Win32api.txt file. The following listing shows the constant values for the scaling and coordinate function parameters:

```
'Graphics Modes
Public Const GM_COMPATIBLE = 1
Public Const GM_ADVANCED = 2
Public Const GM_LAST = 2

'Mapping Modes
Public Const MM_TEXT = 1
Public Const MM_LOMETRIC = 2
Public Const MM_HIMETRIC = 3
Public Const MM_LOENGLISH = 4
Public Const MM_HIENGLISH = 5
Public Const MM_TWIPS = 6
Public Const MM_ISOTROPIC = 7
Public Const MM_ANISOTROPIC = 8

'Min and Max Mapping Mode values
Public Const MM_MIN = MM_TEXT
Public Const MM_MAX = MM_ANISOTROPIC
Public Const MM_MAX_FIXEDSCALE = MM_TWIPS

'xform stuff
Public Const MWT_IDENTITY = 1
Public Const MWT_LEFTMULTIPLY = 2
Public Const MWT_RIGHTMULTIPLY = 3

Public Const MWT_MIN = MWT_IDENTITY
Public Const MWT_MAX = MWT_RIGHTMULTIPLY
```

Table 11–4   Scaling and Coordinate Function Parameters and Descriptions

Parameter	Description
hdc As Long	Handle to the device context (DC).
iMode As Long	Holds GM_ or MWT_ constant.
lpPoint As POINTAPI	Points to first value in a POINTAPI structure to be converted to other form or holding required coordinate information.
lpSize As SIZE	Points to first horz. and vert. extents held in SIZE structure.
lpXform As xform	xform structure to hold World Transform values.
lpxform1 As xform	xform structure holds first transform.
lpxform2 As xform	xform structure holds second transform.
lpxformResult As xform	xform structure holds results of combined transform.
nCount As Long	Number of values in lpPoint array.
nMapMode As Long	Holds one of eight MM_ constants.
nX As Long	Horizontal offset—add to viewport origin.
nXdenom As Long	Current horz. viewport extent times nXnum, then divided by this number.
nXnum As Long	Multiplies horizontal viewport extent by this value.
nY As Long	Vertical offset—add to viewport origin.
nYdenom As Long	Current vert. viewport extent times nYnum, then divided by this number.
nYnum As Long	Multiplies vertical viewport extent by this value.

In addition to the constant values shown, several functions also use structures. Here are the structures used by this group of functions.

```
Type POINTAPI
   x As Long
   y As Long
End Type

Type Size
   cx As Long
   cy As Long
End Type

Type XFORM
   eM11 As Single
   eM12 As Single
   eM21 As Single
   eM22 As Single
   eDx As Single
   eDy As Single
End Type
```

In the next section, you'll see these structures put to use in two separate applications.

Example Applications

The examples in this section illustrate how to use various Windows API functions to manipulate the screen, coordinate system, and viewport. Many other examples in the book take advantage of these same functions.

Manipulating Coordinate Systems

The first project, named Coord1.vbp, illustrates the use of four scaling and coordinate functions available to Windows 95 and NT programmers. In this example a scientific chart will be drawn to the screen. The Windows functions set the number of logical units, the viewport size plotting direction, and the origin.

The following Coord1.bas module file contains the structure definitions and Windows API function declarations used by the program. Chapter 13 contains a more detailed description of the drawing functions used in this example.

```
Type POINTAPI
  x As Long
  y As Long
End Type

Type Size
  cx As Long
  cy As Long
End Type

Declare Function SetMapMode Lib "gdi32" (ByVal hdc As Long,
  ByVal nMapMode As Long) As Long

Declare Function SetViewportExtEx Lib "gdi32"
  (ByVal hdc As Long, ByVal nX As Long, ByVal nY As Long,
  lpSize As Size) As Long

Declare Function SetViewportOrgEx Lib "gdi32"
  (ByVal hdc As Long, ByVal nX As Long, ByVal nY As Long,
  lpPoint As POINTAPI) As Long

Declare Function SetWindowExtEx Lib "gdi32"
  (ByVal hdc As Long, ByVal nX As Long, ByVal nY As Long,
  lpSize As Size) As Long

Declare Function MoveToEx Lib "gdi32" (ByVal hdc As Long,
  ByVal x As Long, ByVal y As Long,
  lpPoint As POINTAPI) As Long

Declare Function LineTo Lib "gdi32" (ByVal hdc As Long,
  ByVal x As Long, ByVal y As Long) As Long
```

The program uses a blank form on which to draw the scientific waveform. Here is the code associated with that form.

```
Private Sub Form_Paint()
      Dim tempSize As Size
      Dim tempPoint As POINTAPI
      Dim r%

      'dummy values
      tempSize.cx = 0
      tempSize.cy = 0
      tempPoint.x = 0
      tempPoint.y = 0

      'pi value for radian numbers
      Const pi = 3.14159

      'Set Map Mode
      r% = SetMapMode(hdc, MM_ISOTROPIC)
      'Set Window Extents to 500 x 500
      r% = SetWindowExtEx(hdc, 500, 500, tempSize)
      'Set Viewport Extents to VGA screen size
        'Positive x is to the right
        'Positive y is up
      r% = SetViewportExtEx(hdc, 640, -480, tempSize)
      'Create a new origin (0,0) at screen position (105,240)
      r% = SetViewportOrgEx(hdc, 640 / 6, 480 / 2, tempPoint)

      'draw x & y coordinate axes
      r% = MoveToEx(hdc, 0, 150, tempPoint)
      r% = LineTo(hdc, 0, -150)
      r% = MoveToEx(hdc, 0, 0, tempPoint)
      r% = LineTo(hdc, 400, 0)
      r% = MoveToEx(hdc, 0, 0, tempPoint)

      'the sine wave
      For i = 0 To 400
        y = -180# * (Exp(-i * 0.01)) *
            Sin(pi * i * (1440# / 400#) / 180#)
        r% = LineTo(hdc, i, y)
      Next i

      'the damping envelope
      r% = MoveToEx(hdc, 0, 0, tempPoint)
      For i = 0 To 400
        y = 180# * (Exp(-i * 0.01))
        r% = LineTo(hdc, i, y)
      Next i
      r% = MoveToEx(hdc, 0, 0, tempPoint)
      For i = 0 To 400
        y = 180# * (Exp(-i * 0.01))
        r% = LineTo(hdc, i, -y)
      Next i
End Sub
```

Study the whole example, but concentrate on the calls to the SetMapMode(), SetWindowExtEx(), SetViewportExtEx(), and SetViewportOrgEx() functions.

The first function call changes the mapping mode from MM_TEXT to MM_ISOTROPIC. The MM_ISOTROPIC mapping mode allows the user to set arbitrary units of measure with equally scaled axes.

```
'Set Map Mode
r% = SetMapMode(hdc, MM_ISOTROPIC)
```

The arbitrary units are set with a call to the SetWindowExtEx() function. The drawing surface will be set to 500 units on the horizontal and 500 units on the vertical regardless of the physical device's resolution.

```
'Set Window Extents to 500 x 500
r% = SetWindowExtEx(hdc, 500, 500, tempSize)
```

The viewport's dimensions are set to a VGA screen size. The *x*-axis is set to 640 and the *y*-axis to −480. A minus sign at this location will allow the *y*-axis values to increase in the vertical direction.

```
'Set Viewport Extents to VGA screen size
  'Positive x is to the right
  'Positive y is up
r% = SetViewportExtEx(hdc, 640, -480, tempSize)
```

The origin is currently at the bottom-left of the screen. For this example, we want the origin at the point where the *x*-axis intersects the *y*-axis on the graph. The SetViewportOrgEx() function moves the origin with the following code:

```
'Create a new origin (0, 0) at screen position (107, 240)
r% = SetViewportOrgEx(hdc, 640 / 6, 480 / 2, tempPoint)
```

Once this call is made, all drawing will be relative to this new origin. For example, the MoveToEx() function does not start at the bottom-left of the screen, now, but at the new origin.

```
'draw x & y coordinate axes
r% = MoveToEx(hdc, 0, 150, tempPoint)
```

When you run this example, you may be a bit surprised as to where the figure has been drawn on the screen. Figure 11–1 shows a typical screen for this application.

If you are running Windows NT, you'll want to examine the following example for additional scaling and coordinate manipulation capabilities.

Manipulating Coordinates with World Coordinate Transformations

The second project, named World1.vbp, illustrates the use of world coordinate transforms available to Windows NT programmers. In this example a simple rectangle will be drawn to the screen multiple times. However, before each drawing

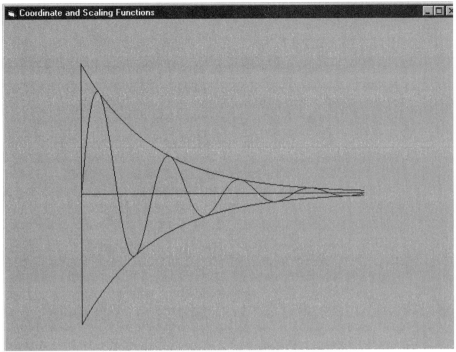

Figure 11–1 This application allows the figure's scaling, viewport, and origin to be changed from the default value.

the *x-y* coordinate system is rotated 45 degrees. The resulting figure, impossible under Windows 95, shows multiple drawings of these rectangles in various positions on the screen. But look at the call to the Rectangle() function. None of the parameters are changed from call to call!

The following World1.bas module file contains the structure definitions and Windows API function declarations used by the program. You can find more information on the Rectangle() function in Chapter 13.

```
Type XFORM
  eM11 As Double
  eM12 As Double
  eM21 As Double
  eM22 As Double
  eDx As Double
  eDy As Double
End Type

Declare Function SetGraphicsMode Lib "gdi32"
  (ByVal hdc As Long, ByVal iMode As Long) As Long

Declare Function SetWorldTransform Lib "gdi32"
  (ByVal hdc As Long, lpXform As XFORM) As Long
```

```
Declare Function Rectangle Lib "gdi32"
   (ByVal hdc As Long, ByVal X1 As Long, ByVal Y1 As Long,
   ByVal X2 As Long, ByVal Y2 As Long) As Long
```

The figure is drawn on an empty form. The code associated with this form is shown in the following listing. As you study this listing, pay particular attention to the multiple calls to the SetWorldTransform() function.

```
Private Sub Form_Paint()
     Dim tempXForm As XFORM
     Dim r%

     '2 * pi value for radian numbers
     Const twopi = 6.28318

     'set graphics mode to advanced
     r% = SetGraphicsMode(hdc, GM_ADVANCED)

     'specify the World Transform
     'work on VGA size screen
      For i = 0 To 180 Step 45
         tempXForm.eM11 = Cos(i * twopi / 360)   'rotation
         tempXForm.eM22 = Cos(i * twopi / 360)   'rotation
         tempXForm.eM21 = Sin(i * twopi / 360)   'rotation
         tempXForm.eM12 = -Sin(i * twopi / 360) 'rotation
         tempXForm.eDx = (640 / 2)               'offset x
         tempXForm.eDy = (480 / 2)               'offset y

         r% = SetWorldTransform(hdc, tempXForm)

         'size figure to fit VGA size screen
         r% = Rectangle(hdc, -640 / 4, -480 / 4, 640 / 4,
                   480 / 4)
      Next i
   End Sub
```

The application is started by setting Window NT's graphics mode to Set-GraphicsMode(hdc, GM_ADVANCED). This will allow the use of the Set-WorldTransform() function.

A **For** loop is created. During each pass through the **For** loop, the values in the XFORM structure will be changed. These values will rotate the *x-y* coordinate axis 45 additional degrees during each pass through the loop.

The transformations are made according to the following equations for each *x,y* point.

```
x (transformed) = ((x * eM11) + (y * eM21)) + eDx
y (transformed) = ((y * eM12) + (y * eM22)) + eDy
```

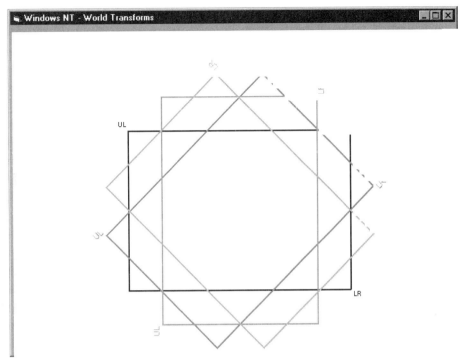

Figure 11–2   The world coordinate system is transformed in this application.

Changing the world coordinates, to simulate rotation, is similar to drawing a fixed rectangle and rotating under it. The rectangle remains fixed, but your rotation gives the illusion that the figure is rotating.

Figure 11–2 shows a typical screen for this application. Letters were added to each corner so you could see how the figures tracked as the coordinates were changed.

Many of these functions will be used again and again throughout the book. For example, Chapter 13 discusses many important drawing primitives.

Chapter 12

Clipping and Region Functions

Clipping and region functions are very important in Windows. These functions are often used to specify a particular region of the screen and protect it from other windows. The default clipping region is the whole window but can be set to any portion of the window.

Clipping and region functions also allow a screen to be divided to areas. Some of these areas might be constantly updated while others remain static, as in the case of a data sampling program.

In the next sections we'll examine all of the popular clipping and region functions and give you brief descriptions for their use. A programming example included in this chapter illustrates how to exclude certain regions from the screen using the ExcludeClipRect() function.

API Clipping and Region Function Names and Descriptions

Table 12–1 shows 37 popular Windows API clipping and region functions and provides a brief description of each.

Table 12–1 Clipping and Region Functions and Descriptions

Function	Description
CombineRgn	Two regions are combined to create a single region.
CreateEllipticRgn	Creates elliptical region in a rectangle specified with X1,Y1 and X2,Y2 diagonal points.
CreateEllipticRgnIndirect	Creates an elliptical region in a bounding rectangle.
CreatePolygonRgn	Creates a region from a series of points.
CreatePolyPolygonRgn	Creates a region from a series of polygons.
CreateRectRgn	Creates rectangular region specified with X1,Y1 and X2,Y2 diagonal points.
CreateRectRgnIndirect	Creates a rectangular region specified by lpRect.
CreateRoundRectRgn	Creates rounded rectangular region specified with X1,Y1 and X2,Y2 diagonal points. Points X3, Y3 give degree of rounding ellipse.
EqualRgn	Determines if regions are equal.
ExcludeClipRect	Excludes rectangular region bound by X1,Y1 and X2,Y2 diagonal points from the clipping area.
ExcludeUpdateRgn	Excludes the region of the window specified from the clipping region.
ExtCreateRegion	Clipping region modified with world transform.
ExtSelectClipRgn	Specified region combined with present clipping region.
FillRgn	Fills region with the given brush.
FrameRgn	Draws a frame around region with the given brush.
GetBoundsRect	Gets the bounding rectangle.
GetClipBox	Smallest rectangle that will hold clipping region.
GetClipRgn	Gets current clipping region.
GetRegionData	Gets region data in a RGNDATA structure.
GetRgnBox	Smallest rectangle that will hold region.
GetUpdateRgn	Gets the update region for window.
GetWindowRgn	Gets the window region.
IntersectClipRect	Finds new clipping region based on intersection of current clipping region and a rectangle bound by X1,Y1 and X2,Y2 diagonal points.
InvalidateRgn	Invalidates a given region.
InvertRgn	Inverts each pixel in a region.
OffsetClipRgn	Offsets the clipping region.
OffsetRgn	Offsets the region by the amount given.
PaintRgn	Fills region with current brush.
PtInRegion	Determines if the point is in the region.
PtVisible	Determines if the point is visible.
RectInRegion	Determines if any part of a rectangle is in region.
RectVisible	Determines if any part of a rectangle is visible.
SelectClipRgn	Selects a clipping region.
SetBoundsRect	Sets the bounding rectangle.
SetRectRgn	Sets region to bounding rectangle given by X1,Y1 and X2,Y2 diagonal points.
SetWindowRgn	Allows nonrectangular regions to be set.
ValidateRgn	Validates a region.

Probably the most frequently used region functions are those for checking, creating, excluding, and offsetting regions with rectangular parameters. This group of functions includes CreateRectRgn(), ExcludeClipRect(), IntersectClipRect(), and SetRectRgn().

The use of the ExcludeClipRect() function will be highlighted in the programming application.

API Clipping and Region Function Declarations

The following listing contains the Window API clipping and region function declarations found in the Win32api.txt file provided with Visual Basic. A number of these functions are closely related to the functions discussed in Chapters 11 and 13.

```
Declare Function CombineRgn Lib "gdi32" Alias
   "CombineRgn" (ByVal hDestRgn As Long,
   ByVal hSrcRgn1 As Long, ByVal hSrcRgn2 As Long,
   ByVal nCombineMode As Long) As Long

Declare Function CreateEllipticRgn Lib "gdi32" Alias
   "CreateEllipticRgn" (ByVal X1 As Long, ByVal Y1 As Long,
   ByVal X2 As Long, ByVal Y2 As Long) As Long

Declare Function CreateEllipticRgnIndirect Lib "gdi32" Alias
   "CreateEllipticRgnIndirect" (lpRect As Rect) As Long

Declare Function CreatePolygonRgn Lib "gdi32" Alias
   "CreatePolygonRgn" (lpPoint As POINTAPI,
   ByVal nCount As Long, ByVal nPolyFillMode As Long) As Long

Declare Function CreatePolyPolygonRgn Lib "gdi32" Alias
   "CreatePolyPolygonRgn" (lpPoint As POINTAPI,
   lpPolyCounts As Long, ByVal nCount As Long,
   ByVal nPolyFillMode As Long) As Long

Declare Function CreateRectRgn Lib "gdi32" Alias
   "CreateRectRgn" (ByVal X1 As Long, ByVal Y1 As Long,
   ByVal X2 As Long, ByVal Y2 As Long) As Long

Declare Function CreateRectRgnIndirect Lib "gdi32" Alias
   "CreateRectRgnIndirect" (lpRect As RECT) As Long

Declare Function CreateRoundRectRgn Lib "gdi32" Alias
   "CreateRoundRectRgn" (ByVal X1 As Long, ByVal Y1 As Long,
   ByVal X2 As Long, ByVal Y2 As Long, ByVal X3 As Long,
   ByVal Y3 As Long) As Long

Declare Function EqualRgn Lib "gdi32" Alias "EqualRgn"
   (ByVal hSrcRgn1 As Long, ByVal hSrcRgn2 As Long) As Long
```

```
Declare Function ExcludeClipRect Lib "gdi32" Alias
   "ExcludeClipRect" (ByVal hdc As Long, ByVal X1 As Long,
   ByVal Y1 As Long, ByVal X2 As Long,
   ByVal Y2 As Long) As Long

Declare Function ExcludeUpdateRgn Lib "user32" Alias
   "ExcludeUpdateRgn" (ByVal hdc As Long,
   ByVal hwnd As Long) As Long

Declare Function ExtCreateRegion Lib "gdi32" Alias
   "ExtCreateRegion" (lpXform As xform, ByVal nCount As Long,
   lpRgnData As RGNDATA) As Long

Declare Function ExtSelectClipRgn Lib "gdi32" Alias
   "ExtSelectClipRgn" (ByVal hdc As Long,
   ByVal hRgn As Long, ByVal fnMode As Long) As Long

Declare Function FillRgn Lib "gdi32" Alias "FillRgn"
   (ByVal hdc As Long, ByVal hRgn As Long,
   ByVal hBrush As Long) As Long

Declare Function FrameRgn Lib "gdi32" Alias "FrameRgn"
   (ByVal hdc As Long, ByVal hRgn As Long,
   ByVal hBrush As Long, ByVal nWidth As Long,
   ByVal nHeight As Long) As Long

Declare Function GetBoundsRect Lib "gdi32" Alias
   "GetBoundsRect" (ByVal hdc As Long, lprcBounds As RECT,
   ByVal flags As Long) As Long

Declare Function GetClipBox Lib "gdi32" Alias "GetClipBox"
   (ByVal hdc As Long, lpRect As RECT) As Long

Declare Function GetClipRgn Lib "gdi32" Alias "GetClipRgn"
   (ByVal hdc As Long, ByVal hRgn As Long) As Long

Declare Function GetRegionData Lib "gdi32" Alias
   "GetRegionDataA" (ByVal hRgn As Long,
   ByVal dwCount As Long, lpRgnData As RgnData) As Long

Declare Function GetRgnBox Lib "gdi32" Alias "GetRgnBox"
   (ByVal hRgn As Long, lpRect As RECT) As Long

Declare Function GetUpdateRgn Lib "user32" Alias
   "GetUpdateRgn" (ByVal hwnd As Long, ByVal hRgn As Long,
   ByVal fErase As Long) As Long

Declare Function GetWindowRgn Lib "user32" Alias
   "GetWindowRgn" (ByVal hWnd As Long,
   ByVal hRgn As Long) As Long

Declare Function IntersectClipRect Lib "gdi32" Alias
   "IntersectClipRect" (ByVal hdc As Long,
   ByVal X1 As Long, ByVal Y1 As Long, ByVal X2 As Long,
   ByVal Y2 As Long) As Long
```

```
Declare Function InvalidateRgn Lib "user32" Alias
  "InvalidateRgn" (ByVal hwnd As Long, ByVal hRgn As Long,
  ByVal bErase As Long) As Long

Declare Function InvertRgn Lib "gdi32" Alias "InvertRgn"
  (ByVal hdc As Long, ByVal hRgn As Long) As Long

Declare Function OffsetClipRgn Lib "gdi32" Alias
  "OffsetClipRgn" (ByVal hdc As Long, ByVal x As Long,
  ByVal y As Long) As Long

Declare Function OffsetRgn Lib "gdi32" Alias "OffsetRgn"
  (ByVal hRgn As Long, ByVal x As Long,
  ByVal y As Long) As Long

Declare Function PaintRgn Lib "gdi32" Alias "PaintRgn"
  (ByVal hdc As Long, ByVal hRgn As Long) As Long

Declare Function PtInRegion Lib "gdi32" Alias "PtInRegion"
  (ByVal hRgn As Long, ByVal x As Long,
  ByVal y As Long) As Long

Declare Function PtVisible Lib "gdi32" Alias "PtVisible"
  (ByVal hdc As Long, ByVal x As Long,
  ByVal y As Long) As Long

Declare Function RectInRegion Lib "gdi32" Alias
  "RectInRegion" (ByVal hRgn As Long,
  lpRect As RECT) As Long

Declare Function RectVisible Lib "gdi32" Alias "RectVisible"
  (ByVal hdc As Long, lpRect As RECT) As Long

Declare Function SelectClipRgn Lib "gdi32" Alias
  "SelectClipRgn" (ByVal hdc As Long,
  ByVal hRgn As Long) As Long

Declare Function SetBoundsRect Lib "gdi32" Alias
  "SetBoundsRect" (ByVal hdc As Long, lprcBounds As RECT,
  ByVal flags As Long) As Long

Declare Function SetRectRgn Lib "gdi32" Alias "SetRectRgn"
  (ByVal hRgn As Long, ByVal X1 As Long, ByVal Y1 As Long,
  ByVal X2 As Long, ByVal Y2 As Long) As Long

Declare Function SetWindowRgn Lib "user32" Alias
  "SetWindowRgn" (ByVal hWnd As Long, ByVal hRgn As Long,
  ByVal bRedraw As Boolean) As Long

Declare Function ValidateRgn Lib "user32" Alias
  "ValidateRgn" (ByVal hwnd As Long,
  ByVal hRgn As Long) As Long
```

Table 12–2 contains a brief description of the parameters used in the various clipping and region functions.

Table 12–2   Clipping and Region Function Parameters and Description

Parameter	Description
bErase As Long	Erase region before update when TRUE.
bRedraw As Boolean	Set to TRUE to immediately redraw window.
dwCount As Long	Size of RGNDATA structure.
fErase As Long	Erase window background when TRUE.
flags As Long	Uses DCB_ constants.
fnMode As Long	Uses RGN_ constants for combining regions.
hBrush As Long	Handle to the selected brush.
hdc As Long	Handle to the device context.
hDestRgn As Long	Handle of region to hold combined regions.
hRgn As Long	Handle to a source region.
hSrcRgn1 As Long	Handle of first region to be combined.
hSrcRgn2 As Long	Handle of second region to be combined.
hwnd As Long	Handle to the window.
lpPoint As POINTAPI	First structure in an array of POINTAPI structures.
lpPolyCounts As Long	First value in an array of Longs. Entries give number of points in each polygon.
lprcBounds As RECT	Structure holds bounding rectangle.
lpRect As RECT	Structure holds the region to create.
lpRgnData As RGNDATA	Structure holds region data.
lpXform As XFORM	Points to XFORM structure holding data to apply to region.
nCombineMode As Long	Uses RGN_ constants for combining regions.
nCount As Long	Number of points for a polygon or size of an lpRgnData structure.
nHeight As Long	Height of horizontal borders.
nPolyFillMode As Long	ALTERNATE or WINDING polygon fill mode.
nWidth As Long	Width of vertical borders.
x As Long	Horizontal offset.
X1, Y1 As Long	First diagonal point on a bounding rectangle.
X2, Y2 As Long	Second diagonal point on a bounding rectangle.
X3 As Long	Width of rounding ellipse.
y As Long	Vertical offset.
Y3 As Long	Height of rounding ellipse.

Many of the parameters described in Table 12–2 use constant values. The Win32api.txt file lists the following constants for these parameters:

```
Public Const DCB_RESET = &H1
Public Const DCB_ACCUMULATE = &H2
Public Const DCB_DIRTY = DCB_ACCUMULATE
Public Const DCB_SET = (DCB_RESET Or DCB_ACCUMULATE)
Public Const DCB_ENABLE = &H4
Public Const DCB_DISABLE = &H8
```

```
' CombineRgn() Styles
Public Const RGN_AND = 1
Public Const RGN_OR = 2
Public Const RGN_XOR = 3
Public Const RGN_DIFF = 4
Public Const RGN_COPY = 5
Public Const RGN_MIN = RGN_AND
Public Const RGN_MAX = RGN_COPY
```

In addition to the constants just listed, these functions make use of a number of structures:

```
Type RECT
  Left As Long
  Top As Long
  Right As Long
  Bottom As Long
End Type

Type POINTAPI
  x As Long
  y As Long
End Type

Type RGNDATAHEADER
  dwSize As Long
  iType As Long
  nCount As Long
  nRgnSize As Long
  rcBound As Rect
End Type

Type RGNDATA
  rdh As RGNDATAHEADER
  Buffer As Byte
End Type

Type XFORM
  eM11 As Double
  eM12 As Double
  eM21 As Double
  eM22 As Double
  eDx As Double
  eDy As Double
End Type
```

The XFORM structure can specify world-space to page-space transformations as shown in Table 12–3.

In the next section, we'll examine an application that makes a unique use of the ExcludeClipRect() function.

Table 12–3   XFORM Parameters

Function Member	When Used For
eM11	scaling: horizontal component. rotation: cosine of angle. reflection: horizontal component.
eM12	shear: horizontal proportionality constant. rotation: sine of angle.
eM21	shear: vertical proportionality constant. rotation: negative sine of angle.
eM22	scaling: vertical component. rotation: cosine of angle. reflection: vertical component.
eDx	Horizontal translation component (offset).
eDy	Vertical translation component (offset).

Example Application

This application makes use of several drawing functions which are explained in more detail in Chapter 13. Without the calls to the ExcludeClipRect() function, all four figures would be drawn on the screen. Figure 12–1 shows this particular case.

In this project, named Region1.vbp, each quarter of the screen will be excluded from drawing after a figure is completed. To exclude a portion of the screen, the ExcludeClipRect() is used three times. Each time it is called, another quarter of the screen will be excluded.

Here is the code required for function declarations. This module file is named Region1.bas.

```
Type POINTAPI
  x As Long
  y As Long
End Type

Declare Function Ellipse Lib "gdi32" (ByVal hdc As Long,
  ByVal X1 As Long, ByVal Y1 As Long, ByVal X2 As Long,
  ByVal Y2 As Long) As Long

Declare Function MoveToEx Lib "gdi32" (ByVal hdc As Long,
  ByVal x As Long, ByVal y As Long,
  lpPoint As POINTAPI) As Long

Declare Function LineTo Lib "gdi32" (ByVal hdc As Long,
  ByVal x As Long, ByVal y As Long) As Long
```

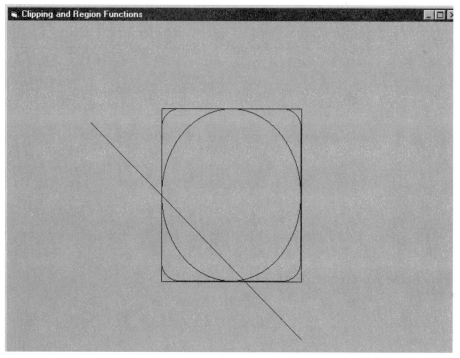

Figure 12–1   Four figures are drawn to the screen without clipping.

```
Declare Function Rectangle Lib "gdi32" (ByVal hdc As Long,
   ByVal X1 As Long, ByVal Y1 As Long, ByVal X2 As Long,
   ByVal Y2 As Long) As Long

Declare Function RoundRect Lib "gdi32" (ByVal hdc As Long,
   ByVal X1 As Long, ByVal Y1 As Long, ByVal X2 As Long,
   ByVal Y2 As Long, ByVal X3 As Long,
   ByVal Y3 As Long) As Long

Declare Function ExcludeClipRect Lib "gdi32"
   (ByVal hdc As Long, ByVal X1 As Long, ByVal Y1 As Long,
   ByVal X2 As Long, ByVal Y2 As Long) As Long
```

The graphics are drawn to a blank form, Region1.frm. Here is the code that supports the drawing to this form.

```
Private Sub Form_Paint()
     Dim tempPoint As POINTAPI
     Dim r&

     'dummy values
     tempPoint.x = 0
     tempPoint.y = 0
```

```
                    'no regions excluded
                    'draw in all four quarters
                    r& = Rectangle(hdc, 220, 120, 420, 360)

                    'exclude first quarter from drawing
                    'draw in 2nd, 3rd and 4th quarters only
                    r& = ExcludeClipRect(hdc, 0, 0, 320, 240)
                    r& = RoundRect(hdc, 220, 120, 420, 360, 50, 50)

                    'now exclude second quarter from drawing
                    'draw in 3rd and 4th quarters only
                    r& = ExcludeClipRect(hdc, 320, 0, 640, 240)
                    r& = Ellipse(hdc, 220, 120, 420, 360)

                    'now exclude third quarter from drawing
                    'draw in 4th quarter only
                    r& = ExcludeClipRect(hdc, 320, 240, 640, 480)
                    r& = MoveToEx(hdc, 120, 140, tempPoint)
                    r& = LineTo(hdc, 420, 440)
          End Sub
```

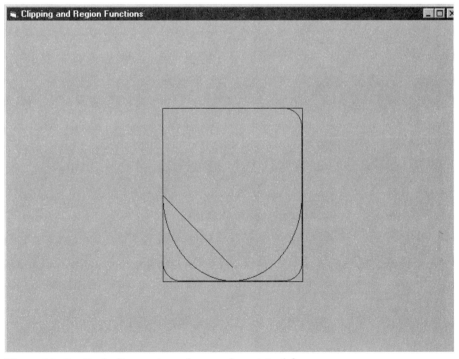

Figure 12–2   Excluding regions changes the original figure.

In this application, the VGA screen is divided into four "invisible" quarters. The Rectangle() function is called to draw a rectangle which crosses into each quarter. Since no clipping regions have been specified or clipping areas eliminated, the full rectangular shape will be present.

Now, the upper-left-hand corner of the VGA screen is excluded and a call is made to the RoundRect() function. This function will only draw in the second, third, and fourth quarters of the screen.

The process continues until the last shape is drawn to the screen. Figure 12–2 shows the resulting graphics drawn to the screen.

Chapter **13**

GDI Drawing Functions

The Windows API functions that encompass the Graphics Device Interface (GDI) are perhaps the most important functions you will encounter. From these simple functions spring all of the graphics drawing shapes available to programmers. Additionally, support functions provide a wealth of brushes and pens styles to suit, well, every palette.

In the following sections you will find the most important GDI functions listed and described. If you don't find your favorite function in this chapter, it may be part of another chapter. For example, functions dealing with metafiles are included in a separate chapter.

GDI Drawing Primitives

There are numerous categories of drawing primitives. Most of these categories are composed of a single function. The most often used categories include functions for drawing arcs, chords, circles, ellipses, lines, pie wedges, polygons, polylines, rectangles, rectangles with rounded corners, single pixels, and techniques for setting cursor positions.

All drawing primitives draw with the current pen style and color and, where applicable, fill the shape with the current brush style and color. Details about pen and brush selections are included later in this chapter.

In the following sections we'll highlight some of the most popular drawing primitives. Once you master how these primitives are called, you'll be able to code other primitives just as easily.

The Arc() and ArcTo() Functions

The Arc() function is used to draw an elliptical arc. The center of the arc is also the center of a bounding rectangle described by the points x_1,y_1 and x_2,y_2, as shown in Figure 13–1.

The actual length of the arc is described as lying between points x_3,y_3 and x_4,y_4, with the drawing performed in a counterclockwise direction. An arc cannot be filled since it is not a closed figure. The Arc() function will not update the coordinates of current point. The handle for the device context is given by hdc. All other parameters are of type Long. This function returns a type Long.

The function can be called by supplying parameters in the following manner:

```
Arc(hdc, x1, y1, x2, y2, x3, y3, x4, y4)
```

For example, the following line of code draws a small arc in the user's window:

```
r% = Arc(hdc, 25, 125, 175, 225, 175, 225, 100, 125)
```

The ArcTo() function, new for Windows NT, is similar to the Arc() function, except that it does update the current point once it is called.

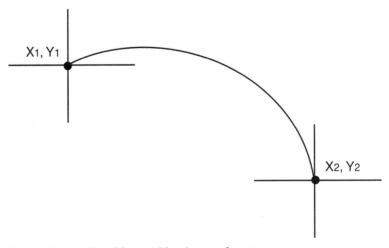

Figure 13–1   Variables used by the Arc function.

The Chord() Function

The Chord() function is identical to the Arc() function, with the added feature that the figure is closed by a line between the two arc points x_3,y_3 and x_4,y_4. Figure 13–2 shows these points.

A chord is filled with the current brush since it is a closed figure. The handle for the device context is given by hdc. All other parameters are of type Long. This function returns a type Long.

The function can be called in the following manner:

```
Chord(hdc, x1, y1, x2, y2, x3, y3, x4, y4)
```

For example, the following line of code draws a small chord in the user's window:

```
r% = Chord(hdc, 125, 125, 275, 225, 275, 225, 200, 125)
```

The Ellipse() (and Circle) Function

The Ellipse() function is used to draw an ellipse or a circle. The center of the ellipse is also the center of an imaginary rectangle described by the points x_1,y_1 and x_2,y_2, as shown in Figure 13–3.

An ellipse is filled since it is a closed figure. The handle for the device context is given by hdc. All other parameters are of type Long. This function returns a type Long.

The function is called with the following parameters:

```
Ellipse(hdc, x1, y1, x2, y2)
```

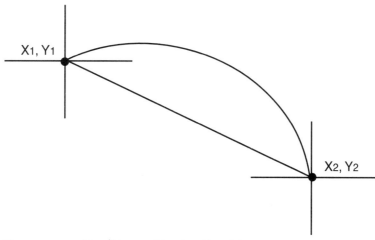

Figure 13–2   Variables used by the Chord function.

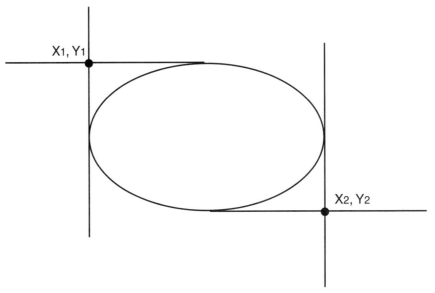

Figure 13–3   Variables used by the Ellipse (circle) function.

For example, the following line of code draws a small ellipse in the user's window:

```
r% = Ellipse(hdc, 275, 300, 200, 250)
```

A special case of the Ellipse() function specifies a circle when the boundary rectangle is a square. The following code draws a circle:

```
r% = Ellipse(hdc, 375, 75, 525, 225)
```

The LineTo() Function

The LineTo() function draws a line from the current point up to, but not including, the specified point. The current point can be set with the MoveToEx() function. The current point will be *x,y* when the function is successful. The handle for the device context is given by hdc. All other parameters are of type Long. This function returns a type Long .

The function can be called with the following parameters:

```
LineTo(hdc, x, y)
```

Here are some values for drawing a diagonal line in the user's window:

```
r% = MoveToEx(hdc, 20, 20, tempPoint)
r% = LineTo(hdc, 100, 100)
```

The MoveToEx() Function

The MoveToEx() function moves the current point to the specified point, and returns the original point to a data structure. The handle for the device context is given by hdc. The *x* and *y* values are of type Long. This function returns a type Long. The *x* and *y* coordinates of the original point are returned in a POINTAPI structure.

This function can be called with the following parameters:

```
MoveToEx(hdc, x, y, tempPoint)
```

The following line of code illustrates a typical call to this function:

```
r% = MoveToEx(hdc, 20, 20, tempPoint)
```

The Pie() Function

The Pie() function is used to draw pie-shaped wedges. The center of the elliptical arc is also the center of an imaginary rectangle described by the points x_1,y_1 and x_2,y_2, as shown in Figure 13–4.

The starting and ending points of the arc are points x_3,y_3 and x_4,y_4. Two lines are drawn from each end point to the center of the rectangle, in a counterclockwise direction. The pie wedge is filled, since it is a closed figure. The handle for the device context is given by hdc. All other parameters are of type Long. This function returns a type Long.

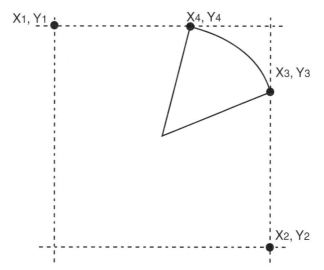

Figure 13–4   Variables used by the Pie function.

This function can be called in the following manner:

```
Pie(hdc, x1, y1, x2, y2, x3, y3, x4, y4)
```

For example, the following line of code draws a small pie-shaped wedge in the user's window:

```
r% = Pie(hdc, 200, 0, 300, 100, 200, 50, 250, 100)
```

The PolyDraw() Function

The PolyDraw() function is a Windows NT function that can be used to draw a set of line segments and Bezier curves. The handle to the device context is given by hdc. The value, lppt, points to an array of type POINTAPI structures. These structures contain the end points for each line and the end points/control points for each Bezier curve. The value, lpbTypes, points to an array of type BYTE. Each value in this array gives the type of corresponding point in the POINTAPI array. The value, cCount, is of type Long containing the number of points. The function returns a type Long.

This function can be called in the following manner:

```
PolyDraw(hdc, lppt, lpbTypes, cCount)
```

The values used by lpbTypes include PT_MOVETO which specifies the start of a disjointed figure. The point also becomes the new current position. PT_LINETO specifies a line from the current position to the given point. The given point then becomes the new current position. PT_BEZIERTO gives a control point or end point for a Bezier curve. The PT_BEZIERTO value occurs only in sets of three. Here the current point specifies the start point for the Bezier curve. The first two PT_BEZIERTO points are used as the control points. The third PT_BEZIERTO point is the end point, and becomes the current position. PT_LINETO or PT_BEZIERTO may be ORed with PT_CLOSEFIGURE to close the figure.

Here is an example of how the PolyDraw() function can be used to draw a small star shape in the user's window.

```
r% = MoveToEx(hdc, 400, 400, tempPoint)
polydpts(0).x = 375
polydpts(0).y = 350
polydpts(1).x = 400
polydpts(1).y = 300
polydpts(2).x = 350
polydpts(2).y = 325
polydpts(3).x = 300
polydpts(3).y = 300
polydpts(4).x = 325
polydpts(4).y = 350
```

```
polydpts(5).x = 300
polydpts(5).y = 400
polydpts(6).x = 350
polydpts(6).y = 375
polydpts(7).x = 400
polydpts(7).y = 400
polydtype(0) = PT_LINETO
polydtype(1) = PT_LINETO
polydtype(2) = PT_LINETO
polydtype(3) = PT_LINETO
polydtype(4) = PT_LINETO
polydtype(5) = PT_LINETO
polydtype(6) = PT_LINETO
polydtype(7) = PT_LINETO
r% = PolyDraw(hdc, polydpts(0), polydtype(0), 8)
```

Care must be used in specifying the parameters of this Windows NT function—one slip and instead of a star you will have a wild graphics display.

The Polygon() Function

The Polygon() function draws a polygon that consists of points connected by lines. How the lines are drawn is dependent on the filling mode. In alternate mode, lines are drawn from the first point to the last. In winding mode, the points are used to calculate a border; then the border is drawn. Both modes use the current pen for drawing and the current brush for filling. The polygon is filled, since it is a closed figure. Figure 13–5 shows an example of a polygon.

The handle for the device context is given by hdc. The location of the data points is held in an array of type POINTAPI in the example that follows. The number of points in the array is a Long. This function returns a type Long.

This function can be called in the following manner:

```
Polygon(hdc, lpPoint, nCount)
```

The following lines of code draw a polygon in the user's window:

```
polygpts(0).x = 40
polygpts(0).y = 200
polygpts(1).x = 100
polygpts(1).y = 270
polygpts(2).x = 80
polygpts(2).y = 290
polygpts(3).x = 20
polygpts(3).y = 220
polygpts(4).x = 40
polygpts(4).y = 200
r% = Polygon(hdc, polygpts(0), 5)
```

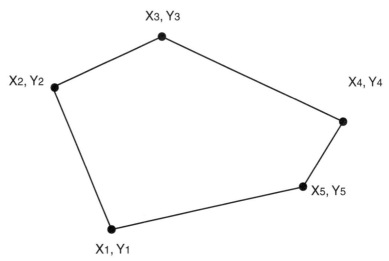

Figure 13–5 An example of a closed polygon.

The Polyline() and PolylineTo() Functions

The Polyline() function draws a group of connected line segments given in a type POINT API array. This function behaves like multiple MoveToEx() and LineTo() function calls, except that the position of the starting point is not changed. A shape drawn by Polyline() is not filled. The handle for the device context is given by hdc. In the example that follows, the location of the data points is held in an array of type POINTAPI. The number of points in the array is a Long. This function returns a type Long.

This function can be called in the following manner:

```
Polyline(hdc, lpPoint, nCount)
```

The following lines of code draw a polyline figure in the user's window:

```
polylpts(0).x = 10
polylpts(0).y = 30
polylpts(1).x = 10
polylpts(1).y = 100
polylpts(2).x = 50
polylpts(2).y = 100
polylpts(3).x = 10
polylpts(3).y = 30
Polyline(hdc, polylpts(0), 4)
```

The PolylineTo() function is similar to the Polyline() function, except that it updates the current point once it is called.

The Rectangle() Function

The Rectangle() function draws a rectangle, or box, described by x_1, y_1 and x_2, y_2. The rectangle is filled since it is a closed shape. The handle for the device context is given by hdc. All other parameters are of type Long. This function returns a type Long.

This function can be called in the following manner:

```
Rectangle(hdc, x1, y1, x2, y2)
```

The following line of code draws a rectangular figure in the user's window:

```
r% = Rectangle(hdc, 25, 300, 150, 375)
```

The RoundRect() Function

The RoundRect() function draws a round-cornered rectangle, or box, described by x_1, y_1 and x_2, y_2. The values x_3 and y_3 specify the width and height of the ellipse used to round the corners. The rounded rectangle is filled since it is a closed figure. The handle for the device context is given by hdc. All other parameters are of type Long. This function returns a type Long.

This function can be called in the following manner:

```
RoundRect(hdc, x1, y1, x2, y2, x3,y3)
```

The following line of code draws a rectangular figure in the user's window:

```
r% = RoundRect(hdc, 350, 250, 400, 290, 20, 20);
```

The SetPixel() and GetPixel() Functions

The SetPixel() function is used to light a pixel at the location specified by x and y. It will select the color closest to that requested. The handle for the device context is given by hdc. The x and y parameters are of type Long. The crColor value is of type Long. This function returns a type Long.

This function can be called in the following manner:

```
SetPixel(hdc, x, y, crColor)
```

The following line of code lights one pixel in the user's window:

```
r% = SetPixel(hdc, 40, 150, 240)
```

The GetPixel() function retrieves the color value at the specified point and returns it as a type Long.

This function can be called in the following manner:

```
r% = GetPixel(hdc, x, y)
```

GDI Tools And Techniques

Windows provides an environment rich in graphical tools and drawing techniques. For example, stock tools can be chosen or special tools can be designed for a particular application. Stock brushes and pens are described in the Win32api.txt file. Stock brushes and pens include

```
WHITE_BRUSH
LTGRAY_BRUSH
GRAY_BRUSH
DKGRAY_BRUSH
BLACK_BRUSH
HOLLOW_BRUSH (or NULL_BRUSH)
WHITE_PEN
BLACK_PEN
NULL_PEN
```

You will learn, shortly, how to select stock pens and brushes and how to create custom pens and brushes that allow you to use dazzling colors for drawing and filling shapes.

Pens

Pens are used to draw the outlines for all GDI graphics functions. Pens can be specified with three attributes: color, style, and width. The default pen is a black pen (BLACK_PEN), which draws a solid line (PS_SOLID), one device pixel wide. Other stock pen color choices include a white pen (WHITE_PEN) and a pen that does not draw (NULL_PEN), which is useful for drawing figures without an outline.

PS_INSIDEFRAME creates a pen that draws inside the frame of closed shapes. The basic stock line styles are

```
PS_SOLID _____
PS_DASH - - - - - - - -
PS_DOT . . . . . . . . . . .
PS_DASHDOT _._._._._._
PS_DASHDOTDOT _.._.._.._..
PS_NULL
PS_INSIDEFRAME Draws a solid rule inside a frame
```

Line widths are specified in logical units as integer numbers. Thus, a width of 10 in the default mode, MM_TEXT, will draw a line 10 pixels wide. All pens greater than one logical unit default to either a null or a solid line style.

Pens are referenced with the use of a handle of type hPen. Stock pens can be obtained with the GetStockObject() function. To change the pen just selected to the current pen, use the SelectObject() function:

```
hPen = SelectObject(hdc, GetStockObject(WHITE_PEN))
```

Creating a customized pen is a little different from creating a stock pen. A custom pen is created and selected with the CreatePen() function, in conjunction with the SelectObject() function. The CreatePen() function creates a logical pen with the syntax

```
CreatePen(nPenStyle, nWidth, crColor)
```

The parameter, nPenStyle, is a type Long and can be specified by any of the values given earlier—for example, PS_SOLID. The value, nWidth, is also of type Long and is described in logical units. The value, crColor, is a type Long. QBColor() values can be used to specify pen colors. For example,

```
hPenRed  = CreatePen(PS_SOLID, 2, Q BColor(12))
newpen = SelectObject(hdc, hPenRed)
```

Stock pens should not be deleted. If multiple pens are desired, they can all be created at the same time and selected individually. When the drawing is complete, the entire group can be deleted.

Brushes

Brushes are used to fill the closed figures created with GDI graphics functions. Brushes can be specified with several attributes. These attributes include colors, brush styles, and hatch styles. The default brush is a white brush (WHITE_ BRUSH) that fills the object with a solid pattern (BS_SOLID). "Solid," in this context, refers to the fill pattern used by the brush, not the "purity" of the color. Other stock brush color choices include LTGRAY_BRUSH, GRAY_BRUSH, DKGRAY_BRUSH, BLACK_BRUSH, and HOLLOW_ BRUSH or NULL_ BRUSH.

The colors of the stock brushes are achieved by dithering. Dithering produces shades of colors. On a monochrome screen, gray shades are obtained by using a block of pixels in which the number of black and white pixels is varied. Varying the number of black and white dots creates the illusion of different shades. A large palette of colors can be obtained in a similar manner. The most frequently used stock fill patterns include those shown in Table 13–1.

Table 13–1   Brush Styles

BS_SOLID	The fill is the color of the brush.
BS_HOLLOW &(BS_NULL)	The color of the brush is ignored.
BS_HATCHED	The hatching is the color of the brush.
BS_PATTERN	The color of the brush is ignored.
BS_INDEXED	The color is selected from a color table.
BS_DIBPATTERN	The color is defined by a device-independent bitmap.

Table 13–2   Cross-Hatch Styles

HS_HORIZONTAL	- - - - -
HS_VERTICAL	||||
HS_FDIAGONAL	/////
HS_BDIAGONAL	\\\\\
HS_CROSS	+++++
HS_DIAGCROSS	xxxxx

Cross-hatching can be selected from the group of hatch patterns shown in Table 13–2.

Other patterns described in the Win32api.txt file include HS_BDIAGO-NAL1, HS_NOSHADE, HS_HALFTONE, HS_FDIAGONAL1, and HS_DENSE1 to HS_DENSE8. Brushes are referenced with the use of a handle of type HBRUSH. Stock brushes can be obtained with the GetStockObject() function. The SelectObject() function changes the brush just selected to the current brush.

```
hBrush = SelectObject(hdc, GetStockObject(LTGRAY_BRUSH))
```

To create and select a customized brush, you must use one of the create brush functions, which include CreateSolidBrush(), CreateHatchBrush(), CreatePatternBrush(), CreateDIBPatternBrush(), and so on. Once created, the brush is selected with the SelectObject() function. Here are two examples:

```
//(a green solid brush)
hGBrush = CreateSolidBrush(QBColor(10)
newbrush = SelectObject(hdc, hGBrush))

//(a red hatched (+++) brush)
hRBrush = CreateHatchBrush(HS_CROSS, QBColor(12))
hRHBrush = SelectObject(hdc, hRBrush)
```

Once a brush is selected, only that brush can be used to fill objects within the device context. To use a brush of another color or pattern the previous brush can be de-selected. This is done by calling the DeleteObject() function. The DeleteObject() function should not be used to delete stock brushes.

If multiple brushes are desired in a program, they can all be created at the same time and selected individually. When the drawing is complete, the entire group of brushes can be deleted.

API Drawing Function Names and Descriptions

Table 13–3 shows 77 popular Windows API drawing functions for the graphics device interface (GDI) and provides a brief description for their use.

Table 13–3   GDI Drawing Functions and Descriptions

Function	Description
AbortPath	Deletes the path from the device context (DC).
AngleArc	Draws an arc with a line segment.
Arc	Draws an arc.
ArcTo	Draws an arc and updates pen position.
BeginPath	Start of a path in the device context.
Chord	Draws a chord, closes with a line segment.
CloseFigure	Closes the path to create a closed figure.
CreateBrushIndirect	LOGBRUSH structure specifies brush.
CreateDIBPatternBrush	Bitmap pattern specifies brush.
CreateDIBPatternBrushPt	Bitmap pattern specifies brush.
CreateHatchBrush	Creates a brush using a hatch pattern.
CreatePatternBrush	Creates a brush using a bitmap pattern.
CreatePen	Creates a drawing pen.
CreatePenIndirect	LOGPEN structure specifies pen.
CreateSolidBrush	Creates a brush using a solid color.
DeleteObject	Deletes a drawing object such as a brush or pen.
DrawEdge	Draws edges of a rectangle in a given style.
DrawFocusRect	Draws an outline of a rectangle to indicate focus.
DrawFrameControl	Draws a control frame.
DrawState	Drawing with advanced drawing capabilities.
Ellipse	Draws an ellipse.
EndPath	End of a path creation.
EnumObjects	Enumerates the device content objects that are available.
ExtCreatePen	Creates a drawing pen with extended characteristics.
ExtFloodFill	Fills a specified area with the current brush.
FillPath	Closes and fills a figure created with a path.
FillRect	Fills a rectangle with the current brush.
FlattenPath	Changes path curves to lines.
FloodFill	Fills a specified area with the current brush.
FrameRect	Draws a frame around a rectangle.
GetArcDirection	Gets drawing direction—clockwise or counterclockwise.
GetBkColor	Gets background color.
GetBkMode	Gets background drawing mode.
GetBrushOrgEx	Gets the brush's origin.
GetCurrentObject	Gets the currently specified object.
GetCurrentPositionEx	Gets the current pen position.
GetMiterLimit	Gets the miter limit for functions using this feature.
GetNearestColor	Gets the nearest available color to one specified.
GetObject	Gets object information.
GetObjectType	Gets type of object.
GetPath	Gets information on a path.
GetPixel	Gets the color of a pixel.
GetPolyFillMode	Gets filling mode for polygon.

(continued)

Table 13–3   GDI Drawing Functions and Descriptions *(Continued)*

Function	Description
GetROP2	Gets line raster mode.
GetStockObject	Gets a stock object, such as a brush or pen.
GetSysColorBrush	Gets a brush for a given system color.
InvertRect	Inverts rectangle's image.
LineDDA	Gets all pixels to be affected by a line.
LineTo	Draws a line and moves pen position.
MoveToEx	Moves the pen position.
PathToRegion	Changes a path into a region.
Pie	Draws a pie wedge.
PolyBezier	Draws a group of Bezier curves.
PolyBezierTo	Draws a group of Bezier curves and moves pen position.
PolyDraw	Draws a group of Bezier curves and lines.
Polygon	Draws a polygon.
Polyline	Draws a group of connected lines.
PolylineTo	Draws a group of connected lines and moves the pen position.
PolyPolygon	Draws a group of polygons.
PolyPolyline	Draws a group of polyline connected lines.
Rectangle	Draws a rectangle.
RoundRect	Draws a rectangle with rounded edges.
SelectClipPath	Combines a path and clipping region.
SelectObject	Selects an object.
SetArcDirection	Sets drawing direction—clockwise or counterclockwise
SetBkColor	Sets the background color.
SetBkMode	Sets the background drawing mode.
SetBrushOrgEx	Sets the brush's origin.
SetMiterLimit	Sets the miter limit for functions using this feature.
SetPixel	Sets the color of a pixel.
SetPixelV	Sets the color of a pixel.
SetPolyFillMode	Sets filling mode for polygon.
SetROP2	Sets line raster mode.
StrokeAndFillPath	Closes and fills figure created by a path.
StrokePath	Draws the segments of a path.
UnrealizeObject	Unrealize an object causing Windows to realize the object before it is used again.
WidenPath	Changes a path into lines.

The most popular drawing functions in this large grouping for drawing graphics to the Device Content (DC) includes the Arc(), Chord(), Ellipse(), LineTo(), Pie(), Rectangle(), and RoundRect() functions. To support these drawing functions, the GDI includes functions for selecting pens to draw the shape's outline and brushes for filling the closed shape's interior.

You'll find these drawing functions used repeatedly throughout the book and in the example application near the end of this chapter.

API Drawing Function Declarations

The following listing contains the Windows API drawing and support function declarations found in the Win32api.txt file provided with Visual Basic. In addition to this large group of functions, you have already learned that the functions discussed in Chapters 10, 11, and 12 are closely related to the use of these functions.

```
Declare Function AbortPath Lib "gdi32" Alias "AbortPath"
   (ByVal hdc As Long) As Long

Declare Function AngleArc Lib "gdi32" Alias "AngleArc"
   (ByVal hdc As Long, ByVal x As Long, ByVal y As Long,
   ByVal dwRadius As Long, ByVal eStartAngle As Double,
   ByVal eSweepAngle As Double) As Long

Declare Function Arc Lib "gdi32" Alias "Arc"
   (ByVal hdc As Long, ByVal X1 As Long, ByVal Y1 As Long,
   ByVal X2 As Long, ByVal Y2 As Long, ByVal X3 As Long,
   ByVal Y3 As Long, ByVal X4 As Long,
   ByVal Y4 As Long) As Long

Declare Function ArcTo Lib "gdi32" Alias "ArcTo"
   (ByVal hdc As Long, ByVal X1 As Long, ByVal Y1 As Long,
   ByVal X2 As Long, ByVal Y2 As Long, ByVal X3 As Long,
   ByVal Y3 As Long, ByVal X4 As Long,
   ByVal Y4 As Long) As Long

Declare Function BeginPath Lib "gdi32" Alias "BeginPath"
   (ByVal hdc As Long) As Long

Declare Function Chord Lib "gdi32" Alias "Chord"
  (ByVal hdc As Long, ByVal X1 As Long, ByVal Y1 As Long,
  ByVal X2 As Long, ByVal Y2 As Long, ByVal X3 As Long,
  ByVal Y3 As Long, ByVal X4 As Long,
  ByVal Y4 As Long) As Long

Declare Function CloseFigure Lib "gdi32" Alias "CloseFigure"
   (ByVal hdc As Long) As Long

Declare Function CreateBrushIndirect Lib "gdi32"
   Alias "CreateBrushIndirect" (lpLogBrush As LOGBRUSH) As Long

Declare Function CreateDIBPatternBrush Lib "gdi32" Alias
   "CreateDIBPatternBrush" (ByVal hPackedDIB As Long,
   ByVal wUsage As Long) As Long

Declare Function CreateDIBPatternBrushPt Lib "gdi32" Alias
   "CreateDIBPatternBrushPt" (lpPackedDIB As Any,
   ByVal iUsage As Long) As Long
```

```
Declare Function CreateHatchBrush Lib "gdi32" Alias
  "CreateHatchBrush" (ByVal nIndex As Long,
  ByVal crColor As Long) As Long

Declare Function CreatePatternBrush Lib "gdi32" Alias
  "CreatePatternBrush" (ByVal hBitmap As Long) As Long

Declare Function CreatePen Lib "gdi32" Alias "CreatePen"
  (ByVal nPenStyle As Long, ByVal nWidth As Long,
  ByVal crColor As Long) As Long

Declare Function CreatePenIndirect Lib "gdi32" Alias
  "CreatePenIndirect" (lpLogPen As LOGPEN) As Long

Declare Function CreateSolidBrush Lib "gdi32" Alias
  "CreateSolidBrush" (ByVal crColor As Long) As Long

Declare Function DeleteObject Lib "gdi32" Alias
  "DeleteObject" (ByVal hObject As Long) As Long

Declare Function DrawEdge Lib "user32" Alias "DrawEdge"
  (ByVal hdc As Long, qrc As RECT, ByVal edge As Long,
  ByVal grfFlags As Long) As Long

Declare Function DrawFocusRect Lib "user32" Alias
  "DrawFocusRect" (ByVal hdc As Long,
  lpRect As RECT) As Long

Declare Function DrawFrameControl Lib "user32" Alias
  "DrawFrameControl" (ByVal hDC As Long, lpRect As RECT,
  ByVal un1 As Long, ByVal un2 As Long) As Long

 Declare Function DrawState Lib "user32" Alias "DrawStateA"
  (ByVal hDC As Long, ByVal hBrush As Long,
  ByVal lpDrawStateProc As Long, ByVal lParam As Long,
  ByVal wParam As Long, ByVal n1 As Long, ByVal n2 As Long,
  ByVal n3 As Long, ByVal n4 As Long,
  ByVal un As Long) As Long

Declare Function Ellipse Lib "gdi32" Alias "Ellipse"
  (ByVal hdc As Long, ByVal X1 As Long, ByVal Y1 As Long,
  ByVal X2 As Long, ByVal Y2 As Long) As Long

Declare Function EndPath Lib "gdi32" Alias "EndPath"
  (ByVal hdc As Long) As Long

Declare Function EnumObjects Lib "gdi32" Alias "EnumObjects"
  (ByVal hDC As Long, ByVal n As Long,
  ByVal lpGOBJEnumProc As Long, lpVoid As Any) As Long

Declare Function ExtCreatePen Lib "gdi32" Alias
  "ExtCreatePen" (ByVal dwPenStyle As Long,
  ByVal dwWidth As Long, lplb As LOGBRUSH,
  ByVal dwStyleCount As Long, lpStyle As Long) As Long
```

```
Declare Function ExtFloodFill Lib "gdi32" Alias
  "ExtFloodFill" (ByVal hdc As Long, ByVal x As Long,
  ByVal y As Long, ByVal crColor As Long,
  ByVal wFillType As Long) As Long

Declare Function FillPath Lib "gdi32" Alias "FillPath"
  (ByVal hdc As Long) As Long

Declare Function FillRect Lib "user32" Alias "FillRect"
  (ByVal hdc As Long, lpRect As RECT,
  ByVal hBrush As Long) As Long

Declare Function FlattenPath Lib "gdi32" Alias "FlattenPath"
  (ByVal hdc As Long) As Long

Declare Function FloodFill Lib "gdi32" Alias "FloodFill"
  (ByVal hdc As Long, ByVal x As Long, ByVal y As Long,
  ByVal crColor As Long) As Long

Declare Function FrameRect Lib "user32" Alias "FrameRect"
  (ByVal hdc As Long, lpRect As RECT,
  ByVal hBrush As Long) As Long

Declare Function GetArcDirection Lib "gdi32" Alias
  "GetArcDirection" (ByVal hdc As Long) As Long

Declare Function GetBkColor Lib "gdi32" Alias "GetBkColor"
  (ByVal hdc As Long) As Long

Declare Function GetBkMode Lib "gdi32" Alias "GetBkMode"
  (ByVal hdc As Long) As Long

Declare Function GetBrushOrgEx Lib "gdi32" Alias
  "GetBrushOrgEx" (ByVal hDC As Long,
  lpPoint As POINTAPI) As Long

Declare Function GetCurrentObject Lib "gdi32" Alias
  "GetCurrentObject" (ByVal hdc As Long,
  ByVal uObjectType As Long) As Long

Declare Function GetCurrentPositionEx Lib "gdi32" Alias
  "GetCurrentPositionEx" (ByVal hdc As Long,
  lpPoint As POINTAPI) As Long

Declare Function GetMiterLimit Lib "gdi32" Alias
  "GetMiterLimit" (ByVal hdc As Long,
  peLimit As Double) As Long

Declare Function GetNearestColor Lib "gdi32" Alias
  "GetNearestColor" (ByVal hdc As Long,
  ByVal crColor As Long) As Long

Declare Function GetObject Lib "gdi32" Alias "GetObjectA"
  (ByVal hObject As Long, ByVal nCount As Long,
  lpObject As Any) As Long
```

```
Declare Function GetObjectType Lib "gdi32" Alias
   "GetObjectType" (ByVal hgdiobj As Long) As Long

Declare Function GetPath Lib "gdi32" Alias "GetPath"
   (ByVal hdc As Long, lpPoint As POINTAPI,
   lpTypes As Byte, ByVal nSize As Long) As Long

Declare Function GetPixel Lib "gdi32" Alias "GetPixel"
   (ByVal hdc As Long, ByVal x As Long,
   ByVal y As Long) As Long

 Declare Function GetPolyFillMode Lib "gdi32" Alias
   "GetPolyFillMode" (ByVal hdc As Long) As Long

Declare Function GetROP2 Lib "gdi32" Alias "GetROP2"
   (ByVal hdc As Long) As Long

Declare Function GetStockObject Lib "gdi32" Alias
   "GetStockObject" (ByVal nIndex As Long) As Long

Declare Function GetSysColorBrush Lib "user32" Alias
   "GetSysColorBrush" (ByVal nIndex As Long) As Long

Declare Function InvertRect Lib "user32" Alias "InvertRect"
   (ByVal hdc As Long, lpRect As RECT) As Long

Declare Function LineDDA Lib "gdi32" Alias "LineDDA"
   (ByVal n1 As Long, ByVal n2 As Long, ByVal n3 As Long,
   ByVal n4 As Long, ByVal lpLineDDAProc As Long,
   ByVal lParam As Long) As Long

Declare Function LineTo Lib "gdi32" Alias "LineTo"
   (ByVal hdc As Long, ByVal x As Long,
   ByVal y As Long) As Long

Declare Function MoveToEx Lib "gdi32" Alias "MoveToEx"
   (ByVal hdc As Long, ByVal x As Long, ByVal y As Long,
   lpPoint As POINTAPI) As Long

Declare Function PathToRegion Lib "gdi32" Alias
   "PathToRegion" (ByVal hdc As Long) As Long

Declare Function Pie Lib "gdi32" Alias "Pie"
   (ByVal hdc As Long, ByVal X1 As Long, ByVal Y1 As Long,
   ByVal X2 As Long, ByVal Y2 As Long, ByVal X3 As Long,
   ByVal Y3 As Long, ByVal X4 As Long,
   ByVal Y4 As Long) As Long

Declare Function PolyBezier Lib "gdi32" Alias "PolyBezier"
   (ByVal hdc As Long, lppt As POINTAPI,
   ByVal cPoints As Long) As Long

Declare Function PolyBezierTo Lib "gdi32" Alias
   "PolyBezierTo" (ByVal hdc As Long, lppt As POINTAPI,
   ByVal cCount As Long) As Long
```

```
Declare Function PolyDraw Lib "gdi32" Alias "PolyDraw"
    (ByVal hdc As Long, lppt As POINTAPI, lpbTypes As Byte,
    ByVal cCount As Long) As Long

Declare Function Polygon Lib "gdi32" Alias "Polygon"
    (ByVal hdc As Long, lpPoint As POINTAPI,
    ByVal nCount As Long) As Long

Declare Function Polyline Lib "gdi32" Alias "Polyline"
    (ByVal hdc As Long, lpPoint As POINTAPI,
    ByVal nCount As Long) As Long

Declare Function PolylineTo Lib "gdi32" Alias "PolylineTo"
    (ByVal hdc As Long, lppt As POINTAPI,
    ByVal cCount As Long) As Long

Declare Function PolyPolygon Lib "gdi32" Alias
    "PolyPolygon" (ByVal hdc As Long, lpPoint As POINTAPI,
    lpPolyCounts As Long, ByVal nCount As Long) As Long

Declare Function PolyPolyline Lib "gdi32" Alias
    "PolyPolyline" (ByVal hdc As Long, lppt As POINTAPI,
    lpdwPolyPoints As Long, ByVal cCount As Long) As Long

Declare Function Rectangle Lib "gdi32" Alias "Rectangle"
    (ByVal hdc As Long, ByVal X1 As Long, ByVal Y1 As Long,
    ByVal X2 As Long, ByVal Y2 As Long) As Long

Declare Function RoundRect Lib "gdi32" Alias "RoundRect"
    (ByVal hdc As Long, ByVal X1 As Long, ByVal Y1 As Long,
    ByVal X2 As Long, ByVal Y2 As Long, ByVal X3 As Long,
    ByVal Y3 As Long) As Long

Declare Function SelectClipPath Lib "gdi32" Alias
    "SelectClipPath" (ByVal hdc As Long,
    ByVal iMode As Long) As Long

Declare Function SelectObject Lib "gdi32" Alias
    "SelectObject" (ByVal hdc As Long,
    ByVal hObject As Long) As Long

Declare Function SetArcDirection Lib "gdi32" Alias
    "SetArcDirection" (ByVal hdc As Long,
    ByVal ArcDirection As Long) As Long

Declare Function SetBkColor Lib "gdi32" Alias "SetBkColor"
    (ByVal hdc As Long, ByVal crColor As Long) As Long

Declare Function SetBkMode Lib "gdi32" Alias "SetBkMode"
    (ByVal hdc As Long, ByVal nBkMode As Long) As Long

Declare Function SetBrushOrgEx Lib "gdi32" Alias
    "SetBrushOrgEx" (ByVal hdc As Long, ByVal nXOrg As Long,
    ByVal nYOrg As Long, lppt As POINTAPI) As Long
```

```
Declare Function SetMiterLimit Lib "gdi32" Alias
   "SetMiterLimit" (ByVal hdc As Long,
   ByVal eNewLimit As Double, peOldLimit As Double) As Long

Declare Function SetPixel Lib "gdi32" Alias "SetPixel"
   (ByVal hdc As Long, ByVal x As Long, ByVal y As Long,
   ByVal crColor As Long) As Long

 Declare Function SetPixelV Lib "gdi32" Alias "SetPixelV"
   (ByVal hdc As Long, ByVal x As Long, ByVal y As Long,
   ByVal crColor As Long) As Long

Declare Function SetPolyFillMode Lib "gdi32" Alias
   "SetPolyFillMode" (ByVal hdc As Long,
   ByVal nPolyFillMode As Long) As Long

Declare Function SetROP2 Lib "gdi32" Alias "SetROP2"
   (ByVal hdc As Long, ByVal nDrawMode As Long) As Long

Declare Function StrokeAndFillPath Lib "gdi32" Alias
   "StrokeAndFillPath" (ByVal hdc As Long) As Long

Declare Function StrokePath Lib "gdi32" Alias "StrokePath"
   (ByVal hdc As Long) As Long

Declare Function UnrealizeObject Lib "gdi32" Alias
   "UnrealizeObject" (ByVal hObject As Long) As Long

Declare Function WidenPath Lib "gdi32" Alias "WidenPath"
   (ByVal hdc As Long) As Long
```

Table 13–4 contains a brief description of the parameters used in the various drawing and support functions.

Table 13–4   GDI Drawing and Support Function Parameters and Descriptions

Parameter	Description
ArcDirection As Long	Uses constants AD_CLOCKWISE or AD_COUNTERCLOCKWISE.
cCount As Long	Size of the lpPoint or lpTypes arrays.
cPoints As Long	Number of points in lppt array.
crColor As Long	RGB color specification.
dwPenStyle As Long	Uses PS_ constants for style.
dwRadius As Long	Radius of graphics shape.
dwStyleCount As Long	Size of lpStyle array.
dwWidth As Long	Pen width.
edge As Long	Uses BDR_ and EDGE_ constants.
eNewLimit As Double	New miter limit.
eStartAngle As Double	Angle (degrees) of line intersection with arc or circle.
eSweepAngle As Double	Angle (degrees) of arc or circle extent.
grfFlags As Long	Uses BF_ constants.
hBitmap As Long	Handle to a bitmap pattern.

**Table 13–4　GDI Drawing and Support Function Parameters
and Descriptions** *(Continued)*

Parameter	Description
hBrush As Long	Handle to a brush.
hdc As Long	Handle to the Device Context (DC).
hgdiobj As Long	An object's handle.
hObject As Long	Handle to drawing object.
hPackedDIB As Long	Handle to portion of memory that holds BITMAPINFO structure and bitmap.
iMode As Long	How path combines with clipping region. Uses RGN_ constants.
iUsage As Long	Uses constant: DIB_PAL_COLORS or DIB_RGB_COLORS.
lParam As Long	Value dependent upon image type.
lpbTypes As Byte	Points to array holding constants of PT_ type.
lpDrawStateProc As Long	Points to a draw function's address.
lpdwPolyPoints As Long	Points to an array holding number of points for polygon.
lpGOBJEnumProc As Long	Points to a function for a given GDI object.
lplb As LOGBRUSH	Structure holds pen color information.
lpLineDDAProc As Long	Points to function address.
lpLogBrush As LOGBRUSH	Structure holds brush information.
lpLogPen As LOGPEN	Structure holds pen information.
lpObject As Any	Points to structure with object data.
lpPackedDIB As Any	Points to portion of memory that holds BITMAPINFO structure and bitmap.
lpPoint As POINTAPI	Structure holds brush origin.
lpPolyCounts As Long	Points to array holding points for polygons.
lppt As POINTAPI	Structure holds poly information.
lpRect As RECT	Structure holds coordinates of rectangle.
lpStyle As Long	Data pairs for PS_USERSTYLE.
lpTypes As Byte	Points to array holding data using PT_ constants.
lpVoid As Any	Value to pass to callback function.
n As Long	Object type: OBJ_PEN or OBJ_BRUSH
n1 As Long	Horizontal image position or (*x*) start of line.
n2 As Long	Vertical image position or (*y*) start of line.
n3 As Long	Image width or (*x*) finish of line.
n4 As Long	Image height or (*y*) finish of line.
nBkMode As Long	Uses constants OPAQUE or TRANSPARENT.
nCount As Long	Number of bytes of data to obtain.
nDrawMode As Long	New drawing mode.
nIndex As Long	Index to hatching pattern, brush style, or pen style. Also used for colors using COLOR_ constant.
nPenStyle As Long	Uses PS_ constant to set style.
nPolyFillMode As Long	Uses constant: ALTERNATE or WINDING.
nSize As Long	Size of lpPoint or lpType array.
nWidth As Long	Pen width (logical units).
nXOrg As Long, nYOrg As Long	New brush origin.

(continued)

**Table 13–4   GDI Drawing and Support Function Parameters
and Descriptions *(Continued)***

Parameter	Description
peLimit As Double	Current miter limit.
peOldLimit As Double	Old miter limit.
qrc As RECT	Structure holds coodinates of rectangle's edges.
un As Long	Type & state. Uses DST_ and DSS_ constants.
un1 As Long	Frame type. Uses DFC_ constants.
un2 As Long	State type. Uses DFCS_ constants.
uObjectType As Long	Uses OBJ_ constant.
wFillType As Long	Uses FLOODFILLBORDER or FLOODFILLSURFACE to fill to border or from given point.
wParam As Long	Value dependent upon image type.
wUsage As Long	Uses DIB_PAL_ or DIB_RGB_ constants.
x As Long, y As Long	Coordinate points for center of graphics shape or starting point for filling.
X1 As Long, Y1 As Long	Upper-left diagonal of bounding rectangle.
X2 As Long, Y2 As Long	Lower-right diagonal of bounding rectangle.
X3 As Long, Y3 As Long	Coordinates of arc starting point or point of line intersection. X_3 can be width of rounding ellipse. Y_3 can be height of rounding ellipse.
X4 As Long, Y4 As Long	Coordinates of arc ending point or point of line intersection.

Many of the parameters described in Table 13–4 use constant values. The win32api.txt file lists the following constants for the drawing and support functions:

```
'Background Modes
Public Const TRANSPARENT = 1
Public Const OPAQUE = 2
Public Const BKMODE_LAST = 2

'Stock Logical Objects
Public Const WHITE_BRUSH = 0
Public Const LTGRAY_BRUSH = 1
Public Const GRAY_BRUSH = 2
Public Const DKGRAY_BRUSH = 3
Public Const BLACK_BRUSH = 4
Public Const NULL_BRUSH = 5
Public Const HOLLOW_BRUSH = NULL_BRUSH
Public Const WHITE_PEN = 6
Public Const BLACK_PEN = 7
Public Const NULL_PEN = 8
Public Const OEM_FIXED_FONT = 10
Public Const ANSI_FIXED_FONT = 11
Public Const ANSI_VAR_FONT = 12
Public Const SYSTEM_FONT = 13
```

```
Public Const DEVICE_DEFAULT_FONT = 14
Public Const DEFAULT_PALETTE = 15
Public Const SYSTEM_FIXED_FONT = 16
Public Const STOCK_LAST = 16

'Drawing Direction
Public Const AD_COUNTERCLOCKWISE = 1
Public Const AD_CLOCKWISE = 2

'DrawEdge Constants
Public Const BDR_RAISEDOUTER = &H1
Public Const BDR_SUNKENOUTER = &H2
Public Const BDR_RAISEDINNER = &H4
Public Const BDR_SUNKENINNER = &H8
Public Const BDR_OUTER = &H3
Public Const BDR_INNER = &HC
Public Const BDR_RAISED = &H5
Public Const BDR_SUNKEN = &HA
Public Const EDGE_RAISED=(BDR_RAISEDOUTER Or BDR_RAISEDINNER)
Public Const EDGE_SUNKEN=(BDR_SUNKENOUTER Or BDR_SUNKENINNER)
Public Const EDGE_ETCHED=(BDR_SUNKENOUTER Or BDR_RAISEDINNER)
Public Const EDGE_BUMP=(BDR_RAISEDOUTER Or BDR_SUNKENINNER)

'Flag Constants
Public Const BF_TOP = &H2
Public Const BF_RIGHT = &H4
Public Const BF_BOTTOM = &H8
Public Const BF_TOPLEFT = (BF_TOP Or BF_LEFT)
Public Const BF_TOPRIGHT = (BF_TOP Or BF_RIGHT)
Public Const BF_BOTTOMLEFT = (BF_BOTTOM Or BF_LEFT)
Public Const BF_BOTTOMRIGHT = (BF_BOTTOM Or BF_RIGHT)
Public Const BF_RECT = (BF_LEFT Or BF_TOP Or
                        BF_RIGHT Or BF_BOTTOM)
Public Const BF_DIAGONAL = &H10
Public Const BF_LEFT = &H1

'For diagonal lines, the BF_RECT flags specify the end
'point of the vector bounded by the rectangle parameter.
Public Const BF_DIAGONAL_ENDTOPRIGHT = (BF_DIAGONAL Or
                                        BF_TOP Or BF_RIGHT)
Public Const BF_DIAGONAL_ENDTOPLEFT = (BF_DIAGONAL Or
                                       BF_TOP Or BF_LEFT)
Public Const BF_DIAGONAL_ENDBOTTOMLEFT = (BF_DIAGONAL Or
                                          BF_BOTTOM Or
                                          BF_LEFT)
Public Const BF_DIAGONAL_ENDBOTTOMRIGHT = (BF_DIAGONAL Or
                                           BF_BOTTOM Or
                                           BF_RIGHT)
Public Const BF_MIDDLE = &H800    'Fill in the middle.
Public Const BF_SOFT = &H1000     'Use for softer buttons.
```

```
Public Const BF_ADJUST = &H2000    'Find left over space.
Public Const BF_FLAT = &H4000      'Flat rather than
                                   '3-D borders.
Public Const BF_MONO = &H8000      'For monochrome borders.

'Brush Styles
Public Const BS_SOLID = 0
Public Const BS_NULL = 1
Public Const BS_HOLLOW = BS_NULL
Public Const BS_HATCHED = 2
Public Const BS_PATTERN = 3
Public Const BS_INDEXED = 4
Public Const BS_DIBPATTERN = 5
Public Const BS_DIBPATTERNPT = 6
Public Const BS_PATTERN8X8 = 7
Public Const BS_DIBPATTERN8X8 = 8

'Color Constants
Public Const COLOR_SCROLLBAR = 0
Public Const COLOR_BACKGROUND = 1
Public Const COLOR_ACTIVECAPTION = 2
Public Const COLOR_INACTIVECAPTION = 3
Public Const COLOR_MENU = 4
Public Const COLOR_WINDOW = 5
Public Const COLOR_WINDOWFRAME = 6
Public Const COLOR_MENUTEXT = 7
Public Const COLOR_WINDOWTEXT = 8
Public Const COLOR_CAPTIONTEXT = 9
Public Const COLOR_ACTIVEBORDER = 10
Public Const COLOR_INACTIVEBORDER = 11
Public Const COLOR_APPWORKSPACE = 12
Public Const COLOR_HIGHLIGHT = 13
Public Const COLOR_HIGHLIGHTTEXT = 14
Public Const COLOR_BTNFACE = 15
Public Const COLOR_BTNSHADOW = 16
Public Const COLOR_GRAYTEXT = 17
Public Const COLOR_BTNTEXT = 18
Public Const COLOR_INACTIVECAPTIONTEXT = 19
Public Const COLOR_BTNHIGHLIGHT = 20

' DIB color table identifiers
Public Const DIB_RGB_COLORS = 0 'color table in RGBs
Public Const DIB_PAL_COLORS = 1 'color table in
                                'palette indices
Public Const DIB_PAL_INDICES = 2 'No color table indices
                                 'into surf palette
Public Const DIB_PAL_PHYSINDICES = 2 'No color table indices
                                     'into surf palette
Public Const DIB_PAL_LOGINDICES = 4 'No color table indices
                                    'into DC palette
```

```
' Hatch Styles
Public Const HS_HORIZONTAL = 0          ' —-
Public Const HS_VERTICAL = 1            ' |||||
Public Const HS_FDIAGONAL = 2           ' \\\\\
Public Const HS_BDIAGONAL = 3           ' /////
Public Const HS_CROSS = 4               ' +++++
Public Const HS_DIAGCROSS = 5           ' xxxxx
Public Const HS_FDIAGONAL1 = 6
Public Const HS_BDIAGONAL1 = 7
Public Const HS_SOLID = 8
Public Const HS_DENSE1 = 9
Public Const HS_DENSE2 = 10
Public Const HS_DENSE3 = 11
Public Const HS_DENSE4 = 12
Public Const HS_DENSE5 = 13
Public Const HS_DENSE6 = 14
Public Const HS_DENSE7 = 15
Public Const HS_DENSE8 = 16
Public Const HS_NOSHADE = 17
Public Const HS_HALFTONE = 18
Public Const HS_SOLIDCLR = 19
Public Const HS_DITHEREDCLR = 20
Public Const HS_SOLIDTEXTCLR = 21
Public Const HS_DITHEREDTEXTCLR = 22
Public Const HS_SOLIDBKCLR = 23
Public Const HS_DITHEREDBKCLR = 24
Public Const HS_API_MAX = 25

'Object Definitions for EnumObjects()
Public Const OBJ_PEN = 1
Public Const OBJ_BRUSH = 2
Public Const OBJ_DC = 3
Public Const OBJ_METADC = 4
Public Const OBJ_PAL = 5
Public Const OBJ_FONT = 6
Public Const OBJ_BITMAP = 7
Public Const OBJ_REGION = 8
Public Const OBJ_METAFILE = 9
Public Const OBJ_MEMDC = 10
Public Const OBJ_EXTPEN = 11
Public Const OBJ_ENHMETADC = 12
Public Const OBJ_ENHMETAFILE = 13

'Pen Styles
Public Const PS_SOLID = 0
Public Const PS_DASH = 1                 ' —-
Public Const PS_DOT = 2                  ' .......
Public Const PS_DASHDOT = 3              ' _._._._
Public Const PS_DASHDOTDOT = 4           ' _.._.._
```

```
Public Const PS_NULL = 5
Public Const PS_INSIDEFRAME = 6
Public Const PS_USERSTYLE = 7
Public Const PS_ALTERNATE = 8
Public Const PS_STYLE_MASK = &HF
Public Const PS_ENDCAP_ROUND = &H0
Public Const PS_ENDCAP_SQUARE = &H100
Public Const PS_ENDCAP_FLAT = &H200
Public Const PS_ENDCAP_MASK = &HF00
Public Const PS_JOIN_ROUND = &H0
Public Const PS_JOIN_BEVEL = &H1000
Public Const PS_JOIN_MITER = &H2000
Public Const PS_JOIN_MASK = &HF000
Public Const PS_COSMETIC = &H0
Public Const PS_GEOMETRIC = &H10000
Public Const PS_TYPE_MASK = &HF0000

'PolyDraw and GetPath point types
Public Const PT_CLOSEFIGURE = &H1
Public Const PT_LINETO = &H2
Public Const PT_BEZIERTO = &H4
Public Const PT_MOVETO = &H6

'CombineRgn() Styles
Public Const RGN_AND = 1
Public Const RGN_OR = 2
Public Const RGN_XOR = 3
Public Const RGN_DIFF = 4
Public Const RGN_COPY = 5
Public Const RGN_MIN = RGN_AND
Public Const RGN_MAX = RGN_COPY
```

The drawing and support parameters often use structures also defined in the win32api.txt file. The following listing contains the structure definitions used by the functions described in this chapter.

```
Type RECT
  Left As Long
  Top As Long
  Right As Long
  Bottom As Long
End Type

Type POINTAPI
  x As Long
  y As Long
End Type
```

```
'Logical Brush (or Pattern)
Type LOGBRUSH
  lbStyle As Long
  lbColor As Long
  lbHatch As Long
End Type

'Logical Pen
Type LOGPEN
  lopnStyle As Long
  lopnWidth As POINTAPI
  lopnColor As Long
End Type

Type EXTLOGPEN
  elpPenStyle As Long
  elpWidth As Long
  elpBrushStyle As Long
  elpColor As Long
  elpHatch As Long
  elpNumEntries As Long
  elpStyleEntry(1) As Long
End Type

Type BITMAPINFO
  bmiHeader As BITMAPINFOHEADER
  bmiColors As RGBQUAD
End Type

Type BITMAPINFOHEADER '40 bytes
  biSize As Long
  biWidth As Long
  biHeight As Long
  biPlanes As Integer
  biBitCount As Integer
  biCompression As Long
  biSizeImage As Long
  biXPelsPerMeter As Long
  biYPelsPerMeter As Long
  biClrUsed As Long
  biClrImportant As Long
End Type

Type RGBQUAD
  rgbBlue As Byte
  rgbGreen As Byte
  rgbRed As Byte
  rgbReserved As Byte
End Type
```

Example Application

The example project for this chapter, GDI1.vbp, will teach you how to draw many graphics primitives with the default pen and several brush colors. Many of the previously discussed drawing primitives are used in this application.

All drawing is done with default settings. The default pen draws a black line. The default brush is white. The default mapping mode is MM_TEXT. The values supplied for the various GDI function parameters are pixel values that will plot on a VGA screen.

The module file used for structure and function declarations is named GDI1.bas. The following listing shows the contents of this file.

```
Public hBrush

Type POINTAPI
  x As Long
  y As Long
End Type

Declare Function Arc Lib "gdi32" (ByVal hdc As Long,
  ByVal X1 As Long, ByVal Y1 As Long, ByVal X2 As Long,
  ByVal Y2 As Long, ByVal X3 As Long, ByVal Y3 As Long,
   ByVal X4 As Long, ByVal Y4 As Long) As Long

Declare Function Chord Lib "gdi32" (ByVal hdc As Long,
  ByVal X1 As Long, ByVal Y1 As Long, ByVal X2 As Long,
  ByVal Y2 As Long, ByVal X3 As Long, ByVal Y3 As Long,
  ByVal X4 As Long, ByVal Y4 As Long) As Long

Declare Function CreateSolidBrush Lib "gdi32"
  (ByVal crColor As Long) As Long

Declare Function Ellipse Lib "gdi32" (ByVal hdc As Long,
  ByVal X1 As Long, ByVal Y1 As Long, ByVal X2 As Long,
  ByVal Y2 As Long) As Long

Declare Function LineTo Lib "gdi32" (ByVal hdc As Long,
  ByVal x As Long, ByVal y As Long) As Long

Declare Function MoveToEx Lib "gdi32" (ByVal hdc As Long,
  ByVal x As Long, ByVal y As Long, lpPoint As POINTAPI) As Long

Declare Function Pie Lib "gdi32" (ByVal hdc As Long,
  ByVal X1 As Long, ByVal Y1 As Long, ByVal X2 As Long,
   ByVal Y2 As Long, ByVal X3 As Long, ByVal Y3 As Long,
  ByVal X4 As Long, ByVal Y4 As Long) As Long

Declare Function Polygon Lib "gdi32" (ByVal hdc As Long,
  lpPoint As POINTAPI, ByVal nCount As Long) As Long
```

```
Declare Function Polyline Lib "gdi32" (ByVal hdc As Long,
   lpPoint As POINTAPI, ByVal nCount As Long) As Long

Declare Function Rectangle Lib "gdi32" (ByVal hdc As Long,
   ByVal X1 As Long, ByVal Y1 As Long, ByVal X2 As Long,
   ByVal Y2 As Long) As Long

Declare Function RoundRect Lib "gdi32" (ByVal hdc As Long,
   ByVal X1 As Long, ByVal Y1 As Long, ByVal X2 As Long,
   ByVal Y2 As Long, ByVal X3 As Long, ByVal Y3 As Long) As Long

Declare Function SelectObject Lib "gdi32" (ByVal hdc As Long,
   ByVal hObject As Long) As Long

Declare Function TextOut Lib "gdi32" Alias "TextOutA"
   (ByVal hdc As Long, ByVal x As Long, ByVal y As Long,
   ByVal lpString As String, ByVal nCount As Long) As Long
```

The project will draw the various graphics shapes on a blank form, named
GDI1.frm. The following listing shows the code required for this form.

```
Private Sub Form_Paint()
      Dim tempPoint As POINTAPI
      Dim r&
      Dim newbrush&
      Dim polylpts(4) As POINTAPI
      Dim polygpts(5) As POINTAPI
      Dim xcoord As Long

      'dummy values
      tempPoint.x = 0
      tempPoint.y = 0

      'draw a diagonal line
      r% = MoveToEx(hdc, 20, 20, tempPoint)
      r% = LineTo(hdc, 100, 100)
      r% = TextOut(hdc, 60, 20, "<- Diagonal Line", 16)

      'draw an arc
      r% = Arc(hdc, 25, 125, 175, 225, 175, 225, 100, 125)
      r% = TextOut(hdc, 70, 150, "Small Arc ->", 12)

      'create a solid dark blue brush
      hBrush = CreateSolidBrush(QBColor(9))
      newbrush = SelectObject(hdc, hBrush)

      'draw a chord
      r% = Chord(hdc, 125, 125, 275, 225, 275, 225, 200, 125)
      r% = TextOut(hdc, 280, 150, "<- Chord", 8)

      'create a solid green brush
      hBrush = CreateSolidBrush(QBColor(10))
      newbrush = SelectObject(hdc, hBrush)
```

```
'draw an ellipse
r% = Ellipse(hdc, 275, 300, 200, 250)
r% = TextOut(hdc, 220, 265, "Ellipse", 7)

'create a solid light blue brush
hBrush = CreateSolidBrush(QBColor(11))
newbrush = SelectObject(hdc, hBrush)

'draw a circle with ellipse function
r% = Ellipse(hdc, 375, 75, 525, 225)
r% = TextOut(hdc, 435, 140, "Circle", 6)

'create a solid red brush
hBrush = CreateSolidBrush(QBColor(12))
newbrush = SelectObject(hdc, hBrush)

'draw a pie wedge
r% = Pie(hdc, 200, 0, 300, 100, 200, 50, 250, 100)
r% = TextOut(hdc, 260, 80, "<- Pie Wedge", 12)

'create a solid magenta brush
hBrush = CreateSolidBrush(QBColor(13))
newbrush = SelectObject(hdc, hBrush)

'draw a rectangle
r% = Rectangle(hdc, 25, 300, 150, 375)
r% = TextOut(hdc, 50, 325, "Rectangle", 9)

'create a solid yellow brush
hBrush = CreateSolidBrush(QBColor(14))
newbrush = SelectObject(hdc, hBrush)

'draw rounded rectangle
r% = RoundRect(hdc, 350, 250, 400, 290, 20, 20)
r% = TextOut(hdc, 410, 270, "<—Rounded Rectangle", 20)

'drawing several lines with Polyline
polylpts(0).x = 10
polylpts(0).y = 30
polylpts(1).x = 10
polylpts(1).y = 100
polylpts(2).x = 50
polylpts(2).y = 100
polylpts(3).x = 10
polylpts(3).y = 30
r% = Polyline(hdc, polylpts(0), 4)
r% = TextOut(hdc, 10, 110, "Polyline", 8)

'create a solid white brush
hBrush = CreateSolidBrush(QBColor(15))
newbrush = SelectObject(hdc, hBrush)

'drawing with Polygon
polygpts(0).x = 40
```

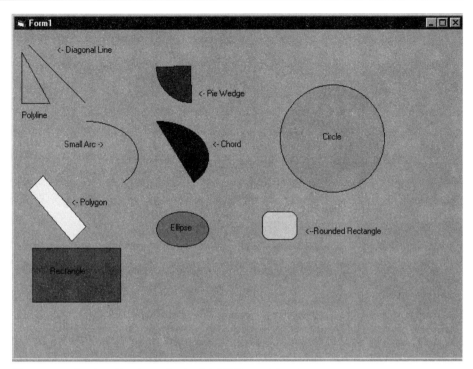

Figure 13–6 A collection of colorful GDI graphics shapes.

```
        polygpts(0).y = 200
        polygpts(1).x = 100
        polygpts(1).y = 270
        polygpts(2).x = 80
        polygpts(2).y = 290
        polygpts(3).x = 20
        polygpts(3).y = 220
        polygpts(4).x = 40
        polygpts(4).y = 200
        r% = Polygon(hdc, polygpts(0), 5)
        r% = TextOut(hdc, 80, 230, "<- Polygon", 10)
End Sub
```

Each of the drawing primitives was discussed previously in this chapter. When you run this application, your screen should appear similar to Figure 13–6.

Continue your study of GDI drawing primitives and support functions by creating your own application with additional GDI drawing primitives. If you are working in the Windows NT environment, be sure to investigate the PolyDraw() function.

Chapter 14

Metafile Functions

Metafile functions are closely associated with the GDI functions discussed in Chapter 13. Metafile functions allow a series of GDI drawing operations to be recorded and played back at a later time. Thus, complex graphics operations can be stored on disk and used to restore a screen at any time.

One of the alternatives to the use of metafiles is the use of bitmaps. Bitmaps, discussed in Chapter 15, are electronic photographics of a whole screen or portion of a screen. The main disadvantage of bitmaps is the large amount of memory they require to save screen images. Since metafiles record and play back a series of GDI functions, they consume less disk space. The GDI functions contained within a metafile, like all GDI drawing functions, are scalable and device independent.

Metafile functions are supported by all versions of Windows. A newer group of enhanced metafile functions are only supported in the 32-bit Windows environment.

API Metafile Function Name and Description

Table 14–1 shows 26 Windows API metafile functions and provides a brief description for their use.

Table 14–1   Metafile Functions and Descriptions

Function	Description
CloseEnhMetaFile	Closes enhanced metafile DC and obtains handle.
CloseMetaFile	Closes metafile DC and obtains handle.
CopyEnhMetaFile	Copies enhanced metafile.
CopyMetaFile	Copies metafile.
CreateEnhMetaFile	Creates an enhanced metafile DC for drawing.
CreateMetaFile	Creates a metafile DC for drawing.
DeleteEnhMetaFile	Deletes an enhanced metafile.
DeleteMetaFile	Deletes a metafile.
EnumEnhMetaFile	Enumerates the records in an enhanced metafile.
EnumMetaFile	Enumerates the records in a metafile.
GdiComment	Adds a comment to an enhanced metafile.
GetEnhMetaFile	Gets enhanced metafile handle.
GetEnhMetaFileBits	Gets enhanced metafile data into memory.
GetEnhMetaFileDescription	Gets enhanced metafile file description.
GetEnhMetaFileHeader	Gets enhanced metafile header information
GetEnhMetaFilePaletteEntries	Gets the palette entries for an enhanced metafile.
GetMetaFile	Gets a metafile handle from a file.
GetMetaFileBitsEx	Gets metafile data into memory.
GetWinMetaFileBits	Converts enhanced metafile into metafile format.
PlayEnhMetaFile	Plays an enhanced metafile.
PlayEnhMetaFileRecord	Plays a single enhanced metafile record.
PlayMetaFile	Plays a metafile.
PlayMetaFileRecord	Plays a single metafile record.
SetEnhMetaFileBits	Creates a handle for a portion of memory with an enhanced metafile.
SetMetaFileBitsEx	Creates a handle for a portion of memory with a metafile.
SetWinMetaFileBits	Converts metafile into enhanced metafile format.

The most frequently used metafile functions include CloseMetaFile(), CreateMetaFile(), DeleteMetaFile(), and PlayMetaFile(). The programming example in this chapter will highlight several important metafile functions.

API Metafile Function Declarations

The following listing contains the Windows API metafile functions declarations found in the Win32api.txt file provided with Visual Basic. As you examine this listing, keep in mind the close association between these functions and the GDI graphics functions discussed in Chapter 13.

```
Declare Function CloseEnhMetaFile Lib "gdi32" Alias
    "CloseEnhMetaFile" (ByVal hdc As Long) As Long
```

```
Declare Function CloseMetaFile Lib "gdi32" Alias
  "CloseMetaFile" (ByVal hMF As Long) As Long

Declare Function CopyEnhMetaFile Lib "gdi32" Alias
  "CopyEnhMetaFileA" (ByVal hemfSrc As Long,
  ByVal lpszFile As String) As Long

Declare Function CopyMetaFile Lib "gdi32" Alias
  "CopyMetaFileA" (ByVal hMF As Long,
  ByVal lpFileName As String) As Long

Declare Function CreateEnhMetaFile Lib "gdi32" Alias
  "CreateEnhMetaFileA" (ByVal hdcRef As Long,
  ByVal lpFileName As String, lpRect As RECT,
  ByVal lpDescription As String) As Long

Declare Function CreateMetaFile Lib "gdi32" Alias
  "CreateMetaFileA" (ByVal lpString As String) As Long

Declare Function DeleteEnhMetaFile Lib "gdi32" Alias
  "DeleteEnhMetaFile" (ByVal hemf As Long) As Long

Declare Function DeleteMetaFile Lib "gdi32" Alias
  "DeleteMetaFile" (ByVal hMF As Long) As Long

Declare Function EnumEnhMetaFile Lib "gdi32" Alias
  "EnumEnhMetaFile" (ByVal hdc As Long, ByVal hemf As Long,
  ByVal lpEnhMetaFunc As Long, lpData As Any,
  lpRect As RECT) As Long

Declare Function EnumMetaFile Lib "gdi32" Alias
  "EnumMetaFile" (ByVal hDC As Long,
  ByVal hMetafile As Long, ByVal lpMFEnumProc As Long,
  ByVal lParam As Long) As Long

Declare Function GdiComment Lib "gdi32" Alias
  "GdiComment" (ByVal hdc As Long, ByVal cbSize As Long,
  lpData As Byte) As Long

Declare Function GetEnhMetaFile Lib "gdi32" Alias
  "GetEnhMetaFileA" (ByVal lpszMetaFile As String) As Long

Declare Function GetEnhMetaFileBits Lib "gdi32" Alias
  "GetEnhMetaFileBits" (ByVal hemf As Long,
  ByVal cbBuffer As Long, lpbBuffer As Byte) As Long

Declare Function GetEnhMetaFileDescription Lib "gdi32" Alias
  "GetEnhMetaFileDescriptionA" (ByVal hemf As Long,
  ByVal cchBuffer As Long,
  ByVal lpszDescription As String) As Long

Declare Function GetEnhMetaFileHeader Lib "gdi32" Alias
  "GetEnhMetaFileHeader" (ByVal hemf As Long,
  ByVal cbBuffer As Long, lpemh As ENHMETAHEADER) As Long
```

```
Declare Function GetEnhMetaFilePaletteEntries Lib
  "gdi32" Alias "GetEnhMetaFilePaletteEntries"
  (ByVal hemf As Long, ByVal cEntries As Long,
  lppe As PALETTEENTRY) As Long

Declare Function GetMetaFile Lib "gdi32" Alias
  "GetMetaFileA" (ByVal lpFileName As String) As Long

Declare Function GetMetaFileBitsEx Lib "gdi32" Alias
  "GetMetaFileBitsEx" (ByVal hMF As Long,
  ByVal nSize As Long,
  lpvData As Any) As Long

Declare Function GetWinMetaFileBits Lib "gdi32" Alias
  "GetWinMetaFileBits" (ByVal hemf As Long,
  ByVal cbBuffer As Long, lpbBuffer As Byte,
  ByVal fnMapMode As Long, ByVal hdcRef As Long) As Long

Declare Function PlayEnhMetaFile Lib "gdi32" Alias
  "PlayEnhMetaFile" (ByVal hdc As Long, ByVal hemf As Long,
  lpRect As RECT) As Long

Declare Function PlayEnhMetaFileRecord Lib "gdi32" Alias
  "PlayEnhMetaFileRecord" (ByVal hdc As Long,
  lpHandletable As HANDLETABLE,
  lpEnhMetaRecord As ENHMETARECORD,
  ByVal nHandles As Long) As Long

Declare Function PlayMetaFile Lib "gdi32" Alias
  "PlayMetaFile" (ByVal hdc As Long,
  ByVal hMF As Long) As Long

Declare Function PlayMetaFileRecord Lib "gdi32" Alias
  "PlayMetaFileRecord" (ByVal hdc As Long,
  lpHandletable As HANDLETABLE, lpMetaRecord As METARECORD,
  ByVal nHandles As Long) As Long

Declare Function SetEnhMetaFileBits Lib "gdi32" Alias
  "SetEnhMetaFileBits" (ByVal cbBuffer As Long,
  lpData As Byte) As Long

Declare Function SetMetaFileBitsEx Lib "gdi32" Alias
  "SetMetaFileBitsEx" (ByVal nSize As Long,
  lpData As Byte) As Long

Declare Function SetWinMetaFileBits Lib "gdi32" Alias
  "SetWinMetaFileBits" (ByVal cbBuffer As Long,
  lpbBuffer As Byte, ByVal hdcRef As Long,
  lpmfp As METAFILEPICT) As Long
```

Table 14–2 contains a brief description of the parameters used in the various metafile functions.

Table 14–2 Metafile Function Parameters and Descriptions

Parameter	Description
cbBuffer As Long	Size of lpbBuffer in bytes.
cbSize As Long	Size of data to place in metafile.
cchBuffer As Long	Size of lpszDescription buffer.
cEntries As Long	Number of entries to obtain.
fnMapMode As Long	MM_ mapping mode (see Chapter 13).
hdc As Long	Handle to the device context (DC).
hdcRef As Long	Handle to reference DC holding screen resolution data.
hemf As Long	Handle to an enhanced metafile.
hemfSrc	Handle to an enhanced metafile.
hMetafile As Long	Handle to a metafile.
hMF As Long	Handle to a metafile device context.
lParam As Long	User-defined parameter.
lpbBuffer As Byte	A buffer used to pass a memory address.
lpData As Any	Pointer to user-defined data.
lpData As Byte	Pointer to user-defined data.
lpDescription As String	Description of metafile: name of program, NULL char, description, NULL char, NULL char.
lpemh As ENHMETAHEADER	Structure holds metafile header data.
lpEnhMetaFunc As Long	Pointer to each metafile command.
lpEnhMetaRecord As ENHMETARECORD	Structure holds enhanced metafile record.
lpFileName As String	Name of file for metafile. NULL for creation in memory.
lpHandletable As HANDLETABLE	Structure holds array of handles.
lpMetaRecord As METARECORD	Structure holds a single metafile record.
lpMFEnumProc As Long	Pointer to each metafile command.
lpmfp As METAFILEPICT	Structure holds additional metafile information.
lppe As PALETTEENTRY	Array of structures that hold palette entries for the enhanced metafile.
lpRect As RECT	Structure holds bounding information for metafile size and location.
lpString As String	File name that holds metafile.
lpszDescription As String	Buffer to hold metafile description.
lpszFile	File name of metafile file. NULL value for metafile in memory.
lpszMetaFile As String	File name of file holding an enhanced metafile.
lpvData As Any	Buffer to hold metafile memory address.
nHandles As Long	Number of handles in table.
nSize As Long	Size of the lpvData buffer.

Many of the parameters in Table 14–2 use structures to hold information. The following listing contains the structures used by the metafile function parameters. These, of course, can also be found in the Win32api.txt file.

```
Type ENHMETAHEADER
   iType As Long
   nSize As Long
   rclBounds As RECTL
   rclFrame As RECTL
   dSignature As Long
   nVersion As Long
   nBytes As Long
   nRecords As Long
   nHandles As Integer
   sReserved As Integer
   nDescription As Long
   offDescription As Long
   nPalEntries As Long
   szlDevice As SIZEL
   szlMillimeters As SIZEL
End Type

Type ENHMETARECORD
   iType As Long
   nSize As Long
   dParm(1) As Long
End Type

' Clipboard Metafile Picture Structure
Type HANDLETABLE
   objectHandle(1) As Long
End Type

Type METARECORD
   rdSize As Long
   rdFunction As Integer
   rdParm(1) As Integer
End Type

Type METAFILEPICT
   mm As Long
   xExt As Long
   yExt As Long
   hMF As Long
End Type

Type PALETTEENTRY
   peRed As Byte
   peGreen As Byte
```

```
      peBlue As Byte
      peFlags As Byte
   End Type

   Type RECT
      Left As Long
      Top As Long
      Right As Long
      Bottom As Long
   End Type
```

In the next section, we'll examine an application that makes use of several metafile functions when drawing to the screen.

Example Application

The example application in this section illustrates the use of three of the most popular metafile functions: CloseMetaFile(), CreateMetaFile(), and PlayMeta File(). In addition to these functions, you'll find several of the GDI functions from Chapter 13 used to complete the example.

This application sets the drawing mode, coordinate system, and viewport parameters for the window. A metafile is created, then several GDI functions are used to draw a damped sine wave image to the metafile. The metafile is then closed. The recorded metafile information is held in a portion of memory since the *vbNullString* value was used during the call to the CreateMetaFile() function. The metafile is then played to the empty viewport using the original coordinates, viewport, and viewport origin. Finally, to illustrate that we are drawing from a metafile, the viewport's origin is shifted and the whole image is drawn once again with just a single call to the PlayMetaFile() function.

The Meta1.vbp project contains two important files. The module file for this application is named Meta1.bas and the source code for the form is named Meta1.frm. The Meta1.bas file contains structure and function definitions copied and pasted from the Win32api.txt file provided with your Visual Basic compiler. The following listing contains the contents of this file:

```
   Type POINTAPI
      x As Long
      y As Long
   End Type

   Type Size
      cx As Long
      cy As Long
   End Type
```

```
Declare Function CloseMetaFile Lib "gdi32"
  (ByVal hMF As Long) As Long

Declare Function CreateMetaFile Lib "gdi32" Alias
  "CreateMetaFileA" (ByVal lpString As String) As Long

Declare Function SetMapMode Lib "gdi32" (ByVal hdc As Long,
  ByVal nMapMode As Long) As Long

Declare Function MoveToEx Lib "gdi32" (ByVal hdc As Long,
  ByVal x As Long, ByVal y As Long,
  lpPoint As POINTAPI) As Long

Declare Function LineTo Lib "gdi32" (ByVal hdc As Long,
  ByVal x As Long, ByVal y As Long) As Long

Declare Function PlayMetaFile Lib "gdi32" (ByVal hdc As Long,
  ByVal hMF As Long) As Long

Declare Function SetWindowExtEx Lib "gdi32"
  (ByVal hdc As Long, ByVal nX As Long, ByVal nY As Long,
  lpSize As Size) As Long

Declare Function SetViewportExtEx Lib "gdi32"
  (ByVal hdc As Long, ByVal nX As Long, ByVal nY As Long,
  lpSize As Size) As Long

Declare Function SetViewportOrgEx Lib "gdi32"
  (ByVal hdc As Long, ByVal nX As Long, ByVal nY As Long,
  lpPoint As POINTAPI) As Long
```

The project will play the metafile image back to a blank form. The code for supporting this application is shown in the following listing of the Meta1.frm file:

```
Private Sub Form_Paint()
    Dim tempSize As Size
    Dim tempPoint As POINTAPI
    Dim r&
    Dim metadc&, hMetafile&

    'dummy values
    tempSize.cx = 0
    tempSize.cy = 0
    tempPoint.x = 0
    tempPoint.y = 0

    'pi value for radian numbers
    Const pi = 3.14159

    'Set Mapping Mode, Viewport, etc.
    r& = SetMapMode(hdc, MM_ANISOTROPIC)
    'Set Window Extents to 500 x 500
    r& = SetWindowExtEx(hdc, 500, 500, tempSize)
```

```
'Set Viewport Extents to VGA screen size
  'Positive x is to the right
  'Positive y is up
r& = SetViewportExtEx(hdc, 640, -480, tempSize)
'Create a new origin (0,0) at screen position (105,240)
r& = SetViewportOrgEx(hdc, 640 / 8, 480 / 4, tempPoint)

'Create and draw to the metafile and close
metadc = CreateMetaFile(vbNullString)
'draw x & y coordinate axes to metafile
r& = MoveToEx(metadc, 0, 100, tempPoint)
r& = LineTo(metadc, 0, -100)
r& = MoveToEx(metadc, 0, 0, tempPoint)
r& = LineTo(metadc, 300, 0)
r& = MoveToEx(metadc, 0, 0, tempPoint)
'draw sine wave to metafile
For i = 0 To 300
  y = -100# * (Exp(-i * 0.01)) * Sin(pi * i * 0.07)
  r& = LineTo(metadc, i, y)
Next i
'close the metafile
hMetafile = CloseMetaFile(metadc)

'Draw the recorded metafile twice
'first, play metafile back to original dc
r& = PlayMetaFile(hdc, hMetafile)
'now move viewport origin by (50, 200)
r& = SetViewportOrgEx(hdc, (640 / 8) + 50,
                           (480 / 4) + 200, tempPoint)
'then, play metafile a second time
r& = PlayMetaFile(hdc, hMetafile)
End Sub
```

In this simple example, the mapping mode, windows extent, viewport extent, and viewport origin are set outside of the metafile with the following portion of code:

```
'Set Mapping Mode, Viewport, etc.
r& = SetMapMode(hdc, MM_ANISOTROPIC)
'Set Window Extents to 500 x 500
r& = SetWindowExtEx(hdc, 500, 500, tempSize)
'Set Viewport Extents to VGA screen size
  'Positive x is to the right
  'Positive y is up
r& = SetViewportExtEx(hdc, 640, -480, tempSize)
'Create a new origin (0,0) at screen position (105, 240)
r& = SetViewportOrgEx(hdc, 640 / 8, 480 / 4, tempPoint)
```

You learned, in Chapter 11, the purpose and use of each of these functions. These function calls establish a unique window in which to create, draw, and play back a metafile. Everything works as predicted because the window and viewport extents do not change. However, imagine that a metafile is recorded under one window and viewport extents are played back under another! In order to prevent problems such as this, programmers have learned a trick. The trick is to create the metafile before calling the previous portion of code. In that manner, it will be possible to embed all of that information in the ENHMETAHEADER structure. Now, when the metafile is played the recorded information can be used to set the coordinate and viewport information.

The metafile is created with the following portion of code:

```
'Create and draw to the metafile and close
metadc = CreateMetaFile(vbNullString)
   .
   .
   .
'close the metafile
hMetafile = CloseMetaFile(metadc)
```

The use of the *vbNullString* value allows us to create the metafile in memory. The GDI graphics functions are then used to draw the graphics shapes. Note in the full listing that the handle for these functions is not the handle to the device context, *hdc*, but the handle to the metafile, *metadc*. Finally, the metafile is closed and the handle information to the metafile is saved in *hMetafile*.

The metafile is then played back without changing any of the coordinate or viewport information. This is achieved with a simple function call:

```
'Draw the recorded metafile twice
'first, play metafile back to original dc
r& = PlayMetaFile(hdc, hMetafile)
```

The PlayMetaFile() is passed the handle to the metafile, *hMetafile*, and the handle to the device context, *hdc*, where the playback is to take place.

In order to prove that the drawing took place with the metafile and not directly from the GDI graphics functions, another image is drawn. The viewport origin is modified slightly in order to translate the second image to a different portion of the window. This is acheived with a second call to the SetViewportOrgExt() function, as you can see in the following listing:

```
'now move viewport origin by (50, 200)
r& = SetViewportOrgEx(hdc, (640 / 8) + 50, (480 / 4) + 200,
                      tempPoint)
'then, play metafile a second time
r& = PlayMetaFile(hdc, hMetafile)
```

When you run this application, your screen appears similar to Figure 14–1.

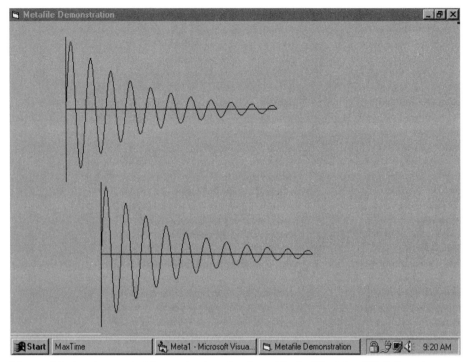

Figure 14–1   A recorded image is played twice with the PlayMetaFile() function.

Remember that when screen images are created with GDI graphics drawing primitives, a metafile is often your best choice for recording the screen image. In Chapter 15 we'll look at the bitmap alternative for saving screen images. Bitmaps are often the best solution when complex images, such as photographic pictures, must be recorded.

Bitmaps, Cursors, and Icon Functions

In the previous chapter you learned how to use metafiles to quickly draw GDI graphics primitives to the screen. Metafiles tend to require less disk space than their bitmap counterparts, but are limited in terms of graphics complexity. Bitmaps, on the other hand, are more like photographs. They can be used to save, store, and reproduce any screen image. The downside to bitmaps is the amount of disk space they require.

In this chapter we will examine a large number of bitmap functions. You'll learn how to read in stock bitmap images then stretch their size with other bitmap functions.

You'll also learn that icons and cursors are really simple bitmap images. We'll investigate several icon and cursor functions.

What are Bitmaps, Cursors, and Icons?

In the final analysis, cursors and icons are just special versions of bitmaps. So what are bitmaps? Bitmaps are created with sets of data that represent pixel locations on the screen. In terms of physical locations, screens can be thought of in terms of a two-dimensional array. Each pixel then has a row and column position. The bitmap, if two-dimensional, can then specify the state of each pixel on the screen.

Saving bitmap images is a relatively simple task until you realize that as screen size has increased and the depth of color rendering has increased, these bitmap files have grown to very large file sizes. The use of bitmap images is therefore limited to those areas where no other technique will work in terms of image storage, such as in a photographic image.

Bitmap images fit into two broad categories: device-dependent bitmaps and device-independent bitmaps. As you look at the function declarations, you will notice that the device-independent bitmaps usually contain the letters "DIB" within the function name. This helps set them apart from their device-dependent counterparts.

A device-dependent bitmap is a GDI Windows object. Because data alignments vary between one physical device and another (video displays, printers, memory, and so on), it is critical that devices are compatible for successful device-dependent bitmap operations. This is why you will see functions, such as CreateCompatibleDC(), used with other device-dependent bitmap functions. Device-dependent bitmaps cannot usually be transferred between different devices, such as a display screen to a printer.

A device-independent bitmap is not a Windows object, but simply data held in a specific data structure. This type of bitmap finds its greatest use when bitmap information must be passed between different types of raster devices, such as from a display screen to a printer.

API Bitmap, Cursor, and Icon Function Names and Descriptions

Table 15–1 shows 40 popular Windows API bitmap, cursor, and icon functions and provides a brief description for their use.

Windows programmers make use of a large number of these functions. The most popular bitmap functions are BitBlt(), CreateBitmap(), and StretchBlt(). The most frequently used cursor functions are CreateCursor() and LoadCursor(). The most popular icon functions are CreateIcon() and LoadIcon().

If you are a Windows NT programmer, you'll want to investigate the use of the MaskBlt() and PlgBlt() functions designed specifically for this environment.

Several bitmap functions are illustrated in the example programs in this chapter.

API Bitmap, Cursor, and Icon Function Declarations

The following listing contains the Windows API bitmap, cursor, and icon function declarations found in the Win32api.txt file provided with Visual Basic.

Table 15–1   Bitmap, Cursor, and Icon Functions and Descriptions

Function	Description
BitBlt	Copies a device-dependent bitmap image from one location to another.
CopyIcon	Copies an icon or cursor image.
CreateBitmap	Creates a device-dependent bitmap.
CreateBitmapIndirect	Creates a device-dependent bitmap based on data in a BITMAP structure.
CreateCompatibleBitmap	Creates a device-dependent bitmap compatible with the device context (DC).
CreateCursor	Creates a cursor image.
CreateDIBitmap	Creates a device-independent bitmap.
CreateDIBSection	Creates a device-independent bitmap object.
CreateIcon	Creates an icon image.
CreateIconFromResource	Creates an icon or cursor from resource bits describing the object.
CreateIconIndirect	Creates an icon image from data in an ICONINFO structure.
DestroyCursor	Destroys a cursor image.
DestroyIcon	Destroys an icon image.
DrawIcon	Draws an icon image.
DrawIconEx	Used additional information to draw an icon image.
ExtractAssociatedIcon	Gets and loads an icon from a file.
ExtractIcon	Gets an icon from an executable file.
ExtractIconEx	Gets an icon from an executable file with additional information.
GetBitmapBits	Get image bits in a device-dependent bitmap.
GetBitmapDimensionEx	Get device-dependent bitmap dimensions.
GetDIBColorTable	Gets color table information for a device-independent bitmap.
GetDIBits	Creates a device-independent bitmap from a device-dependent bitmap's data.
GetIconInfo	Gets icon information.
GetStretchBltMode	Gets how bits or lines are eliminated during stretching of a device-dependent bitmap.
LoadBitmap	Loads a device-dependent bitmap.
LoadCursor	Loads a cursor image.
LoadCursorFromFile	Creates a cursor based on a regular or animated cursor image.
LoadIcon	Loads an icon image.
LoadImage	Loads a bitmap, cursor, or icon image.
MaskBlt	Copies a device-dependent bitmap image from one location to another using a mask under Windows NT.
PatBlt	Fills an area based on a brush pattern.
PlgBlt	Copies an image from one location to another and allows stretching, rotation, and so on under Windows NT.
SetBitmapBits	Sets image bits in a device-dependent bitmap.
SetBitmapDimensionEx	Sets device-dependent bitmap dimensions.
SetDIBColorTable	Sets color table information for a device-independent bitmap.
SetDIBits	Creates a device-dependent bitmap from a device-independent bitmap's data.
SetDIBitsToDevice	Sends device-independent data directly to a specified device.
SetStretchBltMode	Sets how bits or lines are eliminated during stretching.
StretchBlt	Copies a device-dependent image from one location to another and allows stretching.
StretchDIBits	Copies a device-independent image from one location to another and allows stretching

```
Declare Function BitBlt Lib "gdi32" Alias "BitBlt"
  (ByVal hDestDC As Long, ByVal x As Long, ByVal y As Long,
  ByVal nWidth As Long, ByVal nHeight As Long,
  ByVal hSrcDC As Long, ByVal xSrc As Long,
  ByVal ySrc As Long, ByVal dwRop As Long) As Long

Declare Function CopyCursor Lib "user32" Alias "CopyCursor"
  (ByVal hcur As Long) As Long

Declare Function CopyIcon Lib "user32" Alias "CopyIcon"
  (ByVal hIcon As Long) As Long

Declare Function CreateBitmap Lib "gdi32" Alias
  "CreateBitmap" (ByVal nWidth As Long,
  ByVal nHeight As Long, ByVal nPlanes As Long,
  ByVal nBitCount As Long, lpBits As Any) As Long

Declare Function CreateBitmapIndirect Lib "gdi32" Alias
  "CreateBitmapIndirect" (lpBitmap As BITMAP) As Long

Declare Function CreateCompatibleBitmap Lib "gdi32" Alias
  "CreateCompatibleBitmap" (ByVal hdc As Long,
  ByVal nWidth As Long, ByVal nHeight As Long) As Long

Declare Function CreateCursor Lib "user32" Alias
  "CreateCursor" (ByVal hInstance As Long,
  ByVal nXhotspot As Long, ByVal nYhotspot As Long,
  ByVal nWidth As Long, ByVal nHeight As Long,
  lpANDbitPlane As Any, lpXORbitPlane As Any) As Long

Declare Function CreateDIBitmap Lib "gdi32" Alias
  "CreateDIBitmap" (ByVal hdc As Long,
  lpInfoHeader As BITMAPINFOHEADER, ByVal dwUsage As Long,
  lpInitBits As Any, lpInitInfo As BITMAPINFO,
  ByVal wUsage As Long) As Long

Declare Function CreateDIBSection Lib "gdi32" Alias
  "CreateDIBSection" (ByVal hDC As Long,
  pBitmapInfo As BITMAPINFO, ByVal un As Long,
  ByVal lplpVoid As Long, ByVal handle As Long,
  ByVal dw As Long) As Long

Declare Function CreateIcon Lib "user32" Alias
  "CreateIcon" (ByVal hInstance As Long,
  ByVal nWidth As Long, ByVal nHeight As Long,
  ByVal nPlanes As Byte, ByVal nBitsPixel As Byte,
  lpANDbits As Byte, lpXORbits As Byte) As Long

Declare Function CreateIconFromResource Lib "user32"
  Alias "CreateIconFromResource" (presbits As Byte,
  ByVal dwResSize As Long, ByVal fIcon As Long,
  ByVal dwVer As Long) As Long
```

```
Declare Function CreateIconFromResource Lib "user32" Alias
  "CreateIconFromResource" (presbits As Byte,
  ByVal dwResSize As Long, ByVal fIcon As Boolean,
  ByVal dwVer As Long) As Long

Declare Function CreateIconIndirect Lib "user32" Alias
  "CreateIconIndirect" (piconinfo As ICONINFO) As Long

Declare Function DestroyCursor Lib "user32" Alias
  "DestroyCursor" (ByVal hCursor As Long) As Long

Declare Function DestroyIcon Lib "user32" Alias
  "DestroyIcon" (ByVal hIcon As Long) As Long

Declare Function DrawIcon Lib "user32" Alias "DrawIcon"
  (ByVal hdc As Long, ByVal x As Long, ByVal y As Long,
  ByVal hIcon As Long) As Long

Declare Function DrawIconEx Lib "user32" Alias
  "DrawIconEx" (ByVal hdc As Long, ByVal xLeft As Long,
  ByVal yTop As Long, ByVal hIcon As Long,
  ByVal cxWidth As Long, ByVal cyWidth As Long,
  ByVal istepIfAniCur As Long,
  ByVal hbrFlickerFreeDraw As Long,
  ByVal diFlags As Long) As Long

Declare Function ExtractAssociatedIcon Lib
  "shell32.dll" Alias "ExtractAssociateIconA"
  (ByVal hInst As Long, ByVal lpIconPath As String,
  lpiIcon As Long) As Long

Declare Function ExtractIcon Lib "shell32.dll" Alias
  "ExtractIconA" (ByVal hInst As Long,
  ByVal lpszExeFileName As String,
  ByVal nIconIndex As Long) As Long

Declare Function ExtractIconEx Lib "shell32.dll" Alias
  "ExtractIconExA" (ByVal lpszFile As String,
  ByVal nIconIndex As Long, phiconLarge As Long,
  phiconSmall As Long, ByVal nIcons As Long) As Long

Declare Function GetBitmapBits Lib "gdi32" Alias
  "GetBitmapBits" (ByVal hBitmap As Long,
  ByVal dwCount As Long, lpBits As Any) As Long

Declare Function GetBitmapDimensionEx Lib "gdi32" Alias
  "GetBitmapDimensionEx" (ByVal hBitmap As Long,
  lpDimension As SIZE) As Long

Declare Function GetDIBColorTable Lib "gdi32" Alias
  "GetDIBColorTable" (ByVal hDC As Long,
  ByVal un1 As Long, ByVal un2 As Long,
  pRGBQuad As RGBQUAD) As Long
```

```
Declare Function GetDIBits Lib "gdi32" Alias "GetDIBits"
  (ByVal aHDC As Long, ByVal hBitmap As Long,
  ByVal nStartScan As Long, ByVal nNumScans As Long,
  lpBits As Any, lpBI As BITMAPINFO,
  ByVal wUsage As Long) As Long

Declare Function GetIconInfo Lib "user32" Alias
  "GetIconInfo" (ByVal hIcon As Long,
  piconinfo As ICONINFO) As Long

Declare Function GetStretchBltMode Lib "gdi32" Alias
  "GetStretchBltMode" (ByVal hdc As Long) As Long

Declare Function LoadBitmap Lib "user32" Alias
  "LoadBitmapA" (ByVal hInstance As Long,
  ByVal lpBitmapName As String) As Long

Declare Function LoadCursor Lib "user32" Alias
  "LoadCursorA" (ByVal hInstance As Long,
  ByVal lpCursorName As String) As Long

Declare Function LoadCursorFromFile Lib "user32" Alias
  "LoadCursorFromFileA" (ByVal lpFileName As String) As Long

Declare Function LoadIcon Lib "user32" Alias "LoadIconA"
  (ByVal hInstance As Long,
  ByVal lpIconName As String) As Long

Declare Function LoadImage Lib "user32" Alias "LoadImageA"
  (ByVal hInst As Long, ByVal lpsz As String,
  ByVal un1 As Long, ByVal n1 As Long, ByVal n2 As Long,
  ByVal un2 As Long) As Long

Declare Function MaskBlt Lib "gdi32" Alias "MaskBlt"
  (ByVal hdcDest As Long, ByVal nXDest As Long,
  ByVal nYDest As Long, ByVal nWidth As Long,
  ByVal nHeight As Long, ByVal hdcSrc As Long,
  ByVal nXSrc As Long, ByVal nYSrc As Long,
  ByVal hbmMask As Long, ByVal xMask As Long,
  ByVal yMask As Long, ByVal dwRop As Long) As Long

Declare Function PatBlt Lib "gdi32" Alias "PatBlt"
  (ByVal hdc As Long, ByVal x As Long, ByVal y As Long,
  ByVal nWidth As Long, ByVal nHeight As Long,
  ByVal dwRop As Long) As Long

Declare Function PlgBlt Lib "gdi32" Alias "PlgBlt"
  (ByVal hdcDest As Long, lpPoint As POINTAPI,
  ByVal hdcSrc As Long, ByVal nXSrc As Long,
  ByVal nYSrc As Long, ByVal nWidth As Long,
  ByVal nHeight As Long, ByVal hbmMask As Long,
  ByVal xMask As Long, ByVal yMask As Long) As Long
```

```
Declare Function SetBitmapBits Lib "gdi32" Alias
  "SetBitmapBits" (ByVal hBitmap As Long,
  ByVal dwCount As Long, lpBits As Any) As Long

Declare Function SetBitmapDimensionEx Lib "gdi32" Alias
  "SetBitmapDimensionEx" (ByVal hbm As Long,
  ByVal nX As Long, ByVal nY As Long, lpSize As SIZE) As Long

Declare Function SetDIBColorTable Lib "gdi32" Alias
  "SetDIBColorTable" (ByVal hDC As Long,
  ByVal un1 As Long, ByVal un2 As Long,
  pcRGBQuad As RGBQUAD) As Long

Declare Function SetDIBits Lib "gdi32" Alias "SetDIBits"
  (ByVal hdc As Long, ByVal hBitmap As Long,
  ByVal nStartScan As Long, ByVal nNumScans As Long,
  lpBits As Any, lpBI As BITMAPINFO,
  ByVal wUsage As Long) As Long

Declare Function SetDIBitsToDevice Lib "gdi32" Alias
  "SetDIBitsToDevice" (ByVal hdc As Long, ByVal x As Long,
  ByVal y As Long, ByVal dx As Long, ByVal dy As Long,
  ByVal SrcX As Long, ByVal SrcY As Long,
  ByVal Scan As Long, ByVal NumScans As Long,
  Bits As Any, BitsInfo As BITMAPINFO,
  ByVal wUsage As Long) As Long

Declare Function SetStretchBltMode Lib "gdi32" Alias
  "SetStretchBltMode" (ByVal hdc As Long,
  ByVal nStretchMode As Long) As Long

Declare Function StretchBlt Lib "gdi32" Alias "StretchBlt"
  (ByVal hdc As Long, ByVal x As Long, ByVal y As Long,
  ByVal nWidth As Long, ByVal nHeight As Long,
  ByVal hSrcDC As Long, ByVal xSrc As Long,
  ByVal ySrc As Long, ByVal nSrcWidth As Long,
  ByVal nSrcHeight As Long, ByVal dwRop As Long) As Long

Declare Function StretchDIBits Lib "gdi32" Alias
  "StretchDIBits" (ByVal hdc As Long, ByVal x As Long,
  ByVal y As Long, ByVal dx As Long, ByVal dy As Long,
  ByVal SrcX As Long, ByVal SrcY As Long,
  ByVal wSrcWidth As Long, ByVal wSrcHeight As Long,
  lpBits As Any, lpBitsInfo As BITMAPINFO,
  ByVal wUsage As Long, ByVal dwRop As Long) As Long
```

Table 15–2 contains a brief description of the parameters used in the various bitmap, cursor, and icon functions.

Table 15–2 Bitmap, Cursor, and Icon Function Parameters and Descriptions

Parameter	Description
aHDC As Long	Handle to a device context with the device-independent bitmap configuration data.
Bits As Any	Pointer to a buffer that holds device independent bitmap format data.
BitsInfo As BITMAPINFO	Structure holds the format and colors of a device-independent bitmap's bits.
cxWidth As Long, cyWidth As Long	Desired width and height of icon image.
diFlags As Long	Uses DI_ constant.
dw As Long	Displacement for bitmap data.
dwCount As Long	Count of bitmap bytes to copy.
dwResSize As Long	Number of bytes in a bit buffer.
dwRop As Long	Raster operation to use. See Constants listing for more information.
dwUsage As Long	CBM_INIT initializes image to lpInitBits and lpInitInfo parameters. Use zero for no initialization.
dwVer As Long	Windows format version.
dx As Long, dy As Long	Width and height of destination rectangle.
fIcon As Boolean	Icon or cursor flag.
fIcon As Long	Icon or cursor flag.
handle As Long	Handle to the bitmap, cursor, or icon image to be copied.
hBitmap As Long	Handle to a bitmap image.
hbm As Long	Handle to a bitmap image.
hbmMask As Long	Handle to the masking bitmap image.
hbrFlickerFreeDraw As Long	Draws first to memory and then copies to location to reduce flicker.
hcur As Long	Handle to the cursor image to copy.
hCursor As Long	Handle to the cursor image.
hdc As Long	Handle to the Device Context (DC).
hdcDest As Long	Handle to the destination Device Context (DC).
hdcSrc As Long	Handle to the source Device Context (DC).
hDestDC As Long	Handle to the destination Device Context (DC).
hIcon As Long	Handle to the icon (or cursor) image.
hInst As Long	Handle to instance of application.
hInstance As Long	Handle to instance of application owning cursor image.
hSrcDC As Long	Handle to the source Device Context (DC).
istepIfAniCur As Long	Which animated image to draw for cursor.
lpANDbitPlane As Any	Pointer to an AND bitmap.
lpANDbits As Byte	Pointer to the AND bitmap data.
lpBI As BITMAPINFO	Structure holds device-independent bitmap format and color data.
lpBitmap As BITMAP	Structure holds data describing a bitmap.
lpBitmapName As Long	Holds resource identifier of bitmap to load.
lpBitmapName As String	String holds the name of the bitmap to load.
lpBits As Any	Pointer to bitmap data or buffer.
lpBitsInfo As BITMAPINFO	Structure holds format and colors of lpBits in a device-independent bitmap.
lpCursorName As Long	Holds resource identifier of cursor to load.
lpCursorName As String	String holds the name of the cursor to load.

Table 15–2   Bitmap, Cursor, and Icon Function Parameters and Descriptions *(Continued)*

Parameter	Description
lpDimension As SIZE	Structure holds bitmap dimensions.
lpFileName As String	String holds file name for cursor.
LpIconName As Long	Holds resource identifier of icon to load.
lpIconName As String	String holds the name of the icon to load.
lpIconPath As String	String holds file name for icon extraction.
lpiIcon As Long	Holds resource identifier value for the icon to extract.
lpInfoHeader As BITMAPINFOHEADER	Structure holds description of device-independent bitmap image.
lpInitBits As Any	Pointer to device-independent bitmap data given in lpInitInfo parameter.
lpInitInfo As BITMAPINFO	Structure contains device-independent bitmap format and color information.
lplpVoid As Long	Holds memory location of device-independent bitmap data.
lpPoint As POINTAPI	lpPoint is first value in an array of POINTAPI structures holding parallelogram data. Each structure holds four points for parallelogram.
lpSize As SIZE	Structure holds previous bitmap size.
lpsz As String	String holds the name of the image.
lpszExeFileName As String	String holds the program name for the icon to be extracted.
lpszFile As String	Pointer to a string giving the name of an executable file, DLL, or icon file.
lpXORbitPlane As Any	Pointer to an exclusive OR (XOR) bitmap.
lpXORbits As Byte	Pointer to the XOR bitmap data.
n1 As Long, n2 As Long	Width and height of the image (pixels).
nBitCount As Long	Number of bits required to identify a color.
nBitsPixel As Byte	Number of bits / pixel.
nHeight As Long, nWidth As Long	Height and width of bitmap image.
nIconIndex As Long	The index value for the icon to obtain.
nIcons As Long	Gives the number of icons to extract.
nNumScans As Long	Number of scan lines to copy.
nPlanes As Byte	Number of color planes in lpXORbitPlane array.
nPlanes As Long	Number of color planes in image.
nSrcHeight As Long, nSrcWidth As Long	Height and width of image to be copied.
nStartScan As Long	First line number to copy to a device-independent bitmap.
nStretchMode As Long	Uses STRETCH_ constant.
NumScans As Long	Number of lines to copy to a device-independent bitmap.
nX As Long, nY As Long	Bitmap image size given as 1/10 mm.
nXDest As Long, nYDest As Long	Coordinate of upper-left corner of destination image.
nXhotspot As Long, nYhotspot As Long	Coordinate position of cursor hotspot.
nXSrc As Long, nYSrc As Long	Upper-left coordinate of source rectangle.
pBitmapInfo As BITMAPINFO	Structure holds data for bitmap's configuration.

(continued)

**Table 15–2   Bitmap, Cursor, and Icon Function Parameters
and Descriptions (Continued)**

Parameter	Description
pcRGBQuad As RGBQUAD	First entry in an array of RGBQUAD structures. Structures hold color table information.
phiconLarge As Long	Pointer to an array of handles of large icons is returned. This parameter can be NULL.
phiconSmall As Long	Pointer to an array of handles of small icons is returned. This parameter can be NULL.
piconinfo As ICONINFO	Structure holds information on two bitmaps used to create an icon.
presbits As Byte	Pointer to icon or cursor bits.
pRGBQuad As RGBQUAD	This is first value in an array of RGBQUAD structures holding color table data.
Scan As Long	Number of first scan line in lpBits array.
SrcX As Long, SrcY As Long	Pointer to origin of device-independent source rectangle.
un As Long	Uses a DIB_ constant.
un1 As Long	Uses an IMAGE_ constant or holds first entry in the color table.
un2 As Long	Uses an LR_ constant or holds the number of color table entries to obtain.
wSrcHeight As Long, wSrcWidth As Long	Height and width of the source rectangle.
wUsage As Long	Uses a DIB_ constant.
x As Long, y As Long	Upper-left coordinates for destination rectangle.
xLeft As Long, yTop As Long	Coordinate for upper-left corner of icon image.
xMask As Long, yMask As Long	Offset to the masking bitmap image.
xSrc As Long, ySrc As Long	Pointer to the upper-left coordinate or a source rectangle.

Many of the parameters described in Table 15–2 use constant values. The Win32api.txt file lists the following constants for the bitmap, cursor, and icon parameters:

```
'constants for the biCompression field
Public Const BI_RGB = 0&
Public Const BI_RLE8 = 1&
Public Const BI_RLE4 = 2&
Public Const BI_bitfields = 3&

'////////////////////////////////////
'DrawIconEx() flag constants

'Draws the icon or cursor using the system
'default image rather than the user-specified image.
Public Const DI_COMPAT

'Draws the icon or cursor using the width and height
'specified by the system metric values for cursors or icons,
'if the cxWidth and cyWidth parameters are set to zero.
```

```
'If this flag is not specified and cxWidth and cyWidth
'are set to zero, the function uses the actual resource size.

Public Const DI_DEFAULTSIZE

'Draws the icon or cursor using the image.
Public Const DI_IMAGE

'Draws the icon or cursor using the mask.
Public Const DI_MASK

'Combination of DI_IMAGE and DI_MASK.
Public Const DI_NORMAL

'/////////////////////////////////////
'DIB color table identifiers

'color table in RGBs
Public Const DIB_RGB_COLORS = 0

'color table in palette indices
Public Const DIB_PAL_COLORS = 1

'No color table indices into surf palette
Public Const DIB_PAL_INDICES = 2

'No color table indices into surf
Public Const DIB_PAL_PHYSINDICES = 2 palette

'No color table indices into DC
Public Const DIB_PAL_LOGINDICES = 4 palette

'Standard Cursor IDs
Public Const IDC_ARROW = 32512&
Public Const IDC_IBEAM = 32513&
Public Const IDC_WAIT = 32514&
Public Const IDC_CROSS = 32515&
Public Const IDC_UPARROW = 32516&
Public Const IDC_SIZE = 32640&
Public Const IDC_ICON = 32641&
Public Const IDC_SIZENWSE = 32642&
Public Const IDC_SIZENESW = 32643&
Public Const IDC_SIZEWE = 32644&
Public Const IDC_SIZENS = 32645&
Public Const IDC_SIZEALL = 32646&
Public Const IDC_NO = 32648&
Public Const IDC_APPSTARTING = 32650&

'Standard Icon IDs
Public Const IDI_APPLICATION = 32512&
Public Const IDI_HAND = 32513&
Public Const IDI_QUESTION = 32514&
Public Const IDI_EXCLAMATION = 32515&
Public Const IDI_ASTERISK = 32516&
```

```
'Image types
Public Const IMAGE_BITMAP 'Copies a bitmap.
Public Const IMAGE_CURSOR 'Copies a cursor.
Public Const IMAGE_ICON 'Copies an icon.

'//////////////////////////////////////
'hImage flag values
'Deletes the original image after creating the copy.
Public Const LR_COPYDELETEORG

'Creates an exact copy of the image,
'ignoring the cxDesired and cyDesired parameters.
Public Const LR_COPYRETURNORG

'Creates a new monochrome image.
Public Const LR_MONOCHROME

'Tries to reload an icon or cursor resource
'from the original resource file rather than
'simply copying the current image.
'Without this flag, CopyImage stretches the
'original image to the new size.
'If this flag is set, function uses the size in the
'resource file closest to the desired size.
Public Const LR_COPYFROMRESOURCE

'OEM Resource Ordinal Numbers
Public Const OBM_CLOSE = 32754
Public Const OBM_UPARROW = 32753
Public Const OBM_DNARROW = 32752
Public Const OBM_RGARROW = 32751
Public Const OBM_LFARROW = 32750
Public Const OBM_REDUCE = 32749
Public Const OBM_ZOOM = 32748
Public Const OBM_RESTORE = 32747
Public Const OBM_REDUCED = 32746
Public Const OBM_ZOOMD = 32745
Public Const OBM_RESTORED = 32744
Public Const OBM_UPARROWD = 32743
Public Const OBM_DNARROWD = 32742
Public Const OBM_RGARROWD = 32741
Public Const OBM_LFARROWD = 32740
Public Const OBM_MNARROW = 32739
Public Const OBM_COMBO = 32738
Public Const OBM_UPARROWI = 32737
Public Const OBM_DNARROWI = 32736
Public Const OBM_RGARROWI = 32735
Public Const OBM_LFARROWI = 32734
Public Const OBM_OLD_CLOSE = 32767
Public Const OBM_SIZE = 32766
Public Const OBM_OLD_UPARROW = 32765
```

```
Public Const OBM_OLD_DNARROW = 32764
Public Const OBM_OLD_RGARROW = 32763
Public Const OBM_OLD_LFARROW = 32762
Public Const OBM_BTSIZE = 32761
Public Const OBM_CHECK = 32760
Public Const OBM_CHECKBOXES = 32759
Public Const OBM_BTNCORNERS = 32758
Public Const OBM_OLD_REDUCE = 32757
Public Const OBM_OLD_ZOOM = 32756
Public Const OBM_OLD_RESTORE = 32755

'StretchBlt() Modes
Public Const STRETCH_ANDSCANS = 1
Public Const STRETCH_ORSCANS = 2
Public Const STRETCH_DELETESCANS = 3
Public Const STRETCH_HALFTONE = 4

'Binary raster ops
Public Const R2_BLACK = 1          '0
Public Const R2_NOTMERGEPEN = 2    'DPon
Public Const R2_MASKNOTPEN = 3     'DPna
Public Const R2_NOTCOPYPEN = 4     'PN
Public Const R2_MASKPENNOT = 5     'PDna
Public Const R2_NOT = 6            'Dn
Public Const R2_XORPEN = 7         'DPx
Public Const R2_NOTMASKPEN = 8     'DPan
Public Const R2_MASKPEN = 9        'DPa
Public Const R2_NOTXORPEN = 10     'DPxn
Public Const R2_NOP = 11           'D
Public Const R2_MERGENOTPEN = 12   'DPno
Public Const R2_COPYPEN = 13       'P
Public Const R2_MERGEPENNOT = 14   'PDno
Public Const R2_MERGEPEN = 15      'DPo
Public Const R2_WHITE = 16         '1
Public Const R2_LAST = 16

'////////////////////////////////////////
'Ternary raster operations

'(DWORD) dest = source
Public Const SRCCOPY = &HCC0020

'(DWORD) dest = source OR dest
Public Const SRCPAINT = &HEE0086

'(DWORD) dest = source AND dest
Public Const SRCAND = &H8800C6

'(DWORD) dest = source XOR dest
Public Const SRCINVERT = &H660046
```

```
'(DWORD) dest = source AND (NOT dest)
Public Const SRCERASE = &H440328

'(DWORD) dest = (NOT source)
Public Const NOTSRCCOPY = &H330008

'(DWORD) dest = (NOT src) AND (NOT dest)
Public Const NOTSRCERASE = &H1100A6

'(DWORD) dest = (source AND pattern)
Public Const MERGECOPY = &HC000CA

'(DWORD) dest = (NOT source) OR dest
Public Const MERGEPAINT = &HBB0226

'(DWORD) dest = pattern
Public Const PATCOPY = &HF00021

'(DWORD) dest = DPSnoo
Public Const PATPAINT = &HFB0A09

'(DWORD) dest = pattern XOR dest
Public Const PATINVERT = &H5A0049

'(DWORD) dest = (NOT dest)
Public Const DSTINVERT = &H550009

'(DWORD) dest = BLACK
Public Const BLACKNESS = &H42

'(DWORD) dest = WHITE
Public Const WHITENESS = &HFF0062
```

Many of the constants use structures for storing specific system information. Here are the structure definitions, also found in the Win32api.txt file:

```
'Bitmap Header Definition
Type BITMAP '14 bytes
  bmType As Long
  bmWidth As Long
  bmHeight As Long
  bmWidthBytes As Long
  bmPlanes As Integer
  bmBitsPixel As Integer
  bmBits As Long
End Type

'Structures for defining DIBs
Type BITMAPCOREHEADER '12 bytes
  bcSize As Long
  bcWidth As Integer
  bcHeight As Integer
  bcPlanes As Integer
```

```
    bcBitCount As Integer
End Type

Type BITMAPCOREINFO
  bmciHeader As BITMAPCOREHEADER
  bmciColors As RGBTRIPLE
End Type

Type BITMAPFILEHEADER
  bfType As Integer
  bfSize As Long
  bfReserved1 As Integer
  bfReserved2 As Integer
  bfOffBits As Long
End Type

Type BITMAPINFO
  bmiHeader As BITMAPINFOHEADER
  bmiColors As RGBQUAD
End Type

Type BITMAPINFOHEADER '40 bytes
  biSize As Long
  biWidth As Long
  biHeight As Long
  biPlanes As Integer
  biBitCount As Integer
  biCompression As Long
  biSizeImage As Long
  biXPelsPerMeter As Long
  biYPelsPerMeter As Long
  biClrUsed As Long
  biClrImportant As Long
End Type

Type ICONINFO
  fIcon As Long
  xHotspot As Long
  yHotspot As Long
  hbmMask As Long
  hbmColor As Long
End Type

Type POINTAPI
  x As Long
  y As Long
End Type

Type RGBQUAD
  rgbBlue As Byte
  rgbGreen As Byte
  rgbRed As Byte
```

```
      rgbReserved As Byte
End Type

Type Size
   cx As Long
   cy As Long
End Type
```

In the next section, we'll examine two applications that make use of several bitmap and cursor functions.

Example Applications

The two example applications in this section highlight the BitBlt() and Stretch-Blt() bitmap functions. You'll find that the cursor and icon functions are equally easy to use. In both examples, stock bitmap images are loaded and displayed in an empty form. Stock bitmap images, using the constants starting with OBM_, can be identified with sequential numbers. These values can be found in the Win32api.txt file.

When the option exists, you may prefer to work with Visual Basic's LoadPicture() function because of its ease of use.

Working with BitBlt()

The first application is a project named Bitmap1.vbp. This project contains a module file named Bitmap1.bas and a form file named Bitmap1.frm. The following listing shows the contents of the module file which holds structure and function declarations along with several constants used by the application. All of this information was extracted from the Win32api.txt file provided with your Visual Basic compiler.

```
Public Const SRCCOPY = &HCC0020

Type BITMAP
        bmType As Long
        bmWidth As Long
        bmHeight As Long
        bmWidthBytes As Long
        bmPlanes As Integer
        bmBitsPixel As Integer
        bmBits As Long
End Type

'OEM Resource Ordinal Numbers
Public Const OBM_CLOSE = 32754
Public Const OBM_UPARROW = 32753
Public Const OBM_DNARROW = 32752
```

```
Public Const OBM_RGARROW = 32751
Public Const OBM_LFARROW = 32750
Public Const OBM_REDUCE = 32749
Public Const OBM_ZOOM = 32748
Public Const OBM_RESTORE = 32747
Public Const OBM_REDUCED = 32746
Public Const OBM_ZOOMD = 32745
Public Const OBM_RESTORED = 32744
Public Const OBM_UPARROWD = 32743
Public Const OBM_DNARROWD = 32742
Public Const OBM_RGARROWD = 32741
Public Const OBM_LFARROWD = 32740
Public Const OBM_MNARROW = 32739
Public Const OBM_COMBO = 32738
Public Const OBM_UPARROWI = 32737
Public Const OBM_DNARROWI = 32736
Public Const OBM_RGARROWI = 32735
Public Const OBM_LFARROWI = 32734


Declare Function BitBlt Lib "gdi32" (ByVal hDestDC As Long,
   ByVal x As Long, ByVal y As Long, ByVal nWidth As Long,
   ByVal nHeight As Long, ByVal hSrcDC As Long,
   ByVal xSrc As Long, ByVal ySrc As Long,
   ByVal dwRop As Long) As Long
Declare Function CreateCompatibleDC Lib "gdi32"
   (ByVal hdc As Long) As Long
Declare Function DeleteDC Lib "gdi32"
   (ByVal hdc As Long) As Long
Declare Function DeleteObject Lib "gdi32"
   (ByVal hObject As Long) As Long
Declare Function LoadBitmap Lib "user32" Alias
   "LoadBitmapA" (ByVal hInstance As Long,
   ByVal lpBitmapName As String) As Long
Declare Function LoadBitmapModified Lib "user32" Alias
   "LoadBitmapA" (ByVal hInstance As Long,
   ByVal lpBitmapName As Long) As Long
Declare Function GetObject Lib "gdi32" Alias "GetObjectA"
   (ByVal hObject As Long, ByVal nCount As Long,
   lpObject As Any) As Long
Declare Function GetObjectModified Lib "gdi32" Alias
   "GetObjectA" (ByVal hObject As Long, ByVal nCount As Long,
   lpObject As Any) As Long
Declare Function SelectObject Lib "gdi32"
   (ByVal hdc As Long, ByVal hObject As Long) As Long
```

Several bitmap related functions are required for loading and drawing bitmap images with the BitBlt() function.

The project draws the bitmap images on a blank form. The code to support this action is shown in the next listing. This file is named Bitmap1.frm.

```
Private Sub Form_Paint()
        Dim hmdc&
        Dim hBitmap&, r&
        Dim bm As BITMAP

        For i = 0 To 19
          For j = 0 To 20
            'Create a compatible device context for
            'bitmap image
            hmdc& = CreateCompatibleDC(Form1.hdc)

            'Load and display stock bitmaps sequentially using
            'a modified version of LoadBitmap() that accepts
            'an ordinal number for second parameter rather
            'than a string.
            hBitmap& = LoadBitmapModified(0, OBM_LFARROWI + j)

            'Use a modified version of GetObject() that allows
            'three parameters to be passed, as shown below.
            r& = GetObjectModified(hBitmap&, Len(bm), bm)

            'Select the object
            r& = SelectObject(hmdc&, hBitmap)

            'Use BitBlt() to draw multiple versions of
            'these stock bitmaps. Use a 22 x 20 pixel grid
            r& = BitBlt(Form1.hdc, 22 * i, 20 * j, bm.bmWidth,
                        bm.bmHeight, hmdc&, 0, 0, SRCCOPY)

            'Select original object
            r& = SelectObject(hmdc&, r&)

            'Delete object
            r& = DeleteObject(hBitmap&)

            'Delete compatible device context
            r& = DeleteDC(hmdc&)
          Next j
        Next I
    End Sub
```

Examine this listing and notice that several handles are used. The *hmdc* handle serves as a handle to a memory device context. The *hBitmap* handle is the handle to the bitmap. Also notice that *bm* is identified as a type BITMAP. The BITMAP structure was listed in the Bitmap1.bas file.

This application will draw a number of stock bitmap images on the form. The stock bitmap images start sequentially at OBM_LFARROWI = 32734 and end, for our purposes, at OBM_CLOSE = 32754. Two **For** loops will control which bitmap is obtained and how the figures are displayed in the form.

These stock bitmaps are small iconic images, so each one is repeated several times horizontally.

In order to draw a bitmap image, a compatible device context must be created. The CreateCompatibleDC() function is used for this purpose.

```
hmdc& = CreateCompatibleDC(Form1.hdc)
```

The bitmap is loaded with the LoadBitmap() function. However, in this case, instead of using a pointer to a string giving the bitmap name, a numeric index will be used to access stock bitmaps. A modified version of LoadBitmap() named LoadBitmapModified() is used for this purpose.

```
hBitmap& = LoadBitmapModified(0, OBM_LFARROWI + j)
```

Since OBM_LFARROWI is the first bitmap in the sequence, all others can be accessed by simply increasing the constant's value. This is done in a simple **For** loop.

A modified version of GetObject() will allow us to specify the bitmap structure, *bm*, and the size of the bitmap image.

```
r& = GetObjectModified(hBitmap&, Len(bm), bm)
```

The image is then selected into the memory device context with a call to the SelectObject() function:

```
r& = SelectObject(hmdc&, hBitmap)
```

Finally, the bitmap image is drawn to the form with the BitBlt() function. The second and third parameters of this function allow us to place the bitmap images where we desire on the form. These locations are controlled by the two **For** loops. The actual width and height of the bitmap image are given by the fourth and fifth parameters. The two parameters with a zero value specify the upper-left coordinate of where the bitmap starts in memory. For most purposes, these will always be zero, unless you are being creative in your bitmap retrieval. The drawing technique is SRCCOPY. This is the technique where the destination and the source are set equal in terms of the bitmap transfer. Additional drawing techniques are listed under "Ternary raster operations" in the listing dealing with parameter constants for the bitmap, cursor, and icon functions.

```
r& = BitBlt(Form1.hdc, 22 * i, 20 * j, bm.bmWidth,
            bm.bmHeight, hmdc&, 0, 0, SRCCOPY)
```

Once the bitmap is drawn, a little cleanup is done before the next figure is drawn to the screen. Several function calls are used, as you can see in the original listing.

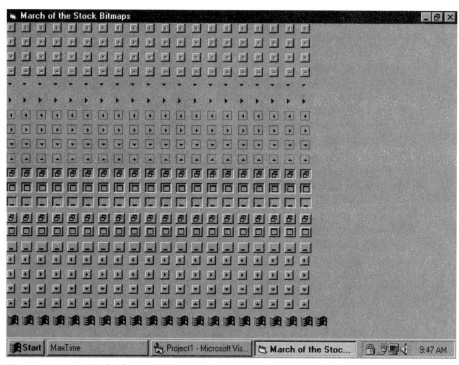

Figure 15–1   Multiple stock bitmap images are drawn to the form.

Figure 15–1 shows the output from this application.

If you find these bitmaps a little small, let's stretch them a bit with the next application.

Working with StretchBlt()

This application is similar to the previous application, but with a slight twist! When the bitmaps are drawn to the screen, they will be magnified by a power of six.

The second application is a project named Bitmap2.vbp. This project contains a module file named Bitmap2.bas and a form file named Bitmap2.frm. The following listing shows the contents of the module file which holds structure and function declarations along with several constants used by the application. Again, all of this information was extracted from the Win32api.txt file provided with your Visual Basic compiler.

```
Public Const SRCCOPY = &HCC0020

Type BITMAP
        bmType As Long
```

```
            bmWidth As Long
            bmHeight As Long
            bmWidthBytes As Long
            bmPlanes As Integer
            bmBitsPixel As Integer
            bmBits As Long
End Type

'OEM Resource Ordinal Numbers
Public Const OBM_CLOSE = 32754
Public Const OBM_UPARROW = 32753
Public Const OBM_DNARROW = 32752
Public Const OBM_RGARROW = 32751
Public Const OBM_LFARROW = 32750
Public Const OBM_REDUCE = 32749
Public Const OBM_ZOOM = 32748
Public Const OBM_RESTORE = 32747
Public Const OBM_REDUCED = 32746
Public Const OBM_ZOOMD = 32745
Public Const OBM_RESTORED = 32744
Public Const OBM_UPARROWD = 32743
Public Const OBM_DNARROWD = 32742
Public Const OBM_RGARROWD = 32741
Public Const OBM_LFARROWD = 32740
Public Const OBM_MNARROW = 32739
Public Const OBM_COMBO = 32738
Public Const OBM_UPARROWI = 32737
Public Const OBM_DNARROWI = 32736
Public Const OBM_RGARROWI = 32735
Public Const OBM_LFARROWI = 32734


Declare Function CreateCompatibleDC Lib "gdi32"
  (ByVal hdc As Long) As Long
Declare Function DeleteDC& Lib "gdi32"
  (ByVal hdc As Long)
Declare Function DeleteObject Lib "gdi32"
  (ByVal hObject As Long) As Long
Declare Function LoadBitmap Lib "user32" Alias
  "LoadBitmapA" (ByVal hInstance As Long,
  ByVal lpBitmapName As String) As Long
Declare Function LoadBitmapModified Lib "user32" Alias
  "LoadBitmapA" (ByVal hInstance As Long,
  ByVal lpBitmapName As Long) As Long
Declare Function GetObject Lib "gdi32" Alias "GetObjectA"
  (ByVal hObject As Long, ByVal nCount As Long,
  lpObject As Any) As Long
Declare Function GetObjectModified Lib "gdi32" Alias
  "GetObjectA" (ByVal hObject As Long, ByVal nCount As Long,
  lpObject As Any) As Long
```

```
Declare Function SelectObject& Lib "gdi32"
  (ByVal hdc As Long, ByVal hObject As Long)
Declare Function StretchBlt Lib "gdi32"
  (ByVal hdc As Long, ByVal x As Long, ByVal y As Long,
  ByVal nWidth As Long, ByVal nHeight As Long,
  ByVal hSrcDC As Long, ByVal xSrc As Long,
  ByVal ySrc As Long, ByVal nSrcWidth As Long,
  ByVal nSrcHeight As Long, ByVal dwRop As Long) As Long
```

The same bitmap-related functions are required for loading and drawing bitmap images with the StretchBlt() function as with the BitBlt() function.

The project draws the magnified bitmap images on a blank form. The code to support this action is shown in the next listing. This file is named Bitmap2.frm.

```
Private Sub Form_Paint()
        Dim hmdc&
        Dim hBitmap&, r&
        Dim bm As BITMAP

        For i = 0 To 4
          'Create a compatible device context for
          'bitmap image
          hmdc& = CreateCompatibleDC(Form1.hdc)

          'Load and display stock bitmaps sequentially
          'using a modified version of LoadBitmap() that
          'accepts an ordinal number for second parameter
          'rather than a string.
          hBitmap& = LoadBitmapModified(0, OBM_UPARROWD + i)

          'Use a modified version of GetObject() that allows
          'three parameters to be passed, as shown below.
          r& = GetObjectModified(hBitmap&, Len(bm), bm)

          'Select the object
          r& = SelectObject(hmdc&, hBitmap)

          'Use StretchBlt() to draw several 6x magnified
          'stock bitmaps. Offset each bitmap by 100 x 100
          'pixels.
          r& = StretchBlt(Form1.hdc, bm.bmWidth + (100 * i),
                      bm.bmHeight + (100 * i),
                      6 * bm.bmWidth, 6 * bm.bmHeight,
                      hmdc&, 0, 0, bm.bmWidth,
                      bm.bmHeight, SRCCOPY)

          'Select original object
          r& = SelectObject(hmdc&, r&)

          'Delete object
          r& = DeleteObject(hBitmap&)
```

```
            'Delete compatible device context
            r& = DeleteDC(hmdc&)
        Next I
End Sub
```

Examine this listing and notice that the code is very similar to the code used in the Bitmap1.vbp project. This project uses one **For** loop since only a few bitmap images will be drawn to the screen. And as you have noticed, the BitBlt() function has been replaced with the StretchBlt() function.

The bitmap images are drawn to the form with the StretchBlt() function. The second and third parameters of this function allow us to place the magnified bitmap images where we desire on the form. These locations are controlled by a single **For** loop. The actual width and height of the magnified bitmap image are given by the fourth and fifth parameters. Here you can see that the original bitmap size is multiplied by the magnification of six in each dimension. The two parameters with a zero value specify the upper-left coordinate of where the bitmap starts in memory. Again, for most purposes, these will usually be the default. The drawing technique is, again, SRCCOPY. This is where the destination and the source are set equal in terms of the bitmap transfer.

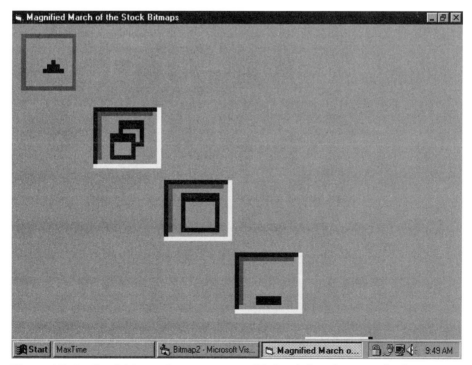

Figure 15–2   Stock bitmap images are magnified and then drawn to the form.

```
r& = StretchBlt(Form1.hdc, bm.bmWidth + (100 * i),
                bm.bmHeight + (100 * i),
                6 * bm.bmWidth, 6 * bm.bmHeight,
                hmdc&, 0, 0, bm.bmWidth,
                bm.bmHeight, SRCCOPY)
```

Figure 15–2 shows the magnified output from this application.

You'll find that working with the cursor and icon functions equally easy. However, for complicated bitmap work, we still recommend Visual Basics picture functions.

Chapter 16

Mouse and Joystick Functions

The Windows API allows access to a small number of functions that allow simulated mouse actions to occur in an application. These functions give the illusion that mouse movement or button action has occurred by simulating their results in an application. If you are interested in accessing physical mouse data, we recommend using Visual Basics MouseDown, MouseUp, and MouseMove events. Cursor functions are often associated with the mouse and are discussed in Chapter 32.

The Windows API also provides full support for joysticks as noted by the numerous joystick functions. If you are developing Visual Basic games or just want to experiment with your computer's game port, you'll want to study the functions in this chapter.

API Mouse and Joystick Function Names and Descriptions

Table 16–1 shows 11 Windows API mouse and joystick functions and provides a brief description for their use.

The most frequently used functions from this group include joyGetDevCaps(), joyGetPosEx(), joyReleaseCapture(), and joySetCapture(). The example application in this chapter will illustrate several of these functions.

Table 16–1   Mouse and Joystick Functions and Descriptions

Function	Description
GetNumberOfConsoleMouseButtons	Gets the number of console mouse buttons.
joyGetDevCaps	Gets a joystick's capabilities.
joyGetNumDevs	Gets the number of joysticks supported by the joystick driver.
joyGetPos	Gets a joystick's position and button status.
joyGetPosEx	Same as joyGetPos() with extended capabilities.
joyGetThreshold	Gets a joystick's current movement threshold.
joyReleaseCapture	Releases a captured joystick.
joySetCapture	Captures a joystick, thus causing its messages to be sent to the given window.
joySetThreshold	Sets a joystick's current movement threshold.
mouse_event	Synthesizes mouse motion and button clicks.
SwapMouseButton	Reverses or restores the meaning of the left and right mouse buttons.

API Mouse and Joystick Function Declarations

The following listing contains the Windows API mouse and joystick function declarations found in the Win32api.txt file provided with Visual Basic. Cursor functions, which are associated with mouse functions, are discussed in Chapter 32.

```
Declare Function GetNumberOfConsoleMouseButtons Lib
   "kernel32" Alias "GetNumberOfConsoleMouseButtons"
   (lpNumberOfMouseButtons As Long) As Long

Declare Function joyGetDevCaps Lib "winmm.dll" Alias
   "joyGetDevCapsA" (ByVal id As Long, lpCaps As JOYCAPS,
   ByVal uSize As Long) As Long

Declare Function joyGetNumDevs Lib "winmm.dll" Alias
   "joyGetNumDev" () As Long

Declare Function joyGetPos Lib "winmm.dll" Alias "joyGetPos"
   (ByVal uJoyID As Long, pji As JOYINFO) As Long

Declare Function joyGetPosEx Lib "winmm.dll" Alias
   "joyGetPosEx" (ByVal uJoyID As Long,
   pji As JOYINFOEX) As Long

Declare Function joyGetThreshold Lib "winmm.dll" Alias
   "joyGetThreshold" (ByVal id As Long,
   lpuThreshold As Long) As Long

Declare Function joyReleaseCapture Lib "winmm.dll"
   Alias "joyReleaseCapture" (ByVal id As Long) As Long
```

```
Declare Function joySetCapture Lib "winmm.dll" Alias
    "joySetCapture" (ByVal hwnd As Long, ByVal uID As Long,
    ByVal uPeriod As Long, ByVal bChanged As Long) As Long

Declare Function joySetThreshold Lib "winmm.dll" Alias
    "joySetThreshold" (ByVal id As Long,
    ByVal uThreshold As Long) As Long

Declare Function SwapMouseButton Lib "user32" Alias
    "SwapMouseButton" (ByVal bSwap As Long) As Long

Declare Sub mouse_event Lib "user32" Alias "mouse_event"
    (ByVal dwFlags As Long, ByVal dx As Long,
    ByVal dy As Long, ByVal cButtons As Long,
    ByVal dwExtraInfo As Long)
```

Table 16–2 contains a brief description of the parameters used in the various mouse and joystick functions.

Table 16–2   Mouse and Joystick Function Parameters and Descriptions

Parameter	Description
bChanged As Long	Change position flag. TRUE to send messages only when the position changes by a value greater than the joystick movement threshold. Else messages are sent at the polling frequency specified in uPeriod.
bSwap As Long	TRUE, the left button generates right-button messages and the right button generates left-button messages. If FALSE, the buttons are restored to their original meanings.
cButtons As Long	Not used.
dwExtraInfo As Long	32 bits of application-defined information.
dwFlags As Long	Mouse or joystick flags specifying various motion/click variants. See JOY_ or MOUSEEVENTF_ constants.
dx As Long	Horizontal mouse position or position change.
dy As Long	Vertical mouse position or position change.
hwnd As Long	Windows handle.
id As Long	Identifier of the joystick (JOYSTICKID1 or JOYSTICKID2).
lpCaps As JOYCAPS	Address of a structure to contain the capabilities of the joystick.
lpNumberOfMouseButtons As Long	Value contains the number of console mouse buttons.
lpuThreshold As Long	New movement threshold.
pji As JOYINFO or JOYINFOEX	Address of structure that holds position or extended position information and button status.
uID As Long	Identifier of the joystick (JOYSTICKID1 or JOYSTICKID2).
uJoyID As Long	Identifier of the joystick (JOYSTICKID1 or JOYSTICKID2) to be captured.
uPeriod As Long	Polling frequency, in milliseconds.
uSize As Long	Size, in bytes, of the JOYCAPS structure.
UThreshold As Long	New movement threshold.

Many of the parameters described in Table 16–2 use constant values. The Win32api.txt file lists the following constants for mouse and joystick functions:

```
'Multimedia Window Messages
Public Const MM_JOY1MOVE = &H3A0 'joystick
Public Const MM_JOY2MOVE = &H3A1
Public Const MM_JOY1ZMOVE = &H3A2
Public Const MM_JOY2ZMOVE = &H3A3
Public Const MM_JOY1BUTTONDOWN = &H3B5
Public Const MM_JOY2BUTTONDOWN = &H3B6
Public Const MM_JOY1BUTTONUP = &H3B7
Public Const MM_JOY2BUTTONUP = &H3B8

Public Const MM_PC_JOYSTICK = 12 'Joystick adapter

'constants used with JOYINFOEX
Public Const JOY_BUTTON5 = &H10&
Public Const JOY_BUTTON6 = &H20&
Public Const JOY_BUTTON7 = &H40&
Public Const JOY_BUTTON8 = &H80&
Public Const JOY_BUTTON9 = &H100&
Public Const JOY_BUTTON10 = &H200&
Public Const JOY_BUTTON11 = &H400&
Public Const JOY_BUTTON12 = &H800&
Public Const JOY_BUTTON13 = &H1000&
Public Const JOY_BUTTON14 = &H2000&
Public Const JOY_BUTTON15 = &H4000&
Public Const JOY_BUTTON16 = &H8000&
Public Const JOY_BUTTON17 = &H10000
Public Const JOY_BUTTON18 = &H20000
Public Const JOY_BUTTON19 = &H40000
Public Const JOY_BUTTON20 = &H80000
Public Const JOY_BUTTON21 = &H100000
Public Const JOY_BUTTON22 = &H200000
Public Const JOY_BUTTON23 = &H400000
Public Const JOY_BUTTON24 = &H800000
Public Const JOY_BUTTON25 = &H1000000
Public Const JOY_BUTTON26 = &H2000000
Public Const JOY_BUTTON27 = &H4000000
Public Const JOY_BUTTON28 = &H8000000
Public Const JOY_BUTTON29 = &H10000000
Public Const JOY_BUTTON30 = &H20000000
Public Const JOY_BUTTON31 = &H40000000
Public Const JOY_BUTTON32 = &H80000000

'constants used with JOYINFOEX structure
Public Const JOY_POVCENTERED = -1
Public Const JOY_POVFORWARD = 0
Public Const JOY_POVRIGHT = 9000
Public Const JOY_POVBACKWARD = 18000
```

```
Public Const JOY_POVLEFT = 27000
Public Const JOY_RETURNX = &H1&
Public Const JOY_RETURNY = &H2&
Public Const JOY_RETURNZ = &H4&
Public Const JOY_RETURNR = &H8&
Public Const JOY_RETURNU = &H10          'axis 5
Public Const JOY_RETURNV = &H20          'axis 6
Public Const JOY_RETURNPOV = &H40&
Public Const JOY_RETURNBUTTONS = &H80&
Public Const JOY_RETURNRAWDATA = &H100&
Public Const JOY_RETURNPOVCTS = &H200&
Public Const JOY_RETURNCENTERED = &H400&
Public Const JOY_USEDEADZONE = &H800&
Public Const JOY_RETURNALL = JOY_RETURNX Or
              JOY_RETURNY Or JOY_RETURNZ Or
              JOY_RETURNR Or JOY_RETURNU Or
              JOY_RETURNV Or JOY_RETURNPOV Or
              JOY_RETURNBUTTONS)
Public Const JOY_CAL_READALWAYS = &H10000
Public Const JOY_CAL_READXYONLY = &H20000
Public Const JOY_CAL_READ3 = &H40000
Public Const JOY_CAL_READ4 = &H80000
Public Const JOY_CAL_READXONLY = &H100000
Public Const JOY_CAL_READYONLY = &H200000
Public Const JOY_CAL_READ5 = &H400000
Public Const JOY_CAL_READ6 = &H800000
Public Const JOY_CAL_READZONLY = &H1000000
Public Const JOY_CAL_READRONLY = &H2000000
Public Const JOY_CAL_READUONLY = &H4000000
Public Const JOY_CAL_READVONLY = &H8000000


'joystick error return values
Public Const JOYERR_NOERROR = 0) 'no error
Public Const JOYERR_PARMS = JOYERR_BASE + 5) 'bad parameters
'request not completed:
Public Const JOYERR_NOCANDO = JOYERR_BASE + 6)
'joystick is unplugged:
Public Const JOYERR_UNPLUGGED = JOYERR_BASE + 7)


'constants used with JOYINFO structure and MM_JOY messages
Public Const JOY_BUTTON1 = &H1
Public Const JOY_BUTTON2 = &H2
Public Const JOY_BUTTON3 = &H4
Public Const JOY_BUTTON4 = &H8
Public Const JOY_BUTTON1CHG = &H100
Public Const JOY_BUTTON2CHG = &H200
Public Const JOY_BUTTON3CHG = &H400
Public Const JOY_BUTTON4CHG = &H800
```

```
'joystick ID constants
Public Const JOYSTICKID1 = 0
Public Const JOYSTICKID2 = 1

'Mouse constants
Public Const WM_NCMOUSEMOVE = &HA0
Public Const WM_NCLBUTTONDOWN = &HA1
Public Const WM_NCLBUTTONUP = &HA2
Public Const WM_NCLBUTTONDBLCLK = &HA3
Public Const WM_NCRBUTTONDOWN = &HA4
Public Const WM_NCRBUTTONUP = &HA5
Public Const WM_NCRBUTTONDBLCLK = &HA6
Public Const WM_NCMBUTTONDOWN = &HA7
Public Const WM_NCMBUTTONUP = &HA8
Public Const WM_NCMBUTTONDBLCLK = &HA9

Public Const WM_MOUSEFIRST = &H200
Public Const WM_MOUSEMOVE = &H200
Public Const WM_LBUTTONDOWN = &H201
Public Const WM_LBUTTONUP = &H202
Public Const WM_LBUTTONDBLCLK = &H203
Public Const WM_RBUTTONDOWN = &H204
Public Const WM_RBUTTONUP = &H205
Public Const WM_RBUTTONDBLCLK = &H206
Public Const WM_MBUTTONDOWN = &H207
Public Const WM_MBUTTONUP = &H208
Public Const WM_MBUTTONDBLCLK = &H209
Public Const WM_MOUSELAST = &H209

'WM_NCHITTEST and MOUSEHOOKSTRUCT Mouse Position Codes
Public Const HTERROR = -2)
Public Const HTTRANSPARENT = -1)
Public Const HTNOWHERE = 0
Public Const HTCLIENT = 1
Public Const HTCAPTION = 2
Public Const HTSYSMENU = 3
Public Const HTGROWBOX = 4
Public Const HTSIZE = HTGROWBOX
Public Const HTMENU = 5
Public Const HTHSCROLL = 6
Public Const HTVSCROLL = 7
Public Const HTMINBUTTON = 8
Public Const HTMAXBUTTON = 9
Public Const HTLEFT = 10
Public Const HTRIGHT = 11
Public Const HTTOP = 12
Public Const HTTOPLEFT = 13
Public Const HTTOPRIGHT = 14
```

```
Public Const HTBOTTOM = 15
Public Const HTBOTTOMLEFT = 16
Public Const HTBOTTOMRIGHT = 17
Public Const HTBORDER = 18
Public Const HTREDUCE = HTMINBUTTON
Public Const HTZOOM = HTMAXBUTTON
Public Const HTSIZEFIRST = HTLEFT
Public Const HTSIZELAST = HTBOTTOMRIGHT

'WM_MOUSEACTIVATE Return Codes
Public Const MA_ACTIVATE = 1
Public Const MA_ACTIVATEANDEAT = 2
Public Const MA_NOACTIVATE = 3
Public Const MA_NOACTIVATEANDEAT = 4

'Key State Masks for Mouse Messages
Public Const MK_LBUTTON = &H1
Public Const MK_RBUTTON = &H2
Public Const MK_SHIFT = &H4
Public Const MK_CONTROL = &H8
Public Const MK_MBUTTON = &H10

Public Const MOUSEEVENTF_MOVE = &H1 'mouse move
Public Const MOUSEEVENTF_LEFTDOWN = &H2 'left button down
Public Const MOUSEEVENTF_LEFTUP = &H4 'left button up
Public Const MOUSEEVENTF_RIGHTDOWN = &H8 'right button down
Public Const MOUSEEVENTF_RIGHTUP = &H10 'right button up
Public Const MOUSEEVENTF_MIDDLEDOWN = &H20 'middle button down
Public Const MOUSEEVENTF_MIDDLEUP = &H40 'middle button up
Public Const MOUSEEVENTF_ABSOLUTE = &H8000 'absolute move
'ButtonState flags
Public Const FROM_LEFT_1ST_BUTTON_PRESSED = &H1
Public Const RIGHTMOST_BUTTON_PRESSED = &H2
Public Const FROM_LEFT_2ND_BUTTON_PRESSED = &H4
Public Const FROM_LEFT_3RD_BUTTON_PRESSED = &H8
Public Const FROM_LEFT_4TH_BUTTON_PRESSED = &H10

'EventFlags
Public Const MOUSE_MOVED = &H1
Public Const DOUBLE_CLICK = &H2
```

A number of unique structures are also associated with these mouse and joystick parameters. The following structures are also listed in the Win32api.txt file:

```
Type JOYCAPS
   wMid As Integer
   wPid As Integer
   szPname As String * MAXPNAMELEN
   wXmin As Integer
   wXmax As Integer
```

```
      wYmin As Integer
      wYmax As Integer
      wZmin As Integer
      wZmax As Integer
      wNumButtons As Integer
      wPeriodMin As Integer
      wPeriodMax As Integer
   End Type

   Type JOYINFO
      wXpos As Integer
      wYpos As Integer
      wZpos As Integer
      wButtons As Integer
   End Type

   Type JOYINFOEX
      dwSize As Long          'size of structure
      dwFlags As Long         'flags to indicate what to return
      dwXpos As Long          'x position
      dwYpos As Long          'y position
      dwZpos As Long          'z position
      dwRpos As Long          'rudder/4th axis position
      dwUpos As Long          '5th axis position
      dwVpos As Long          '6th axis position
      dwButtons As Long       'button states
      dwButtonNumber As Long 'current button number pressed
      dwPOV As Long           'point of view state
      dwReserved1 As Long 'reserved for communication between
                          'winmm driver
      dwReserved2 As Long 'reserved for future expansion
   End Type

   Type MOUSE_EVENT_RECORD
    dwMousePosition As COORD
    dwButtonState As Long
    dwControlKeyState As Long
    dwEventFlags As Long
   End Type

   Type MOUSEHOOKSTRUCT
    pt As POINTAPI
    hwnd As Long
    wHitTestCode As Long
    dwExtraInfo As Long
   End Type
```

In the next section we'll examine an application that makes use of several of these functions.

Example Application

This section contains a simple application that polls the joystick for various pieces of data including depressed buttons, axis position values, and rudder positions. Our joystick only provided X-Y axis movements, but the application also tests for movements in the Z axis direction.

This Visual Basic project is named Joy1, and contains a form for drawing text information on and a module file for function declarations. Here are the contents of the Joy1.bas module file. The constant, structure, and function declarations are simply copied and pasted into this file from the Win32api.txt file provided with your Visual Basic compiler.

```
Type JOYINFOEX
   dwSize As Long 'size of structure
   dwFlags As Long 'flags to indicate what to return
   dwXpos As Long 'x position
   dwYpos As Long 'y position
   dwZpos As Long 'z position
   dwRpos As Long 'rudder/4th axis position
   dwUpos As Long '5th axis position
   dwVpos As Long '6th axis position
   dwButtons As Long 'button states
   dwButtonNumber As Long 'current button number pressed
   dwPOV As Long 'point of view state
   dwReserved1 As Long 'reserved for communication between
   'winmm driver
   dwReserved2 As Long 'reserved for future expansion
End Type

'joystick ID constants
Public Const JOYSTICKID1 = 0
Public Const JOYSTICKID2 = 1

'constants used with JOYINFOEX structure
Public Const JOY_POVCENTERED = -1
Public Const JOY_POVFORWARD = 0
Public Const JOY_POVRIGHT = 9000
Public Const JOY_POVBACKWARD = 18000
Public Const JOY_POVLEFT = 27000
Public Const JOY_RETURNX = &H1&
Public Const JOY_RETURNY = &H2&
Public Const JOY_RETURNZ = &H4&
Public Const JOY_RETURNR = &H8&
Public Const JOY_RETURNU = &H10      'axis 5
Public Const JOY_RETURNV = &H20      'axis 6
Public Const JOY_RETURNPOV = &H40&
Public Const JOY_RETURNBUTTONS = &H80&
```

```
Public Const JOY_RETURNRAWDATA = &H100&
Public Const JOY_RETURNPOVCTS = &H200&
Public Const JOY_RETURNCENTERED = &H400&
Public Const JOY_USEDEADZONE = &H800&
Public Const JOY_RETURNALL = (JOY_RETURNX Or JOY_RETURNY Or
                              JOY_RETURNZ Or JOY_RETURNR Or
                              JOY_RETURNU Or JOY_RETURNV Or
                              JOY_RETURNPOV Or
                              JOY_RETURNBUTTONS)
Public Const JOY_CAL_READALWAYS = &H10000
Public Const JOY_CAL_READXYONLY = &H20000
Public Const JOY_CAL_READ3 = &H40000
Public Const JOY_CAL_READ4 = &H80000
Public Const JOY_CAL_READXONLY = &H100000
Public Const JOY_CAL_READYONLY = &H200000
Public Const JOY_CAL_READ5 = &H400000
Public Const JOY_CAL_READ6 = &H800000
Public Const JOY_CAL_READZONLY = &H1000000
Public Const JOY_CAL_READRONLY = &H2000000
Public Const JOY_CAL_READUONLY = &H4000000
Public Const JOY_CAL_READVONLY = &H8000000

Declare Function joyGetPosEx Lib "winmm.dll"
  (ByVal uJoyID As Long, pji As JOYINFOEX) As Long
Declare Function joyReleaseCapture Lib "winmm.dll"
  (ByVal id As Long) As Long
Declare Function joySetCapture Lib "winmm.dll"
  (ByVal hWnd As Long, ByVal uID As Long,
  ByVal uPeriod As Long, ByVal bChanged As Long) As Long
```

The application makes use of the joySetCapture(), joyReleaseCapture(), and joyGetPosEx() functions. Joystick data is returned to a JOYINFOEX structure where it is later accessed by the application.

The project's form, Joy1.frm, contains a Form_Load() and Timer1_Timer() subroutine as you can see in the following listing:

```
Private Sub Form_Load()
  Dim r&
  Dim hWnd&

  r& = joySetCapture(hWnd, JOYSTICKID1, 1, 0)
  r& = joyReleaseCapture(JOYSTICKID1)
End Sub

Private Sub Timer1_Timer()
  Dim myJoy As JOYINFOEX

  myJoy.dwSize = 64
  myJoy.dwFlags = JOY_RETURNALL
```

```
        r& = joyGetPosEx(JOYSTICKID1, myJoy)
        Label8.Caption = myJoy.dwButtons
        Label9.Caption = myJoy.dwXpos
        Label10.Caption = myJoy.dwYpos
        Label11.Caption = myJoy.dwZpos
        Label12.Caption = myJoy.dwRpos
        Label13.Caption = myJoy.dwUpos
        Label14.Caption = myJoy.dwVpos
    End Sub
```

The form for this application is shown in Figure 16–1.

This form contains 14 label controls. The label control captions in the left column describe the value to be returned for the joystick. The label control captions in the right column are left blank and will be used to report specific joystick values. In addition to the label controls, notice the inclusion of a timer control. The timer is used to set up the polling interval for the joystick. For this application it is set to 100 milliseconds. You can find this value in the Timer's properties window shown earlier in Figure 16–1.

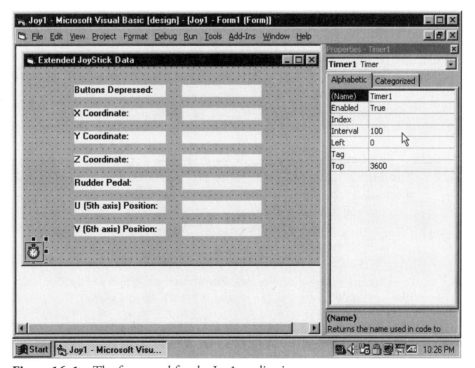

Figure 16–1 The form used for the Joy1 application.

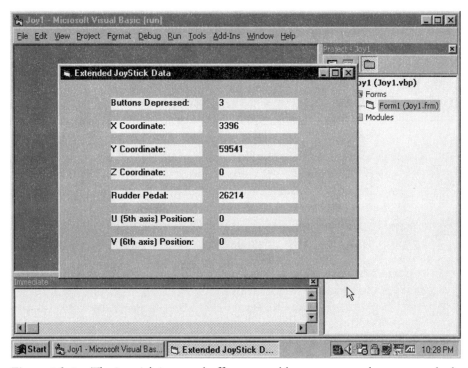

Figure 16–2   The joystick is moved off center and buttons one and two are pushed.

A flag value indicating what values are to be returned must be initialized before the joyGetPosEx() function is called. In this case the JOY_RETURNALL constant is used.

The joyGetPosEx() function reports button positions in a unique manner. The first button returns a value of 1 when depressed, the second button a 2, the third button a 4, and the fourth button an 8. Do you know what's happening? (Hint: If you push all four buttons, a value of 15 is reported—15_{10} is equal to 1111_2.)

The coordinate values returned for the joystick are dependent on the default (or set) movement threshold values and the number of axes. In our case, your joystick had only two degrees of movement along the X-Y axis and a rudder control.

Figure 16–2 shows one data sample when the first and second buttons are simultaneously pushed and the joystick is positioned slightly off center.

The joyGetPosEx() function is preferred over the older joyGetPos() function since newer joysticks perform more actions than earlier joysticks.

Chapter 17

Font Functions

The Windows API allows access to a wide variety of fonts, including TrueType fonts. With Windows API font functions, you can create fonts by altering a wide variety of font properties, such as *orientation* and *escapement*. These two font properties allow you to rotate individual characters in a string or the whole string. If you are developing charting applications, you will probably want to create labels for a vertical chart axis. If this is the case, the Windows API functions are just what you need.

Many font functions are used in conjunction with the text functions described in Chapter 20. You'll want to examine this chapter for additional font capabilities and examples.

What Is a Font?

It is relatively easy to draw text on the screen using Visual Basic functions. These font functions work well for the majority of applications, However, when several fonts and/or font orientations are required, Windows API font functions must be used.

A *font* can be defined as a complete set of characters of the same typeface and size. Fonts include letters, punctuation marks, and additional symbols. The physical size of a font is measured in points. For example, 12-point Courier, 12-point Times New Roman, 14-point Times New Roman, and 12-point Lucida Bright are all different fonts. A *point* is the smallest unit of measure used in typography. There are 12 points in a *pica* and 72 points (6 picas) in an inch.

A *typeface* is a basic character design that is defined by a stroke width and a serif (a smaller line used to finish off a main stroke of a letter). A font represents a complete set of characters from one specific typeface, all with a certain size and style, such as italics or bold. Usually the system owns all of the font resources and shares them with application programs. Fonts are not usually compiled into the final executable version of a program.

Applications treat fonts like other drawing objects. Windows supplies several fonts: System, Terminal, Courier, Helvetica, Modern, Roman, Script, and Times Roman, as well as several TrueType fonts. These are called *GDI_supplied fonts*.

The Windows API CreateFont() function is often used to select a logical font from the GDI's pool of physical fonts that most closely matches the characteristics specified by the developer in the function call. Once created, this logical font can be selected by any device. You'll see, shortly, that using the CreateFont() function, with its 14 parameters, requires quite a bit of skill. For example, an application may require the function to use the following parameter values:

```
Height = 14
Width  = 14
Escapement = 0
Orientation = 0
Weight = FW_BOLD
Italic = FALSE
Underline = FALSE
StrikeOut = FALSE
CharSet = OEM_CHARSET
OutputPrecision = OUT_DEFAULT_PRECIS
ClipPrecision = CLIP_DEFAULT_PRECIS
Quality = DEFAULT_QUALITY
PitchAndFamily = VARIABLE_PITCH|FF_ROMAN
Facename = "Roman"
```

An attempt will then be made by the Windows API to find a font to match the preceding specifications. This font could then be used to print a horizontal string of text in the window. However, the application may require an additional font. The next time the CreateFont() function is called, the parameters might be set to the following values:

```
Height = 14
Width  = 14
```

```
Escapement = 900
Orientation = 900
Weight = FW_BOLD
Italic = FALSE
Underline = FALSE
StrikeOut = FALSE
CharSet = OEM_CHARSET
OutputPrecision = OUT_DEFAULT_PRECIS
ClipPrecision = CLIP_DEFAULT_PRECIS
Quality = DEFAULT_QUALITY
PitchAndFamily = VARIABLE_PITCH|FF_ROMAN
Facename = "Roman"
```

Again, an attempt will be made by the Windows API to find a match to the preceding specifications. In the previous specification only *Escapement* and *Orientation* were changed. Both of these parameters use angle values specified in tenths of a degree. Thus, 900 represents an angle of 90.0 degrees. The *Escapement* parameter rotates the line of text from horizontal to vertical. *Orientation* rotates each character, in this example, by 90.0 degrees. This font could then be used to print a vertical axis label in the application.

API Font Function Name and Description

Table 17–1 shows 21 popular Windows API font functions and provides a brief description for their use.

Perhaps the two functions that are used most frequently when manipulating fonts are the CreateFont() and CreateFontIndirect() functions. The example applications in this chapter will illustrate their use.

API Font Function Declarations

The following listing contains the Windows API font function declarations found in the Win32api.txt file provided with Visual Basic. As we mentioned earlier, there are additional functions related to font manipulations that are described in Chapter 20.

```
Declare Function AddFontResource Lib "gdi32" Alias
   "AddFontResourceA" (ByVal lpFileName As String) As Long

Declare Function CreateFont Lib "gdi32" Alias "CreateFontA"
   (ByVal H As Long, ByVal W As Long, ByVal E As Long,
   ByVal O As Long, ByVal W As Long, ByVal I As Long,
   ByVal u As Long, ByVal S As Long, ByVal C As Long,
   ByVal OP As Long, ByVal CP As Long, ByVal Q As Long,
   ByVal PAF As Long, ByVal F As String) As Long
```

Table 17–1   Font Functions and Descriptions

Function	Description
AddFontResource	Adds a new font resource to application.
CreateFont	Directly creates a logical font.
CreateFontIndirect	Indirectly creates a logical font.
CreateScalableFontResource	Makes a resource file for a TrueType font.
EnumFontFamilies	Enumerates all fonts for all platforms. Device based on LOGFONT info.
EnumFontFamiliesEx	Enumerates all fonts for 32-bit platforms based on LOGFONT info.
EnumFonts	Enumerates all fonts for all platforms. (Use of EnumFontFamilies preferred.)
GetAspectRatioFilterEx	Gets aspect ratio for the selection process when using SetMapperFlags function.
GetCharABCWidths	Gets the A|B|C dimensions of a TrueType font character(s).
GetCharABCWidthsFloat	Gets the A|B|C dimensions of an NT TrueType font character(s).
GetCharWidth	Gets the width of character(s) in a font.
GetCharWidth32	Gets the width of character(s) in a Win32 font.
GetCharWidthFloat	Gets the width of character(s) in an NT font.
GetFontLanguageInfo	Gets current font family information.
GetKerningPairs	Gets kerning information for font.
GetOutlineTextMetrics	Gets internal characteristics for TrueType font.
GetRasterizerCaps	Gets information regarding device support for scalable fonts.
GetTextFace	Gets typeface name for a font.
GetTextMetrics	Gets information for the current physical font.
RemoveFontResource	Removes the selected font resource.
SetMapperFlags	Uses aspect ratio to match raster font selection.

```
Declare Function CreateFontIndirect Lib "gdi32" Alias
   "CreateFontIndirectA" (lpLogFont As LOGFONT) As Long

Declare Function CreateScalableFontResource Lib
   "gdi32" Alias "CreateScalableFontResourceA"
   (ByVal fHidden As Long, ByVal lpszResourceFile As String,
   ByVal lpszFontFile As String,
   ByVal lpszCurrentPath As String) As Long

Declare Function EnumFontFamilies Lib "gdi32" Alias
   "EnumFontFamiliesA" (ByVal hdc As Long, ByVal lpszFamily
   As String, ByVal lpEnumFontFamProc As Long,
   ByVal lParam As Long) As Long

Declare Function EnumFontFamiliesEx Lib "gdi32" Alias
   "EnumFontFamiliesExA" (ByVal hdc As Long,
   lpLogFont As LOGFONT, ByVal lpEnumFontProc As Long,
   ByVal lParam As Long, ByVal dw As Long) As Long

Declare Function EnumFonts Lib "gdi32" Alias
   "EnumFontsA" (ByVal hDC As Long, ByVal lpsz As String,
   ByVal lpFontEnumProc As Long, ByVal lParam As Long) As Long
```

```
Declare Function GetAspectRatioFilterEx Lib "gdi32" Alias
   "GetAspectRatioFilterEx" (ByVal hdc As Long,
   lpAspectRatio As SIZE) As Long

Declare Function GetCharABCWidths Lib "gdi32" Alias
   "GetCharABCWidthsA" (ByVal hdc As Long,
   ByVal uFirstChar As Long, ByVal uLastChar As Long,
   lpabc As ABC) As Long

Declare Function GetCharABCWidthsFloat Lib "gdi32" Alias
   "GetCharABCWidthsFloatA" (ByVal hdc As Long,
   ByVal iFirstChar As Long, ByVal iLastChar As Long,
   lpABCF As ABCFLOAT) As Long

Declare Function GetCharWidth Lib "gdi32" Alias
   "GetCharWidthA" (ByVal hDC As Long, ByVal un1 As Long,
   ByVal un2 As Long, lpn As Long) As Long

Declare Function GetCharWidth32 Lib "gdi32" Alias
   "GetCharWidth32A" (ByVal hdc As Long,
   ByVal iFirstChar As Long, ByVal iLastChar As Long,
   lpBuffer As Long) As Long

Declare Function GetCharWidthFloat Lib "gdi32" Alias
   "GetCharWidthFloatA" (ByVal hdc As Long,
   ByVal iFirstChar As Long, ByVal iLastChar As Long,
   pxBuffer As Double) As Long

Declare Function GetFontLanguageInfo Lib "gdi32" Alias
   "GetFontLanguageInfo" (ByVal hdc As Long) As Long

Declare Function GetKerningPairs Lib "gdi32" Alias
   "GetKerningPairsA" (ByVal hdc As Long, ByVal cPairs As Long,
   lpkrnpair As KERNINGPAIR) As Long

Declare Function GetOutlineTextMetrics Lib "gdi32" Alias
   "GetOutlineTextMetricsA" (ByVal hdc As Long,
   ByVal cbData As Long, lpotm As OUTLINETEXTMETRIC) As Long

Declare Function GetRasterizerCaps Lib "gdi32" Alias
   "GetRasterizerCaps" (lpraststat As RASTERIZER_STATUS,
   ByVal cb As Long) As Long

Declare Function GetTextFace Lib "gdi32" Alias
   "GetTextFaceA" (ByVal hdc As Long, ByVal nCount As Long,
   ByVal lpFacename As String) As Long

Declare Function GetTextMetrics Lib "gdi32" Alias
   "GetTextMetricsA" (ByVal hdc As Long,
   lpMetrics As TEXTMETRIC) As Long

Declare Function RemoveFontResource Lib "gdi32" Alias
   "RemoveFontResourceA" (ByVal lpFileName As String) As Long
```

```
Declare Function SetMapperFlags Lib "gdi32" Alias
   "SetMapperFlags" (ByVal hdc As Long,
   ByVal dwFlag As Long) As Long
```

Table 17–2 contains a brief description of the parameters used in the various font functions.

Table 17–2   Font Function Parameters and Descriptions

Parameter	Description
C As Long	lfCharSet.
cb As Long	Number of bytes to copy to lpraststat structure.
CP As Long	lpClipPrecision.
cPairs As Long	Number of kerning pairs.
dw As Long	Reserved (use 0).
dwFlag As Long	ASPECT_FILTERING constant matches selected fonts with device aspect ratio.
E As Long	lfEscapement.
F As String	lfFaceName.
fHidden As Long	0 creates a normal font resource, 1 creates a read-only resource.
H As Long	lfHeight.
hdc As Long	Handle to the device context.
I As Long	lfItalic.
iFirstChar As Long	ASCII value of first character to hold width values.
iLastChar As Long	ASCII value of last character to hold width values.
lpabc As ABC	First entry in array of ABC structures to fill with values of character(s) dimensions.
lpABCF As ABCFLOAT	First entry in array of ABCFLOAT structures to fill with values of character(s) dimensions.
lParam As Long	Value, defined by user, to pass to the callback function.
lpAspectRatio As SIZE	Structure holds the aspect ratio.
lpBuffer As Long	First entry in array of long values to fill with the character widths.
lpEnumFontFamProc As Long	Function address to call.
lpEnumFontProc As Long	Function address to call.
lpFacename As String	Strings holds Facename for current font.
lpFileName As String	String holds FileName for current font file.
lpFontEnumProc As Long	Function address to call.
lpkrnpair As KERNINGPAIR	First entry in the array of KERNINGPAIR structures.
lpLogFont As LOGFONT	Structure holds attributes for logical font.
lpMetrics As TEXTMETRIC	Structure holds metrics for current physical font.
lpn As Long	See lpBuffer.
lpotm As OUTLINETEXTMETRIC	Structure holds textmetric font outline data.
lpraststat As RASTERIZER_STATUS	Structure contains rasterized data.
lpsz As String	Font family to be enumerated.
lpszCurrentPath As String	Current file path, used by lpszFontFile parameter.

Table 17–2   Font Function Parameters and Descriptions *(Continued)*

Parameter	Description
lpszFamily As String	Font family to be enumerated.
lpszFontFile As String	TrueType font file name
lpszResourceFile As String	Resource file name (.FOT for normal, .FOR for RO).
nCount As Long	lpFacename size.
O As Long	lfOrientation.
OP As Long	lfOutputPrecision.
PAF As Long	lfPitchNadFamily.
pxBuffer As Double	First entry in array of double values to fill with character widths.
Q As Long	lfQuality.
S As Long	lfStrikeOut.
u As Long	lfUnderline.
uFirstChar As Long	ASCII value of first character for A|B|C values.
uLastChar As Long	ASCII value of last character for A|B|C values.
un1 As Long	Value of first character to hold width values.
un2 As Long	Value of last character to hold width values.
W As Long	lpWeight.
wFirstChar As Long	Value of first character to hold width values.
wLastChar As Long	Value of last character to hold width values.

Many of the parameters described in Table 17–2 use constant values. The Win32api.txt file list the following constants for font parameters:

```
Public Const OUT_DEFAULT_PRECIS = 0
Public Const OUT_STRING_PRECIS = 1
Public Const OUT_CHARACTER_PRECIS = 2
Public Const OUT_STROKE_PRECIS = 3
Public Const OUT_TT_PRECIS = 4
Public Const OUT_DEVICE_PRECIS = 5
Public Const OUT_RASTER_PRECIS = 6
Public Const OUT_TT_ONLY_PRECIS = 7
Public Const OUT_OUTLINE_PRECIS = 8

Public Const CLIP_DEFAULT_PRECIS = 0
Public Const CLIP_CHARACTER_PRECIS = 1
Public Const CLIP_STROKE_PRECIS = 2
Public Const CLIP_MASK = &HF
Public Const CLIP_LH_ANGLES = 16
Public Const CLIP_TT_ALWAYS = 32
Public Const CLIP_EMBEDDED = 128

Public Const DEFAULT_QUALITY = 0
Public Const DRAFT_QUALITY = 1
Public Const PROOF_QUALITY = 2
```

```
Public Const DEFAULT_PITCH = 0
Public Const FIXED_PITCH = 1
Public Const VARIABLE_PITCH = 2

Public Const ANSI_CHARSET = 0
Public Const DEFAULT_CHARSET = 1
Public Const SYMBOL_CHARSET = 2
Public Const SHIFTJIS_CHARSET = 128
Public Const HANGEUL_CHARSET = 129
Public Const CHINESEBIG5_CHARSET = 136
Public Const OEM_CHARSET = 255

' Font Families
'
Public Const FF_DONTCARE = 0      ' Don't care or don't know.
Public Const FF_ROMAN = 16        ' Variable stroke width, serifed.

' Times Roman, Century Schoolbook, etc.
Public Const FF_SWISS = 32        ' Variable stroke width, sans-
                                    serifed.

' Helvetica, Swiss, etc.
Public Const FF_MODERN = 48       ' Constant stroke width, serifed
or sans-serifed.

' Pica, Elite, Courier, etc.
Public Const FF_SCRIPT = 64       ' Cursive, etc.
Public Const FF_DECORATIVE = 80 ' Old English, etc.

' Font Weights
Public Const FW_DONTCARE = 0
Public Const FW_THIN = 100
Public Const FW_EXTRALIGHT = 200
Public Const FW_LIGHT = 300
Public Const FW_NORMAL = 400
Public Const FW_MEDIUM = 500
Public Const FW_SEMIBOLD = 600
Public Const FW_BOLD = 700
Public Const FW_EXTRABOLD = 800
Public Const FW_HEAVY = 900

Public Const FW_ULTRALIGHT = FW_EXTRALIGHT
Public Const FW_REGULAR = FW_NORMAL
Public Const FW_DEMIBOLD = FW_SEMIBOLD
Public Const FW_ULTRABOLD = FW_EXTRABOLD
Public Const FW_BLACK = FW_HEAVY
```

In the next section, we'll examine two applications that make use of Windows API font functions.

Example Applications

This section contains two programming examples that will serve to illustrate the use of two important font functions: CreateFont() and CreateFontIndirect(). You'll see that using the other functions listed in this chapter are just as easy once you master the techniques in these two examples.

Using CreateFont()

The CreateFont() function is very easy to use. When compared to CreateFontIndirect(), you will notice that it does not require the use of a separate data structure. This is just the function you need to create and implement a font quickly.

This Visual Basic project is named Font1 and contains a form for drawing text on and a module file for function declarations. Here are the contents of the Font1.bas module file. The function declarations are simply copied and pasted into this file from the Win32api.txt file provided with your Visual Basic compiler.

```
Declare Function CreateFont Lib "gdi32" Alias "CreateFontA"
   (ByVal H As Long, ByVal W As Long, ByVal E As Long,
   ByVal O As Long, ByVal W As Long, ByVal I As Long,
   ByVal u As Long, ByVal S As Long, ByVal C As Long,
   ByVal OP As Long, ByVal CP As Long, ByVal Q As Long,
   ByVal PAF As Long, ByVal F As String) As Long

Declare Function SelectObject Lib "gdi32"
   (ByVal hdc As Long, ByVal hObject As Long) As Long

Declare Function TextOut Lib "gdi32" Alias "TextOutA"
   (ByVal hdc As Long, ByVal x As Long, ByVal y As Long,
   ByVal lpString As String, ByVal nCount As Long) As Long
```

As you can see from the listing, this project will access the CreateFont(), SelectObject(), and TextOut() Windows API functions.

The project's form contains a Form_Load() and Form_Paint() subroutine. Examine the following listing for Font1.frm:

```
Dim hnFont&, hoFont&
Dim r&

Private Sub Form_Load()
 Form1.Show
End Sub

Private Sub Form_Paint()
  hnFont = CreateFont(48, 48, 450, 0, FW_BOLD, False, False, False,
                  OEM_CHARSET, OUT_DEFAULT_PRECIS,
                  CLIP_DEFAULT_PRECIS, DEFAULT_QUALITY,
                  34, "Arial")
```

```
    hoFont = SelectObject(hdc, hnFont)
    r& = TextOut(hdc, 50, 450, "This is text," 12)
End Sub
```

In this example, a new font is created with a call to the CreateFont() function. The font is selected as the current font with a call to the SelectObject() function. A text string is printed to the screen with a call to the TextOut() function.

Here the CreateFont() function is being requested to generate a 48-point bold Arial font. The escapement parameter is set to 450, which will produce a font at a 45-degree angle. Escapement values are the angle values in degrees multiplied by a factor of 10.

The TextOut() function prints the specified string starting at the point (50,450) on the screen. Figure 17–1 shows the output from this application.

This is just the function you want to use when your project uses only a few fonts and you have specifications for the font that cannot be handled by normal Visual Basic font functions.

If your project requires many fonts, the CreateFont() function would be a burden to use because of the long list of parameters that must be specified each time

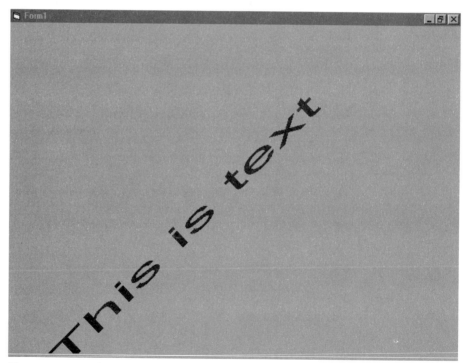

Figure 17–1   The CreateFont() function is used to draw a bold Arial font at a 45-degree angle.

the function is called. A better solution, in this situation, is to use the Create-FontIndirect() function.

Using CreateFontIndirect()

The CreateFontIndirect() function is a good function to use when your project requires many fonts. This function uses a structure to specify the font characteristics. While including this structure adds a small level of complexity to the project, its use will save you a great deal of programming effort.

This Visual Basic project is named Font2, and contains a form for drawing text on and a module file for function and structure declarations. Here are the contents of the Font2.bas module file. The function declarations and structures are simply copied and pasted into this file from the Win32api.txt file.

```
Public Const LF_FACESIZE = 32
Public Const LF_FULLFACESIZE = 64

Type LOGFONT
  lfHeight As Long
  lfWidth As Long
  lfEscapement As Long
  lfOrientation As Long
  lfWeight As Long
  lfItalic As Byte
  lfUnderline As Byte
  lfStrikeOut As Byte
  lfCharSet As Byte
  lfOutPrecision As Byte
  lfClipPrecision As Byte
  lfQuality As Byte
  lfPitchAndFamily As Byte
  lfFaceName(LF_FACESIZE) As Byte
End Type

Declare Function CreateFontIndirect Lib "gdi32"
  Alias "CreateFontIndirectA" (lpLogFont As LOGFONT) As Long

Declare Function SelectObject Lib "gdi32" (ByVal hdc As Long,
  ByVal hObject As Long) As Long

Declare Function TextOut Lib "gdi32" Alias "TextOutA"
  (ByVal hdc As Long, ByVal x As Long, ByVal y As Long,
  ByVal lpString As String, ByVal nCount As Long) As Long
```

As you can see from the listing, this project will access the CreateFontIndirect(), SelectObject(), and TextOut() Windows API functions. In addition, the CreateFontIndirect() function will use the LOGFONT structure declared in this file.

The project's form contains a Form_Load() and Form_Paint() subroutine. Examine the following listing for Font2.frm:

```
Dim hnFont&, hoFont&
Dim lf As LOGFONT
Dim r&

Private Sub Form_Load()
  Form1.Show
End Sub

Private Sub Form_Paint()
  lf.lfHeight = 40
  For I = 0 To 315 Step 45
    lf.lfEscapement = I * 10
    hnFont = CreateFontIndirect(lf)
    hoFont = SelectObject(hdc, hnFont)
    r& = TextOut(hdc, 320, 240, "  Totally Cool", 15)
  Next I
End Sub
```

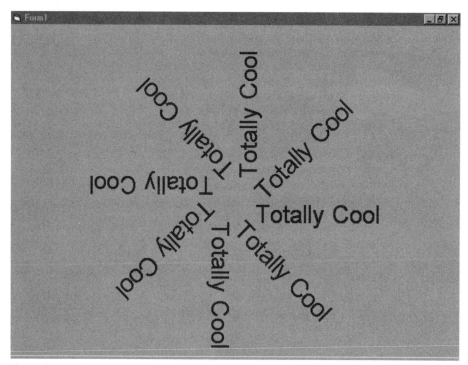

Figure 17–2   The CreateFontIndirect() function is used to create multiple fonts for the screen.

In this example, a new font is created with each pass through the **For** loop. A call is made to the CreateFontIndirect() function with each pass. The new font is then selected as the current font with a call to the SelectObject() function. A text string is printed to the screen during each pass with a call to the TextOut() function.

Here the CreateFontIndirect() function is requested to generate a 40-point system default font. The escapement parameter is incremented with each pass to create a new font at angles of 0, 45, 90, 135, 270, and 315 degrees.

The TextOut() function prints the specified string starting at the point (320,240) on the screen. Figure 17–2 shows the output from this application.

The CreateFontIndirect() function is the best choice when your project contains many fonts and where only one or two parameters change for the font from one instance to another.

Complete your study of this chapter by creating your own Visual Basic project and experimenting with other Windows API font functions.

Chapter 18

Menu Functions

Menus are very important to most applications. Visual Basic provides a menu editor that will automatically generate Windows style menus and create click events for menu items. The Windows API also allows access to a wide variety of menu capabilities. Without the use of subclassing techniques it is very difficult to generate and process new menu item event information. Most menu activity, using the Windows API, revolves around modifying previously created Visual Basic menus. With the Windows API it is easy to, for example, change a menu default, check a menu item, disable a menu item, get a menu string, and so on.

You'll want to investigate these capabilities to gain total control over your application menus.

API Menu Function Names and Descriptions

Table 18–1 shows 35 popular Windows API menu functions and provides a brief description for their use.

Many of the functions described in Table 18–1 are used frequently in Visual Basic applications. Of particular interest are the GetMenu(), GetMenuItem-Count(), GetMenuItemID(), CheckMenuItem(), SetMenuDefaultItem(), Get-

Table 18–1 Menu Functions and Descriptions

Function	Description
AppendMenu	Appends an item to the end of the menu bar, drop-down menu, submenu, or shortcut menu.
CheckMenuItem	Checks or unchecks a menu item.
CheckMenuRadioItem	Checks or unchecks a radio button item.
CreateMenu	Creates a new menu.
CreatePopupMenu	Creates a pop-up style menu.
DeleteMenu	Deletes a menu.
DestroyMenu	Destroys a menu.
DrawMenuBar	Draws a menu for a specific window.
EnableMenuItem	Enable or disable a menu item.
GetMenu	Gets a menu's handle.
GetMenuCheckMarkDimensions	Gets a checkmark's dimensions.
GetMenuContextHelpId	Gets the ID associated with the help context of a menu.
GetMenuDefaultItem	Gets the default menu item.
GetMenuItemCount	Gets the number of menu items.
GetMenuItemID	Gets the ID of the menu item.
GetMenuItemInfo	Uses MENUITEMINFO to hold specific menu item information.
GetMenuItemRect	Loads a rectangle using the menu item screen coordinates.
GetMenuState	Gets a menu item's state information.
GetMenuString	Gets a string for a menu item.
GetSubMenu	Gets a submenu handle.
GetSystemMenu	Gets the system menu handle.
HiliteMenuItem	Sets or removes the highlight from a top-level menu item.
InsertMenu	Inserts a new menu item into a menu, moving other items down.
InsertMenuItem	Inserts a menu item, using information in MENUITEMINFO.
IsMenu	Finds if a handle is a menu handle.
LoadMenu	Loads a menu.
LoadMenuIndirect	Loads a menu using MENUITEMTERMPLATE information.
MenuItemFromPoint	Determines which menu item holds a specific point.
ModifyMenu	Modifies a menu.
RemoveMenu	Removes a menu.
SetMenuContextHelpId	Sets the ID associated with the help context of a menu.
SetMenuDefaultItem	Sets the default menu item.
SetMenuItemBitmaps	Replaces a checkmark with a small bitmap image.
SetMenuItemInfo	Uses MENUITEMINFO to hold specific menu item information.
TrackPopupMenu	Displays a shortcut menu at the location and tracks the selection of items on the menu.
TrackPopupMenuEx	Same as TrackPopupMenu() with extended capabilities.

MenuString(), DeleteMenu(), and EnableMenuItem() functions. You'll see all of these used in the sample application provided at the end of this chapter.

API Menu Function Declarations

The following listing contains the Windows API menu function declarations found in the Win32api.txt file provided with Visual Basic.

```
Declare Function AppendMenu Lib "user32" Alias "AppendMenuA"
   (ByVal hMenu As Long,
   ByVal wFlags As Long,
   ByVal wIDNewItem As Long,
   ByVal lpNewItem As Any) As Long

Declare Function CheckMenuItem Lib "user32" Alias
   "CheckMenuItem" (ByVal hMenu As Long,
   ByVal wIDCheckItem As Long,
   ByVal wCheck As Long) As Long

Declare Function CheckMenuRadioItem Lib "user32" Alias
   "CheckMenuRadioItem" (ByVal hMenu As Long,
   ByVal un1 As Long,
   ByVal un2 As Long,
   ByVal un3 As Long,
   ByVal un4 As Long) As Long

Declare Function CreateMenu Lib "user32" Alias
   "CreateMenu" () As Long

Declare Function CreatePopupMenu Lib "user32" Alias
   "CreatePopupMenu" () As Long

Declare Function DeleteMenu Lib "user32" Alias "DeleteMenu"
   (ByVal hMenu As Long,
   ByVal nPosition As Long,
   ByVal wFlags As Long) As Long

Declare Function DestroyMenu Lib "user32" Alias "DestroyMenu"
   (ByVal hMenu As Long) As Long

Declare Function DrawMenuBar Lib "user32" Alias "DrawMenuBar"
   (ByVal hwnd As Long) As Long

Declare Function EnableMenuItem Lib "user32" Alias
   "EnableMenuItem" (ByVal hMenu As Long,
   ByVal wIDEnableItem As Long,
   ByVal wEnable As Long) As Long

Declare Function GetMenu Lib "user32" Alias "GetMenu"
   (ByVal hwnd As Long) As Long
```

```
Declare Function GetMenuCheckMarkDimensions Lib "user32"
  Alias "GetMenuCheckMarkDimensions" () As Long

Declare Function GetMenuContextHelpId Lib "user32" Alias
  "GetMenuContextHelpId" (ByVal hMenu As Long) As Long

Declare Function GetMenuDefaultItem Lib "user32" Alias
  "GetMenuDefaultItem" (ByVal hMenu As Long,
  ByVal fByPos As Long,
  ByVal gmdiFlags As Long) As Long

Declare Function GetMenuItemCount Lib "user32" Alias
  "GetMenuItemCount" (ByVal hMenu As Long) As Long

Declare Function GetMenuItemID Lib "user32" Alias
  "GetMenuItemID" (ByVal hMenu As Long,
  ByVal nPos As Long) As Long

Declare Function GetMenuItemInfo Lib "user32" Alias
  "GetMenuItemInfoA" (ByVal hMenu As Long,
  ByVal un As Long,
  ByVal b As Boolean,
  lpMenuItemInfo As MENUITEMINFO) As Long

Declare Function GetMenuItemRect Lib "user32" Alias
  "GetMenuItemRect" (ByVal hWnd As Long,
  ByVal hMenu As Long,
  ByVal uItem As Long,
  lprcItem As RECT) As Long

Declare Function GetMenuState Lib "user32" Alias
  "GetMenuState" (ByVal hMenu As Long,
  ByVal wID As Long,
  ByVal wFlags As Long) As Long

Declare Function GetMenuString Lib "user32" Alias
  "GetMenuStringA" (ByVal hMenu As Long,
  ByVal wIDItem As Long,
  ByVal lpString As String,
  ByVal nMaxCount As Long,
  ByVal wFlag As Long) As Long

Declare Function GetSubMenu Lib "user32" Alias "GetSubMenu"
  (ByVal hMenu As Long,
  ByVal nPos As Long) As Long

Declare Function GetSystemMenu Lib "user32" Alias
  "GetSystemMenu" (ByVal hwnd As Long,
  ByVal bRevert As Long) As Long

Declare Function HiliteMenuItem Lib "user32" Alias
  "HiliteMenuItem" (ByVal hwnd As Long,
  ByVal hMenu As Long,
```

```
    ByVal wIDHiliteItem As Long,
    ByVal wHilite As Long) As Long

Declare Function InsertMenu Lib "user32" Alias "InsertMenuA"
    (ByVal hMenu As Long,
    ByVal nPosition As Long,
    ByVal wFlags As Long,
    ByVal wIDNewItem As Long,
    ByVal lpNewItem As Any) As Long

Declare Function InsertMenuItem Lib "user32" Alias
    "InsertMenuItemA" (ByVal hMenu As Long,
    ByVal un As Long,
    ByVal bool As Boolean,
    ByVal lpcMenuItemInfo As MENUITEMINFO) As Long

Declare Function IsMenu Lib "user32" Alias "IsMenu"
    (ByVal hMenu As Long) As Long

Declare Function LoadMenu Lib "user32" Alias "LoadMenuA"
    (ByVal hInstance As Long,
    ByVal lpString As String) As Long

Declare Function LoadMenuIndirect Lib "user32" Alias
    "LoadMenuIndirectA" (ByVal lpMenuTemplate As Long) As Long

Declare Function MenuItemFromPoint Lib "user32" Alias
    "MenuItemFromPoint" (ByVal hWnd As Long,
    ByVal hMenu As Long,
    ByVal ptScreen As POINTAPI) As Long

Declare Function ModifyMenu Lib "user32" Alias "ModifyMenuA"
    (ByVal hMenu As Long,
    ByVal nPosition As Long,
    ByVal wFlags As Long,
    ByVal wIDNewItem As Long,
    ByVal lpString As Any) As Long

Declare Function RemoveMenu Lib "user32" Alias "RemoveMenu"
    (ByVal hMenu As Long,
    ByVal nPosition As Long,
    ByVal wFlags As Long) As Long

Declare Function SetMenuContextHelpId Lib "user32" Alias
    "SetMenuContextHelpId" (ByVal hMenu As Long,
    ByVal dw As Long) As Long

Declare Function SetMenuDefaultItem Lib "user32" Alias
    "SetMenuDefaultItem" (ByVal hMenu As Long,
    ByVal uItem As Long,
    ByVal fByPos As Long) As Long

Declare Function SetMenuItemBitmaps Lib "user32" Alias
    "SetMenuItemBitmaps" (ByVal hMenu As Long,
```

```
      ByVal nPosition As Long,
      ByVal wFlags As Long,
      ByVal hBitmapUnchecked As Long,
      ByVal hBitmapChecked As Long) As Long

   Declare Function SetMenuItemInfo Lib "user32" Alias
      "SetMenuItemInfoA" (ByVal hMenu As Long,
      ByVal un As Long,
      ByVal bool As Boolean,
      lpcMenuItemInfo As MENUITEMINFO) As Long

   Declare Function TrackPopupMenu Lib "user32" Alias
      "TrackPopupMenu" (ByVal hMenu As Long,
      ByVal wFlags As Long,
      ByVal x As Long,
      ByVal y As Long,
      ByVal nReserved As Long,
      ByVal hwnd As Long,
      lprc As Rect) As Long

   Declare Function TrackPopupMenuEx Lib "user32" Alias
      "TrackPopupMenuEx" (ByVal hMenu As Long,
      ByVal un As Long,
      ByVal n1 As Long,
      ByVal n2 As Long,
      ByVal hWnd As Long,
      lpTPMParams As TPMPARAMS) As Long
```

Table 18–2 contains a brief description of the parameters used in the various menu functions.

Table 18–2   Menu Function Parameters and Descriptions

Parameter	Description
b As Boolean	TRUE—position of item FALSE—for menu ID.
bool As Boolean	TRUE—position of item FALSE—for menu ID.
bRevert As Long	TRUE restores original system menu.
dw As Long	ID of help context.
fByPos As Long	TRUE—gets item position; FALSE gets menu ID.
gmdiFlags As Long	Uses GMDI_GOINTOPOPUPS or GMDI_USEDISABLED constant.
HBitmapChecked As Long	Handle of bitmap to use when menu item checked.
HBitmapUnchecked As Long	Handle of bitmap to use when menu item unchecked.
hInstance As Long	Handle for DLL or menu resource file.
hMenu As Long	Handle for menu.

(continued)

Table 18–2   Menu Function Parameters and Descriptions *(Continued)*

Parameter	Description
hwnd As Long	Handle of window containing menu.
LpMenuItemInfo As MENUITEMINFO	Structure holds requested menu item information.
LpMenuTemplate As Long	Uses a MENUITEMTEMPLATEHEADER structure and MENUITEMTEMPLATE structure.
lpNewItem As Any	MF_STRING in wflags sets a string. MF_BITMAP in wflags sets a bitmap.
lprc As RECT	Structure holds rectangle's coordinates.
lprcItem As RECT	Structure holds rectangular coordinates for menu item.
lpString As Any	Buffer holds menu item string.
lpTPMParams As TPMPARAMS	Structure holds rectangle NOT to cover with pop-up.
n1 As Long	Pop-up menu location in screen coordinates.
n2 As Long	
nMaxCount As Long	Number of characters to load into lpString + 1.
nPos As Long	Menu item position.
nPosition As Long	ID of menu item to delete or change.
nReserved As Long	Not used.
ptScreen As POINTAPI	Structure holds x,y menu position.
uItem As Long	ID or position of menu item.
un As Long	ID or position of menu item.
un1 As Long	First menu ID or position.
un2 As Long	Last menu ID or position.
un3 As Long	Menu ID or position to check.
un4 As Long	MF_BYPOSITION or MF_BYCOMMAND.
wCheck As Long	A combination of MF_ constants.
wEnable As Long	A combination of MF_ constants.
wFlag As Long	Use MF_BYCOMMAND or MF_BYPOSITION constant. Mouse tracking flags include TPM_ constants.
wFlags As Long	A combination of MF_ constants.
wHilite As Long	Uses MF_HILITE or MF_UNHILITE constant along with MF_BYCOMMAND or MF_BYPOSITION.
wID As Long	ID of menu item.
wIDCheckItem As Long	ID value for the menu item to check or uncheck.
wIDEnableItem As Long	ID value of menu item to enable or disable.
wIDHiliteItem As Long	ID of menu item to highlight or un-highlight.
wIDItem As Long	ID of menu item string.
WIDNewItem As Long	ID value for the menu item.
X As Long	x and y menu position.
y As Long	

Many of the parameters described in Table 18–2 use constant values. The win32api.txt file lists the following constants for menu parameters:

```
'Flags for TrackPopupMenu
Public Const TPM_LEFTBUTTON = &H0&
Public Const TPM_RIGHTBUTTON = &H2&
Public Const TPM_LEFTALIGN = &H0&
Public Const TPM_CENTERALIGN = &H4&
Public Const TPM_RIGHTALIGN = &H8&

'Menu flags for Add/Check/EnableMenuItem()
Public Const MF_INSERT = &H0&
Public Const MF_CHANGE = &H80&
Public Const MF_APPEND = &H100&
Public Const MF_DELETE = &H200&
Public Const MF_REMOVE = &H1000&
Public Const MF_BYCOMMAND = &H0&
Public Const MF_BYPOSITION = &H400&
Public Const MF_SEPARATOR = &H800&
Public Const MF_ENABLED = &H0&
Public Const MF_GRAYED = &H1&
Public Const MF_DISABLED = &H2&
Public Const MF_UNCHECKED = &H0&
Public Const MF_CHECKED = &H8&
Public Const MF_USECHECKBITMAPS = &H200&
Public Const MF_STRING = &H0&
Public Const MF_BITMAP = &H4&
Public Const MF_OWNERDRAW = &H100&
Public Const MF_POPUP = &H10&
Public Const MF_MENUBARBREAK = &H20&
Public Const MF_MENUBREAK = &H40&
Public Const MF_UNHILITE = &H0&
Public Const MF_HILITE = &H80&
Public Const MF_SYSMENU = &H2000&
Public Const MF_HELP = &H4000&
Public Const MF_MOUSESELECT = &H8000&
Public Const MF_END = &H80
```

Many of the menu parameters use unique data structures to store returned information. Here are the structures unique to menu function parameters.

```
Type MENUITEMINFO
  cbSize As Long
  fMask As Long
  fType As Long
  fState As Long
  wID As Long
  hSubMenu As Long
  hbmpChecked As Long
```

```
      hbmpUnchecked As Long
      dwItemData As Long
      dwTypeData As String
      cch As Long
End Type

'Menu item resource format
Type MENUITEMTEMPLATEHEADER
   versionNumber As Integer
   offset As Integer
End Type

Type MENUITEMTEMPLATE
   mtOption As Integer
   mtID As Integer
   mtString As Byte
End Type

Type POINTAPI
   x As Long
   y As Long
End Type

Type RECT
   Left As Long
   Top As Long
   Right As Long
   Bottom As Long
End Type

Type TPMPARAMS
     cbSize As Long
     rcExclude As Rect
End Type
```

In the next section we'll examine an application that illustrates the use of several of the Windows API menu functions.

Example Application

This application is designed to modify an existing Visual Basic menu that was created using the Visual Basic Menu Editor. The project is named Menu1.vbp and contains a module file and a simple form with six label controls as shown in Figure 18–1.

The application will make use of several MF_ constants and function declarations as you can see in the Menu1.bas module file. All of this information is available in the Win32api.txt file provided with your Visual Basic compiler.

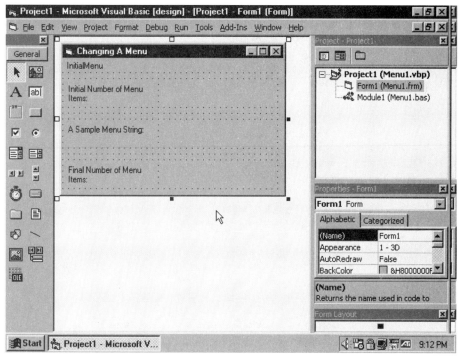

Figure 18–1 Placement of six label controls on the project's form.

```
'Menu flags for Add/Check/EnableMenuItem()
Public Const MF_INSERT = &H0&
Public Const MF_CHANGE = &H80&
Public Const MF_APPEND = &H100&
Public Const MF_DELETE = &H200&
Public Const MF_REMOVE = &H1000&
Public Const MF_BYCOMMAND = &H0&
Public Const MF_BYPOSITION = &H400&
Public Const MF_SEPARATOR = &H800&
Public Const MF_ENABLED = &H0&
Public Const MF_GRAYED = &H1&
Public Const MF_DISABLED = &H2&
Public Const MF_UNCHECKED = &H0&
Public Const MF_CHECKED = &H8&
Public Const MF_USECHECKBITMAPS = &H200&
Public Const MF_STRING = &H0&
Public Const MF_BITMAP = &H4&
Public Const MF_OWNERDRAW = &H100&
Public Const MF_POPUP = &H10&
Public Const MF_MENUBARBREAK = &H20&
Public Const MF_MENUBREAK = &H40&
```

```
Public Const MF_UNHILITE = &H0&
Public Const MF_HILITE = &H80&
Public Const MF_SYSMENU = &H2000&
Public Const MF_HELP = &H4000&
Public Const MF_MOUSESELECT = &H8000&
Public Const MF_END = &H80


Declare Function CheckMenuItem Lib "user32"
  (ByVal hmenu As Long,
  ByVal wIDCheckItem As Long,
  ByVal wCheck As Long) As Long
Declare Function DeleteMenu Lib "user32"
  (ByVal hmenu As Long,
  ByVal nPosition As Long,
  ByVal wFlags As Long) As Long
Declare Function EnableMenuItem Lib "user32"
  (ByVal hmenu As Long,
  ByVal wIDEnableItem As Long,
  ByVal wEnable As Long) As Long
Declare Function GetMenu Lib "user32"
  (ByVal hWnd As Long) As Long
Declare Function GetMenuItemCount Lib "user32"
  (ByVal hmenu As Long) As Long
Declare Function GetMenuItemID Lib "user32"
  (ByVal hmenu As Long,
  ByVal nPos As Long) As Long
Declare Function GetMenuString Lib "user32"
  Alias "GetMenuStringA" (ByVal hmenu As Long,
  ByVal wIDItem As Long,
  ByVal lpString As String,
  ByVal nMaxCount As Long,
  ByVal wFlag As Long) As Long
Declare Function GetSubMenu Lib "user32"
  (ByVal hmenu As Long,
  ByVal nPos As Long) As Long
Declare Function IsMenu Lib "user32"
  (ByVal hmenu As Long) As Long
Declare Function LoadMenuMod Lib "user32"
  Alias "LoadMenuA" (ByVal hInstance As Long,
  lpValue As Long) As Long
Declare Function SetMenuDefaultItem Lib "user32"
  (ByVal hmenu As Long,
  ByVal uItem As Long,
  ByVal fByPos As Long) As Long
```

The project's form contains six label controls. Three are used to create labels within the form. The remaining three will report data in the form of a label caption. All computation is done within a Form_Load() subroutine. The contents of Menu1.frm are shown in the following listing:

```
Private Sub Form_Load()
  Dim r&, hSubMenu&, hInitMenu&
  Dim orgmenulen&, newmenulen&
  Dim Idvalue&

  hInitMenu& = GetMenu(hWnd)
  hSubMenu& = GetSubMenu(hInitMenu&, 0)

  'Get initial number of items in menu.
  orgmenulen& = GetMenuItemCount(hSubMenu)
  Label4.Caption = orgmenulen&

  'Check "Item Two" in the menu.
  'Index value starts zero.
  IDvalue& = GetMenuItemID(hSubMenu, 1)
  r& = CheckMenuItem(hSubMenu, IDvalue&, MF_CHECKED)
  'Now make it the default selection (Bold)
  r& = SetMenuDefaultItem(hSubMenu, 1, True)

  'Get and print a menu item string
  'Use the 5th entry. Index starts at zero
  datastring$ = String(64, 0)
  IDvalue& = GetMenuItemID(hSubMenu, 4)
  r& = GetMenuString(hInitMenu, IDvalue&, datastring, 63, MF_BYCOMMAND)
  Label5.Caption = datastring$

  'Delete a menu entry by position
  r& = DeleteMenu(hSubMenu, 5, MF_BYPOSITION)

  'Disable and gray "Item One"
  r& = EnableMenuItem(hSubMenu, 2, MF_GRAYED)

  'Get final number of items in menu
  newmenulen& = GetMenuItemCount(hSubMenu)
  'determine how many items were added
  Label6.Caption = newmenulen&
End Sub

Private Sub ItemOne_Click(Index As Integer)
  MsgBox "Here is 1"
End Sub

Private Sub ItemTwo_Click(Index As Integer)
  MsgBox "Here is 2"
End Sub

Private Sub ItemThree_Click(Index As Integer)
  MsgBox "Here is 3"
End Sub
```

```
Private Sub ItemFour_Click(Index As Integer)
  MsgBox "Here is 4"
End Sub

Private Sub ItemFive_Click(Index As Integer)
  MsgBox "Here is 5"
End Sub

Private Sub ItemSix_Click(Index As Integer)
  MsgBox "Here is 6"
End Sub

Private Sub ItemSeven_Click(Index As Integer)
  MsgBox "Here is 7"
End Sub
```

The application is straightforward. During the design phase, the Menu Editor
is used to create a single menu with seven menu items, as shown in Figure 18–2.

The count of the original number of menu items is returned by a call to the
GetMenuItemCount() function and reported to the caption property of the
Label4 control.

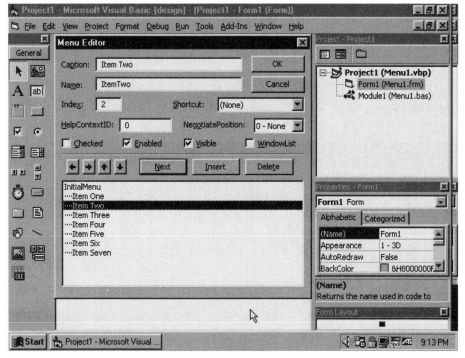

Figure 18–2   The initial menu being designed in the Visual Basic Menu Editor.

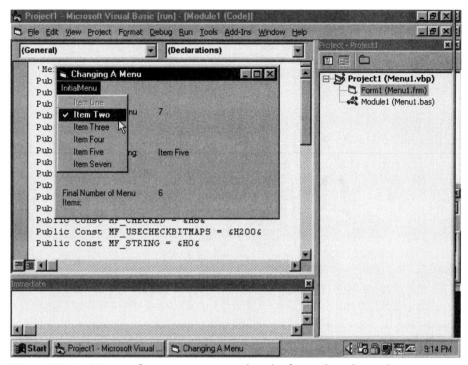

Figure 18–3   Menu information is returned to the form when the application is executed.

Next the menu item "Item Two" is both checked and set as the menu default. This is achieved with a call to the CheckMenuItem() and SetMenuDefaultItem() functions.

The menu string for the fifth menu entry is then returned to the caption property of the Label5 control. This is obtained by using the GetMenuString() function.

A menu entry is deleted with a call to DeleteMenu() and an entry is disabled with the use of the EnableMenuItem() function.

Finally, the GetMenuItemCount() function is called again, and the new menu item count is reported to the caption property of Label6. This value is, of course, one less than the starting count since one item was deleted.

Figure 18–3 shows the data reported to the caption properties when the application is executed.

Chapter 19

Message Box and Dialog Functions

In most books dealing with the Windows API, a chapter on dialog boxes immediately follows the chapter on menus. As you have learned from the previous chapter, Visual Basic handles menus in a manner uniquely different from other programming languages such as C, C++, and Java. Dialog boxes fit into the same category. Visual Basic creates traditional looking Windows dialog boxes with the use of additional Visual Basic forms or by using ActiveX components.

If you scan the Win32api.txt file, provided with your Visual Basic compiler, you will discover that there are numerous dialog box functions, structures, and constants listed. However, the use of these functions is not recommended when attempting to control dialog box resources in a Visual Basic program. To further seal their fate, the Win32api.txt file lists the common dialog box functions for Color, Fonts, and File I/O but includes several ActiveX components to achieve the same functionality. The ActiveX approach is, of course, the preferred method.

In this chapter we're going to break with our usual style and divide the chapter into three broad areas: Message Boxes, common dialog boxes, and regular dialog boxes. In each section, we'll give you the best solution to adding these components to your Visual Basic application. However, we warned that two of these categories will not use the Windows API in their approach.

API Message Box Function Names and Descriptions

Message Boxes are, perhaps, the simplest dialog boxes that can be created with the Windows API. Table 19–1 shows two Windows API Message Box functions and provides a brief description for their use.

Visual Basic provides the MsgBox() function for creating Message Boxes. You can use the Windows API functions, shown in Table 19–1, in place of this Visual Basic function. MsgBox() and MessageBox() have almost identical capabilities. However, you'll also see that the MessageBoxEx() function provides a language identifier parameter that allows the text inside the Message Box to be printed in a specific language.

Message Box Function Declarations

The following listing contains the Windows API Message Box function declarations found in the Win32api.txt file provided with Visual Basic. Successful function calls return a dialog box command value.

```
Declare Function MessageBox Lib "user32" Alias "MessageBoxA"
    (ByVal hwnd As Long, ByVal lpText As String,
    ByVal lpCaption As String, ByVal wType As Long) As Long

Declare Function MessageBoxEx Lib "user32" Alias
    "MessageBoxExA" (ByVal hwnd As Long,
    ByVal lpText As String, ByVal lpCaption As String,
    ByVal uType As Long, ByVal wLanguageId As Long) As Long
```

Table 19–2 contains a brief description of the parameters used in the two Message Box functions.

Two of the parameters described in Table 19–2 use constant values. The Win32api.txt file lists the following constants for message box parameters.

```
'Dialog Box Command IDs
Public Const IDOK = 1
Public Const IDCANCEL = 2
Public Const IDABORT = 3
Public Const IDRETRY = 4
Public Const IDIGNORE = 5
```

Table 19–1   Message Box Functions and Descriptions

Function	Description
MessageBox	Creates a Message Box.
MessageBoxEx	Creates a Message Box with extended capabilities.

Table 19–2 Message Box Function Parameters and Descriptions

Parameter	Description
hwnd As Long	Windows handle.
LpCaption As String	String contains the Message Box caption.
LpText As String	String contains the Message Box text.
uType As Long, wType As Long	Uses a MB_ constant to describe the desired action.
WLanguageId As Long	Uses a language ID to specify a particular language. (See language ID constant.)

```
Public Const IDYES = 6
Public Const IDNO = 7

'  Calculate the byte offset of a field in a structure
'  of type type.
'  *  Language IDs.
'  *
'  *  The following two combinations of primary language ID
'  *  and sublanguage ID have special semantics:
'  *
'  *  Primary ID   Sublanguage ID     Result
'  *  ----------   --------------     ----------------------
'  *  LANG_NEUTRAL SUBLANG_NEUTRAL     Language neutral
'  *  LANG_NEUTRAL SUBLANG_DEFAULT     User default language
'  *  LANG_NEUTRAL SUBLANG_SYS_DEFAULT System default lang.
'  */
'
'  *  Primary language IDs.
'  */
Public Const LANG_NEUTRAL = &H0

Public Const LANG_BULGARIAN = &H2
Public Const LANG_CHINESE = &H4
Public Const LANG_CROATIAN = &H1A
Public Const LANG_CZECH = &H5
Public Const LANG_DANISH = &H6
Public Const LANG_DUTCH = &H13
Public Const LANG_ENGLISH = &H9
Public Const LANG_FINNISH = &HB
Public Const LANG_FRENCH = &HC
Public Const LANG_GERMAN = &H7
Public Const LANG_GREEK = &H8
Public Const LANG_HUNGARIAN = &HE
Public Const LANG_ICELANDIC = &HF
Public Const LANG_ITALIAN = &H10
Public Const LANG_JAPANESE = &H11
```

```
Public Const LANG_KOREAN = &H12
Public Const LANG_NORWEGIAN = &H14
Public Const LANG_POLISH = &H15
Public Const LANG_PORTUGUESE = &H16
Public Const LANG_ROMANIAN = &H18
Public Const LANG_RUSSIAN = &H19
Public Const LANG_SLOVAK = &H1B
Public Const LANG_SLOVENIAN = &H24
Public Const LANG_SPANISH = &HA
Public Const LANG_SWEDISH = &H1D
Public Const LANG_TURKISH = &H1F


'
'   * Sublanguage IDs.
'   *
'   * The name immediately following SUBLANG_ dictates which
'   * primary language ID that sublanguage ID can be combined
'   * with to form a valid language ID.
'   */
Public Const SUBLANG_NEUTRAL = &H0      'language neutral
Public Const SUBLANG_DEFAULT = &H1      'user default
Public Const SUBLANG_SYS_DEFAULT = &H2 'system default
'Chinese (Taiwan):
Public Const SUBLANG_CHINESE_TRADITIONAL = &H1
'Chinese (PR China):
Public Const SUBLANG_CHINESE_SIMPLIFIED = &H2
'Chinese (Hong Kong):
Public Const SUBLANG_CHINESE_HONGKONG = &H3
'Chinese (Singapore):
Public Const SUBLANG_CHINESE_SINGAPORE = &H4
Public Const SUBLANG_DUTCH = &H1 'Dutch
Public Const SUBLANG_DUTCH_BELGIAN = &H2 'Dutch (Belgian)
Public Const SUBLANG_ENGLISH_US = &H1 'English (USA)
Public Const SUBLANG_ENGLISH_UK = &H2 'English (UK)
Public Const SUBLANG_ENGLISH_AUS = &H3 'English (Australian)
Public Const SUBLANG_ENGLISH_CAN = &H4 'English (Canadian)
Public Const SUBLANG_ENGLISH_NZ = &H5 'English (New Zealand)
Public Const SUBLANG_ENGLISH_EIRE = &H6 'English (Irish)
Public Const SUBLANG_FRENCH = &H1 'French
Public Const SUBLANG_FRENCH_BELGIAN = &H2 'French (Belgian)
Public Const SUBLANG_FRENCH_CANADIAN = &H3 'French (Canadian)
Public Const SUBLANG_FRENCH_SWISS = &H4 'French (Swiss)
Public Const SUBLANG_GERMAN = &H1 'German
Public Const SUBLANG_GERMAN_SWISS = &H2 'German (Swiss)
Public Const SUBLANG_GERMAN_AUSTRIAN = &H3 'German (Austrian)
Public Const SUBLANG_ITALIAN = &H1 'Italian
Public Const SUBLANG_ITALIAN_SWISS = &H2 'Italian (Swiss)
'Norwegian (Bokma):
Public Const SUBLANG_NORWEGIAN_BOKMAL = &H1
```

```
'Norwegian (Nynorsk):
Public Const SUBLANG_NORWEGIAN_NYNORSK = &H2
Public Const SUBLANG_PORTUGUESE = &H2 'Portuguese
'Portuguese (Brazilian):
Public Const SUBLANG_PORTUGUESE_BRAZILIAN = &H1
Public Const SUBLANG_SPANISH = &H1 'Spanish (Castilian)
Public Const SUBLANG_SPANISH_MEXICAN = &H2 'Spanish (Mexican)
Public Const SUBLANG_SPANISH_MODERN = &H3 'Spanish (Modern)

'
'   * Sorting IDs.
'   *
'   */
Public Const SORT_DEFAULT = &H0 'sorting default

Public Const SORT_JAPANESE_XJIS = &H0 'Japanese0xJIS
Public Const SORT_JAPANESE_UNICODE = &H1 'Japanese Unicode

Public Const SORT_CHINESE_BIG5 = &H0 'Chinese BIG5
Public Const SORT_CHINESE_UNICODE = &H1 'Chinese Unicode

Public Const SORT_KOREAN_KSC = &H0 'Korean KSC
Public Const SORT_KOREAN_UNICODE = &H1 'Korean Unicode

'MessageBox() Flags
Public Const MB_OK = &H0&
Public Const MB_OKCANCEL = &H1&
Public Const MB_ABORTRETRYIGNORE = &H2&
Public Const MB_YESNOCANCEL = &H3&
Public Const MB_YESNO = &H4&
Public Const MB_RETRYCANCEL = &H5&

Public Const MB_ICONHAND = &H10&
Public Const MB_ICONQUESTION = &H20&
Public Const MB_ICONEXCLAMATION = &H30&
Public Const MB_ICONASTERISK = &H40&

Public Const MB_ICONINFORMATION = MB_ICONASTERISK
Public Const MB_ICONSTOP = MB_ICONHAND

Public Const MB_DEFBUTTON1 = &H0&
Public Const MB_DEFBUTTON2 = &H100&
Public Const MB_DEFBUTTON3 = &H200&

Public Const MB_APPLMODAL = &H0&
Public Const MB_SYSTEMMODAL = &H1000&
Public Const MB_TASKMODAL = &H2000&

Public Const MB_NOFOCUS = &H8000&
Public Const MB_SETFOREGROUND = &H10000
Public Const MB_DEFAULT_DESKTOP_ONLY = &H20000

Public Const MB_TYPEMASK = &HF&
Public Const MB_ICONMASK = &HF0&
```

```
Public Const MB_DEFMASK = &HF00&
Public Const MB_MODEMASK = &H3000&
Public Const MB_MISCMASK = &HC000&
```

In the next section we'll illustrate the MessageBox() function with a simple application.

Message Box Application

The MessageBox() function can be used quite easily in Visual Basic. The sample project for this section is named Message1.vbp. This project contains a module file named Message1.bas that contains the constant and function declarations. The contents of this file are shown in the following listing. Both the constant declarations and function declarations were copied from the Win32api.txt file.

```
'MessageBox() Flags
Public Const MB_OK = &H0&
Public Const MB_OKCANCEL = &H1&
Public Const MB_ABORTRETRYIGNORE = &H2&
Public Const MB_YESNOCANCEL = &H3&
Public Const MB_YESNO = &H4&
Public Const MB_RETRYCANCEL = &H5&
Public Const MB_ICONHAND = &H10&
Public Const MB_ICONQUESTION = &H20&
Public Const MB_ICONEXCLAMATION = &H30&
Public Const MB_ICONASTERISK = &H40&
Public Const MB_ICONINFORMATION = MB_ICONASTERISK
Public Const MB_ICONSTOP = MB_ICONHAND
Public Const MB_DEFBUTTON1 = &H0&
Public Const MB_DEFBUTTON2 = &H100&
Public Const MB_DEFBUTTON3 = &H200&
Public Const MB_APPLMODAL = &H0&
Public Const MB_SYSTEMMODAL = &H1000&
Public Const MB_TASKMODAL = &H2000&
Public Const MB_NOFOCUS = &H8000&
Public Const MB_SETFOREGROUND = &H10000
Public Const MB_DEFAULT_DESKTOP_ONLY = &H20000
Public Const MB_TYPEMASK = &HF&
Public Const MB_ICONMASK = &HF0&
Public Const MB_DEFMASK = &HF00&
Public Const MB_MODEMASK = &H3000&
Public Const MB_MISCMASK = &HC000&

'Dialog Box Command IDs
Public Const IDOK = 1
Public Const IDCANCEL = 2
Public Const IDABORT = 3
Public Const IDRETRY = 4
```

```
Public Const IDIGNORE = 5
Public Const IDYES = 6
Public Const IDNO = 7

Declare Function MessageBox Lib "user32" Alias "MessageBoxA"
  (ByVal hwnd As Long, ByVal lpText As String,
  ByVal lpCaption As String, ByVal wType As Long) As Long
```

The application uses the Form_Load subroutine to launch the first message box. This message box provides a message box caption, text, and icon as you can see from the following listing:

```
Private Sub Form_Load()
  Dim r&

  r& = MessageBox(hwnd, "Warning: Message Boxes Work!",
                  "A Windows Message Box",
                  MB_OKCANCLAMATION Or MB_ICONEXCLAMATION)
  If r& = IDOK Then
    r& = MessageBox(hwnd, "Yep - it worked.", "", MB_OK)
  End If

End Sub
```

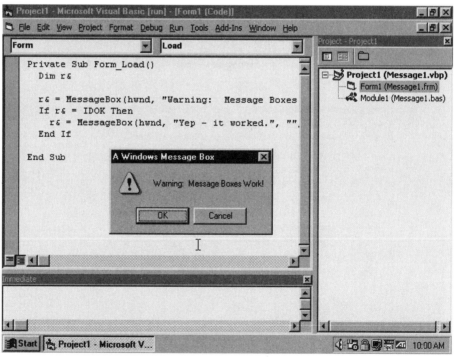

Figure 19–1   A message box produced with a call to the MessageBox() function.

If the user clicks the "OK" button, a second dialog box will appear indicating that the first dialog box operated successfully and returned an IDOK command value. Otherwise, the user can select the "Cancel" button and return to an empty form.

Figure 19–1 shows the first Message Box as it appears on the screen.

Common Dialog Boxes

As you have already learned, Visual Basic provides access to common dialog boxes such as Color, Font, and File I/O selection through ActiveX controls. In this section we'll illustrate how to access the Color dialog box. This application, however, does not employ the Windows API.

To create this demonstration application, start with a new Visual Basic Project and use the Project | Components menu selection to add the ActiveX control.

Figure 19–2 shows the Microsoft Common Dialog Control 5.0 being selected from the list of optional controls.

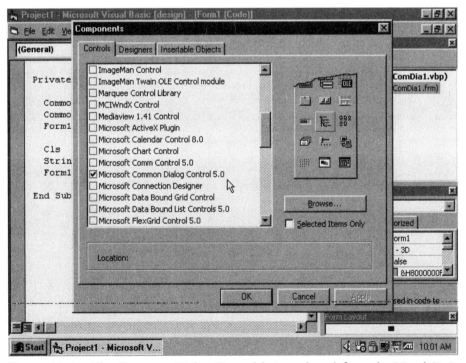

Figure 19–2 The Common Dialog Control being selected from the Visual Basic Components list.

When selected, the Common Dialog Control will be added to the Visual Basic Toolbox, as you can see in Figure 19–3.

Our application is named ComDia1.vbp. The project's form contains a single command button.

Add the following code to the click event for the command button:

```
Private Sub Command1_Click()


    CommonDialog1.flags = cdlCCRGBInit
    CommonDialog1.ShowColor
    Form1.BackColor = CommonDialog1.Color


    Cls
    String1$ = "Push TEST to select a background color"
    Form1.Print String1$

End Sub
```

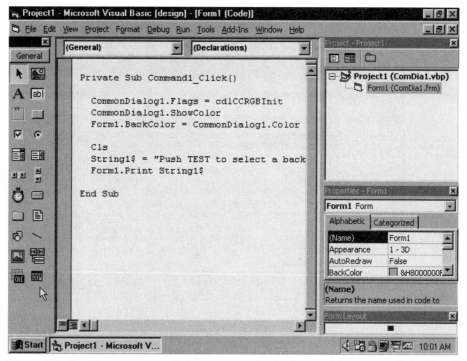

Figure 19–3   The new control's icon appears in the lower-right corner of the Visual Basic Toolbox.

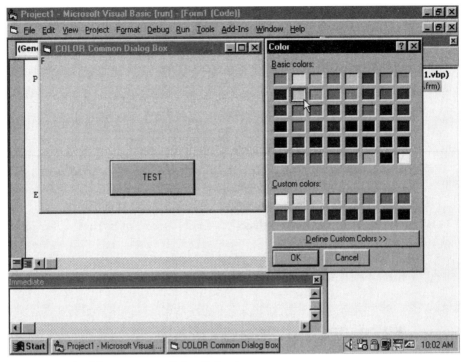

Figure 19–4 The common Color dialog box.

When the command button is selected, the common Color dialog box will appear, as shown in Figure 19–4.

Visual Basic provides additional details via its help facility regarding the common Color dialog box. The various parameters used in the example are explained there.

Visual Basic Dialog Boxes

Windows programmers using C or C++ know that dialog boxes are just a form of child window that is typically used for user input. Visual Basic programmers, on the other hand, don't usually distinguish one type of window from another. Usually, Visual Basic programmers have been using forms to add text boxes, command buttons, and so on since they have been programming.

A simple charting application is used here to illustrate this concept better. The pie chart application is a straightforward Visual Basic programming project and therefore is not explained in detail. In this application, you'll see one form used to draw the graphics and one form used as a dialog box to gather user data. Note that this application does not make use of the Windows API.

A Pie Chart

The pie chart project will allow the user to enter pie labels for an optional legend, enter a chart title, and enter a number of pie wedge values. Once the data have been entered in the dialog box, the project will allow the user to save the chart to a bitmap file and clip and paste chart information to the Windows clipboard.

The project, named PieCht1.vbp, uses several forms. The data entry form (dialog box) is shown in Figure 19–5 and is named PieCht1.frm.

The file save form (dialog box) is shown in Figure 19–6 and is named PieCht3.frm.

The form on which the pie chart is drawn is shown in Figure 19–7, and is named PieCht2.frm.

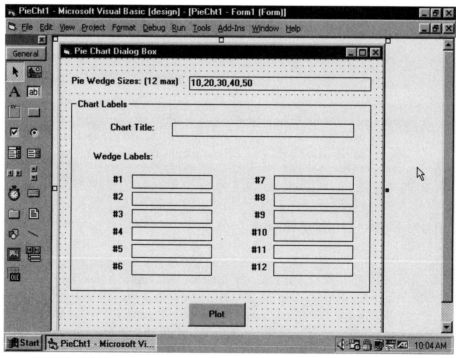

Figure 19–5 The data entry form (dialog box) for the pie chart project.

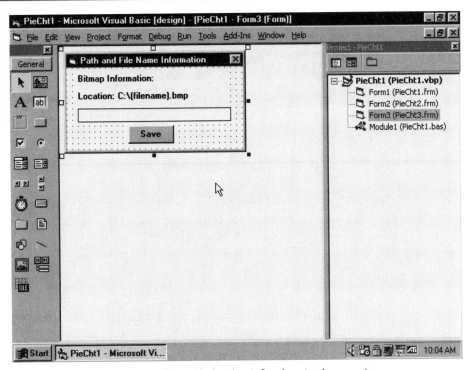

Figure 19–6 The file save form (dialog box) for the pie chart project.

Coding the Pie Chart

As you have learned, the pie chart project uses a total of three forms. The following is a list of global variables found in the module file named PieCht1.bas:

```
DefInt A-Z
Global I, TNums, SPos, FPos, NLen
Global LabelWidth, LabelHeight
Global NArray(20) As Single, ScaledNArray(20) As Single
Global SAngle As Single, FAngle As Single
Global PWTotal As Single, X1 As Single, Y1 As Single
Global Leg(20) As String
Global Title As String
```

Here the string array *Leg()* will be used for legend labels.

The Pie Chart Data Entry Form   The pie chart project is started by entering values on the data entry form (dialog box) and clicking the command button named Plot.

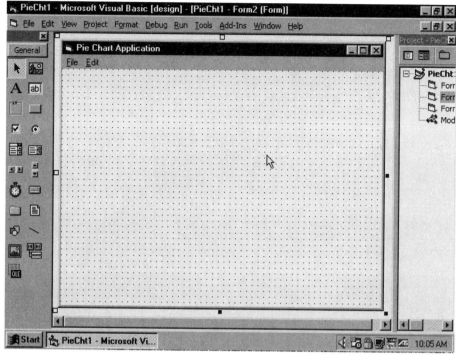

Figure 19–7   The project's form where the pie chart will be drawn.

The value for PI is entered in the general declarations section for the first form.

```
Const PI = 3.141

Private Sub Command1_Click ()
  ProcessData
  ScaleData
  Form2.Show
End Sub

Private Sub ProcessData ()
  'numbers in string equal commas+1
  TNums = 1
  For I = 1 To Len(Text1.Text)
    PCh$ = Mid$(Text1.Text, I, 1)
    If PCh$ = "," Then TNums = TNums + 1
  Next I

  'limit number of wedges
  If TNums > 12 Then TNums = 12

  'convert each group to a pie wedge number
  PNewStr$ = Text1.Text + ","
```

```
    SPos = 0
    For I = 1 To TNums
      FPos = InStr(SPos + 1, PNewStr$, Chr$(44))
      NLen = (FPos - SPos) - 1
      NArray(I) = Val(Mid$(PNewStr$, SPos + 1, NLen))
      SPos = FPos
    Next I

    'prepare title and legend labels
    Title = Text2.Text
    Leg(1) = Text3.Text
    Leg(2) = Text4.Text
    Leg(3) = Text5.Text
    Leg(4) = Text6.Text
    Leg(5) = Text7.Text
    Leg(6) = Text8.Text
    Leg(7) = Text9.Text
    Leg(8) = Text10.Text
    Leg(9) = Text11.Text
    Leg(10) = Text12.Text
    Leg(11) = Text13.Text
    Leg(12) = Text14.Text
  End Sub
```

The value for pi is specified to just a few decimal places. The value 3.141 was chosen so that the whole pie was just a bit shy of 360 degrees or 2 x pi radians. This is needed in order for the closing angle to be larger than the starting angle. This would not be true if we returned, full circle, to 0 degrees. Read the details on the Circle() function using the Visual Basic help facility.

```
  Private Sub ScaleData ()
    'add all pie slice sizes together
    PWTotal = 0
    For I = 1 To TNums
      PWTotal = PWTotal + NArray(I)
    Next I

    'scale all pie slices to fit in whole pie
    For I = 1 To TNums
      ScaledNArray(I) = NArray(I) * 2 * PI / PWTotal
    Next I
  End Sub
```

Data are scaled to fit the circle by scaling all slices in proportion to the total of all individual slice values. An appropriate angle is then assigned to these calculated values. For example, suppose a user enters the following data values: 15, 20, 25. The data are processed in the following manner:

```
  15 + 20 + 25 = 60  (total of all slice values)
  15 / 60 = .25    ->   .25   x (2 x PI) = 1.5705
```

```
20 / 60 = .333333   ->   .333333 x (2 x PI) = 2.094
25 / 60 = .41667    ->   .41667 x (2 x PI) = 2.6175
```

The sum of the final values should add up to the number of radians in a full circle (2 x PI = 6.282).

```
1.5705 + 2.094 + 2.6175 = 6.282
```

You will find that this technique works for any set of data values entered by the user.

The Pie Charting Code   The origin (0,0) for this coordinate system is placed at the center of the pie. (The origin is 0,0 when the legend is not printed.)

```
Private Sub PiePlot ()
  'set chart constants
  ScaleLeft = -800
  ScaleTop = 800
  ScaleWidth = 1600
  ScaleHeight = -1600

  Cls
  AutoRedraw = -1
  DrawWidth = 1
  FillStyle = 0
    .
    .
    .
```

The Circle() function must use a value, other than zero, to work properly. The first value is set to a very small number.

```
    .
    .
    .
'a small seed number is needed
'for the initial angle
SAngle = 0.0000001
    .
    .
    .
```

If a legend is being drawn, the pie is shifted slightly to the left of center screen with the following code:

```
    .
    .
    .
SAngle = 0
If Leg(1) = "" Then
```

```
      X1 = 0
   Else X1 = -250
   End If
      .
      .
      .
```

A **For** loop is used for drawing the pie slices and selecting the fill color. The brighter Quick Basic colors start at an index value of 8, so this pie chart starts its color selection there. A modulo operator is used in case more than eight pie wedges are needed.

```
      .
      .
      .
   For I = 1 To TNums
     FillColor = QBColor((I + 8) Mod 16)
     FAngle = SAngle + ScaledNArray(I)
     Circle (X1, 0), 400, , -SAngle, -FAngle
     SAngle = FAngle
   Next I
      .
      .
      .
```

The starting points for the circle are fixed (except the offset value). The radius is 400 and the outline color value is black—the default. A wedge will be drawn when using the Circle() function since *SAngle* is smaller than *FAngle*. The negative sign (–) in front of each value extends a line from the tip of the curve to the center of the circle

Legend values and a chart title, where appropriate, are drawn next.

```
      .
      .
      .
   'print legend boxes and labels
   If Leg(1) <> "" Then
     X1 = 250
     Y1 = 400
     FontSize = Height / 600
     For I = 1 To TNums
       FillColor = QBColor((I + 8) Mod 16)
       Line (X1, Y1)-(X1 + 50, Y1 + 50),
             QBColor((I + 8) Mod 16), BF
       Print " " + Leg(I)
          Y1 = Y1 - 75
```

```
      Next I
    End If

  'print pie chart title
  If Title <> "" Then
    ForeColor = QBColor(11)
    FontSize = Height / 200
    LabelWidth = TextWidth(Title) / 2
    LabelHeight = TextHeight(Title) / 2
    CurrentX = -LabelWidth
    CurrentY = LabelHeight - ScaleHeight * 9 / 16
    Print Title
  End If
End Sub
```

Since sizing affects the chart, the PiePlot() function just discussed is called from the Form_Resize() subroutine:

```
Private Sub Form_Resize ()
  Call PiePlot
End Sub
```

The menu options for saving the bitmap file or clipping and pasting from the clipboard are handled with a small additional amount of code:

```
Private Sub MCopy_Click ()
  'copy image to clipboard as a bitmap
  Clipboard.SetData Form2.Image, 2
End Sub

Private Sub MPaste_Click ()
  'paste a bitmap picture from clipboard
  Form2.Picture = Clipboard.GetData(2)
End Sub

Private Sub MSave_Click ()
  'show form for name and file path
  Form3.Show
End Sub
```

Saving to a File   If the file save option is selected, an additional form permits the user to specify the path and file name for the bitmap file.

```
Private Sub Command1_Click ()
  If Form3.Text1.Text <> "" Then
   FileSave$ = Form3.Text1.Text
   SavePicture Form2.Image, FileSave$
  End If
  Form3.Hide
End Sub
```

The dialog box form is hidden, once the file is saved.

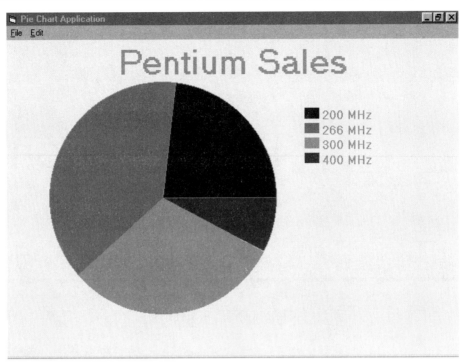

Figure 19–8 The pie chart plotted with default values.

A Unique Chart

Figure 19–8 shows a unique pie chart plotted with this application.

Hopefully this application illustrates Visual Basic's approach to handling dialog box information via additional forms.

Chapter 20

Text Functions

The Windows API provides a large number of functions specifically created to handle strings and characters. Working in conjunction with the font functions, discussed in Chapter 17, the string and character functions provide a quick and easy way to get and set character parameters and to draw strings on the screen.

The string functions, such as TextOut(), draw strings in the currently selected font. By manipulating font characteristics such as orientation and escapement (see Chapter 17), you will be able to draw text at any angle and rotate individual characters. This feature, alone, will allow you to create graphs and charts with vertical axis labels and fancy TrueType fonts.

API Character and Text Function Names and Descriptions

Table 20–1 shows 21 popular Windows API character and text functions and provides a brief description of their use.

In this group of functions, DrawText() and TextOut() rank as the most frequently used functions for drawing text to the screen. Two example applications in this chapter will illustrate their use.

Table 20–1 Character and Text Function Descriptions

Function	Description
DrawText	Draws text in the given rectangular area.
DrawTextEx	Similar to DrawText() but includes additional parameters given in DRAWTEXTPARAMS structure.
ExtTextOut	Similar to TextOut() but allows additional manipulation with ETO_ parameters.
GetCharacterPlacement	Returns information for displaying a string with a specified font.
GetTabbedTextExtent	Returns information an a string's extent, including tab information.
GetTextAlign	Returns the text alignment flag for the device context.
GetTextCharacterExtra	Returns the extra character spacing value.
GetTextCharset	Returns the character set identifier for the selected font in the device context.
GetTextCharsetInfo	Returns information on the character set for the current font.
GetTextColor	Returns the foreground text color.
GetTextExtentExPoint	Returns the number of characters capable of fitting into a given area.
GetTextExtentPoint	Uses GetTextExtentPoint32().
GetTextExtentPoint32	Returns the extents of a string.
GrayString	Draws a "grayed" string to indicate disabled status.
PolyTextOut	Draws multiple strings.
SetTextAlign	Sets the text alignment for the specified device context.
SetTextCharacterExtra	Sets the space used between characters when drawing strings.
SetTextColor	Sets the text foreground color.
SetTextJustification	Sets line justification.
TabbedTextOut	Similar to TextOut() with tab support.
TextOut	Draws a text string in the device context.

API Character and Text Declarations

The following listing contains the Windows API character and text function declarations found in the Win32api.txt file provided with Visual Basic. As we mentioned earlier, there are additional functions related to font manipulation that are described in Chapter 17.

```
Declare Function DrawText Lib "user32" Alias "DrawTextA"
   (ByVal hdc As Long, ByVal lpStr As String,
   ByVal nCount As Long, lpRect As RECT, ByVal wFormat
   As Long) As Long

Declare Function DrawTextEx Lib "user32" Alias "DrawTextExA"
   (ByVal hDC As Long, ByVal lpsz As String, ByVal n As Long,
   lpRect As RECT, ByVal un As Long,
   lpDrawTextParams As DRAWTEXTPARAMS) As Long
```

```
Declare Function ExtTextOut Lib "gdi32" Alias "ExtTextOutA"
  (ByVal hdc As Long, ByVal x As Long, ByVal y As Long,
  ByVal wOptions As Long, lpRect As Rect,
  ByVal lpString As String, ByVal nCount As Long,
  lpDx As Long) As Long

Declare Function GetCharacterPlacement Lib "gdi32" Alias
  "GetCharacterPlacementA" (ByVal hdc As Long,
  ByVal lpsz As String, ByVal n1 As Long,
  ByVal n2 As Long, lpGcpResults As GCP_RESULTS,
  ByVal dw As Long) As Long

Declare Function GetTabbedTextExtent Lib "user32" Alias
  "GetTabbedTextExtentA" (ByVal hdc As Long,
  ByVal lpString As String, ByVal nCount As Long,
  ByVal nTabPositions As Long,
  lpnTabStopPositions As Long) As Long

Declare Function GetTextAlign Lib "gdi32" Alias
  "GetTextAlign" (ByVal hdc As Long) As Long

Declare Function GetTextCharacterExtra Lib "gdi32" Alias
  "GetTextCharacterExtraA" (ByVal hdc As Long) As Long

Declare Function GetTextCharset Lib "gdi32" Alias
  "GetTextCharset" (ByVal hdc As Long) As Long

Declare Function GetTextCharsetInfo Lib "gdi32" Alias
  "GetTextCharsetInfo" (ByVal hdc As Long,
  lpSig As FONTSIGNATURE, ByVal dwFlags As Long) As Long

Declare Function GetTextColor Lib "gdi32" Alias
  "GetTextColor" (ByVal hdc As Long) As Long

Declare Function GetTextExtentExPoint Lib "gdi32" Alias
  "GetTextExtentExPointA" (ByVal hdc As Long,
  ByVal lpszStr As String, ByVal cchString As Long,
  ByVal nMaxExtent As Long, lpnFit As Long, alpDx As Long,
  lpSize As SIZE) As Long

Declare Function GetTextExtentPoint Lib "gdi32" Alias
  "GetTextExtentPointA" (ByVal hdc As Long,
  ByVal lpszString As String, ByVal cbString As Long,
  lpSize As SIZE) As Long

Declare Function GetTextExtentPoint32 Lib "gdi32" Alias
  "GetTextExtentPoint32A" (ByVal hdc As Long,
  ByVal lpsz As String, ByVal cbString As Long,
  lpSize As SIZE) As Long

Declare Function GrayString Lib "user32" Alias "GrayStringA"
  (ByVal hDC As Long, ByVal hBrush As Long,
  ByVal lpOutputFunc As Long, ByVal lpData As Long,
```

```
      ByVal nCount As Long, ByVal x As Long, ByVal y As Long,
      ByVal nWidth As Long, ByVal nHeight As Long) As Long

Declare Function PolyTextOut Lib "gdi32" Alias
   "PolyTextOutA" (ByVal hdc As Long, pptxt As POLYTEXT,
   cStrings As Long) As Long

Declare Function SetTextAlign Lib "gdi32" Alias
   "SetTextAlign" (ByVal hdc As Long,
   ByVal wFlags As Long) As Long

Declare Function SetTextCharacterExtra Lib "gdi32" Alias
   "SetTextCharacterExtraA" (ByVal hdc As Long,
   ByVal nCharExtra As Long) As Long

Declare Function SetTextColor Lib "gdi32" Alias
   "SetTextColor" (ByVal hdc As Long,
   ByVal crColor As Long) As Long

Declare Function SetTextJustification Lib "gdi32" Alias
   "SetTextJustification" (ByVal hdc As Long,
   ByVal nBreakExtra As Long,
   ByVal nBreakCount As Long) As Long

Declare Function TabbedTextOut Lib "user32" Alias
   "TabbedTextOutA" (ByVal hdc As Long, ByVal x As Long,
   ByVal y As Long, ByVal lpString As String,
   ByVal nCount As Long, ByVal nTabPositions As Long,
   lpnTabStopPositions As Long,
   ByVal nTabOrigin As Long) As Long

Declare Function TextOut Lib "gdi32" Alias "TextOutA"
   (ByVal hdc As Long, ByVal x As Long, ByVal y As Long,
   ByVal lpString As String, ByVal nCount As Long) As Long
```

Table 20–2 contains a brief description of the parameters used in the various character and text functions.

Table 20–2   Character and Text Function Parameters and Descriptions

Parameter	Description
alpDx As Long	Initial value in array of cchString values. Array contains distance in logical units for each character measured from the start of the string.
cbString As Long	Number of characters in the lpzStr string.
cchString As Long	Number of characters in the lpszStr string.
crColor As Long	Foreground text color.
cStrings As Long	Number of items in the pptxt array.
dw As Long	Uses an ORed combination of GCP_ parameters for character placement and control.
dwFlags As Long	Use zero (0)—reserved value.

(continued)

Table 20–2   Character and Text Function Parameters and Descriptions *(Continued)*

Parameter	Description
hBrush As Long	Brush for graying. Use zero (0) for current brush.
hdc As Long	Handle to the device context.
lpData As Long	Points the string to gray or a variable to pass to the Windows callback function.
lpDrawTextParams As DRAWTEXTPARAMS	Additional drawing parameters contained in a DRAWTEXTPARAMS structure.
lpDx As Long	Pointer to an array giving the spacing between pairs of characters. Logical units are used.
lpGcpResults As GCP_RESULTS	Holds information in a GCP_RESULTS structure determined for the string.
lpnFit As Long	Number of characters that will fit in the given extent.
lpnTabStopPositions As Long	Initial value in array of tab stop positions.
lpOutputFunc As Long	Pointer to a function where text will be sent. Use zero (0) for TextOut(), etc.
lpRect As RECT	A formatting rectangle using RECT structure.
lpSig As FONTSIGNATURE	Character set information contained in a FONTSIGNATURE structure.
lpSize As SIZE	String extents stored in a SIZE structure.
lpStr As String	Text string.
lpString As String	Text string.
lpsz As String	Text string.
lpszStr As String	Text string to have extents measured.
lpszString As String	Text string to have extents measured.
n As Long	Number of characters in string. If drawing all characters, use (-1).
n1 As Long	Number of characters in string.
n2 As Long	Used with GCP_MAXEXTENT to stop character processing once this value is met.
nBreakCount As Long	Count of break characters used to provide extra space.
nBreakExtra As Long	Extra space added to string.
nCharExtra As Long	Extra space added between characters in a string.
nCount As Long	Number of characters in string. If drawing all characters, use (-1).
nHeight As Long	Height of a bounding rectangle for a string.
nMaxExtent As Long	Horizontal extent for a string in logical units.
nTabOrigin As Long	Tab start origin.
nTabPositions As Long	Number of tabs in lpnTabStopPositions array.
nWidth As Long	Width of a bounding rectangle for a string.
pptxt As POLYTEXT	Initial entry in an array of POLYTEXT structures. Used to place and draw strings.
un As Long	Contains an array of flag bits that specify how a string will be drawn.
wFlags As Long	ORed combination of TA_ parameters used for text alignment.
wFormat	Contains an array of flag bits that specify how a string will be drawn.
wOptions As Long	ORed combination of ETO_ parameters for extended capabilities.
x As Long	Starting horizontal logical coordinate for drawing a string.
y As Long	Starting vertical logical coordinate for drawing a string.
X As Long	Horizontal coordinate of a bounding rectangle.
Y As Long	Vertical coordinate of a bounding rectangle.

Many of the parameters described in Table 20–2 use constant values. The Win32api.txt file lists the following constants for these parameters:

```
' DrawText() Format Flags
Public Const DT_TOP = &H0
Public Const DT_LEFT = &H0
Public Const DT_CENTER = &H1
Public Const DT_RIGHT = &H2
Public Const DT_VCENTER = &H4
Public Const DT_BOTTOM = &H8
Public Const DT_WORDBREAK = &H10
Public Const DT_SINGLELINE = &H20
Public Const DT_EXPANDTABS = &H40
Public Const DT_TABSTOP = &H80
Public Const DT_NOCLIP = &H100
Public Const DT_EXTERNALLEADING = &H200
Public Const DT_CALCRECT = &H400
Public Const DT_NOPREFIX = &H800
Public Const DT_INTERNAL = &H1000

Public Const ETO_CLIPPED = 4
Public Const ETO_GRAYED = 1
Public Const ETO_OPAQUE = 2

Public Const GCP_CLASSIN = &H80000
Public Const GCP_DBCS = &H1
Public Const GCP_DIACRITIC = &H100
Public Const GCP_DISPLAYZWG = &H400000
Public Const GCP_ERROR = &H8000
Public Const GCP_GLYPHSHAPE = &H10
Public Const GCP_JUSTIFY = &H10000
Public Const GCP_JUSTIFYIN = &H200000
Public Const GCP_KASHIDA = &H400
Public Const GCP_LIGATE = &H20
Public Const GCP_MAXEXTENT = &H100000
Public Const GCP_NEUTRALOVERRIDE = &H2000000
Public Const GCP_NODIACRITICS = &H20000
Public Const GCP_NUMERICOVERRIDE = &H1000000
Public Const GCP_NUMERICSLATIN = &H4000000
Public Const GCP_NUMERICSLOCAL = &H8000000
Public Const GCP_REORDER = &H2
Public Const GCP_SYMSWAPOFF = &H800000
Public Const GCP_USEKERNING = &H8

Public Const TA_BASELINE = 24
Public Const TA_BOTTOM = 8
Public Const TA_CENTER = 6
Public Const TA_LEFT = 0
Public Const TA_MASK = (TA_BASELINE+TA_CENTER+TA_UPDATECP)
Public Const TA_NOUPDATECP = 0
```

```
Public Const TA_RIGHT = 2
Public Const TA_TOP = 0
Public Const TA_UPDATECP = 1
```

In the next section, we'll examine two applications that make use of Windows API character and text functions.

Example Applications

This section contains two programming examples that will illustrate several important text handling functions: DrawText(), SetTextColor(), and TextOut(). The DrawText() function makes use of the RECT structure found in the Win32api.txt file.

Using the DrawText() Function

In order to use the DrawText() function, your project will need to include a module file that provides the declarations for the Win API functions and any required constants and structures. Remember that all of this information is located in the Win32api.txt file and can simply be copied and pasted into your project. Here are the contents of the Text1.bas module file for this project.

```
Type RECT
  Left As Long
  Top As Long
  Right As Long
  Bottom As Long
End Type

Declare Function DrawText Lib "user32" Alias "DrawTextA"
  (ByVal hdc As Long, ByVal lpStr As String,
  ByVal nCount As Long, lpRect As RECT,
  ByVal wFormat As Long) As Long

Declare Function SetTextColor Lib "gdi32"
  (ByVal hdc As Long, ByVal crColor As Long) As Long
```

This project will draw text on an empty form. Your project should include a form, named Text1.frm. The code for this form is shown in the following listing:

```
Dim rc As RECT
Dim str As String
Dim r&

Private Sub Form_Load()
  Form1.Show
End Sub
```

```
Private Sub Form_Paint()
  rc.Left = 100
  rc.Top = 220
  rc.Right = 640
  rc.Bottom = 260

  str = "Drawing text is easy with the DrawText() function"

  'Set text color to blue
  r& = SetTextColor(hdc, RGB(0, 0, 255))
  'Left justify and draw whole string
  r& = DrawText(hdc, str, -1, rc, DT_LEFT)
End Sub
```

The output for the project is shown in Figure 20–1.

This project sets the drawing rectangle for the DrawText() function and then draws a string of text in a blue color. Recall that a -1 when used as the string length draws the whole string to the rectangle.

Both the SetTextColor() and DrawText() functions are easy to use. In the next example, we'll examine a more extensive programming example using the TextOut() function.

Figure 20–1 The SetTextColor() and DrawText() functions are easy to use.

A Charting Application Using TextOut()

This application takes advantage of the CreateFont() function and TextOut() function to create a variety of fonts for a complete chart application. Details of the CreateFont() function can be found in Chapter 17.

This application used a module file, named Text2.bas, to hold global and function declarations. The next listing shows the contents of the Text2.bas module file.

```
DefInt A-Z
Global I, J, TNums, SPos, FPos, NLen
Global NArray(50, 50) As Single,
  ScaledNArray(50, 50) As Single
Global PtXMax As Single, PtYMax As Single
Global X1 As Single, Y1 As Single
Global X2 As Single, Y2 As Single

Declare Function CreateFont Lib "gdi32" Alias "CreateFontA"
  (ByVal H As Long, ByVal W As Long, ByVal E As Long,
  ByVal O As Long, ByVal W As Long, ByVal I As Long,
  ByVal u As Long, ByVal S As Long, ByVal C As Long,
  ByVal OP As Long, ByVal CP As Long, ByVal Q As Long,
  ByVal PAF As Long, ByVal F As String) As Long

Declare Function SelectObject Lib "gdi32"
  (ByVal hdc As Long, ByVal hObject As Long) As Long

Declare Function TextOut Lib "gdi32" Alias "TextOutA"
  (ByVal hdc As Long, ByVal x As Long, ByVal y As Long,
  ByVal lpString As String, ByVal nCount As Long) As Long
```

The project also used two forms. Text2a.frm is used as a data entry form for the line chart project. Figure 20–2 shows the data entry form for the Text2 project.

The following listing contains the code for this form (Form1). Again, this form is named Text2a.frm for this project.

```
Private Sub Command1_Click()
  ProcessData
  ScaleData
  Form2.Show
End Sub

Private Sub ProcessData()
  'the numbers in string equal number of commas + 1
  TNums = 1
  For I = 1 To Len(Text1.Text)
    XCh$ = Mid$(Text1.Text, I, 1)
    YCh$ = Mid$(Text2.Text, I, 1)
```

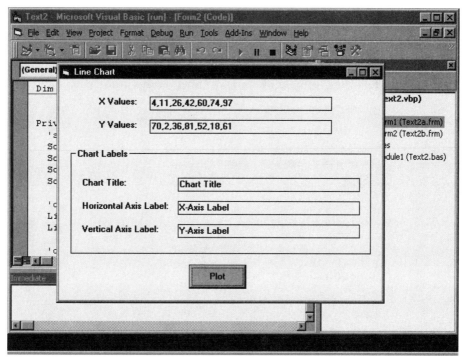

Figure 20–2   The data entry form for the line chart project.

```
   If XCh$ = "," Then TNums = TNums + 1
Next I

'now convert each group to a X number
XNewStr$ = Text1.Text + ","
SPos = 0
J = 0
For I = 1 To TNums
  FPos = InStr(SPos + 1, XNewStr$, Chr$(44))
  NLen = (FPos - SPos) - 1
  NArray(I, J) = Val(Mid$(XNewStr$, SPos + 1, NLen))
  SPos = FPos
Next I

'now convert each group to a Y number
YNewStr$ = Text2.Text + ","
SPos = 0
J = 1
For I = 1 To TNums
  FPos = InStr(SPos + 1, YNewStr$, Chr$(44))
  NLen = (FPos - SPos) - 1
  NArray(I, J) = Val(Mid$(YNewStr$, SPos + 1, NLen))
```

```
      SPos = FPos
   Next I
End Sub
```

The chart is drawn to a blank form (Form2). This form is named Text2b.frm. The following listing is the code required for this form:

```
Dim hnFont&, hoFont&
Dim r&

Private Sub Form_GotFocus()
  'set chart size parameters
  ScaleLeft = -200
  ScaleTop = 1400
  ScaleWidth = 1400
  ScaleHeight = -1700

  'draw horizontal and vertical axes
  Line (0, 0)-(1000, 0)
  Line (0, 0)-(0, 1000)

  'draw chart tic marks
   For I = 100 To 1000 Step 100
     Line (I, -5)-(I, 15) 'x tic
     Line (-5, I)-(6, I) 'y tic
   Next I

  DrawStyle = 3 'use dash-dot line style
  'draw lines between each pair of data points
  For I = 1 To TNums - 1
    X1 = ScaledNArray(I, 0): Y1 = ScaledNArray(I, 1)
    X2 = ScaledNArray(I + 1, 0): Y2 = ScaledNArray(I + 1, 1)
    Line (X1, Y1)-(X2, Y2), QBColor(1)
  Next I

  DrawStyle = 0
  'draw a "+" mark at each data point
  For I = 1 To TNums
    X1 = ScaledNArray(I, 0)
    Y1 = ScaledNArray(I, 1)
    Line (X1 - 9, Y1)-(X1 + 11, Y1), QBColor(11)  'x width
    Line (X1, Y1 - 15)-(X1, Y1 + 15), QBColor(11) 'y width
  Next I

  'draw the chart title
  hnFont = CreateFont(60, 0, 0, 0, FW_BOLD, False, False,
                   False, OEM_CHARSET, OUT_DEFAULT_PRECIS,
                   CLIP_DEFAULT_PRECIS, DEFAULT_QUALITY,
                   34, "Arial")
  hoFont = SelectObject(hdc, hnFont)
  sStr$ = Form1.Text3.Text
```

```
        r& = TextOut(Form2.hdc, 320 - (Len(sStr$) * 15), 15, sStr$,
                Len(sStr$))

        'draw the horizontal axis label
        hnFont = CreateFont(16, 0, 0, 0, FW_Normal, False, False,
                        False, OEM_CHARSET, OUT_DEFAULT_PRECIS,
                        CLIP_DEFAULT_PRECIS, DEFAULT_QUALITY,
                        34, "Arial")
        hoFont = SelectObject(hdc, hnFont)
        sStr$ = Form1.Text4.Text
        r& = TextOut(Form2.hdc, 320 - (Len(sStr$) * 4), 400, sStr$,
                Len(sStr$))

        'determine and draw the max and min X values
        sStr$ = Str$(PtXMax)
        r& = TextOut(Form2.hdc, 90, 375, "0", 1)
        r& = TextOut(Form2.hdc, 555 - (Len(sStr$) * 4), 375, sStr$,
                Len(sStr$))

        'determine and draw the max and min Y values
        sStr$ = Str$(PtYMax)
        r& = TextOut(Form2.hdc, 60, 350, "0", 1)
        r& = TextOut(Form2.hdc, 60, 100, sStr$, Len(sStr$))

        'draw the vertical axis label
        hnFont = CreateFont(16, 0, 900, 900, FW_Normal, False,
                        False, False, OEM_CHARSET,
                        OUT_DEFAULT_PRECIS,
                        CLIP_DEFAULT_PRECIS, DEFAULT_QUALITY,
                        34, "Arial")
        hoFont = SelectObject(hdc, hnFont)
        sStr$ = Form1.Text5.Text
        r& = TextOut(Form2.hdc, 40, 250 + (Len(sStr$) * 4),
                sStr$, Len(sStr$))
End Sub
```

Figure 20–3 shows the default line chart for this project.

Use the data entry form to customize a line chart to suite your needs. Figure 20–4 shows a typical chart.

Chart Capabilities

If you study the Visual Basic code, you will find that this application will allow the user

- to enter chart labels.
- to enter coordinate (*x,y*) values for several data points.

When all the values have been entered, the application will

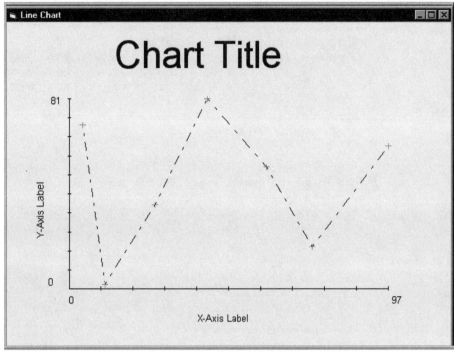

Figure 20–3   The Text2 project produces a default line chart.

- divide each axis with several tic marks.
- draw a line between each data point entered by the user.
- draw a symbol (+) at the location of each data point.
- draw an *X*- and *Y*-axis on a form.
- draw the chart labels using Windows API function calls.
- print the Max and Min values for each axis.
- scale the data points to the chart size.

In this application, each data point has an *X* and corresponding *Y* coordinate point. These points must be entered in pairs. Chart labels are optional, but this project provides three default values. The chart can be drawn by clicking the command button named Plot.

The Data Entry Form

The line chart is created when the command button is pushed on the data entry form (Form1). Pushing this button initiates a series of events; ProcessData, Scale-Data, and Form2.Show.

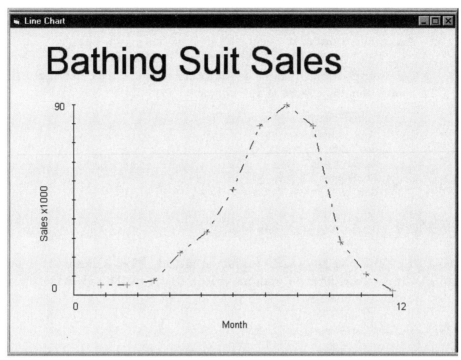

Figure 20–4   A custom line chart created with the Text2 project.

Examine the code for Form1 (Text1a.frm) and notice that this example reads *X* and *Y* data pairs from separate text boxes, converts them to numeric values, and stores them in a two-dimensional array, *NArray*.

The array information is then scaled so that the maximum value data value becomes the chart's upper value. All other data values are scaled as a fractional part of the maximum value. The program scales each array point to the maximum data point and also to the size of the axis it is plotted on. This project uses an *X*- and *Y*-axis with a 1,000-point extent. For example, if the user enters the values 20, 10, 50 as original data, the values will be processed in the following manner.

First, the program will select 30 as the maximum data value. All other points are then proportionally scaled to this value.

```
20 * 1000 / 50 = 400
10 * 1000 / 50 = 200
50 * 1000 / 50 = 1000
```

On the line chart, 50 will be scaled and drawn to the maximum scale size of 1,000 units. This technique works for any values entered by the user.

Examining the Charting Code

A custom coordinate system is created for drawing the line chart. The 0 point on the *X*-axis is 200 units from the left edge. The *Y*-axis is created so that chart values increase positively from the bottom of the screen. The 0 point on the *Y*-axis is 300 units from the bottom of the window.

```
Private Sub Form_GotFocus ()
  'set chart constants
  ScaleLeft = -200
  ScaleTop = 1400
  ScaleWidth = 1400
  ScaleHeight = -1700
    .
    .
    .
```

An *X*- and *Y*-axis is needed for the line chart. This is drawn (1,000 units) in the appropriate direction from the chart origin (0,0). The advantage to using a custom coordinate system is to avoid the need of offsetting each data point on the chart. If the origin of the chart is 0,0, then every data point can be drawn directly.

```
    .
    .
    .
  'draw horizontal and vertical axes
  Line (0, 0)-(1000, 0)
  Line (0, 0)-(0, 1000)
    .
    .
    .
```

This chart will draw tic marks on each axis. Tic marks are small symbols used to divide an axis. Tic marks are used to divide both the *X*- and *Y*-axis every 100 units.

```
    .
    .
    .
  'draw tic marks
  For I = 100 To 1000 Step 100
     Line (I, -5)-(I, 15) 'x tic
     Line (-5, I)-(6, I) 'y tic
  Next I
    .
    .
    .
```

Next, a **For** loop is used to draw each data point and then draw a line between each point. A dash-dot line style is used instead of the default solid line style for drawing each line.

```
        .
        .
        .
DrawStyle = 3 'dash-dot style
'draw lines between data points
For I = 1 To TNums - 1
    X1 = ScaledNArray(I, 0)
    Y1 = ScaledNArray(I, 1)
    X2 = ScaledNArray(I + 1, 0)
    Y2 = ScaledNArray(I + 1, 1)
    Line (X1, Y1)-(X2,Y2), QBColor(1)
Next I
        .
        .
        .
```

Small marker symbols, in the form of a "+", are drawn after the lines are drawn.

```
        .
        .
        .
DrawStyle = 0
'draw a "+" marker at each point plotted
For I = 1 To TNums
    X1 = ScaledNArray(I, 0)
    Y1 = ScaledNArray(I, 1)
    Line (X1 - 9, Y1)-(X1 + 11, Y1), QBColor(11) 'x width
    Line (X1, Y1 - 15)-(X1, Y1 + 15), QBColor(11) 'y width
Next I
        .
        .
        .
```

The CreateFont(), SelectObject(), and TextOut() functions are used to draw the chart labels. In the first portion of code, a bold font size of 60 is requested for the chart title.

NOTE: Several function calls in the following listing have been wrapped to a second line of code. They should be entered on a single program line.

```
                          .
                          .
                          .
            'draw the chart title
            hnFont = CreateFont(60, 0, 0, 0, FW_BOLD, False, False,
                                False, OEM_CHARSET, OUT_DEFAULT_PRECIS,
                                CLIP_DEFAULT_PRECIS, DEFAULT_QUALITY,
                                34, "Arial")
            hoFont = SelectObject(hdc, hnFont)
            sStr$ = Form1.Text3.Text
            r& = TextOut(Form2.hdc, 320 - (Len(sStr$) * 15), 15, sStr$,
                    Len(sStr$))

            'draw the horizontal axis label
            hnFont = CreateFont(16, 0, 0, 0, FW_Normal, False, False,
                                False, OEM_CHARSET, OUT_DEFAULT_PRECIS,
                                CLIP_DEFAULT_PRECIS, DEFAULT_QUALITY,
                                34, "Arial")
            hoFont = SelectObject(hdc, hnFont)
            sStr$ = Form1.Text4.Text
            r& = TextOut(Form2.hdc, 320 - (Len(sStr$) * 4), 400, sStr$,
                    Len(sStr$))

            'determine and draw the max and min X values
            sStr$ = Str$(PtXMax)
            r& = TextOut(Form2.hdc, 90, 375, "0", 1)
            r& = TextOut(Form2.hdc, 555 - (Len(sStr$) * 4), 375, sStr$,
                    Len(sStr$))

            'determine and draw the max and min Y values
            sStr$ = Str$(PtYMax)
            r& = TextOut(Form2.hdc, 60, 350, "0", 1)
            r& = TextOut(Form2.hdc, 60, 100, sStr$, Len(sStr$))

            'draw the vertical axis label
            hnFont = CreateFont(16, 0, 900, 900, FW_Normal, False,
                                False, False, OEM_CHARSET,
                                OUT_DEFAULT_PRECIS,
                                CLIP_DEFAULT_PRECIS, DEFAULT_QUALITY,
                                34, "Arial")
            hoFont = SelectObject(hdc, hnFont)
            sStr$ = Form1.Text5.Text
            r& = TextOut(Form2.hdc, 40, 250 + (Len(sStr$) * 4),
                    sStr$, Len(sStr$))
            End Sub
```

The remaining text is printed to the form in a 16-pt normal font. This font label information is printed on the line chart as it is produced. Notice, in the previous listing, that a special font is created for drawing the vertical axis label. The label will be drawn vertically.

Chapter **21**

Printing: Devices, Documents, and Properties

The Windows API provides a wide variety of functions relating to printers. In this chapter and Chapter 22, the most frequently used functions are examined. This chapter addresses those functions that are associated with printers, documents, and device properties. Chapter 22 addresses print functions relating to forms, jobs, and ports.

Several of the print functions are highlighted in a simple programming example in the last section of this chapter.

API Print Function Names and Descriptions

Table 21–1 shows 22 popular Windows API print functions associated with print devices, documents, and properties. Table 21–1 also provides a brief description of their use.

The OpenPrinter() function is used frequently to obtain the handle to the current default printer. Once a printer handle is available, functions such as Printer-Properties() can be used to retrieve additional data on a current printer by displaying the Printer Properties dialog box. You'll see both of these functions used in a simple application at the end of this chapter.

285

Table 21–1   Print Functions and Descriptions

Function	Description
AbortDoc	Aborts printing the current document.
AdvancedDocumentProperties	Dialog box for document interfacing.
ClosePrinter	Closes the printer object.
ConnectToPrinterDlg	Dialog box for network printer interfacing.
DeviceCapabilities	Use to find printer capabilities.
DocumentProperties	Get and set printer configuration for a document.
EndDocPrinter	Document printing is ended.
EndPage	End of page signal.
EndPagePrinter	End of page signal.
Escape	Sends raw data to printer.
OpenPrinter	Obtains a handle identifying the printer or print server.
PrinterMessageBox	Message box for displaying printer error messages under Windows NT.
PrinterProperties	Dialog box for printer property interfacing.
ReadPrinter	Read printer information.
ResetDC	Document device mode settings are reset.
ResetPrinter	Sets printer to default printer settings under Windows NT.
SetAbortProc	Procedure that permits print jobs to be aborted.
StartDoc	Start of document signal.
StartDocPrinter	Spools a new document.
StartPage	Start of page signal.
StartPagePrinter	New page signal to spooler.
WritePrinter	Spooled data sent to printer.

API Print Function Declarations

The following listing contains the Windows API print function declarations for devices, documents, and properties found in the Win32api.txt file provided with Visual Basic. Remember that Chapter 22 contains additional print functions that you'll want to examine, too.

```
Declare Function AbortDoc
   "gdi32" Alias "AbortDoc" (ByVal hdc As Long) As Long

Declare Function AdvancedDocumentProperties
   "winspool.drv" Alias "AdvancedDocumentPropertiesA"
   (ByVal hwnd As Long, ByVal hPrinter As Long,
   ByVal pDeviceName As String, pDevModeOutput As DEVMODE,
   pDevModeInput As DEVMODE) As Long

Declare Function ClosePrinter
   "winspool.drv" Alias "ClosePrinter"
   (ByVal hPrinter As Long) As Long
```

```
Declare Function ConnectToPrinterDlg
  "winspool.drv" Alias "ConnectToPrinterDlg"
  (ByVal hwnd As Long, ByVal flags As Long) As Long

Declare Function DeviceCapabilities
  "winspool.drv" Alias "DeviceCapabilitiesA"
  (ByVal lpDeviceName As String, ByVal lpPort As String,
  ByVal iIndex As Long, ByVal lpOutput As String,
  lpDevMode As DEVMODE) As Long

Declare Function DocumentProperties
  "winspool.drv" Alias "DocumentPropertiesA"
  (ByVal hwnd As Long, ByVal hPrinter As Long,
  ByVal pDeviceName As String, pDevModeOutput As DEVMODE,
  pDevModeInput As DEVMODE, ByVal fMode As Long) As Long

Declare Function EndDocPrinter
  "winspool.drv" Alias "EndDocPrinter"
  (ByVal hPrinter As Long) As Long

Declare Function EndPage
  "gdi32" Alias "EndPage" (ByVal hdc As Long) As Long

Declare Function EndPagePrinter
  "winspool.drv" Alias "EndPagePrinter"
  (ByVal hPrinter As Long) As Long

Declare Function Escape
  "gdi32" Alias "Escape" (ByVal hdc As Long,
  ByVal nEscape As Long, ByVal nCount As Long,
  ByVal lpInData As String, lpOutData As Any) As Long

Declare Function OpenPrinter
  "winspool.drv" Alias "OpenPrinterA"
  (ByVal pPrinterName As String, phPrinter As Long,
  pDefault As PRINTER_DEFAULTS) As Long

Declare Function PrinterMessageBox
  "winspool.drv" Alias "PrinterMessageBoxA"
  (ByVal hPrinter As Long, ByVal error As Long,
  ByVal hwnd As Long, ByVal pText As String,
  ByVal pCaption As String, ByVal dwType As Long) As Long

Declare Function PrinterProperties
  "winspool.drv" Alias "PrinterProperties"
  (ByVal hwnd As Long, ByVal hPrinter As Long) As Long

Declare Function ReadPrinter
  "winspool.drv" Alias "ReadPrinter"
  (ByVal hPrinter As Long, pBuf As Any, ByVal cdBuf As Long,
  pNoBytesRead As Long) As Long
```

```
Declare Function ResetDC
  "gdi32" Alias "ResetDCA" (ByVal hdc As Long,
  lpInitData As DEVMODE) As Long

Declare Function ResetPrinter
  "winspool.drv" Alias "ResetPrinterA"
  (ByVal hPrinter As Long,
  pDefault As PRINTER_DEFAULTS) As Long

Declare Function SetAbortProc
  "gdi32" Alias "SetAbortProc" (ByVal hDC As Long,
  ByVal lpAbortProc As Long) As Long

Declare Function StartDoc
  "gdi32" Alias "StartDocA" (ByVal hdc As Long,
  lpdi As DOCINFO) As Long

Declare Function StartDocPrinter
  "winspool.drv" Alias "StartDocPrinterA"
  (ByVal hPrinter As Long, ByVal Level As Long,
  pDocInfo As Byte) As Long

Declare Function StartPage
  "gdi32" Alias "StartPage" (ByVal hdc As Long) As Long

Declare Function StartPagePrinter
  "winspool.drv" Alias "StartPagePrinter"
  (ByVal hPrinter As Long) As Long

Declare Function WritePrinter
  "winspool.drv" Alias "WritePrinter"
  (ByVal hPrinter As Long, pBuf As Any, ByVal cdBuf As Long,
  pcWritten As Long) As Long
```

Table 21–2 constants a brief description of the parameters used in the various print functions.

Table 21–2   Print Function Parameters and Descriptions

Parameter	Description
cdBuf As Long	Holds number of bytes to read or the size of the buffer.
dwType As Long	Message box flag. Uses MB_ constants.
error As Long	Uses specific ERROR_ constants.
flags As Long	Set to "0"; reserved value.
fMode As Long	Operation mode flags (see DM_).
hdc As Long	Handle to the Device Context (DC).
hPrinter As Long	Handle to a printer object.
hwnd As Long	Handle to the window.
iIndex As Long	Uses specific DC_ constants.
Level As Long	Value is set to "1" or "2."

Table 21–2   Print Function Parameters and Descriptions *(Continued)*

Parameter	Description
lpAbortProc As Long	Pointer to the abort function.
lpDeviceName As String	Name of device as string.
lpDevMode As DEVMODE	Structure holds device information if present.
lpdi As DOCINFO	Structure used to define a document.
lpInData As String	Pointer to variable holding escape value for QUERYESCSUPPORT or a portion of data containing the number of bytes to send for PASSTHROUGH.
lpInitData As DEVMODE	Structure holds initial device information.
lpOutData As Any	Usually a NULL value.
lpOutput As String	Pointer to buffer containing device capabilities.
lpPort As String	Name of port as string.
nCount As Long	Size (bytes) of lpInData parameter.
nEscape As Long	Escape number.
pBuf As Any	Buffer holds printer data.
pCaption As String	Caption to be displayed in message box.
pcWritten As Long	Holds number of bytes actually written.
pDefault As PRINTER_DEFAULTS	Structure holds default printer information.
pDeviceName As String	Printer name.
pDevModeInput As DEVMODE	Structure uses DM_ constants.
pDevModeOutput As DEVMODE	Structure uses DM_ constants.
pDocInfo As Byte	Uses a DOC_INFO structure for data.
phPrinter As Long	Printer handle.
pNoBytesRead As Long	Actual number of bytes read.
pPrinterName As String	Printer to open.
pText As String	Text to be displayed in message box.

Many of the parameters described in Table 21–2 use constant values. The Win32api.txt file lists the following constants for these print parameters.

Note: There may be additional ERROR_ constants available. Check specific circumstances in the Win32api.txt file.

```
'device capabilities indices
Public Const DC_FIELDS = 1
Public Const DC_PAPERS = 2
Public Const DC_PAPERSIZE = 3
Public Const DC_MINEXTENT = 4
Public Const DC_MAXEXTENT = 5
Public Const DC_BINS = 6
Public Const DC_DUPLEX = 7
Public Const DC_SIZE = 8
Public Const DC_EXTRA = 9
Public Const DC_VERSION = 10
Public Const DC_DRIVER = 11
```

```
Public Const DC_BINNAMES = 12
Public Const DC_ENUMRESOLUTIONS = 13
Public Const DC_FILEDEPENDENCIES = 14
Public Const DC_TRUETYPE = 15
Public Const DC_PAPERNAMES = 16
Public Const DC_ORIENTATION = 17
Public Const DC_COPIES = 18
Public Const DC_BINADJUST = 19
Public Const DC_EMF_COMPLIANT = 20
Public Const DC_DATATYPE_PRODUCED = 21
Public Const DC_COLLATE = 22

'return values for DC_BINADJUST
Public Const DCBA_FACEUPNONE = &H0
Public Const DCBA_FACEUPCENTER = &H1
Public Const DCBA_FACEUPLEFT = &H2
Public Const DCBA_FACEUPRIGHT = &H3
Public Const DCBA_FACEDOWNNONE = &H100
Public Const DCBA_FACEDOWNCENTER = &H101
Public Const DCBA_FACEDOWNLEFT = &H102
Public Const DCBA_FACEDOWNRIGHT = &H103

'mode selections for the device mode function
Public Const DM_UPDATE = 1
Public Const DM_COPY = 2
Public Const DM_PROMPT = 4
Public Const DM_MODIFY = 8
Public Const DM_IN_BUFFER = DM_MODIFY
Public Const DM_IN_PROMPT = DM_PROMPT
Public Const DM_OUT_BUFFER = DM_COPY
Public Const DM_OUT_DEFAULT = DM_UPDATE

'The device is not ready.
Public Const ERROR_NOT_READY = 21&

'The printer is out of paper.
Public Const ERROR_OUT_OF_PAPER = 28&

'The printer queue is full.
Public Const ERROR_PRINTQ_FULL = 61&

'Space to store the file waiting to be printed is
'not available on the server.
Public Const ERROR_NO_SPOOL_SPACE = 62&

'Your file waiting to be printed was deleted.
Public Const ERROR_PRINT_CANCELLED = 63&
```

In addition to the constants used by these functions, several unique structures are also accessed. The following listing gives the structures used by these functions.

```
'size of a device name string
Public Const CCHDEVICENAME = 32

'size of a form name string
Public Const CCHFORMNAME = 32

Type DEVMODE
  dmDeviceName As String * CCHDEVICENAME
  dmSpecVersion As Integer
  dmDriverVersion As Integer
  dmSize As Integer
  dmDriverExtra As Integer
  dmFields As Long
  dmOrientation As Integer
  dmPaperSize As Integer
  dmPaperLength As Integer
  dmPaperWidth As Integer
  dmScale As Integer
  dmCopies As Integer
  dmDefaultSource As Integer
  dmPrintQuality As Integer
  dmColor As Integer
  dmDuplex As Integer
  dmYResolution As Integer
  dmTTOption As Integer
  dmCollate As Integer
  dmFormName As String * CCHFORMNAME
  dmUnusedPadding As Integer
  dmBitsPerPel As Integer
  dmPelsWidth As Long
  dmPelsHeight As Long
  dmDisplayFlags As Long
  dmDisplayFrequency As Long
End Type

Type DOC_INFO_1
  pDocName As String
  pOutputFile As String
  pDatatype As String
End Type

Type PRINTER_DEFAULTS
  pDatatype As String
  pDevMode As DEVMODE
  DesiredAccess As Long
End Type
```

In the next section, we'll examine several of these print functions in a simple application.

Example Application

This section contains a programming example that will serve to illustrate the general approach to using the print functions contained in this chapter.

In order to access printer data, information on the default printer is obtained with a call to the GetProfileString() function. This printer information is obtained in the form of a Null terminated string. The information returned in this string contains the printer name, driver, and port value. If you wish to view each part of the data string separately, the string must be parsed. String elements are separated by a comma and a blank, so parsing is fairly simple. This simple application will display these three pieces of information on a form and then allow the Printer Properties dialog box to be viewed. The dialog box is accessed with a simple call to the PrinterProperties() function.

This Visual Basic project is named Print1.vbp and contains a form for drawing the data and a module file for constants, structures, and function declarations. All of this information can be copied from the Win32api.txt file supplied with your Visual Basic compiler. Here is the file listing for the Print1.bas file.

```
Public Const PRINTER_ACCESS_USE = &H8

'Modified pDevMode from As DEVMODE to As Long
Type PRINTER_DEFAULTS
  pDatatype As String
  pDevMode As Long
  DesiredAccess As Long
End Type


Declare Function GetProfileString Lib "kernel32" Alias
  "GetProfileStringA" (ByVal lpAppName As String,
  ByVal lpKeyName As String, ByVal lpDefault As String,
  ByVal lpReturnedString As String,
  ByVal nSize As Long) As Long
Declare Function OpenPrinter Lib "winspool.drv" Alias
  "OpenPrinterA" (ByVal pPrinterName As String,
  phPrinter As Long, pDefault As PRINTER_DEFAULTS) As Long
Declare Function PrinterProperties Lib "winspool.drv"
  (ByVal hwnd As Long, ByVal hPrinter As Long) As Long
```

The project's form contains six label controls. Three label controls are used for simple labels. The remaining three accept, as a caption property, returned information on the default printer.

The programming code that supports this display is shown in the following code listing for Print1.frm.

```
Private Sub Form_Load()
  Dim r&
  Dim ptrnampos%, drvnampos%, tempstart%, tempfinish%
  Dim hPtr&
  Dim profile$, PrinterName$, PrinterDriver$, PrinterPort$
  Dim ptrdefault As PRINTER_DEFAULTS

  'profile of default printer info as null terminated string
  profile$ = String$(128, 0)
  r& = GetProfileString("WINDOWS", "DEVICE", "",
                        profile$, 128)
  'string length less null terminator
  tempstart% = InStr(profile$, Chr$(0)) - 1
  profile$ = Left$(profile$, tempstart%)

  'Parse string into three pieces of information
  'Get Printer Name - left portion of string
  ptrnampos% = InStr(profile$, ",")
  tempstart% = ptrnampos% - 1
  PrinterName$ = Left$(profile$, tempstart%)
  Label4.Caption = PrinterName$

  'Get Driver Name - middle portion of string
  drvnampos% = InStr(ptrnampos% + 1, profile$, ",")
  tempstart% = ptrnampos% + 1
  tempfinish% = drvnampos% - ptrnampos% - 1
  PrinterDriver$ = Mid$(profile$, tempstart%, tempfinish%)
  Label5.Caption = PrinterDriver$

  'Get Port - final portion of string
  tempstart% = drvnampos% + 1
  PrinterPort$ = Mid$(profile$, tempstart%)
  Label6.Caption = PrinterPort$

  'Open Printer to retrieve handle
  ptrdefault.pDatatype = vbNullString
  ptrdefault.pDevMode = 0
  ptrdefault.DesiredAccess = PRINTER_ACCESS_USE
  r& = OpenPrinter(PrinterName$, hPtr, ptrdefault)

  'Display Printer Properties Dialog Box
  r& = PrinterProperties(hwnd, hPtr)
End Sub
```

This application uses the information obtained from the GetProfileString() function to provide data on the printer name, driver name, and port location. The OpenPrinter() function is then called to obtain a printer handle for the eventual call to the PrinterProperties() function. This function will display the Windows Printer Properties dialog box on the screen for the given printer.

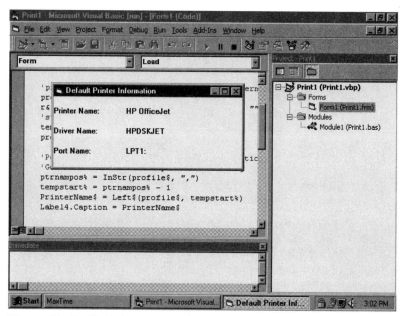

Figure 21–1   Default printer information is returned with the GetProfileString() function.

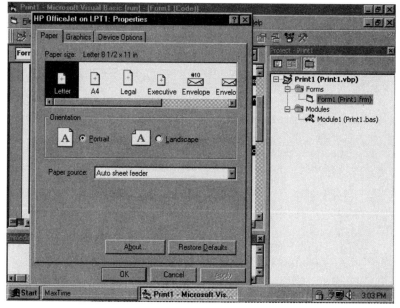

Figure 21–2   The Printer Properties dialog box is viewed with a call to the PrinterProperties() function.

Figure 21–1 shows the project's form with the current default printer name, driver, and port location.

Figure 21–2 shows the Printer Properties dialog box that is displayed with a call to the PrinterProperties() function.

Chapter 22 contains additional print functions dealing with forms, jobs, and ports.

Printing: Forms, Jobs, Ports, and Printers

This chapter describes additional functions relating to printers. In this chapter and Chapter 21, the most frequently used functions are examined. This chapter addresses those functions that are associated with forms, jobs, ports, and printers. Chapter 21 addresses print functions relating to devices, documents, and properties.

Several of the print functions are highlighted in a simple programming example in the last section of this chapter.

API Print Function Names and Descriptions

Table 22–1 shows 42 Windows API print functions related to forms, jobs, ports, and printers. This table contains the function name and a brief description of their use.

Several of the functions in this table are used quite frequently. For example the enumeration functions, those starting with "Enum" can be used to list current printers, drivers, jobs, and so on. The ConfigurePort() function, illustrated in this chapter's application, allows the user to set port configurations via the standard Windows Configure Port dialog box.

Table 22-1 Form, Job, Port, and Printer Functions and Descriptions

Function	Description
AbortPrinter	Printer's spooling file is deleted.
AddForm	Adds a form to the Windows NT form list.
AddJob	Adds a spool file.
AddMonitor	Adds a printer monitor.
AddPort	Port is made available.
AddPrinter	Adds a printer.
AddPrinterConnection	Adds a printer connection.
AddPrinterDriver	Adds a printer driver.
AddPrintProcessor	Adds a print processor.
AddPrintProvidor	Adds a print provider.
ConfigurePort	Shows port-configuration dialog box for a port.
DeleteForm	Deletes a form from the Windows NT form list.
DeleteMonitor	Deletes a printer monitor.
DeletePort	Port is made unavailable.
DeletePrinter	Deletes a printer.
DeletePrinterConnection	Deletes a printer connection.
DeletePrinterDriver	Deletes a printer driver.
DeletePrintProcessor	Deletes a print processor.
DeletePrintProvidor	Deletes a print provider.
EnumForms	Enumerates available Windows NT forms.
EnumJobs	Enumerates print jobs.
EnumMonitors	Enumerates printer monitors.
EnumPorts	Enumerates ports.
EnumPrinterDrivers	Enumerates printer drivers.
EnumPrinters	Enumerates printers.
EnumPrintProcessorDatatypes	Enumerates data types for print processor support.
EnumPrintProcessors	Enumerates print processors.
FindClosePrinterChangeNotification	Closes a Windows NT printer notification object.
FindFirstPrinterChangeNotification	Finds a Windows NT printer notification object.
FindNextPrinterChangeNotification	Finds information about a Windows NT printer notification change.
GetForm	Initializes a Windows NT FORM_INFO_1 structure with data describing the form.
GetJob	Gets print job information.
GetPrinter	Gets printer information.
GetPrinterData	Gets printer configuration information.
GetPrinterDriver	Gets printer driver information.
GetPrinterDriverDirectory	Gets DLL directory for printer drivers.
GetPrintProcessorDirectory	Gets DLL directory for print processors.
ScheduleJob	Schedules a print job.
SetForm	Sets a Windows NT printer's form.
SetJob	Sets print job control.
SetPrinter	Sets a printer's control.
SetPrinterData	Sets configuration information into registry for a printer.

API Print Function Declarations

The following listing contains the Windows API print functions relating to forms, jobs, ports, and printers as found in the Win32api.txt file provided with Visual Basic. Chapter 21 contains additional print functions that you may wish to examine.

```
Declare Function AbortPrinter Lib "winspool.drv" Alias
    "AbortPrinter" (ByVal hPrinter As Long) As Long

Declare Function AddForm Lib "winspool.drv" Alias
    "AddFormA" (ByVal hPrinter As Long,
    ByVal Level As Long, pForm As Byte) As Long

Declare Function AddJob Lib "winspool.drv" Alias
    "AddJobA" (ByVal hPrinter As Long, ByVal Level As Long,
    pData As Byte, ByVal cdBuf As Long, pcbNeeded As Long) As Long

Declare Function AddMonitor Lib "winspool.drv" Alias
    "AddMonitorA" (ByVal pName As String, ByVal Level As Long,
    pMonitors As Byte) As Long

Declare Function AddPort Lib "winspool.drv" Alias
    "AddPortA" (ByVal pName As String, ByVal hwnd As Long,
    ByVal pMonitorName As String) As Long

Declare Function AddPrinter Lib "winspool.drv" Alias
    "AddPrinterA" (ByVal pName As String, ByVal Level As Long,
    pPrinter As Any) As Long

Declare Function AddPrinterConnection Lib "winspool.drv"
    Alias "AddPrinterConnectionA"
    (ByVal pName As String) As Long

Declare Function AddPrinterDriver Lib "winspool.drv" Alias
    "AddPrinterDriverA" (ByVal pName As String,
    ByVal Level As Long, pDriverInfo As Any) As Long

Declare Function AddPrintProcessor Lib "winspool.drv" Alias
    "AddPrintProcessorA" (ByVal pName As String,
    ByVal pEnvironment As String, ByVal pPathName As String,
    ByVal pPrintProcessorName As String) As Long

Declare Function AddPrintProvidor Lib "winspool.drv"
    Alias "AddPrintProvidorA" (ByVal pName As String,
    ByVal Level As Long, pProvidorInfo As Byte) As Long

Declare Function ConfigurePort Lib "winspool.drv" Alias
    "ConfigurePortA" (ByVal pName As String,
    ByVal hwnd As Long, ByVal pPortName As String) As Long
```

```
Declare Function DeleteForm Lib "winspool.drv" Alias
   "DeleteFormA" (ByVal hPrinter As Long,
   ByVal pFormName As String) As Long

Declare Function DeleteMonitor Lib "winspool.drv" Alias
   "DeleteMonitorA" (ByVal pName As String,
   ByVal pEnvironment As String,
   ByVal pMonitorName As String) As Long

Declare Function DeletePort Lib "winspool.drv" Alias
   "DeletePortA" (ByVal pName As String, ByVal hwnd As Long,
   ByVal pPortName As String) As Long

Declare Function DeletePrinter Lib "winspool.drv" Alias
   "DeletePrinter" (ByVal hPrinter As Long) As Long

Declare Function DeletePrinterConnection Lib
   "winspool.drv" Alias
   "DeletePrinterConnectionA" (ByVal pName As String) As Long

Declare Function DeletePrinterDriver Lib "winspool.drv"
   Alias "DeletePrinterDriverA" (ByVal pName As String,
   ByVal pEnvironment As String,
   ByVal pDriverName As String) As Long

Declare Function DeletePrintProcessor Lib "winspool.drv"
   Alias "DeletePrintProcessorA" (ByVal pName As String,
   ByVal pEnvironment As String,
   ByVal pPrintProcessorName As String) As Long

Declare Function DeletePrintProvidor Lib "winspool.drv"
   Alias "DeletePrintProvidorA" (ByVal pName As String,
   ByVal pEnvironment As String,
   ByVal pPrintProvidorName As String) As Long

Declare Function EnumForms Lib "winspool.drv" Alias
   "EnumFormsA" (ByVal hPrinter As Long, ByVal Level As Long,
   pForm As Byte, ByVal cbBuf As Long, pcbNeeded As Long,
   pcReturned As Long) As Long

Declare Function EnumJobs Lib "winspool.drv" Alias
   "EnumJobsA" (ByVal hPrinter As Long,
   ByVal FirstJob As Long, ByVal NoJobs As Long,
   ByVal Level As Long, pJob As Byte, ByVal cdBuf As Long,
   pcbNeeded As Long, pcReturned As Long) As Long

Declare Function EnumMonitors Lib "winspool.drv" Alias
   "EnumMonitorsA" (ByVal pName As String,
   ByVal Level As Long, pMonitors As Byte,
   ByVal cbBuf As Long, pcbNeeded As Long,
   pcReturned As Long) As Long

Declare Function EnumPorts Lib "winspool.drv" Alias
   "EnumPortsA" (ByVal pName As String, ByVal Level As Long,
```

```
      ByVal lpbPorts As Long, ByVal cbBuf As Long,
      pcbNeeded As Long, pcReturned As Long) As Long

  Declare Function EnumPrinterDrivers Lib "winspool.drv"
      Alias "EnumPrinterDriversA" (ByVal pName As String,
      ByVal pEnvironment As String, ByVal Level As Long,
      pDriverInfo As Byte, ByVal cdBuf As Long,
      pcbNeeded As Long, pcReturned As Long) As Long

  Declare Function EnumPrinters Lib "winspool.drv" Alias
      "EnumPrintersA" (ByVal flags As Long,
      ByVal name As String, ByVal Level As Long,
      pPrinterEnum As Byte, ByVal cdBuf As Long,
      pcbNeeded As Long, pcReturned As Long) As Long

  Declare Function EnumPrintProcessorDatatypes Lib
      "winspool.drv" Alias "EnumPrintProcessorDatatypesA"
      (ByVal pName As String,
      ByVal pPrintProcessorName As String,
      ByVal Level As Long, pDatatypes As Byte,
      ByVal cdBuf As Long, pcbNeeded As Long,
      pcReturned As Long) As Long

  Declare Function EnumPrintProcessors Lib "winspool.drv"
      Alias "EnumPrintProcessorsA" (ByVal pName As String,
      ByVal pEnvironment As String, ByVal Level As Long,
      pPrintProcessorInfo As Byte, ByVal cdBuf As Long,
      pcbNeeded As Long, pcReturned As Long) As Long

  Declare Function FindClosePrinterChangeNotification Lib
      "winspool.drv" Alias "FindClosePrinterChangeNotification"
      (ByVal hChange As Long) As Long

  Declare Function FindFirstPrinterChangeNotification Lib
      "winspool.drv" Alias "FindFirstPrinterChangeNotification"
      (ByVal hPrinter As Long, ByVal fdwFlags As Long,
      ByVal fdwOptions As Long,
      ByVal pPrinterNotifyOptions As Byte) As Long

  Declare Function FindNextPrinterChangeNotification Lib
      "winspool.drv" Alias "FindNextPrinterChangeNotification"
      (ByVal hChange As Long, pdwChange As Long,
      ByVal pvReserved As Long,
      ByVal ppPrinterNotifyInfo As Long) As Long

  Declare Function GetForm Lib "winspool.drv" Alias "GetFormA"
      (ByVal hPrinter As Long, ByVal pFormName As String,
      ByVal Level As Long, pForm As Byte, ByVal cbBuf As Long,
      pcbNeeded As Long) As Long

  Declare Function GetJob Lib "winspool.drv" Alias "GetJobA"
      (ByVal hPrinter As Long, ByVal JobId As Long,
```

```
    ByVal Level As Long, pJob As Byte, ByVal cdBuf As Long,
    pcbNeeded As Long) As Long

Declare Function GetPrinter Lib "winspool.drv" Alias
    "GetPrinterA" (ByVal hPrinter As Long,
    ByVal Level As Long, pPrinter As Any, ByVal cbBuf As Long,
    pcbNeeded As Long) As Long

Declare Function GetPrinterData Lib "winspool.drv" Alias
    "GetPrinterDataA" (ByVal hPrinter As Long,
    ByVal pValueName As String, pType As Long,
    pData As Byte, ByVal nSize As Long,
    pcbNeeded As Long) As Long

Declare Function GetPrinterDriver Lib "winspool.drv" Alias
    "GetPrinterDriverA" (ByVal hPrinter As Long,
    ByVal pEnvironment As String, ByVal Level As Long,
    pDriverInfo As Byte, ByVal cdBuf As Long,
    pcbNeeded As Long) As Long

Declare Function GetPrinterDriverDirectory Lib
    "winspool.drv" Alias "GetPrinterDriverDirectoryA"
    (ByVal pName As String, ByVal pEnvironment As String,
    ByVal Level As Long, pDriverDirectory As Byte,
    ByVal cdBuf As Long, pcbNeeded As Long) As Long

Declare Function GetPrintProcessorDirectory Lib
    "winspool.drv" Alias "GetPrintProcessorDirectoryA"
    (ByVal pName As String, ByVal pEnvironment As String,
    ByVal Level As Long, ByVal pPrintProcessorInfo As String,
    ByVal cdBuf As Long, pcbNeeded As Long) As Long

Declare Function ScheduleJob Lib "winspool.drv" Alias
    "ScheduleJob" (ByVal hPrinter As Long,
    ByVal JobId As Long) As Long

Declare Function SetForm Lib "winspool.drv" Alias "SetFormA"
    (ByVal hPrinter As Long, ByVal pFormName As String,
    ByVal Level As Long, pForm As Byte) As Long

Declare Function SetJob Lib "winspool.drv" Alias "SetJobA"
    (ByVal hPrinter As Long, ByVal JobId As Long,
    ByVal Level As Long, pJob As Byte,
    ByVal Command As Long) As Long

Declare Function SetPrinter Lib "winspool.drv" Alias
    "SetPrinterA" (ByVal hPrinter As Long,
    ByVal Level As Long, pPrinter As Byte,
    ByVal Command As Long) As Long

Declare Function SetPrinterData Lib "winspool.drv" Alias
    "SetPrinterDataA" (ByVal hPrinter As Long,
    ByVal pValueName As String, ByVal dwType As Long,
    pData As Byte, ByVal cbData As Long) As Long
```

Table 22–2 contains a brief description of the parameters used in the various print functions and a brief description of their purpose.

Table 22–2   Print Function Parameters and Descriptions

Parameter	Description
cbBuf As Long	Holds number of bytes to read or the size of the buffer.
Command As Long	Uses a JOB_CONTROL_ constant to cancel, pause, restart, or resume a job.
dwType As Long	Uses REG_ constants.
fdwFlags As Long	Uses PRINTER_CHANGE_ constants.
fdwOptions As Long	Set to "0" as a reserved value.
FirstJob As Long	First job in list.
flags As Long	Set to "0" as a reserved value or PRINTER_ENUM_ constant where appropriate.
hChange As Long	Handle to object to change or close.
hPrinter As Long	Handle to a printer object.
hwnd As Long	Handle to the window.
JobId As Long	Job number.
Level As Long	Level value can be set to 1, 2, 3, 4, or 5 dependent upon function.
lpbPorts As Long	Buffer holds PORT_INFO_1 or PORT_INFO_2 structures.
name As String	Name for enumerated printers.
NoJobs As Long	Number of jobs.
nSize As Long	Size of array, in bytes.
pcbNeeded As Long	Pointer to variable to be loaded with actual bytes read or needed buffer size.
pcReturned As Long	Number of structures returned where appropriate.
pData As Byte	References an ADDJOB_INFO_1 structure.
pDatatypes As Byte	Buffer holds DATATYPES_INFO_1 structures.
pDriverDirectory As Byte	Buffer holds path to printer driver directory.
pDriverInfo As Any	Buffer holds DRIVER_INFO_1 or DRIVER_INFO_2 structures.
pDriverInfo As Byte	Buffer holds DRIVER_INFO_ structures.
pDriverName As String	Driver name.
pdwChange As Long	Uses PRINTER_CHANGE_ constants.
pEnvironment As String	Environment of processor, driver, provider, or monitor.
pForm As Byte	References a FORM_INFO_1 structure.
pFormName As String	Form name.
pJob As Byte	Buffer holds JOB_INFO_1 or JOB_INFO_2 structures.
pMonitorName As String	Name of the monitor.
pMonitors As Byte	Buffer holds MONITOR_INFO_1 or MONITOR_INFO_2 structures.
pName As String	Name of the printer or server.
pPathName As String	Path to file holding print processor.
pPortName As String	Port name.
ppPrinterNotifyInfo As Long	Address of buffer containing PRINTER_NOTIFY_INTO and PRINTER_NOTIFY_INFO_DATA structures.
pPrinter As Any	Pointer to structure holding PRINTER_INFO_ data.
pPrinter As Byte	First byte of structure holding PRINTER_INFO_ data structure.
pPrinterEnum As Byte	Buffer contains PRINTER_ENUM_ structures for data.

Table 22–2   Print Function Parameters and Descriptions *(Continued)*

Parameter	Description
pPrinterNotifyOptions As Byte	Buffer holds PRINTER_NOTIFY_OPTIONS structures.
pPrintProcessorInfo As Byte	First byte of structure holding PROVIDER_INFO_1 data.
pPrintProcessorInfo As String	Name of print processor or path of print processor directory.
pPrintProcessorName As String	Print processor name.
pPrintProvidorName As String	Print provider name.
pProvidorInfo As Byte	Buffer holds PROVIDER_INFO_1 structure.
pType As Long	Uses REG_ constants.
pValueName As String	Registry value.
pvReserved As Long	Holds address of PRINTER_NOTIFY_OPTIONS structure.

Many of the parameters described in Table 22–2 use constant values. The Win32api.txt file lists the following constants for the print functions in this chapter.

```
Public Const JOB_CONTROL_DELETE = 5
Public Const JOB_CONTROL_PAUSE = 1
Public Const JOB_CONTROL_RESUME = 2
Public Const JOB_CONTROL_CANCEL = 3
Public Const JOB_CONTROL_RESTART = 4

JOB_NOTIFY_TYPE     'Indicates that the fields specified
                    'in the pFields array are
                    'JOB_NOTIFY_FIELD_* constants.

'Port type constants
Public Const PORT_TYPE_WRITE = &H1
Public Const PORT_TYPE_READ = &H2
Public Const PORT_TYPE_REDIRECTED = &H4
Public Const PORT_TYPE_NET_ATTACHED = &H8

'Printer change constants
Public Const PRINTER_CHANGE_ADD_PRINTER = &H1
Public Const PRINTER_CHANGE_SET_PRINTER = &H2
Public Const PRINTER_CHANGE_DELETE_PRINTER = &H4
Public Const PRINTER_CHANGE_PRINTER = &HFF
Public Const PRINTER_CHANGE_ADD_JOB = &H100
Public Const PRINTER_CHANGE_SET_JOB = &H200
Public Const PRINTER_CHANGE_DELETE_JOB = &H400
Public Const PRINTER_CHANGE_WRITE_JOB = &H800
Public Const PRINTER_CHANGE_JOB = &HFF00
Public Const PRINTER_CHANGE_ADD_FORM = &H10000
Public Const PRINTER_CHANGE_SET_FORM = &H20000
Public Const PRINTER_CHANGE_DELETE_FORM = &H40000
Public Const PRINTER_CHANGE_FORM = &H70000
```

```
Public Const PRINTER_CHANGE_ADD_PORT = &H100000
Public Const PRINTER_CHANGE_CONFIGURE_PORT = &H200000
Public Const PRINTER_CHANGE_DELETE_PORT = &H400000
Public Const PRINTER_CHANGE_PORT = &H700000
Public Const PRINTER_CHANGE_ADD_PRINT_PROCESSOR = &H1000000
Public Const PRINTER_CHANGE_DELETE_PRINT_PROCESSOR = &H4000000
Public Const PRINTER_CHANGE_PRINT_PROCESSOR = &H7000000
Public Const PRINTER_CHANGE_ADD_PRINTER_DRIVER = &H10000000
Public Const PRINTER_CHANGE_DELETE_PRINTER_DRIVER = &H40000000
Public Const PRINTER_CHANGE_PRINTER_DRIVER = &H70000000
Public Const PRINTER_CHANGE_TIMEOUT = &H80000000
Public Const PRINTER_CHANGE_ALL = &H7777FFFF

'Printer enumeration constants
Public Const PRINTER_ENUM_DEFAULT = &H1
Public Const PRINTER_ENUM_LOCAL = &H2
Public Const PRINTER_ENUM_CONNECTIONS = &H4
Public Const PRINTER_ENUM_FAVORITE = &H4
Public Const PRINTER_ENUM_NAME = &H8
Public Const PRINTER_ENUM_REMOTE = &H10
Public Const PRINTER_ENUM_SHARED = &H20
Public Const PRINTER_ENUM_NETWORK = &H40
Public Const PRINTER_ENUM_EXPAND = &H4000
Public Const PRINTER_ENUM_CONTAINER = &H8000
Public Const PRINTER_ENUM_ICONMASK = &HFF0000
Public Const PRINTER_ENUM_ICON1 = &H10000
Public Const PRINTER_ENUM_ICON2 = &H20000
Public Const PRINTER_ENUM_ICON3 = &H40000
Public Const PRINTER_ENUM_ICON4 = &H80000
Public Const PRINTER_ENUM_ICON5 = &H100000
Public Const PRINTER_ENUM_ICON6 = &H200000
Public Const PRINTER_ENUM_ICON7 = &H400000
Public Const PRINTER_ENUM_ICON8 = &H800000

PRINTER_NOTIFY_TYPE      'Indicates that the fields specified
                         'in the pFields array are
                         'PRINTER_NOTIFY_FIELD_* constants.

'Reg Data Types
Public Const REG_NONE =   0 'No value type
Public Const REG_SZ = 1      'Unicode nul terminated string
Public Const REG_EXPAND_SZ = 2 'Unicode nul terminated string
Public Const REG_BINARY = 3    'Free form binary
Public Const REG_DWORD = 4     '32-bit number
Public Const REG_DWORD_LITTLE_ENDIAN = 4 '32-bit number
Public Const REG_DWORD_BIG_ENDIAN = 5    '32-bit number
Public Const REG_LINK = 6      'Symbolic Link (unicode)
Public Const REG_MULTI_SZ = 7  'Multiple Unicode strings
Public Const REG_RESOURCE_LIST = 8 'Resource list in res map
' Resource list in the hardware description
```

```
Public Const REG_FULL_RESOURCE_DESCRIPTOR = 9
Public Const REG_RESOURCE_REQUIREMENTS_LIST = 10
Public Const REG_CREATED_NEW_KEY = &H1    'Key created
Public Const REG_OPENED_EXISTING_KEY = &H2 'Key opened
'Restore whole hive volatile
Public Const REG_WHOLE_HIVE_VOLATILE = &H1
Public Const REG_REFRESH_HIVE = &H2        'Unwind changes
Public Const REG_NOTIFY_CHANGE_NAME = &H1    'Create or delete
Public Const REG_NOTIFY_CHANGE_ATTRIBUTES = &H2
Public Const REG_NOTIFY_CHANGE_LAST_SET = &H4 'Time stamp
Public Const REG_NOTIFY_CHANGE_SECURITY = &H8
Public Const REG_LEGAL_CHANGE_FILTER =
  (REG_NOTIFY_CHANGE_NAME Or
  REG_NOTIFY_CHANGE_ATTRIBUTES Or
  REG_NOTIFY_CHANGE_LAST_SET Or
  REG_NOTIFY_CHANGE_SECURITY)
Public Const REG_LEGAL_OPTION =
  (REG_OPTION_RESERVED Or
  REG_OPTION_NON_VOLATILE Or
  REG_OPTION_VOLATILE Or
  REG_OPTION_CREATE_LINK Or REG_OPTION_BACKUP_RESTORE)

' Reg Create Type Values...
Public Const REG_OPTION_RESERVED = 0       'reserved
Public Const REG_OPTION_NON_VOLATILE = 0 'key preserved
Public Const REG_OPTION_VOLATILE = 1       'key not preserved
Public Const REG_OPTION_CREATE_LINK = 2   'key is symbolic link
Public Const REG_OPTION_BACKUP_RESTORE = 4 'backup or restore
```

In addition to the constants in the previous listing, the print functions in this chapter use several unique structures. The next listing contains those structures unique to these functions.

```
Type ADDJOB_INFO_1
  Path As String
  JobId As Long
End Type

Type DATATYPES_INFO_1
  pName As String
End Type

Type DRIVER_INFO_1
  pName As String
End Type

Type DRIVER_INFO_2
  cVersion As Long
  pName As String
  pEnvironment As String
  pDriverPath As String
```

```
    pDataFile As String
    pConfigFile As String
End Type

Type FORM_INFO_1
    pName As String
    Size As SIZEL
    ImageableArea As RECTL
End Type

Type JOB_INFO_1
    JobId As Long
    pPrinterName As String
    pMachineName As String
    pUserName As String
    pDocument As String
    pDatatype As String
    pStatus As String
    Status As Long
    Priority As Long
    Position As Long
    TotalPages As Long
    PagesPrinted As Long
    Submitted As SYSTEMTIME
End Type

Type JOB_INFO_2
    JobId As Long
    pPrinterName As String
    pMachineName As String
    pUserName As String
    pDocument As String
    pNotifyName As String
    pDatatype As String
    pPrintProcessor As String
    pParameters As String
    pDriverName As String
    pDevMode As DEVMODE
    pStatus As String
    pSecurityDescriptor As SECURITY_DESCRIPTOR
    Status As Long
    Priority As Long
    Position As Long
    StartTime As Long
    UntilTime As Long
    TotalPages As Long
    Size As Long
    Submitted As SYSTEMTIME
    time As Long
    PagesPrinted As Long
End Type
```

```
Type MONITOR_INFO_1
  pName As String
End Type

Type MONITOR_INFO_2
  pName As String
  pEnvironment As String
  pDLLName As String
End Type

Type PRINTER_INFO_1
  flags As Long
  pDescription As String
  pName As String
  pComment As String
End Type

Type PRINTER_INFO_2
  pServerName As String
  pPrinterName As String
  pShareName As String
  pPortName As String
  pDriverName As String
  pComment As String
  pLocation As String
  pDevMode As DEVMODE
  pSepFile As String
  pPrintProcessor As String
  pDatatype As String
  pParameters As String
  pSecurityDescriptor As SECURITY_DESCRIPTOR
  Attributes As Long
  Priority As Long
  DefaultPriority As Long
  StartTime As Long
  UntilTime As Long
  Status As Long
  cJobs As Long
  AveragePPM As Long
End Type

Type PRINTER_INFO_3
  pSecurityDescriptor As SECURITY_DESCRIPTOR
End Type
Type PORT_INFO_1
  pName As String
End Type

Type PORT_INFO_2
  pPortName As String
  pMonitorName As String
  pDescription As String
```

```
        fPortType As Long
        Reserved As Long
    End Type


    Type PROVIDOR_INFO_1
      pName As String
      pEnvironment As String
      pDLLName As String
    End Type


    Type _PRINTER_NOTIFY_OPTIONS {
        Version As Long
        Flags As Long
        Count As Long
        pTypes As PPRINTER_NOTIFY_OPTIONS_TYPE
    End Type


    Type _PRINTER_NOTIFY_OPTIONS_TYPE {
        Type As Integer   'PRINTER_NOTIFY_TYPE or
                          'JOB_NOTIFY_TYPE
        Reserved0 As Integer
        Reserved1 As Long
        Reserved2 As Long
        Count As Long
        pFields As String
    End Type
```

In the next section, we'll examine an application that makes use of several Windows API print functions. Recall that many print functions were discussed in Chapter 21, too.

Example Application

The programming application in this section is a modified variation of the application developed in Chapter 21.

In this application, the ConfigurePort() function is highlighted. The ConfigurePort() function calls the Windows Configure Port dialog box allowing certain port options to be set. All that is needed, in addition to the window handle, is the port information if local ports are to be queried. The null string, *vbNullString*, is used for this purpose.

This Visual Basic project is named Print2.vbp and contains a form for drawing text on and a module file for function declarations. Here are the contents of the Print2.bas module file. The function declarations are simply copied and pasted into this file from the Win32api.txt file provided with your Visual Basic compiler.

```
Declare Function GetProfileString Lib "kernel32" Alias
   "GetProfileStringA" (ByVal lpAppName As String,
   ByVal lpKeyName As String, ByVal lpDefault As String,
   ByVal lpReturnedString As String,
   ByVal nSize As Long) As Long
Declare Function PrinterProperties Lib "winspool.drv"
   (ByVal hwnd As Long, ByVal hPrinter As Long) As Long
Declare Function ConfigurePort Lib "winspool.drv" Alias
   "ConfigurePortA" (ByVal pName As String,
   ByVal hwnd As Long, ByVal pPortName As String) As Long
```

The application uses a form similar to the application in Chapter 21. Information regarding the default printer is entered into the caption fields of three label controls. The port information is also sent to the ConfigurePort() function. Here is the form's supporting code. The file is named Print2.frm.

```
Private Sub Form_Load()
   Dim r&
   Dim ptrnampos%, drvnampos%, tempstart%, tempfinish%
   Dim hPtr&
   Dim profile$, PrinterName$, PrinterDriver$, PrinterPort$

   'profile of default printer info as null terminated string
   profile$ = String$(128, 0)
   r& = GetProfileString("WINDOWS", "DEVICE", "",
                          profile$, 128)
   'string length less null terminator
   tempstart% = InStr(profile$, Chr$(0)) - 1
   profile$ = Left$(profile$, tempstart%)

   'Parse string into three pieces of information
   'Get Printer Name - left portion of string
   ptrnampos% = InStr(profile$, ",")
   tempstart% = ptrnampos% - 1
   PrinterName$ = Left$(profile$, tempstart%)
   Label4.Caption = PrinterName$

   'Get Driver Name - middle portion of string
   drvnampos% = InStr(ptrnampos% + 1, profile$, ",")
   tempstart% = ptrnampos% + 1
   tempfinish% = drvnampos% - ptrnampos% - 1
   PrinterDriver$ = Mid$(profile$, tempstart%, tempfinish%)
   Label5.Caption = PrinterDriver$

   'Get Port - final portion of string
   tempstart% = drvnampos% + 1
   PrinterPort$ = Mid$(profile$, tempstart%)
   Label6.Caption = PrinterPort$

   'Get local port configuration information
   r& = ConfigurePort(vbNullString, hwnd, PrinterPort$)
End Sub
```

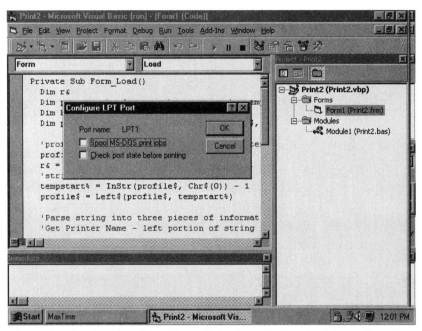

Figure 22–1   The Configure Port dialog box displayed with a call to ConfigurePort().

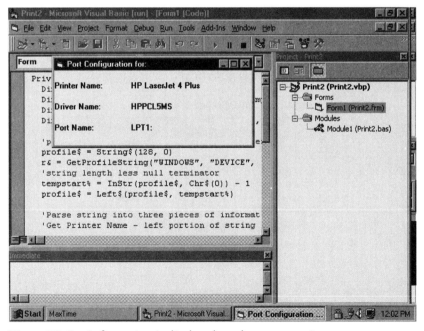

Figure 22–2   Information is displayed on the current printer.

Figure 22–1 shows the Configure Port dialog box.

The printer information is displayed on a small form, as shown in Figure 22–2.

In this and the last chapter you have learned how to obtain the basic information regarding a printer. As an exercise, experiment with other functions such as the functions starting with "Enum." These functions enumerate objects for jobs, monitors, ports, drivers, and printers.

Chapter 23

File: Drive, Directory, and Time

The Windows API provides access to a large number of powerful high-level and low-level functions related to files. In the next three chapters, we'll examine these functions as they relate to Visual Basic programming.

This chapter will investigate those functions most closely associated with file drives, directories, paths, dates, and times. Chapter 24 will investigate registry functions and examine the role they play with file functions. Finally, Chapter 25 will investigate a large number of standard file functions, such as OpenFile(), CloseFile(), ReadFile(), WriteFile(), and so on.

You'll need to study all three chapters to gain a comprehensive understanding of how Windows handles files.

API Drive, Directory, and Time Function Names and Descriptions

Table 23–1 shows 27 popular Windows API drive, directory, path, and file time and date functions. Table 23–1 also provides a brief description to each function's use.

Table 23–1 Drive, Directory, and Time Functions and Descriptions

Function	Description
CompareFileTime	Compares data in FILETIME structures.
CreateDirectory	Creates a directory.
CreateDirectoryEx	Creates a directory with additional capabilities.
DeviceIoControl	Low-level disk operations.
DosDateTimeToFileTime	Converts DOS file info. to FILETIME structure info.
FileTimeToDosDateTime	Converts FILETIME structure info. to DOS file info.
FileTimeToLocalFileTime	Converts FILETIME structure info. to local time format.
FileTimeToSystemTime	Converts FILETIME structure info. to SYSTEMTIME structure info.
GetCurrentDirectory	Gets current directory info.
GetDiskFreeSpace	Gets free space available on disk.
GetDriveType	Gets drive type.
GetFileTime	Gets file date/time information.
GetFullPathName	Gets complete path info. for a file.
GetLogicalDrives	Gets names of all logical drives.
GetLogicalDriveStrings	Gets names of all logical drives.
GetShortPathName	Gets short path info. for a file.
GetSystemDirectory	Gets path to Windows system directory.
GetTempFileName	Gets name of temporary file.
GetTempPath	Gets path info. for temporary file.
GetVolumeInformation	Gets disk volume information.
GetWindowsDirectory	Gets path to Windows directory.
RemoveDirectory	Deletes an empty directory.
SearchPath	Uses Windows search techniques for finding a file.
SetCurrentDirectory	Sets the current directory.
SetFileTime	Sets file date/time information.
SetVolumeLabel	Sets the volume name.
SystemTimeToFileTime	Converts SYSTEMTIME structure info. to FILETIME structure info.

Time and date functions, as they relate to files and directories, are covered in this chapter.

A programming example at the end of this chapter will show you how to use various drive, directory, and path functions to return information on the disk free space, drive type, system directory, logical drives and the Windows directory, and temporary file path.

API Drive, Directory, and Time Function Declarations

The following listing contains the Windows API drive, directory, and time function declarations found in the Win32api.txt file provided with Visual Basic. As we mentioned earlier, there are additional functions related to file operations that are described in Chapters 24 and 25.

```
Declare Function CompareFileTime Lib "kernel32" Alias
  "CompareFileTime" (lpFileTime1 As FILETIME,
  lpFileTime2 As FILETIME) As Long

Declare Function CreateDirectory Lib "kernel32" Alias
  "CreateDirectoryA" (ByVal lpPathName As String,
  lpSecurityAttributes As SECURITY_ATTRIBUTES) As Long

Declare Function CreateDirectoryEx Lib "kernel32" Alias
  "CreateDirectoryExA" (ByVal lpTemplateDirectory As String,
  ByVal lpNewDirectory As String,
  lpSecurityAttributes As SECURITY_ATTRIBUTES) As Long

Declare Function DeviceIoControl Lib "kernel32" Alias
  "DeviceIoControl" (ByVal hDevice As Long,
  ByVal dwIoControlCode As Long, lpInBuffer As Any,
  ByVal nInBufferSize As Long, lpOutBuffer As Any,
  ByVal nOutBufferSize As Long, lpBytesReturned As Long,
  lpOverlapped As OVERLAPPED) As Long

Declare Function DosDateTimeToFileTime Lib "kernel32" Alias
  "DosDateTimeToFileTime" (ByVal wFatDate As Long,
  ByVal wFatTime As Long, lpFileTime As FILETIME) As Long

Declare Function FileTimeToDosDateTime Lib "kernel32" Alias
  "FileTimeToDosDateTime" (lpFileTime As FILETIME,
  ByVal lpFatDate As Long, ByVal lpFatTime As Long) As Long

Declare Function FileTimeToLocalFileTime Lib "kernel32" Alias
  "FileTimeToLocalFileTime" (lpFileTime As FILETIME,
  lpLocalFileTime As FILETIME) As Long

Declare Function FileTimeToSystemTime Lib "kernel32" Alias
  "FileTimeToSystemTime" (lpFileTime As FILETIME,
  lpSystemTime As SYSTEMTIME) As Long

Declare Function GetCurrentDirectory Lib "kernel32" Alias
  "GetCurrentDirectory" (ByVal nBufferLength As Long,
  ByVal lpBuffer As String) As Long

Declare Function GetDiskFreeSpace Lib "kernel32" Alias
  "GetDiskFreeSpaceA" (ByVal lpRootPathName As String,
  lpSectorsPerCluster As Long, lpBytesPerSector As Long,
  lpNumberOfFreeClusters As Long,
  lpTotalNumberOfClusters As Long) As Long

Declare Function GetDriveType Lib "kernel32" Alias
  "GetDriveTypeA" (ByVal nDrive As String) As Long

Declare Function GetFileTime Lib "kernel32" Alias
  "GetFileTime" (ByVal hFile As Long,
```

```
    lpCreationTime As FILETIME, lpLastAccessTime As FILETIME,
    lpLastWriteTime As FILETIME) As Long

Declare Function GetFullPathName Lib "kernel32" Alias
    "GetFullPathNameA" (ByVal lpFileName As String,
    ByVal nBufferLength As Long, ByVal lpBuffer As String,
    ByVal lpFilePart As String) As Long

Declare Function GetLogicalDrives Lib "kernel32" Alias
    "GetLogicalDrives" () As Long

Declare Function GetLogicalDriveStrings Lib "kernel32" Alias
    "GetLogicalDriveStringsA" (ByVal nBufferLength As Long,
    ByVal lpBuffer As String) As Long

Declare Function GetShortPathName Lib "kernel32" Alias
    "GetShortPathName" (ByVal lpszLongPath As String,
    ByVal lpszShortPath As String,
    ByVal cchBuffer As Long) As Long

Declare Function GetSystemDirectory Lib "kernel32" Alias
    "GetSystemDirectoryA" (ByVal lpBuffer As String,
    ByVal nSize As Long) As Long

Declare Function GetTempFileName Lib "kernel32" Alias
    "GetTempFileNameA" (ByVal lpszPath As String,
    ByVal lpPrefixString As String, ByVal wUnique As Long,
    ByVal lpTempFileName As String) As Long

Declare Function GetTempPath Lib "kernel32" Alias
    "GetTempPathA" (ByVal nBufferLength As Long,
    ByVal lpBuffer As String) As Long

Declare Function GetVolumeInformation Lib "kernel32" Alias
    "GetVolumeInformationA" (ByVal lpRootPathName As String,
    ByVal lpVolumeNameBuffer As String,
    ByVal nVolumeNameSize As Long,
    lpVolumeSerialNumber As Long,
    lpMaximumComponentLength As Long,
    lpFileSystemFlags As Long,
    ByVal lpFileSystemNameBuffer As String,
    ByVal nFileSystemNameSize As Long) As Long

Declare Function GetWindowsDirectory Lib "kernel32" Alias
    "GetWindowsDirectoryA" (ByVal lpBuffer As String,
    ByVal nSize As Long) As Long

Declare Function RemoveDirectory Lib "kernel32" Alias
    "RemoveDirectoryA" (ByVal lpPathName As String) As Long

Declare Function SearchPath Lib "kernel32" Alias
    "SearchPathA" (ByVal lpPath As String,
    ByVal lpFileName As String, ByVal lpExtension As String,
```

```
   ByVal nBufferLength As Long, ByVal lpBuffer As String,
   ByVal lpFilePart As String) As Long

Declare Function SetCurrentDirectory Lib "kernel32" Alias
   "SetCurrentDirectoryA" (ByVal lpPathName As String) As Long

Declare Function SetCurrentDirectory Lib "kernel32" Alias
   "SetCurrentDirectoryA" (ByVal lpPathName As String) As Long

Declare Function SetFileTime Lib "kernel32" Alias
   "SetFileTime" (ByVal hFile As Long,
   lpCreationTime As FILETIME, lpLastAccessTime As FILETIME,
   lpLastWriteTime As FILETIME) As Long

Declare Function SetVolumeLabel Lib "kernel32" Alias
   "SetVolumeLabelA" (ByVal lpRootPathName As String,
   ByVal lpVolumeName As String) As Long

Declare Function SystemTimeToFileTime Lib "kernel32" Alias
   "SystemTimeToFileTime" (lpSystemTime As SYSTEMTIME,
   lpFileTime As FILETIME) As Long
```

Table 23–2 contains a brief description of the parameters used in the various drive, directory, and time functions.

Table 23–2 Drive, Directory, and Time Function Parameters and Descriptions

Parameter	Description
cchBuffer As Long	Size of lpszShortPath string.
dwIoControlCode As Long	Uses FSCTL_ constants. (See Table 23–3.)
hDevice As Long	Handle for the device.
hFile As Long	Handle to file.
lpBuffer As String	String to hold current directory info.
lpBytesPerSector As Long	Number of disk bytes/sector.
lpBytesReturned As Long	Number of bytes loaded into output buffer.
lpCreationTime As FILETIME	Structure holds a file's creation time and date info.
lpExtension As String	String holds file extension information.
lpFatDate As Long	Holds file date information.
lpFatTime As Long	Holds file time information.
lpFileName As String	String holds file name.
lpFilePart As String	Holds address of file's file name.
lpFileSystemFlags As Long	Uses FS_ constants.
lpFileSystemNameBuffer As String	String holds file system name.
lpFileTime As FILETIME	Information stored in FILETIME structure.
lpFileTime1 As FILETIME	Information in first structure is compared to that in second.
lpFileTime2 As FILETIME	Information in first structure is compared to that in second.
lpInBuffer As Any	Input buffer used by dwIoControlCode parameter.
lpLastAccessTime As FILETIME	Structure holds file's last access time and date info.
lpLastWriteTime As FILETIME	Structure holds file's last write time and date info.
lpLocalFileTime As FILETIME	Structure holds local time formatted data.

(continued)

Table 23–2   Drive, Directory, and Time Function Parameters and Descriptions *(Continued)*

Parameter	Description
lpMaximumComponentLength As Long	Holds all components of a file name.
lpNewDirectory As String	New directory name.
lpNumberOfFreeClusters As Long	Number of disk clusters free.
lpOutBuffer As Any	Output buffer used by dwIoControlCode parameter.
lpOverlapped As OVERLAPPED	Structure holds data for overlapped device operations.
lpPath As String	Search path. vbNullString used when desiring Windows search path.
lpPathName As String	String holds path to current directory.
lpPrefixString As String	String holds file prefix (i.e., .exe, .bas, etc.).
lpRootPathName As String	Strings holds root path for the disk.
lpSectorsPerCluster As Long	Number of disk sectors/cluster.
lpSecurityAttributes As SECURITY_ATTRIBUTES	Structure holds security information for the directory.
lpSystemTime As SYSTEMTIME	Structure holds system time formatted data.
lpszLongPath As String	String holds file's long path and name.
lpszPath As String	String holds directory information for temporary file.
lpszShortPath As String	String holds file's short path and name.
lpTempFileName As String	String holds temporary file name.
lpTemplateDirectory As String	Directory location from which to copy template. Use vbNullString for none.
lpTotalNumberOfClusters As Long	Number of disk total clusters.
lpVolumeName As String	String holds volume name. vbNullString for none.
lpVolumeNameBuffer As String	String holds name of disk volume.
lpVolumeSerialNumber As Long	Serial number of disk volume.
nBufferLength As Long	lpBuffer length.
nDrive As String	String holds path to root directory.
nFileSystemNameSize As Long	Size of lpFileSystemName.
nInBufferSize As Long	Length of input buffer used by dwIoControlCode parameter.
nOutBufferSize As Long	Length of output buffer used by dwIoControlCode parameter.
nSize As Long	lpBuffer maximum size.
nVolumeNameSize As Long	Size of lpVolumeNameBuffer.
wFatDate As Long	DOS format date data.
wFatTime As Long	DOS format time data.
wUnique As Long	Number appended to prefix string to prevent similar file names.

Many of the parameters described in Table 23–2 use constant values. The Win32api.txt file lists the following constants for these functions:

```
'GetDriveType return values
Public Const DRIVE_REMOVABLE = 2
Public Const DRIVE_FIXED = 3
Public Const DRIVE_REMOTE = 4
```

```
Public Const DRIVE_CDROM = 5
Public Const DRIVE_RAMDISK = 6

'file type
Public Const FILE_TYPE_UNKNOWN = &H0
Public Const FILE_TYPE_DISK = &H1
Public Const FILE_TYPE_CHAR = &H2
Public Const FILE_TYPE_PIPE = &H3
Public Const FILE_TYPE_REMOTE = &H8000

Public Const FS_CASE_IS_PRESERVED = FILE_CASE_PRESERVED_NAMES
Public Const FS_CASE_SENSITIVE = FILE_CASE_SENSITIVE_SEARCH
Public Const FS_UNICODE_STORED_ON_DISK = FILE_UNICODE_ON_DISK
Public Const FS_PERSISTENT_ACLS = FILE_PERSISTENT_ACLS
```

In addition to the constants in the previous listing, several FSTCL_ device constants are described in Table 23–3.

Table 23–3   Device Control Codes and Parameters

Control Codes and Parameters	Description
dwIoControlCode = **FSCTL_DISMOUNT_VOLUME**	Operation code.
lpInBuffer = NULL	Pointer to input buffer; not used; must be (ByVal 0).
nInBufferSize = 0	Size of input buffer; not used; must be zero.
lpOutBuffer	Pointer to output. buffer; not used; must be (ByVal 0).
nOutBufferSize	Size of output buffer; not used; must be zero.
lpBytesReturned	Pointer to DWORD used by Device IoControl function.
dwIoControlCode = **FSCTL_GET_COMPRESSION**	Operation code.
lpInBuffer = NULL	Pointer to input buffer; not used; must be (ByVal 0).
nInBufferSize = 0	Size of input buffer; not used; must be zero.
lpOutBuffer	Pointer to output buffer.
nOutBufferSize	Size of output buffer.
lpBytesReturned	Pointer to actual bytes of output.
dwIoControlCode = **FSCTL_LOCK_VOLUME**	Operation code.
lpInBuffer = NULL	Pointer to input buffer; not used; must be (ByVal 0).
nInBufferSize = 0	Size of input buffer; not used; must be zero.
lpOutBuffer	Pointer to output buffer; not used; must be (ByVal 0).

(continued)

Table 23–3   Device Control Codes and Parameters *(Continued)*

Control Codes and Parameters	Description
nOutBufferSize	Size of output buffer; not used; must be zero.
lpBytesReturned	Pointer to DWORD used by Device IoControl function.
dwIoControlCode = **FSCTL_SET_COMPRESSION**	Operation code.
lpInBuffer	Pointer to input buffer.
nInBufferSize	Size of input buffer.
lpOutBuffer = NULL	Pointer to output buffer; not used; must be (ByVal 0).
nOutBufferSize = 0	Size of output buffer; not used; must be zero.
lpBytesReturned	Pointer to DWORD used by Device IoControl function.
dwIoControlCode = **FSCTL_UNLOCK_VOLUME**	Operation code.
lpInBuffer = NULL	Pointer to input buffer; not used; must be (ByVal 0).
nInBufferSize = 0	Size of input buffer; not used; must be zero.
lpOutBuffer	Pointer to output buffer; not used; must be (ByVal 0).
nOutBufferSize	Size of output buffer; not used; must be zero.
lpBytesReturned	Pointer to DWORD used by Device IoControl function.
dwIoControlCode = **IOCTL_STORAGE_CHECK_VERIFY**	Operation code.
lpInBuffer = NULL	Address of input buffer; not used; must be (ByVal 0).
nInBufferSize = 0	Size of input buffer; not used; must be zero.
lpOutBuffer = NULL	Address of output buffer; not used; must be (ByVal 0).
nOutBufferSize = 0	Size of output buffer; not used; must be zero.
lpBytesReturned	Address of actual bytes of output.
dwIoControlCode = **IOCTL_STORAGE_EJECT_MEDIA**	Operation code.
lpInBuffer = NULL	Address of input buffer; not used; must be (ByVal 0).
nInBufferSize = 0	Size of input buffer; not used; must be zero.

(continued)

Table 23–3   Device Control Codes and Parameters *(Continued)*

Control Codes and Parameters	Description
lpOutBuffer = NULL	Address of output buffer; not used; must be (ByVal 0).
nOutBufferSize = 0	Size of output buffer; not used; must be zero.
lpBytesReturned	Address of actual bytes of output.
dwIoControlCode = **IOCTL_DISK_FORMAT_TRACKS**	Operation code.
lpInBuffer	Address of input buffer.
nInBufferSize	Size of input buffer.
lpOutBuffer = NULL	Address of output buffer; not used; must be (ByVal 0).
nOutBufferSize = 0	Size of output buffer; not used; must be zero.
lpBytesReturned	Address of actual bytes of output.
dwIoControlCode = **IOCTL_DISK_GET_DRIVE_GEOMETRY**	Operation code.
lpInBuffer = NULL	Address of input buffer; not used; must be (ByVal 0).
nInBufferSize = 0	Size of input buffer; not used; must be zero.
lpOutBuffer	Address of output buffer.
nOutBufferSize	Size of output buffer.
lpBytesReturned	Address of actual bytes of output.
dwIoControlCode = **IOCTL_DISK_GET_DRIVE_LAYOUT**	Operation code.
lpInBuffer = NULL	Address of input buffer; not used; must be (ByVal 0).
nInBufferSize = 0	Size of input buffer; not used; must be zero.
lpOutBuffer	Address of output buffer.
nOutBufferSize	Size of output buffer.
lpBytesReturned	Address of actual bytes of output.
dwIoControlCode = **IOCTL_STORAGE_GET_MEDIA_TYPES**	Operation code.
lpInBuffer = NULL	Address of input buffer; not used; must be (ByVal 0).
nInBufferSize = 0	Size of input buffer; not used; must be zero.
lpOutBuffer	Address of output buffer.
nOutBufferSize	Size of output buffer.
lpBytesReturned	Address of actual bytes of output.
dwIoControlCode = **IOCTL_DISK_GET_PARTITION_INFO**	Operation code.
lpInBuffer = NULL	Address of input buffer; not used; must be (ByVal 0).

(continued)

Table 23–3   Device Control Codes and Parameters *(Continued)*

Control Codes and Parameters	Description
nInBufferSize = 0	Size of input buffer; not used; must be zero.
lpOutBuffer	Address of output buffer.
nOutBufferSize	Size of output buffer.
lpBytesReturned	Address of actual bytes of output.
dwIoControlCode = **IOCTL_STORAGE_LOAD_MEDIA**	Operation code.
lpInBuffer = NULL	Address of input buffer; not used; must be (ByVal 0).
nInBufferSize = 0	Size of input buffer; not used; must be zero.
lpOutBuffer = NULL	Address of output buffer; not used; must be (ByVal 0).
nOutBufferSize = 0	Size of output buffer; not used; must be zero.
lpBytesReturned	Address of actual bytes of output.
dwIoControlCode = **IOCTL_STORAGE_MEDIA_REMOVAL**	Operation code.
lpInBuffer	Address of input buffer.
nInBufferSize	Size of input buffer.
lpOutBuffer = NULL	Address of output buffer; not used; must be (ByVal 0).
nOutBufferSize = 0	Size of output buffer; not used; must be zero.
lpBytesReturned	Address of actual bytes of output.
dwIoControlCode = **IOCTL_DISK_PERFORMANCE**	Operation code.
lpInBuffer = NULL	Address of input buffer; not used; must be (ByVal 0).
nInBufferSize = 0	Size of input buffer; not used; must be zero.
lpOutBuffer	Address of output buffer.
nOutBufferSize	Size of output buffer.
lpBytesReturned	Address of actual bytes of output.
dwIoControlCode = **IOCTL_DISK_REASSIGN_BLOCKS**	Operation code.
lpInBuffer	Address of input buffer.
nInBufferSize	Size of input buffer.
lpOutBuffer = NULL	Address of output buffer; not used; must be (ByVal 0).
nOutBufferSize = 0	Size of output buffer; not used; must be zero.
lpBytesReturned	Address of actual bytes of output.

(continued)

Table 23–3 Device Control Codes and Parameters *(Continued)*

Control Codes and Parameters	Description
dwIoControlCode = **IOCTL_DISK_SET_DRIVE_LAYOUT**	Operation code.
lpInBuffer	Address of input buffer.
nInBufferSize	Size of input buffer.
lpOutBuffer = NULL	Address of output buffer; not used; must be (ByVal 0).
nOutBufferSize = 0	Size of output buffer; not used; must be zero.
lpBytesReturned	Address of actual bytes of output.
dwIoControlCode = **IOCTL_DISK_SET_PARTITION_INFO**	Operation code.
lpInBuffer	Address of input buffer.
nInBufferSize	Size of input buffer.
lpOutBuffer = NULL	Address of output buffer; not used; must be (ByVal 0).
nOutBufferSize = 0	Size of output buffer; not used; must be zero.
lpBytesReturned	Address of actual bytes of output.
dwIoControlCode = **IOCTL_DISK_VERIFY**	Operation code.
lpInBuffer	Address of input buffer.
nInBufferSize	Size of input buffer.
lpOutBuffer = NULL	Address of output buffer; not used; must be (ByVal 0).
nOutBufferSize = 0	Size of output buffer; not used; must be zero.
lpBytesReturned	Address of actual bytes of output.
dwIoControlCode = **IOCTL_SERIAL_LSRMST_INSERT**	Operation code.
lpInBuffer	Address of input buffer.
nInBufferSize	Size of input buffer.
lpOutBuffer = NULL	Address of output buffer; not used; must be (ByVal 0).
nOutBufferSize = 0	Size of output buffer; not used; must be zero.
lpBytesReturned	Address of actual bytes of output.

The functions make use of several structures for accessing and storing information. The Win32api.txt file provides the following structure declarations as shown in the next listing.

```
Type FILETIME
   dwLowDateTime As Long
   dwHighDateTime As Long
End Type
```

```
Type SYSTEMTIME
  wYear As Integer
  wMonth As Integer
  wDayOfWeek As Integer
  wDay As Integer
  wHour As Integer
  wMinute As Integer
  wSecond As Integer
  wMilliseconds As Integer
End Type

Type OVERLAPPED
  Internal As Long
  InternalHigh As Long
  Offset As Long
  OffsetHigh As Long
  hEvent As Long
End Type

Type SECURITY_ATTRIBUTES
  nLength As Long
  lpSecurityDescriptor As Long
  bInheritHandle As Long
End Type
```

In the next section, a simple application will illustrate the use of several of these functions.

Example Application

This section contains a programming example that will serve to illustrate the use of six functions selected from the previous sections. These functions return information on the disk free space, drive type, system directory, logical drives, and the Windows directory and temporary file path.

This Visual Basic project is named File1.vbp and uses a form with several label controls for reporting data. The project also uses a module file for declaring constants and functions. The constants and functions shown in the File1.bas module file are copied from the Win32api.txt file provided with your Visual Basic compiler.

```
'GetDriveType return values
Public Const DRIVE_REMOVABLE = 2
Public Const DRIVE_FIXED = 3
Public Const DRIVE_REMOTE = 4
Public Const DRIVE_CDROM = 5
Public Const DRIVE_RAMDISK - 6
```

```
Declare Function GetDiskFreeSpace Lib "kernel32" Alias
  "GetDiskFreeSpaceA" (ByVal lpRootPathName As String,
  lpSectorsPerCluster As Long, lpBytesPerSector As Long,
  lpNumberOfFreeClusters As Long,
  lpTtoalNumberOfClusters As Long) As Long
Declare Function GetDriveType Lib "kernel32" Alias
  "GetDriveTypeA" (ByVal nDrive As String) As Long
Declare Function GetLogicalDrives Lib "kernel32" () As Long
Declare Function GetSystemDirectory Lib "kernel32" Alias
  "GetSystemDirectoryA" (ByVal lpBuffer As String,
  ByVal nSize As Long) As Long
Declare Function GetTempPath Lib "kernel32" Alias
  "GetTempPathA" (ByVal nBufferLength As Long,
  ByVal lpBuffer As String) As Long
Declare Function GetWindowsDirectory Lib "kernel32" Alias
  "GetWindowsDirectoryA" (ByVal lpBuffer As String,
  ByVal nSize As Long) As Long
```

As you can see from the previous listing, this application will use six important functions in order to return system information: GetDiskFreeSpace(), GetDrive-Type(), GetLogicalDrives(), GetSystemDirectory(), GetTempPath(), and GetWin-dowsDirectory().

This project's form contains a Form_Load() subroutine. Six label controls are used to report data to the form via the label's caption property. Note: The form also uses six label controls as labels for each output value. Here is the code that supports these six functions. This file is File1.frm.

```
Private Sub Form_Load()
  Dim r&
  Dim dirdata$, drvdata$
  Dim sectorspercluster&, bytespercluster&
  Dim freeclusters&, totalclusters&
  Dim nBytes As Byte

  nBytes = 255
  dirdata$ = String$(nBytes, 0)
  drvdata$ = String$(nBytes, 0)

  'find Windows directory
  r& = GetWindowsDirectory(dirdata$, nBytes - 1)
  Label7.Caption = dirdata$

  'determine C:\ drives free disk space
  r& = GetDiskFreeSpace("c:\", sectorspercluster,
                        bytespercluster, freeclusters,
                        totalclusters)
  Label8.Caption = Str$(sectorspercluster *
                        bytespercluster * freeclusters)
```

```
'determine C:\ drive type
r& = GetDriveType("c:\")
If r& = DRIVE_REMOVABLE Then
  Label9.Caption = "Removable Drive"
ElseIf r& = DRIVE_FIXED Then
  Label9.Caption = "Fixed Drive"
ElseIf r& = DRIVE_REMOTE Then
  Label9.Caption = "Remote Drive"
ElseIf r& = DRIVE_CDROM Then
  Label9.Caption = "CD-ROM Drive"
End If


'find Windows system directory location
r& = GetSystemDirectory(dirdata$, nBytes - 1)
Label10.Caption = dirdata$


'determine logical drive letters
r& = GetLogicalDrives()
If r& And 1 Then
  drvdata$ = "A"
End If
'build list of drives
If r& And 2 Then
  drvdata$ = drvdata$ + ", B"
End If
If r& And 4 Then
  drvdata$ = drvdata$ + ", C"
End If
If r& And 8 Then
  drvdata$ = drvdata$ + ", D"
End If
If r& And 16 Then
  drvdata$ = drvdata$ + ", E"
End If
If r& And 32 Then
  drvdata$ = drvdata$ + ", F"
End If
If r& And 64 Then
  drvdata$ = drvdata$ + ", G"
End If
Label11.Caption = drvdata$


'find path to Windows temporary directory
r& = GetTempPath(nBytes - 1, dirdata$)
Label12.Caption = dirdata$
End Sub
```

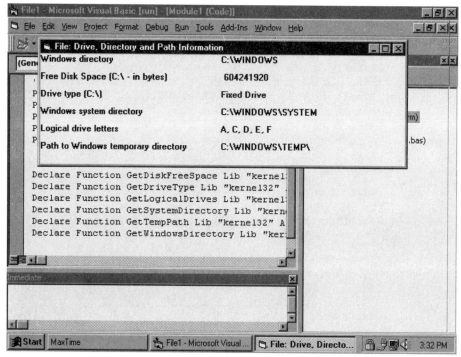

Figure 23–1   Drive, directory, and path information is returned for a typical computer.

The use of each of these functions is straightforward. Experiment with this application and find out information on other drives and directories used by your system. Figure 23–1 shows the information returned for a typical computer.

Chapter 24 continues the study of Windows API file functions by looking at registry functions.

File: Registry Information

The Windows API provides access to a large number of powerful high-level and low-level functions related to files. The previous chapter, this chapter, and the following chapter examine these functions as they relate to Visual Basic programming.

Chapter 23 investigated file drives, directories, paths, dates, and times. This chapter will investigate those functions most closely associated with the Windows registry as they relate to file operations. Chapter 25 will examine a large number of standard file functions, such as OpenFile(), CloseFile(), ReadFile(), WriteFile(), and so on.

You'll need to study all three chapters to gain a comprehensive understanding of how Windows handles files.

API Registry Function Names and Descriptions

Table 24–1 shows 25 popular Windows API registry functions and provides a brief description for their use.

The example application, at the end of this chapter, will illustrate how to open, enumerate, and close a key. The registry contains descriptions for system software

Table 24–1   Registry Functions and Descriptions

Function	Description
RegCloseKey	Closes a key.
RegConnectRegistry	Opens a remote system key.
RegCreateKey	Creates a key.
RegCreateKeyEx	Creates a key with optional security and disposition options.
RegDeleteKey	Deletes a key.
RegDeleteValue	Deletes a key's values.
RegEnumKey	Enumerates subkeys.
RegEnumKeyEx	Enumerates subkeys with optional FILETIME structure data.
RegEnumValue	Enumerates the values of a key.
RegFlushKey	Forces a key change to disk.
RegGetKeySecurity	Gets security data for a key.
RegLoadKey	Loads key registry information.
RegNotifyChangeKeyValue	Notification of a key's value change.
RegOpenKey	Opens a key.
RegOpenKeyEx	Opens a key with optional options.
RegQueryInfoKey	Querys for key information.
RegQueryValue	Querys for a key's values.
RegQueryValueEx	Querys for a key's value with subkey options.
RegReplaceKey	Replaces a key's registry information from a file.
RegRestoreKey	Restores a key's registry information from a file.
RegSaveKey	Saves a key's registry information to a file.
RegSetKeySecurity	Sets a key's security.
RegSetValue	Sets the values for a key.
RegSetValueEx	Sets the values for a key with specific data options.
RegUnLoadKey	Unloads a remote system's key.

and hardware. This application will list the first three PCMCIA devices installed on a computer.

API Registry Function Declarations

The following listing contains the Windows API registry function declarations found in the Win32api.txt file provided with Visual Basic. You will need to study the functions provided in Chapters 23 and 25 to gain a complete understanding of file operations.

```
Declare Function RegCloseKey Lib "advapi32.dll" Alias
   "RegCloseKey" (ByVal hKey As Long) As Long

Declare Function RegConnectRegistry Lib "advapi32.dll"
   Alias "RegConnectRegistryA" (ByVal lpMachineName As String,
   ByVal hKey As Long, phkResult As Long) As Long
```

```
Declare Function RegCreateKey Lib "advapi32.dll" Alias
  "RegCreateKeyA" (ByVal hKey As Long,
  ByVal lpSubKey As String, phkResult As Long) As Long

Declare Function RegCreateKeyEx Lib "advapi32.dll" Alias
  "RegCreateKeyExA" (ByVal hKey As Long,
  ByVal lpSubKey As String, ByVal Reserved As Long,
  ByVal lpClass As String, ByVal dwOptions As Long,
  ByVal samDesired As Long,
  lpSecurityAttributes As SECURITY_ATTRIBUTES,
  phkResult As Long, lpdwDisposition As Long) As Long

Declare Function RegDeleteKey Lib "advapi32.dll" Alias
  "RegDeleteKeyA" (ByVal hKey As Long,
  ByVal lpSubKey As String) As Long

Declare Function RegDeleteValue Lib "advapi32.dll" Alias
  "RegDeleteValueA" (ByVal hKey As Long,
  ByVal lpValueName As String) As Long

Declare Function RegEnumKey Lib "advapi32.dll" Alias
  "RegEnumKeyA" (ByVal hKey As Long, ByVal dwIndex As Long,
  ByVal lpName As String, ByVal cbName As Long) As Long

Declare Function RegEnumKeyEx Lib "advapi32.dll" Alias
  "RegEnumKeyExA" (ByVal hKey As Long, ByVal dwIndex As Long,
  ByVal lpName As String, lpcbName As Long, lpReserved As Long,
  ByVal lpClass As String, lpcbClass As Long,
  lpftLastWriteTime As FILETIME) As Long

Declare Function RegEnumValue Lib "advapi32.dll" Alias
  "RegEnumValueA" (ByVal hKey As Long, ByVal dwIndex As Long,
  ByVal lpValueName As String, lpcbValueName As Long,
  lpReserved As Long, lpType As Long, lpData As Byte,
  lpcbData As Long) As Long

Declare Function RegFlushKey Lib "advapi32.dll" Alias
  "RegFlushKey" (ByVal hKey As Long) As Long

Declare Function RegGetKeySecurity Lib "advapi32.dll" Alias
  "RegGetKeySecurity" (ByVal hKey As Long,
  ByVal SecurityInformation As Long,
  pSecurityDescriptor As SECURITY_DESCRIPTOR,
  lpcbSecurityDescriptor As Long) As Long

Declare Function RegLoadKey Lib "advapi32.dll" Alias
  "RegLoadKeyA" (ByVal hKey As Long,
  ByVal lpSubKey As String, ByVal lpFile As String) As Long

Declare Function RegNotifyChangeKeyValue Lib "advapi32.dll"
  Alias "RegNotifyChangeKeyValue" (ByVal hKey As Long,
  ByVal bWatchSubtree As Long, ByVal dwNotifyFilter As Long,
  ByVal hEvent As Long, ByVal fAsynchronus As Long) As Long
```

```
Declare Function RegOpenKey Lib "advapi32.dll" Alias
  "RegOpenKeyA" (ByVal hKey As Long, ByVal lpSubKey As String,
  phkResult As Long) As Long

Declare Function RegOpenKeyEx Lib "advapi32.dll" Alias
  "RegOpenKeyExA" (ByVal hKey As Long,
  ByVal lpSubKey As String, ByVal ulOptions As Long,
  ByVal samDesired As Long, phkResult As Long) As Long

Declare Function RegQueryInfoKey Lib "advapi32.dll" Alias
  "RegQueryInfoKeyA" (ByVal hKey As Long,
  ByVal lpClass As String, lpcbClass As Long,
  lpReserved As Long, lpcSubKeys As Long,
  lpcbMaxSubKeyLen As Long, lpcbMaxClassLen As Long,
  lpcValues As Long, lpcbMaxValueNameLen As Long,
  lpcbMaxValueLen As Long, lpcbSecurityDescriptor As Long,
  lpftLastWriteTime As FILETIME) As Long

Declare Function RegQueryValue Lib "advapi32.dll" Alias
  "RegQueryValueA" (ByVal hKey As Long,
  ByVal lpSubKey As String, ByVal lpValue As String,
  lpcbValue As Long) As Long

Declare Function RegQueryValueEx Lib "advapi32.dll" Alias
  "RegQueryValueExA" (ByVal hKey As Long,
  ByVal lpValueName As String, ByVal lpReserved As Long,
  lpType As Long, lpData As Any, lpcbData As Long) As Long

Declare Function RegReplaceKey Lib "advapi32.dll" Alias
  "RegReplaceKeyA" (ByVal hKey As Long,
  ByVal lpSubKey As String, ByVal lpNewFile As String,
  ByVal lpOldFile As String) As Long

Declare Function RegRestoreKey Lib "advapi32.dll" Alias
  "RegRestoreKeyA" (ByVal hKey As Long,
  ByVal lpFile As String, ByVal dwFlags As Long) As Long

Declare Function RegSaveKey Lib "advapi32.dll" Alias
  "RegSaveKeyA" (ByVal hKey As Long, ByVal lpFile As String,
  lpSecurityAttributes As SECURITY_ATTRIBUTES) As Long

Declare Function RegSetKeySecurity Lib "advapi32.dll" Alias
  "RegSetKeySecurity" (ByVal hKey As Long,
  ByVal SecurityInformation As Long,
  pSecurityDescriptor As SECURITY_DESCRIPTOR) As Long

Declare Function RegSetValue Lib "advapi32.dll" Alias
  "RegSetValueA" (ByVal hKey As Long,
  ByVal lpSubKey As String, ByVal dwType As Long,
  ByVal lpData As String, ByVal cbData As Long) As Long

Declare Function RegSetValueEx Lib "advapi32.dll" Alias
  "RegSetValueExA" (ByVal hKey As Long,
```

```
     ByVal lpValueName As String, ByVal Reserved As Long,
     ByVal dwType As Long, lpData As Any,
     ByVal cbData As Long) As Long

  Declare Function RegUnLoadKey Lib "advapi32.dll" Alias
     "RegUnLoadKeyA" (ByVal hKey As Long,
     ByVal lpSubKey As String) As Long
```

Table 24–2 contains a brief desciption of the parameters used in the various registry functions.

Table 24–2   Registry Function Parameters and Descriptions

Parameter	Description
bWatchSubtree As Long	If TRUE, watch key and subkeys.
cbData As Long	Value holds length of lpData string.
cbName As Long	Value holds length of lpName string.
dwFlags As Long	Uses either REG_WHOLE_HIVE_VOLATILE or zero for normal file operation.
dwIndex As Long	The subkey's index. Index starts at 0.
dwNotifyFilter As Long	Uses REG_NOTIFY_CHANGE_ constants, such as NAME, ATTRIBUTES, LAST_SET, or SECURITY.
dwOptions As Long	Uses one of the following constants: REG_OPTION_NON_ VOLATILE, REG_OPTION_VOLATILE, or REG_OPTION_BACKUP_RESTORE.
dwType As Long	Set to REG_SZ constant.
fAsynchronus As Long	hEvent is signaled immediately if nonzero. If zero, hEvent is signaled upon a change only.
hEvent As Long	Handle of event.
hKey As Long	Handle of key or HKEY_CLASSES_ROOT, HKEY_CURRENT_USER, HKEY_LOCAL_MACHINE, HKEY_USERS.
lpcbClass As Long	Value holds length of lpClass string.
lpcbData As Long	Holds length of lpData string. Return value holds actual string length loaded.
lpcbMaxClassLen As Long	Holds length of longest class name.
lpcbMaxSubKeyLen As Long	Holds length of longest subkey name.
lpcbMaxValueLen As Long	Value holds largest data value for key.
lpcbMaxValueNameLen As Long	Value holds length of longest subkey name.
lpcbName As Long	Holds length of lpName string. Return value holds actual string length loaded.
lpcbSecurityDescriptor As Long	Holds length of pSecurityDescriptor buffer. Return value holds actual bytes loaded.
lpcbValue As Long	Holds length of lpValue string. Return value holds actual string length loaded.
lpcbValueName As Long	Holds length of lpValueName string. Return value holds actual string length loaded.

(continued)

Table 24–2   Registry Function Parameters and Descriptions *(Continued)*

Parameter	Description
lpClass As String	Key's class name.
lpcSubKeys As Long	Value holds number of subkeys.
lpcValues As Long	Value holds number of values for key.
lpData As Any	Value holds data for function.
lpData As String	String holds data for function.
lpdwDisposition As Long	Uses REG_CREATED_NEW_KEY or REG_OPENED_EXISTING_ KEY constant.
lpFile As String	String holds registration information.
lpftLastWriteTime As FILETIME	Structure holds data for last file update.
lpMachineName As String	String holds system name for connection.
lpName As String	String holds key name.
lpNewFile As String	String holds new file registration info.
lpOldFile As String	String holds present file registration info.
lpReserved As Long	Reserved value; set to 0.
lpSecurityAttributes As SECURITY_ATTRIBUTES	Structure holds Windows NT security description for key.
lpSubKey As String	String holds name of subkey.
lpType As Long	Holds type code: REG_BINARY, REG_DWORD, REG_DWORD_ LITTLE_ENDIAN, REG_DWORD_BIG_ENDIAN, REG_EX- PAND_SZ, REG_LINK, REG_MULTI_SZ, REG_NONE, REG_RESOURCE_LIST, or REG_SZ.
lpValue As String	String holds value for key.
lpValueName As String	String holds name of value.
phkResult As Long	Holds handle of subkey.
pSecurityDescriptor As SECURITY_DESCRIPTOR	Structure holds key's security information.
Reserved As Long	Set to 0; reserved value.
samDesired As Long	Uses KEY_ constant.
SecurityInformation As Long	Flag used to request information; OWNER_SECURITY_ INFORMATION, GROUP_SECURITY_INFORMATION, DACL_SECURITY_INFORMATION, SACL_SECURITY_INFORMATION.
ulOptions As Long	Reserved value; set to 0.

Many of the parameters described in Table 24–2 use constant values. The Win32api.txt file lists the following constants for registry functions.

```
'constants for Windows 32-bit Registry API
Public Const HKEY_CLASSES_ROOT = &H80000000
Public Const HKEY_CURRENT_USER = &H80000001
Public Const HKEY_LOCAL_MACHINE = &H80000002
Public Const HKEY_USERS = &H80000003
```

```
Public Const HKEY_PERFORMANCE_DATA = &H80000004
Public Const HKEY_CURRENT_CONFIG = &H80000005
Public Const HKEY_DYN_DATA = &H80000006

'Reg Key Security Options
Public Const READ_CONTROL = &H20000
Public Const KEY_QUERY_VALUE = &H1
Public Const KEY_SET_VALUE = &H2
Public Const KEY_CREATE_SUB_KEY = &H4
Public Const KEY_ENUMERATE_SUB_KEYS = &H8
Public Const KEY_NOTIFY = &H10
Public Const KEY_CREATE_LINK = &H20
Public Const KEY_READ = ((STANDARD_RIGHTS_READ Or
                         KEY_QUERY_VALUE Or
                         KEY_ENUMERATE_SUB_KEYS Or
                         KEY_NOTIFY) And (Not SYNCHRONIZE))
Public Const KEY_WRITE = ((STANDARD_RIGHTS_WRITE Or
                         KEY_SET_VALUE Or
                         KEY_CREATE_SUB_KEY) And
                         (Not SYNCHRONIZE))
Public Const KEY_EXECUTE = (KEY_READ)
Public Const KEY_ALL_ACCESS = ((STANDARD_RIGHTS_ALL Or
                             KEY_QUERY_VALUE Or
                             KEY_SET_VALUE Or
                             KEY_CREATE_SUB_KEY Or
                             KEY_ENUMERATE_SUB_KEYS Or
                             KEY_NOTIFY Or
                             KEY_CREATE_LINK) And
                             (Not SYNCHRONIZE))
Public Const STANDARD_RIGHTS_READ = (READ_CONTROL)
Public Const STANDARD_RIGHTS_WRITE = (READ_CONTROL)
Public Const KEY_EXECUTE = ((KEY_READ) And (Not SYNCHRONIZE))

'Registry API Constants
'Reg Data Types...
Public Const REG_NONE = 0    'No value type
Public Const REG_SZ = 1      'Unicode nul terminated string
Public Const REG_EXPAND_SZ = 2 'Unicode nul terminated string
Public Const REG_BINARY = 3 'Free form binary
Public Const REG_DWORD = 4   '32-bit number
'32-bit number (same as REG_DWORD)

Public Const REG_DWORD_LITTLE_ENDIAN = 4
Public Const REG_DWORD_BIG_ENDIAN = 5    '32-bit number
Public Const REG_LINK = 6            'Symbolic Link (unicode)
Public Const REG_MULTI_SZ = 7       'Multiple Unicode strings
'Resource list in the resource map
Public Const REG_RESOURCE_LIST = 8
'Resource list in the hardware description
```

```
Public Const REG_FULL_RESOURCE_DESCRIPTOR = 9
Public Const REG_RESOURCE_REQUIREMENTS_LIST = 10
'New Registry Key created
Public Const REG_CREATED_NEW_KEY = &H1
'Existing Key opened
Public Const REG_OPENED_EXISTING_KEY = &H2
'Restore whole hive volatile
Public Const REG_WHOLE_HIVE_VOLATILE = &H1
'Unwind changes to last flush
Public Const REG_REFRESH_HIVE = &H2
'Create or delete (child)
Public Const REG_NOTIFY_CHANGE_NAME = &H1

Public Const REG_NOTIFY_CHANGE_ATTRIBUTES = &H2
Public Const REG_NOTIFY_CHANGE_LAST_SET = &H4      'Time stamp
Public Const REG_NOTIFY_CHANGE_SECURITY = &H8
Public Const REG_LEGAL_CHANGE_FILTER=(REG_NOTIFY_CHANGE_NAME
                         Or REG_NOTIFY_CHANGE_ATTRIBUTES
                         Or REG_NOTIFY_CHANGE_LAST_SET
                         Or REG_NOTIFY_CHANGE_SECURITY)
Public Const REG_LEGAL_OPTION = (REG_OPTION_RESERVED Or
                         REG_OPTION_NON_VOLATILE Or
                         REG_OPTION_VOLATILE Or
                         REG_OPTION_CREATE_LINK Or
                         REG_OPTION_BACKUP_RESTORE)
'Reg Create Type Values...
'Parameter is reserved
Public Const REG_OPTION_RESERVED = 0
'Key is preserved when system is rebooted
Public Const REG_OPTION_NON_VOLATILE = 0
'Key is not preserved when system is rebooted
Public Const REG_OPTION_VOLATILE = 1
'Created key is a symbolic link
Public Const REG_OPTION_CREATE_LINK = 2
'open for backup or restore
Public Const REG_OPTION_BACKUP_RESTORE = 4

'Current security descriptor revision value
Public Const SECURITY_DESCRIPTOR_REVISION = (1)
Public Const SECURITY_DESCRIPTOR_REVISION1 = (1)

Public Const SECURITY_DESCRIPTOR_MIN_LENGTH = (20)

Public Const SE_OWNER_DEFAULTED = &H1
Public Const SE_GROUP_DEFAULTED = &H2
Public Const SE_DACL_PRESENT = &H4
Public Const SE_DACL_DEFAULTED = &H8
Public Const SE_SACL_PRESENT = &H10
```

```
Public Const SE_SACL_DEFAULTED = &H20
Public Const SE_SELF_RELATIVE = &H8000


'SE_OWNER_DEFAULTED - This boolean flag, when set, indicates
'that the SID pointed to by the Owner field was provided by a
'defaulting mechanism rather than explicitly provided by the
'original provider of the security descriptor. This may
'affect the treatment of the SID with respect to inheritance
'of an owner.
'
'SE_GROUP_DEFAULTED - This boolean flag, when set, indicates
'that the SID in the Group field was provided by a defaulting
'mechanism rather than explicitly provided by the original
'provider of the security descriptor. This may affect the
'treatment of the SID with respect to inheritance of a
'primary group.
'
'SE_DACL_PRESENT - This boolean flag, when set, indicates
'that the security descriptor contains a discretionary ACL.
'If this flag is set and the Dacl field of the
'SECURITY_DESCRIPTOR is null, then a null ACL is explicitly
'being specified.
'
'SE_DACL_DEFAULTED - This boolean flag, when set, indicates
'that the ACL pointed to by the Dacl field was provided by a
'defaulting mechanism rather than explicitly provided by the
'original provider of the security descriptor. This may
'affect the treatment of the ACL with respect to inheritance
'of an ACL. This flag is ignored if the DaclPresent flag is
'not set.
'
'SE_SACL_PRESENT - This boolean flag, when set, indicates
'that the security descriptor contains a system ACL pointed
'to by the Sacl field. If this flag is set and the Sacl
'field of the SECURITY_DESCRIPTOR is null, then an empty
'(but present) ACL is being specified.
'
'SE_SACL_DEFAULTED - This boolean flag, when set, indicates
'that the ACL pointed to by the Sacl field was provided by a
'defaulting mechanism rather than explicitly provided by the
'original provider of the security descriptor. This may
'affect the treatment of the ACL with respect to inheritance
'of an ACL. This flag is ignored if the SaclPresent flag is
'not set.
'
'SE_SELF_RELATIVE - This boolean flag, when set, indicates
'that the security descriptor is in self-relative form. In
```

```
'this form, all fields of the security descriptor are
'contiguous in memory and all pointer fields are expressed
'as offsets from the beginning of the security descriptor.
'This form is useful for treating security descriptors as
'opaque data structures for transmission in communication
'protocol or for storage on secondary media.
```

These functions also use several structures which can also be found in the Win32api.txt file. The following listing contains the structures for the functions in this chapter.

```
Type FILETIME
   dwLowDateTime As Long
   dwHighDateTime As Long
End Type

Type SECURITY_ATTRIBUTES
   nLength As Long
   lpSecurityDescriptor As Long
   bInheritHandle As Long
End Type

Type SECURITY_DESCRIPTOR
   Revision As Byte
   Sbz1 As Byte
   Control As Long
   Owner As Long
   Group As Long
   Sacl As ACL
   Dacl As ACL
End Type

'Where:
'
'Revision - Contains the revision level of the security
'descriptor. This allows this structure to be passed between
'systems or stored on disk even though it is expected to
'change in the future.
'
'Control - A set of flags which qualify the meaning of the
'security descriptor or individual fields of the security
'descriptor.
'
'Owner - is a pointer to an SID representing an object's
'owner. If this field is null, then no owner SID is
'present in the security descriptor. If the security
'descriptor is in self-relative form, then this field
'contains an offset to the SID, rather than a pointer.
'
'Group - is a pointer to an SID representing an object's
```

```
'primary group. If this field is null, then no primary
'group SID is present in the security descriptor. If the
'security descriptor is in self-relative form, then this
'field contains an offset to the SID, rather than a pointer.
'
'Sacl - is a pointer to a system ACL. This field value is
'only valid if the DaclPresent control flag is set. If the
'SaclPresent flag is set and this field is null, then a null
'ACL is specified. If the security descriptor is in
'self-relative form, then this field contains an offset to
'the ACL, rather than a pointer.
'
'Dacl - is a pointer to a discretionary ACL. This field
'value is only valid if the DaclPresent control flag is set.
'If the DaclPresent flag is set and this field is null, then
'a null ACL (unconditionally granting access) is specified.
'If the security descriptor is in self-relative form, then
'this field contains an offset to the ACL, rather than a
'pointer.
```

In the next section, a simple application will illustrate the use of several of these functions.

Example Application

This application will illustrate how to open, enumerate, and close a key. The registry contains descriptions for system software and hardware. This application will list the first three PCMCIA devices installed on a computer. Other registry items that can be enumerated include installed fonts, software, ports, printers, and so on.

This Visual Basic project is named File2.vbp and uses a form with several label controls for reporting data. The project also uses a module file for declaring constants and functions. The constants and functions shown in the File2.bas module file are copied from the Win32api.txt file provided with your Visual Basic compiler.

```
Type FILETIME
   dwLowDateTime As Long
   dwHighDateTime As Long
End Type

'--------
'ADVAPI32
'--------
'function prototypes, constants, and type definitions
'for Windows 32-bit Registry API
```

```
'HKEY_ types
Public Const HKEY_CLASSES_ROOT = &H80000000
Public Const HKEY_CURRENT_USER = &H80000001
Public Const HKEY_LOCAL_MACHINE = &H80000002
Public Const HKEY_USERS = &H80000003
Public Const HKEY_PERFORMANCE_DATA = &H80000004
Public Const HKEY_CURRENT_CONFIG = &H80000005
Public Const HKEY_DYN_DATA = &H80000006

Public Const SYNCHRONIZE = &H100000

'Reg Key Security Options
Public Const READ_CONTROL = &H20000
Public Const KEY_QUERY_VALUE = &H1
Public Const KEY_SET_VALUE = &H2
Public Const KEY_CREATE_SUB_KEY = &H4
Public Const KEY_ENUMERATE_SUB_KEYS = &H8
Public Const KEY_NOTIFY = &H10
Public Const KEY_CREATE_LINK = &H20
Public Const KEY_READ = ((READ_CONTROL Or KEY_QUERY_VALUE Or
KEY_ENUMERATE_SUB_KEYS Or KEY_NOTIFY) And (Not SYNCHRONIZE))
Public Const KEY_WRITE = ((STANDARD_RIGHTS_WRITE Or
KEY_SET_VALUE Or KEY_CREATE_SUB_KEY) And (Not SYNCHRONIZE))
Public Const KEY_EXECUTE = (KEY_READ)
Public Const STANDARD_RIGHTS_READ = (READ_CONTROL)
Public Const STANDARD_RIGHTS_WRITE = (READ_CONTROL)

Declare Function RegCloseKey Lib "advapi32.dll"
  (ByVal hKey As Long) As Long
Declare Function RegEnumKeyEx Lib "advapi32.dll" Alias
  "RegEnumKeyExA" (ByVal hKey As Long, ByVal dwIndex As Long,
  ByVal lpName As String, lpcbName As Long,
  lpReserved As Long, ByVal lpClass As String,
  lpcbClass As Long, lpftLastWriteTime As FILETIME) As Long
Declare Function RegOpenKeyEx Lib "advapi32.dll" Alias
  "RegOpenKeyExA" (ByVal hKey As Long,
  ByVal lpSubKey As String, ByVal ulOptions As Long,
  ByVal samDesired As Long, phkResult As Long) As Long
```

As you can see from the previous listing, this application will use three important functions in order to return information from the registry: RegCloseKey(), RegEnumKeyEx(), and RegOpenKeyEx().

This project's form contains a Form_Load() subroutine. Three label controls are used to report data to the form via the label's caption property. Note: The form also uses three label controls as labels for each output value. Here is the code that supports the registry function calls. This file is File2.frm

```
Private Sub Form_Load()
    Dim r&
```

```
Dim hKey&, res&
Dim KeyName$, ClassName$
Dim KeySize&, ClassSize&
Dim FileTimeDate As FILETIME

KeySize& = 64
ClassSize& = 64
KeyName$ = String$(KeySize, 0)
ClassName$ = String$(ClassSize, 0)

'open key to installed PCMCIA device area
r& = RegOpenKeyEx(HKEY_CURRENT_CONFIG, "Enum\PCMCIA",
                  0, KEY_READ, hKey&)

'if exists, get first PCMCIA device
r& = RegEnumKeyEx(hKey&, 0, KeyName$, KeySize, res&,
                  ClassName$, ClassSize, FileTimeDate)
If r& = 0 Then Label7.Caption = KeyName$
  Else Label7.Caption = "(none)"

'if exists, get second PCMCIA device
r& = RegEnumKeyEx(hKey&, 1, KeyName$, KeySize, res&,
                  ClassName$, ClassSize, FileTimeDate)
```

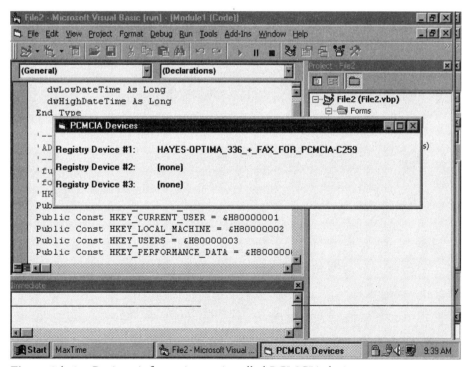

Figure 24–1 Registry information on installed PCMCIA devices.

```
    If r& = 0 Then Label8.Caption = KeyName$
      Else Label8.Caption = "(none)"

    'if exists, get third PCMCIA device
    r& = RegEnumKeyEx(hKey&, 2, KeyName$, KeySize, res&,
                      ClassName$, ClassSize, FileTimeDate)
    If r& = 0 Then Label9.Caption = KeyName$
      Else Label9.Caption = "(none)"

    RegCloseKey (hKey&)
End Sub
```

The use of each of these registry functions is straightforward. You'll notice that the enumeration index values are "hard wired" into the function call. This function could be placed in a loop, with the index value being replaced with a variable.

Test your understanding of this application by using a different registry key to enumerate fonts or installed software. Figure 24–1 shows the information returned for a typical computer.

Chapter 25 continues the study of Windows API file functions. In this chapter we'll examine standard functions that open, close, read, and write to standard Windows files.

Chapter **25**

File: File Operation
Functions

As you have learned in the previous two chapters, the Windows API provides access to a large number of powerful high-level and low-level functions related to files. The previous two chapters and this chapter examine these functions as they relate to Visual Basic programming.

Chapter 23 investigated file drives, directories, paths, dates, and times. Chapter 24 examined those functions most closely associated with the Windows registry as they relate to file operations. This chapter will look at a large number of standard file functions, such as CreateFile(), CloseHandle(), ReadFile(), WriteFile(), and so on.

You'll need to study all three chapters to gain a comprehensive understanding of how Windows handles files.

API File Function Names and Descriptions

Table 25–1 shows 50 frequently used Windows API registry functions and provides a brief description for their use. A number of 16-bit functions are provided in the Win32api.txt file for compatibility purposes. In this book, only Win32 functions are discussed. For example, CreateFile() should be used in place of the

Win16 OpenFile() function and CloseHandle() in place of the Win16 CloseFile() function.

Table 25–1   File Operation Functions and Descriptions

Function	Description
CloseHandle	Closes objects such as files, mappings, and so on.
CopyFile	Copies a file.
CreateFile	Creates a file.
CreateFileMapping	Creates a file mapping object.
DeleteFile	Deletes a file.
DuplicateHandle	Duplicates an object handle.
FindClose	Closes a FindFirstFile() search handle.
FindFirstFile	Finds the first file matching a file name.
FindNextFile	Finds the next file matching a file name.
FlushFileBuffers	Flushes the file buffer.
FlushViewOfFile	Flushes file mapping buffer data.
GetBinaryType	Finds if a file is executable.
GetCompressedFileSize	Gets compressed files size in bytes.
GetExpandedName	Gets full name of a compressed file.
GetFileAttributes	Gets a file's attributes.
GetFileInformationByHandle	Gets file information into a data structure.
GetFileSize	Gets a file's size.
GetFileType	Gets a file's type.
GetFileVersionInfo	Gets a file's version information.
GetFileVersionInfoSize	Gets the size of a buffer needed to hold a file's version information.
GetOverlappedResult	Gets the state of the overlapped operation.
LockFile	Locks a region in a file preventing other processes from accessing the region.
LockFileEx	Same as LockFile() with extended capabilities.
LZClose	Closes a file opened by LZOpenFile().
LZCopy	Copies a file. Compressed files are decompressed during copy operation.
LZInit	Initializes buffers needed for file decompression.
LZOpenFile	Creates, opens, reopens, or deletes the file or compressed file.
LZRead	Reads data from file into a buffer.
LZSeek	Sets the position for a file read or write operation.
MapViewOfFile	Maps a view of a file into the address space of the calling process.
MapViewOfFileEx	Same as MapViewOfFile() with extended capabilities.
MoveFile	Moves a file.
MoveFileEx	Same as MoveFile() with extended capabilities.
OpenFileMapping	Opens a file-mapping object.
QueryDosDevice	Applications can obtain information about MS-DOS device names.
ReadFile	Reads data from a file.
ReadFileEx	Same as ReadFile() with extended capabilities.
SetEndOfFile	Sets the end of file position.
SetFileAttributes	Sets a file's attributes.
SetFilePointer	Sets the pointer position for read and write operations.
UnlockFile	Unlocks a region in an open file allowing other processes to access the region.

Table 25–1   File Operation Functions and Descriptions *(Continued)*

Function	Description
UnlockFileEx	Same as UnlockFile() with extended capabilities.
UnmapViewOfFile	Unmaps a mapped view of a file from the calling process's address space.
UnmapViewOfFile	Same as UnmapViewOfFile() with extended capabilities.
VerFindFile	Finds where to install a file based on whether it locates another version of the file in the system.
VerInstallFile	Tries to install the file based on information returned from the VerFindFile() function.
VerLanguageName	Gets a description string for the language associated with a binary Microsoft language identifier.
VerQueryValue	Gets selected version information from the version-information resource.
WriteFile	Writes data to a file. Designed for both synchronous and asynchronous operation.
WriteFileEx	Similar to WriteFile() with extended capabilities.

The most frequently used functions from this extensive list include Create-File(), CloseHandle(), ReadFile(), WriteFile(), and others. The example application at the end of this chapter will illustrate several of these functions.

API File Operation Function Declarations

The following listing contains the Windows API file operation function declarations found in the Win32api.txt file provided with Visual Basic. As we mentioned earlier, there are additional functions related to file operations that are described in Chapters 23 and 24.

```
Declare Function CloseHandle Lib "kernel32" Alias
  "CloseHandle" (ByVal hObject As Long) As Long

Declare Function CopyFile Lib "kernel32" Alias
  "CopyFileA" (ByVal lpExistingFileName As String,
  ByVal lpNewFileName As String,
  ByVal bFailIfExists As Long) As Long

Declare Function CreateFile Lib "kernel32" Alias
  "CreateFileA" (ByVal lpFileName As String,
  ByVal dwDesiredAccess As Long, ByVal dwShareMode As Long,
  lpSecurityAttributes As SECURITY_ATTRIBUTES,
  ByVal dwCreationDisposition As Long,
  ByVal dwFlagsAndAttributes As Long,
  ByVal hTemplateFile As Long) As Long
```

```
Declare Function CreateFileMapping Lib "kernel32" Alias
  "CreateFileMappingA" (ByVal hFile As Long,
  lpFileMappigAttributes As SECURITY_ATTRIBUTES,
  ByVal flProtect As Long, ByVal dwMaximumSizeHigh As Long,
  ByVal dwMaximumSizeLow As Long,
  ByVal lpName As String) As Long

Declare Function DeleteFile Lib "kernel32" Alias
  "DeleteFileA" (ByVal lpFileName As String) As Long

Declare Function DuplicateHandle Lib "kernel32" Alias
  "DuplicateHandle" (ByVal hSourceProcessHandle As Long,
  ByVal hSourceHandle As Long, ByVal

Declare Function FindClose Lib "kernel32" Alias
  "FindClose" (ByVal hFindFile As Long) As Long

Declare Function FindFirstFile Lib "kernel32" Alias
  "FindFirstFileA" (ByVal lpFileName As String,
  lpFindFileData As WIN32_FIND_DATA) As Long

Declare Function FindNextFile Lib "kernel32" Alias
  "FindNextFileA" (ByVal hFindFile As Long,
  lpFindFileData As WIN32_FIND_DATA) As Long

Declare Function FlushFileBuffers Lib "kernel32" Alias
  "FlushFileBuffers" (ByVal hFile As Long) As Long

Declare Function FlushViewOfFile Lib "kernel32" Alias
  "FlushViewOfFile" (lpBaseAddress As Any,
  ByVal dwNumberOfBytesToFlush As Long) As Long

Declare Function GetBinaryType Lib "kernel32" Alias
  "GetBinaryTypeA" (ByVal lpApplicationName As String,
  lpBinaryType As Long) As Long

Declare Function GetCompressedFileSize Lib "kernel32"
  Alias "GetCompressedFileSizeA" (ByVal lpFileName As String,
  lpFileSizeHigh As Long) As Long

Declare Function GetExpandedName Lib "lz32.dll" Alias
  "GetExpandedNameA" (ByVal lpszSource As String,
  ByVal lpszBuffer As String) As Long

Declare Function GetFileAttributes Lib "kernel32" Alias
  "GetFileAttributesA" (ByVal lpFileName As String) As Long

Declare Function GetFileInformationByHandle Lib "kernel32"
  Alias "GetFileInformationByHandle" (ByVal hFile As Long,
  lpFileInformation As BY_HANDLE_FILE_INFORMATION) As Long

Declare Function GetFileSize Lib "kernel32" Alias
  "GetFileSize" (ByVal hFile As Long,
  lpFileSizeHigh As Long) As Long
```

```
Declare Function GetFileType Lib "kernel32" Alias
  "GetFileType" (ByVal hFile As Long) As Long

Declare Function GetFileVersionInfo Lib "version.dll"
  Alias "GetFileVersionInfoA"
  (ByVal lptstrFilename As String, ByVal dwHandle As Long,
  ByVal dwLen As Long, lpData As Any) As Long

Declare Function GetFileVersionInfoSize Lib "version.dll"
  Alias "GetFileVersionInfoSizeA"
  (ByVal lptstrFilename As String,
  lpdwHandle As Long) As Long

Declare Function GetOverlappedResult Lib "kernel32" Alias
  "GetOverlappedResult" (ByVal hFile As Long,
  lpOverlapped As OVERLAPPED,
  lpNumberOfBytesTransferred As Long,
  ByVal bWait As Long) As Long

Declare Function LockFile Lib "kernel32" Alias "LockFile"
  (ByVal hFile As Long, ByVal dwFileOffsetLow As Long,
  ByVal dwFileOffsetHigh As Long,
  ByVal nNumberOfBytesToLockLow As Long,
  ByVal nNumberOfBytesToLockHigh As Long) As Long

Declare Function LockFileEx Lib "kernel32" Alias "LockFileEx"
  (ByVal hFile As Long, ByVal dwFlags As Long,
  ByVal dwReserved As Long,
  ByVal nNumberOfBytesToLockLow As Long,
  ByVal nNumberOfBytesToLockHigh As Long,
  lpOverlapped As OVERLAPPED) As Long

Declare Sub LZClose Lib "lz32.dll"
  Alias "LZClose" (ByVal hfFile As Long)

Declare Function LZCopy Lib "lz32.dll" Alias "LZCopy"
  (ByVal hfSource As Long, ByVal hfDest As Long) As Long

Declare Function LZInit Lib "lz32.dll" Alias "LZInit"
  (ByVal hfSrc As Long) As Long

Declare Function LZOpenFile Lib "lz32.dll" Alias
  "LZOpenFileA" (ByVal lpszFile As String,
  lpOf As OFSTRUCT, ByVal style As Long) As Long

Declare Function LZRead Lib "lz32.dll" Alias "LZRead"
  (ByVal hfFile As Long, ByVal lpvBuf As String,
  ByVal cbread As Long) As Long

Declare Function LZSeek Lib "lz32.dll" Alias "LZSeek"
  (ByVal hfFile As Long, ByVal lOffset As Long,
  ByVal nOrigin As Long) As Long
```

```
Declare Function MapViewOfFile Lib "kernel32"
  Alias "MapViewOfFile" (ByVal hFileMappingObject As Long,
  ByVal dwDesiredAccess As Long,
  ByVal dwFileOffsetHigh As Long,
  ByVal dwFileOffsetLow As Long,
  ByVal dwNumberOfBytesToMap As Long) As Long

Declare Function MapViewOfFileEx Lib "kernel32"
  Alias "MapViewOfFileEx" (ByVal hFileMappingObject As Long,
  ByVal dwDesiredAccess As Long,
  ByVal dwFileOffsetHigh As Long,
  ByVal dwFileOffsetLow As Long,
  ByVal dwNumberOfBytesToMap As Long,
  lpBaseAddress As Any) As Long

Declare Function MoveFile Lib "kernel32"
  Alias "MoveFileA" (ByVal lpExistingFileName As String,
  ByVal lpNewFileName As String) As Long

Declare Function MoveFileEx Lib "kernel32"
  Alias "MoveFileExA" (ByVal lpExistingFileName As String,
  ByVal lpNewFileName As String,
  ByVal dwFlags As Long) As Long

Declare Function OpenFileMapping Lib "kernel32"
  Alias "OpenFileMappingA" (ByVal dwDesiredAccess As Long,
  ByVal bInheritHandle As Long,
  ByVal lpName As String) As Long

Declare Function QueryDosDevice Lib "kernel32"
  Alias "QueryDosDeviceA" (ByVal lpDeviceName As String,
  ByVal lpTargetPath As String,
  ByVal ucchMax As Long) As Long

Declare Function ReadFile Lib "kernel32"
  Alias "ReadFile" (ByVal hFile As Long,
  lpBuffer As Any, ByVal nNumberOfBytesToRead As Long,
  lpNumberOfBytesRead As Long,
  lpOverlapped As OVERLAPPED) As Long

Declare Function ReadFileEx Lib "kernel32"
  Alias "ReadFileEx" (ByVal hFile As Long,
  lpBuffer As Any, ByVal nNumberOfBytesToRead As Long,
  lpOverlapped As OVERLAPPED,
  ByVal lpCompletionRoutine As Long) As Long

Declare Function SetEndOfFile Lib "kernel32"
  Alias "SetEndOfFile" (ByVal hFile As Long) As Long

Declare Function SetFileAttributes Lib "kernel32"
  Alias "SetFileAttributesA" (ByVal lpFileName As String,
  ByVal dwFileAttributes As Long) As Long
```

```
Declare Function SetFilePointer Lib "kernel32"
  Alias "SetFilePointer" (ByVal hFile As Long,
  ByVal lDistanceToMove As Long,
  lpDistanceToMoveHigh As Long,
  ByVal dwMoveMethod As Long) As Long

Declare Function UnlockFile Lib "kernel32"
  Alias "UnlockFile" (ByVal hFile As Long,
  ByVal dwFileOffsetLow As Long,
  ByVal dwFileOffsetHigh As Long,
  ByVal nNumberOfBytesToUnlockLow As Long,
  ByVal nNumberOfBytesToUnlockHigh As Long) As Long

Declare Function UnlockFileEx Lib "kernel32"
  Alias "UnlockFileEx" (ByVal hFile As Long,
  ByVal dwReserved As Long,
  ByVal nNumberOfBytesToUnlockLow As Long,
  ByVal nNumberOfBytesToUnlockHigh As Long,
  lpOverlapped As OVERLAPPED) As Long

Declare Function UnmapViewOfFile Lib "kernel32"
  Alias "UnmapViewOfFile" (lpBaseAddress As Any) As Long

Declare Function UnmapViewOfFile Lib "kernel32"
  Alias "UnmapViewOfFile" (lpBaseAddress As Any) As Long

Declare Function VerFindFile Lib "version.dll"
  Alias "VerFindFileA" (ByVal uFlags As Long,
  ByVal szFileName As String, ByVal szWinDir As String,
  ByVal szAppDir As String, ByVal szCurDir As String,
  lpuCurDirLen As Long, ByVal szDestDir As String,
  lpuDestDirLen As Long) As Long

Declare Function VerInstallFile Lib "version.dll"
  Alias " VerInstallFileA" (ByVal uFlags As Long,
  ByVal szSrcFileName As String,
  ByVal szDestFileName As String,
  ByVal szSrcDir As String, ByVal szDestDir As String,
  ByVal szCurDir As String, ByVal szTmpFile As String,
  lpuTmpFileLen As Long) As Long

Declare Function VerLanguageName Lib "kernel32"
  Alias "VerLanguageNameA" (ByVal wLang As Long,
  ByVal szLang As String, ByVal nSize As Long) As Long

Declare Function VerQueryValue Lib "version.dll"
  Alias "VerQueryValue" (pBlock As Any,
  ByVal lpSubBlock As String, ByVal lplpBuffer As Long,
  puLen As Long) As Long

Declare Function WriteFile Lib "kernel32"
  Alias "WriteFile" (ByVal hFile As Long,
  lpBuffer As Any,
```

```
     ByVal nNumberOfBytesToWrite As Long,
     lpNumberOfBytesWritten As Long,
     lpOverlapped As OVERLAPPED) As Long

  Declare Function WriteFileEx Lib "kernel32"
     Alias "WriteFileEx" (ByVal hFile As Long,
     lpBuffer As Any,
     ByVal nNumberOfBytesToWrite As Long,
     lpOverlapped As OVERLAPPED,
     ByVal lpCompletionRoutine As Long) As Long
```

Table 25–2 contains a brief description of the parameters used in the various file operations functions.

Table 25–2   File Operation Function Parameters and Descriptions

Parameter	Description
bFailIfExists As Long	Boolean flag. TRUE (nonzero); else FALSE (zero).
bInheritHandle As Long	Boolean flag. TRUE (nonzero) if handle can be inherited, else FALSE (zero).
bWait As Long	Boolean flag. TRUE (nonzero) wait for asynchronous operation to finish; else FALSE (zero) to return immediately.
cbread As Long	lpvBuf size.
dwCreationDisposition As Long	Operation uses CREATE_ALWAYS, CREATE_NEW, OPEN_ALWAYS, OPEN_EXISTING, or TRUNCATE_EXISTING constant.
dwDesiredAccess As Long	Operation uses GENERIC_READ and/or GENERIC_WRITE constant. Use "0" for device information only.
dwFileAttributes As Long	Uses FILE_ATTRIBUTE_ constants.
dwFileOffsetHigh As Long	High 32-bit offset of region.
dwFileOffsetLow As Long	Low 32-bit offset of region.
dwFlags As Long	Uses a LOCKFILE_ or MOVEFILE_ constant for appropriate function call.
dwFlagsAndAttributes As Long	Operation uses a FILE_ATTRIBUTE_, FILE_FLAG_, or SECURITY_ constant.
dwHandle As Long	Not used by Win32.
dwLen As Long	Size of byte array.
dwMaximumSizeHigh As Long	Maximum file mapping size in high 32 bits.
dwMaximumSizeLow As Long	Maximum file mapping size in low 32 bits.
dwMoveMethod As Long	Uses a FILE_BEGIN, FILE_CURRENT, or FILE_END constant.
dwNumberOfBytesToFlush As Long	Number of bytes to flush.
dwNumberOfBytesToMap As Long	Number of bytes to map.
dwReserved As Long	Use "0" under Win32.
dwShareMode As Long	Operation uses FILE_SHARE_READ and/or FILE_SHARE_WRITE constant. Use "0" for no sharing.
flProtect As Long	Uses PAGE_ or SEC_ constants.
hfDest As Long	Handle of destination file.
hfFile As Long	Handle of file to close.

Table 25–2   File Operation Function Parameters and Descriptions *(Continued)*

Parameter	Description
hFile As Long	Handle of file for finding or mapping.
hFileMappingObject As Long	Handle to a file mapping object.
hFindFile As Long	Handle for search file.
hfSource As Long	Handle of source file.
hfSrc As Long	Handle to a file.
hObject As Long	Handle of an object, such as a file.
hTemplateFile As Long	Handle of file containing extended attributes.
lDistanceToMove As Long	File offset in bytes.
lpApplicationName As String	String holds file's path name information.
lpAppName As String	String holds name of section to set.
lpBaseAddress As Any	Pointer to a base address.
lpBinaryType As Long	Uses an SCS_ constant.
lpBuffer As Any	Pointer to memory area for read or write operation.
lpCompletionRoutine As Long	Pointer to completion routine called when the read operation is complete and the calling thread is in an alertable wait state.
lpData As Any	First location in buffer to hold version information.
lpDistanceToMoveHigh As Long	Long composes of high double word offset.
lpdwHandle As Long	Use "0" under Win32.
lpExistingFileName As String	String containing a source file name.
lpFileInformation As BY_HANDLE_ FILE_INFORMATION	Structure holds file information.
lpFileMappingAttributes As SECURITY_ATTRIBUTES	Structure holds security mapping information.
lpFileName As String	String containing a file name.
lpFileSizeHigh As Long	High 32 bits of a file size.
lpFindFileData As WIN32_FIND_DATA	Structure holds data on found file.
lpKeyName As String	The key name to set.
lplpBuffer As Long	Address of buffer to load with version information.
lpName As String	String holds name of file mapping object.
lpNewFileName As String	String containing a destination file name.
lpNumberOfBytesRead As Long	Number of bytes read from a file.
lpNumberOfBytesTransferred As Long	Number of bytes transferred.
lpNumberOfBytesWritten As Long	Number of bytes actually written.
lpOf As OFSTRUCT	Structure holds file information.
lpOverlapped As OVERLAPPED	Structure holds data for overlapped or I/O operation.
lpSecurityAttributes As SECURITY_ATTRIBUTES	Structure holds file's security definition.
lpString As Any	Holds group of key and value strings.
lpSubBlock As String	Use \ for root block. Function gets pointer to the VS_ FIXEDFILEINFO structure.
	Use \VarFileInfo\Translation. Gives the translation table in the variable information structure.

(continued)

Table 25–2   File Operation Function Parameters and Descriptions *(Continued)*

Parameter	Description
	Use \StringFileInfo\lang-charset\string-name. Gives a value in a language-specific structure. The name is a concatenation of a language and character-set identifier pair found in the translation table for the resource.
lpszBuffer As String	String buffer holds expanded file name information.
lpszFile As String	String holds a file name.
lpszKeyName As String	The key name to set.
lpszSection As String	Section where new string is written.
lpszSource As String	String holds a compressed source file name.
lpszString As String	The value written for the key.
lptstrFilename As String	String holds file name.
lpuCurDirLen As Long	Length of szCurrDir string buffer.
lpuDestDirLen As Long	Length of szDestDir string buffer.
lpuTmpFileLen As Long	Length of temporary file buffer.
lpvBuf As String	Pointer to memory location for read or write operations.
nNumberOfBytesToLockHigh As Long	High 32 bits of value in locked region.
nNumberOfBytesToLockLow As Long	Low 32 bits of value in locked region.
nNumberOfBytesToRead As Long	Number of bytes to read.
nNumberOfBytesToUnlockHigh As Long	High 32 bits of value in locked region.
nNumberOfBytesToUnlockLow As Long	Low 32 bits of value in locked region.
nNumberOfBytesToWrite As Long	Number of bytes to write.
nSize As Long	SzLang buffer length.
pBlock As Any	First location in memory holding version information.
puLen As Long	Length of data accessed by lplpBuffer.
style As Long	Uses OF_ constant.
szAppDir As String	String holds path name of application's directory.
szCurDir As String	String holds directory for file's location.
szDestDir As String	String holds directory for destination file.
szDestFileName As String	String holds a valid destination file name.
szFileName As String	String holds a valid file name.
szLang As String	String holds name of an actual language.
szSrcDir As String	Strings holds source directory name.
szSrcFileName As String	String contains a valid file name.
szTmpFile As String	String holds name of temporary file copy.
szWinDir As String	String holds Windows directory.
uFlags As Long	Use VFFF_ISSHAREDFILE to indicate sharable file. Install file function can use VIFF_FORCEINSTALL or VIFF_DONT-DELETEOLD.
wBytes As Long	Number of bytes to read or write.
wLang As Long	Language identification value. Uses LANG_ constant.

Many of the parameters described in Table 25–2 use constant values. The Win32api.txt file lists the following constants for file operation parameters:

```
Public Const CREATE_NEW = 1
Public Const CREATE_ALWAYS = 2
Public Const OPEN_EXISTING = 3
Public Const OPEN_ALWAYS = 4
Public Const TRUNCATE_EXISTING = 5

Public Const FILE_ATTRIBUTE_READONLY = &H1
Public Const FILE_ATTRIBUTE_HIDDEN = &H2
Public Const FILE_ATTRIBUTE_SYSTEM = &H4
Public Const FILE_ATTRIBUTE_DIRECTORY = &H10
Public Const FILE_ATTRIBUTE_ARCHIVE = &H20
Public Const FILE_ATTRIBUTE_NORMAL = &H80
Public Const FILE_ATTRIBUTE_TEMPORARY = &H100
Public Const FILE_ATTRIBUTE_COMPRESSED = &H800

Public Const FILE_FLAG_WRITE_THROUGH = &H80000000
Public Const FILE_FLAG_OVERLAPPED = &H40000000
Public Const FILE_FLAG_NO_BUFFERING = &H20000000
Public Const FILE_FLAG_RANDOM_ACCESS = &H10000000
Public Const FILE_FLAG_SEQUENTIAL_SCAN = &H8000000
Public Const FILE_FLAG_DELETE_ON_CLOSE = &H4000000
Public Const FILE_FLAG_BACKUP_SEMANTICS = &H2000000
Public Const FILE_FLAG_POSIX_SEMANTICS = &H1000000

Public Const FILE_BEGIN = 0
Public Const FILE_CURRENT = 1
Public Const FILE_END = 2

Public Const GENERIC_READ = &H80000000
Public Const GENERIC_WRITE = &H40000000
Public Const GENERIC_EXECUTE = &H20000000
Public Const GENERIC_ALL = &H10000000

'Primary language IDs.
Public Const LANG_NEUTRAL = &H0
Public Const LANG_BULGARIAN = &H2
Public Const LANG_CHINESE = &H4
Public Const LANG_CROATIAN = &H1A
Public Const LANG_CZECH = &H5
Public Const LANG_DANISH = &H6
Public Const LANG_DUTCH = &H13
Public Const LANG_ENGLISH = &H9
Public Const LANG_FINNISH = &HB
Public Const LANG_FRENCH = &HC
Public Const LANG_GERMAN = &H7
Public Const LANG_GREEK = &H8
Public Const LANG_HUNGARIAN = &HE
Public Const LANG_ICELANDIC = &HF
```

```
Public Const LANG_ITALIAN = &H10
Public Const LANG_JAPANESE = &H11
Public Const LANG_KOREAN = &H12
Public Const LANG_NORWEGIAN = &H14
Public Const LANG_POLISH = &H15
Public Const LANG_PORTUGUESE = &H16
Public Const LANG_ROMANIAN = &H18
Public Const LANG_RUSSIAN = &H19
Public Const LANG_SLOVAK = &H1B
Public Const LANG_SLOVENIAN = &H24
Public Const LANG_SPANISH = &HA
Public Const LANG_SWEDISH = &H1D
Public Const LANG_TURKISH = &H1F

'Sublanguage IDs.
'The name immediately following SUBLANG_ dictates which
'primary language ID that sublanguage ID can be combined
'with to form a valid language ID.
Public Const SUBLANG_NEUTRAL = &H0      'language neutral
Public Const SUBLANG_DEFAULT = &H1      'user default
Public Const SUBLANG_SYS_DEFAULT = &H2 'system default
'Chinese (Taiwan):
Public Const SUBLANG_CHINESE_TRADITIONAL = &H1
'Chinese (PR China):
Public Const SUBLANG_CHINESE_SIMPLIFIED = &H2
'Chinese (Hong Kong):
Public Const SUBLANG_CHINESE_HONGKONG = &H3
'Chinese (Singapore):
Public Const SUBLANG_CHINESE_SINGAPORE = &H4
Public Const SUBLANG_DUTCH = &H1   'Dutch
Public Const SUBLANG_DUTCH_BELGIAN = &H2 'Dutch (Belgian)
Public Const SUBLANG_ENGLISH_US = &H1  'English (USA)
Public Const SUBLANG_ENGLISH_UK = &H2  'English (UK)
Public Const SUBLANG_ENGLISH_AUS = &H3 'English (Australian)
Public Const SUBLANG_ENGLISH_CAN = &H4 'English (Canadian)
Public Const SUBLANG_ENGLISH_NZ = &H5  'English (New Zealand)
Public Const SUBLANG_ENGLISH_EIRE = &H6 'English (Irish)
Public Const SUBLANG_FRENCH = &H1       'French
Public Const SUBLANG_FRENCH_BELGIAN = &H2 'French (Belgian)
Public Const SUBLANG_FRENCH_CANADIAN = &H3 'French (Canadian)
Public Const SUBLANG_FRENCH_SWISS = &H4   'French (Swiss)
Public Const SUBLANG_GERMAN = &H1           'German
Public Const SUBLANG_GERMAN_SWISS = &H2    'German (Swiss)
Public Const SUBLANG_GERMAN_AUSTRIAN = &H3 'German (Austrian)
Public Const SUBLANG_ITALIAN = &H1          'Italian
Public Const SUBLANG_ITALIAN_SWISS = &H2   'Italian (Swiss)
'Norwegian (Bokma):
Public Const SUBLANG_NORWEGIAN_BOKMAL = &H1
'Norwegian (Nynorsk):
```

```
Public Const SUBLANG_NORWEGIAN_NYNORSK = &H2
Public Const SUBLANG_PORTUGUESE = &H2      'Portuguese
'Portuguese (Brazilian):
Public Const SUBLANG_PORTUGUESE_BRAZILIAN = &H1
Public Const SUBLANG_SPANISH = &H1     'Spanish (Castilian)
Public Const SUBLANG_SPANISH_MEXICAN = &H2 'Spanish (Mexican)
Public Const SUBLANG_SPANISH_MODERN = &H3   'Spanish (Modern)

Public Const LOCKFILE_FAIL_IMMEDIATELY = &H1
Public Const LOCKFILE_EXCLUSIVE_LOCK = &H2

Public Const MOVEFILE_REPLACE_EXISTING = &H1
Public Const MOVEFILE_COPY_ALLOWED = &H2
Public Const MOVEFILE_DELAY_UNTIL_REBOOT = &H4

'OpenFile() Flags
Public Const OF_READ = &H0
Public Const OF_WRITE = &H1
Public Const OF_READWRITE = &H2
Public Const OF_SHARE_COMPAT = &H0
Public Const OF_SHARE_EXCLUSIVE = &H10
Public Const OF_SHARE_DENY_WRITE = &H20
Public Const OF_SHARE_DENY_READ = &H30
Public Const OF_SHARE_DENY_NONE = &H40
Public Const OF_PARSE = &H100
Public Const OF_DELETE = &H200
Public Const OF_VERIFY = &H400
Public Const OF_CANCEL = &H800
Public Const OF_CREATE = &H1000
Public Const OF_PROMPT = &H2000
Public Const OF_EXIST = &H4000
Public Const OF_REOPEN = &H8000

'ImmSetCompositionString Capability bits
Public Const SCS_CAP_COMPSTR = &H1
Public Const SCS_CAP_MAKEREAD = &H2

Public Const SECURITY_NULL_RID = &H0
Public Const SECURITY_WORLD_RID = &H0
Public Const SECURITY_LOCAL_RID = &H0
Public Const SECURITY_CREATOR_OWNER_RID = &H0
Public Const SECURITY_CREATOR_GROUP_RID = &H1

Public Const SECURITY_DIALUP_RID = &H1
Public Const SECURITY_NETWORK_RID = &H2
Public Const SECURITY_BATCH_RID = &H3
Public Const SECURITY_INTERACTIVE_RID = &H4
Public Const SECURITY_SERVICE_RID = &H6
Public Const SECURITY_ANONYMOUS_LOGON_RID = &H7
Public Const SECURITY_LOGON_IDS_RID = &H5
Public Const SECURITY_LOCAL_SYSTEM_RID = &H12
```

```
Public Const SECURITY_NT_NON_UNIQUE = &H15
Public Const SECURITY_BUILTIN_DOMAIN_RID = &H20

'VerInstallFile() flags:
Public Const VIFF_FORCEINSTALL = &H1
Public Const VIFF_DONTDELETEOLD = &H2
Public Const VIF_TEMPFILE = &H1&
Public Const VIF_MISMATCH = &H2&
Public Const VIF_SRCOLD = &H4&
Public Const VIF_DIFFLANG = &H8&
Public Const VIF_DIFFCODEPG = &H10&
Public Const VIF_DIFFTYPE = &H20&
Public Const VIF_WRITEPROT = &H40&
Public Const VIF_FILEINUSE = &H80&
Public Const VIF_OUTOFSPACE = &H100&
Public Const VIF_ACCESSVIOLATION = &H200&
Public Const VIF_SHARINGVIOLATION = &H400&
Public Const VIF_CANNOTCREATE = &H800&
Public Const VIF_CANNOTDELETE = &H1000&
Public Const VIF_CANNOTRENAME = &H2000&
Public Const VIF_CANNOTDELETECUR = &H4000&
Public Const VIF_OUTOFMEMORY = &H8000&
Public Const VIF_CANNOTREADSRC = &H10000
Public Const VIF_CANNOTREADDST = &H20000
Public Const VIF_BUFFTOOSMALL = &H40000
```

The file operation functions also incorporate a number of unique structures for returning and storing data. The following listing contains the structures unique to the file operations functions:

```
Type BY_HANDLE_FILE_INFORMATION
  dwFileAttributes As Long
  ftCreationTime As FILETIME
  ftLastAccessTime As FILETIME
  ftLastWriteTime As FILETIME
  dwVolumeSerialNumber As Long
  nFileSizeHigh As Long
  nFileSizeLow As Long
  nNumberOfLinks As Long
  nFileIndexHigh As Long
  nFileIndexLow As Long
End Type

'OpenFile() Structure
Type OFSTRUCT
  cBytes As Byte
  fFixedDisk As Byte
  nErrCode As Integer
  Reserved1 As Integer
  Reserved2 As Integer
```

```
      szPathName(OFS_MAXPATHNAME) As Byte
End Type

Type OVERLAPPED
  Internal As Long
  InternalHigh As Long
  Offset As Long
  OffsetHigh As Long
  hEvent As Long
End Type

Type SECURITY_ATTRIBUTES
  nLength As Long
  lpSecurityDescriptor As Long
  bInheritHandle As Long
End Type

Type VS_FIXEDFILEINFO
  dwSignature As Long
  dwStrucVersion As Long    'e.g. 0x00000042 = "0.42"
  dwFileVersionMS As Long   'e.g. 0x00030075 = "3.75"
  dwFileVersionLS As Long   'e.g. 0x00000031 = "0.31"
  dwProductVersionMS As Long 'e.g. 0x00030010 = "3.10"
  dwProductVersionLS As Long 'e.g. 0x00000031 = "0.31"
  dwFileFlagsMask As Long   '= 0x3F for version "0.42"
  dwFileFlags As Long       'e.g. VFF_DEBUG Or VFF_PRERELEASE
  dwFileOS As Long          'e.g. VOS_DOS_WINDOWS16
  dwFileType As Long        'e.g. VFT_DRIVER
  dwFileSubtype As Long     'e.g. VFT2_DRV_KEYBOARD
  dwFileDateMS As Long      'e.g. 0
  dwFileDateLS As Long      'e.g. 0
End Type

Type WIN32_FIND_DATA
  dwFileAttributes As Long
  ftCreationTime As FILETIME
  ftLastAccessTime As FILETIME
  ftLastWriteTime As FILETIME
  nFileSizeHigh As Long
  nFileSizeLow As Long
  dwReserved0 As Long
  dwReserved1 As Long
  cFileName As String * MAX_PATH
  cAlternate As String * 14
End Type
```

In the next section we'll examine an application that will demonstrate the use of several file operation functions.

Example Application

This section contains a programming example that illustrates the use of the Close-Handle(), CreateFile(), and WriteFile() file operation functions.

This Visual Basic project is named File3.vbp and contains a blank form and a module file for constants and function declarations. Here are the contents of the File3.bas module file. The constant and function declarations are simply copied and pasted into this file from the Win32api.txzt file provided with your Visual Basic compiler.

```
Public Const CREATE_ALWAYS = 2
Public Const FILE_ATTRIBUTE_NORMAL = &H80
Public Const GENERIC_WRITE = &H40000000

Declare Function CloseHandle Lib "kernel32"
  (ByVal hObject As Long) As Long

'CreateFile() modified to allow a NULL to be passed
'to lpSecurityAttributes parameter.
Declare Function CreateFile Lib "kernel32" Alias
  "CreateFileA" (ByVal lpFileName As String,
  ByVal dwDesiredAccess As Long, ByVal dwShareMode As Long,
  ByVal lpSecurityAttributes As Long,
  ByVal dwCreationDisposition As Long,
  ByVal dwFlagsAndAttributes As Long,
  ByVal hTemplateFile As Long) As Long

'WriteFile() modified to allow a NULL to be passed
'to lpOverlapped parameter.
Declare Function WriteFile Lib "kernel32"
  (ByVal hFile As Long, lpBuffer As Any,
  ByVal nNumberOfBytesToWrite As Long,
  lpNumberOfBytesWritten As Long,
  ByVal lpOverlapped As Long) As Long
```

As you can see from the previous listing, the application will access three file operation functions.

The project's form, while not visible, contains a Form_Load() subroutine as shown in the following listing. This file is named File3.frm.

```
Private Sub Form_Load()
  Dim r&
  Dim hFile&, datasent&
  Dim FileName$, FileData$

  Form1.Hide  'no need to show blank form.

  FileName$="c:\Sample.txt"
  FileData$="This is text that will be written to the file."
```

```
    'Create new file and get file handle
    hFile = CreateFile(FileName$, GENERIC_WRITE, 0,
                        0, CREATE_ALWAYS,
                        FILE_ATTRIBUTE_NORMAL, 0)

    'Write the string to the new file
    r& = WriteFile(hFile, ByVal FileData$,
                    Len(FileData$), datasent&, 0)

    'Close the file
    r& = CloseHandle(hFile)
End Sub
```

This application will create a file named Sample.txt in the root directory of the C: drive. The CreateFile() file function is used to return a file handle, *hFile*. If you examine the previous listing, note that the function declaration has been modified slightly to permit a NULL value (0) to be passed ByVal as the dwFlagsAndAttributes parameter. Windows 95 does not support security checking.

A short string of data is written to the empty file by using the WriteFile() function. This function was also modified to allow a NULL value to be passed as its last parameter, since the write operation will not occur asynchronously.

Finally, the file is closed by calling the CloseHandle() function.

After the program executes, check your root directory on the C: drive for the file. Since this is a text file, it can be read with a generic word processor or printed to the screen or printer.

You can extend this simple application by using the ReadFile() function to read the contents of the same file and write them to the current form.

For further practice, experiment with the GetFileVersionInfo() and GetFile-Type() functions. They can provide interesting and useful information on files you read or write to.

Chapter 26

Character and String Functions

The Windows API allows access to a large number of character and string functions designed to handle ANSI, Unicode, and wide-character formats.

In the next section we'll list and describe the functions available to the Visual Basic programmer.

API Character and String Function Names and Descriptions

Table 26–1 shows 31 Windows API character and string functions and provides a brief description for their use.

In the example application included at the end of this chapter we'll examine the use of the CharLower(), CharUpper(), IsCharAlpha(), IsCharAlphaNumeric(), Is CharLower(), and IsCharUpper() functions.

Table 26–1 Character and String Functions and Descriptions

Function	Description
CharLower	Converts a character string or a single character to lowercase. This function replaces AnsiLower().
CharLowerBuff	Converts uppercase characters in a buffer to lowercase characters. This function replaces AnsiLowerBuff().
CharNext	Returns a pointer to the next character in a string. This function replaces AnsiNext().
CharPrev	Returns a pointer to the preceding character in a string. This function replaces AnsiPrev().
CharToOem	Converts a string into the OEM-defined character set. This function replaces AnsiToOem().
CharToOemBuff	Converts a specified number of characters in a string into the OEM-defined character set. This function replaces AnsiToOemBuff().
CharUpper	Converts a character string or a single character to uppercase. If the operand is a character string, characters are converted in place. This function replaces AnsiUpper().
CharUpperBuff	Converts lowercase characters in a buffer to uppercase characters. Characters are converted in place. The function replaces AnsiUpperBuff().
CompareString	Compares two character strings, using the locale given by the identifier as the basis for the comparison.
FoldString	Maps one string to another while performing a transformation option.
GetStringTypeA	Gets character-type information for the ANSI characters in the source string. The function sets one or more bits in the corresponding 16-bit element of the output array for each string. Here each bit is used to identify a given character type such as letter, digit, or neither.
GetStringTypeEx	Same as GetStringTypeA with extended capabilities.
GetStringTypeW	Gets character-type information for the Unicode characters in the source string. The function sets one or more bits in the corresponding 16-bit element of the output array for each string. Here each bit is used to identify a given character type such as letter, digit, or neither.
IsCharAlpha	Finds if a character is an alphabetic character.
IsCharAlphaNumeric	Finds if a character is either an alphabetic or a numeric character.
IsCharLower	Finds if a character is lowercase.
IsCharUpper	Finds if a character is uppercase.
IsDBCSLeadByte	Finds if a character is a lead byte (the first byte of a character in a double-byte character set).
IsTextUnicode	Finds if a buffer contains Unicode text. The function uses various mathematical methods to make the decision under the control of flags passed the lpi parameter. If the tests are passed, the function returns TRUE; otherwise it returns FALSE.
LCMapString	Maps one character string to another, performing a locale-dependent transformation. This function can also generate a sort key for the input string.
Lstrcat	Appends one string to another.
Lstrcmp	Compares two character strings. The comparison is case-sensitive.
Lstrcmpi	Compares two character strings. The comparison is not case-sensitive.

(continued)

Table 26–1   Character and String Functions and Descriptions *(Continued)*

Function	Description
Lstrcpy	Copies a string to a buffer.
Lstrcpyn	Copies a given number of characters from a source string into a buffer.
Lstrlen	Gets the length in bytes (ANSI version) or characters (unicode version) of the string. Does not include the null character terminator.
MultiByteToWideChar	Maps a character string to a wide-character unicode string. The character string is not necessarily from a multibyte character set.
OemToChar	Translates a string from the OEM-defined character set into an ANSI or a wide-character string. This function replaces OemToAnsi().
OemToCharBuff	Translates a number of characters in a string from the OEM-defined character set into either an ANSI or a wide-character string. This function replaces OemToAnsiBuff().
WideCharToMultiByte	Maps a wide-character string to a new character string. The new character string is not necessarily from a multibyte character set.

API Character and String Function Declarations

The following listing contains the Windows API character and string function declarations found in the Win32api.txt file provided with Visual Basic:

```
Declare Function CharLower Lib "user32" Alias
   "CharLowerA" (ByVal lpsz As String) As String

Declare Function CharLowerBuff Lib "user32" Alias
   "CharLowerBuffA" (ByVal lpsz As String,
   ByVal cchLength As Long) As Long

Declare Function CharNext Lib "user32" Alias
   "CharNextA" (ByVal lpsz As String) As String

Declare Function CharPrev Lib "user32" Alias
   "CharPrevA" (ByVal lpszStart As String,
   ByVal lpszCurrent As String) As String

Declare Function CharToOem Lib "user32" Alias
   "CharToOemA" (ByVal lpszSrc As String,
   ByVal lpszDst As String) As Long

Declare Function CharToOemBuff Lib "user32" Alias
   "CharToOemBuffA" (ByVal lpszSrc As String,
   ByVal lpszDst As String,
   ByVal cchDstLength As Long) As Long

Declare Function CharUpper Lib "user32" Alias
   "CharUpperA" (ByVal lpsz As String) As String
```

```
Declare Function CharUpperBuff Lib "user32" Alias
   "CharUpperBuffA" (ByVal lpsz As String,
   ByVal cchLength As Long) As Long

Declare Function CompareString Lib "kernel32" Alias
   "CompareStringA" (ByVal Locale As Long,
   ByVal dwCmpFlags As Long, ByVal lpString1 As String,
   ByVal cchCount1 As Long, ByVal lpString2 As String,
   ByVal cchCount2 As Long) As Long

Declare Function FoldString Lib "kernel32" Alias
   "FoldStringA" (ByVal dwMapFlags As Long,
   ByVal lpSrcStr As String, ByVal cchSrc As Long,
   ByVal lpDestStr As String,
   ByVal cchDest As Long) As Long

Declare Function GetStringTypeA Lib "kernel32" Alias
   "GetStringTypeA" (ByVal lcid As Long,
   ByVal dwInfoType As Long, ByVal lpSrcStr As String,
   ByVal cchSrc As Long, lpCharType As Long) As Long

Declare Function GetStringTypeEx Lib "kernel32" Alias
   "GetStringTypeExA" (ByVal Locale As Long,
   ByVal dwInfoType As Long, ByVal lpSrcStr As String,
   ByVal cchSrc As Long, lpCharType As Integer) As Long

Declare Function GetStringTypeW Lib "kernel32" Alias
   "GetStringTypeW" (ByVal dwInfoType As Long,
   ByVal lpSrcStr As String, ByVal cchSrc As Long,
   lpCharType As Integer) As Long

Declare Function IsCharAlpha Lib "user32" Alias
   "IsCharAlphaA" (ByVal cChar As Byte) As Long

Declare Function IsCharAlphaNumeric Lib "user32" Alias
   "IsCharAlphaNumericA" (ByVal cChar As Byte) As Long

Declare Function IsCharLower Lib "user32" Alias
   "IsCharLowerA" (ByVal cChar As Byte) As Long

Declare Function IsCharUpper Lib "user32" Alias
   "IsCharUpperA" (ByVal cChar As Byte) As Long

Declare Function IsDBCSLeadByte Lib "kernel32" Alias
   "IsDBCSLeadByte" (ByVal bTestChar As Byte) As Long

Declare Function IsTextUnicode Lib "advapi32" Alias
   "IsTextUnicode" (lpBuffer As Any, ByVal cb As Long,
   lpi As Long) As Long

Declare Function LCMapString Lib "kernel32" Alias
   "LCMapStringA" (ByVal Locale As Long,
   ByVal dwMapFlags As Long, ByVal lpSrcStr As String,
```

```
    ByVal cchSrc As Long, ByVal lpDestStr As String,
    ByVal cchDest As Long) As Long

Declare Function lstrcat Lib "kernel32" Alias
    "lstrcatA" (ByVal lpString1 As String,
    ByVal lpString2 As String) As Long

Declare Function lstrcmp Lib "kernel32" Alias
    "lstrcmpA" (ByVal lpString1 As String,
    ByVal lpString2 As String) As Long

Declare Function lstrcmpi Lib "kernel32" Alias
    "lstrcmpiA" (ByVal lpString1 As String,
    ByVal lpString2 As String) As Long

Declare Function lstrcpy Lib "kernel32" Alias
    "lstrcpyA" (ByVal lpString1 As String,
    ByVal lpString2 As String) As Long

Declare Function lstrcpyn Lib "kernel32" Alias
    "lstrcpynA" (ByVal lpString1 As String,
    ByVal lpString2 As String,
    ByVal iMaxLength As Long) As Long

Declare Function lstrlen Lib "kernel32" Alias
    "lstrlenA" (ByVal lpString As String) As Long

Declare Function MultiByteToWideChar Lib "kernel32" Alias
    "MultiByteToWideChar" (ByVal CodePage As Long,
    ByVal dwFlags As Long, ByVal lpMultiByteStr As String,
    ByVal cchMultiByte As Long, ByVal lpWideCharStr As String,
    ByVal cchWideChar As Long) As Long

Declare Function OemToChar Lib "user32" Alias
    "OemToCharA" (ByVal lpszSrc As String,
    ByVal lpszDst As String) As Long

Declare Function OemToCharBuff Lib "user32" Alias
    "OemToCharBuffA" (ByVal lpszSrc As String,
    ByVal lpszDst As String,
    ByVal cchDstLength As Long) As Long

Declare Function WideCharToMultiByte Lib "kernel32" Alias
    "WideCharToMultiByte" (ByVal CodePage As Long,
    ByVal dwFlags As Long, ByVal lpWideCharStr As String,
    ByVal cchWideChar As Long, ByVal lpMultiByteStr As String,
    ByVal cchMultiByte As Long, ByVal lpDefaultChar As String,
    ByVal lpUsedDefaultChar As Long) As Long
```

Table 26–2 contains a brief description of the parameters used in the various character and string functions.

Table 26–2   Character and String Function Parameters and Descriptions

Parameter	Description
bTestChar As Byte	The character to be tested.
cb As Long	Gives the size (bytes) of the input buffer pointed to by the lpBuffer parameter.
cChar As Byte	Character to test.
CchCount1 As Long	Gives the size (bytes for the ANSI version or characters for the unicode version) of the string pointed to by the lpString1 parameter. When this parameter is (-1), the string is assumed to be null terminated and the length is calculated automatically.
CchCount2 As Long	Gives the size (bytes for the ANSI version or characters for the unicode version) of the string pointed to by the lpString2 parameter. When this parameter is (-1), the string is assumed to be null terminated and the length is calculated automatically.
CchDest As Long	Gives the size (bytes for ANSI version or characters for unicode version) of the lpDestStr buffer. When cchDest is zero, the function returns the number of bytes or characters required to hold the mapped string. In this case the buffer, pointed to by lpDestStr, is not used.
CchDstLength As Long	Gives the number of characters to translate in the string identified by the lpszSrc parameter.
CchLength As Long	Gives the size (bytes for ANSI version or characters for unicode version) of the buffer pointed to by the lpsz parameter.
CchMultiByte As Long	Gives the size (bytes) of the string pointed to by the lpMultiByteStr parameter. If (-1), the string is assumed to be null terminated and the length is automatically calculated.
CchSrc As Long	Gives the size (bytes for ANSI version or characters for unicode version) of the lpSrcStr buffer. If cchSrc is (-1), lpSrcStr buffer should be null terminated. The length is then calculated automatically.
CchWideChar As Long	Gives the size (wide characters) of the buffer pointed to by the lpWideCharStr parameter. If (0) the function returns the buffer size, in wide characters ignoring the lpWideCharStr buffer.
CodePage As Long	Gives the code page to be used to perform the conversion. Uses CP_ constants.
DwCmpFlags As Long	Used to indicate how the function compares two strings. The flags are not set by default. Uses the NORM_ constants or SORT_STRINGSORT.
DwFlags As Long	Uses flags that indicate whether to translate to precomposed or composite-wide characters, to use glyph characters in place of control characters, and how to deal with invalid characters. Use MB_ constants.
	Or
	A set of bit flags that specify the handling of unmapped characters. Here WC_ constants are used.
DwInfoType As Long	Gives the type of character information to retrieve. The various types are indicated by CT_ constants.
DwMapFlags As Long	Uses flags to indicate the type of transformation to be used during mapping. Flags use LCMAP_, MAP_, NORM_, or SORT_STRINGSORT constants.

(continued)

Table 26–2   Character and String Function Parameters and Descriptions *(Continued)*

Parameter	Description
IMaxLength As Long	Gives the number bytes (ANSI version) or characters (unicode version) to be copied from lpString2 into the lpString1 buffer. Count includes a null character terminator.
Locale As Long	Gives the locale used for the comparison. This parameter can be LOCALE_SYSTEM_DEFAULT for the system default locale or LOCALE_USER_DEFAULT for the user's default locale.
LpBuffer As Any	Pointer to the input buffer to be examined.
LpCharType As Integer	Points to an array of 16-bit values. The length of this array receives a 16-bit value for each character in the source string. When the function returns, this array contains one word corresponding to each character in the source string.
LpCharType As Long	Points to an array of 16-bit values. The array holds one 16-bit value for each character in the source string. The array holds one word corresponding to each character in the source string when the function returns.
LpDefaultChar As String	Points to the character used if a wide character cannot be represented in the code page. If NULL, a system default value is used.
LpDestStr As String	Points to the buffer to store the mapped string.
lpi As Long	Pointer to a value that initially contains a set of flags that specify the tests to be applied to the input buffer text. Upon exit the same value holds a set of bit flags indicating the results of the tests. A (1) indicates the buffer pass a test while a (0) indicates failure. Test flags are combinations of the IS_TEXT_UNICODE_ constants.
LpMultiByteStr As String	Points to the character string to be converted.
LpSrcStr As String	Points to the string. For functions using the cchSrc parameter; when the value is (-1), the string is assumed to be null terminated. This must be a unicode string if the function uses the W version of this function and an ANSI string for the A version of the function.
LpString As String	Points to a null-terminated string.
LpString1 As String	Points to the first string to be compared or appended. If lpString2 is appended, lpString1 must be large enough to hold both.
LpString2 As String	Points to the second string to be compared or appended to the string in lpString1.
lpsz As String	Can be a pointer to a buffer containing one or more characters to process, a pointer to a string or a single character. When the high-order word of this parameter is zero, the low-order word must contain a single character to convert.
LpszCurrent As String	Pointer to a character in a null-terminated string.
LpszDst As String	Pointer to the buffer for the translated string.
LpszSrc As String	Pointer to the null-terminated string to translate.
LpszStart As String	Pointer to the beginning of the string.
LpUsedDefaultChar As Long	Points to a flag that indicates whether a default character was used. The flag is set to TRUE if one or more wide characters in the source string cannot be represented in the code page.
LpWideCharStr As String	Points to a buffer that receives the translated string.

Many of the parameters described in Table 26–2 use constant values. The win32api.txt file lists the following constants for character and string parameters:

```
'Code Page Default Values.
Public Const CP_ACP = 0    'default to ANSI code page
Public Const CP_OEMCP = 1 'default to OEM code page

'Character Type Flags.
Public Const CT_CTYPE1 = &H1 'ctype 1 information
Public Const CT_CTYPE2 = &H2 'ctype 2 information
Public Const CT_CTYPE3 = &H4 'ctype 3 information

'lpi's bit flags (NOT listed as part of win32api.txt):
'text is Unicode:
  IS_TEXT_UNICODE_ASCII16
'text is Unicode, byte reversed:
  IS_TEXT_UNICODE_REVERSE_ASCII16
'text is probably Unicode:
  IS_TEXT_UNICODE_STATISTICS
'text is probably Unicode, byte reversed:
  IS_TEXT_UNICODE_REVERSE_STATISTICS
'text contains Unicode non-printing characters -
'RETURN, LINEFEED, SPACE, CJK_SPACE, TAB:
  IS_TEXT_UNICODE_CONTROLS
'text contains Unicode non-printing — characters:
'RETURN, LINEFEED, SPACE, CJK_SPACE, TAB,
'but byte-reversed.
'IS_TEXT_UNICODE_REVERSE_CONTROLS
'too few characters analysis:
  IS_TEXT_UNICODE_BUFFER_TOO_SMALL
'contains the Unicode byte-order mark (BOM):
  IS_TEXT_UNICODE_SIGNATURE
'contains the Unicode byte-reversed byte order mark
'(Reverse BOM):
  IS_TEXT_UNICODE_REVERSE_SIGNATURE
'contains one of these Unicode-illegal characters -
'embedded Reverse BOM, UNICODE_NUL, CRLF
'(packed into one WORD), or 0xFFFF:
  IS_TEXT_UNICODE_ILLEGAL_CHARS
'number of characters in the string is odd:
  IS_TEXT_UNICODE_ODD_LENGTH
'contains null bytes, which indicate non-ASCII text:
  IS_TEXT_UNICODE_NULL_BYTES
'a combination of IS_TEXT_UNICODE_ASCII16,
'IS_TEXT_UNICODE_STATISTICS,
'IS_TEXT_UNICODE_CONTROLS,
'IS_TEXT_UNICODE_SIGNATURE:
  IS_TEXT_UNICODE_UNICODE_MASK
'a combination of
```

```
'IS_TEXT_UNICODE_REVERSE_ASCII16,
'IS_TEXT_UNICODE_REVERSE_STATISTICS,
'IS_TEXT_UNICODE_REVERSE_CONTROLS,
'IS_TEXT_UNICODE_REVERSE_SIGNATURE:
  IS_TEXT_UNICODE_REVERSE_MASK
'a combination of
'IS_TEXT_UNICODE_ILLEGAL_CHARS,
'IS_TEXT_UNICODE_ODD_LENGTH,
'and two currently unused bit flags:
  IS_TEXT_UNICODE_NOT_UNICODE_MASK
'a combination of
'IS_TEXT_UNICODE_NULL_BYTES and
'three currently unused bit flags.
  IS_TEXT_UNICODE_NOT_ASCII_MASK

'Locale Dependent Mapping Flags.
Public Const LCMAP_LOWERCASE = &H100 'lower case letters
Public Const LCMAP_UPPERCASE = &H200 'upper case letters
Public Const LCMAP_SORTKEY = &H400   'WC sort key (normalize)
Public Const LCMAP_BYTEREV = &H800   'byte reversal

'Locale Independent Mapping Flags.
'fold compatibility zone chars:
Public Const MAP_FOLDCZONE = &H10
'convert to precomposed chars:

Public Const MAP_PRECOMPOSED = &H20
'convert to composite chars:

Public Const MAP_COMPOSITE = &H40
Public Const MAP_FOLDDIGITS = &H80   'all digits to ASCII 0-9

'MBCS and Unicode Translation Flags.
Public Const MB_PRECOMPOSED = &H1    'use precomposed chars
Public Const MB_COMPOSITE = &H2      'use composite chars
Public Const MB_USEGLYPHCHARS = &H4  'use glyph chars
                                     'not ctrl chars

'String Flags.
Public Const NORM_IGNORECASE = &H1      'ignore case
Public Const NORM_IGNORENONSPACE = &H2 'ignore nonspacing
                                        'chars
Public Const NORM_IGNORESYMBOLS = &H4   'ignore symbols

Public Const WC_DEFAULTCHECK = &H100  'check for default char
Public Const WC_COMPOSITECHECK = &H200 'convert composite to
                                        'precomposed
Public Const WC_DISCARDNS = &H10    'discard non-spacing chars
Public Const WC_SEPCHARS = &H20     'generate separate chars
Public Const WC_DEFAULTCHAR = &H40 'replace w/ default char
```

In the next section, we'll examine an application that makes use of several of the windows API character and string functions.

Example Application

The example application included in this section uses the CharLower(), CharUpper(), IsCharAlpha(), IsCharAlphaNumeric(), Is CharLower(), and IsCharUpper() functions.

This simple application demonstrates how character information can be handled in Visual Basic with Windows API functions. The project, named Char1.vbp, contains a module file for function declarations. The module file is named Char1.bas and is shown in the following listing:

```
Declare Function CharLower Lib "user32" Alias
  "CharLowerA" (ByVal lpsz As String) As String
Declare Function CharUpper Lib "user32" Alias
  "CharUpperA" (ByVal lpsz As String) As String
Declare Function IsCharAlpha Lib "user32" Alias
  "IsCharAlphaA" (ByVal cChar As Byte) As Long
Declare Function IsCharAlphaNumeric Lib "user32" Alias
  "IsCharAlphaNumericA" (ByVal cChar As Byte) As Long
Declare Function IsCharLower Lib "user32" Alias
  "IsCharLowerA" (ByVal cChar As Byte) As Long
Declare Function IsCharUpper Lib "user32" Alias
  "IsCharUpperA" (ByVal cChar As Byte) As Long
```

The project uses a form, Char1.frm, for reporting information to the user. This form contains 12 label controls. Six of the controls use their caption property to label the output result. The remaining 6 labels will have information returned to their label property from the various Windows API functions.

The code for manipulating character information is shown next.

```
Private Sub Form_Load()
  Dim teststr As String
  Dim r&

  'convert "A" to "a"
  teststr = CharLower("A")
  Label7.Caption = teststr

  'convert "b" to "B"
  teststr = CharUpper("b")
  Label8.Caption = teststr

  'Is "5" an alpha character?
  'Decimal 53 is ASCII equivalent of "5"
  r& = IsCharAlpha(53)
```

```
If r& <> 0 Then
  Label9.Caption = "Is alpha"
Else
  Label9.Caption = "Is not alpha"
End If

'Is "5" an alphanumeric character?
'Decimal 53 is ASCII equivalent of "5"
r& = IsCharAlphaNumeric(53)
Label10.Caption = r&
If r& <> 0 Then
  Label10.Caption = "Is alphanumeric"
Else
  Label10.Caption = "Is not alphanumeric"
End If

'Is "C" a lower-case character?
'Decimal 67 is ASCII equivalent of "C"
r& = IsCharLower(67)
If r& <> 0 Then
  Label11.Caption = "Is lower-case"
Else
```

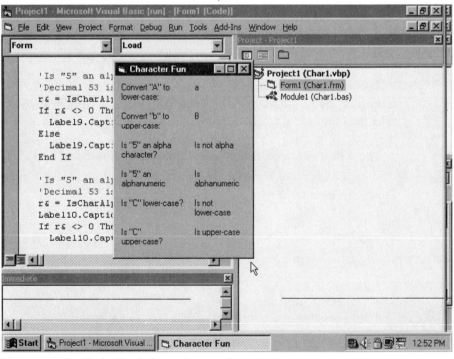

Figure 26–1   Gathering information on characters.

```
      Label11.Caption = "Is not lower-case"
   End If

   'Is "C" an upper-case character?
   'Decimal 67 is ASCII equivalent of "C"
   r& = IsCharUpper(67)
   If r& <> 0 Then
      Label12.Caption = "Is upper-case"
   Else
      Label12.Caption = "Is not upper-case"
   End If
End Sub
```

The use of each of these functions is straightforward. For this example, the results returned should be similar to those shown in Figure 26–1.

One special note: The IsCharAlpha(), IsCharAlphaNumeric(), IsCharLower(), and IsCharUpper() use parameters that are passed as byte values. In this application we just used the ASCII equivalent of the character information we wished to pass.

Chapter 27

Memory Allocation Functions

The Windows API allows access to a number of memory functions. These memory functions fall into four groups; global, heap, local, and virtual. Under Win32, however, memory is treated in a linear fashion and global and local function groups produce identical results.

The global memory functions allow manipulation of three basic categories of memory: fixed, movable, and discardable. Fixed memory represents a portion of memory that cannot be moved once an address is obtained for it. Movable memory is memory that can be moved once it is allocated by Windows. Discardable memory is memory that can be discarded when Windows determines it is needed by another process.

Heap functions allow you to control private heaps of allocated memory and to protect that memory in situations where multiple threads may manipulate the heap.

Virtual memory functions allow access to memory areas without the need to specifically allocate physical memory. Under Win32 this is useful because of the large memory allocated to each process.

API Memory Function Names and Descriptions

Table 27–1 shows 35 Windows API memory functions and provides a brief description for their use. Under Win32, the global and local functions behave in an identical manner, so actually only 27 unique functions are discussed in this chapter.

An example application at the end of this chapter will illustrate the use of the GlobalAlloc(), GlobalLock(), GlobalSize(), and GlobalUnlock() functions.

Table 27–1 Memory Functions and Descriptions

Function	Description
GetProcessHeap	Gets a handle to the heap of the calling process. The handle can then be used by the HeapAlloc(), HeapReAlloc(), HeapFree(), and HeapSize() functions.
GlobalAlloc	Allocates a number of bytes from the heap. With Win32, there is no difference between the local heap and the global heap.
GlobalFlags	Gets information about the global memory object.
GlobalFree	Frees the global memory object and invalidates the handle.
GlobalHandle	Gets the handle associated with the pointer to a global memory block.
GlobalLock	Locks a global memory object and returns a pointer to the first byte of the object's memory block. The memory block cannot be moved or discarded. If the memory object is allocated using the GMEM_MOVEABLE flag, the function will increment the lock count associated with the memory object.
GlobalReAlloc	Reallocates the size (increase or decrease) or attributes of a global memory object.
GlobalSize	Gets the current size (bytes) of the global memory object.
GlobalUnlock	Decrements the lock count associated with a memory object obtained with the GMEM_MOVEABLE flag constant. This function will have no effect on memory objects if they were allocated using the GMEM_FIXED flag constant.
HeapAlloc	Allocates a block of memory from a heap. The allocated memory is not movable.
HeapCompact	Attempts to compact a heap. The heap is compacted by coalescing adjacent free blocks of memory and decommitting large free blocks of memory.
HeapCreate	Creates a heap object that can be used by the calling process. The function reserves a contiguous block in the virtual address space of the process and assigns physical storage for an initial portion of the block.
HeapDestroy	Destroys the heap object. The function decommits and releases all the pages of a private heap object.
HeapFree	Frees a memory block allocated from a heap using the HeapAlloc() or HeapReAlloc() functions.
HeapLock	Attempts to acquire the critical section object or lock associated with a heap.
HeapReAlloc	Reallocates a block of memory from a heap. Use the function to resize a memory block and change memory block properties. The allocated memory is not movable.
HeapSize	Gets the size (bytes) of a memory block allocated from a heap by either the HeapAlloc() or HeapReAlloc() function.
HeapUnlock	Frees ownership of the critical section object, or lock, associated with a heap.

(continued)

Table 27–1   Memory Functions and Descriptions

Function	Description
HeapValidate	Attempts to validate a heap by scanning all memory blocks in the heap and verifying that the heap control structures are in a consistent state.
LocalAlloc	Use GlobalAlloc() under Win32.
LocalFlags	Use GlobalFlags() under Win32.
LocalFree	Use GlobalFree() under Win32.
LocalHandle	Use GlobalHandle() under Win32.
LocalLock	Use GlobalLock() under Win32.
LocalReAlloc	Use GlobalReAlloc() under Win32.
LocalSize	Use GlobalSine() under Win32.
LocalUnlock	Use GlobalUnlock() under win32.
VirtualAlloc	Reserves or allocates a region of pages in the virtual address space of the calling process. The memory allocated is automatically initialized to zero.
VirtualFree	Frees or decommits a region of pages within the virtual address space of the calling process.
VirtualLock	Locks the region of the process's virtual address space into memory. Subsequent access to the region will not incur a page fault.
VirtualProtect	Changes the access protection on a region of committed pages in the virtual address space of the calling process.
VirtualProtectEx	Changes the access protection on a region of committed pages in the virtual address space of the any process.
VirtualQuery	Obtains information about a range of pages in the virtual address space of the calling process.
VirtualQueryEx	Obtains information about a range of pages within the virtual address space of any process.
VirtualUnlock	Unlocks a range of pages in the virtual address space of a process. This allows the system to swap the pages out to the paging file if needed.

API Memory Function Declarations

The following listing contains the Windows API memory function declarations found in the Win32api.txt file provided with Visual Basic. As we mentioned earlier, the global and local memory functions produce identical results under Win32, so the local memory prototypes are not listed.

```
Declare Function GetProcessHeap Lib "kernel32"
    Alias "GetProcessHeap" () As Long

Declare Function GlobalAlloc Lib "kernel32"
    Alias "GlobalAlloc" (ByVal wFlags As Long,
    ByVal dwBytes As Long) As Long
```

```
Declare Function GlobalFlags Lib "kernel32"
  Alias "GlobalFlags" (ByVal hMem As Long) As Long

Declare Function GlobalFree Lib "kernel32"
  Alias "GlobalFree" (ByVal hMem As Long) As Long

Declare Function GlobalHandle Lib "kernel32"
  Alias "GlobalHandle" (wMem As Any) As Long

Declare Function GlobalLock Lib "kernel32"
  Alias "GlobalLock" (ByVal hMem As Long) As Long

Declare Function GlobalReAlloc Lib "kernel32"
  Alias "GlobalReAlloc" (ByVal hMem As Long,
  ByVal dwBytes As Long,
  ByVal wFlags As Long) As Long

Declare Function GlobalSize Lib "kernel32"
  Alias "GlobalSize" (ByVal hMem As Long) As Long

Declare Function GlobalUnlock Lib "kernel32"
  Alias "GlobalUnlock" (ByVal hMem As Long) As Long

Declare Function HeapAlloc Lib "kernel32"
  Alias "HeapAlloc" (ByVal hHeap As Long,
  ByVal dwFlags As Long,
  ByVal dwBytes As Long) As Long

Declare Function HeapCompact Lib "kernel32"
  Alias "HeapCompact" (ByVal hHeap As Long,
  ByVal dwFlags As Long) As Long

Declare Function HeapCreate Lib "kernel32"
  Alias "HeapCreate" (ByVal flOptions As Long,
  ByVal dwInitialSize As Long,
  ByVal dwMaximumSize As Long) As Long

Declare Function HeapDestroy Lib "kernel32"
  Alias "HeapDestroy" (ByVal hHeap As Long) As Long

Declare Function HeapFree Lib "kernel32"
  Alias "HeapFree" (ByVal hHeap As Long,
  ByVal dwFlags As Long, lpMem As Any) As Long

Declare Function HeapLock Lib "kernel32"
  Alias "HeapLock" (ByVal hHeap As Long) As Long

Declare Function HeapReAlloc Lib "kernel32"
  Alias "HeapReAlloc" (ByVal hHeap As Long,
  ByVal dwFlags As Long, lpMem As Any,
  ByVal dwBytes As Long) As Long
```

```
Declare Function HeapSize Lib "kernel32"
  Alias "HeapSize" (ByVal hHeap As Long,
  ByVal dwFlags As Long, lpMem As Any) As Long

Declare Function HeapUnlock Lib "kernel32"
  Alias "HeapUnlock" (ByVal hHeap As Long) As Long

Declare Function HeapValidate Lib "kernel32"
  Alias "HeapValidate" (ByVal hHeap As Long,
  ByVal dwFlags As Long, lpMem As Any) As Long

Declare Function VirtualAlloc Lib "kernel32"
  Alias "VirtualAlloc" (lpAddress As Any,
  ByVal dwSize As Long, ByVal flAllocationType As Long,
  ByVal flProtect As Long) As Long

Declare Function VirtualFree Lib "kernel32"
  Alias "VirtualFree" (lpAddress As Any,
  ByVal dwSize As Long,
  ByVal dwFreeType As Long) As Long

Declare Function VirtualLock Lib "kernel32"
  Alias "VirtualLock" (lpAddress As Any,
  ByVal dwSize As Long) As Long

Declare Function VirtualProtect Lib "kernel32"
  Alias "VirtualProtect" (lpAddress As Any,
  ByVal dwSize As Long, ByVal flNewProtect As Long,
  lpflOldProtect As Long) As Long

Declare Function VirtualProtectEx Lib "kernel32"
  Alias "VirtualProtectEx" (ByVal hProcess As Long,
  lpAddress As Any, ByVal dwSize As Long,
  ByVal flNewProtect As Long, lpflOldProtect As Long) As Long

Declare Function VirtualQuery Lib "kernel32"
  Alias "VirtualQuery" (lpAddress As Any,
  lpBuffer As MEMORY_BASIC_INFORMATION,
  ByVal dwLength As Long) As Long

Declare Function VirtualQueryEx Lib "kernel32"
  Alias "VirtualQueryEx" (ByVal hProcess As Long,
  lpAddress As Any, lpBuffer As MEMORY_BASIC_INFORMATION,
  ByVal dwLength As Long) As Long

Declare Function VirtualUnlock Lib "kernel32"
  Alias "VirtualUnlock" (lpAddress As Any,
  ByVal dwSize As Long) As Long
```

Table 27–2 contains a brief description of the parameters used in the various memory functions.

Table 27–2   Memory Function Parameters and Descriptions

Parameter	Description
dwBytes As Long	Gives the number of bytes allocated. When zero and the uFlags parameter uses the GMEM_MOVEABLE flag constant, the function returns a handle to a memory object that is marked as discarded. When uFlags uses the GMEM_MODIFY flag constant, this parameter is ignored.
dwFlags As Long	A set of bit flags that control heap access during function operation. Uses HEAP_ constants.
dwFreeType As Long	Gives the type of free operation. Can use MEM_DECOMMIT to specify the region of committed pages or MEM_RELEASE to specify the region of reserved pages.
dwInitialSize As Long	The initial size (bytes) of the heap. This value represents the initial amount of physical storage for the heap, rounded up to the next page boundary.
dwLength As Long	Gives the size (bytes) of the buffer pointed to by the lpBuffer parameter.
dwMaximumSize As Long	When dwMaximumSize <> 0, it gives the maximum size (bytes) of the heap. If dwMaximumSize <> 0, the heap cannot grow.
	If dwMaximumSize = 0, it means the heap can grow.
dwSize As Long	Gives the size (bytes) of the region. The region of affected pages includes all pages containing one or more bytes in the range from the lpAddress parameter to (lpAddress+dwSize).
flAllocationType As Long	Specifies the type of allocation using MEM_ constants.
flNewProtect As Long	Gives the new access protection. Uses PAGE_ constants.
flOptions As Long	Optional attributes for the heap. These HEAP_ flag constants will affect subsequent access to the heap through calls to various heap functions.
flProtect As Long	Gives the type of access protection using PAGE_ constants.
hHeap As Long	Handle to the heap.
hMem As Long	Handle for the global memory object returned by the GlobalAlloc() or GlobalReAlloc() functions.
hProcess As Long	Handle to a process.
lpAddress As Any	Gives the starting address of the region to allocate, freed or locked. The address is rounded down to the next 64 kilobyte boundary when memory is being reserved. When memory is already reserved and is being committed the address is rounded down to the next page boundary.
lpBuffer As MEMORY_ BASIC_INFORMATION	Structure holds information about the page range.
LpflOldProtect As Long	Points to a variable that the function sets to the previous access protection value of the first page in the region of pages.
lpMem As Any	Points to the memory block. This pointer is returned by the HeapAlloc() or HeapReAlloc() functions.
wFlags As Long	Uses GMEM_, GPTR_ and GHND_ constants.
wMem As Any	Points to the first byte of the global memory block. This pointer is returned by the GlobalLock() function.

Many of the parameters described in Table 27–2 use constant values. The Win32api.txt file lists the following constants for this group of memory functions:

```
'Global Memory Flags
Public Const GMEM_FIXED = &H0
Public Const GMEM_MOVEABLE = &H2
Public Const GMEM_NOCOMPACT = &H10
Public Const GMEM_NODISCARD = &H20
Public Const GMEM_ZEROINIT = &H40
Public Const GMEM_MODIFY = &H80
Public Const GMEM_DISCARDABLE = &H100
Public Const GMEM_NOT_BANKED = &H1000
Public Const GMEM_SHARE = &H2000
Public Const GMEM_DDESHARE = &H2000
Public Const GMEM_NOTIFY = &H4000
Public Const GMEM_LOWER = GMEM_NOT_BANKED
Public Const GMEM_VALID_FLAGS = &H7F72
Public Const GMEM_INVALID_HANDLE = &H8000
Public Const GHND = (GMEM_MOVEABLE Or GMEM_ZEROINIT)
Public Const GPTR = (GMEM_FIXED Or GMEM_ZEROINIT)

'Flags returned by GlobalFlags
'(in addition to GMEM_DISCARDABLE)
Public Const GMEM_DISCARDED = &H4000
Public Const GMEM_LOCKCOUNT = &HFF

'Heap constants not declared in Win32api.txt
'operating system will raise an exception to indicate
'a function failure:
HEAP_GENERATE_EXCEPTIONS

'mutual exclusion will not be used while this
'function is accessing the heap:
HEAP_NO_SERIALIZE

'The allocated memory will be initialized to zero:
HEAP_ZERO_MEMORY

'Page constants not declared in Win32api.txt.
'Enables read access to the committed region of pages:
PAGE_READONLY

'Enables both read and write access to the committed
'region of pages:
PAGE_READWRITE

'Enables execute access to the committed region of pages:
PAGE_EXECUTE

'Enables execute and read access to the committed
'region of pages:
PAGE_EXECUTE_READ
```

```
'Enables execute, read, and write access to the committed
'region of pages.
PAGE_EXECUTE_READWRITE

'Pages in the region become guard pages. Any attempt
'to read from or write to a guard page causes the
'operating system to raise a STATUS_GUARD_PAGE
'exception and turn off the guard page status:
PAGE_GUARD

'Disables all access to the committed region of pages.
PAGE_NOACCESS

'Allows no caching of the committed regions of pages.
'The hardware attributes for the physical memory
'should be specified as "no cache."
PAGE_NOCACHE

'Memory constants not declared in Win32api.txt file.
'Allocates physical storage in memory or in the paging
'file on disk for the specified region of pages.
MEM_COMMIT

'Reserves a range of the process's virtual address
'space without allocating any physical storage.
MEM_RESERVE

'Allocates memory at the highest possible address.
MEM_TOP_DOWN
```

The lpBuffer parameter uses a MEMORY_BASIC_INFORMATION structure in which to store information. Here is the structure, as listed in the Win32api.txt file:

```
Type MEMORY_BASIC_INFORMATION
  BaseAddress as Long
  AllocationBase as Long
  AllocationProtect As Long
  RegionSize As Long
  State As Long
  Protect As Long
  lType As Long
End Type
```

In the following section we'll look at a simple programming example that will illustrate the use of several of these Win32 API memory functions.

Example Application

The following application is named Memory1.vbp. The project contains one form (Memory1.frm) and one module (Memory1.bas). The module contains the GMEM_ constant declarations as well as four global memory functions. All of this information was copied from the Win32api.txt file. Here is the listing for the Memory1.bas file.

```
'Global Memory Flags
Public Const GMEM_FIXED = &H0
Public Const GMEM_MOVEABLE = &H2
Public Const GMEM_NOCOMPACT = &H10
Public Const GMEM_NODISCARD = &H20
Public Const GMEM_ZEROINIT = &H40
Public Const GMEM_MODIFY = &H80
Public Const GMEM_DISCARDABLE = &H100
Public Const GMEM_NOT_BANKED = &H1000
Public Const GMEM_SHARE = &H2000
Public Const GMEM_DDESHARE = &H2000
Public Const GMEM_NOTIFY = &H4000
Public Const GMEM_LOWER = GMEM_NOT_BANKED
Public Const GMEM_VALID_FLAGS = &H7F72
Public Const GMEM_INVALID_HANDLE = &H8000
Public Const GHND = (GMEM_MOVEABLE Or GMEM_ZEROINIT)
Public Const GPTR = (GMEM_FIXED Or GMEM_ZEROINIT)
'Flags returned by GlobalFlags
'(in addition to GMEM_DISCARDABLE)
Public Const GMEM_DISCARDED = &H4000
Public Const GMEM_LOCKCOUNT = &HFF

Declare Function GlobalAlloc Lib "kernel32" (ByVal wFlags As
  Long, ByVal dwBytes As Long) As Long
Declare Function GlobalLock Lib "kernel32" (ByVal hMem As Long)
  As Long
Declare Function GlobalSize Lib "kernel32" (ByVal hMem As Long)
  As Long
Declare Function GlobalUnlock Lib "kernel32" (ByVal hMem As Long)
  As Long
```

The application uses one form. The Form_Load() subroutine houses the code for globally allocating several blocks of movable and fixed memory. The block size is optional, but 512 was used for each block in this example.

```
Private Sub Form_Load()
  Dim hMem(6) As Long
  Dim pMem(6) As Long
  Dim lFree(6) As Long

  'Allocate moveable and fixed memory
  hMem(0) = GlobalAlloc(GMEM_MOVEABLE, 512)
  hMem(1) = GlobalAlloc(GMEM_MOVEABLE, 512)
  hMem(2) = GlobalAlloc(GMEM_MOVEABLE, 512)
  hMem(3) = GlobalAlloc(GMEM_FIXED, 512)
  hMem(4) = GlobalAlloc(GMEM_FIXED, 512)
  hMem(5) = GlobalAlloc(GMEM_FIXED, 512)
```

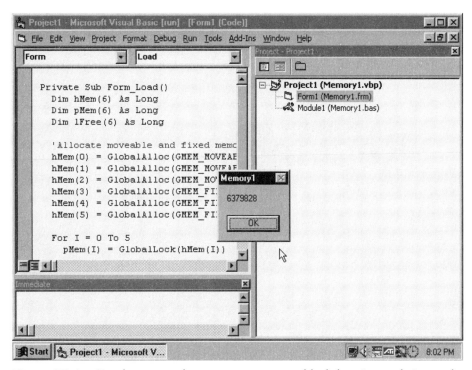

Figure 27–1   Simple message boxes return memory block location and size to the user.

```
   For I = 0 To 5
     pMem(I) = GlobalLock(hMem(I))
     lFree(I) = GlobalSize(hMem(I))
     MsgBox (pMcm(I)) 'Print Block Location
     MsgBox (lFree(I)) 'Print Memory Object Size
     GlobalUnlock (hMem(I))
   Next I
End Sub
```

Once the global memory is allocated, the GlobalLock() function locks the memory object and returns a pointer to the first byte of the memory block. The value is then printed to a message box using the MsgBox() function. The Global-Size() function gets the current size, in bytes, of the global memory object. This information is then printed to the screen with another MsgBox().

Each mouse click on the message box button brings the next message box to the screen until all 12 message boxes have been viewed.

Figure 27–1 is an example of a memory block's location as reported by the MsgBox() function.

Chapter 28

Rectangle and Point Functions

The Windows API provides a number of functions designed to manipulate rectangles. Rectangles, as you know, form the foundation for many GDI drawing primitives and are also the basic building block for designing all rectangular Windows screens. Rectangles always exist along horizontal and vertical X and Y coordinate positions. The only time you'll see a rectangle rotated from this position is when special Windows NT coordinate functions, described earlier in Chapter 11, are used.

This is not our first look at functions that involve the use of rectangles. You'll find functions that reference the rectangular structure in Chapters 8, 11, 13, 14, and 15. This chapter is unique in that it deals with rectangle and point functions that are more involved with the manipulation of portions of a Windows than they are with drawing or filling rectangular shapes.

API Rectangle and Point Function Names and Descriptions

Table 28–1 shows 11 Windows API rectangle and point functions and provides a brief description for their use. Other functions, dealing with rectangles, are scattered in the chapters previous mentioned. For a complete understanding of rectangles and their use, you'll want to study these chapters also.

Table 28–1   Rectangle and Point Functions and Descriptions

Function	Description
CopyRect	Copies one rectangle into another rectangle.
EqualRect	Determines if two rectangles are equivalent.
InflateRect	Inflates or deflates a rectangle's size.
IntersectRect	Creates a rectangle based on the intersection of two separate rectangles. The new rectangle's size is determined by the points common to both of the originating rectangles.
IsRectEmpty	Determines if the rectangle is empty.
OffsetRect	Displaces a rectangle by the given offset.
PtInRect	Determines if a point is within a rectangle.
SetRect	Sets the coordinates of the rectangle. This is equivalent to assigning the left, top, right, and bottom arguments to the appropriate members of the RECT structure.
SetRectEmpty	Creates an empty rectangle where all coordinates are set to zero.
SubtractRect	Gets the coordinates of a rectangle by subtracting one rectangle from another rectangle.
UnionRect	Creates the union of two rectangles. The union is the smallest rectangle that contains both original rectangles.

We'll illustrate the use of some of these functions in an application contained at the end of this chapter.

API Rectangle and Point Function Declarations

The following listing contains the Windows API rectangle and point function declarations found in the Win32api.txt file provided with Visual Basic. As we mentioned earlier, there are numerous functions scattered throughout the book that also involve rectangles. You'll want to study these chapters too.

```
Declare Function CopyRect Lib "user32" Alias
   "CopyRect" (lpDestRect As RECT,
   lpSourceRect As RECT) As Long

Declare Function EqualRect Lib "user32" Alias
   "EqualRect" (lpRect1 As RECT,
   lpRect2 As RECT) As Long

Declare Function InflateRect Lib "user32" Alias
   "InflateRect" (lpRect As RECT, ByVal x As Long,
   ByVal y As Long) As Long
```

```
Declare Function IntersectRect Lib "user32" Alias
  "IntersectRect" (lpDestRect As RECT,
  lpSrc1Rect As RECT, lpSrc2Rect As RECT) As Long

Declare Function IsRectEmpty Lib "user32" Alias
  "IsRectEmpty" (lpRect As RECT) As Long

Declare Function OffsetRect Lib "user32" Alias
  "OffsetRect" (lpRect As RECT,
  ByVal x As Long, ByVal y As Long) As Long

Declare Function PtInRect Lib "user32" Alias
  "PtInRect" (lpRect As RECT, pt As POINTAPI) As Long

Declare Function SetRect Lib "user32" Alias
  "SetRect" (lpRect As RECT, ByVal X1 As Long,
  ByVal Y1 As Long, ByVal X2 As Long,
  ByVal Y2 As Long) As Long

Declare Function SetRectEmpty Lib "user32" Alias
  "SetRectEmpty" (lpRect As RECT) As Long

Declare Function SubtractRect Lib "user32" Alias
  "SubtractRect" (lprcDst As RECT,
  lprcSrc1 As RECT, lprcSrc2 As RECT) As Long

Declare Function UnionRect Lib "user32" Alias
  "UnionRect" (lpDestRect As RECT,
  lpSrc1Rect As RECT, lpSrc2Rect As RECT) As Long
```

Table 28–2 contains a brief description of the parameters used in the various rectangle and point functions.

Many of the parameters described in Table 28–2 return information to structures. These structures are also described in the Win32api.txr file. The following listing shows the structures related to the rectangle and point function in this chapter.

```
Type RECT
  Left As Long
  Top As Long
  Right As Long
  Bottom As Long
End Type

Type POINTAPI
  x As Long
  y As Long
End Type
```

In the next section, we'll examine an application that makes use of several rectangle functions.

Table 28–2 Rectangle and Point Function Parameters and Descriptions

Parameter	Description
lpDestRect As RECT	Structure holds
lprcDst As RECT	Points to a RECT structure that containing results of the operation involving the rectangles pointed to by the lprcSrc1 and lprcSrc2 parameters.
lprcSrc1 As RECT	Points to the RECT structure that contains the first source rectangle.
lprcSrc2 As RECT	Points to the RECT structure that contains the second source rectangle.
lpRect As RECT	Points to the RECT structure that contains the coordinates of the rectangle.
lpRect1 As RECT	Points to a RECT structure that contains the logical coordinates of the first rectangle.
lpRect2 As RECT	Points to a RECT structure that contains the logical coordinates of the second rectangle.
lpSourceRect As RECT	Points to the RECT structure whose coordinates are to be copied.
lpSrc1Rect As RECT	Points to the RECT structure that contains the first source rectangle.
lpSrc2Rect As RECT	Points to the RECT structure that contains the second source rectangle.
pt As POINTAPI	Specifies a POINT structure that contains the given point.
X As Long	Gives the amount to move the rectangle left or right. This parameter must be a negative value to move the rectangle to the left.
	(or)
	Gives the amount to increase or decrease the rectangle width. This parameter must be negative to decrease the width.
X1 As Long	Gives the X coordinate of the rectangle's upper-left corner.
X2 As Long	Gives the X coordinate of the rectangle's lower-right corner.
Y As Long	Gives the amount to move the rectangle up or down. This parameter must be a negative value to move the rectangle up.
	(or)
	Gives the amount to increase or decrease the rectangle height. This parameter must be negative to decrease the height.
Y1 As Long	Gives the Y coordinate of the rectangle's upper-left corner.
Y2 As Long	Gives the Y coordinate of the rectangle's lower-right corner.

Example Application

This group of functions is very easy to use. We'll illustrate their use with a simple example that creates and draws two rectangles to the screen. The intersection of the two rectangles will then be made, and the resulting rectangle will be drawn to the screen in a different color.

The Visual Basic project is named Rect1.vbp. The project contains one module (Rect1.bas) for declaring the structure and functions and a simple form for drawing (Rect1.frm).

The contents of the module file are shown in the following listing. Notice the use of some additional functions for this project that have been discussed in previous chapters.

```
Type RECT
  Left As Long
  Top As Long
  Right As Long
  Bottom As Long
End Type

'Rectangle functions to use
Declare Function IntersectRect Lib "user32"
  (lpDestRect As RECT, lpSrc1Rect As RECT,
  lpSrc2Rect As RECT) As Long
Declare Function SetRect Lib "user32"
  (lpRect As RECT, ByVal X1 As Long,
  ByVal Y1 As Long, ByVal X2 As Long,
  ByVal Y2 As Long) As Long

'Functions used in previous chapters
Declare Function Rectangle Lib "gdi32"
  (ByVal hdc As Long, ByVal X1 As Long,
  ByVal Y1 As Long, ByVal X2 As Long,
  ByVal Y2 As Long) As Long
Declare Function CreateSolidBrush Lib "gdi32"
  (ByVal crColor As Long) As Long
Declare Function SelectObject Lib "gdi32"
  (ByVal hdc As Long, ByVal hObject As Long) As Long
```

The project uses the Form_Paint() subroutine for drawing to the screen. Here is the code for determining the intersection of the two specified rectangles.

```
Private Sub Form_Paint()
  Dim r&
  Dim newbrush&
  Dim lpRect1 As RECT
  Dim lpRect2 As RECT
  Dim lpRectInter As RECT

  'Define the first rectangle
  r& = SetRect(lpRect1, 0, 0, 200, 200)
  'create a solid light green brush
  hBrush = CreateSolidBrush(QBColor(10))
  newbrush = SelectObject(hdc, hBrush)
  'draw the first rectangle
  r& = Rectangle(hdc, lpRect1.Left, lpRect1.Top,
                 lpRect1.Right, lpRect1.Bottom)

  'Define the second rectangle
  r& = SetRect(lpRect2, 150, 150, 400, 400)
```

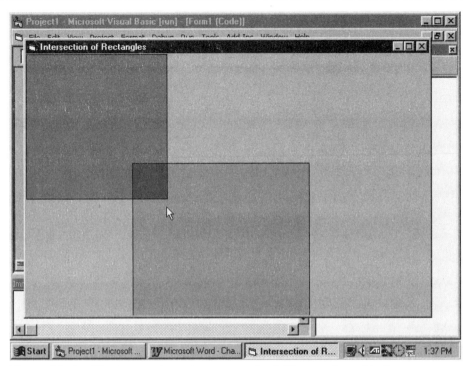

Figure 28–1 The intersection of two rectangles is illustrated graphically.

```
'create a solid light blue brush
hBrush = CreateSolidBrush(QBColor(11))
newbrush = SelectObject(hdc, hBrush)
'draw the second rectangle
r& = Rectangle(hdc, lpRect2.Left, lpRect2.Top,
               lpRect2.Right, lpRect2.Bottom)

r& = IntersectRect(lpRectInter, lpRect1, lpRect2)
'create a solid magenta brush
hBrush = CreateSolidBrush(QBColor(13))
newbrush = SelectObject(hdc, hBrush)
'draw the intersection of the original rectangles
r& = Rectangle(hdc, lpRectInter.Left, lpRectInter.Top,
               lpRectInter.Right, lpRectInter.Bottom)
End Sub
```

When the application is run, you should see a screen similar to Figure 28–1.

You can modify this application to experiment with the subtraction of two rectangles or with the union of two rectangles. Give it a try. The results might surprise you.

Chapter 29

Cursor and Caret Functions

The Windows API allows manipulation of cursors and carets. Cursors and carets are actually small bitmapped images that are used to indicate positions within a window or on the screen. Cursors usually track mouse movements. Carets are typically used within text controls and word processors to indicate the current position within a line, paragraph, or page of text.

API Cursor and Caret Function Names and Descriptions

Table 29–1 shows 20 Windows API cursor and caret functions and provides a brief description for their use.

The Visual Basic application, provided at the end of this chapter, illustrates the use of several caret functions.

API Cursor and Caret Function Declarations

The following listing contains the Windows API function declarations found in the Win32api.txt file provided with Visual Basic:

Table 29–1   Cursor and Caret Functions and Descriptions

Function	Description
ClipCursor	Restricts the cursor to a rectangular area on the screen.
CopyCursor	Copies a cursor.
CreateCaret	Creates a new system caret. The specified window becomes the caret's owner.
CreateCursor	Creates a cursor having the given size, bit patterns, and hot spot location.
DestroyCaret	Destroys the caret's shape, frees the caret from the window, and removes the caret from the screen. When the caret is a bitmapped image, the function does not free the bitmapped image.
DestroyCursor	Destroys a cursor created by CreateCursor() and frees any memory. Cannot be used to destroy a cursor created by any function except CreateCursor().
GetCaretBlinkTime	Gets the elapsed time (milliseconds) needed to invert the caret's pixels.
GetCaretPos	Gets the caret's position (client coordinates).
GetClipCursor	Gets the screen coordinates of the rectangular area to which the cursor is confined.
GetCursor	Gets the handle of the cursor.
GetCursorPos	Gets the cursor's position, in screen coordinates.
HideCaret	Hides the caret. The caret's shape or insertion point is not affected.
LoadCursor	Loads the cursor resource from the executable file.
SetCaretBlinkTime	Sets the elapsed time (milliseconds) needed to invert the caret's pixels.
SetCaretPos	Sets the caret's position (client coordinates).
SetCursor	Establishes the cursor shape. Under Win 95: The width and height of the cursor must be the values returned by GetSystemMetrics() for SM_CXCURSOR and SM_CYCURSOR.
SetCursorPos	Sets the cursor's position in screen coordinates.
SetSystemCursor	Replaces the contents of the system cursor with the contents of the cursor specified by the handle.
ShowCaret	Makes the caret visible.
ShowCursor	Shows or hides the cursor.

```
Declare Function ClipCursor Lib "user32" Alias
   "ClipCursor" (lpRect As Any) As Long

Declare Function CopyCursor Lib "user32" Alias
   "CopyCursor" (ByVal hcur As Long) As Long

Declare Function CreateCaret Lib "user32" Alias
   "CreateCaret" (ByVal hwnd As Long,
   ByVal hBitmap As Long, ByVal nWidth As Long,
   ByVal nHeight As Long) As Long

Declare Function CreateCursor Lib "user32" Alias
   "CreateCursor" (ByVal hInstance As Long,
   ByVal nXhotspot As Long, ByVal nYhotspot As Long,
   ByVal nWidth As Long, ByVal nHeight As Long,
   lpANDbitPlane As Any, lpXORbitPlane As Any) As Long
```

```
Declare Function DestroyCaret Lib "user32" Alias
  "DestroyCaret" () As Long

Declare Function DestroyCursor Lib "user32" Alias
  "DestroyCursor" (ByVal hCursor As Long) As Long

Declare Function GetCaretBlinkTime Lib "user32" Alias
  "GetCaretBlinkTime" () As Long

Declare Function GetCaretPos Lib "user32" Alias
  "GetCaretPos" (lpPoint As POINTAPI) As Long

Declare Function GetClipCursor Lib "user32" Alias
  "GetClipCursor" (lprc As RECT) As Long

Declare Function GetCursor Lib "user32" Alias
  "GetCursor" () As Long

Declare Function GetCursorPos Lib "user32" Alias
  "GetCursorPos" (lpPoint As POINTAPI) As Long

Declare Function HideCaret Lib "user32" Alias
  "HideCaret" (ByVal hwnd As Long) As Long

Declare Function LoadCursor Lib "user32" Alias
  "LoadCursorA" (ByVal hInstance As Long,
  ByVal lpCursorName As String) As Long

Declare Function SetCaretBlinkTime Lib "user32" Alias
  "SetCaretBlinkTime" (ByVal wMSeconds As Long) As Long

Declare Function SetCaretPos Lib "user32" Alias
  "SetCaretPos" (ByVal x As Long,
  ByVal y As Long) As Long

Declare Function SetCursor Lib "user32" Alias
  "SetCursor" (ByVal hCursor As Long) As Long

Declare Function SetCursorPos Lib "user32" Alias
  "SetCursorPos" (ByVal x As Long,
  ByVal y As Long) As Long

Declare Function SetSystemCursor Lib "user32" Alias
  "SetSystemCursor" (ByVal hcur As Long,
  ByVal id As Long) As Long

Declare Function ShowCaret Lib "user32" Alias
  "ShowCaret" (ByVal hwnd As Long) As Long

Declare Function ShowCursor Lib "user32" Alias
  "ShowCursor" (ByVal bShow As Long) As Long
```

Table 29–2 contains a brief description of the parameters used in the various cursor and caret functions.

Table 29–2   Cursor and Caret Function Parameters and Descriptions

Parameter	Description
bshow As Long	Determines if the internal display counter is incremented or decremented. If TRUE, the display count is incremented. If FALSE, the display count is decremented.
hbitmap As Long	Handle that identifies the bitmapped caret shape. When NULL, the caret is solid. When 1, the caret is gray. When a bitmap handle, the caret is assigned the bitmapped image. Handles are created with calls to CreateBitmap(), CreateDIBitmap(), or LoadBitmap(). When a bitmap handle is used, the width and height parameters are ignored.
hcur As Long	Handle of cursor.
hcursor As Long	Handle of cursor.
hinstance As Long	Handle of instance.
hwnd As Long	Handle of window.
id As Long	A system cursor ID. Uses OCR_ constants.
lpANDbitPlane As Any	Points to an array of bytes that contains the bit values for the AND bitmask of the cursor.
lpCursorName As String	Points to a string that holds the name, or identifier, of the cursor resource to be loaded. Can use IDC_ constants, too.
lpPoint As POINTAPI	Structure holds the client coordinates of the caret.
lprc As RECT	Structure receives the screen coordinates of the confining rectangle or the whole screen if the cursor is not confined.
lpXORbitPlane As Any	Points to an array of bytes that contains the bit values for the XOR bitmask of the cursor.
nheight As Long	The height of the image in logical units. If a caret: When 0, the height is the system-defined window border height.
nwidth As Long	The width of the image in logical units. If a caret: When 0, the width is the system-defined window border width.
nXhotspot As Long	The horizontal position of the cursor's hot spot.
nYhotspot As Long	The vertical position of the cursor's hot spot.
wMSeconds As Long	Caret blink time in milliseconds.
x As Long	Gives the new X coordinate of the caret.
y As Long	Gives the new Y coordinate of the caret.

Many of the parameters described in Table 29–2 use constant values. The Win32api.txt file lists the following constants for cursor and caret parameters.

```
'Standard Cursor IDs
Public Const IDC_ARROW = 32512&
Public Const IDC_IBEAM = 32513&
Public Const IDC_WAIT = 32514&
Public Const IDC_CROSS = 32515&
Public Const IDC_UPARROW = 32516&
Public Const IDC_SIZE = 32640&
Public Const IDC_ICON = 32641&
```

```
Public Const IDC_SIZENWSE = 32642&
Public Const IDC_SIZENESW = 32643&
Public Const IDC_SIZEWE = 32644&
Public Const IDC_SIZENS = 32645&
Public Const IDC_SIZEALL = 32646&
Public Const IDC_NO = 32648&
Public Const IDC_APPSTARTING = 32650&

'OEM Resource Ordinal Numbers
'relating to cursors.
Public Const OCR_NORMAL = 32512
Public Const OCR_IBEAM = 32513
Public Const OCR_WAIT = 32514
Public Const OCR_CROSS = 32515
Public Const OCR_UP = 32516
Public Const OCR_SIZE = 32640
Public Const OCR_ICON = 32641
Public Const OCR_SIZENWSE = 32642
Public Const OCR_SIZENESW = 32643
Public Const OCR_SIZEWE = 32644
Public Const OCR_SIZENS = 32645
Public Const OCR_SIZEALL = 32646
Public Const OCR_ICOCUR = 32647
Public Const OCR_NO = 32648 ' not in win3.1
```

In addition to the constants just listed, a structure is required by two functions. The structure declarations are also found in the Win32api.txt file.

```
Type RECT
  Left As Long
  Top As Long
  Right As Long
  Bottom As Long
End Type

Type POINTAPI
  x As Long
  y As Long
End Type
```

In the next section we'll investigate an application that makes use of several caret functions.

Example Application

In this section we'll investigate the use of four caret functions built into a simple Visual Basic application. The functions will allow the caret shape and blink rate to be changed. Also, the option to make the caret visible or hidden will be provided.

This project, named Caret1.vbp, uses a single form with a text control and four command buttons. A module file, named Caret1.bas, contains the function declarations for the four caret functions. Here are the contents of Caret1.bas.

```
Declare Function CreateCaret Lib "user32"
  (ByVal hwnd As Long, ByVal hBitmap As Long,
  ByVal nWidth As Long, ByVal nHeight As Long) As Long

Declare Function HideCaret Lib "user32"
  (ByVal hwnd As Long) As Long

Declare Function SetCaretBlinkTime Lib "user32"
  (ByVal wMSeconds As Long) As Long

Declare Function ShowCaret Lib "user32"
  (ByVal hwnd As Long) As Long
```

The form, Caret1.frm, uses command button click events to change various caret properties. Here is the code used to support the various caret options.

```
Private Sub Command1_Click()
  Dim r&

  'Faster blinking caret
  r& = CreateCaret(Text1.hwnd, 1, 10, 25)
  r& = ShowCaret(Text1.hwnd)
  r& = SetCaretBlinkTime(10)
  r& = ShowCaret(Text1.hwnd)
End Sub

Private Sub Command2_Click()
  Dim r&

  'Slower blinking caret
  r& = CreateCaret(Text1.hwnd, 1, 10, 25)
  r& = ShowCaret(Text1.hwnd)
  r& = SetCaretBlinkTime(200)
  r& = ShowCaret(Text1.hwnd)
End Sub

Private Sub Command3_Click()
  Dim r&

  'Show the caret
  r& = ShowCaret(Text1.hwnd)
End Sub

Private Sub Command4_Click()
  Dim r&

  'Hide the caret
  r& = HideCaret(Text1.hwnd)
End Sub
```

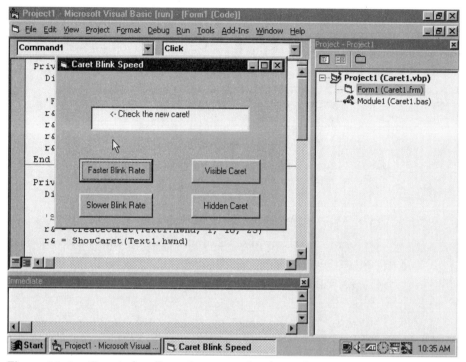

Figure 29–1   Caret1.vbp allows the caret to be changed and its blink rate altered.

```
Private Sub Form_Load()
  Dim r&

  'Create initial caret
  Form1.Show
  r& = CreateCaret(Text1.hwnd, 1, 10, 25)
  r& = ShowCaret(Text1.hwnd)
End Sub
```

The shape of the caret is changed to a light gray 10x25 block. If a 0 is used as the second parameter in the CreateCaret() function, the new caret will be black. Visual Basic and Windows often interact in a strange manner with regard to carets so the CreateCaret() function is repeated each time the blink rate is changed.

You'll notice as you examine the code that the fast blink rate is set to 10 milliseconds and the slower blink rate to 200 milliseconds.

Figure 29–1 shows the application with a fast blink rate and the caret visible. Of course, you'll just have to imagine how fast it is blinking until you try the application yourself.

Win32 API
Function and
Subroutine Prototypes

The following listing contains the complete listing of over 1,500 function and subroutine prototypes contained in the Win32api.txt file. If you study the Win32api.txt file, you'll quickly appreciate this alphabetical listing; the Win32api.txt file does not list functions or subroutines in an alphabetical order.

A
AbortDoc
AbortPath
AbortPrinter
AbortSystemShutdown
AccessCheck
AccessCheckAndAuditAlarm
ActivateKeyboardLayout
AddAccessAllowedAce
AddAccessDeniedAce
AddAce
AddAtom
AddAuditAccessAce
AddFontResource
AddForm
AddJob

AddMonitor
AddPort
AddPrinter
AddPrinterConnection
AddPrinterDriver
AddPrintProcessor
AddPrintProvidor
AdjustTokenGroups
AdjustTokenPrivileges
AdjustWindowRect
AdjustWindowRectEx
AdvancedDocumentProperties
AllocateAndInitializeSid
AllocateLocallyUniqueId
AllocConsole

AngleArc
AnimatePalette
AnyPopup
AppendMenu
Arc
ArcTo
AreAllAccessesGranted
AreAnyAccessesGranted

B
BackupEventLog
BackupRead
BackupSeek
BackupWrite
Beep
BeginDeferWindowPos
BeginPaint

C
CallMsgFilter
CallNamedPipe
CallNextHookEx
CallWindowProc
CancelDC
CascadeWindows
ChangeClipboardChain
ChangeMenu
ChangeServiceConfig
CharLower
CharLowerBuff
CharNext
CharPrev
CharToOem
CharToOemBuff
CharUpper
CharUpperBuff
CheckColorsInGamut
CheckDlgButton
CheckMenuItem
CheckMenuRadioItem
CheckRadioButton
ChildWindowFromPoint
ChildWindowFromPointEx
ChooseColor
ChooseFont
ChoosePixelFormat
Chord
ClearCommBreak
ClearCommError

ArrangeIconicWindows
AttachThreadInput
auxGetDevCaps
auxGetNumDevs
auxGetVolume
auxOutMessage
auxSetVolume

BeginPath
BeginUpdateResource
BitBlt
BringWindowToTop
BroadcastSystemMessage
BuildCommDCB
BuildCommDCBAndTimeouts

ClearEventLog
ClientToScreen
ClipCursor
CloseClipboard
CloseDesktop
CloseDriver
CloseEnhMetaFile
CloseEventLog
CloseFigure
CloseHandle
CloseMetaFile
ClosePrinter
CloseServiceHandle
CloseWindow
CloseWindowStation
ColorMatchToTarget
CombineRgn
CombineTransform
CommandLineToArgv
CommConfigDialog
CommDlgExtendedError
CompareFileTime
CompareString
ConfigurePort
ConnectNamedPipe
ConnectToPrinterDlg
ContinueDebugEvent
ControlService
ConvertDefaultLocale
CopyAcceleratorTable

CopyCursor
CopyEnhMetaFile
CopyFile
CopyIcon
CopyImage
CopyLZFile
CopyMetaFile
CopyRect
CopySid
CountClipboardFormats
CreateAcceleratorTable
CreateBitmap
CreateBitmapIndirect
CreateBrushIndirect
CreateCaret
CreateColorSpace
CreateCompatibleBitmap
CreateCompatibleDC
CreateConsoleScreenBuffer
CreateCursor
CreateDC
CreateDesktop
CreateDialogIndirectParam
CreateDialogParam
CreateDIBitmap
CreateDIBPatternBrush
CreateDIBPatternBrushPt
CreateDIBSection
CreateDirectory
CreateDirectoryEx
CreateDiscardableBitmap
CreateEllipticRgn
CreateEllipticRgnIndirect
CreateEnhMetaFile
CreateEvent
CreateFile
CreateFileMapping
CreateFont

CreateFontIndirect
CreateHalftonePalette
CreateHatchBrush
CreateIC
CreateIcon
CreateIconFromResource
CreateIconFromResource
CreateIconIndirect
CreateIoCompletionPort
CreateMailslot
CreateMDIWindow
CreateMenu
CreateMetaFile
CreateMutex
CreateNamedPipe
CreatePalette
CreatePatternBrush
CreatePen
CreatePenIndirect
CreatePipe
CreatePolygonRgn
CreatePolyPolygonRgn
CreatePopupMenu
CreatePrivateObjectSecurity
CreateProcess
CreateProcessAsUser
CreateRectRgn
CreateRectRgnIndirect
CreateRemoteThread
CreateRoundRectRgn
CreateScalableFontResource
CreateSemaphore
CreateService
CreateSolidBrush
CreateTapePartition
CreateThread
CreateWindowEx

D
DdeAbandonTransaction
DdeAccessData
DdeAddData
DdeClientTransaction
DdeCmpStringHandles
DdeConnect
DdeConnectList
DdeCreateDataHandle
DdeCreateStringHandle

DdeDisconnect
DdeDisconnectList
DdeEnableCallback
DdeFreeDataHandle
DdeFreeStringHandle
DdeFreeStringHandle
DdeFreeStringHandle
DdeGetLastError
DdeImpersonateClient

DdeInitialize
DdeKeepStringHandle
DdeNameService
DdePostAdvise
DdeQueryConvInfo
DdeQueryNextServer
DdeQueryString
DdeReconnect
DdeSetQualityOfService
DdeSetUserHandle
DdeUnaccessData
DdeUninitialize
DebugActiveProcess
DebugBreak
DefDlgProc
DefDriverProc
DeferWindowPos
DefFrameProc
DefineDosDevice
DefMDIChildProc
DefWindowProc
DeleteAce
DeleteAtom
DeleteColorSpace
DeleteCriticalSection
DeleteDC
DeleteEnhMetaFile
DeleteFile
DeleteForm
DeleteMenu
DeleteMetaFile
DeleteMonitor
DeleteObject
DeletePort
DeletePrinter
DeletePrinterConnection
DeletePrinterDriver
DeletePrintProcessor
DeletePrintProvidor
DeleteService
DeregisterEventSource
DescribePixelFormat
DestroyAcceleratorTable

E
Ellipse
EmptyClipboard
EnableMenuItem
EnableScrollBar

DestroyCaret
DestroyCursor
DestroyIcon
DestroyMenu
DestroyPrivateObjectSecurity
DestroyWindow
DeviceCapabilities
DeviceIoControl
DialogBoxIndirectParam
DisableThreadLibraryCalls
DisconnectNamedPipe
DispatchMessage
DlgDirList
DlgDirListComboBox
DlgDirSelectComboBoxExDlgDir
    SelectEx
DocumentProperties
DoEnvironmentSubst
DosDateTimeToFileTime
DPtoLP
DragAcceptFiles
DragDetect
DragFinish
DragObject
DragQueryFile
DragQueryPoint
DrawAnimatedRects
DrawCaption
DrawEdge
DrawEscape
DrawFocusRect
DrawFrameControl
DrawIcon
DrawIconEx
DrawMenuBar
DrawState
DrawText
DrawTextEx
DrvGetModuleHandle
DuplicateHandle
DuplicateIcon
DuplicateToken

EnableWindow
EndDeferWindowPos
EndDialog
EndDoc

EndDoc
EndDocPrinter
EndPage
EndPagePrinter
EndPaint
EndPath
EndUpdateResource
EnterCriticalSection
EnumCalendarInfo
EnumChildWindows
EnumClipboardFormats
EnumDateFormats
EnumDependentServices
EnumDesktops
EnumDesktopWindows
EnumEnhMetaFile
EnumFontFamilies
EnumFontFamiliesEx
EnumFonts
EnumForms
EnumICMProfiles
EnumJobs
EnumMetaFile
EnumMonitors
EnumObjects
EnumPorts
EnumPrinterDrivers
EnumPrinterPropertySheets
EnumPrinters
EnumPrintProcessorDatatypes
EnumPrintProcessors
EnumProps
EnumPropsEx

EnumResourceLanguages
EnumResourceNames
EnumResourceTypes
EnumServicesStatus
EnumSystemCodePages
EnumSystemLocales
EnumThreadWindows
EnumTimeFormats
EnumWindowStations
EqualPrefixSid
EqualRect
EqualRgn
EqualSid
EraseTape
Escape
EscapeCommFunction
ExcludeClipRect
ExcludeUpdateRgn
ExitProcess
ExitThread
ExitWindows
ExitWindowsEx
ExpandEnvironmentStrings
ExtCreatePen
ExtCreateRegion
ExtEscape
ExtFloodFill
ExtractAssociatedIcon
ExtractIcon
ExtractIconEx
ExtSelectClipRgn
ExtTextOut

F
FatalAppExit
FatalExit
FileTimeToDosDateTime
FileTimeToLocalFileTime
FileTimeToSystemTime
FillConsoleOutputAttribute
FillConsoleOutputCharacter
FillPath
FillRect
FillRgn
FindAtom
FindClose
FindCloseChangeNotification

FindClosePrinterChangeNotification
FindEnvironmentString
FindExecutable
FindFirstChangeNotification
FindFirstFile
FindFirstFreeAce
FindFirstPrinterChangeNotification
FindNextChangeNotification
FindNextFile
FindNextPrinterChangeNotification
FindResource
FindResourceEx
FindText

FindWindow
FindWindowEx
FixBrushOrgEx
FlashWindow
FlattenPath
FloodFill
FlushConsoleInputBuffer
FlushFileBuffers
FlushInstructionCache
FlushViewOfFile
FoldString

FormatMessage
FrameRect
FrameRgn
FreeConsole
FreeDDElParam
FreeEnvironmentStrings
FreeLibrary
FreeLibraryAndExitThread
FreeResource
FreeSid

G
GdiComment
GdiFlush
GdiGetBatchLimit
GdiSetBatchLimit
GenerateConsoleCtrlEvent
GetAce
GetAclInformation
GetACP
GetActiveWindow
GetArcDirection
GetAspectRatioFilterEx
GetAsyncKeyState
GetAtomName
GetBinaryType
GetBitmapBits
GetBitmapDimensionEx
GetBkColor
GetBkMode
GetBoundsRect
GetBrushOrgEx
GetCapture
GetCaretBlinkTime
GetCaretPos
GetCharABCWidths
GetCharABCWidthsFloat
GetCharacterPlacement
GetCharWidth
GetCharWidth32
GetCharWidthFloat
GetClassInfo
GetClassLong
GetClassName
GetClassWord
GetClientRect
GetClipboardData
GetClipboardFormatName

GetClipboardOwner
GetClipboardViewer
GetClipBox
GetClipCursor
GetClipRgn
GetColorAdjustment
GetColorSpace
GetCommandLine
GetCommConfig
GetCommMask
GetCommModemStatus
GetCommProperties
GetCommState
GetCommTimeouts
GetCompressedFileSize
GetComputerName
GetConsoleCP
GetConsoleCursorInfo
GetConsoleMode
GetConsoleOutputCP
GetConsoleScreenBufferInfo
GetConsoleTitle
GetCPInfo
GetCurrencyFormat
GetCurrentDirectory
GetCurrentObject
GetCurrentPositionEx
GetCurrentProcess
GetCurrentProcessId
GetCurrentThread
GetCurrentThreadId
GetCursor
GetCursorPos
GetDateFormat
GetDC
GetDCEx

GetDCOrgEx
GetDefaultCommConfig
GetDesktopWindow
GetDeviceCaps
GetDeviceGammaRamp
GetDialogBaseUnits
GetDIBColorTable
GetDIBits
GetDiskFreeSpace
GetDlgCtrlID
GetDlgItem
GetDlgItemInt
GetDlgItemText
GetDoubleClickTime
GetDriverModuleHandle
GetDriveType
GetEnhMetaFile
GetEnhMetaFileBits
GetEnhMetaFileDescription
GetEnhMetaFileHeader
GetEnhMetaFilePaletteEntries
GetEnvironmentStrings
GetEnvironmentVariable
GetExitCodeProcess
GetExitCodeThread
GetExpandedName
GetFileAttributes
GetFileInformationByHandle
GetFileSecurity
GetFileSize
GetFileTime
GetFileTitle
GetFileType
GetFileVersionInfo
GetFileVersionInfoSize
GetFocus
GetFontData
GetFontLanguageInfo
GetForegroundWindow
GetForm
GetFullPathName
GetGlyphOutline
GetGraphicsMode
GetHandleInformation
GetICMProfile
GetIconInfo
GetInputState
GetJob

GetKBCodePage
GetKernelObjectSecurity
GetKerningPairs
GetKeyboardLayout
GetKeyboardLayoutList
GetKeyboardLayoutName
GetKeyboardState
GetKeyboardType
GetKeyNameText
GetKeyState
GetLargestConsoleWindowSize
GetLastActivePopup
GetLastError
GetLengthSid
GetLocaleInfo
GetLocalTime
GetLogColorSpace
GetLogicalDrives
GetLogicalDriveStrings
GetMailslotInfo
GetMapMode
GetMenu
GetMenuCheckMarkDimensions
GetMenuContextHelpId
GetMenuDefaultItem
GetMenuItemCount
GetMenuItemID
GetMenuItemInfo
GetMenuItemRect
GetMenuState
GetMenuString
GetMessage
GetMessageExtraInfo
GetMessagePos
GetMessageTime
GetMetaFile
GetMetaFileBitsEx
GetMetaRgn
GetMiterLimit
GetModuleFileName
GetModuleHandle
GetNamedPipeHandleState
GetNamedPipeInfo
GetNearestColor
GetNearestPaletteIndex
GetNextDlgGroupItem
GetNextDlgTabItem
GetNextWindow

GetNumberFormat

GetNumberOfConsoleInputEvents

GetNumberOfConsoleMouseButtons

GetNumberOfEventLogRecords

GetObject

GetObjectType

GetOEMCP

GetOldestEventLogRecord

GetOpenClipboardWindow

GetOpenFileName

GetOutlineTextMetrics

GetOverlappedResult

GetPaletteEntries

GetParent

GetPath

GetPixel

GetPixelFormat

GetPolyFillMode

GetPrinter

GetPrinterData

GetPrinterDriver

GetPrinterDriverDirectory

GetPrintProcessorDirectory

GetPriorityClass

GetPriorityClipboardFormat

GetPrivateObjectSecurity

GetPrivateProfileInt

GetPrivateProfileSection

GetPrivateProfileString

GetProcAddress

GetProcessAffinityMask

GetProcessHeap

GetProcessHeaps

GetProcessShutdownParameters

GetProcessTimes

GetProcessWindowStation

GetProcessWorkingSetSize

GetProfileInt

GetProfileSection

GetProfileString

GetProp

GetQueuedCompletionStatus

GetQueueStatus

GetRasterizerCaps

GetRegionData

GetRgnBox

GetROP2

GetSaveFileName

GetScrollInfo

GetScrollPos

GetScrollRange

GetSecurityDescriptorControl

GetSecurityDescriptorDacl

GetSecurityDescriptorGroup

GetSecurityDescriptorLength

GetSecurityDescriptorOwner

GetSecurityDescriptorSacl

GetServiceDisplayName

GetServiceKeyName

GetShortPathName

GetSidIdentifierAuthority

GetSidLengthRequired

GetSidSubAuthority

GetSidSubAuthorityCount

GetStartupInfo

GetStdHandle

GetStockObject

GetStretchBltMode

GetStringTypeA

GetStringTypeEx

GetStringTypeW

GetSubMenu

GetSysColor

GetSysColorBrush

GetSystemDefaultLangID

GetSystemDefaultLCID

GetSystemDirectory

GetSystemInfo

GetSystemMenu

GetSystemMetrics

GetSystemPaletteEntries

GetSystemPaletteUse

GetSystemPowerStatus

GetSystemTime

GetSystemTimeAdjustment

GetTabbedTextExtent

GetTapeParameters

GetTapePosition

GetTapeStatus

GetTempFileName

GetTempPath

GetTextAlign

GetTextCharacterExtra

GetTextCharset

GetTextCharsetInfo

GetTextColor

GetTextExtentExPoint
GetTextExtentPoint
GetTextExtentPoint32
GetTextFace
GetTextMetrics
GetThreadContext
GetThreadDesktop
GetThreadLocale
GetThreadPriority
GetThreadSelectorEntry
GetThreadTimes
GetTickCount
GetTimeFormat
GetTimeZoneInformation
GetTokenInformation
GetTopWindow
GetUpdateRect
GetUpdateRgn
GetUserDefaultLangID
GetUserDefaultLCID
GetUserName
GetUserObjectInformation
GetUserObjectSecurity
GetVersion
GetVersionEx
GetViewportExtEx
GetViewportOrgEx
GetVolumeInformation
GetWindow
GetWindowContextHelpId
GetWindowDC
GetWindowExtEx

GetWindowLong
GetWindowOrgEx
GetWindowPlacement
GetWindowRect
GetWindowRgn
GetWindowsDirectory
GetWindowText
GetWindowTextLength
GetWindowThreadProcessId
GetWindowWord
GetWinMetaFileBits
GetWorldTransform
GlobalAddAtom
GlobalAlloc
GlobalCompact
GlobalDeleteAtom
GlobalFindAtom
GlobalFix
GlobalFlags
GlobalFree
GlobalGetAtomName
GlobalHandle
GlobalLock
GlobalMemoryStatus
GlobalReAlloc
GlobalSize
GlobalUnfix
GlobalUnlock
GlobalUnWire
GlobalWire
GrayString

H
HeapAlloc
HeapCompact
HeapCreate
HeapDestroy
HeapFree
HeapLock
HeapReAlloc

HeapSize
HeapUnlock
HeapValidate
HideCaret
HiliteMenuItem
hread
hwrite

I
ImmAssociateContext
ImmConfigureIME
ImmCreateContext
ImmDestroyContext
ImmEnumRegisterWord
ImmEscape

ImmGetCandidateList
ImmGetCandidateListCount
ImmGetCandidateWindow
ImmGetCompositionFont
ImmGetCompositionString
ImmGetCompositionWindow

ImmGetContext
ImmGetConversionList
ImmGetConversionStatus
ImmGetDefaultIMEWnd
ImmGetDescription
ImmGetGuideLine
ImmGetIMEFileName
ImmGetOpenStatus
ImmGetProperty
ImmGetRegisterWordStyle
ImmGetStatusWindowPos
ImmGetVirtualKey
ImmInstallIME
ImmIsIME
ImmIsUIMessage
ImmNotifyIME
ImmRegisterWord
ImmReleaseContext
ImmSetCandidateWindow
ImmSetCompositionFont
ImmSetCompositionString
ImmSetCompositionWindow
ImmSetConversionStatus
ImmSetOpenStatus
ImmSetStatusWindowPos
ImmSimulateHotKey
ImmUnregisterWord
ImpersonateDdeClientWindow
ImpersonateLoggedOnUser
ImpersonateNamedPipeClient
ImpersonateSelf
InflateRect
InitAtomTable
InitializeAcl
InitializeCriticalSection
InitializeSecurityDescriptor
InitializeSid
InitiateSystemShutdown
InSendMessage
InsertMenu

J
joyGetDevCaps
joyGetNumDevs
joyGetPos
joyGetPosEx

K
keybd_event

InsertMenuItem
InterlockedDecrement
InterlockedExchange
InterlockedIncrement
IntersectClipRect
IntersectRect
InvalidateRect
InvalidateRgn
InvertRect
InvertRgn
IsBadCodePtr
IsBadHugeReadPtr
IsBadHugeWritePtr
IsBadReadPtr
IsBadStringPtr
IsBadWritePtr
IsCharAlpha
IsCharAlphaNumeric
IsCharLower
IsCharUpper
IsChild
IsClipboardFormatAvailable
IsDBCSLeadByte
IsDialogMessage
IsDlgButtonChecked
IsIconic
IsMenu
IsRectEmpty
IsTextUnicode
IsValidAcl
IsValidCodePage
IsValidLocale
IsValidSecurityDescriptor
IsValidSid
IsWindow
IsWindowEnabled
IsWindowUnicode
IsWindowVisible
IsZoomed

joyGetThreshold
joyReleaseCapture
joySetCapture
joySetThreshold

KillTimer

L

lclose	LockFile
LCMapString	LockFileEx
lcreat	LockResource
LeaveCriticalSection	LockServiceDatabase
LineDDA	LockWindowUpdate
LineTo	LogonUser
llseek	LookupAccountName
LoadAccelerators	LookupAccountSid
LoadBitmap	LookupIconIdFromDirectory
LoadCursor	LookupIconIdFromDirectoryEx
LoadCursorFromFile	LookupPrivilegeDisplayName
LoadIcon	LookupPrivilegeName
LoadImage	LookupPrivilegeValue
LoadKeyboardLayout	lopen
LoadLibrary	LPtoDP
LoadLibraryEx	lread
LoadMenu	lstrcat
LoadMenuIndirect	lstrcmp
LoadModule	lstrcmpi
LoadResource	lstrcpy
LoadString	lstrcpyn
LocalAlloc	lstrlen
LocalCompact	lwrite
LocalFileTimeToFileTime	LZClose
LocalFlags	LZCopy
LocalFree	LZDone
LocalHandle	LZInit
LocalLock	LZOpenFile
LocalReAlloc	LZRead
LocalShrink	LZSeek
LocalSize	LZStart
LocalUnlock	

M

MakeAbsoluteSD	mciGetErrorString
MakeSelfRelativeSD	mciGetYieldProc
MapDialogRect	mciSendCommand
MapGenericMask	mciSendString
MapViewOfFile	mciSetYieldProc
MapViewOfFileEx	MenuItemFromPoint
MapVirtualKey	MessageBeep
MapVirtualKeyEx	MessageBox
MapWindowPoints	MessageBoxEx
MaskBlt	MessageBoxIndirect
mciExecute	midiConnect
mciGetCreatorTask	midiDisconnect
mciGetDeviceID	midiInAddBuffer
mciGetDeviceIDFromElementID	midiInClose

midiInGetDevCaps
midiInGetErrorText
midiInGetID
midiInGetNumDevs
midiInMessage
midiInOpen
midiInPrepareHeader
midiInReset
midiInStart
midiInStop
midiInUnprepareHeader
midiOutCacheDrumPatches
midiOutCachePatches
midiOutClose
midiOutGetDevCaps
midiOutGetErrorText
midiOutGetID
midiOutGetNumDevs
midiOutGetVolume
midiOutLongMsg
midiOutMessage
midiOutOpen
midiOutPrepareHeader
midiOutReset
midiOutSetVolume
midiOutShortMsg
midiOutUnprepareHeader
midiStreamClose
midiStreamOpen
midiStreamOut
midiStreamPause
midiStreamPosition
midiStreamProperty
midiStreamRestart
midiStreamStop
mixerClose

mixerGetControlDetails
mixerGetDevCaps
mixerGetID
mixerGetLineControls
mixerGetLineInfo
mixerGetNumDevs
mixerMessage
mixerOpen
mixerSetControlDetails
mmioAdvance
mmioAscend
mmioClose
mmioCreateChunk
mmioDescend
mmioFlush
mmioGetInfo
mmioInstallIOProcA
mmioOpen
mmioRead
mmioRename
mmioSeek
mmioSendMessage
mmioSetInfo
mmioStringToFOURCC
mmioWrite
mmsystemGetVersion
ModifyMenu
ModifyWorldTransform
mouse_event
MoveFile
MoveFileEx
MoveToEx
MoveWindow
MsgWaitForMultipleObjects
MulDiv
MultiByteToWideChar

N
Netbios
NotifyBootConfigStatus

NotifyChangeEventLog

O
ObjectCloseAuditAlarm
ObjectOpenAuditAlarm
ObjectPrivilegeAuditAlarm
OemKeyScan
OemToChar
OemToCharBuff

OffsetClipRgn
OffsetRect
OffsetRgn
OffsetViewportOrgEx
OffsetWindowOrgEx
OpenBackupEventLog

OpenClipboard
OpenDesktop
OpenDriver
OpenEvent
OpenEventLog
OpenFile
OpenFileMapping
OpenIcon
OpenInputDesktop
OpenMutex

OpenPrinter
OpenProcess
OpenProcessToken
OpenSCManager
OpenSemaphore
OpenService
OpenThreadToken
OpenWindowStation
OutputDebugStr
OutputDebugString

P
PackDDElParam
PageSetupDlg
PaintDesktop
PaintRgn
PatBlt
PathToRegion
PeekMessage
PeekNamedPipe
Pie
PlayEnhMetaFile
PlayEnhMetaFileRecord
PlayMetaFile
PlayMetaFileRecord
PlaySound
PlgBlt
PolyBezier
PolyBezierTo
PolyDraw
Polygon

Polyline
PolylineTo
PolyPolygon
PolyPolyline
PolyTextOut
PostMessage
PostQuitMessage
PostThreadMessage
PrepareTape
PrintDlg
PrinterMessageBox
PrinterProperties
PrivilegeCheck
PrivilegedServiceAuditAlarm
PtInRect
PtInRegion
PtVisible
PulseEvent
PurgeComm

Q
QueryDosDevice
QueryPerformanceCounter
QueryPerformanceFrequency
QueryServiceConfig

QueryServiceLockStatus
QueryServiceObjectSecurity
QueryServiceStatus

R
RaiseException
ReadConsole
ReadConsoleOutput
ReadConsoleOutputAttribute
ReadConsoleOutputCharacter
ReadEventLog
ReadFile
ReadFileEx
ReadPrinter

ReadProcessMemory
RealizePalette
Rectangle
RectInRegion
RectVisible
RedrawWindow
RegCloseKey
RegConnectRegistry
RegCreateKey

RegCreateKeyEx
RegDeleteKey
RegDeleteValue
RegEnumKey
RegEnumKeyEx
RegEnumValue
RegFlushKey
RegGetKeySecurity
RegisterClass
RegisterClassEx
RegisterClipboardFormat
RegisterEventSource
RegisterHotKey
RegisterServiceCtrlHandler
RegisterWindowMessage
RegLoadKey
RegNotifyChangeKeyValue
RegOpenKey
RegOpenKeyEx
RegQueryInfoKey
RegQueryValue
RegQueryValueEx
RegReplaceKey
RegRestoreKey
RegSaveKey

RegSetKeySecurity
RegSetValue
RegSetValueEx
RegUnLoadKey
ReleaseCapture
ReleaseDC
ReleaseMutex
ReleaseSemaphore
RemoveDirectory
RemoveFontResource
RemoveMenu
RemoveProp
ReplaceText
ReplyMessage
ReportEvent
ResetDC
ResetEvent
ResetPrinter
ResizePalette
RestoreDC
ResumeThread
ReuseDDElParam
RevertToSelf
RoundRect

S
SaveDC
ScaleViewportExtEx
ScaleWindowExtEx
ScheduleJob
ScreenToClient
ScrollConsoleScreenBuffer
ScrollDC
ScrollWindow
ScrollWindowEx
SearchPath
SelectClipPath
SelectClipRgn
SelectObject
SelectPalette
SendDlgItemMessage
SendDriverMessage
SendMessage
SendMessageCallback
SendMessageTimeout
SendNotifyMessage
SetAbortProc
SetAclInformation

SetActiveWindow
SetArcDirection
SetBitmapBits
SetBitmapDimensionEx
SetBkColor
SetBkMode
SetBoundsRect
SetBrushOrgEx
SetCapture
SetCaretBlinkTime
SetCaretPos
SetClassLong
SetClassWord
SetClipboardData
SetClipboardViewer
SetColorAdjustment
SetColorSpace
SetCommBreak
SetCommConfig
SetCommMask
SetCommState
SetCommTimeouts

SetComputerName
SetConsoleActiveScreenBuffer
SetConsoleCP
SetConsoleCtrlHandler
SetConsoleCursorInfo
SetConsoleCursorPosition
SetConsoleMode
SetConsoleOutputCP
SetConsoleScreenBufferSize
SetConsoleTextAttribute
SetConsoleTitle
SetConsoleWindowInfo
SetCurrentDirectory
SetCursor
SetCursorPos
SetDebugErrorLevel
SetDefaultCommConfig
SetDeviceGammaRamp
SetDIBColorTable
SetDIBits
SetDIBitsToDevice
SetDlgItemInt
SetDlgItemText
SetDoubleClickTime
SetEndOfFile
SetEnhMetaFileBits
SetEnvironmentVariable
SetErrorMode
SetEvent
SetFileApisToANSI
SetFileApisToOEM
SetFileAttributes
SetFilePointer
SetFileSecurity
SetFileTime
SetFocus
SetForegroundWindow
SetForm
SetGraphicsMode
SetHandleCount
SetHandleInformation
SetICMMode
SetICMProfile
SetJob
SetKernelObjectSecurity
SetKeyboardState
SetLastError
SetLastErrorEx

SetLocaleInfo
SetLocalTime
SetMailslotInfo
SetMapMode
SetMapperFlags
SetMenu
SetMenuContextHelpId
SetMenuDefaultItem
SetMenuItemBitmaps
SetMenuItemInfo
SetMessageExtraInfo
SetMessageQueue
SetMetaFileBitsEx
SetMetaRgn
SetMiterLimit
SetNamedPipeHandleState
SetPaletteEntries
SetParent
SetPixel
SetPixelFormat
SetPixelV
SetPolyFillMode
SetPrinter
SetPrinterData
SetPriorityClass
SetPrivateObjectSecurity
SetProcessShutdownParameters
SetProcessWindowStation
SetProcessWorkingSetSize
SetProp
SetRect
SetRectEmpty
SetRectRgn
SetROP2
SetScrollInfo
SetScrollPos
SetScrollRange
SetSecurityDescriptorDacl
SetSecurityDescriptorGroup
SetSecurityDescriptorOwner
SetSecurityDescriptorSacl
SetServiceBits
SetServiceObjectSecurity
SetServiceStatus
SetStdHandle
SetStretchBltMode
SetSysColors
SetSystemCursor

SetSystemPaletteUse
SetSystemPowerState
SetSystemTime
SetSystemTimeAdjustment
SetTapeParameters
SetTapePosition
SetTextAlign
SetTextCharacterExtra
SetTextColor
SetTextJustification
SetThreadAffinityMask
SetThreadContext
SetThreadDesktop
SetThreadLocale
SetThreadPriority
SetThreadToken
SetTimer
SetTimeZoneInformation
SetTokenInformation
SetUnhandledExceptionFilter
SetupComm
SetUserObjectInformation
SetUserObjectSecurity
SetViewportExtEx
SetViewportOrgEx
SetVolumeLabel
SetWindowContextHelpId
SetWindowExtEx
SetWindowLong
SetWindowOrgEx
SetWindowPlacement
SetWindowPos
SetWindowRgn
SetWindowsHook
SetWindowsHookEx
SetWindowText
SetWindowWord
SetWinMetaFileBits

T
TabbedTextOut
TerminateProcess
TerminateThread
TextOut
TileWindows
timeBeginPeriod
timeEndPeriod
timeGetDevCaps
timeGetSystemTime

SetWorldTransform
SHAppBarMessage
Shell_NotifyIcon
ShellAbout
ShellExecute
SHFileOperation
SHFreeNameMappings
SHGetFileInfo
SHGetNewLinkInfo
ShowCaret
ShowCursor
ShowOwnedPopups
ShowScrollBar
ShowWindow
ShowWindowAsync
SizeofResource
Sleep
SleepEx
sndPlaySound
StartDoc
StartDocPrinter
StartPage
StartPagePrinter
StartService
StartServiceCtrlDispatcher
StretchBlt
StretchDIBits
StrokeAndFillPath
StrokePath
SubtractRect
SuspendThread
SwapBuffers
SwapMouseButton
SwitchDesktop
SystemParametersInfo
SystemTimeToFileTime
SystemTimeToTzSpecificLocalTime

timeGetTime
timeKillEvent
timeSetEvent
TlsAlloc
TlsFree
TlsGetValue
TlsSetValue
ToAscii
ToAsciiEx

ToUnicode
TrackPopupMenu
TrackPopupMenuEx
TransactNamedPipe
TranslateAccelerator

TranslateCharsetInfo
TranslateMDISysAccel
TranslateMessage
TransmitCommChar

U

UnhandledExceptionFilter
UnhookWindowsHook
UnhookWindowsHookEx
UnionRect
UnloadKeyboardLayout
UnlockFile
UnlockFileEx
UnlockServiceDatabase

UnmapViewOfFile
UnpackDDElParam
UnrealizeObject
UnregisterClass
UnregisterHotKey
UpdateColors
UpdateResource
UpdateWindow

V

ValidateRect
ValidateRgn
VerFindFile
VerInstallFile
VerLanguageName
VerQueryValue
VirtualAlloc
VirtualFree

VirtualLock
VirtualProtect
VirtualProtectEx
VirtualQuery
VirtualQueryEx
VirtualUnlock
VkKeyScan
VkKeyScanEx

W

WaitCommEvent
WaitForInputIdle
WaitForMultipleObjects
WaitForMultipleObjectsEx
WaitForPrinterChange
WaitForSingleObject
WaitForSingleObjectEx
WaitMessage
WaitNamedPipe
waveInAddBuffer
waveInClose
waveInGetDevCaps
waveInGetErrorText
waveInGetID
waveInGetNumDevs
waveInGetPosition
waveInMessage
waveInOpen
waveInPrepareHeader
waveInReset
waveInStart
waveInStop
waveInUnprepareHeader

waveOutBreakLoop
waveOutClose
waveOutGetDevCaps
waveOutGetErrorText
waveOutGetID
waveOutGetNumDevs
waveOutGetPitch
waveOutGetPlaybackRate
waveOutGetPosition
waveOutGetVolume
waveOutMessage
waveOutOpen
waveOutPause
waveOutPrepareHeader
waveOutReset
waveOutRestart
waveOutSetPitch
waveOutSetPlaybackRate
waveOutSetVolume
waveOutUnprepareHeader
waveOutWrite
WideCharToMultiByte
WidenPath

```
WindowFromDC                    WNetGetUser
WindowFromPoint                 WNetOpenEnum
WinExec                         WriteConsole
WinExecError                    WriteConsoleOutput
WinHelp                         WriteConsoleOutputAttribute
WNetAddConnection               WriteConsoleOutputCharacter
WNetAddConnection2              WriteFile
WNetCancelConnection            WriteFileEx
WNetCancelConnection2           WritePrinter
WNetCloseEnum                   WritePrivateProfileSection
WNetConnectionDialog            WritePrivateProfileString
WNetDisconnectDialog            WriteProcessMemory
WNetEnumResource                WriteProfileSection
WNetGetConnection               WriteProfileString
WNetGetLastError                WriteTapemark
WNetGetUniversalName
```

Win32 API Structure Declarations

The following listing contains the complete listing of over 400 declarations for various structures used by Win32 API functions and subroutines. Like their function and subroutine counterparts, the structure declarations are scattered within the Win32api.txt file. This alphabetical listing will help you locate any structure declaration you might need.

```
Type ABC
   abcA As Long
   abcB As Long
   abcC As Long
End Type

Type ABCFLOAT
   abcfA As Double
   abcfB As Double
   abcfC As Double
End Type

Type ACCEL
   fVirt As Byte
   key As Integer
   cmd As Integer
End Type
```

```
Type ACCESS_ALLOWED_ACE
  Header As ACE_HEADER
  Mask As Long
  SidStart As Long
End Type

Type ACCESS_DENIED_ACE
  Header As ACE_HEADER
  Mask As Long
  SidStart As Long
End Type

Type ACE_HEADER
  AceType As Byte
  AceFlags As Byte
  AceSize As Long
End Type

Type ACL
  AclRevision As Byte
  Sbz1 As Byte
  AclSize As Integer
  AceCount As Integer
  Sbz2 As Integer
End Type

Type ACL_REVISION_INFORMATION
  AclRevision As Long
End Type

Type ACL_SIZE_INFORMATION
  AceCount As Long
  AclBytesInUse As Long
  AclBytesFree As Long
End Type

Type ACTION_HEADER
  transport_id As Long
  action_code As Integer
  Reserved As Integer
End Type

Type ADAPTER_STATUS
  adapter_address As String * 6
  rev_major As Integer
  reserved0 As Integer
  adapter_type As Integer
  rev_minor As Integer
  duration As Integer
  frmr_recv As Integer
  frmr_xmit As Integer
  iframe_recv_err As Integer
```

```
          xmit_aborts As Integer
          xmit_success As Long
          recv_success As Long
          iframe_xmit_err As Integer
          recv_buff_unavail As Integer
          t1_timeouts As Integer
          ti_timeouts As Integer
          Reserved1 As Long
          free_ncbs As Integer
          max_cfg_ncbs As Integer
          max_ncbs As Integer
          xmit_buf_unavail As Integer
          max_dgram_size As Integer
          pending_sess As Integer
          max_cfg_sess As Integer
          max_sess As Integer
          max_sess_pkt_size As Integer
          name_count As Integer
        End Type

        Type ADDJOB_INFO_1
          Path As String
          JobId As Long
        End Type

        Type ANIMATIONINFO
          cbSize As Long
          iMinAnimate As Long
        End Type

        Type APPBARDATA
          cbSize As Long
          hwnd As Long
          uCallbackMessage As Long
          uEdge As Long
          rc As Rect
          lParam As Long 'message specific
        End Type

        Type AUXCAPS
          wMid As Integer
          wPid As Integer
          vDriverVersion As Long
          szPname As String * MAXPNAMELEN
          wTechnology As Integer
          dwSupport As Long
        End Type

        Type BITMAP '14 bytes
          bmType As Long
          bmWidth As Long
```

```
    bmHeight As Long
    bmWidthBytes As Long
    bmPlanes As Integer
    bmBitsPixel As Integer
    bmBits As Long
End Type

Type BITMAPCOREHEADER '12 bytes
    bcSize As Long
    bcWidth As Integer
    bcHeight As Integer
    bcPlanes As Integer
    bcBitCount As Integer
End Type

Type BITMAPCOREINFO
    bmciHeader As BITMAPCOREHEADER
    bmciColors As RGBTRIPLE
End Type

Type BITMAPFILEHEADER
    bfType As Integer
    bfSize As Long
    bfReserved1 As Integer
    bfReserved2 As Integer
    bfOffBits As Long
End Type

Type BITMAPINFO
    bmiHeader As BITMAPINFOHEADER
    bmiColors As RGBQUAD
End Type

Type BITMAPINFOHEADER '40 bytes
    biSize As Long
    biWidth As Long
    biHeight As Long
    biPlanes As Integer
    biBitCount As Integer
    biCompression As Long
    biSizeImage As Long
    biXPelsPerMeter As Long
    biYPelsPerMeter As Long
    biClrUsed As Long
    biClrImportant As Long
End Type

Type BITMAPV4HEADER
    bV4Size As Long
    bV4Width As Long
    bV4Height As Long
    bV4Planes As Integer
    bV4BitCount As Integer
```

```
    bV4V4Compression As Long
    bV4SizeImage As Long
    bV4XPelsPerMeter As Long
    bV4YPelsPerMeter As Long
    bV4ClrUsed As Long
    bV4ClrImportant As Long
    bV4RedMask As Long
    bV4GreenMask As Long
    bV4BlueMask As Long
    bV4AlphaMask As Long
    bV4CSType As Long
    bV4Endpoints As Long
    bV4GammaRed As Long
    bV4GammaGreen As Long
    bV4GammaBlue As Long
End Type

Type BY_HANDLE_FILE_INFORMATION
    dwFileAttributes As Long
    ftCreationTime As FILETIME
    ftLastAccessTime As FILETIME
    ftLastWriteTime As FILETIME
    dwVolumeSerialNumber As Long
    nFileSizeHigh As Long
    nFileSizeLow As Long
    nNumberOfLinks As Long
    nFileIndexHigh As Long
    nFileIndexLow As Long
End Type

Type CANDIDATEFORM
    dwIndex As Long
    dwStyle As Long
    ptCurrentPos As POINTAPI
    rcArea As Rect
End Type

Type CANDIDATELIST
    dwSize As Long
    dwStyle As Long
    dwCount As Long
    dwSelection As Long
    dwPageStart As Long
    dwPageSize As Long
    dwOffset(1) As Long
End Type

Type CBT_CREATEWND
    lpcs As CREATESTRUCT
    hWndInsertAfter As Long
End Type
```

```
Type CBTACTIVATESTRUCT
  fMouse As Long
  hWndActive As Long
End Type

Type CHAR_INFO
  Char As Integer
  Attributes As Integer          ,
End Type

Type CHARSETINFO
  ciCharset As Long
  ciACP As Long
  fs As FONTSIGNATURE
End Type

Type CHOOSECOLOR
  lStructSize As Long
  hwndOwner As Long
  hInstance As Long
  rgbResult As Long
  lpCustColors As Long
  flags As Long
  lCustData As Long
  lpfnHook As Long
  lpTemplateName As String
End Type

Type CHOOSEFONT
  lStructSize As Long
  hwndOwner As Long    'caller's window handle
  hdc As Long     'printer DC/IC or NULL
  lpLogFont As LOGFONT    'ptr. to a LOGFONT struct
  iPointSize As Long  '10 * size in points of selected font
  flags As Long        'enum. type flags
  rgbColors As Long     'returned text color
  lCustData As Long     'data passed to hook fn.
  lpfnHook As Long      'ptr. to hook function
  lpTemplateName As String   'custom template name
  hInstance As Long       'instance handle of.EXE that
            ' contains cust. dlg. template
  lpszStyle As String     'return the style field here
            'must be LF_FACESIZE or bigger
  nFontType As Integer  'same value reported to the EnumFonts
            ' call back with the extra FONTTYPE_
            ' bits added
  MISSING_ALIGNMENT As Integer
  nSizeMin As Long      'minimum pt size allowed &
  nSizeMax As Long      'max pt size allowed if
            ' CF_LIMITSIZE is used
End Type
```

```
Type CIEXYZ
  ciexyzX As Long
  ciexyzY As Long
  ciexyzZ As Long
End Type

Type CIEXYZTRIPLE
  ciexyzRed As CIEXYZ
  ciexyzGreen As CIEXYZ
  ciexyBlue As CIEXYZ
End Type

Type CLIENTCREATESTRUCT
  hWindowMenu As Long
  idFirstChild As Long
End Type

Type COLORADJUSTMENT
  caSize As Integer
  caFlags As Integer
  caIlluminantIndex As Integer
  caRedGamma As Integer
  caGreenGamma As Integer
  caBlueGamma As Integer
  caReferenceBlack As Integer
  caReferenceWhite As Integer
  caContrast As Integer
  caBrightness As Integer
  caColorfulness As Integer
  caRedGreenTint As Integer
End Type

Type COMMCONFIG
  dwSize As Long
  wVersion As Integer
  wReserved As Integer
  dcbx As DCB
  dwProviderSubType As Long
  dwProviderOffset As Long
  dwProviderSize As Long
  wcProviderData As Byte
End Type

Type COMMPROP
  wPacketLength As Integer
  wPacketVersion As Integer
  dwServiceMask As Long
  dwReserved1 As Long
  dwMaxTxQueue As Long
  dwMaxRxQueue As Long
  dwMaxBaud As Long
```

```
      dwProvSubType As Long
      dwProvCapabilities As Long
      dwSettableParams As Long
      dwSettableBaud As Long
      wSettableData As Integer
      wSettableStopParity As Integer
      dwCurrentTxQueue As Long
      dwCurrentRxQueue As Long
      dwProvSpec1 As Long
      dwProvSpec2 As Long
      wcProvChar(1) As Integer
   End Type

   Type COMMTIMEOUTS
      ReadIntervalTimeout As Long
      ReadTotalTimeoutMultiplier As Long
      ReadTotalTimeoutConstant As Long
      WriteTotalTimeoutMultiplier As Long
      WriteTotalTimeoutConstant As Long
   End Type

   Type COMPAREITEMSTRUCT
      CtlType As Long
      CtlID As Long
      hwndItem As Long
      itemID1 As Long
      itemData1 As Long
      itemID2 As Long
      itemData2 As Long
   End Type

   Type COMPOSITIONFORM
      dwStyle As Long
      ptCurrentPos As POINTAPI
      rcArea As Rect
   End Type

   Type COMSTAT
      fBitFields As Long 'See Comment in Win32API.Txt
      cbInQue As Long
      cbOutQue As Long
   End Type

   Type CONSOLE_CURSOR_INFO
      dwSize As Long
      bVisible As Long
   End Type

   Type CONSOLE_SCREEN_BUFFER_INFO
      dwSize As COORD
      dwCursorPosition As COORD
```

```
      wAttributes As Integer
      srWindow As SMALL_RECT
      dwMaximumWindowSize As COORD
End Type

Type CONTEXT
   FltF0 As Double
   FltF1 As Double
   FltF2 As Double
   FltF3 As Double
   FltF4 As Double
   FltF5 As Double
   FltF6 As Double
   FltF7 As Double
   FltF8 As Double
   FltF9 As Double
   FltF10 As Double
   FltF11 As Double
   FltF12 As Double
   FltF13 As Double
   FltF14 As Double
   FltF15 As Double
   FltF16 As Double
   FltF17 As Double
   FltF18 As Double
   FltF19 As Double
   FltF20 As Double
   FltF21 As Double
   FltF22 As Double
   FltF23 As Double
   FltF24 As Double
   FltF25 As Double
   FltF26 As Double
   FltF27 As Double
   FltF28 As Double
   FltF29 As Double
   FltF30 As Double
   FltF31 As Double

   IntV0 As Double
   IntT0 As Double
   IntT1 As Double
   IntT2 As Double
   IntT3 As Double
   IntT4 As Double
   IntT5 As Double
   IntT6 As Double
   IntT7 As Double
   IntS0 As Double
```

```
        IntS1 As Double
        IntS2 As Double
        IntS3 As Double
        IntS4 As Double
        IntS5 As Double
        IntFp As Double
        IntA0 As Double
        IntA1 As Double
        IntA2 As Double
        IntA3 As Double
        IntA4 As Double
        IntA5 As Double
        IntT8 As Double
        IntT9 As Double
        IntT10 As Double
        IntT11 As Double
        IntRa As Double
        IntT12 As Double
        IntAt As Double
        IntGp As Double
        IntSp As Double
        IntZero As Double

        Fpcr As Double
        SoftFpcr As Double

        Fir As Double
        Psr As Long

        ContextFlags As Long
        Fill(4) As Long
    End Type

    Type CONVCONTEXT
      cb As Long
      wFlags As Long
      wCountryID As Long
      iCodePage As Long
      dwLangID As Long
      dwSecurity As Long
      qos As SECURITY_QUALITY_OF_SERVICE
    End Type

    Type CONVINFO
      cb As Long
      hUser As Long
      hConvPartner As Long
      hszSvcPartner As Long
      hszServiceReq As Long
      hszTopic As Long
```

```
    hszItem As Long
    wFmt As Long
    wType As Long
    wStatus As Long
    wConvst As Long
    wLastError As Long
    hConvList As Long
    ConvCtxt As CONVCONTEXT
    hwnd As Long
    hwndPartner As Long
End Type

Type COORD
  x As Integer
  y As Integer
End Type

Type COPYDATASTRUCT
  dwData As Long
  cbData As Long
  lpData As Long
End Type

Type CPINFO
  MaxCharSize As Long          'max length (Byte) of a char
  DefaultChar(MAX_DEFAULTCHAR) As Byte   'default character
  LeadByte(MAX_LEADBYTES) As Byte    'lead byte ranges
End Type

Type NUMBERFMT
  NumDigits As Long        'number of decimal digits
  LeadingZero As Long 'if leading zero in decimal fields
  Grouping As Long 'group size left of decimal
  lpDecimalSep As String    'ptr to decimal separator string
  lpThousandSep As String   'ptr to thousand separator string
  NegativeOrder As Long 'negative number ordering
End Type

Type CREATE_PROCESS_DEBUG_INFO
  hFile As Long
  hProcess As Long
  hThread As Long
  lpBaseOfImage As Long
  dwDebugInfoFileOffset As Long
  nDebugInfoSize As Long
  lpThreadLocalBase As Long
  lpStartAddress As Long
  lpImageName As Long
  fUnicode As Integer
End Type
```

```
Type CREATE_THREAD_DEBUG_INFO
  hThread As Long
  lpThreadLocalBase As Long
  lpStartAddress As Long
End Type

Type CREATESTRUCT
  lpCreateParams As Long
  hInstance As Long
  hMenu As Long
  hWndParent As Long
  cy As Long
  cx As Long
  y As Long
  x As Long
  style As Long
  lpszName As String
  lpszClass As String
  ExStyle As Long
End Type

Type CRGB
  bRed As Byte
  bGreen As Byte
  bBlue As Byte
  bExtra As Byte
End Type

Type CRITICAL_SECTION
  dummy As Long
End Type

Type CURRENCYFMT
  NumDigits As Long 'number of decimal digits
  LeadingZero As Long 'if leading zero in decimal fields
  Grouping As Long 'group size left of decimal
  lpDecimalSep As String  'ptr to decimal separator string
  lpThousandSep As String 'ptr to thousand separator string
  NegativeOrder As Long 'negative currency ordering
  PositiveOrder As Long 'positive currency ordering
  lpCurrencySymbol As String 'ptr to currency symbol string
End Type

Type CWPSTRUCT
  lParam As Long
  wParam As Long
  message As Long
  hwnd As Long
End Type
```

```
Type DATATYPES_INFO_1
  pName As String
End Type

Type DCB
  DCBlength As Long
  BaudRate As Long
  fBitFields As Long 'See Comments in Win32API.Txt
  wReserved As Integer
  XonLim As Integer
  XoffLim As Integer
  ByteSize As Byte
  Parity As Byte
  StopBits As Byte
  XonChar As Byte
  XoffChar As Byte
  ErrorChar As Byte
  EofChar As Byte
  EvtChar As Byte
  wReserved1 As Integer 'Reserved; Do Not Use
End Type

Type DDEACK
  bAppReturnCode As Integer
  Reserved As Integer
  fbusy As Integer
  fack As Integer
End Type

Type DDEADVISE
  Reserved As Integer
  fDeferUpd As Integer
  fAckReq As Integer
  cfFormat As Integer
End Type

Type DDEDATA
  unused As Integer
  fresponse As Integer
  fRelease As Integer
  Reserved As Integer
  fAckReq As Integer
  cfFormat As Integer
  Value(1) As Byte
End Type

Type DDELN
  unused As Integer
  fRelease As Integer
  fDeferUpd As Integer
```

```
    fAckReq As Integer
    cfFormat As Integer
End Type

Type DDEML_MSG_HOOK_DATA    'new for NT
    uiLo As Long  'unpacked lo and hi parts of lParam
    uiHi As Long
    cbData As Long  'amount of data in message, if any.
    Data(8) As Long 'data peeking limited to 32 bytes.
End Type

Type DDEPOKE
    unused As Integer
    fRelease As Integer
    fReserved As Integer
    cfFormat As Integer
    Value(1) As Byte
End Type

Type DDEUP
    unused As Integer
    fAck As Integer
    fRelease As Integer
    fReserved As Integer
    fAckReq As Integer
    cfFormat As Integer
    rgb(1) As Byte
End Type

Type DEBUGHOOKINFO
    hModuleHook As Long
    Reserved As Long
    lParam As Long
    wParam As Long
    code As Long
End Type

Type DELETEITEMSTRUCT
    CtlType As Long
    CtlID As Long
    itemID As Long
    hwndItem As Long
    itemData As Long
End Type

Type DEVMODE
    dmDeviceName As String * CCHDEVICENAME
    dmSpecVersion As Integer
    dmDriverVersion As Integer
    dmSize As Integer
    dmDriverExtra As Integer
```

```
        dmFields As Long
        dmOrientation As Integer
        dmPaperSize As Integer
        dmPaperLength As Integer
        dmPaperWidth As Integer
        dmScale As Integer
        dmCopies As Integer
        dmDefaultSource As Integer
        dmPrintQuality As Integer
        dmColor As Integer
        dmDuplex As Integer
        dmYResolution As Integer
        dmTTOption As Integer
        dmCollate As Integer
        dmFormName As String * CCHFORMNAME
        dmUnusedPadding As Integer
        dmBitsPerPel As Integer
        dmPelsWidth As Long
        dmPelsHeight As Long
        dmDisplayFlags As Long
        dmDisplayFrequency As Long
    End Type

    Type DEVNAMES
      wDriverOffset As Integer
      wDeviceOffset As Integer
      wOutputOffset As Integer
      wDefault As Integer
    End Type

    Type DLGITEMTEMPLATE
      style As Long
      dwExtendedStyle As Long
      x As Integer
      y As Integer
      cx As Integer
      cy As Integer
      id As Integer
    End Type

    Type DLGTEMPLATE
      style As Long
      dwExtendedStyle As Long
      cdit As Integer
      x As Integer
      y As Integer
      cx As Integer
      cy As Integer
    End Type
```

```
Type DOC_INFO_1
  pDocName As String
  pOutputFile As String
  pDatatype As String
End Type

Type DOC_INFO_2
  pDocName As String
  pOutputFile As String
  pDatatype As String
  dwMode As Long
  JobId As Long
End Type

Type DOCINFO
  cbSize As Long
  lpszDocName As String
  lpszOutput As String
End Type

Type DRAGINFO
  uSize As Long        'init with sizeof(DRAGINFO)
  pt As POINTAPI
  fNC As Long
  lpFileList As String
  grfKeyState As Long
End Type

Type DRAWITEMSTRUCT
  CtlType As Long
  CtlID As Long
  itemID As Long
  itemAction As Long
  itemState As Long
  hwndItem As Long
  hdc As Long
  rcItem As Rect
  itemData As Long
End Type

Type DRAWTEXTPARAMS
  cbSize As Long
  iTabLength As Long
  iLeftMargin As Long
  iRightMargin As Long
  uiLengthDrawn As Long
End Type

Type DRIVER_INFO_1
  pName As String
End Type
```

```
Type DRIVER_INFO_2
  cVersion As Long
  pName As String
  pEnvironment As String
  pDriverPath As String
  pDataFile As String
  pConfigFile As String
End Type

Type DRIVER_INFO_3
  cVersion As Long
  pName As String          'QMS 810
  pEnvironment As String      'Win32 x86
  pDriverPath As String         'c:\drivers\pscript.dll
  pDataFile As String       'c:\drivers\QMS810.PPD
  pConfigFile As String        'c:\drivers\PSCRPTUI.DLL
  pHelpFile As String      'c:\drivers\PSCRPTUI.HLP
  pDependentFiles As String      '
  pMonitorName As String       '"PJL monitor"
  pDefaultDataType As String    '"EMF"
End Type

Type DRVCONFIGINFO
  dwDCISize As Long
  lpszDCISectionName As String
  lpszDCIAliasName As String
  dnDevNode As Long
End Type

Type emr
  iType As Long
  nSize As Long
End Type

Type EMRABORTPATH
  pEmr As emr
End Type

Type EMRANGLEARC
  pEmr As emr
  ptlCenter As POINTL
  nRadius As Long
  eStartAngle As Double
  eSweepAngle As Double
End Type

Type EMRARC
  pEmr As emr
  rclBox As RECTL
  ptlStart As POINTL
  ptlEnd As POINTL
End Type
```

```
Type EMRARCTO
  pEmr As emr
  rclBox As RECTL
  ptlStart As POINTL
  ptlEnd As POINTL
End Type

Type EMRBEGINPATH
  pEmr As emr
End Type

Type EMRBITBLT
  pEmr As emr
  rclBounds As RECTL
  xDest As Long
  yDest As Long
  cxDest As Long
  cyDest As Long
  dwRop As Long
  xSrc As Long
  ySrc As Long
  xformSrc As xform
  crBkColorSrc As Long
  iUsageSrc As Long
  offBmiSrc As Long
  cbBmiSrc As Long
  offBitsSrc As Long
  cbBitsSrc As Long
End Type

Type EMRCHORD
  pEmr As emr
  rclBox As RECTL
  ptlStart As POINTL
  ptlEnd As POINTL
End Type

Type EMRCLOSEFIGURE
  pEmr As emr
End Type

Type EMRCREATEBRUSHINDIRECT
  pEmr As emr
  ihBrush As Long
  lb As LOGBRUSH
End Type

Type EMRCREATECOLORSPACE
  pEmr As emr
  ihCS As Long 'ColorSpace handle index
  lcs As LOGCOLORSPACE
End Type
```

```
Type EMRCREATEDIBPATTERNBRUSHPT
  pEmr As emr
  ihBursh As Long
  iUsage As Long
  offBmi As Long
  cbBmi As Long
  offBits As Long
  cbBits As Long
End Type

Type EMRCREATEMONOBRUSH
  pEmr As emr
  ihBrush As Long
  iUsage As Long
  offBmi As Long
  cbBmi As Long
  offBits As Long
  cbBits As Long
End Type

Type EMRCREATEPALETTE
  pEmr As emr
  ihPal As Long
  lgpl As LOGPALETTE
End Type

Type EMRCREATEPEN
  pEmr As emr
  ihPen As Long
  lopn As LOGPEN
End Type

Type EMRDELETEOBJECT
  pEmr As emr
  ihObject As Long
End Type

Type EMRELLIPSE
  pEmr As emr
  rclBox As RECTL
End Type

Type EMREMRSAVEDC
  pEmr As emr
End Type

Type EMRENDPATH
  pEmr As emr
End Type

Type EMREOF
  pEmr As emr
```

```
      nPalEntries As Long
      offPalEntries As Long
      nSizeLast As Long
   End Type

   Type EMREXCLUDECLIPRECT
     pEmr As emr
     rclClip As RECTL
   End Type

   Type EMREXTCREATEFONTINDIRECT
     pEmr As emr
     ihFont As Long
     elfw As EXTLOGFONT
   End Type

   Type EMREXTCREATEPEN
     pEmr As emr
     ihPen As Long
     offBmi As Long
     cbBmi As Long
     offBits As Long
     cbBits As Long
     elp As EXTLOGPEN
   End Type

   Type EMREXTFLOODFILL
     pEmr As emr
     ptlStart As POINTL
     crColor As Long
     iMode As Long
   End Type

   Type EMREXTSELECTCLIPRGN
     pEmr As emr
     cbRgnData As Long
     iMode As Long
     RgnData(1) As Integer
   End Type

   Type EMREXTTEXTOUT
     pEmr As emr
     rclBounds As RECTL
     iGraphicsMode As Long
     exScale As Double
     eyScale As Double
     emrtext As emrtext
   End Type

   Type EMRFILLPATH
     pEmr As emr
     rclBounds As RECTL
   End Type
```

```
Type EMRFILLRGN
  pEmr As emr
  rclBounds As RECTL
  cbRgnData As Long
  ihBrush As Long
  RgnData(1) As Integer
End Type

Type EMRFLATTENPATH
  pEmr As emr
End Type

Type EMRFRAMERGN
  pEmr As emr
  rclBounds As RECTL
  cbRgnData As Long
  ihBrush As Long
  szlStroke As SIZEL
  RgnData(1) As Integer
End Type

Type EMRGDICOMMENT
  pEmr As emr
  cbData As Long
  Data(1) As Integer
End Type

Type EMRINTERSECTCLIPRECT
  pEmr As emr
  rclClip As RECTL
End Type

Type EMRINVERTRGN
  pEmr As emr
  rclBounds As RECTL
  cbRgnData As Long
  RgnData(1) As Integer
End Type

Type EMRLINETO
  pEmr As emr
  ptl As POINTL
End Type

Type EMRMASKBLT
  pEmr As emr
  rclBounds As RECTL
  xDest As Long
  yDest As Long
  cxDest As Long
  cyDest As Long
  dwRop As Long
```

```
        xSrc2 As Long
        cyDest2 As Long
        dwRop2 As Long
        xSrc As Long
        ySrc As Long
        xformSrc As XFORM
        crBkColorSrc As Long
        iUsageSrc As Long
        offBmiSrc As Long
        cbBmiSrc As Long
        offBitsSrc As Long
        cbBitsSrc As Long
        xMask As Long
        yMask As Long
        iUsageMask As Long
        offBmiMask As Long
        cbBmiMask As Long
        offBitsMask As Long
        cbBitsMask As Long
    End Type

    Type EMRMODIFYWORLDTRANSFORM
        pEmr As emr
        xform As XFORM
        iMode As Long
    End Type

    Type EMRMOVETOEX
        pEmr As emr
        ptl As POINTL
    End Type

    Type EMROFFSETCLIPRGN
        pEmr As emr
        ptlOffset As POINTL
    End Type

    Type EMRPAINTRGN
        pEmr As emr
        rclBounds As RECTL
        cbRgnData As Long
        RgnData(1) As Integer
    End Type

    Type EMRPIE
        pEmr As emr
        rclBox As RECTL
        ptlStart As POINTL
        ptlEnd As POINTL
    End Type
```

```
Type EMRPLGBLT
  pEmr As emr
  rclBounds As RECTL
  aptlDest(3) As POINTL
  xSrc As Long
  ySrc As Long
  cxSrc As Long
  cySrc As Long
  xformSrc As XFORM
  crBkColorSrc As Long
  iUsageSrc As Long
  offBmiSrc As Long
  cbBmiSrc As Long
  offBitsSrc As Long
  cbBitsSrc As Long
  xMask As Long
  yMask As Long
  iUsageMask As Long
  offBmiMask As Long
  cbBmiMask As Long
  offBitsMask As Long
  cbBitsMask As Long
End Type

Type EMRPLOYBEZIERTO16
  pEmr As emr
  rclBounds As RECTL
  cpts As Long
  apts(1) As POINTS
End Type

Type EMRPOLYBEZIER
  pEmr As emr
  rclBounds As RECTL
  cptl As Long
  aptl(1) As POINTL
End Type

Type EMRPOLYBEZIER16
  pEmr As emr
  rclBounds As RECTL
  cpts As Long
  apts(1) As POINTS
End Type

Type EMRPOLYBEZIERTO
  pEmr As emr
  rclBounds As RECTL
  cptl As Long
  aptl(1) As POINTL
End Type
```

```
Type EMRPOLYDRAW
  pEmr As emr
  rclBounds As RECTL
  cptl As Long
  aptl(1) As POINTL
  abTypes(1) As Integer
End Type

Type EMRPOLYDRAW16
  pEmr As emr
  rclBounds As RECTL
  cpts As Long
  apts(1) As POINTS
  abTypes(1) As Integer
End Type

Type EMRPOLYGON
  pEmr As emr
  rclBounds As RECTL
  cptl As Long
  aptl(1) As POINTL
End Type

Type EMRPOLYGON16
  pEmr As emr
  rclBounds As RECTL
  cpts As Long
  apts(1) As POINTS
End Type

Type EMRPOLYLINE
  pEmr As emr
  rclBounds As RECTL
  cptl As Long
  aptl(1) As POINTL
End Type

Type EMRPOLYLINE16
  pEmr As emr
  rclBounds As RECTL
  cpts As Long
  apts(1) As POINTS
End Type

Type EMRPOLYLINETO16
  pEmr As emr
  rclBounds As RECTL
  cpts As Long
  apts(1) As POINTS
End Type
```

```
Type EMRPOLYPOLYGON
  pEmr As emr
  rclBounds As RECTL
  nPolys As Long
  cptl As Long
  aPolyCounts(1) As Long
  aptl(1) As POINTL
End Type

Type EMRPOLYPOLYGON16
  pEmr As emr
  rclBounds As RECTL
  nPolys As Long
  cpts As Long
  aPolyCounts(1) As Long
  apts(1) As POINTS
End Type

Type EMRPOLYPOLYLINE
  pEmr As emr
  rclBounds As RECTL
  nPolys As Long
  cptl As Long
  aPolyCounts(1) As Long
  aptl(1) As POINTL
End Type

Type EMRPOLYPOLYLINE16
  pEmr As emr
  rclBounds As RECTL
  nPolys As Long
  cpts As Long
  aPolyCounts(1) As Long
  apts(1) As POINTS
End Type

Type EMRREALIZEPALETTE
  pEmr As emr
End Type

Type EMRRECTANGLE
  pEmr As emr
  rclBox As RECTL
End Type

Type EMRRESIZEPALETTE
  pEmr As emr
  ihPal As Long
  cEntries As Long
End Type
```

```
Type EMRRESTOREDC
  pEmr As emr
  iRelative As Long
End Type

Type EMRROUNDRECT
  pEmr As emr
  rclBox As RECTL
  szlCorner As SIZEL
End Type

Type EMRSCALEVIEWPORTEXTEX
  pEmr As emr
  xNum As Long
  xDenom As Long
  yNum As Long
  yDemon As Long
End Type

Type EMRSCALEWINDOWEXTEX
  pEmr As emr
  xNum As Long
  xDenom As Long
  yNum As Long
  yDemon As Long
End Type

Type EMRSELECTCLIPPATH
  pEmr As emr
  iMode As Long
End Type

Type EMRSELECTCOLORSPACE
  pEmr As emr
  ihCS As Long          'ColorSpace handle index
End Type

Type EMRSELECTOBJECT
  pEmr As emr
  ihObject As Long
End Type

Type EMRSELECTPALETTE
  pEmr As emr
  ihPal As Long
End Type

Type EMRSETARCDIRECTION
  pEmr As emr
  iArcDirection As Long
End Type
```

```
Type EMRSETBKCOLOR
  pEmr As emr
  crColor As Long
End Type

Type EMRSETBKMODE
  pEmr As emr
  iMode As Long
End Type

Type EMRSETBRUSHORGEX
  pEmr As emr
  ptlOrigin As POINTL
End Type

Type EMRSETCOLORADJUSTMENT
  pEmr As emr
  ColorAdjustment As ColorAdjustment
End Type

Type EMRSETDIBITSTODEVICE
  pEmr As emr
  rclBounds As RECTL
  xDest As Long
  yDest As Long
  xSrc As Long
  ySrc As Long
  cxSrc As Long
  cySrc As Long
  offBmiSrc As Long
  cbBmiSrc As Long
  offBitsSrc As Long
  cbBitsSrc As Long
  iUsageSrc As Long
  iStartScan As Long
  cScans As Long
End Type

Type EMRSETMAPMODE
  pEmr As emr
  iMode As Long
End Type

Type EMRSETMAPPERFLAGS
  pEmr As emr
  dwFlags As Long
End Type

Type EMRSETMETARGN
  pEmr As emr
End Type
```

```
Type EMRSETMITERLIMIT
  pEmr As emr
  eMiterLimit As Double
End Type

Type EMRSETPALETTEENTRIES
  pEmr As emr
  ihPal As Long
  iStart As Long
  cEntries As Long
  aPalEntries(1) As PALETTEENTRY
End Type

Type EMRSETPIXELV
  pEmr As emr
  ptlPixel As POINTL
  crColor As Long
End Type

Type EMRSETPOLYFILLMODE
  pEmr As emr
  iMode As Long
End Type

Type EMRSETROP2
  pEmr As emr
  iMode As Long
End Type

Type EMRSETSTRETCHBLTMODE
  pEmr As emr
  iMode As Long
End Type

Type EMRSETTEXTALIGN
  pEmr As emr
  iMode As Long
End Type

Type EMRSETTEXTCOLOR
  pEmr As emr
  crColor As Long
End Type

Type EMRSETVIEWPORTEXTEX
  pEmr As emr
  szlExtent As SIZEL
End Type

Type EMRSETVIEWPORTORGEX
  pEmr As emr
  ptlOrigin As POINTL
End Type
```

```
Type EMRSETWINDOWEXTEX
  pEmr As emr
  szlExtent As SIZEL
End Type

Type EMRSETWINDOWORGEX
  pEmr As emr
  ptlOrigin As POINTL
End Type

Type EMRSETWORLDTRANSFORM
  pEmr As emr
  xform As XFORM
End Type

Type EMRSTRETCHBLT
  pEmr As emr
  rclBounds As RECTL
  xDest As Long
  yDest As Long
  cxDest As Long
  cyDest As Long
  dwRop As Long
  xSrc As Long
  ySrc As Long
  xformSrc As xform
  crBkColorSrc As Long
  iUsageSrc As Long
  offBmiSrc As Long
  cbBmiSrc As Long
  offBitsSrc As Long
  cbBitsSrc As Long
  cxSrc As Long
  cySrc As Long
End Type

Type EMRSTRETCHDIBITS
  pEmr As emr
  rclBounds As RECTL
  xDest As Long
  yDest As Long
  xSrc As Long
  ySrc As Long
  cxSrc As Long
  cySrc As Long
  offBmiSrc As Long
  cbBmiSrc As Long
  offBitsSrc As Long
  cbBitsSrc As Long
  iUsageSrc As Long
```

```
      dwRop As Long
      cxDest As Long
      cyDest As Long
    End Type

    Type EMRSTROKEANDFILLPATH
      pEmr As emr
      rclBounds As RECTL
    End Type

    Type EMRSTROKEPATH
      pEmr As emr
      rclBounds As RECTL
    End Type

    Type emrtext
      ptlReference As POINTL
      nchars As Long
      offString As Long
      fOptions As Long
      rcl As RECTL
      offDx As Long
    End Type

    Type EMRWIDENPATH
      pEmr As emr
    End Type

    Type ENHMETAHEADER
      iType As Long
      nSize As Long
      rclBounds As RECTL
      rclFrame As RECTL
      dSignature As Long
      nVersion As Long
      nBytes As Long
      nRecords As Long
      nHandles As Integer
      sReserved As Integer
      nDescription As Long
      offDescription As Long
      nPalEntries As Long
      szlDevice As SIZEL
      szlMillimeters As SIZEL
    End Type

    Type ENHMETARECORD
      iType As Long
      nSize As Long
      dParm(1) As Long
    End Type
```

```
Type ENUM_SERVICE_STATUS
  lpServiceName As String
  lpDisplayName As String
  ServiceStatus As SERVICE_STATUS
End Type

Type ENUMLOGFONT
  elfLogFont As LOGFONT
  elfFullName(LF_FULLFACESIZE) As Byte
  elfStyle(LF_FACESIZE) As Byte
End Type

Type ENUMLOGFONTEX
  elfLogFont As LOGFONT
  elfFullName(LF_FULLFACESIZE) As Byte
  elfStyle(LF_FACESIZE) As Byte
  elfScript(LF_FACESIZE) As Byte
End Type

Type EVENTLOGRECORD
  Length as Long        'Length of full record
  Reserved as Long      'Used by the service
  RecordNumber as Long      'Absolute record number
  TimeGenerated as Long      'Seconds since 1-1-1970
  TimeWritten as Long       'Seconds since 1-1-1970
  EventID as Long
  EventType as Integer
  NumStrings as Integer
  EventCategory as Integer
  ReservedFlags as Integer     'For use with paired events
(auditing)
  ClosingRecordNumber as Long  'For use with paired events
(auditing)
  StringOffset as Long      'Offset from beginning of record
  UserSidLength as Long
  UserSidOffset as Long
  DataLength as Long
  DataOffset as Long       'Offset from beginning of record
End Type

Type EVENTMSG
  message As Long
  paramL As Long
  paramH As Long
  time As Long
  hwnd As Long
End Type

Type EXCEPTION_DEBUG_INFO
  pExceptionRecord As EXCEPTION_RECORD
  dwFirstChance As Long
End Type
```

```
Type EXCEPTION_POINTERS
  pExceptionRecord As EXCEPTION_RECORD
  ContextRecord As CONTEXT
End Type

Type EXCEPTION_RECORD
  ExceptionCode As Long
  ExceptionFlags As Long
  pExceptionRecord As Long ' Pointer to an EXCEPTION_RECORD
structure
  ExceptionAddress As Long
  NumberParameters As Long
  ExceptionInformation(EXCEPTION_MAXIMUM_PARAMETERS) As Long
End Type

Type EXIT_PROCESS_DEBUG_INFO
  dwExitCode As Long
End Type

Type EXIT_THREAD_DEBUG_INFO
  dwExitCode As Long
End Type

Type EXTLOGFONT
  elfLogFont As LOGFONT
  elfFullName(LF_FULLFACESIZE) As Byte
  elfStyle(LF_FACESIZE) As Byte
  elfVersion As Long
  elfStyleSize As Long
  elfMatch As Long
  elfReserved As Long
  elfVendorId(ELF_VENDOR_SIZE) As Byte
  elfCulture As Long
  elfPanose As PANOSE
End Type

Type EXTLOGPEN
  elpPenStyle As Long
  elpWidth As Long
  elpBrushStyle As Long
  elpColor As Long
  elpHatch As Long
  elpNumEntries As Long
  elpStyleEntry(1) As Long
End Type

Type FILETIME
  dwLowDateTime As Long
  dwHighDateTime As Long
End Type

Type FIND_NAME_BUFFER
  Length As Integer
```

```
    access_control As Integer
    frame_control As Integer
    destination_addr(6) As Integer
    source_addr(6) As Integer
    routing_info(18) As Integer
End Type

Type FIND_NAME_HEADER
  node_count As Integer
  Reserved As Integer
  unique_group As Integer
End Type

Type FINDREPLACE
  lStructSize As Long    'size of this struct 0x20
  hwndOwner As Long      'handle to owner's window
  hInstance As Long      'instance handle of.EXE that
           ' contains cust. dlg. template
  flags As Long          'one or more of the FR_??
  lpstrFindWhat As String     'ptr. to search string
  lpstrReplaceWith As String   'ptr. to replace string
  wFindWhatLen As Integer      'size of find buffer
  wReplaceWithLen As Integer    'size of replace buffer
  lCustData As Long     'data passed to hook fn.
  lpfnHook As Long      'ptr. to hook fn. or NULL
  lpTemplateName As String    'custom template name
End Type

Type FIXED
  fract As Integer
  Value As Integer
End Type

Type FOCUS_EVENT_RECORD
  bSetFocus As Long
End Type

Type FONTSIGNATURE
  fsUsb(4) As Long
  fsCsb(2) As Long
End Type

Type FORM_INFO_1
  pName As String
  Size As SIZEL
  ImagableArea As RECTL
End Type

Type GCP_RESULTS
  lStructSize As Long
  lpOutString As String
  lpOrder As Long
```

```
        lpDX As Long
        lpCaretPos As Long
        lpClass As String
        lpGlyphs As String
        nGlyphs As Long
        nMaxFit As Long
End Type

Type GENERIC_MAPPING
    GenericRead As Long
    GenericWrite As Long
    GenericExecute As Long
    GenericAll As Long
End Type

Type GLYPHMETRICS
    gmBlackBoxX As Long
    gmBlackBoxY As Long
    gmptGlyphOrigin As POINTAPI
    gmCellIncX As Integer
    gmCellIncY As Integer
End Type

Type HANDLETABLE
    objectHandle(1) As Long
End Type

Type HELPINFO
        cbSize As Long
        iContextType As Long
        iCtrlId As Long
        hItemHandle As Long
        dwContextId As Long
        MousePos As POINTAPI
End Type

Type HELPWININFO
    wStructSize As Long
    x As Long
    y As Long
    dx As Long
    dy As Long
    wMax As Long
    rgchMember As String * 2
End Type

Type HSZPAIR
    hszSvc As Long
    hszTopic As Long
End Type
```

```
Type ICONINFO
  fIcon As Long
  xHotspot As Long
  yHotspot As Long
  hbmMask As Long
  hbmColor As Long
End Type

Type ICONMETRICS
  cbSize As Long
  iHorzSpacing As Long
  iVertSpacing As Long
  iTitleWrap As Long
  lfFont As LOGFONT
End Type

Type JOB_INFO_1
  JobId As Long
  pPrinterName As String
  pMachineName As String
  pUserName As String
  pDocument As String
  pDatatype As String
  pStatus As String
  Status As Long
  Priority As Long
  Position As Long
  TotalPages As Long
  PagesPrinted As Long
  Submitted As SYSTEMTIME
End Type

Type JOB_INFO_2
  JobId As Long
  pPrinterName As String
  pMachineName As String
  pUserName As String
  pDocument As String
  pNotifyName As String
  pDatatype As String
  pPrintProcessor As String
  pParameters As String
  pDriverName As String
  pDevMode As DEVMODE
  pStatus As String
  pSecurityDescriptor As SECURITY_DESCRIPTOR
  Status As Long
  Priority As Long
  Position As Long
```

```
      StartTime As Long
      UntilTime As Long
      TotalPages As Long
      Size As Long
      Submitted As SYSTEMTIME
      time As Long
      PagesPrinted As Long
  End Type

  Type JOYCAPS
    wMid As Integer
    wPid As Integer
    szPname As String * MAXPNAMELEN
    wXmin As Integer
    wXmax As Integer
    wYmin As Integer
    wYmax As Integer
    wZmin As Integer
    wZmax As Integer
    wNumButtons As Integer
    wPeriodMin As Integer
    wPeriodMax As Integer
  End Type

  Type JOYINFO
    wXpos As Integer
    wYpos As Integer
    wZpos As Integer
    wButtons As Integer
  End Type

  Type JOYINFOEX
     dwSize As Long       'size of structure
     dwFlags As Long       'flags to indicate what to return
     dwXpos As Long      'x position
     dwYpos As Long      'y position
     dwZpos As Long      'z position
     dwRpos As Long       'rudder/4th axis position
     dwUpos As Long       '5th axis position
     dwVpos As Long       '6th axis position
     dwButtons As Long       'button states
     dwButtonNumber As Long  'current button number pressed
     dwPOV As Long       'point of view state
     dwReserved1 As Long 'reserved for comm. between winmm driver
     dwReserved2 As Long      'reserved for future expansion
  End Type

  Type KERNINGPAIR
    wFirst As Integer
    wSecond As Integer
```

```
      iKernAmount As Long
End Type

Type KEY_EVENT_RECORD
  bKeyDown As Long
  wRepeatCount As Integer
  wVirtualKeyCode As Integer
  wVirtualScanCode As Integer
  uChar As Integer
  dwControlKeyState As Long
End Type

Type LANA_ENUM
  Length As Integer
  lana(MAX_LANA) As Integer
End Type

Type LARGE_INTEGER
  lowpart As Long
  highpart As Long
End Type

Type LDT_BYTES   ' Defined for use in LDT_ENTRY Type
  BaseMid As Byte
  Flags1 As Byte
  Flags2 As Byte
  BaseHi As Byte
End Type

Type LDT_ENTRY
  LimitLow As Integer
  BaseLow As Integer
  HighWord As Long    ' Can use LDT_BYTES Type
End Type

Type LOAD_DLL_DEBUG_INFO
  hFile As Long
  lpBaseOfDll As Long
  dwDebugInfoFileOffset As Long
  nDebugInfoSize As Long
  lpImageName As Long
  fUnicode As Integer
End Type

Type LOCALESIGNATURE
  lsUsb(4) As Long
  lsCsbDefault(2) As Long
  lsCsbSupported(2) As Long
End Type

Type LOGBRUSH
  lbStyle As Long
```

```
      lbColor As Long
      lbHatch As Long
    End Type

    Type LOGCOLORSPACE
      lcsSignature As Long
      lcsVersion As Long
      lcsSize As Long
      lcsCSType As Long
      lcsIntent As Long
      lcsEndPoints As CIEXYZTRIPLE
      lcsGammaRed As Long
      lcsGammaGreen As Long
      lcsGammaBlue As Long
      lcsFileName As String * MAX_PATH
    End Type

    Type LOGFONT
      lfHeight As Long
      lfWidth As Long
      lfEscapement As Long
      lfOrientation As Long
      lfWeight As Long
      lfItalic As Byte
      lfUnderline As Byte
      lfStrikeOut As Byte
      lfCharSet As Byte
      lfOutPrecision As Byte
      lfClipPrecision As Byte
      lfQuality As Byte
      lfPitchAndFamily As Byte
      lfFaceName(LF_FACESIZE) As Byte
    End Type

    Type LOGPALETTE
      palVersion As Integer
      palNumEntries As Integer
      palPalEntry(1) As PALETTEENTRY
    End Type

    Type LOGPEN
      lopnStyle As Long
      lopnWidth As POINTAPI
      lopnColor As Long
    End Type

    Type LUID
      LowPart As Long
      HighPart As Long
    End Type
```

```
Type LUID_AND_ATTRIBUTES
  pLuid As LUID
  Attributes As Long
End Type

Type MAT2
  eM11 As FIXED
  eM12 As FIXED
  eM21 As FIXED
  eM22 As FIXED
End Type

Type MCI_ANIM_OPEN_PARMS
  dwCallback As Long
  wDeviceID As Long
  lpstrDeviceType As String
  lpstrElementName As String
  lpstrAlias As String
  dwStyle As Long
  hWndParent As Long
End Type

Type MCI_ANIM_PLAY_PARMS
  dwCallback As Long
  dwFrom As Long
  dwTo As Long
  dwSpeed As Long
End Type

Type MCI_ANIM_RECT_PARMS
  dwCallback As Long
  rc As Rect
End Type

Type MCI_ANIM_STEP_PARMS
  dwCallback As Long
  dwFrames As Long
End Type

Type MCI_ANIM_UPDATE_PARMS
  dwCallback As Long
  rc As Rect
  hdc As Long
End Type

Type MCI_ANIM_WINDOW_PARMS
  dwCallback As Long
  hwnd As Long
  nCmdShow As Long
  lpstrText As String
End Type
```

```
Type MCI_BREAK_PARMS
  dwCallback As Long
  nVirtKey As Long
  hwndBreak As Long
End Type

Type MCI_GENERIC_PARMS
  dwCallback As Long
End Type

Type MCI_GETDEVCAPS_PARMS
  dwCallback As Long
  dwReturn As Long
  dwIten As Long
End Type

Type MCI_INFO_PARMS
  dwCallback As Long
  lpstrReturn As String
  dwRetSize As Long
End Type

Type MCI_LOAD_PARMS
  dwCallback As Long
  lpFileName As String
End Type

Type MCI_OPEN_PARMS
  dwCallback As Long
  wDeviceID As Long
  lpstrDeviceType As String
  lpstrElementName As String
  lpstrAlias As String
End Type

Type MCI_OVLY_LOAD_PARMS
  dwCallback As Long
  lpFileName As String
  rc As Rect
End Type

Type MCI_OVLY_OPEN_PARMS
  dwCallback As Long
  wDeviceID As Long
  lpstrDeviceType As String
  lpstrElementName As String
  lpstrAlias As String
  dwStyle As Long
  hWndParent As Long
End Type
```

```
Type MCI_OVLY_RECT_PARMS
  dwCallback As Long
  rc As Rect
End Type

Type MCI_OVLY_SAVE_PARMS
  dwCallback As Long
  lpFileName As String
  rc As Rect
End Type

Type MCI_OVLY_WINDOW_PARMS
  dwCallback As Long
  hwnd As Long
  nCmdShow As Long
  lpstrText As String
End Type

Type MCI_PLAY_PARMS
  dwCallback As Long
  dwFrom As Long
  dwTo As Long
End Type

Type MCI_RECORD_PARMS
  dwCallback As Long
  dwFrom As Long
  dwTo As Long
End Type

Type MCI_SAVE_PARMS
  dwCallback As Long
  lpFileName As String
End Type

Type MCI_SEEK_PARMS
  dwCallback As Long
  dwTo As Long
End Type

Type MCI_SEQ_SET_PARMS
  dwCallback As Long
  dwTimeFormat As Long
  dwAudio As Long
  dwTempo As Long
  dwPort As Long
  dwSlave As Long
  dwMaster As Long
  dwOffset As Long
End Type
```

```
Type MCI_SET_PARMS
  dwCallback As Long
  dwTimeFormat As Long
  dwAudio As Long
End Type

Type MCI_SOUND_PARMS
  dwCallback As Long
  lpstrSoundName As String
End Type

Type MCI_STATUS_PARMS
  dwCallback As Long
  dwReturn As Long
  dwItem As Long
  dwTrack As Integer
End Type

Type MCI_SYSINFO_PARMS
  dwCallback As Long
  lpstrReturn As String
  dwRetSize As Long
  dwNumber As Long
  wDeviceType As Long
End Type

Type MCI_VD_ESCAPE_PARMS
  dwCallback As Long
  lpstrCommand As String
End Type

Type MCI_VD_PLAY_PARMS
  dwCallback As Long
  dwFrom As Long
  dwTo As Long
  dwSpeed As Long
End Type

Type MCI_VD_STEP_PARMS
  dwCallback As Long
  dwFrames As Long
End Type

Type MCI_WAVE_DELETE_PARMS
  dwCallback As Long
  dwFrom As Long
  dwTo As Long
End Type

Type MCI_WAVE_OPEN_PARMS
  dwCallback As Long
  wDeviceID As Long
```

```
        lpstrDeviceType As String
        lpstrElementName As String
        lpstrAlias As String
        dwBufferSeconds As Long
    End Type

    Type MCI_WAVE_SET_PARMS
        dwCallback As Long
        dwTimeFormat As Long
        dwAudio As Long
        wInput As Long
        wOutput As Long
        wFormatTag As Integer
        wReserved2 As Integer
        nChannels As Integer
        wReserved3 As Integer
        nSamplesPerSec As Long
        nAvgBytesPerSec As Long
        nBlockAlign As Integer
        wReserved4 As Integer
        wBitsPerSample As Integer
        wReserved5 As Integer
    End Type

    Type MDICREATESTRUCT
        szClass As String
        szTitle As String
        hOwner As Long
        x As Long
        y As Long
        cx As Long
        cy As Long
        style As Long
        lParam As Long
    End Type

    Type MEASUREITEMSTRUCT
        CtlType As Long
        CtlID As Long
        itemID As Long
        itemWidth As Long
        itemHeight As Long
        itemData As Long
    End Type

    Type MEMORY_BASIC_INFORMATION
        BaseAddress as Long
        AllocationBase as Long
        AllocationProtect As Long
        RegionSize As Long
```

```
    State As Long
    Protect As Long
    lType As Long
End Type

Type MEMORYSTATUS
    dwLength As Long
    dwMemoryLoad As Long
    dwTotalPhys As Long
    dwAvailPhys As Long
    dwTotalPageFile As Long
    dwAvailPageFile As Long
    dwTotalVirtual As Long
    dwAvailVirtual As Long
End Type

Type MENU_EVENT_RECORD
    dwCommandId As Long
End Type

Type MENUITEMINFO
    cbSize As Long
    fMask As Long
    fType As Long
    fState As Long
    wID As Long
    hSubMenu As Long
    hbmpChecked As Long
    hbmpUnchecked As Long
    dwItemData As Long
    dwTypeData As String
    cch As Long
End Type

Type MENUITEMTEMPLATE
    mtOption As Integer
    mtID As Integer
    mtString As Byte
End Type

Type MENUITEMTEMPLATEHEADER
    versionNumber As Integer
    offset As Integer
End Type

Type METAFILEPICT
    mm As Long
    xExt As Long
    yExt As Long
    hMF As Long
End Type
```

```
Type METAHEADER
  mtType As Integer
  mtHeaderSize As Integer
  mtVersion As Integer
  mtSize As Long
  mtNoObjects As Integer
  mtMaxRecord As Long
  mtNoParameters As Integer
End Type

Type METARECORD
  rdSize As Long
  rdFunction As Integer
  rdParm(1) As Integer
End Type

Type midi
  songptrpos As Long
End Type

Type MIDIEVENT
  dwDeltaTime As Long      'Ticks since last event
  dwStreamID As Long       'Reserved; must be zero
  dwEvent As Long          'Event type and parameters
  dwParms(1) As Long       'Parameters if this is a long event
End Type

Type MIDIHDR
  lpData As String
  dwBufferLength As Long
  dwBytesRecorded As Long
  dwUser As Long
  dwFlags As Long
  lpNext As Long
  Reserved As Long
End Type

Type MIDIINCAPS
  wMid As Integer
  wPid As Integer
  vDriverVersion As Long
  szPname As String * MAXPNAMELEN
End Type

Type MIDIOUTCAPS
  wMid As Integer
  wPid As Integer
  vDriverVersion As Long
  szPname As String * MAXPNAMELEN
  wTechnology As Integer
  wVoices As Integer
```

```
    wNotes As Integer
    wChannelMask As Integer
    dwSupport As Long
End Type

Type MIDIPROPTEMPO
  cbStruct As Long
  dwTempo As Long
End Type

Type MIDIPROPTIMEDIV
  cbStruct As Long
  dwTimeDiv As Long
End Type

Type MIDISTRMBUFFVER
  dwVersion As Long       'Stream buffer format version
  dwMid As Long           'Manufacturer ID as defined in MMREG.H
  dwOEMVersion As Long    'Manufacturer version for custom ext
End Type

Type MINIMIZEDMETRICS
  cbSize As Long
  iWidth As Long
  iHorzGap As Long
  iVertGap As Long
  iArrange As Long
  lfFont As LOGFONT
End Type

Type MINMAXINFO
  ptReserved As POINTAPI
  ptMaxSize As POINTAPI
  ptMaxPosition As POINTAPI
  ptMinTrackSize As POINTAPI
  ptMaxTrackSize As POINTAPI
End Type

Type MIXERCAPS
  wMid As Integer         'manufacturer id
  wPid As Integer         'product id
  vDriverVersion As Long      'version of the driver
  szPname As String * MAXPNAMELEN 'product name
  fdwSupport As Long         'misc. support bits
  cDestinations As Long       'count of destinations
End Type

Type MIXERCONTROL
  cbStruct As Long        'size in Byte of MIXERCONTROL
  dwControlID As Long     'unique control id for mixer device
  dwControlType As Long     'MIXERCONTROL_CONTROLTYPE_xxx
  fdwControl As Long        'MIXERCONTROL_CONTROLF_xxx
```

```
      cMultipleItems As Long 'MIXERCONTROL_CONTROLF_MULTIPLE set
      szShortName As String * MIXER_SHORT_NAME_CHARS
      szName As String * MIXER_LONG_NAME_CHARS
      Bounds As Double
      Metrics As Long
   End Type

   Type MIXERCONTROLDETAILS
      cbStruct As Long        'size in Byte of MIXERCONTROLDETAILS
      dwControlID As Long     'control id to get/set details on
      cChannels As Long       'number of channels in paDetails array
      item As Long            ' hwndOwner or cMultipleItems
      cbDetails As Long       'size of _one_ details_XX struct
      paDetails As Long       'pointer to array of details_XX structs
   End Type

   Type MIXERCONTROLDETAILS_BOOLEAN
      fValue As Long
   End Type

   Type MIXERCONTROLDETAILS_LISTTEXT
      dwParam1 As Long
      dwParam2 As Long
      szName As String * MIXER_LONG_NAME_CHARS
   End Type

   Type MIXERCONTROLDETAILS_SIGNED
      lValue As Long
   End Type

   Type MIXERCONTROLDETAILS_UNSIGNED
      dwValue As Long
   End Type

   Type MIXERLINE
      cbStruct As Long          'size of MIXERLINE structure
      dwDestination As Long     'zero based destination index
      dwSource As Long          'zero based source index (if source)
      dwLineID As Long          'unique line id for mixer device
      fdwLine As Long         'state/information about line
      dwUser As Long          'driver specific information
      dwComponentType As Long 'component type line connects to
      cChannels As Long         'number of channels line supports
      cConnections As Long      'number of connections (possible)
      cControls As Long         'number of controls at this line
      szShortName As String * MIXER_SHORT_NAME_CHARS
      szName As String * MIXER_LONG_NAME_CHARS
      lpTarget As Target
   End Type

   Type MIXERLINECONTROLS
      cbStruct As Long        'size in Byte of MIXERLINECONTROLS
```

```
    dwLineID As Long      'line id (from MIXERLINE.dwLineID)
                 'MIXER_GETLINECONTROLSF_ONEBYID or
    dwControl As Long   'MIXER_GETLINECONTROLSF_ONEBYTYPE
    cControls As Long      'count of controls pmxctrl points to
    cbmxctrl As Long       'size in Byte of _one_ MIXERCONTROL
    pamxctrl As MIXERCONTROL 'pointer to MIXERCONTROL array
End Type

Type MMCKINFO
  ckid As Long
  ckSize As Long
  fccType As Long
  dwDataOffset As Long
  dwFlags As Long
End Type

Type MMIOINFO
  dwFlags As Long
  fccIOProc As Long
  pIOProc As Long
  wErrorRet As Long
  htask As Long
  cchBuffer As Long
  pchBuffer As String
  pchNext As String
  pchEndRead As String
  pchEndWrite As String
  lBufOffset As Long
  lDiskOffset As Long
  adwInfo(4) As Long
  dwReserved1 As Long
  dwReserved2 As Long
  hmmio As Long
End Type

Type MMTIME
  wType As Long
  u As Long
End Type

Type MODEMDEVCAPS
  dwActualSize As Long
  dwRequiredSize As Long
  dwDevSpecificOffset As Long
  dwDevSpecificSize As Long

   'product and version identification
  dwModemProviderVersion As Long
  dwModemManufacturerOffset As Long
  dwModemManufacturerSize As Long
  dwModemModelOffset As Long
```

```
    dwModemModelSize As Long
    dwModemVersionOffset As Long
    dwModemVersionSize As Long

     'local option capabilities
    dwDialOptions As Long      'bitmap of supported values
    dwCallSetupFailTimer As Long  'maximum in seconds
    dwInactivityTimeout As Long   'maximum in seconds
    dwSpeakerVolume As Long    'bitmap of supported values
    dwSpeakerMode As Long      'bitmap of supported values
    dwModemOptions As Long     'bitmap of supported values
    dwMaxDTERate As Long       'maximum value in bit/s
    dwMaxDCERate As Long       'maximum value in bit/s

     'Variable portion for proprietary expansion
    abVariablePortion(1) As Byte
End Type

Type MODEMSETTINGS
   dwActualSize As Long
   dwRequiredSize As Long
   dwDevSpecificOffset As Long
   dwDevSpecificSize As Long

     'static local options (read/write)
    dwCallSetupFailTimer As Long      'seconds
    dwInactivityTimeout As Long  'seconds
    dwSpeakerVolume As Long      'level
    dwSpeakerMode As Long        'mode
    dwPreferredModemOptions As Long    'bitmap

     'negotiated options (read only) for current or last call
    dwNegotiatedModemOptions As Long  'bitmap
    dwNegotiatedDCERate As Long  'bit/s

     'Variable portion for proprietary expansion
    abVariablePortion(1) As Byte
End Type

Type MONCBSTRUCT
   cb As Long
   dwTime As Long
   htask As Long
   dwRet As Long
   wType As Long
   wFmt As Long
   hConv As Long
   hsz1 As Long
   hsz2 As Long
   hData As Long
   dwData1 As Long
   dwData2 As Long
```

```
   cc As CONVCONTEXT      'new for NT for XTYP_CONNECT callbacks
   cbData As Long         'new for NT for data peeking
   Data(8) As Long        'new for NT for data peeking
End Type

Type MONCONVSTRUCT
  cb As Long
  fConnect As Long
  dwTime As Long
  htask As Long
  hszSvc As Long
  hszTopic As Long
  hConvClient As Long    'unique value != apps local hConv
  hConvServer As Long    'unique value != apps local hConv
End Type

Type MONERRSTRUCT
  cb As Long
  wLastError As Long
  dwTime As Long
  htask As Long
End Type

Type MONHSZSTRUCT
  cb As Long
  fsAction As Long 'MH_ value
  dwTime As Long
  hsz As Long
  htask As Long
  str As Byte
End Type

Type MONITOR_INFO_1
  pName As String
End Type

Type MONITOR_INFO_2
  pName As String
  pEnvironment As String
  pDLLName As String
End Type

Type MONLINKSTRUCT
  cb As Long
  dwTime As Long
  htask As Long
  fEstablished As Long
  fNoData As Long
  hszSvc As Long
  hszTopic As Long
  hszItem As Long
```

```
    wFmt As Long
    fServer As Long
    hConvServer As Long
    hConvClient As Long
End Type

Type MONMSGSTRUCT
    cb As Long
    hwndTo As Long
    dwTime As Long
    htask As Long
    wMsg As Long
    wParam As Long
    lParam As Long
    dmhd As DDEML_MSG_HOOK_DATA      'new for NT
End Type

Type MOUSE_EVENT_RECORD
    dwMousePosition As COORD
    dwButtonState As Long
    dwControlKeyState As Long
    dwEventFlags As Long
End Type

Type MOUSEHOOKSTRUCT
    pt As POINTAPI
    hwnd As Long
    wHitTestCode As Long
    dwExtraInfo As Long
End Type

Type MSG
    hwnd As Long
    message As Long
    wParam As Long
    lParam As Long
    time As Long
    pt As POINTAPI
End Type

Type MSGBOXPARAMS
    cbSize As Long
    hwndOwner As Long
    hInstance As Long
    lpszText As String
    lpszCaption As String
    dwStyle As Long
    lpszIcon As String
    dwContextHelpId As Long
    lpfnMsgBoxCallback As Long
    dwLanguageId As Long
End Type
```

```
Type MULTIKEYHELP
  mkSize As Long
  mkKeylist As Byte
  szKeyphrase As String * 253 ' Array length is arbitrary
End Type

Type NAME_BUFFER
  name  As String * NCBNAMSZ
  name_num As Integer
  name_flags As Integer
End Type

Type NCB
  ncb_command As Integer
  ncb_retcode As Integer
  ncb_lsn As Integer
  ncb_num As Integer
  ncb_buffer As String
  ncb_length As Integer
  ncb_callname As String * NCBNAMSZ
  ncb_name As String * NCBNAMSZ
  ncb_rto As Integer
  ncb_sto As Integer
  ncb_post As Long
  ncb_lana_num As Integer
  ncb_cmd_cplt As Integer
  ncb_reserve(10) As Byte    ' Reserved, must be 0
  ncb_event As Long
End Type

Type NETRESOURCE
  dwScope As Long
  dwType As Long
  dwDisplayType As Long
  dwUsage As Long
  lpLocalName As String
  lpRemoteName As String
  lpComment As String
  lpProvider As String
End Type

Type NEWTEXTMETRIC
  tmHeight As Long
  tmAscent As Long
  tmDescent As Long
  tmInternalLeading As Long
  tmExternalLeading As Long
  tmAveCharWidth As Long
  tmMaxCharWidth As Long
  tmWeight As Long
```

```
       tmOverhang As Long
       tmDigitizedAspectX As Long
       tmDigitizedAspectY As Long
       tmFirstChar As Byte
       tmLastChar As Byte
       tmDefaultChar As Byte
       tmBreakChar As Byte
       tmItalic As Byte
       tmUnderlined As Byte
       tmStruckOut As Byte
       tmPitchAndFamily As Byte
       tmCharSet As Byte
       ntmFlags As Long
       ntmSizeEM As Long
       ntmCellHeight As Long
       ntmAveWidth As Long
   End Type

   Type NEWTEXTMETRICEX
     ntmTm As NEWTEXTMETRIC
     ntmFontSig As FONTSIGNATURE
   End Type

   Type NMHDR
      hwndFrom As Long
      idfrom As Long
      code As Long
   End Type

   Type NONCLIENTMETRICS
     cbSize As Long
     iBorderWidth As Long
     iScrollWidth As Long
     iScrollHeight As Long
     iCaptionWidth As Long
     iCaptionHeight As Long
     lfCaptionFont As LOGFONT
     iSMCaptionWidth As Long
     iSMCaptionHeight As Long
     lfSMCaptionFont As LOGFONT
     iMenuWidth As Long
     iMenuHeight As Long
     lfMenuFont As LOGFONT
     lfStatusFont As LOGFONT
     lfMessageFont As LOGFONT
   End Type

   Type NOTIFYICONDATA
     cbSize As Long
     hwnd As Long
```

```
    uID As Long
    uFlags As Long
    uCallbackMessage As Long
    hIcon As Long
    szTip As String * 64
End Type

Type OFNOTIFY
  hdr As NMHDR
  lpOFN As OPENFILENAME
  pszFile As String   'May be NULL
End Type

Type OFSTRUCT
  cBytes As Byte
  fFixedDisk As Byte
  nErrCode As Integer
  Reserved1 As Integer
  Reserved2 As Integer
  szPathName(OFS_MAXPATHNAME) As Byte
End Type

Type OPENFILENAME
  lStructSize As Long
  hwndOwner As Long
  hInstance As Long
  lpstrFilter As String
  lpstrCustomFilter As String
  nMaxCustFilter As Long
  nFilterIndex As Long
  lpstrFile As String
  nMaxFile As Long
  lpstrFileTitle As String
  nMaxFileTitle As Long
  lpstrInitialDir As String
  lpstrTitle As String
  flags As Long
  nFileOffset As Integer
  nFileExtension As Integer
  lpstrDefExt As String
  lCustData As Long
  lpfnHook As Long
  lpTemplateName As String
End Type

Type OSVERSIONINFO
  dwOSVersionInfoSize As Long
  dwMajorVersion As Long
  dwMinorVersion As Long
  dwBuildNumber As Long
  dwPlatformId As Long
```

```
      szCSDVersion As String * 128 'Maintenance string PSS usage
End Type

Type OUTLINETEXTMETRIC
   otmSize As Long
   otmTextMetrics As TEXTMETRIC
   otmFiller As Byte
   otmPanoseNumber As PANOSE
   otmfsSelection As Long
   otmfsType As Long
   otmsCharSlopeRise As Long
   otmsCharSlopeRun As Long
   otmItalicAngle As Long
   otmEMSquare As Long
   otmAscent As Long
   otmDescent As Long
   otmLineGap As Long
   otmsCapEmHeight As Long
   otmsXHeight As Long
   otmrcFontBox As Rect
   otmMacAscent As Long
   otmMacDescent As Long
   otmMacLineGap As Long
   otmusMinimumPPEM As Long
   otmptSubscriptSize As POINTAPI
   otmptSubscriptOffset As POINTAPI
   otmptSuperscriptSize As POINTAPI
   otmptSuperscriptOffset As POINTAPI
   otmsStrikeoutSize As Long
   otmsStrikeoutPosition As Long
   otmsUnderscorePosition As Long
   otmsUnderscoreSize As Long
   otmpFamilyName As String
   otmpFaceName As String
   otmpStyleName As String
   otmpFullName As String
End Type

Type OUTPUT_DEBUG_STRING_INFO
   lpDebugStringData As String
   fUnicode As Integer
   nDebugStringLength As Integer
End Type

Type OVERLAPPED
   Internal As Long
   InternalHigh As Long
   offset As Long
   OffsetHigh As Long
   hEvent As Long
End Type
```

```
Type PAGESETUPDLG
  lStructSize As Long
  hwndOwner As Long
  hDevMode As Long
  hDevNames As Long
  flags As Long
  ptPaperSize As POINTAPI
  rtMinMargin As Rect
  rtMargin As Rect
  hInstance As Long
  lCustData As Long
  lpfnPageSetupHook As Long
  lpfnPagePaintHook As Long
  lpPageSetupTemplateName As String
  hPageSetupTemplate As Long
End Type

Type PAINTSTRUCT
  hdc As Long
  fErase As Long
  rcPaint As Rect
  fRestore As Long
  fIncUpdate As Long
  rgbReserved As Byte
End Type

Type PALETTEENTRY
  peRed As Byte
  peGreen As Byte
  peBlue As Byte
  peFlags As Byte
End Type

Type PANOSE
  ulculture As Long
  bFamilyType As Byte
  bSerifStyle As Byte
  bWeight As Byte
  bProportion As Byte
  bContrast As Byte
  bStrokeVariation As Byte
  bArmStyle As Byte
  bLetterform As Byte
  bMidline As Byte
  bXHeight As Byte
End Type

Type PCMWAVEFORMAT
  wf As WAVEFORMAT
  wBitsPerSample As Integer
End Type
```

```
Type PELARRAY
  paXCount As Long
  paYCount As Long
  paXExt As Long
  paYExt As Long
  paRGBs As Integer
End Type

Type PERF_COUNTER_BLOCK
  ByteLength As Long
End Type

Type PERF_COUNTER_DEFINITION
  ByteLength As Long
  CounterNameTitleIndex As Long
  CounterNameTitle As String
  CounterHelpTitleIndex As Long
  CounterHelpTitle As String
  DefaultScale As Long
  DetailLevel As Long
  CounterType As Long
  CounterSize As Long
  CounterOffset As Long
End Type

Type PERF_DATA_BLOCK
  Signature As String * 4
  LittleEndian As Long
  Version As Long
  Revision As Long
  TotalByteLength As Long
  HeaderLength As Long
  NumObjectTypes As Long
  DefaultObject As Long
  SystemTime As SYSTEMTIME
  PerfTime As LARGE_INTEGER
  PerfFreq As LARGE_INTEGER
  PerTime100nSec As LARGE_INTEGER
  SystemNameLength As Long
  SystemNameOffset As Long
End Type

Type PERF_INSTANCE_DEFINITION
  ByteLength As Long
  ParentObjectTitleIndex As Long
  ParentObjectInstance As Long
  UniqueID As Long
  NameOffset As Long
  NameLength As Long
End Type
```

```
Type PERF_OBJECT_TYPE
  TotalByteLength As Long
  DefinitionLength As Long
  HeaderLength As Long
  ObjectNameTitleIndex As Long
  ObjectNameTitle As String
  ObjectHelpTitleIndex As Long
  ObjectHelpTitle As String
  DetailLevel As Long
  NumCounters As Long
  DefaultCounter As Long
  NumInstances As Long
  CodePage As Long
  PerfTime As LARGE_INTEGER
  PerfFreq As LARGE_INTEGER
End Type

Type PIXELFORMATDESCRIPTOR
  nSize As Integer
  nVersion As Integer
  dwFlags As Long
  iPixelType As Byte
  cColorBits As Byte
  cRedBits As Byte
  cRedShift As Byte
  cGreenBits As Byte
  cGreenShift As Byte
  cBlueBits As Byte
  cBlueShift As Byte
  cAlphaBits As Byte
  cAlphaShift As Byte
  cAccumBits As Byte
  cAccumRedBits As Byte
  cAccumGreenBits As Byte
  cAccumBlueBits As Byte
  cAccumAlphaBits As Byte
  cDepthBits As Byte
  cStencilBits As Byte
  cAuxBuffers As Byte
  iLayerType As Byte
  bReserved As Byte
  dwLayerMask As Long
  dwVisibleMask As Long
  dwDamageMask As Long
End Type

Type POINTAPI
  x As Long
  y As Long
End Type
```

```
Type POINTFX
  x As FIXED
  y As FIXED
End Type

Type POINTL
  x As Long
  y As Long
End Type

Type POINTS
  x  As Integer
  y  As Integer
End Type

Type POLYTEXT
  x As Long
  y As Long
  n As Long
  lpStr As String
  uiFlags As Long
  rcl As Rect
  pdx As Long
End Type

Type PORT_INFO_1
  pName As String
End Type

Type PORT_INFO_2
  pPortName As String
  pMonitorName As String
  pDescription As String
  fPortType As Long
  Reserved As Long
End Type

Type PRINTDLG
  lStructSize As Long
  hwndOwner As Long
  hDevMode As Long
  hDevNames As Long
  hdc As Long
  flags As Long
  nFromPage As Integer
  nToPage As Integer
  nMinPage As Integer
  nMaxPage As Integer
  nCopies As Integer
  hInstance As Long
  lCustData As Long
```

```
        lpfnPrintHook As Long
        lpfnSetupHook As Long
        lpPrintTemplateName As String
        lpSetupTemplateName As String
        hPrintTemplate As Long
        hSetupTemplate As Long
End Type

Type PRINTER_DEFAULTS
    pDatatype As String
    pDevMode As DEVMODE
    DesiredAccess As Long
End Type

Type PRINTER_INFO_1
    flags As Long
    pDescription As String
    pName As String
    pComment As String
End Type

Type PRINTER_INFO_2
    pServerName As String
    pPrinterName As String
    pShareName As String
    pPortName As String
    pDriverName As String
    pComment As String
    pLocation As String
    pDevMode As DEVMODE
    pSepFile As String
    pPrintProcessor As String
    pDatatype As String
    pParameters As String
    pSecurityDescriptor As SECURITY_DESCRIPTOR
    Attributes As Long
    Priority As Long
    DefaultPriority As Long
    StartTime As Long
    UntilTime As Long
    Status As Long
    cJobs As Long
    AveragePPM As Long
End Type

Type PRINTER_INFO_3
    pSecurityDescriptor As SECURITY_DESCRIPTOR
End Type

Type PRINTER_INFO_4
    pPrinterName As String
```

```
    pServerName As String
    Attributes As Long
End Type

Type PRINTER_INFO_5
  pPrinterName As String
  pPortName As String
  Attributes As Long
  DeviceNotSelectedTimeout As Long
  TransmissionRetryTimeout As Long
End Type

Type PRINTPROCESSOR_INFO_1
  pName As String
End Type

Type PRIVILEGE_SET
  PrivilegeCount As Long
  Control As Long
  Privilege(ANYSIZE_ARRAY) As LUID_AND_ATTRIBUTES
End Type

Type PROCESS_INFORMATION
  hProcess As Long
  hThread As Long
  dwProcessId As Long
  dwThreadId As Long
End Type

Type PROVIDOR_INFO_1
  pName As String
  pEnvironment As String
  pDLLName As String
End Type

Type QUERY_SERVICE_CONFIG
  dwServiceType As Long
  dwStartType As Long
  dwErrorControl As Long
  lpBinaryPathName As String
  lpLoadOrderGroup As String
  dwTagId As Long
  lpDependencies As String
  lpServiceStartName As String
  lpDisplayName As String
End Type

Type QUERY_SERVICE_LOCK_STATUS
  fIsLocked As Long
  lpLockOwner As String
  dwLockDuration As Long
End Type
```

```
Type RASTERIZER_STATUS
  nSize As Integer
  wFlags As Integer
  nLanguageID As Integer
End Type

Type RECT
  Left As Long
  Top As Long
  Right As Long
  Bottom As Long
End Type

Type RECTL
  Left As Long
  Top As Long
  Right As Long
  Bottom As Long
End Type

Type RGBQUAD
  rgbBlue As Byte
  rgbGreen As Byte
  rgbRed As Byte
  rgbReserved As Byte
End Type

Type RGBTRIPLE
  rgbtBlue As Byte
  rgbtGreen As Byte
  rgbtRed As Byte
End Type

Type RGNDATA
  rdh As RGNDATAHEADER
  Buffer As Byte
End Type

Type RGNDATAHEADER
  dwSize As Long
  iType As Long
  nCount As Long
  nRgnSize As Long
  rcBound As Rect
End Type

Type RIP_INFO
  dwError As Long
  dwType As Long
End Type
```

```
Type SCROLLINFO
  cbSize As Long
  fMask As Long
  nMin As Long
  nMax As Long
  Page As Long
  nPos As Long
  nTrackPos As Long
End Type

Type SECURITY_ATTRIBUTES
  nLength As Long
  lpSecurityDescriptor As Long
  bInheritHandle As Long
End Type

Type SECURITY_DESCRIPTOR
  Revision As Byte
  Sbz1 As Byte
  Control As Long
  Owner As Long
  Group As Long
  Sacl As ACL
  Dacl As ACL
End Type

Type SECURITY_QUALITY_OF_SERVICE
  Length As Long
  Impersonationlevel As Integer
  ContextTrackingMode As Integer
  EffectiveOnly As Long
End Type

Type SERVICE_STATUS
  dwServiceType As Long
  dwCurrentState As Long
  dwControlsAccepted As Long
  dwWin32ExitCode As Long
  dwServiceSpecificExitCode As Long
  dwCheckPoint As Long
  dwWaitHint As Long
End Type

Type SERVICE_TABLE_ENTRY
  lpServiceName As String
  lpServiceProc As Long
End Type

Type SESSION_BUFFER
  lsn As Integer
```

```
      State As Integer
      local_name As String * NCBNAMSZ
      remote_name As String * NCBNAMSZ
      rcvs_outstanding As Integer
      sends_outstanding As Integer
    End Type

    Type SESSION_HEADER
      sess_name As Integer
      num_sess As Integer
      rcv_dg_outstanding As Integer
      rcv_any_outstanding As Integer
    End Type

    Type SHELLEXECUTEINFO
      cbSize As Long
      fMask As Long
      hwnd As Long
      lpVerb As String
      lpFile As String
      lpParameters As String
      lpDirectory As String
      nShow As Long
      hInstApp As Long
      'Optional fields
      lpIDList As Long
      lpClass As String
      hkeyClass As Long
      dwHotKey As Long
      hIcon As Long
      hProcess As Long
    End Type

    Type SHFILEINFO
      hIcon As Long          'out: icon
      iIcon As Long     'out: icon index
      dwAttributes As Long        'out: SFGAO_ flags
      szDisplayName As String * MAX_PATH 'out: name (or path)
      szTypeName As String * 80    'out: type name
    End Type

    Type SHFILEOPSTRUCT
      hwnd As Long
      wFunc As Long
      pFrom As String
      pTo As String
      fFlags As Integer
      fAnyOperationsAborted As Long
      hNameMappings As Long
      lpszProgressTitle As String 'only for FOF_SIMPLEPROGRESS
    End Type
```

```
Type SHNAMEMAPPING
  pszOldPath As String
  pszNewPath As String
  cchOldPath As Long
  cchNewPath As Long
End Type

Type SID_AND_ATTRIBUTES
  Sid As Long
  Attributes As Long
End Type

Type SID_IDENTIFIER_AUTHORITY
  Value(6) As Byte
End Type

Type Size
  cx As Long
  cy As Long
End Type

Type SIZEL
  cx As Long
  cy As Long
End Type

Type SMALL_RECT
  Left As Integer
  Top As Integer
  Right As Integer
  Bottom As Integer
End Type

Type smpte
  hour As Byte
  min As Byte
  sec As Byte
  frame As Byte
  fps As Byte
  dummy As Byte
  pad(2) As Byte
End Type

Type STARTUPINFO
  cb As Long
  lpReserved As String
  lpDesktop As String
  lpTitle As String
  dwX As Long
  dwY As Long
  dwXSize As Long
  dwYSize As Long
```

```
    dwXCountChars As Long
    dwYCountChars As Long
    dwFillAttribute As Long
    dwFlags As Long
    wShowWindow As Integer
    cbReserved2 As Integer
    lpReserved2 As Byte
    hStdInput As Long
    hStdOutput As Long
    hStdError As Long
End Type

Type STYLEBUF
  dwStyle As Long
  szDescription As String * STYLE_DESCRIPTION_SIZE
End Type

Type SYSTEM_ALARM_ACE
  Header As ACE_HEADER
  Mask As Long
  SidStart As Long
End Type

Type SYSTEM_AUDIT_ACE
  Header As ACE_HEADER
  Mask As Long
  SidStart As Long
End Type

Type SYSTEM_INFO
  dwOemID As Long
  dwPageSize As Long
  lpMinimumApplicationAddress As Long
  lpMaximumApplicationAddress As Long
  dwActiveProcessorMask As Long
  dwNumberOrfProcessors As Long
  dwProcessorType As Long
  dwAllocationGranularity As Long
  dwReserved As Long
End Type

Type SYSTEM_POWER_STATUS
  ACLineStatus As Byte
  BatteryFlag As Byte
  BatteryLifePercent As Byte
  Reserved1 As Byte
  BatteryLifeTime As Long
  BatteryFullLifeTime As Long
End Type
```

```
Type SYSTEMTIME
  wYear As Integer
  wMonth As Integer
  wDayOfWeek As Integer
  wDay As Integer
  wHour As Integer
  wMinute As Integer
  wSecond As Integer
  wMilliseconds As Integer
End Type

Type Target 'use in MIXERLINE and embedded structure
  dwType As Long       'MIXERLINE_TARGETTYPE_xxxx
  dwDeviceID As Long 'target device ID of device type
  wMid As Integer      'of target device
  wPid As Integer      '    "
  vDriverVersion As Long      '    "
  szPname As String * MAXPNAMELEN
End Type

Type TEXTMETRIC
  tmHeight As Long
  tmAscent As Long
  tmDescent As Long
  tmInternalLeading As Long
  tmExternalLeading As Long
  tmAveCharWidth As Long
  tmMaxCharWidth As Long
  tmWeight As Long
  tmOverhang As Long
  tmDigitizedAspectX As Long
  tmDigitizedAspectY As Long
  tmFirstChar As Byte
  tmLastChar As Byte
  tmDefaultChar As Byte
  tmBreakChar As Byte
  tmItalic As Byte
  tmUnderlined As Byte
  tmStruckOut As Byte
  tmPitchAndFamily As Byte
  tmCharSet As Byte
End Type

Type TIME_ZONE_INFORMATION
  Bias As Long
  StandardName(32) As Integer
  StandardDate As SYSTEMTIME
  StandardBias As Long
  DaylightName(32) As Integer
```

```
    DaylightDate As SYSTEMTIME
    DaylightBias As Long
End Type

Type TIMECAPS
  wPeriodMin As Long
  wPeriodMax As Long
End Type

Type TOKEN_GROUPS
  GroupCount As Long
  Groups(ANYSIZE_ARRAY) As SID_AND_ATTRIBUTES
End Type

Type TOKEN_PRIVILEGES
  PrivilegeCount As Long
  Privileges(ANYSIZE_ARRAY) As LUID_AND_ATTRIBUTES
End Type

Type TPMPARAMS
  cbSize As Long
  rcExclude As Rect
End Type

Type TTPOLYCURVE
  wType As Integer
  cpfx As Integer
  apfx As POINTFX
End Type

Type TTPOLYGONHEADER
  cb As Long
  dwType As Long
  pfxStart As POINTFX
End Type

Type UNLOAD_DLL_DEBUG_INFO
  lpBaseOfDll As Long
End Type

Type VS_FIXEDFILEINFO
  dwSignature As Long
  dwStrucVersion As Long    'e.g. 0x00000042 = "0.42"
  dwFileVersionMS As Long   'e.g. 0x00030075 = "3.75"
  dwFileVersionLS As Long   'e.g. 0x00000031 = "0.31"
  dwProductVersionMS As Long   'e.g. 0x00030010 = "3.10"
  dwProductVersionLS As Long   'e.g. 0x00000031 = "0.31"
  dwFileFlagsMask As Long   '= 0x3F for version "0.42"
  dwFileFlags As Long       'e.g. VFF_DEBUG Or VFF_PRERELEASE
  dwFileOS As Long          'e.g. VOS_DOS_WINDOWS16
  dwFileType As Long        'e.g. VFT_DRIVER
  dwFileSubtype As Long     'e.g. VFT2_DRV_KEYBOARD
```

```
      dwFileDateMS As Long     'e.g. 0
      dwFileDateLS As Long     'e.g. 0
    End Type

    Type WAVEFORMAT
      wFormatTag As Integer
      nChannels As Integer
      nSamplesPerSec As Long
      nAvgBytesPerSec As Long
      nBlockAlign As Integer
    End Type

    Type WAVEHDR
      lpData As String
      dwBufferLength As Long
      dwBytesRecorded As Long
      dwUser As Long
      dwFlags As Long
      dwLoops As Long
      lpNext As Long
      Reserved As Long
    End Type

    Type WAVEINCAPS
      wMid As Integer
      wPid As Integer
      vDriverVersion As Long
      szPname As String * MAXPNAMELEN
      dwFormats As Long
      wChannels As Integer
    End Type

    Type WAVEOUTCAPS
      wMid As Integer
      wPid As Integer
      vDriverVersion As Long
      szPname As String * MAXPNAMELEN
      dwFormats As Long
      wChannels As Integer
      dwSupport As Long
    End Type

    Type WIN32_FIND_DATA
      dwFileAttributes As Long
      ftCreationTime As FILETIME
      ftLastAccessTime As FILETIME
      ftLastWriteTime As FILETIME
      nFileSizeHigh As Long
      nFileSizeLow As Long
      dwReserved0 As Long
      dwReserved1 As Long
```

```
      cFileName As String * MAX_PATH
      cAlternate As String * 14
   End Type

   Type WIN32_STREAM_ID
      dwStreamID As Long
      dwStreamAttributes As Long
      dwStreamSizeLow As Long
      dwStreamSizeHigh As Long
      dwStreamNameSize As Long
      cStreamName As Byte
   End Type

   Type WINDOW_BUFFER_SIZE_RECORD
      dwSize As COORD
   End Type

   Type WINDOWPLACEMENT
      Length As Long
      flags As Long
      showCmd As Long
      ptMinPosition As POINTAPI
      ptMaxPosition As POINTAPI
      rcNormalPosition As Rect
   End Type

   Type WINDOWPOS
      hwnd As Long
      hWndInsertAfter As Long
      x As Long
      y As Long
      cx As Long
      cy As Long
      flags As Long
   End Type

   Type WNDCLASS
      style As Long
      lpfnwndproc As Long
      cbClsextra As Long
      cbWndExtra2 As Long
      hInstance As Long
      hIcon As Long
      hCursor As Long
      hbrBackground As Long
      lpszMenuName As String
      lpszClassName As String
   End Type

   Type WNDCLASSEX
      cbSize As Long
```

```
      style As Long
      lpfnWndProc As Long
      cbClsExtra As Long
      cbWndExtra As Long
      hInstance As Long
      hIcon As Long
      hCursor As Long
      hbrBackground As Long
      lpszMenuName As String
      lpszClassName As String
      hIconSm As Long
End Type

Type XFORM
   eM11 As Single
   eM12 As Single
   eM21 As Single
   eM22 As Single
   eDx As Single
   eDy As Single
End Type
```

Appendix C

Win32 API Constant Declarations

The following listing contains the complete listing of the Win32 constants used by the various functions and subroutines. This alphabetical grouping should help you quickly find the constant or group of constants needed for your Visual Basic applications.

```
A
ABE_BOTTOM=3
ABE_LEFT=0
ABE_RIGHT=2
ABE_TOP=1
ABM_ACTIVATE=&H6 'lParam == TRUE/FALSE means act/deact
ABM_GETAUTOHIDEBAR=&H7
ABM_GETSTATE=&H4
ABM_GETTASKBARPOS=&H5
ABM_NEW=&H0
ABM_QUERYPOS=&H2
ABM_REMOVE=&H1
ABM_SETAUTOHIDEBAR=&H8 'this can fail at any time.
ABM_SETPOS=&H3
ABM_WINDOWPOSCHANGED=&H9
ABN_FULLSCREENAPP=&H2
ABN_POSCHANGED=&H1
```

```
ABN_STATECHANGE=&H0
ABN_WINDOWARRANGE=&H3  'lParam == TRUE means hide
AbortDocC=2
ABS_ALWAYSONTOP=&H2
ABS_AUTOHIDE=&H1
ABSOLUTE=1
AC_LINE_BACKUP_POWER=&H2
AC_LINE_OFFLINE=&H0
AC_LINE_ONLINE=&H1
AC_LINE_UNKNOWN=&HFF
ACCESS_ALLOWED_ACE_TYPE=&H0
ACCESS_DENIED_ACE_TYPE=&H1
ACCESS_SYSTEM_SECURITY=&H1000000
ACL_REVISION=(2)
ACL_REVISION1=(1)
ACL_REVISION2=(2)
AclRevisionInformation=1
AclSizeInformation=2
AD_CLOCKWISE=2
AD_COUNTERCLOCKWISE=1
ALL_TRANSPORTS="M\0\0\0"
ALTERNATE=1
ANSI_CHARSET=0
ANSI_FIXED_FONT=11
ANSI_VAR_FONT=12
ANYSIZE_ARRAY=1
APPCLASS_MASK=&HF&
APPCLASS_MONITOR=&H1&
APPCLASS_STANDARD=&H0&
APPCMD_CLIENTONLY=&H10&
APPCMD_FILTERINITS=&H20&
APPCMD_MASK=&HFF0&
APPLICATION_ERROR_MASK=&H20000000
ARABIC_CHARSET=178
ASPECT_FILTERING=&H1
ASPECTX=40 'Length of the X leg
ASPECTXY=44 'Length of the hypotenuse
ASPECTY=42 'Length of the Y leg
ASYNCH=&H80   'high bit set == asynchronous
ATTR_CONVERTED=&H2
ATTR_INPUT=&H0
ATTR_INPUT_ERROR=&H4
ATTR_TARGET_CONVERTED=&H1
ATTR_TARGET_NOTCONVERTED=&H3
AUX_MAPPER=-1&
AUXCAPS_AUXIN=2   'audio from auxiliary input jacks
AUXCAPS_CDAUDIO=1   'audio from internal CD-ROM drive
```

```
AUXCAPS_LRVOLUME=&H2 'separate left-right volume control
AUXCAPS_VOLUME=&H1 'supports volume control

B
BACKGROUND_BLUE=&H10 'background color contains blue.
BACKGROUND_GREEN=&H20 'background color contains green.
BACKGROUND_INTENSITY=&H80 'background color is intensified.
BACKGROUND_RED=&H40 'background color contains red.
BACKUP_ALTERNATE_DATA=&H4
BACKUP_DATA=&H1
BACKUP_EA_DATA=&H2
BACKUP_LINK=&H5
BACKUP_SECURITY_DATA=&H3
BALTIC_CHARSET=186
BANDINFO=24
BATTERY_FLAG_CHARGING=&H8
BATTERY_FLAG_CRITICAL=&H4
BATTERY_FLAG_HIGH=&H1
BATTERY_FLAG_LOW=&H2
BATTERY_FLAG_NO_BATTERY=&H80
BATTERY_FLAG_UNKNOWN=&HFF
BATTERY_LIFE_UNKNOWN=&HFFFF
BATTERY_PERCENTAGE_UNKNOWN=&HFF
BAUD_075=&H1&
BAUD_110=&H2&
BAUD_115200=&H20000
BAUD_1200=&H40&
BAUD_128K=&H10000
BAUD_134_5=&H4&
BAUD_14400=&H1000&
BAUD_150=&H8&
BAUD_1800=&H80&
BAUD_19200=&H2000&
BAUD_2400=&H100&
BAUD_300=&H10&
BAUD_38400=&H4000&
BAUD_4800=&H200&
BAUD_56K=&H8000&
BAUD_57600=&H40000
BAUD_600=&H20&
BAUD_7200=&H400&
BAUD_9600=&H800&
BAUD_USER=&H10000000
BDR_INNER=&HC
BDR_OUTER=&H3
BDR_RAISED=&H5
BDR_RAISEDINNER=&H4
BDR_RAISEDOUTER=&H1
```

```
BDR_SUNKEN=&HA
BDR_SUNKENINNER=&H8
BDR_SUNKENOUTER=&H2
BEGIN_PATH=4096
BF_ADJUST=&H2000 'Calculate the space left over.
BF_BOTTOM=&H8
BF_BOTTOMLEFT=(BF_BOTTOM Or BF_LEFT)
BF_BOTTOMRIGHT=(BF_BOTTOM Or BF_RIGHT)
BF_DIAGONAL=&H10
BF_DIAGONAL_ENDBOTTOMLEFT=(BF_DIAGONAL Or BF_BOTTOM Or BF_LEFT)
BF_DIAGONAL_ENDBOTTOMRIGHT=(BF_DIAGONAL Or BF_BOTTOM Or BF_RIGHT)
BF_DIAGONAL_ENDTOPLEFT=(BF_DIAGONAL Or BF_TOP Or BF_LEFT)
BF_DIAGONAL_ENDTOPRIGHT=(BF_DIAGONAL Or BF_TOP Or BF_RIGHT)
BF_FLAT=&H4000 'For flat rather than 3-D borders.
BF_LEFT=&H1
BF_MIDDLE=&H800 'Fill in the middle.
BF_MONO=&H8000 'For monochrome borders.
BF_RECT=(BF_LEFT Or BF_TOP Or BF_RIGHT Or BF_BOTTOM)
BF_RIGHT=&H4
BF_SOFT=&H1000 'Use for softer buttons.
BF_TOP=&H2
BF_TOPLEFT=(BF_TOP Or BF_LEFT)
BF_TOPRIGHT=(BF_TOP Or BF_RIGHT)
BI_bitfields=3&
BI_RGB=0&
BI_RLE4=2&
BI_RLE8=1&
BITSPIXEL=12 'Number of bits per pixel
BKMODE_LAST=2
BLACK_BRUSH=4
BLACK_PEN=7
BLACKNESS=&H42 '(DWORD) dest=BLACK
BLACKONWHITE=1
BM_GETCHECK=&HF0
BM_GETSTATE=&HF2
BM_SETCHECK=&HF1
BM_SETSTATE=&HF3
BM_SETSTYLE=&HF4
BN_CLICKED=0
BN_DISABLE=4
BN_DOUBLECLICKED=5
BN_HILITE=2
BN_PAINT=1
BN_UNHILITE=3
BOLD_FONTTYPE=&H100
BS_3STATE=&H5&
BS_AUTO3STATE=&H6&
BS_AUTOCHECKBOX=&H3&
```

```
BS_AUTORADIOBUTTON=&H9&
BS_CHECKBOX=&H2&
BS_DEFPUSHBUTTON=&H1&
BS_DIBPATTERN=5
BS_DIBPATTERN8X8=8
BS_DIBPATTERNPT=6
BS_GROUPBOX=&H7&
BS_HATCHED=2
BS_HOLLOW=BS_NULL
BS_INDEXED=4
BS_LEFTTEXT=&H20&
BS_NULL=1
BS_OWNERDRAW=&HB&
BS_PATTERN=3
BS_PATTERN8X8=7
BS_PUSHBUTTON=&H0&
BS_RADIOBUTTON=&H4&
BS_SOLID=0
BS_USERBUTTON=&H8&


C
C1_ALPHA=&H100 'any letter
C1_BLANK=&H40 'blank characters
C1_CNTRL=&H20 'control characters
C1_DIGIT=&H4 'decimal digits
C1_LOWER=&H2 'lowercase
C1_PUNCT=&H10 'punctuation characters
C1_SPACE=&H8 'spacing characters
C1_TRANSPARENT=&H1 'new raster cap
C1_UPPER=&H1 'uppercase
C1_XDIGIT=&H80 'other digits
C2_ARABICNUMBER=&H6 'Arabic number
C2_BLOCKSEPARATOR=&H8 'block separator
C2_COMMONSEPARATOR=&H7 'common numeric separator
C2_EUROPENUMBER=&H3 'European number, digit
C2_EUROPESEPARATOR=&H4 'European numeric separator
C2_EUROPETERMINATOR=&H5 'European numeric terminator
C2_LEFTTORIGHT=&H1 'left to right
C2_NOTAPPLICABLE=&H0 'no implicit directionality
C2_OTHERNEUTRAL=&HB 'other neutrals
C2_RIGHTTOLEFT=&H2 'right to left
C2_SEGMENTSEPARATOR=&H9 'segment separator
C2_WHITESPACE=&HA 'white space
C3_DIACRITIC=&H2 'diacritic mark
C3_NONSPACING=&H1 'nonspacing character
C3_NOTAPPLICABLE=&H0 'ctype 3 is not applicable
C3_SYMBOL=&H8 'symbols
C3_VOWELMARK=&H4 'vowel mark
```

```
CA_LOG_FILTER=&H2
CA_NEGATIVE=&H1
CACHE_E_FIRST=&H80040170
CACHE_E_LAST=&H8004017F
CACHE_E_NOCACHE_UPDATED=&H80040170
CACHE_S_FIRST=&H40170
CACHE_S_FORMATETC_NOTSUPPORTED=&H40170
CACHE_S_LAST=&H4017F
CACHE_S_SAMECACHE=&H40171
CACHE_S_SOMECACHES_NOTUPDATED=&H40172
CADV_LATEACK=&HFFFF
CAL_GREGORIAN=1 'Gregorian (localized) calendar
CAL_GREGORIAN_US=2 'Gregorian (U.S.) calendar
CAL_ICALINTVALUE=&H1 'calendar type
CAL_IYEAROFFSETRANGE=&H3 'starting years of eras
CAL_JAPAN=3 'Japanese Emperor Era calendar
CAL_KOREA=5 'Korean Tangun Era calendar
CAL_SABBREVDAYNAME1=&HE 'abbreviated name for Monday
CAL_SABBREVDAYNAME2=&HF 'abbreviated name for Tuesday
CAL_SABBREVDAYNAME3=&H10 'abbreviated name for Wednesday
CAL_SABBREVDAYNAME4=&H11 'abbreviated name for Thursday
CAL_SABBREVDAYNAME5=&H12 'abbreviated name for Friday
CAL_SABBREVDAYNAME6=&H13 'abbreviated name for Saturday
CAL_SABBREVDAYNAME7=&H14 'abbreviated name for Sunday
CAL_SABBREVMONTHNAME1=&H22 'abbreviated name for January
CAL_SABBREVMONTHNAME10=&H2B 'abbreviated name for October
CAL_SABBREVMONTHNAME11=&H2C 'abbreviated name for November
CAL_SABBREVMONTHNAME12=&H2D 'abbreviated name for December
CAL_SABBREVMONTHNAME13=&H2E 'abbreviated name for 13th month
CAL_SABBREVMONTHNAME2=&H23 'abbreviated name for February
CAL_SABBREVMONTHNAME3=&H24 'abbreviated name for March
CAL_SABBREVMONTHNAME4=&H25 'abbreviated name for April
CAL_SABBREVMONTHNAME5=&H26 'abbreviated name for May
CAL_SABBREVMONTHNAME6=&H27 'abbreviated name for June
CAL_SABBREVMONTHNAME7=&H28 'abbreviated name for July
CAL_SABBREVMONTHNAME8=&H29 'abbreviated name for August
CAL_SABBREVMONTHNAME9=&H2A 'abbreviated name for September
CAL_SCALNAME=&H2 'native name of calendar
CAL_SDAYNAME1=&H7 'native name for Monday
CAL_SDAYNAME2=&H8 'native name for Tuesday
CAL_SDAYNAME3=&H9 'native name for Wednesday
CAL_SDAYNAME4=&HA 'native name for Thursday
CAL_SDAYNAME5=&HB 'native name for Friday
CAL_SDAYNAME6=&HC 'native name for Saturday
CAL_SDAYNAME7=&HD 'native name for Sunday
CAL_SERASTRING=&H4 'era name for IYearOffsetRanges
CAL_SLONGDATE=&H6 'long date format string
CAL_SMONTHNAME1=&H15 'native name for January
```

```
CAL_SMONTHNAME10=&H1E 'native name for October
CAL_SMONTHNAME11=&H1F 'native name for November
CAL_SMONTHNAME12=&H20 'native name for December
CAL_SMONTHNAME13=&H21 'native name for 13th month (if any)
CAL_SMONTHNAME2=&H16 'native name for February
CAL_SMONTHNAME3=&H17 'native name for March
CAL_SMONTHNAME4=&H18 'native name for April
CAL_SMONTHNAME5=&H19 'native name for May
CAL_SMONTHNAME6=&H1A 'native name for June
CAL_SMONTHNAME7=&H1B 'native name for July
CAL_SMONTHNAME8=&H1C 'native name for August
CAL_SMONTHNAME9=&H1D 'native name for September
CAL_SSHORTDATE=&H5 'Integer date format string
CAL_TAIWAN=4 'Republic of China Era calendar
CALL_PENDING=&H2
CALLBACK_FUNCTION=&H30000 'dwCallback is a FARPROC
CALLBACK_NULL=&H0 'no callback
CALLBACK_TASK=&H20000 'dwCallback is a HTASK
CALLBACK_TYPEMASK=&H70000 'callback type mask
CALLBACK_WINDOW=&H10000 'dwCallback is a HWND
CAPS1=94 'other caps
CAPSLOCK_ON=&H80 'the capslock light is on.
CB_ADDSTRING=&H143
CB_DELETESTRING=&H144
CB_DIR=&H145
CB_ERR=(-1)
CB_ERRSPACE=(-2)
CB_FINDSTRING=&H14C
CB_FINDSTRINGEXACT=&H158
CB_GETCOUNT=&H146
CB_GETCURSEL=&H147
CB_GETDROPPEDCONTROLRECT=&H152
CB_GETDROPPEDSTATE=&H157
CB_GETEDITSEL=&H140
CB_GETEXTENDEDUI=&H156
CB_GETITEMDATA=&H150
CB_GETITEMHEIGHT=&H154
CB_GETLBTEXT=&H148
CB_GETLBTEXTLEN=&H149
CB_GETLOCALE=&H15A
CB_INSERTSTRING=&H14A
CB_LIMITTEXT=&H141
CB_MSGMAX=&H15B
CB_OKAY=0
CB_RESETCONTENT=&H14B
CB_SELECTSTRING=&H14D
CB_SETCURSEL=&H14E
CB_SETEDITSEL=&H142
```

```
CB_SETEXTENDEDUI=&H155
CB_SETITEMDATA=&H151
CB_SETITEMHEIGHT=&H153
CB_SETLOCALE=&H159
CB_SHOWDROPDOWN=&H14F
CBF_FAIL_ADVISES=&H4000
CBF_FAIL_ALLSVRXACTIONS=&H3F000
CBF_FAIL_CONNECTIONS=&H2000
CBF_FAIL_EXECUTES=&H8000
CBF_FAIL_POKES=&H10000
CBF_FAIL_REQUESTS=&H20000
CBF_FAIL_SELFCONNECTIONS=&H1000
CBF_SKIP_ALLNOTIFICATIONS=&H3C0000
CBF_SKIP_CONNECT_CONFIRMS=&H40000
CBF_SKIP_DISCONNECTS=&H200000
CBF_SKIP_REGISTRATIONS=&H80000
CBF_SKIP_UNREGISTRATIONS=&H100000
CBM_CREATEDIB=&H2 'create DIB bitmap
CBM_INIT=&H4 'initialize bitmap
CBN_CLOSEUP=8
CBN_DBLCLK=2
CBN_DROPDOWN=7
CBN_EDITCHANGE=5
CBN_EDITUPDATE=6
CBN_ERRSPACE=(-1)
CBN_KILLFOCUS=4
CBN_SELCHANGE=1
CBN_SELENDCANCEL=10
CBN_SELENDOK=9
CBN_SETFOCUS=3
CBR_110=110
CBR_115200=115200
CBR_1200=1200
CBR_128000=128000
CBR_14400=14400
CBR_19200=19200
CBR_2400=2400
CBR_256000=256000
CBR_300=300
CBR_38400=38400
CBR_4800=4800
CBR_56000=56000
CBR_57600=57600
CBR_600=600
CBR_9600=9600
CBR_BLOCK=&HFFFF
CBS_AUTOHSCROLL=&H40&
CBS_DISABLENOSCROLL=&H800&
```

```
CBS_DROPDOWN=&H2&
CBS_DROPDOWNLIST=&H3&
CBS_HASSTRINGS=&H200&
CBS_NOINTEGRALHEIGHT=&H400&
CBS_OEMCONVERT=&H80&
CBS_OWNERDRAWFIXED=&H10&
CBS_OWNERDRAWVARIABLE=&H20&
CBS_SIMPLE=&H1&
CBS_SORT=&H100&
CC_ANYCOLOR=&H100
CC_CHORD=4 'Can do chord arcs
CC_CIRCLES=1 'Can do circles
CC_ELLIPSES=8 'Can do ellipse
CC_ENABLEHOOK=&H10
CC_ENABLETEMPLATE=&H20
CC_ENABLETEMPLATEHANDLE=&H40
CC_FULLOPEN=&H2
CC_INTERIORS=128 'Can do interiors
CC_NONE=0   'Curves not supported
CC_PIE=2 'Can do pie wedges
CC_PREVENTFULLOPEN=&H4
CC_RGBINIT=&H1
CC_ROUNDRECT=256 '
CC_SHOWHELP=&H8
CC_SOLIDCOLOR=&H80
CC_STYLED=32 'Can do styled lines
CC_WIDE=16 'Can do wide lines
CC_WIDESTYLED=64 'Can do wide styled lines
CCERR_CHOOSECOLORCODES=&H5000
CCHDEVICENAME=32
CCHFORMNAME=32
CD_LBSELADD=2
CD_LBSELCHANGE=0
CD_LBSELNOITEMS=-1
CD_LBSELSUB=1
CDERR_DIALOGFAILURE=&HFFFF
CDERR_FINDRESFAILURE=&H6
CDERR_GENERALCODES=&H0
CDERR_INITIALIZATION=&H2
CDERR_LOADRESFAILURE=&H7
CDERR_LOADSTRFAILURE=&H5
CDERR_LOCKRESFAILURE=&H8
CDERR_MEMALLOCFAILURE=&H9
CDERR_MEMLOCKFAILURE=&HA
CDERR_NOHINSTANCE=&H4
CDERR_NOHOOK=&HB
CDERR_NOTEMPLATE=&H3
CDERR_REGISTERMSGFAIL=&HC
```

```
CDERR_STRUCTSIZE=&H1
CDM_FIRST=(WM_USER+100)
CDM_GETFILEPATH=(CDM_FIRST+&H1)
CDM_GETFOLDERIDLIST=(CDM_FIRST+&H3)
CDM_GETFOLDERPATH=(CDM_FIRST+&H2)
CDM_GETSPEC=(CDM_FIRST+&H0)
CDM_HIDECONTROL=(CDM_FIRST+&H5)
CDM_LAST=(WM_USER+200)
CDM_SETCONTROLTEXT=(CDM_FIRST+&H4)
CDM_SETDEFEXT=(CDM_FIRST+&H6)
CE_BREAK=&H10  'Break Detected
CE_DNS=&H800 'LPTx Device not selected
CE_FRAME=&H8 'Receive Framing error
CE_IOE=&H400 'LPTx I/O Error
CE_MODE=&H8000 'Requested mode unsupported
CE_OOP=&H1000  'LPTx Out-Of-Paper
CE_OVERRUN=&H2 'Receive Overrun Error
CE_PTO=&H200 'LPTx Timeout
CE_RXOVER=&H1  'Receive Queue overflow
CE_RXPARITY=&H4 'Receive Parity Error
CE_TXFULL=&H100 'TX Queue is full
CF_ANSIONLY=&H400&
CF_APPLY=&H200&
CF_BITMAP=2
CF_BOTH=(CF_SCREENFONTS Or CF_PRINTERFONTS)
CF_DIB=8
CF_DIF=5
CF_DSPBITMAP=&H82
CF_DSPENHMETAFILE=&H8E
CF_DSPMETAFILEPICT=&H83
CF_DSPTEXT=&H81
CF_EFFECTS=&H100&
CF_ENABLEHOOK=&H8&
CF_ENABLETEMPLATE=&H10&
CF_ENABLETEMPLATEHANDLE=&H20&
CF_ENHMETAFILE=14
CF_FIXEDPITCHONLY=&H4000&
CF_FORCEFONTEXIST=&H10000
CF_GDIOBJFIRST=&H300
CF_GDIOBJLAST=&H3FF
CF_INITTOLOGFONTSTRUCT=&H40&
CF_LIMITSIZE=&H2000&
CF_METAFILEPICT=3
CF_NOFACESEL=&H80000
CF_NOOEMFONTS=CF_NOVECTORFONTS
CF_NOSCRIPTSEL=&H800000
CF_NOSIMULATIONS=&H1000&
CF_NOSIZESEL=&H200000
```

```
CF_NOSTYLESEL=&H100000
CF_NOVECTORFONTS=&H800&
CF_NOVERTFONTS=&H1000000
CF_OEMTEXT=7
CF_OWNERDISPLAY=&H80
CF_PALETTE=9
CF_PENDATA=10
CF_PRINTERFONTS=&H2
CF_PRIVATEFIRST=&H200
CF_PRIVATELAST=&H2FF
CF_RIFF=11
CF_SCALABLEONLY=&H20000
CF_SCREENFONTS=&H1
CF_SCRIPTSONLY=CF_ANSIONLY
CF_SELECTSCRIPT=&H400000
CF_SHOWHELP=&H4&
CF_SYLK=4
CF_TEXT=1
CF_TIFF=6
CF_TTONLY=&H40000
CF_UNICODETEXT=13
CF_USESTYLE=&H80&
CF_WAVE=12
CF_WYSIWYG=&H8000 'must have CF_SCREENFONTS CF_PRINTERFONTS
CFERR_CHOOSEFONTCODES=&H2000
CFERR_MAXLESSTHANMIN=&H2002
CFERR_NOFONTS=&H2001
CFS_CANDIDATEPOS=&H40
CFS_DEFAULT=&H0
CFS_EXCLUDE=&H80
CFS_FORCE_POSITION=&H20
CFS_POINT=&H2
CFS_RECT=&H1
CFS_SCREEN=&H4
CFSEPCHAR="+"  'compound file name separator char.
CHINESEBIG5_CHARSET=136
chx1=&H410
chx10=&H419
chx11=&H41A
chx12=&H41B
chx13=&H41C
chx14=&H41D
chx15=&H41E
chx16=&H41D
chx2=&H411
chx3=&H412
chx4=&H413
chx5=&H414
```

```
chx6=&H415
chx7=&H416
chx8=&H417
chx9=&H418
CLASS_E_CLASSNOTAVAILABLE=&H80040111
CLASS_E_NOAGGREGATION=&H80040110
CLASSFACTORY_E_FIRST=&H80040110
CLASSFACTORY_E_LAST=&H8004011F
CLASSFACTORY_S_FIRST=&H40110
CLASSFACTORY_S_LAST=&H4011F
CLIENTSITE_E_FIRST=&H80040190
CLIENTSITE_E_LAST=&H8004019F
CLIENTSITE_S_FIRST=&H40190
CLIENTSITE_S_LAST=&H4019F
CLIP_CHARACTER_PRECIS=1
CLIP_DEFAULT_PRECIS=0
CLIP_EMBEDDED=128
CLIP_LH_ANGLES=16
CLIP_MASK=&HF
CLIP_STROKE_PRECIS=2
CLIP_TO_PATH=4097
CLIP_TT_ALWAYS=32
CLIPBRD_E_BAD_DATA=&H800401D3
CLIPBRD_E_CANT_CLOSE=&H800401D4
CLIPBRD_E_CANT_EMPTY=&H800401D1
CLIPBRD_E_CANT_OPEN=&H800401D0
CLIPBRD_E_CANT_SET=&H800401D2
CLIPBRD_E_FIRST=&H800401D0
CLIPBRD_E_LAST=&H800401DF
CLIPBRD_S_FIRST=&H401D0
CLIPBRD_S_LAST=&H401DF
CLIPCAPS=36 'Clipping capabilities
CLOSECHANNEL=4112
CLR_INVALID=&HFFFF
CLRBREAK=9 'Clear the device break line
CLRDTR=6 'Set DTR low
CLRRTS=4 'Set RTS low
cmb1=&H470
cmb10=&H479
cmb11=&H47A
cmb12=&H47B
cmb13=&H47C
cmb14=&H47D
cmb15=&H47E
cmb16=&H47F
cmb2=&H471
cmb3=&H472
cmb4=&H473
```

```
cmb5=&H474
cmb6=&H475
cmb7=&H476
cmb8=&H477
cmb9=&H478
CN_EVENT=&H4
CN_RECEIVE=&H1
CN_TRANSMIT=&H2
CO_E_ALREADYINITIALIZED=&H800401F1
CO_E_APPDIDNTREG=&H800401FE
CO_E_APPNOTFOUND=&H800401F5
CO_E_APPSINGLEUSE=&H800401F6
CO_E_BAD_PATH=&H80080004
CO_E_CANTDETERMINECLASS=&H800401F2
CO_E_CLASS_CREATE_FAILED=&H80080001
CO_E_CLASSSTRING=&H800401F3
CO_E_DLLNOTFOUND=&H800401F8
CO_E_ERRORINAPP=&H800401F7
CO_E_ERRORINDLL=&H800401F9
CO_E_FIRST=&H800401F0
CO_E_IIDSTRING=&H800401F4
CO_E_INIT_CLASS_CACHE=&H80004009
CO_E_INIT_MEMORY_ALLOCATOR=&H80004008
CO_E_INIT_ONLY_SINGLE_THREADED=&H80004012
CO_E_INIT_RPC_CHANNEL=&H8000400A
CO_E_INIT_SCM_EXEC_FAILURE=&H80004011
CO_E_INIT_SCM_FILE_MAPPING_EXISTS=&H8000400F
CO_E_INIT_SCM_MAP_VIEW_OF_FILE=&H80004010
CO_E_INIT_SCM_MUTEX_EXISTS=&H8000400E
CO_E_INIT_SHARED_ALLOCATOR=&H80004007
CO_E_INIT_TLS=&H80004006
CO_E_INIT_TLS_CHANNEL_CONTROL=&H8000400C
CO_E_INIT_TLS_SET_CHANNEL_CONTROL=&H8000400B
CO_E_INIT_UNACCEPTED_USER_ALLOCATOR=&H8000400D
CO_E_LAST=&H800401FF
CO_E_NOTINITIALIZED=&H800401F0
CO_E_OBJISREG=&H800401FC
CO_E_OBJNOTCONNECTED=&H800401FD
CO_E_OBJNOTREG=&H800401FB
CO_E_OBJSRV_RPC_FAILURE=&H80080006
CO_E_RELEASED=&H800401FF
CO_E_SCM_ERROR=&H80080002
CO_E_SCM_RPC_FAILURE=&H80080003
CO_E_SERVER_EXEC_FAILURE=&H80080005
CO_E_SERVER_STOPPING=&H80080008
CO_E_WRONGOSFORAPP=&H800401FA
CO_S_FIRST=&H401F0
CO_S_LAST=&H401FF
```

```
COLOR_ACTIVEBORDER=10
COLOR_ACTIVECAPTION=2
COLOR_ADJ_MAX=100
COLOR_ADJ_MIN=-100 'shorts
COLOR_APPWORKSPACE=12
COLOR_BACKGROUND=1
COLOR_BTNFACE=15
COLOR_BTNHIGHLIGHT=20
COLOR_BTNSHADOW=16
COLOR_BTNTEXT=18
COLOR_CAPTIONTEXT=9
COLOR_GRAYTEXT=17
COLOR_HIGHLIGHT=13
COLOR_HIGHLIGHTTEXT=14
COLOR_INACTIVEBORDER=11
COLOR_INACTIVECAPTION=3
COLOR_INACTIVECAPTIONTEXT=19
COLOR_MENU=4
COLOR_MENUTEXT=7
COLOR_SCROLLBAR=0
COLOR_WINDOW=5
COLOR_WINDOWFRAME=6
COLOR_WINDOWTEXT=8
COLOROKSTRING="commdlg_ColorOK"
COLORONCOLOR=3
COLORRES=108 'Actual color resolution
COMPLEXREGION=3
CONNECT_UPDATE_PROFILE=&H1
CONSOLE_TEXTMODE_BUFFER=1
CONTAINER_INHERIT_ACE=&H2
CONVERT10_E_FIRST=&H800401C0
CONVERT10_E_LAST=&H800401CF
CONVERT10_E_OLESTREAM_BITMAP_TO_DIB=&H800401C3
CONVERT10_E_OLESTREAM_FMT=&H800401C2
CONVERT10_E_OLESTREAM_GET=&H800401C0
CONVERT10_E_OLESTREAM_PUT=&H800401C1
CONVERT10_E_STG_DIB_TO_BITMAP=&H800401C6
CONVERT10_E_STG_FMT=&H800401C4
CONVERT10_E_STG_NO_STD_STREAM=&H800401C5
CONVERT10_S_FIRST=&H401C0
CONVERT10_S_LAST=&H401CF
CONVERT10_S_NO_PRESENTATION=&H401C0
CP_ACP=0   'default to ANSI code page
CP_NONE=0   'No clipping of output
CP_OEMCP=1   'default to OEM  code page
CP_RECTANGLE=1 'Output clipped to rects
CP_REGION=2 '
CP_WINANSI=1004   'default codepage for windows old DDE convs.
```

```
CP_WINUNICODE=1200
CPS_CANCEL=&H4
CPS_COMPLETE=&H1
CPS_CONVERT=&H2
CPS_REVERT=&H3
CREATE_ALWAYS=2
CREATE_NEW=1
CREATE_NEW_CONSOLE=&H10
CREATE_NEW_PROCESS_GROUP=&H200
CREATE_NO_WINDOW=&H8000000
CREATE_PROCESS_DEBUG_EVENT=3
CREATE_SUSPENDED=&H4
CREATE_THREAD_DEBUG_EVENT=2
CS_BYTEALIGNCLIENT=&H1000
CS_BYTEALIGNWINDOW=&H2000
CS_CLASSDC=&H40
CS_DBLCLKS=&H8
CS_HREDRAW=&H2
CS_INSERTCHAR=&H2000
CS_KEYCVTWINDOW=&H4
CS_NOCLOSE=&H200
CS_NOKEYCVT=&H100
CS_NOMOVECARET=&H4000
CS_OWNDC=&H20
CS_PARENTDC=&H80
CS_PUBLICCLASS=&H4000
CS_SAVEBITS=&H800
CS_VREDRAW=&H1
CT_CTYPE1=&H1 'ctype 1 information
CT_CTYPE2=&H2 'ctype 2 information
CT_CTYPE3=&H4 'ctype 3 information
CTLCOLOR_BTN=3
CTLCOLOR_DLG=4
CTLCOLOR_EDIT=1
CTLCOLOR_LISTBOX=2
CTLCOLOR_MAX=8 'three bits max
CTLCOLOR_MSGBOX=0
CTLCOLOR_SCROLLBAR=5
CTLCOLOR_STATIC=6
ctlFirst=&H400
ctlLast=&H4FF
CTRL_BREAK_EVENT=1
CTRL_C_EVENT=0
CTRL_CLOSE_EVENT=2
CTRL_LOGOFF_EVENT=5
CTRL_SHUTDOWN_EVENT=6
CTRY_AUSTRALIA=61 'Australia
CTRY_AUSTRIA=43  'Austria
```

```
CTRY_BELGIUM=32   'Belgium
CTRY_BRAZIL=55   'Brazil
CTRY_CANADA=2   'Canada
CTRY_DEFAULT=0
CTRY_DENMARK=45   'Denmark
CTRY_FINLAND=358   'Finland
CTRY_FRANCE=33   'France
CTRY_GERMANY=49   'Germany
CTRY_ICELAND=354   'Iceland
CTRY_IRELAND=353   'Ireland
CTRY_ITALY=39   'Italy
CTRY_JAPAN=81   'Japan
CTRY_MEXICO=52   'Mexico
CTRY_NETHERLANDS=31   'Netherlands
CTRY_NEW_ZEALAND=64   'New Zealand
CTRY_NORWAY=47   'Norway
CTRY_PORTUGAL=351   'Portugal
CTRY_PRCHINA=86   'PR China
CTRY_SOUTH_KOREA=82   'South Korea
CTRY_SPAIN=34   'Spain
CTRY_SWEDEN=46   'Sweden
CTRY_SWITZERLAND=41   'Switzerland
CTRY_TAIWAN=886   'Taiwan
CTRY_UNITED_KINGDOM=44   'United Kingdom
CTRY_UNITED_STATES=1   'United States
CURVECAPS=28 'Curve capabilities
CW_USEDEFAULT=&H80000000

D
DATA_E_FIRST=&H80040130
DATA_E_LAST=&H8004013F
DATA_S_FIRST=&H40130
DATA_S_LAST=&H4013F
DATA_S_SAMEFORMATETC=&H40130
DATABITS_16=&H10&
DATABITS_16X=&H20&
DATABITS_5=&H1&
DATABITS_6=&H2&
DATABITS_7=&H4&
DATABITS_8=&H8&
DATE_LONGDATE=&H2 'use long date picture
DATE_SHORTDATE=&H1 'use short date picture
DC_BINADJUST=19
DC_BINNAMES=12
DC_BINS=6
DC_COLLATE=22
DC_COPIES=18
DC_DATATYPE_PRODUCED=21
```

```
DC_DRIVER=11
DC_DUPLEX=7
DC_EMF_COMPLIANT=20
DC_ENUMRESOLUTIONS=13
DC_EXTRA=9
DC_FIELDS=1
DC_FILEDEPENDENCIES=14
DC_HASDEFID=&H534 '0x534B
DC_MAXEXTENT=5
DC_MINEXTENT=4
DC_ORIENTATION=17
DC_PAPERNAMES=16
DC_PAPERS=2
DC_PAPERSIZE=3
DC_SIZE=8
DC_TRUETYPE=15
DC_VERSION=10
DCB_ACCUMULATE=&H2
DCB_DIRTY=DCB_ACCUMULATE
DCB_DISABLE=&H8
DCB_ENABLE=&H4
DCB_RESET=&H1
DCB_SET=(DCB_RESET Or DCB_ACCUMULATE)
DCBA_FACEDOWNCENTER=&H101
DCBA_FACEDOWNLEFT=&H102
DCBA_FACEDOWNNONE=&H100
DCBA_FACEDOWNRIGHT=&H103
DCBA_FACEUPCENTER=&H1
DCBA_FACEUPLEFT=&H2
DCBA_FACEUPNONE=&H0
DCBA_FACEUPRIGHT=&H3
DCTT_BITMAP=&H1&
DCTT_DOWNLOAD=&H2&
DCTT_DOWNLOAD_OUTLINE=&H8&
DCTT_SUBDEV=&H4&
DCX_CACHE=&H2&
DCX_CLIPCHILDREN=&H8&
DCX_CLIPSIBLINGS=&H10&
DCX_EXCLUDERGN=&H40&
DCX_EXCLUDEUPDATE=&H100&
DCX_INTERSECTRGN=&H80&
DCX_INTERSECTUPDATE=&H200&
DCX_LOCKWINDOWUPDATE=&H400&
DCX_NORECOMPUTE=&H100000
DCX_NORESETATTRS=&H4&
DCX_PARENTCLIP=&H20&
DCX_VALIDATE=&H200000
DCX_WINDOW=&H1&
```

```
DDD_EXACT_MATCH_ON_REMOVE=&H4
DDD_RAW_TARGET_PATH=&H1
DDD_REMOVE_DEFINITION=&H2
DDE_FACK=&H8000
DDE_FACKREQ=&H8000
DDE_FACKRESERVED=(Not (DDE_FACK Or DDE_FBUSY Or DDE_FAPPSTATUS))
DDE_FADVRESERVED=(Not (DDE_FACKREQ Or DDE_FDEFERUPD))
DDE_FAPPSTATUS=&HFF
DDE_FBUSY=&H4000
DDE_FDATRESERVED=(Not (DDE_FACKREQ Or DDE_FRELEASE Or
                       DDE_FREQUESTED))
DDE_FDEFERUPD=&H4000
DDE_FNOTPROCESSED=&H0
DDE_FPOKRESERVED=(Not (DDE_FRELEASE))
DDE_FRELEASE=&H2000
DDE_FREQUESTED=&H1000
DDL_ARCHIVE=&H20
DDL_DIRECTORY=&H10
DDL_DRIVES=&H4000
DDL_EXCLUSIVE=&H8000
DDL_HIDDEN=&H2
DDL_POSTMSGS=&H2000
DDL_READONLY=&H1
DDL_READWRITE=&H0
DDL_SYSTEM=&H4
DEBUG_ONLY_THIS_PROCESS=&H2
DEBUG_PROCESS=&H1
DEF_PRIORITY=1
DEFAULT_CHARSET=1
DEFAULT_GUI_FONT=17
DEFAULT_PALETTE=15
DEFAULT_PITCH=0
DEFAULT_QUALITY=0
DELETE=&H10000
DEREGISTERED=&H5
DESKTOP_CREATEMENU=&H4&
DESKTOP_CREATEWINDOW=&H2&
DESKTOP_ENUMERATE=&H40&
DESKTOP_HOOKCONTROL=&H8&
DESKTOP_JOURNALPLAYBACK=&H20&
DESKTOP_JOURNALRECORD=&H10&
DESKTOP_READOBJECTS=&H1&
DESKTOP_WRITEOBJECTS=&H80&
DETACHED_PROCESS=&H8
DEVICE_DEFAULT_FONT=14
DEVICE_FONTTYPE=&H2
DEVICEDATA=19
DI_CHANNEL=1 'start direct read/write channel,
```

```
DI_READ_SPOOL_JOB=3
DIALOPTION_BILLING=&H40 'Supports wait for bong "$"
DIALOPTION_DIALTONE=&H100 'Supports wait for dial tone "W"
DIALOPTION_QUIET=&H80 'Supports wait for quiet "@"
DIB_PAL_COLORS=1 'color in palette indices
DIB_PAL_INDICES=2 'No color indices into surf palette
DIB_PAL_LOGINDICES=4 'No color indices into DC palette
DIB_PAL_PHYSINDICES=2 'No color indices into surf palette
DIB_RGB_COLORS=0 'color table in RGBs
DISP_E_ARRAYISLOCKED=&H8002000D
DISP_E_BADCALLEE=&H80020010
DISP_E_BADINDEX=&H8002000B
DISP_E_BADPARAMCOUNT=&H8002000E
DISP_E_BADVARTYPE=&H80020008
DISP_E_EXCEPTION=&H80020009
DISP_E_MEMBERNOTFOUND=&H80020003
DISP_E_NONAMEDARGS=&H80020007
DISP_E_NOTACOLLECTION=&H80020011
DISP_E_OVERFLOW=&H8002000A
DISP_E_PARAMNOTFOUND=&H80020004
DISP_E_PARAMNOTOPTIONAL=&H8002000F
DISP_E_TYPEMISMATCH=&H80020005
DISP_E_UNKNOWNINTERFACE=&H80020001
DISP_E_UNKNOWNLCID=&H8002000C
DISP_E_UNKNOWNNAME=&H80020006
DKGRAY_BRUSH=3
DLGC_BUTTON=&H2000 'Button item: can be checked
DLGC_DEFPUSHBUTTON=&H10 'Default pushbutton
DLGC_HASSETSEL=&H8 'Understands EM_SETSEL message
DLGC_RADIOBUTTON=&H40 'Radio button
DLGC_STATIC=&H100  'Static item: don't include
DLGC_UNDEFPUSHBUTTON=&H20 'Non-default pushbutton
DLGC_WANTALLKEYS=&H4 'Control wants all keys
DLGC_WANTARROWS=&H1 'Control wants arrow keys
DLGC_WANTCHARS=&H80 'Want WM_CHAR messages
DLGC_WANTMESSAGE=&H4 'Pass message to control
DLGC_WANTTAB=&H2 'Control wants tab keys
DLGWINDOWEXTRA=30 'extra bytes for private dialog classes
DM_COLLATE As Long=&H8000
DM_COLOR=&H800&
DM_COPIES=&H100&
DM_COPY=2
DM_DEFAULTSOURCE=&H200&
DM_DITHERTYPE=&H10000000
DM_DUPLEX=&H1000&
DM_FORMNAME As Long=&H10000
DM_GETDEFID=WM_USER+0
DM_GRAYSCALE=&H1
```

```
DM_ICMINTENT=&H4000000
DM_ICMMETHOD=&H2000000
DM_IN_BUFFER=DM_MODIFY
DM_IN_PROMPT=DM_PROMPT
DM_INTERLACED=&H2
DM_MEDIATYPE=&H8000000
DM_MODIFY=8
DM_ORIENTATION=&H1&
DM_OUT_BUFFER=DM_COPY
DM_OUT_DEFAULT=DM_UPDATE
DM_PAPERLENGTH=&H4&
DM_PAPERSIZE=&H2&
DM_PAPERWIDTH=&H8&
DM_PRINTQUALITY=&H400&
DM_PROMPT=4
DM_RESERVED1=&H800000
DM_RESERVED2=&H1000000
DM_SCALE=&H10&
DM_SETDEFID=WM_USER+1
DM_SPECVERSION=&H320
DM_TTOPTION=&H4000&
DM_UPDATE=1
DM_YRESOLUTION=&H2000&
DMBIN_AUTO=7
DMBIN_CASSETTE=14
DMBIN_ENVELOPE=5
DMBIN_ENVMANUAL=6
DMBIN_FIRST=DMBIN_UPPER
DMBIN_LARGECAPACITY=11
DMBIN_LARGEFMT=10
DMBIN_LAST=DMBIN_CASSETTE
DMBIN_LOWER=2
DMBIN_MANUAL=4
DMBIN_MIDDLE=3
DMBIN_ONLYONE=1
DMBIN_SMALLFMT=9
DMBIN_TRACTOR=8
DMBIN_UPPER=1
DMBIN_USER=256 'device specific bins start here
DMCOLLATE_FALSE=0
DMCOLLATE_TRUE=1
DMCOLOR_COLOR=2
DMCOLOR_MONOCHROME=1
DMDITHER_COARSE=2 'Dither with a coarse brush
DMDITHER_FINE=3 'Dither with a fine brush
DMDITHER_GRAYSCALE=5 'Device does grayscaling
DMDITHER_LINEART=4 'LineArt dithering
DMDITHER_NONE=1 'No dithering
```

```
DMDITHER_USER=256 'Device-specific dithers start here
DMDUP_HORIZONTAL=3
DMDUP_SIMPLEX=1
DMDUP_VERTICAL=2
DMICM_COLORMETRIC=3 'Use specific color metric
DMICM_CONTRAST=2 'Maximize color contrast
DMICM_SATURATE=1 'Maximize color saturation
DMICM_USER=256 'Device-specific intents start here
DMICMMETHOD_DEVICE=4 'ICM handled by device
DMICMMETHOD_DRIVER=3 'ICM handled by driver
DMICMMETHOD_NONE=1 'ICM disabled
DMICMMETHOD_SYSTEM=2 'ICM handled by system
DMICMMETHOD_USER=256 'Device-specific methods start here
DMLERR_ADVACKTIMEOUT=&H4000
DMLERR_BUSY=&H4001
DMLERR_DATAACKTIMEOUT=&H4002
DMLERR_DLL_NOT_INITIALIZED=&H4003
DMLERR_DLL_USAGE=&H4004
DMLERR_EXECACKTIMEOUT=&H4005
DMLERR_FIRST=&H4000
DMLERR_INVALIDPARAMETER=&H4006
DMLERR_LAST=&H4011
DMLERR_LOW_MEMORY=&H4007
DMLERR_MEMORY_ERROR=&H4008
DMLERR_NO_CONV_ESTABLISHED=&H400A
DMLERR_NO_ERROR=0 'must be 0
DMLERR_NOTPROCESSED=&H4009
DMLERR_POKEACKTIMEOUT=&H400B
DMLERR_POSTMSG_FAILED=&H400C
DMLERR_REENTRANCY=&H400D
DMLERR_SERVER_DIED=&H400E
DMLERR_SYS_ERROR=&H400F
DMLERR_UNADVACKTIMEOUT=&H4010
DMLERR_UNFOUND_QUEUE_ID=&H4011
DMMEDIA_GLOSSY=2 'Glossy paper
DMMEDIA_STANDARD=1 'Standard paper
DMMEDIA_TRANSPARENCY=3 'Transparency
DMMEDIA_USER=256 'Device-specific media start here
DMORIENT_LANDSCAPE=2
DMORIENT_PORTRAIT=1
DMPAPER_10X11=45 '10 x 11 in
DMPAPER_10X14=16 '10 x 14 in
DMPAPER_11X17=17 '11 x 17 in
DMPAPER_15X11=46 '15 x 11 in
DMPAPER_9X11=44 '9 x 11 in
DMPAPER_A_PLUS=57 'SuperA/SuperA/A4 227 x 356 mm
DMPAPER_A2=66 'A2 420 x 594 mm
DMPAPER_A3=8 'A3 297 x 420 mm
```

```
DMPAPER_A3_EXTRA=63 'A3 Extra 322 x 445 mm
DMPAPER_A3_EXTRA_TRANSVERSE=68 'A3 Extra Transverse 322 x 445 mm
DMPAPER_A3_TRANSVERSE=67 'A3 Transverse 297 x 420 mm
DMPAPER_A4=9 'A4 210 x 297 mm
DMPAPER_A4_EXTRA=53 'A4 Extra 9.27 x 12.69 in
DMPAPER_A4_PLUS=60 'A4 Plus 210 x 330 mm
DMPAPER_A4_TRANSVERSE=55 'A4 Transverse 210 x 297 mm
DMPAPER_A4SMALL=10 'A4 Small 210 x 297 mm
DMPAPER_A5=11 'A5 148 x 210 mm
DMPAPER_A5_EXTRA=64 'A5 Extra 174 x 235 mm
DMPAPER_A5_TRANSVERSE=61 'A5 Transverse 148 x 210 mm
DMPAPER_B_PLUS=58   'SuperB/SuperB/A3 305 x 487 mm
DMPAPER_B4=12 'B4 250 x 354
DMPAPER_B5=13 'B5 182 x 257 mm
DMPAPER_B5_EXTRA=65 'B5 (ISO) Extra 201 x 276 mm
DMPAPER_B5_TRANSVERSE=62 'B5 (JIS) Transverse 182 x 257 mm
DMPAPER_CSHEET=24   'C size sheet
DMPAPER_DSHEET=25   'D size sheet
DMPAPER_ENV_10=20   'Envelope #10 4 1/8 x 9 1/2
DMPAPER_ENV_11=21   'Envelope #11 4 1/2 x 10 3/8
DMPAPER_ENV_12=22   'Envelope #12 4 \276 x 11
DMPAPER_ENV_14=23   'Envelope #14 5 x 11 1/2
DMPAPER_ENV_9=19    'Envelope #9 3 7/8 x 8 7/8
DMPAPER_ENV_B4=33   'Envelope B4   250 x 353 mm
DMPAPER_ENV_B5=34   'Envelope B5   176 x 250 mm
DMPAPER_ENV_B6=35   'Envelope B6   176 x 125 mm
DMPAPER_ENV_C3=29   'Envelope C3   324 x 458 mm
DMPAPER_ENV_C4=30   'Envelope C4   229 x 324 mm
DMPAPER_ENV_C5=28   'Envelope C5 162 x 229 mm
DMPAPER_ENV_C6=31   'Envelope C6   114 x 162 mm
DMPAPER_ENV_C65=32 'Envelope C65 114 x 229 mm
DMPAPER_ENV_DL=27   'Envelope DL 110 x 220mm
DMPAPER_ENV_INVITE=47 'Envelope Invite 220 x 220 mm
DMPAPER_ENV_ITALY=36 'Envelope 110 x 230 mm
DMPAPER_ENV_MONARCH=37 'Envelope Monarch 3.875 x 7.5 in
DMPAPER_ENV_PERSONAL=38 '6 3/4 Envelope 3 5/8 x 6 1/2 in
DMPAPER_ESHEET=26   'E size sheet
DMPAPER_EXECUTIVE=7 'Executive 7 1/4 x 10 1/2 in
DMPAPER_FANFOLD_LGL_GERMAN=41 'German Legal Fanfold 8 1/2 x 13 in
DMPAPER_FANFOLD_STD_GERMAN=40 'German Std Fanfold 8 1/2 x 12 in
DMPAPER_FANFOLD_US=39 'US Std Fanfold 14 7/8 x 11 in
DMPAPER_FIRST=DMPAPER_LETTER
DMPAPER_FOLIO=14 'Folio 8 1/2 x 13 in
DMPAPER_ISO_B4=42   'B4 (ISO) 250 x 353 mm
DMPAPER_JAPANESE_POSTCARD=43 'Japanese Postcard 100 x 148 mm
DMPAPER_LAST=DMPAPER_FANFOLD_LGL_GERMAN
DMPAPER_LEDGER=4 'Ledger 17 x 11 in
DMPAPER_LEGAL=5 'Legal 8 1/2 x 14 in
```

```
DMPAPER_LEGAL_EXTRA=51 'Legal Extra 9 \275 x 15 in
DMPAPER_LETTER=1
DMPAPER_LETTER_EXTRA=50 'Letter Extra 9 \275 x 12 in
DMPAPER_LETTER_EXTRA_TRANSVERSE=56 'Transverse 9\275 x 12 in
DMPAPER_LETTER_PLUS=59 'Letter Plus 8.5 x 12.69 in
DMPAPER_LETTER_TRANSVERSE=54 'Letter Transverse 8 \275 x 11 in
DMPAPER_LETTERSMALL=2 'Letter Small 8 1/2 x 11 in
DMPAPER_NOTE=18 'Note 8 1/2 x 11 in
DMPAPER_QUARTO=15  'Quarto 215 x 275 mm
DMPAPER_RESERVED_48=48 'RESERVED—DO NOT USE
DMPAPER_RESERVED_49=49 'RESERVED—DO NOT USE
DMPAPER_STATEMENT=6 'Statement 5 1/2 x 8 1/2 in
DMPAPER_TABLOID=3  'Tabloid 11 x 17 in
DMPAPER_TABLOID_EXTRA=52 'Tabloid Extra 11.69 x 18 in
DMPAPER_USER=256
DMRES_DRAFT=(-1)
DMRES_HIGH=(-4)
DMRES_LOW=(-2)
DMRES_MEDIUM=(-3)
DMTT_BITMAP=1 'print TT fonts as graphics
DMTT_DOWNLOAD=2 'download TT fonts as soft fonts
DMTT_DOWNLOAD_OUTLINE=4 'download TT fonts as outline fonts
DMTT_SUBDEV=3 'substitute device fonts for TT fonts
DN_DEFAULTPRN=&H1
DNS_FILTEROFF=&H8
DNS_FILTERON=&H4
DNS_REGISTER=&H1
DNS_UNREGISTER=&H2
DOMAIN_ALIAS_RID_ACCOUNT_OPS=&H224
DOMAIN_ALIAS_RID_ADMINS=&H220
DOMAIN_ALIAS_RID_BACKUP_OPS=&H227
DOMAIN_ALIAS_RID_GUESTS=&H222
DOMAIN_ALIAS_RID_POWER_USERS=&H223
DOMAIN_ALIAS_RID_PRINT_OPS=&H226
DOMAIN_ALIAS_RID_REPLICATOR=&H228
DOMAIN_ALIAS_RID_SYSTEM_OPS=&H225
DOMAIN_ALIAS_RID_USERS=&H221
DOMAIN_GROUP_RID_ADMINS=&H200
DOMAIN_GROUP_RID_GUESTS=&H202
DOMAIN_GROUP_RID_USERS=&H201
DOMAIN_USER_RID_ADMIN=&H1F4
DOMAIN_USER_RID_GUEST=&H1F5
DONT_RESOLVE_DLL_REFERENCES=&H1
DOUBLE_CLICK=&H2
DOWNLOADFACE=514
DOWNLOADHEADER=4111
DRAFT_QUALITY=1
DRAFTMODE=7
```

```
DRAGDROP_E_ALREADYREGISTERED=&H80040101
DRAGDROP_E_FIRST=&H80040100
DRAGDROP_E_INVALIDHWND=&H80040102
DRAGDROP_E_LAST=&H8004010F
DRAGDROP_E_NOTREGISTERED=&H80040100
DRAGDROP_S_CANCEL=&H40101
DRAGDROP_S_DROP=&H40100
DRAGDROP_S_FIRST=&H40100
DRAGDROP_S_LAST=&H4010F
DRAGDROP_S_USEDEFAULTCURSORS=&H40102
DRAWPATTERNRECT=25
DRIVE_CDROM=5
DRIVE_FIXED=3
DRIVE_RAMDISK=6
DRIVE_REMOTE=4
DRIVE_REMOVABLE=2
DRIVERVERSION=0 'Device driver version
DRV_CANCEL=DRVCNF_CANCEL
DRV_CLOSE=&H4
DRV_CONFIGURE=&H7
DRV_DISABLE=&H5
DRV_ENABLE=&H2
DRV_EXITSESSION=&HB
DRV_FREE=&H6
DRV_INSTALL=&H9
DRV_LOAD=&H1
DRV_MCI_FIRST=DRV_RESERVED
DRV_MCI_LAST=DRV_RESERVED+&HFFF
DRV_OK=DRVCNF_OK
DRV_OPEN=&H3
DRV_POWER=&HF
DRV_QUERYCONFIGURE=&H8
DRV_REMOVE=&HA
DRV_RESERVED=&H800
DRV_RESTART=DRVCNF_RESTART
DRV_USER=&H4000
DRVCNF_CANCEL=&H0
DRVCNF_OK=&H1
DRVCNF_RESTART=&H2
DS_ABSALIGN=&H1&
DS_LOCALEDIT=&H20 'Edit items get Local storage.
DS_MODALFRAME=&H80 'Can be combined with WS_CAPTION
DS_NOIDLEMSG=&H100 'WM_ENTERIDLE message will not be sent
DS_SETFONT=&H40 'User specified font for Dlg controls
DS_SETFOREGROUND=&H200 'not in win3.1
DS_SYSMODAL=&H2&
DSTINVERT=&H550009 '(DWORD) dest=(NOT dest)
DT_BOTTOM=&H8
```

```
DT_CALCRECT=&H400
DT_CENTER=&H1
DT_CHARSTREAM=4 'Character-stream, PLP
DT_DISPFILE=6 'Display-file
DT_EXPANDTABS=&H40
DT_EXTERNALLEADING=&H200
DT_INTERNAL=&H1000
DT_LEFT=&H0
DT_METAFILE=5 'Metafile, VDM
DT_NOCLIP=&H100
DT_NOPREFIX=&H800
DT_PLOTTER=0 'Vector plotter
DT_RASCAMERA=3 'Raster camera
DT_RASDISPLAY=1 'Raster display
DT_RASPRINTER=2 'Raster printer
DT_RIGHT=&H2
DT_SINGLELINE=&H20
DT_TABSTOP=&H80
DT_TOP=&H0
DT_VCENTER=&H4
DT_WORDBREAK=&H10
DTR_CONTROL_DISABLE=&H0
DTR_CONTROL_ENABLE=&H1
DTR_CONTROL_HANDSHAKE=&H2
DUPLICATE=&H6
DUPLICATE_CLOSE_SOURCE=&H1
DUPLICATE_DEREG=&H7
DUPLICATE_SAME_ACCESS=&H2
DV_E_CLIPFORMAT=&H8004006A
DV_E_DVASPECT=&H8004006B
DV_E_DVTARGETDEVICE=&H80040065
DV_E_DVTARGETDEVICE_SIZE=&H8004006C
DV_E_FORMATETC=&H80040064
DV_E_LINDEX=&H80040068
DV_E_NOIVIEWOBJECT=&H8004006D
DV_E_STATDATA=&H80040067
DV_E_STGMEDIUM=&H80040066
DV_E_TYMED=&H80040069
DWL_DLGPROC=4
DWL_MSGRESULT=0
DWL_USER=8

E
E_ABORT=&H80004004
E_ACCESSDENIED=&H80070005
E_FAIL=&H80004005
E_HANDLE=&H80070006
E_INVALIDARG=&H80070057
```

```
E_NOINTERFACE=&H80004002
E_NOTIMPL=&H80004001
E_OUTOFMEMORY=&H8007000E
E_POINTER=&H80004003
E_UNEXPECTED=&H8000FFFF
EASTEUROPE_CHARSET=238
EC_DISABLE=ST_BLOCKED
EC_ENABLEALL=0
EC_ENABLEONE=ST_BLOCKNEXT
EC_QUERYWAITING=2
EDGE_BUMP=(BDR_RAISEDOUTER Or BDR_SUNKENINNER)
EDGE_ETCHED=(BDR_SUNKENOUTER Or BDR_RAISEDINNER)
EDGE_RAISED=(BDR_RAISEDOUTER Or BDR_RAISEDINNER)
EDGE_SUNKEN=(BDR_SUNKENOUTER Or BDR_SUNKENINNER)
edt1=&H480
edt10=&H489
edt11=&H48A
edt12=&H48B
edt13=&H48C
edt14=&H48D
edt15=&H48E
edt16=&H48F
edt2=&H481
edt3=&H482
edt4=&H483
edt5=&H484
edt6=&H485
edt7=&H486
edt8=&H487
edt9=&H488
EIRESID=-1
ELF_CULTURE_LATIN=0
ELF_VENDOR_SIZE=4
ELF_VERSION=0
EM_CANUNDO=&HC6
EM_EMPTYUNDOBUFFER=&HCD
EM_FMTLINES=&HC8
EM_GETFIRSTVISIBLELINE=&HCE
EM_GETHANDLE=&HBD
EM_GETLINE=&HC4
EM_GETLINECOUNT=&HBA
EM_GETMODIFY=&HB8
EM_GETPASSWORDCHAR=&HD2
EM_GETRECT=&HB2
EM_GETSEL=&HB0
EM_GETTHUMB=&HBE
EM_GETWORDBREAKPROC=&HD1
EM_LIMITTEXT=&HC5
```

```
EM_LINEFROMCHAR=&HC9
EM_LINEINDEX=&HBB
EM_LINELENGTH=&HC1
EM_LINESCROLL=&HB6
EM_REPLACESEL=&HC2
EM_SCROLL=&HB5
EM_SCROLLCARET=&HB7
EM_SETHANDLE=&HBC
EM_SETMODIFY=&HB9
EM_SETPASSWORDCHAR=&HCC
EM_SETREADONLY=&HCF
EM_SETRECT=&HB3
EM_SETRECTNP=&HB4
EM_SETSEL=&HB1
EM_SETTABSTOPS=&HCB
EM_SETWORDBREAKPROC=&HD0
EM_UNDO=&HC7
EMR_ABORTPATH=68
EMR_ANGLEARC=41
EMR_ARC=45
EMR_ARCTO=55
EMR_BEGINPATH=59
EMR_BITBLT=76
EMR_CHORD=46
EMR_CLOSEFIGURE=61
EMR_CREATEBRUSHINDIRECT=39
EMR_CREATECOLORSPACE=99
EMR_CREATEDIBPATTERNBRUSHPT=94
EMR_CREATEMONOBRUSH=93
EMR_CREATEPALETTE=49
EMR_CREATEPEN=38
EMR_DELETECOLORSPACE=101
EMR_DELETEOBJECT=40
EMR_ELLIPSE=42
EMR_ENDPATH=60
EMR_EOF=14
EMR_EXCLUDECLIPRECT=29
EMR_EXTCREATEFONTINDIRECTW=82
EMR_EXTCREATEPEN=95
EMR_EXTFLOODFILL=53
EMR_EXTSELECTCLIPRGN=75
EMR_EXTTEXTOUTA=83
EMR_EXTTEXTOUTW=84
EMR_FILLPATH=62
EMR_FILLRGN=71
EMR_FLATTENPATH=65
EMR_FRAMERGN=72
EMR_GDICOMMENT=70
```

```
EMR_HEADER=1
EMR_INTERSECTCLIPRECT=30
EMR_INVERTRGN=73
EMR_LINETO=54
EMR_MASKBLT=78
EMR_MAX=97
EMR_MIN=1
EMR_MODIFYWORLDTRANSFORM=36
EMR_MOVETOEX=27
EMR_OFFSETCLIPRGN=26
EMR_PAINTRGN=74
EMR_PIE=47
EMR_PLGBLT=79
EMR_POLYBEZIER=2
EMR_POLYBEZIER16=85
EMR_POLYBEZIERTO=5
EMR_POLYBEZIERTO16=88
EMR_POLYDRAW=56
EMR_POLYDRAW16=92
EMR_POLYGON=3
EMR_POLYGON16=86
EMR_POLYLINE=4
EMR_POLYLINE16=87
EMR_POLYLINETO=6
EMR_POLYLINETO16=89
EMR_POLYPOLYGON=8
EMR_POLYPOLYGON16=91
EMR_POLYPOLYLINE=7
EMR_POLYPOLYLINE16=90
EMR_POLYTEXTOUTA=96
EMR_POLYTEXTOUTW=97
EMR_REALIZEPALETTE=52
EMR_RECTANGLE=43
EMR_RESIZEPALETTE=51
EMR_RESTOREDC=34
EMR_ROUNDRECT=44
EMR_SAVEDC=33
EMR_SCALEVIEWPORTEXTEX=31
EMR_SCALEWINDOWEXTEX=32
EMR_SELECTCLIPPATH=67
EMR_SELECTOBJECT=37
EMR_SELECTPALETTE=48
EMR_SETARCDIRECTION=57
EMR_SETBKCOLOR=25
EMR_SETBKMODE=18
EMR_SETBRUSHORGEX=13
EMR_SETCOLORADJUSTMENT=23
EMR_SETCOLORSPACE=100
```

```
EMR_SETDIBITSTODEVICE=80
EMR_SETICMMODE=98
EMR_SETMAPMODE=17
EMR_SETMAPPERFLAGS=16
EMR_SETMETARGN=28
EMR_SETMITERLIMIT=58
EMR_SETPALETTEENTRIES=50
EMR_SETPIXELV=15
EMR_SETPOLYFILLMODE=19
EMR_SETROP2=20
EMR_SETSTRETCHBLTMODE=21
EMR_SETTEXTALIGN=22
EMR_SETTEXTCOLOR=24
EMR_SETVIEWPORTEXTEX=11
EMR_SETVIEWPORTORGEX=12
EMR_SETWINDOWEXTEX=9
EMR_SETWINDOWORGEX=10
EMR_SETWORLDTRANSFORM=35
EMR_STRETCHBLT=77
EMR_STRETCHDIBITS=81
EMR_STROKEANDFILLPATH=63
EMR_STROKEPATH=64
EMR_WIDENPATH=66
EN_CHANGE=&H300
EN_ERRSPACE=&H500
EN_HSCROLL=&H601
EN_KILLFOCUS=&H200
EN_MAXTEXT=&H501
EN_SETFOCUS=&H100
EN_UPDATE=&H400
EN_VSCROLL=&H602
ENABLE_ECHO_INPUT=&H4
ENABLE_LINE_INPUT=&H2
ENABLE_MOUSE_INPUT=&H10
ENABLE_PROCESSED_INPUT=&H1
ENABLE_PROCESSED_OUTPUT=&H1
ENABLE_WINDOW_INPUT=&H8
ENABLE_WRAP_AT_EOL_OUTPUT=&H2
ENABLEDUPLEX=28
ENABLEPAIRKERNING=769
ENABLERELATIVEWIDTHS=768
ENCAPSULATED_POSTSCRIPT=4116
END_PATH=4098
EndDocC=11
ENHANCED_KEY=&H100 'the key is enhanced.
ENHMETA_SIGNATURE=&H464D4520
ENHMETA_STOCK_OBJECT=&H80000000
ENUM_ALL_CALENDARS=&HFFFF   'enumerate all calendars
```

```
ENUM_E_FIRST=&H800401B0
ENUM_E_LAST=&H800401BF
ENUM_S_FIRST=&H401B0
ENUM_S_LAST=&H401BF
ENUMPAPERBINS=31
ENUMPAPERMETRICS=34
EPSPRINTING=33
EPT_S_CANT_CREATE=1899&
EPT_S_CANT_PERFORM_OP=1752&
EPT_S_INVALID_ENTRY=1751&
EPT_S_NOT_REGISTERED=1753&
ERROR_ACCESS_DENIED=5&
ERROR_ACCOUNT_DISABLED=1331&
ERROR_ACCOUNT_EXPIRED=1793&
ERROR_ACCOUNT_RESTRICTION=1327&
ERROR_ADAP_HDW_ERR=57&
ERROR_ALIAS_EXISTS=1379&
ERROR_ALLOTTED_SPACE_EXCEEDED=1344&
ERROR_ALREADY_ASSIGNED=85&
ERROR_ALREADY_EXISTS=183&
ERROR_ALREADY_RUNNING_LKG=1074&
ERROR_ALREADY_WAITING=1904&
ERROR_ARENA_TRASHED=7&
ERROR_ARITHMETIC_OVERFLOW=534&
ERROR_ATOMIC_LOCKS_NOT_SUPPORTED=174&
ERROR_AUTODATASEG_EXCEEDS_64k=199&
ERROR_BAD_ARGUMENTS=160&
ERROR_BAD_COMMAND=22&
ERROR_BAD_DESCRIPTOR_FORMAT=1361&
ERROR_BAD_DEV_TYPE=66&
ERROR_BAD_DEVICE=1200&
ERROR_BAD_DRIVER=2001
ERROR_BAD_DRIVER_LEVEL=119&
ERROR_BAD_ENVIRONMENT=10&
ERROR_BAD_EXE_FORMAT=193&
ERROR_BAD_FORMAT=11&
ERROR_BAD_IMPERSONATION_LEVEL=1346&
ERROR_BAD_INHERITANCE_ACL=1340&
ERROR_BAD_LENGTH=24&
ERROR_BAD_LOGON_SESSION_STATE=1365&
ERROR_BAD_NET_NAME=67&
ERROR_BAD_NET_RESP=58&
ERROR_BAD_NETPATH=53&
ERROR_BAD_PATHNAME=161&
ERROR_BAD_PIPE=230&
ERROR_BAD_PROFILE=1206&
ERROR_BAD_PROVIDER=1204&
ERROR_BAD_REM_ADAP=60&
```

```
ERROR_BAD_THREADID_ADDR=159&
ERROR_BAD_TOKEN_TYPE=1349&
ERROR_BAD_UNIT=20&
ERROR_BAD_USERNAME=2202&
ERROR_BAD_VALIDATION_CLASS=1348&
ERROR_BADDB=1009&
ERROR_BADKEY=1010&
ERROR_BEGINNING_OF_MEDIA=1102&
ERROR_BOOT_ALREADY_ACCEPTED=1076&
ERROR_BROKEN_PIPE=109&
ERROR_BUFFER_OVERFLOW=111&
ERROR_BUS_RESET=1111&
ERROR_BUSY=170&
ERROR_BUSY_DRIVE=142&
ERROR_CALL_NOT_IMPLEMENTED=120&
ERROR_CAN_NOT_COMPLETE=1003&
ERROR_CAN_NOT_DEL_LOCAL_WINS=4001
ERROR_CANCEL_VIOLATION=173&
ERROR_CANNOT_COPY=266&
ERROR_CANNOT_FIND_WND_CLASS=1407&
ERROR_CANNOT_IMPERSONATE=1368&
ERROR_CANNOT_MAKE=82&
ERROR_CANNOT_OPEN_PROFILE=1205&
ERROR_CANT_ACCESS_DOMAIN_INFO=1351&
ERROR_CANT_DISABLE_MANDATORY=1310&
ERROR_CANT_OPEN_ANONYMOUS=1347&
ERROR_CANTOPEN=1011&
ERROR_CANTREAD=1012&
ERROR_CANTWRITE=1013&
ERROR_CHILD_MUST_BE_VOLATILE=1021&
ERROR_CHILD_NOT_COMPLETE=129&
ERROR_CHILD_WINDOW_MENU=1436&
ERROR_CIRCULAR_DEPENDENCY=1059&
ERROR_CLASS_ALREADY_EXISTS=1410&
ERROR_CLASS_DOES_NOT_EXIST=1411&
ERROR_CLASS_HAS_WINDOWS=1412&
ERROR_CLIPBOARD_NOT_OPEN=1418&
ERROR_CLIPPING_NOT_SUPPORTED=2005
ERROR_CONNECTION_UNAVAIL=1201&
ERROR_CONTROL_ID_NOT_FOUND=1421&
ERROR_COUNTER_TIMEOUT=1121&
ERROR_CRC=23&
ERROR_CURRENT_DIRECTORY=16&
ERROR_DATABASE_DOES_NOT_EXIST=1065&
ERROR_DC_NOT_FOUND=1425&
ERROR_DEPENDENT_SERVICES_RUNNING=1051&
ERROR_DESTROY_OBJECT_OF_OTHER_THREAD=1435&
ERROR_DEV_NOT_EXIST=55 'dderror
```

```
ERROR_DEVICE_ALREADY_REMEMBERED=1202&
ERROR_DEVICE_IN_USE=2404&
ERROR_DEVICE_NOT_PARTITIONED=1107&
ERROR_DIR_NOT_EMPTY=145&
ERROR_DIR_NOT_ROOT=144&
ERROR_DIRECT_ACCESS_HANDLE=130&
ERROR_DIRECTORY=267&
ERROR_DISCARDED=157&
ERROR_DISK_CHANGE=107&
ERROR_DISK_CORRUPT=1393&
ERROR_DISK_FULL=112&
ERROR_DISK_OPERATION_FAILED=1127&
ERROR_DISK_RECALIBRATE_FAILED=1126&
ERROR_DISK_RESET_FAILED=1128&
ERROR_DLL_INIT_FAILED=1114&
ERROR_DOMAIN_EXISTS=1356&
ERROR_DOMAIN_LIMIT_EXCEEDED=1357&
ERROR_DOMAIN_TRUST_INCONSISTENT=1810&
ERROR_DRIVE_LOCKED=108&
ERROR_DUP_DOMAINNAME=1221&
ERROR_DUP_NAME=52&
ERROR_DUPLICATE_SERVICE_NAME=1078&
ERROR_DYNLINK_FROM_INVALID_RING=196&
ERROR_EA_ACCESS_DENIED=994&
ERROR_EA_FILE_CORRUPT=276&
ERROR_EA_LIST_INCONSISTENT=255&
ERROR_EA_TABLE_FULL=277&
ERROR_EAS_DIDNT_FIT=275&
ERROR_EAS_NOT_SUPPORTED=282&
ERROR_END_OF_MEDIA=1100&
ERROR_ENVVAR_NOT_FOUND=203&
ERROR_EOM_OVERFLOW=1129&
ERROR_EVENTLOG_CANT_START=1501&
ERROR_EVENTLOG_FILE_CHANGED=1503&
ERROR_EVENTLOG_FILE_CORRUPT=1500&
ERROR_EXCEPTION_IN_SERVICE=1064&
ERROR_EXCL_SEM_ALREADY_OWNED=101&
ERROR_EXE_MARKED_INVALID=192&
ERROR_EXTENDED_ERROR=1208&
ERROR_FAIL_I24=83&
ERROR_FAILED_SERVICE_CONTROLLER_CONNECT=1063&
ERROR_FILE_CORRUPT=1392&
ERROR_FILE_EXISTS=80&
ERROR_FILE_INVALID=1006&
ERROR_FILE_NOT_FOUND=2&
ERROR_FILEMARK_DETECTED=1101&
ERROR_FILENAME_EXCED_RANGE=206&
ERROR_FLOPPY_BAD_REGISTERS=1125&
```

```
ERROR_FLOPPY_ID_MARK_NOT_FOUND=1122&
ERROR_FLOPPY_UNKNOWN_ERROR=1124&
ERROR_FLOPPY_WRONG_CYLINDER=1123&
ERROR_FULL_BACKUP=4004
ERROR_FULLSCREEN_MODE=1007&
ERROR_GEN_FAILURE=31&
ERROR_GENERIC_NOT_MAPPED=1360&
ERROR_GROUP_EXISTS=1318&
ERROR_HANDLE_DISK_FULL=39&
ERROR_HANDLE_EOF=38&
ERROR_HOOK_NEEDS_HMOD=1428&
ERROR_HOOK_NOT_INSTALLED=1431&
ERROR_HOTKEY_ALREADY_REGISTERED=1409&
ERROR_HOTKEY_NOT_REGISTERED=1419&
ERROR_HWNDS_HAVE_DIFF_PARENT=1441&
ERROR_ILL_FORMED_PASSWORD=1324&
ERROR_INC_BACKUP=4003
ERROR_INFLOOP_IN_RELOC_CHAIN=202&
ERROR_INSUFFICIENT_BUFFER=122 'dderror
ERROR_INTERNAL_DB_CORRUPTION=1358&
ERROR_INTERNAL_DB_ERROR=1383&
ERROR_INTERNAL_ERROR=1359&
ERROR_INVALID_ACCEL_HANDLE=1403&
ERROR_INVALID_ACCESS=12&
ERROR_INVALID_ACCOUNT_NAME=1315&
ERROR_INVALID_ACL=1336&
ERROR_INVALID_ADDRESS=487&
ERROR_INVALID_AT_INTERRUPT_TIME=104&
ERROR_INVALID_BLOCK=9&
ERROR_INVALID_BLOCK_LENGTH=1106&
ERROR_INVALID_CATEGORY=117&
ERROR_INVALID_COMBOBOX_MESSAGE=1422&
ERROR_INVALID_COMPUTERNAME=1210&
ERROR_INVALID_CURSOR_HANDLE=1402&
ERROR_INVALID_DATA=13&
ERROR_INVALID_DATATYPE=1804&
ERROR_INVALID_DOMAIN_ROLE=1354&
ERROR_INVALID_DOMAIN_STATE=1353&
ERROR_INVALID_DOMAINNAME=1212&
ERROR_INVALID_DRIVE=15&
ERROR_INVALID_DWP_HANDLE=1405&
ERROR_INVALID_EA_HANDLE=278&
ERROR_INVALID_EA_NAME=254&
ERROR_INVALID_EDIT_HEIGHT=1424&
ERROR_INVALID_ENVIRONMENT=1805&
ERROR_INVALID_EVENT_COUNT=151&
ERROR_INVALID_EVENTNAME=1211&
ERROR_INVALID_EXE_SIGNATURE=191&
```

```
ERROR_INVALID_FILTER_PROC=1427&
ERROR_INVALID_FLAG_NUMBER=186&
ERROR_INVALID_FLAGS=1004&
ERROR_INVALID_FORM_NAME=1902&
ERROR_INVALID_FORM_SIZE=1903&
ERROR_INVALID_FUNCTION=1 'dderror
ERROR_INVALID_GROUP_ATTRIBUTES=1345&
ERROR_INVALID_GROUPNAME=1209&
ERROR_INVALID_GW_COMMAND=1443&
ERROR_INVALID_HANDLE=6&
ERROR_INVALID_HOOK_FILTER=1426&
ERROR_INVALID_HOOK_HANDLE=1404&
ERROR_INVALID_ICON_HANDLE=1414&
ERROR_INVALID_ID_AUTHORITY=1343&
ERROR_INVALID_INDEX=1413&
ERROR_INVALID_LB_MESSAGE=1432&
ERROR_INVALID_LEVEL=124&
ERROR_INVALID_LIST_FORMAT=153&
ERROR_INVALID_LOGON_HOURS=1328&
ERROR_INVALID_LOGON_TYPE=1367&
ERROR_INVALID_MEMBER=1388&
ERROR_INVALID_MENU_HANDLE=1401&
ERROR_INVALID_MESSAGE=1002&
ERROR_INVALID_MESSAGEDEST=1218&
ERROR_INVALID_MESSAGENAME=1217&
ERROR_INVALID_MINALLOCSIZE=195&
ERROR_INVALID_MODULETYPE=190&
ERROR_INVALID_MSGBOX_STYLE=1438&
ERROR_INVALID_NAME=123&
ERROR_INVALID_NETNAME=1214&
ERROR_INVALID_ORDINAL=182&
ERROR_INVALID_OWNER=1307&
ERROR_INVALID_PARAMETER=87 'dderror
ERROR_INVALID_PASSWORD=86&
ERROR_INVALID_PASSWORDNAME=1216&
ERROR_INVALID_PIXEL_FORMAT=2000
ERROR_INVALID_PRIMARY_GROUP=1308&
ERROR_INVALID_PRINTER_COMMAND=1803&
ERROR_INVALID_PRINTER_NAME=1801&
ERROR_INVALID_PRINTER_STATE=1906&
ERROR_INVALID_PRIORITY=1800&
ERROR_INVALID_SCROLLBAR_RANGE=1448&
ERROR_INVALID_SECURITY_DESCR=1338&
ERROR_INVALID_SEGDPL=198&
ERROR_INVALID_SEGMENT_NUMBER=180&
ERROR_INVALID_SEPARATOR_FILE=1799&
ERROR_INVALID_SERVER_STATE=1352&
ERROR_INVALID_SERVICE_ACCOUNT=1057&
```

```
ERROR_INVALID_SERVICE_CONTROL=1052&
ERROR_INVALID_SERVICE_LOCK=1071&
ERROR_INVALID_SERVICENAME=1213&
ERROR_INVALID_SHARENAME=1215&
ERROR_INVALID_SHOWWIN_COMMAND=1449&
ERROR_INVALID_SID=1337&
ERROR_INVALID_SIGNAL_NUMBER=209&
ERROR_INVALID_SPI_VALUE=1439&
ERROR_INVALID_STACKSEG=189&
ERROR_INVALID_STARTING_CODESEG=188&
ERROR_INVALID_SUB_AUTHORITY=1335&
ERROR_INVALID_TARGET_HANDLE=114&
ERROR_INVALID_THREAD_ID=1444&
ERROR_INVALID_TIME=1901&
ERROR_INVALID_USER_BUFFER=1784&
ERROR_INVALID_VERIFY_SWITCH=118&
ERROR_INVALID_WINDOW_HANDLE=1400&
ERROR_INVALID_WINDOW_STYLE=2002
ERROR_INVALID_WORKSTATION=1329&
ERROR_IO_DEVICE=1117&
ERROR_IO_INCOMPLETE=996&
ERROR_IO_PENDING=997 'dderror
ERROR_IOPL_NOT_ENABLED=197&
ERROR_IRQ_BUSY=1119&
ERROR_IS_JOIN_PATH=147&
ERROR_IS_JOIN_TARGET=133&
ERROR_IS_JOINED=134&
ERROR_IS_SUBST_PATH=146&
ERROR_IS_SUBST_TARGET=149&
ERROR_IS_SUBSTED=135&
ERROR_ITERATED_DATA_EXCEEDS_64k=194&
ERROR_JOIN_TO_JOIN=138&
ERROR_JOIN_TO_SUBST=140&
ERROR_JOURNAL_HOOK_SET=1430&
ERROR_KEY_DELETED=1018&
ERROR_KEY_HAS_CHILDREN=1020&
ERROR_LABEL_TOO_LONG=154&
ERROR_LAST_ADMIN=1322&
ERROR_LB_WITHOUT_TABSTOPS=1434&
ERROR_LISTBOX_ID_NOT_FOUND=1416&
ERROR_LM_CROSS_ENCRYPTION_REQUIRED=1390&
ERROR_LOCAL_USER_SESSION_KEY=1303&
ERROR_LOCK_FAILED=167&
ERROR_LOCK_VIOLATION=33&
ERROR_LOCKED=212&
ERROR_LOG_FILE_FULL=1502&
ERROR_LOGON_FAILURE=1326&
ERROR_LOGON_NOT_GRANTED=1380&
```

```
ERROR_LOGON_SESSION_COLLISION=1366&
ERROR_LOGON_SESSION_EXISTS=1363&
ERROR_LOGON_TYPE_NOT_GRANTED=1385&
ERROR_LUIDS_EXHAUSTED=1334&
ERROR_MAPPED_ALIGNMENT=1132&
ERROR_MAX_THRDS_REACHED=164&
ERROR_MEDIA_CHANGED=1110&
ERROR_MEMBER_IN_ALIAS=1378&
ERROR_MEMBER_IN_GROUP=1320&
ERROR_MEMBER_NOT_IN_ALIAS=1377&
ERROR_MEMBER_NOT_IN_GROUP=1321&
ERROR_MEMBERS_PRIMARY_GROUP=1374&
ERROR_META_EXPANSION_TOO_LONG=208&
ERROR_METAFILE_NOT_SUPPORTED=2003
ERROR_MOD_NOT_FOUND=126&
ERROR_MORE_DATA=234 'dderror
ERROR_MORE_WRITES=1120&
ERROR_MR_MID_NOT_FOUND=317&
ERROR_NEGATIVE_SEEK=131&
ERROR_NESTING_NOT_ALLOWED=215&
ERROR_NET_WRITE_FAULT=88&
ERROR_NETLOGON_NOT_STARTED=1792&
ERROR_NETNAME_DELETED=64&
ERROR_NETWORK_ACCESS_DENIED=65&
ERROR_NETWORK_BUSY=54&
ERROR_NO_BROWSER_SERVERS_FOUND=6118&
ERROR_NO_DATA=232&
ERROR_NO_DATA_DETECTED=1104&
ERROR_NO_IMPERSONATION_TOKEN=1309&
ERROR_NO_INHERITANCE=1391&
ERROR_NO_LOG_SPACE=1019&
ERROR_NO_LOGON_SERVERS=1311&
ERROR_NO_MEDIA_IN_DRIVE=1112&
ERROR_NO_MORE_FILES=18&
ERROR_NO_MORE_ITEMS=259&
ERROR_NO_MORE_SEARCH_HANDLES=113&
ERROR_NO_NET_OR_BAD_PATH=1203&
ERROR_NO_NETWORK=1222&
ERROR_NO_PROC_SLOTS=89&
ERROR_NO_QUOTAS_FOR_ACCOUNT=1302&
ERROR_NO_SCROLLBARS=1447&
ERROR_NO_SECURITY_ON_OBJECT=1350&
ERROR_NO_SHUTDOWN_IN_PROGRESS=1116&
ERROR_NO_SIGNAL_SENT=205&
ERROR_NO_SPOOL_SPACE=62&
ERROR_NO_SUCH_ALIAS=1376&
ERROR_NO_SUCH_DOMAIN=1355&
ERROR_NO_SUCH_GROUP=1319&
```

```
ERROR_NO_SUCH_LOGON_SESSION=1312&
ERROR_NO_SUCH_MEMBER=1387&
ERROR_NO_SUCH_PACKAGE=1364&
ERROR_NO_SUCH_PRIVILEGE=1313&
ERROR_NO_SUCH_USER=1317&
ERROR_NO_SYSTEM_MENU=1437&
ERROR_NO_TOKEN=1008&
ERROR_NO_TRUST_LSA_SECRET=1786&
ERROR_NO_TRUST_SAM_ACCOUNT=1787&
ERROR_NO_UNICODE_TRANSLATION=1113&
ERROR_NO_USER_SESSION_KEY=1394&
ERROR_NO_VOLUME_LABEL=125&
ERROR_NO_WILDCARD_CHARACTERS=1417&
ERROR_NOACCESS=998&
ERROR_NOLOGON_INTERDOMAIN_TRUST_ACCOUNT=1807&
ERROR_NOLOGON_SERVER_TRUST_ACCOUNT=1809&
ERROR_NOLOGON_WORKSTATION_TRUST_ACCOUNT=1808&
ERROR_NON_MDICHILD_WINDOW=1445&
ERROR_NONE_MAPPED=1332&
ERROR_NOT_ALL_ASSIGNED=1300&
ERROR_NOT_CHILD_WINDOW=1442&
ERROR_NOT_CONNECTED=2250&
ERROR_NOT_CONTAINER=1207&
ERROR_NOT_DOS_DISK=26&
ERROR_NOT_ENOUGH_MEMORY=8 'dderror
ERROR_NOT_ENOUGH_QUOTA=1816&
ERROR_NOT_ENOUGH_SERVER_MEMORY=1130&
ERROR_NOT_JOINED=136&
ERROR_NOT_LOCKED=158&
ERROR_NOT_LOGON_PROCESS=1362&
ERROR_NOT_OWNER=288&
ERROR_NOT_READY=21&
ERROR_NOT_REGISTRY_FILE=1017&
ERROR_NOT_SAME_DEVICE=17&
ERROR_NOT_SUBSTED=137&
ERROR_NOT_SUPPORTED=50&
ERROR_NOTIFY_ENUM_DIR=1022&
ERROR_NT_CROSS_ENCRYPTION_REQUIRED=1386&
ERROR_NULL_LM_PASSWORD=1304&
ERROR_OPEN_FAILED=110&
ERROR_OPEN_FILES=2401&
ERROR_OPERATION_ABORTED=995&
ERROR_OUT_OF_PAPER=28&
ERROR_OUT_OF_STRUCTURES=84&
ERROR_OUTOFMEMORY=14&
ERROR_PARTITION_FAILURE=1105&
ERROR_PASSWORD_EXPIRED=1330&
ERROR_PASSWORD_RESTRICTION=1325&
```

```
ERROR_PATH_BUSY=148&
ERROR_PATH_NOT_FOUND=3&
ERROR_PIPE_BUSY=231&
ERROR_PIPE_CONNECTED=535&
ERROR_PIPE_LISTENING=536&
ERROR_PIPE_NOT_CONNECTED=233&
ERROR_POPUP_ALREADY_ACTIVE=1446&
ERROR_POSSIBLE_DEADLOCK=1131&
ERROR_PRINT_CANCELLED=63&
ERROR_PRINT_MONITOR_ALREADY_INSTALLED=3006
ERROR_PRINT_PROCESSOR_ALREADY_INSTALLED=3005
ERROR_PRINTER_ALREADY_EXISTS=1802&
ERROR_PRINTER_DELETED=1905&
ERROR_PRINTER_DRIVER_ALREADY_INSTALLED=1795&
ERROR_PRINTER_DRIVER_IN_USE=3001
ERROR_PRINTQ_FULL=61&
ERROR_PRIVATE_DIALOG_INDEX=1415&
ERROR_PRIVILEGE_NOT_HELD=1314&
ERROR_PROC_NOT_FOUND=127&
ERROR_PROCESS_ABORTED=1067&
ERROR_PUBLIC_ONLY_HOOK=1429&
ERROR_READ_FAULT=30&
ERROR_REC_NON_EXISTENT=4005
ERROR_REDIR_PAUSED=72&
ERROR_REDIRECTOR_HAS_OPEN_HANDLES=1794&
ERROR_REGISTRY_CORRUPT=1015&
ERROR_REGISTRY_IO_FAILED=1016&
ERROR_REGISTRY_RECOVERED=1014&
ERROR_RELOC_CHAIN_XEEDS_SEGLIM=201&
ERROR_REM_NOT_LIST=51&
ERROR_REMOTE_SESSION_LIMIT_EXCEEDED=1220&
ERROR_REQ_NOT_ACCEP=71&
ERROR_RESOURCE_DATA_NOT_FOUND=1812&
ERROR_RESOURCE_LANG_NOT_FOUND=1815&
ERROR_RESOURCE_NAME_NOT_FOUND=1814&
ERROR_RESOURCE_TYPE_NOT_FOUND=1813&
ERROR_REVISION_MISMATCH=1306&
ERROR_RING2_STACK_IN_USE=207&
ERROR_RING2SEG_MUST_BE_MOVABLE=200&
ERROR_RPL_NOT_ALLOWED=4006
ERROR_RXACT_COMMIT_FAILURE=1370&
ERROR_RXACT_INVALID_STATE=1369&
ERROR_SAME_DRIVE=143&
ERROR_SCREEN_ALREADY_LOCKED=1440&
ERROR_SECRET_TOO_LONG=1382&
ERROR_SECTOR_NOT_FOUND=27&
ERROR_SEEK=25&
ERROR_SEEK_ON_DEVICE=132&
```

```
ERROR_SEM_IS_SET=102&
ERROR_SEM_NOT_FOUND=187&
ERROR_SEM_OWNER_DIED=105&
ERROR_SEM_TIMEOUT=121&
ERROR_SEM_USER_LIMIT=106&
ERROR_SERIAL_NO_DEVICE=1118&
ERROR_SERVER_DISABLED=1341&
ERROR_SERVER_HAS_OPEN_HANDLES=1811&
ERROR_SERVER_NOT_DISABLED=1342&
ERROR_SERVICE_ALREADY_RUNNING=1056&
ERROR_SERVICE_CANNOT_ACCEPT_CTRL=1061&
ERROR_SERVICE_DATABASE_LOCKED=1055&
ERROR_SERVICE_DEPENDENCY_DELETED=1075&
ERROR_SERVICE_DEPENDENCY_FAIL=1068&
ERROR_SERVICE_DISABLED=1058&
ERROR_SERVICE_DOES_NOT_EXIST=1060&
ERROR_SERVICE_EXISTS=1073&
ERROR_SERVICE_LOGON_FAILED=1069&
ERROR_SERVICE_MARKED_FOR_DELETE=1072&
ERROR_SERVICE_NEVER_STARTED=1077&
ERROR_SERVICE_NO_THREAD=1054&
ERROR_SERVICE_NOT_ACTIVE=1062&
ERROR_SERVICE_REQUEST_TIMEOUT=1053&
ERROR_SERVICE_SPECIFIC_ERROR=1066&
ERROR_SERVICE_START_HANG=1070&
ERROR_SESSION_CREDENTIAL_CONFLICT=1219&
ERROR_SETCOUNT_ON_BAD_LB=1433&
ERROR_SETMARK_DETECTED=1103&
ERROR_SEVERITY_ERROR=&HC0000000
ERROR_SEVERITY_INFORMATIONAL=&H40000000
ERROR_SEVERITY_SUCCESS=&H0
ERROR_SEVERITY_WARNING=&H80000000
ERROR_SHARING_BUFFER_EXCEEDED=36&
ERROR_SHARING_PAUSED=70&
ERROR_SHARING_VIOLATION=32&
ERROR_SHUTDOWN_IN_PROGRESS=1115&
ERROR_SIGNAL_PENDING=162&
ERROR_SIGNAL_REFUSED=156&
ERROR_SOME_NOT_MAPPED=1301&
ERROR_SPECIAL_ACCOUNT=1371&
ERROR_SPECIAL_GROUP=1372&
ERROR_SPECIAL_USER=1373&
ERROR_SPL_NO_ADDJOB=3004
ERROR_SPL_NO_STARTDOC=3003
ERROR_SPOOL_FILE_NOT_FOUND=3002
ERROR_STACK_OVERFLOW=1001&
ERROR_STATIC_INIT=4002
ERROR_SUBST_TO_JOIN=141&
```

```
ERROR_SUBST_TO_SUBST=139&
ERROR_SUCCESS=0&
ERROR_SWAPERROR=999&
ERROR_SYSTEM_TRACE=150&
ERROR_THREAD_1_INACTIVE=210&
ERROR_TLW_WITH_WSCHILD=1406&
ERROR_TOKEN_ALREADY_IN_USE=1375&
ERROR_TOO_MANY_CMDS=56&
ERROR_TOO_MANY_CONTEXT_IDS=1384&
ERROR_TOO_MANY_LUIDS_REQUESTED=1333&
ERROR_TOO_MANY_MODULES=214&
ERROR_TOO_MANY_MUXWAITERS=152&
ERROR_TOO_MANY_NAMES=68&
ERROR_TOO_MANY_OPEN_FILES=4&
ERROR_TOO_MANY_POSTS=298&
ERROR_TOO_MANY_SECRETS=1381&
ERROR_TOO_MANY_SEM_REQUESTS=103&
ERROR_TOO_MANY_SEMAPHORES=100&
ERROR_TOO_MANY_SESS=69&
ERROR_TOO_MANY_SIDS=1389&
ERROR_TOO_MANY_TCBS=155&
ERROR_TRANSFORM_NOT_SUPPORTED=2004
ERROR_TRUST_FAILURE=1790&
ERROR_TRUSTED_DOMAIN_FAILURE=1788&
ERROR_TRUSTED_RELATIONSHIP_FAILURE=1789&
ERROR_UNABLE_TO_LOCK_MEDIA=1108&
ERROR_UNABLE_TO_UNLOAD_MEDIA=1109&
ERROR_UNEXP_NET_ERR=59&
ERROR_UNKNOWN_PORT=1796&
ERROR_UNKNOWN_PRINT_MONITOR=3000
ERROR_UNKNOWN_PRINTER_DRIVER=1797&
ERROR_UNKNOWN_PRINTPROCESSOR=1798&
ERROR_UNKNOWN_REVISION=1305&
ERROR_UNRECOGNIZED_MEDIA=1785&
ERROR_UNRECOGNIZED_VOLUME=1005&
ERROR_USER_EXISTS=1316&
ERROR_VC_DISCONNECTED=240&
ERROR_WAIT_NO_CHILDREN=128&
ERROR_WINDOW_NOT_COMBOBOX=1423&
ERROR_WINDOW_NOT_DIALOG=1420&
ERROR_WINDOW_OF_OTHER_THREAD=1408&
ERROR_WINS_INTERNAL=4000
ERROR_WRITE_FAULT=29&
ERROR_WRITE_PROTECT=19&
ERROR_WRONG_DISK=34&
ERROR_WRONG_PASSWORD=1323&
ERRORAPI=0
ES_AUTOHSCROLL=&H80&
```

```
ES_AUTOVSCROLL=&H40&
ES_CENTER=&H1&
ES_LEFT=&H0&
ES_LOWERCASE=&H10&
ES_MULTILINE=&H4&
ES_NOHIDESEL=&H100&
ES_OEMCONVERT=&H400&
ES_PASSWORD=&H20&
ES_READONLY=&H800&
ES_RIGHT=&H2&
ES_UPPERCASE=&H8&
ES_WANTRETURN=&H1000&
ESB_DISABLE_BOTH=&H3
ESB_DISABLE_DOWN=&H2
ESB_DISABLE_LEFT=&H1
ESB_DISABLE_LTUP=ESB_DISABLE_LEFT
ESB_DISABLE_RIGHT=&H2
ESB_DISABLE_RTDN=ESB_DISABLE_RIGHT
ESB_DISABLE_UP=&H1
ESB_ENABLE_BOTH=&H0
ETO_CLIPPED=4
ETO_GRAYED=1
ETO_OPAQUE=2
EV_BREAK=&H40   'BREAK received
EV_CTS=&H8 'CTS changed state
EV_DSR=&H10 'DSR changed state
EV_ERR=&H80 'Line status error occurred
EV_EVENT1=&H800 'Provider specific event 1
EV_EVENT2=&H1000 'Provider specific event 2
EV_PERR=&H200   'Printer error occured
EV_RING=&H100   'Ring signal detected
EV_RLSD=&H20 'RLSD changed state
EV_RX80FULL=&H400 'Receive buffer is 80 percent full
EV_RXCHAR=&H1   'Any Character received
EV_RXFLAG=&H2   'Received certain character
EV_TXEMPTY=&H4 'Transmitt Queue Empty
EVENPARITY=2
EWX_FORCE=4
EWX_LOGOFF=0
EWX_REBOOT=2
EWX_SHUTDOWN=1
EXCEPTION_CONTINUE_EXECUTION=-1
EXCEPTION_CONTINUE_SEARCH=0
EXCEPTION_DEBUG_EVENT=1
EXCEPTION_EXECUTE_HANDLER=1
EXCEPTION_MAXIMUM_PARAMETERS=15
EXIT_PROCESS_DEBUG_EVENT=5
EXIT_THREAD_DEBUG_EVENT=4
```

```
EXT_DEVICE_CAPS=4099
ExtTextOutC=512


F
FACILITY_NT_BIT=&H10000000
FAILED_ACCESS_ACE_FLAG=&H80
FALT=&H10
FCONTROL=&H8
FF_DECORATIVE=80 'Old English, etc.
FF_DONTCARE=0 'Don't care or don't know.
FF_MODERN=48 'Constant stroke width, serifed or sans-serifed.
FF_ROMAN=16 'Variable stroke width, serifed.
FF_SCRIPT=64 'Cursive, etc.
FF_SWISS=32 'Variable stroke width, sans-serifed.
FILE_ADD_FILE=(&H2) 'directory
FILE_ADD_SUBDIRECTORY=(&H4) 'directory
FILE_ALL_ACCESS=(STANDARD_RIGHTS_REQUIRED Or
                    SYNCHRONIZE Or &H1FF)
FILE_APPEND_DATA=(&H4) 'file
FILE_ATTRIBUTE_ARCHIVE=&H20
FILE_ATTRIBUTE_COMPRESSED=&H800
FILE_ATTRIBUTE_DIRECTORY=&H10
FILE_ATTRIBUTE_HIDDEN=&H2
FILE_ATTRIBUTE_NORMAL=&H80
FILE_ATTRIBUTE_READONLY=&H1
FILE_ATTRIBUTE_SYSTEM=&H4
FILE_ATTRIBUTE_TEMPORARY=&H100
FILE_BEGIN=0
FILE_CASE_PRESERVED_NAMES=&H2
FILE_CASE_SENSITIVE_SEARCH=&H1
FILE_CREATE_PIPE_INSTANCE=(&H4) 'named pipe
FILE_CURRENT=1
FILE_DELETE_CHILD=(&H40) 'directory
FILE_END=2
FILE_EXECUTE=(&H20) 'file
FILE_FILE_COMPRESSION=&H10
FILE_FLAG_BACKUP_SEMANTICS=&H2000000
FILE_FLAG_DELETE_ON_CLOSE=&H4000000
FILE_FLAG_NO_BUFFERING=&H20000000
FILE_FLAG_OVERLAPPED=&H40000000
FILE_FLAG_POSIX_SEMANTICS=&H1000000
FILE_FLAG_RANDOM_ACCESS=&H10000000
FILE_FLAG_SEQUENTIAL_SCAN=&H8000000
FILE_FLAG_WRITE_THROUGH=&H80000000
FILE_GENERIC_EXECUTE=(STANDARD_RIGHTS_EXECUTE Or
                       FILE_READ_ATTRIBUTES Or
                       FILE_EXECUTE Or SYNCHRONIZE)
```

```
FILE_GENERIC_READ=(STANDARD_RIGHTS_READ Or
                   FILE_READ_DATA Or FILE_READ_ATTRIBUTES Or
                   FILE_READ_EA Or SYNCHRONIZE)
FILE_GENERIC_WRITE=(STANDARD_RIGHTS_WRITE Or
                    FILE_WRITE_DATA Or FILE_WRITE_ATTRIBUTES Or
                    FILE_WRITE_EA Or FILE_APPEND_DATA Or
                    SYNCHRONIZE)
FILE_LIST_DIRECTORY=(&H1)  'directory
FILE_MAP_ALL_ACCESS=SECTION_ALL_ACCESS
FILE_MAP_COPY=SECTION_QUERY
FILE_MAP_READ=SECTION_MAP_READ
FILE_MAP_WRITE=SECTION_MAP_WRITE
FILE_NOTIFY_CHANGE_ATTRIBUTES=&H4
FILE_NOTIFY_CHANGE_DIR_NAME=&H2
FILE_NOTIFY_CHANGE_FILE_NAME=&H1
FILE_NOTIFY_CHANGE_LAST_WRITE=&H10
FILE_NOTIFY_CHANGE_SECURITY=&H100
FILE_NOTIFY_CHANGE_SIZE=&H8
FILE_PERSISTENT_ACLS=&H8
FILE_READ_ATTRIBUTES=(&H80) 'all
FILE_READ_DATA=(&H1) 'file pipe
FILE_READ_EA=(&H8) 'file directory
FILE_READ_PROPERTIES=FILE_READ_EA
FILE_SHARE_READ=&H1
FILE_SHARE_WRITE=&H2
FILE_TRAVERSE=(&H20) 'directory
FILE_TYPE_CHAR=&H2
FILE_TYPE_DISK=&H1
FILE_TYPE_PIPE=&H3
FILE_TYPE_REMOTE=&H8000
FILE_TYPE_UNKNOWN=&H0
FILE_UNICODE_ON_DISK=&H4
FILE_VOLUME_IS_COMPRESSED=&H8000
FILE_WRITE_ATTRIBUTES=(&H100) 'all
FILE_WRITE_DATA=(&H2) 'file pipe
FILE_WRITE_EA=(&H10) 'file directory
FILE_WRITE_PROPERTIES=FILE_WRITE_EA
FILEOKSTRING="commdlg_FileNameOK"
FILEOPENORD=1536
FINDDLGORD=1540
FINDMSGSTRING="commdlg_FindReplace"
FIXED_PITCH=1
FLI_GLYPHS=&H40000
FLI_MASK=&H103B
FLOODFILLBORDER=0
FLOODFILLSURFACE=1
FLUSHOUTPUT=6
FNERR_BUFFERTOOSMALL=&H3003
```

```
FNERR_FILENAMECODES=&H3000
FNERR_INVALIDFILENAME=&H3002
FNERR_SUBCLASSFAILURE=&H3001
FNOINVERT=&H2
FO_COPY=&H2
FO_DELETE=&H3
FO_MOVE=&H1
FO_RENAME=&H4
FOCUS_EVENT=&H10 'event contains focus change
FOF_ALLOWUNDO=&H40
FOF_CONFIRMMOUSE=&H2
FOF_FILESONLY=&H80 'on *.*, do only files
FOF_MULTIDESTFILES=&H1
FOF_NOCONFIRMATION=&H10 'Don't prompt the user.
FOF_NOCONFIRMMKDIR=&H200 'don't confirm making needed dirs
FOF_RENAMEONCOLLISION=&H8
FOF_SILENT=&H4 'don't create progress/report
FOF_SIMPLEPROGRESS=&H100 'means don't show names of files
FOF_WANTMAPPINGHANDLE=&H20 'SHFILEOPSTRUCT.hNameMappings
FONTDLGORD=1542
FONTMAPPER_MAX=10
FOREGROUND_BLUE=&H1 'text color contains blue.
FOREGROUND_GREEN=&H2 'text color contains green.
FOREGROUND_INTENSITY=&H8 'text color is intensified.
FOREGROUND_RED=&H4 'text color contains red.
FORM_BUILTIN=&H1
FORMAT_MESSAGE_ALLOCATE_BUFFER=&H100
FORMAT_MESSAGE_ARGUMENT_ARRAY=&H2000
FORMAT_MESSAGE_FROM_HMODULE=&H800
FORMAT_MESSAGE_FROM_STRING=&H400
FORMAT_MESSAGE_FROM_SYSTEM=&H1000
FORMAT_MESSAGE_IGNORE_INSERTS=&H200
FORMAT_MESSAGE_MAX_WIDTH_MASK=&HFF
FORMATDLGORD30=1544
FORMATDLGORD31=1543
FR_DIALOGTERM=&H40
FR_DOWN=&H1
FR_ENABLEHOOK=&H100
FR_ENABLETEMPLATE=&H200
FR_ENABLETEMPLATEHANDLE=&H2000
FR_FINDNEXT=&H8
FR_HIDEMATCHCASE=&H8000
FR_HIDEUPDOWN=&H4000
FR_HIDEWHOLEWORD=&H10000
FR_MATCHCASE=&H4
FR_NOMATCHCASE=&H800
FR_NOUPDOWN=&H400
FR_NOWHOLEWORD=&H1000
```

```
FR_REPLACE=&H10
FR_REPLACEALL=&H20
FR_SHOWHELP=&H80
FR_WHOLEWORD=&H2
FRERR_BUFFERLENGTHZERO=&H4001
FRERR_FINDREPLACECODES=&H4000
frm1=&H434
frm2=&H435
frm3=&H436
frm4=&H437
FROM_LEFT_1ST_BUTTON_PRESSED=&H1
FROM_LEFT_2ND_BUTTON_PRESSED=&H4
FROM_LEFT_3RD_BUTTON_PRESSED=&H8
FROM_LEFT_4TH_BUTTON_PRESSED=&H10
FS_ARABIC=&H40&
FS_BALTIC=&H80&
FS_CASE_IS_PRESERVED=FILE_CASE_PRESERVED_NAMES
FS_CASE_SENSITIVE=FILE_CASE_SENSITIVE_SEARCH
FS_CHINESESIMP=&H40000
FS_CHINESETRAD=&H100000
FS_CYRILLIC=&H4&
FS_GREEK=&H8&
FS_HEBREW=&H20&
FS_JISJAPAN=&H20000
FS_JOHAB=&H200000
FS_LATIN1=&H1&
FS_LATIN2=&H2&
FS_PERSISTENT_ACLS=FILE_PERSISTENT_ACLS
FS_SYMBOL=&H80000000
FS_THAI=&H10000
FS_TURKISH=&H10&
FS_UNICODE_STORED_ON_DISK=FILE_UNICODE_ON_DISK
FS_WANSUNG=&H80000
FSHIFT=&H4
FVIRTKEY=True 'Assumed to be == TRUE
FW_BLACK=FW_HEAVY
FW_BOLD=700
FW_DEMIBOLD=FW_SEMIBOLD
FW_DONTCARE=0
FW_EXTRABOLD=800
FW_EXTRALIGHT=200
FW_HEAVY=900
FW_LIGHT=300
FW_MEDIUM=500
FW_NORMAL=400
FW_REGULAR=FW_NORMAL
FW_SEMIBOLD=600
FW_THIN=100
```

```
FW_ULTRABOLD=FW_EXTRABOLD
FW_ULTRALIGHT=FW_EXTRALIGHT

G
GCL_CBCLSEXTRA=(-20)
GCL_CBWNDEXTRA=(-18)
GCL_CONVERSION=&H1
GCL_HBRBACKGROUND=(-10)
GCL_HCURSOR=(-12)
GCL_HICON=(-14)
GCL_HMODULE=(-16)
GCL_MENUNAME=(-8)
GCL_REVERSE_LENGTH=&H3
GCL_REVERSECONVERSION=&H2
GCL_STYLE=(-26)
GCL_WNDPROC=(-24)
GCP_CLASSIN=&H80000
GCP_DBCS=&H1
GCP_DIACRITIC=&H100
GCP_DISPLAYZWG=&H400000
GCP_ERROR=&H8000
GCP_GLYPHSHAPE=&H10
GCP_JUSTIFY=&H10000
GCP_JUSTIFYIN=&H200000
GCP_KASHIDA=&H400
GCP_LIGATE=&H20
GCP_MAXEXTENT=&H100000
GCP_NEUTRALOVERRIDE=&H2000000
GCP_NODIACRITICS=&H20000
GCP_NUMERICOVERRIDE=&H1000000
GCP_NUMERICSLATIN=&H4000000
GCP_NUMERICSLOCAL=&H8000000
GCP_REORDER=&H2
GCP_SYMSWAPOFF=&H800000
GCP_USEKERNING=&H8
GCPCLASS_ARABIC=2
GCPCLASS_HEBREW=2
GCPCLASS_LATIN=1
GCPCLASS_LATINNUMBER=5
GCPCLASS_LATINNUMERICSEPARATOR=7
GCPCLASS_LATINNUMERICTERMINATOR=6
GCPCLASS_LOCALNUMBER=4
GCPCLASS_NEUTRAL=3
GCPCLASS_NUMERICSEPARATOR=8
GCPCLASS_PREBOUNDLTR=&H40
GCPCLASS_PREBOUNDRTL=&H80
GCS_COMPATTR=&H10
GCS_COMPCLAUSE=&H20
```

```
GCS_COMPREADATTR=&H2
GCS_COMPREADCLAUSE=&H4
GCS_COMPREADSTR=&H1
GCS_COMPSTR=&H8
GCS_CURSORPOS=&H80
GCS_DELTASTART=&H100
GCS_RESULTCLAUSE=&H1000
GCS_RESULTREADCLAUSE=&H400
GCS_RESULTREADSTR=&H200
GCS_RESULTSTR=&H800
GCW_ATOM=(-32)
GDI_ERROR=&HFFFF
GENERIC_ALL=&H10000000
GENERIC_EXECUTE=&H20000000
GENERIC_READ=&H80000000
GENERIC_WRITE=&H40000000
GET_TAPE_DRIVE_INFORMATION=1
GET_TAPE_MEDIA_INFORMATION=0
GETCOLORTABLE=5
GETDEVICEUNITS=42
GETEXTENDEDTEXTMETRICS=256
GETEXTENTTABLE=257
GETFACENAME=513
GETPAIRKERNTABLE=258
GETPENWIDTH=16
GETPHYSPAGESIZE=12
GETPRINTINGOFFSET=13
GETSCALINGFACTOR=14
GETSETPAPERBINS=29
GETSETPAPERMETRICS=35
GETSETPRINTORIENT=30
GETSETSCREENPARAMS=3072
GETTECHNOLGY=20
GETTECHNOLOGY=20
GETTRACKKERNTABLE=259
GETVECTORBRUSHSIZE=27
GETVECTORPENSIZE=26
GGL_INDEX=&H2
GGL_LEVEL=&H1
GGL_PRIVATE=&H4
GGL_STRING=&H3
GGO_BITMAP=1
GGO_GLYPH_INDEX=&H80
GGO_GRAY2_BITMAP=4
GGO_GRAY4_BITMAP=5
GGO_GRAY8_BITMAP=6
GGO_METRICS=0
GGO_NATIVE=2
```

```
GHND=(GMEM_MOVEABLE Or GMEM_ZEROINIT)
GL_ID_CANNOTSAVE=&H11
GL_ID_CHOOSECANDIDATE=&H28
GL_ID_INPUTCODE=&H26
GL_ID_INPUTRADICAL=&H25
GL_ID_INPUTREADING=&H24
GL_ID_INPUTSYMBOL=&H27
GL_ID_NOCONVERT=&H20
GL_ID_NODICTIONARY=&H10
GL_ID_NOMODULE=&H1
GL_ID_PRIVATE_FIRST=&H8000
GL_ID_PRIVATE_LAST=&HFFFF
GL_ID_READINGCONFLICT=&H23
GL_ID_REVERSECONVERSION=&H29
GL_ID_TOOMANYSTROKE=&H22
GL_ID_TYPINGERROR=&H21
GL_ID_UNKNOWN=&H0
GL_LEVEL_ERROR=&H2
GL_LEVEL_FATAL=&H1
GL_LEVEL_INFORMATION=&H4
GL_LEVEL_NOGUIDELINE=&H0
GL_LEVEL_WARNING=&H3
GM_ADVANCED=2
GM_COMPATIBLE=1
GM_LAST=2
GMEM_DDESHARE=&H2000
GMEM_DISCARDABLE=&H100
GMEM_DISCARDED=&H4000
GMEM_FIXED=&H0
GMEM_INVALID_HANDLE=&H8000
GMEM_LOCKCOUNT=&HFF
GMEM_LOWER=GMEM_NOT_BANKED
GMEM_MODIFY=&H80
GMEM_MOVEABLE=&H2
GMEM_NOCOMPACT=&H10
GMEM_NODISCARD=&H20
GMEM_NOT_BANKED=&H1000
GMEM_NOTIFY=&H4000
GMEM_SHARE=&H2000
GMEM_VALID_FLAGS=&H7F72
GMEM_ZEROINIT=&H40
GPTR=(GMEM_FIXED Or GMEM_ZEROINIT)
GRAY_BRUSH=2
GREEK_CHARSET=161
GROUP_NAME=&H80
grp1=&H430
grp2=&H431
grp3=&H432
```

```
grp4=&H433
GW_CHILD=5
GW_HWNDFIRST=0
GW_HWNDLAST=1
GW_HWNDNEXT=2
GW_HWNDPREV=3
GW_MAX=5
GW_OWNER=4
GWL_EXSTYLE=(-20)
GWL_HINSTANCE=(-6)
GWL_HWNDPARENT=(-8)
GWL_ID=(-12)
GWL_STYLE=(-16)
GWL_USERDATA=(-21)
GWL_WNDPROC=(-4)

H
HALFTONE=4
HANGEUL_CHARSET=129
HANGUP_COMPLETE=&H5
HANGUP_PENDING=&H4
HC_ACTION=0
HC_GETNEXT=1
HC_NOREM=HC_NOREMOVE
HC_NOREMOVE=3
HC_SKIP=2
HC_SYSMODALOFF=5
HC_SYSMODALON=4
HCBT_ACTIVATE=5
HCBT_CLICKSKIPPED=6
HCBT_CREATEWND=3
HCBT_DESTROYWND=4
HCBT_KEYSKIPPED=7
HCBT_MINMAX=1
HCBT_MOVESIZE=0
HCBT_QS=2
HCBT_SETFOCUS=9
HCBT_SYSCOMMAND=8
HDATA_APPOWNED=&H1
HEBREW_CHARSET=177
HELP_COMMAND=&H102&
HELP_CONTENTS=&H3&
HELP_CONTEXT=&H1 'Display topic in ulTopic
HELP_CONTEXTPOPUP=&H8&
HELP_FORCEFILE=&H9&
HELP_HELPONHELP=&H4 'Display help on using help
HELP_INDEX=&H3 'Display index
HELP_KEY=&H101 'Display topic for keyword in offabData
```

```
HELP_MULTIKEY=&H201&
HELP_PARTIALKEY=&H105&
HELP_QUIT=&H2 'Terminate help
HELP_SETCONTENTS=&H5&
HELP_SETINDEX=&H5 'Set current Index for multiindex help
HELP_SETWINPOS=&H203&
HELPMSGSTRING="commdlg_help"
HGDI_ERROR=&HFFFF
HIDE_WINDOW=0
HIGH_PRIORITY_CLASS=&H80
HKEY_CLASSES_ROOT=&H80000000
HKEY_CURRENT_CONFIG=&H80000005
HKEY_CURRENT_USER=&H80000001
HKEY_DYN_DATA=&H80000006
HKEY_LOCAL_MACHINE=&H80000002
HKEY_PERFORMANCE_DATA=&H80000004
HKEY_USERS=&H80000003
HKL_NEXT=1
HKL_PREV=0
HOLLOW_BRUSH=NULL_BRUSH
HORZRES=8 'Horizontal width in pixels
HORZSIZE=4 'Horizontal size in millimeters
HS_API_MAX=25
HS_BDIAGONAL=3 '/////
HS_BDIAGONAL1=7
HS_CROSS=4 '+++++
HS_DENSE1=9
HS_DENSE2=10
HS_DENSE3=11
HS_DENSE4=12
HS_DENSE5=13
HS_DENSE6=14
HS_DENSE7=15
HS_DENSE8=16
HS_DIAGCROSS=5 'xxxxx
HS_DITHEREDBKCLR=24
HS_DITHEREDCLR=20
HS_DITHEREDTEXTCLR=22
HS_FDIAGONAL=2 '\\\\\
HS_FDIAGONAL1=6
HS_HALFTONE=18
HS_HORIZONTAL=0 '—-
HS_NOSHADE=17
HS_SOLID=8
HS_SOLIDBKCLR=23
HS_SOLIDCLR=19
HS_SOLIDTEXTCLR=21
HS_VERTICAL=1  '|||||
```

```
HSHELL_ACTIVATESHELLWINDOW=3
HSHELL_WINDOWCREATED=1
HSHELL_WINDOWDESTROYED=2
HTBORDER=18
HTBOTTOM=15
HTBOTTOMLEFT=16
HTBOTTOMRIGHT=17
HTCAPTION=2
HTCLIENT=1
HTERROR=(-2)
HTGROWBOX=4
HTHSCROLL=6
HTLEFT=10
HTMAXBUTTON=9
HTMENU=5
HTMINBUTTON=8
HTNOWHERE=0
HTREDUCE=HTMINBUTTON
HTRIGHT=11
HTSIZE=HTGROWBOX
HTSIZEFIRST=HTLEFT
HTSIZELAST=HTBOTTOMRIGHT
HTSYSMENU=3
HTTOP=12
HTTOPLEFT=13
HTTOPRIGHT=14
HTTRANSPARENT=(-1)
HTVSCROLL=7
HTZOOM=HTMAXBUTTON
HWND_BOTTOM=1
HWND_BROADCAST=&HFFFF&
HWND_DESKTOP=0
HWND_NOTOPMOST=-2
HWND_TOP=0
HWND_TOPMOST=-1

I
ICM_OFF=1
ICM_ON=2
ICM_QUERY=3
ico1=&H43C
ico2=&H43D
ico3=&H43E
ico4=&H43F
IDABORT=3
IDC_APPSTARTING=32650&
IDC_ARROW=32512&
IDC_CROSS=32515&
```

```
IDC_IBEAM=32513&
IDC_ICON=32641&
IDC_NO=32648&
IDC_SIZE=32640&
IDC_SIZEALL=32646&
IDC_SIZENESW=32643&
IDC_SIZENS=32645&
IDC_SIZENWSE=32642&
IDC_SIZEWE=32644&
IDC_UPARROW=32516&
IDC_WAIT=32514&
IDCANCEL=2
IDHOT_SNAPDESKTOP=(-2) 'PRINTSCRN
IDHOT_SNAPWINDOW=(-1) 'SHIFT-PRINTSCRN
IDI_APPLICATION=32512&
IDI_ASTERISK=32516&
IDI_EXCLAMATION=32515&
IDI_HAND=32513&
IDI_QUESTION=32514&
IDIGNORE=5
IDLE_PRIORITY_CLASS=&H40
IDNO=7
IDOK=1
IDRETRY=4
IDYES=6
IE_BADID=(-1)  'Invalid or unsupported id
IE_BAUDRATE=(-12) 'Unsupported BaudRate
IE_BYTESIZE=(-11) 'Illegal Byte Size
IE_DEFAULT=(-5) 'Error in default parameters
IE_HARDWARE=(-10) 'Hardware Not Present
IE_MEMORY=(-4) 'Unable to allocate queues
IE_NOPEN=(-3)  'Device Not Open
IE_OPEN=(-2) 'Device Already Open
IGNORE=0 'Ignore signal
IGP_CONVERSION=&H8
IGP_PROPERTY=&H4
IGP_SELECT=&H18
IGP_SENTENCE=&HC
IGP_SETCOMPSTR=&H14
IGP_UI=&H10
ILLUMINANT_A=1
ILLUMINANT_B=2
ILLUMINANT_C=3
ILLUMINANT_D50=4
ILLUMINANT_D55=5
ILLUMINANT_D65=6
ILLUMINANT_D75=7
ILLUMINANT_DAYLIGHT=ILLUMINANT_C
```

```
ILLUMINANT_DEVICE_DEFAULT=0
ILLUMINANT_F2=8
ILLUMINANT_FLUORESCENT=ILLUMINANT_F2
ILLUMINANT_MAX_INDEX=ILLUMINANT_F2
ILLUMINANT_NTSC=ILLUMINANT_C
ILLUMINANT_TUNGSTEN=ILLUMINANT_A
IMC_CLOSESTATUSWINDOW=&H21
IMC_GETCANDIDATEPOS=&H7
IMC_GETCOMPOSITIONFONT=&H9
IMC_GETCOMPOSITIONWINDOW=&HB
IMC_GETSTATUSWINDOWPOS=&HF
IMC_OPENSTATUSWINDOW=&H22
IMC_SETCANDIDATEPOS=&H8
IMC_SETCOMPOSITIONFONT=&HA
IMC_SETCOMPOSITIONWINDOW=&HC
IMC_SETSTATUSWINDOWPOS=&H10
IME_CAND_CODE=&H2
IME_CAND_MEANING=&H3
IME_CAND_RADICAL=&H4
IME_CAND_READ=&H1
IME_CAND_STROKE=&H5
IME_CAND_UNKNOWN=&H0
IME_CHOTKEY_IME_NONIME_TOGGLE=&H10
IME_CHOTKEY_SHAPE_TOGGLE=&H11
IME_CHOTKEY_SYMBOL_TOGGLE=&H12
IME_CMODE_ALPHANUMERIC=&H0
IME_CMODE_CHARCODE=&H20
IME_CMODE_CHINESE=IME_CMODE_NATIVE
IME_CMODE_EUDC=&H200
IME_CMODE_FULLSHAPE=&H8
IME_CMODE_HANGEUL=IME_CMODE_NATIVE
IME_CMODE_HANJACONVERT=&H40
IME_CMODE_JAPANESE=IME_CMODE_NATIVE
IME_CMODE_KATAKANA=&H2 'only effect under IME_CMODE_NATIVE
IME_CMODE_LANGUAGE=&H3
IME_CMODE_NATIVE=&H1
IME_CMODE_NOCONVERSION=&H100
IME_CMODE_ROMAN=&H10
IME_CMODE_SOFTKBD=&H80
IME_CMODE_SYMBOL=&H400
IME_CONFIG_GENERAL=1
IME_CONFIG_REGISTERWORD=2
IME_CONFIG_SELECTDICTIONARY=3
IME_ESC_GET_EUDC_DICTIONARY=&H1003
IME_ESC_HANJA_MODE=&H1008
IME_ESC_IME_NAME=&H1006
IME_ESC_MAX_KEY=&H1005
IME_ESC_PRIVATE_FIRST=&H800
```

```
IME_ESC_PRIVATE_LAST=&HFFF
IME_ESC_QUERY_SUPPORT=&H3
IME_ESC_RESERVED_FIRST=&H4
IME_ESC_RESERVED_LAST=&H7FF
IME_ESC_SEQUENCE_TO_INTERNAL=&H1001
IME_ESC_SET_EUDC_DICTIONARY=&H1004
IME_ESC_SYNC_HOTKEY=&H1007
IME_HOTKEY_DSWITCH_FIRST=&H100
IME_HOTKEY_DSWITCH_LAST=&H11F
IME_ITHOTKEY_PREVIOUS_COMPOSITION=&H201
IME_ITHOTKEY_RESEND_RESULTSTR=&H200
IME_ITHOTKEY_UISTYLE_TOGGLE=&H202
IME_JHOTKEY_CLOSE_OPEN=&H30
IME_KHOTKEY_ENGLISH=&H52
IME_KHOTKEY_HANJACONVERT=&H51
IME_KHOTKEY_SHAPE_TOGGLE=&H50
IME_PROP_AT_CARET=&H10000
IME_PROP_CANDLIST_START_FROM_1=&H40000
IME_PROP_SPECIAL_UI=&H20000
IME_PROP_UNICODE=&H80000
IME_REGWORD_STYLE_EUDC=&H1
IME_REGWORD_STYLE_USER_FIRST=&H80000000
IME_REGWORD_STYLE_USER_LAST=&HFFFF
IME_SMODE_AUTOMATIC=&H4
IME_SMODE_NONE=&H0
IME_SMODE_PHRASEPREDICT=&H8
IME_SMODE_PLAURALCLAUSE=&H1
IME_SMODE_SINGLECONVERT=&H2
IME_THOTKEY_IME_NONIME_TOGGLE=&H70
IME_THOTKEY_SHAPE_TOGGLE=&H71
IME_THOTKEY_SYMBOL_TOGGLE=&H72
IMM_ERROR_GENERAL=(-2)
IMM_ERROR_NODATA=(-1)
IMN_CHANGECANDIDATE=&H3
IMN_CLOSECANDIDATE=&H4
IMN_CLOSESTATUSWINDOW=&H1
IMN_GUIDELINE=&HD
IMN_OPENCANDIDATE=&H5
IMN_OPENSTATUSWINDOW=&H2
IMN_PRIVATE=&HE
IMN_SETCANDIDATEPOS=&H9
IMN_SETCOMPOSITIONFONT=&HA
IMN_SETCOMPOSITIONWINDOW=&HB
IMN_SETCONVERSIONMODE=&H6
IMN_SETOPENSTATUS=&H8
IMN_SETSENTENCEMODE=&H7
IMN_SETSTATUSWINDOWPOS=&HC
INFINITE=&HFFFF 'Infinite timeout
```

```
INHERIT_ONLY_ACE=&H8
INPLACE_E_FIRST=&H800401A0
INPLACE_E_LAST=&H800401AF
INPLACE_E_NOTOOLSPACE=&H800401A1
INPLACE_E_NOTUNDOABLE=&H800401A0
INPLACE_S_FIRST=&H401A0
INPLACE_S_LAST=&H401AF
INPLACE_S_TRUNCATED=&H401A0
INVALID_HANDLE_VALUE=-1
IO_COMPLETION_ALL_ACCESS=(STANDARD_RIGHTS_REQUIRED Or
                                SYNCHRONIZE Or &H3)
IO_COMPLETION_MODIFY_STATE=&H2
ISC_SHOWUIALL=&HC000000F
ISC_SHOWUIALLCANDIDATEWINDOW=&HF
ISC_SHOWUICANDIDATEWINDOW=&H1
ISC_SHOWUICOMPOSITIONWINDOW=&H80000000
ISC_SHOWUIGUIDELINE=&H40000000
ITALIC_FONTTYPE=&H200


J
JOB_ACCESS_ADMINISTER=&H10
JOB_ALL_ACCESS=(STANDARD_RIGHTS_REQUIRED Or
                   JOB_ACCESS_ADMINISTER)
JOB_CONTROL_CANCEL=3
JOB_CONTROL_DELETE=5
JOB_CONTROL_PAUSE=1
JOB_CONTROL_RESTART=4
JOB_CONTROL_RESUME=2
JOB_EXECUTE=(STANDARD_RIGHTS_EXECUTE Or
               JOB_ACCESS_ADMINISTER)
JOB_POSITION_UNSPECIFIED=0
JOB_READ=(STANDARD_RIGHTS_READ Or
             JOB_ACCESS_ADMINISTER)
JOB_STATUS_DELETING=&H4
JOB_STATUS_ERROR=&H2
JOB_STATUS_OFFLINE=&H20
JOB_STATUS_PAPEROUT=&H40
JOB_STATUS_PAUSED=&H1
JOB_STATUS_PRINTED=&H80
JOB_STATUS_PRINTING=&H10
JOB_STATUS_SPOOLING=&H8
JOB_STATUS_USER_INTERVENTION=&H10000
JOB_WRITE=(STANDARD_RIGHTS_WRITE Or JOB_ACCESS_ADMINISTER)
JOHAB_CHARSET=130
JOY_BUTTON1=&H1
JOY_BUTTON10=&H200&
JOY_BUTTON11=&H400&
JOY_BUTTON12=&H800&
```

```
JOY_BUTTON13=&H1000&
JOY_BUTTON14=&H2000&
JOY_BUTTON15=&H4000&
JOY_BUTTON16=&H8000&
JOY_BUTTON17=&H10000
JOY_BUTTON18=&H20000
JOY_BUTTON19=&H40000
JOY_BUTTON1CHG=&H100
JOY_BUTTON2=&H2
JOY_BUTTON20=&H80000
JOY_BUTTON21=&H100000
JOY_BUTTON22=&H200000
JOY_BUTTON23=&H400000
JOY_BUTTON24=&H800000
JOY_BUTTON25=&H1000000
JOY_BUTTON26=&H2000000
JOY_BUTTON27=&H4000000
JOY_BUTTON28=&H8000000
JOY_BUTTON29=&H10000000
JOY_BUTTON2CHG=&H200
JOY_BUTTON3=&H4
JOY_BUTTON30=&H20000000
JOY_BUTTON31=&H40000000
JOY_BUTTON32=&H80000000
JOY_BUTTON3CHG=&H400
JOY_BUTTON4=&H8
JOY_BUTTON4CHG=&H800
JOY_BUTTON5=&H10&
JOY_BUTTON6=&H20&
JOY_BUTTON7=&H40&
JOY_BUTTON8=&H80&
JOY_BUTTON9=&H100&
JOY_CAL_READ3=&H40000
JOY_CAL_READ4=&H80000
JOY_CAL_READ5=&H400000
JOY_CAL_READ6=&H800000
JOY_CAL_READALWAYS=&H10000
JOY_CAL_READRONLY=&H2000000
JOY_CAL_READUONLY=&H4000000
JOY_CAL_READVONLY=&H8000000
JOY_CAL_READXONLY=&H100000
JOY_CAL_READXYONLY=&H20000
JOY_CAL_READYONLY=&H200000
JOY_CAL_READZONLY=&H1000000
JOY_POVBACKWARD=18000
JOY_POVCENTERED=-1
JOY_POVFORWARD=0
JOY_POVLEFT=27000
```

```
JOY_POVRIGHT=9000
JOY_RETURNALL=(JOY_RETURNX Or JOY_RETURNY Or
                   JOY_RETURNZ Or JOY_RETURNR Or
                   JOY_RETURNU Or JOY_RETURNV Or
                   JOY_RETURNPOV Or JOY_RETURNBUTTONS)
JOY_RETURNBUTTONS=&H80&
JOY_RETURNCENTERED=&H400&
JOY_RETURNPOV=&H40&
JOY_RETURNPOVCTS=&H200&
JOY_RETURNR=&H8&
JOY_RETURNRAWDATA=&H100&
JOY_RETURNU=&H10   'axis 5
JOY_RETURNV=&H20   'axis 6
JOY_RETURNX=&H1&
JOY_RETURNY=&H2&
JOY_RETURNZ=&H4&
JOY_USEDEADZONE=&H800&
JOYERR_BASE=160
JOYERR_NOCANDO=(JOYERR_BASE+6) 'request not completed
JOYERR_NOERROR=(0)  'no error
JOYERR_PARMS=(JOYERR_BASE+5) 'bad parameters
JOYERR_UNPLUGGED=(JOYERR_BASE+7) 'joystick is unplugged
JOYSTICKID1=0
JOYSTICKID2=1


K
KEY_ALL_ACCESS=((STANDARD_RIGHTS_ALL Or
                   KEY_QUERY_VALUE Or KEY_SET_VALUE Or
                   KEY_CREATE_SUB_KEY Or
                   KEY_ENUMERATE_SUB_KEYS Or KEY_NOTIFY Or
                   KEY_CREATE_LINK) And (Not SYNCHRONIZE))
KEY_CREATE_LINK=&H20
KEY_CREATE_SUB_KEY=&H4
KEY_ENUMERATE_SUB_KEYS=&H8
KEY_EVENT=&H1 'Event contains key event record
KEY_EXECUTE=((KEY_READ) And (Not SYNCHRONIZE))
KEY_EXECUTE=(KEY_READ)
KEY_NOTIFY=&H10
KEY_QUERY_VALUE=&H1
KEY_READ=((STANDARD_RIGHTS_READ Or KEY_QUERY_VALUE Or
            KEY_ENUMERATE_SUB_KEYS Or KEY_NOTIFY) And
            (Not SYNCHRONIZE))
KEY_SET_VALUE=&H2
KEY_WRITE=((STANDARD_RIGHTS_WRITE Or KEY_SET_VALUE Or
              KEY_CREATE_SUB_KEY) And (Not SYNCHRONIZE))
KEYEVENTF_EXTENDEDKEY=&H1
KEYEVENTF_KEYUP=&H2
KF_ALTDOWN=&H2000
```

```
KF_DLGMODE=&H800
KF_EXTENDED=&H100
KF_MENUMODE=&H1000
KF_REPEAT=&H4000
KF_UP=&H8000
KL_NAMELENGTH=9
KLF_ACTIVATE=&H1
KLF_REORDER=&H8
KLF_SUBSTITUTE_OK=&H2
KLF_UNLOADPREVIOUS=&H4

L
LANG_BULGARIAN=&H2
LANG_CHINESE=&H4
LANG_CROATIAN=&H1A
LANG_CZECH=&H5
LANG_DANISH=&H6
LANG_DUTCH=&H13
LANG_ENGLISH=&H9
LANG_FINNISH=&HB
LANG_FRENCH=&HC
LANG_GERMAN=&H7
LANG_GREEK=&H8
LANG_HUNGARIAN=&HE
LANG_ICELANDIC=&HF
LANG_ITALIAN=&H10
LANG_JAPANESE=&H11
LANG_KOREAN=&H12
LANG_NEUTRAL=&H0
LANG_NORWEGIAN=&H14
LANG_POLISH=&H15
LANG_PORTUGUESE=&H16
LANG_ROMANIAN=&H18
LANG_RUSSIAN=&H19
LANG_SLOVAK=&H1B
LANG_SLOVENIAN=&H24
LANG_SPANISH=&HA
LANG_SWEDISH=&H1D
LANG_TURKISH=&H1F
LB_ADDFILE=&H196
LB_ADDSTRING=&H180
LB_CTLCODE=0&
LB_DELETESTRING=&H182
LB_DIR=&H18D
LB_ERR=(-1)
LB_ERRSPACE=(-2)
LB_FINDSTRING=&H18F
LB_FINDSTRINGEXACT=&H1A2
```

```
LB_GETANCHORINDEX=&H19D
LB_GETCARETINDEX=&H19F
LB_GETCOUNT=&H18B
LB_GETCURSEL=&H188
LB_GETHORIZONTALEXTENT=&H193
LB_GETITEMDATA=&H199
LB_GETITEMHEIGHT=&H1A1
LB_GETITEMRECT=&H198
LB_GETLOCALE=&H1A6
LB_GETSEL=&H187
LB_GETSELCOUNT=&H190
LB_GETSELITEMS=&H191
LB_GETTEXT=&H189
LB_GETTEXTLEN=&H18A
LB_GETTOPINDEX=&H18E
LB_INSERTSTRING=&H181
LB_MSGMAX=&H1A8
LB_OKAY=0
LB_RESETCONTENT=&H184
LB_SELECTSTRING=&H18C
LB_SELITEMRANGE=&H19B
LB_SELITEMRANGEEX=&H183
LB_SETANCHORINDEX=&H19C
LB_SETCARETINDEX=&H19E
LB_SETCOLUMNWIDTH=&H195
LB_SETCOUNT=&H1A7
LB_SETCURSEL=&H186
LB_SETHORIZONTALEXTENT=&H194
LB_SETITEMDATA=&H19A
LB_SETITEMHEIGHT=&H1A0
LB_SETLOCALE=&H1A5
LB_SETSEL=&H185
LB_SETTABSTOPS=&H192
LB_SETTOPINDEX=&H197
LBN_DBLCLK=2
LBN_ERRSPACE=(-2)
LBN_KILLFOCUS=5
LBN_SELCANCEL=3
LBN_SELCHANGE=1
LBN_SETFOCUS=4
LBS_DISABLENOSCROLL=&H1000&
LBS_EXTENDEDSEL=&H800&
LBS_HASSTRINGS=&H40&
LBS_MULTICOLUMN=&H200&
LBS_MULTIPLESEL=&H8&
LBS_NODATA=&H2000&
LBS_NOINTEGRALHEIGHT=&H100&
LBS_NOREDRAW=&H4&
```

```
LBS_NOTIFY=&H1&
LBS_OWNERDRAWFIXED=&H10&
LBS_OWNERDRAWVARIABLE=&H20&
LBS_SORT=&H2&
LBS_STANDARD=(LBS_NOTIFY Or LBS_SORT Or
                WS_VSCROLL Or WS_BORDER)
LBS_USETABSTOPS=&H80&
LBS_WANTKEYBOARDINPUT=&H400&
LBSELCHSTRING="commdlg_LBSelChangedNotify"
LC_INTERIORS=128 'Can do interiors
LC_MARKER=4 'Can do markers
LC_NONE=0   'Lines not supported
LC_POLYLINE=2 'Can do polylines
LC_POLYMARKER=8 'Can do polymarkers
LC_STYLED=32 'Can do styled lines
LC_WIDE=16 'Can do wide lines
LC_WIDESTYLED=64 'Can do wide styled lines
LCMAP_BYTEREV=&H800 'byte reversal
LCMAP_LOWERCASE=&H100 'lowercase letters
LCMAP_SORTKEY=&H400 'WC sort key (normalize)
LCMAP_UPPERCASE=&H200 'uppercase letters
LEFT_ALT_PRESSED=&H2 'the left alt key is pressed.
LEFT_CTRL_PRESSED=&H8 'the left ctrl key is pressed.
LF_FACESIZE=32
LF_FULLFACESIZE=64
LHND=(LMEM_MOVEABLE+LMEM_ZEROINIT)
LINECAPS=30 'Line capabilities
LISTEN_OUTSTANDING=&H1
LMEM_DISCARDABLE=&HF00
LMEM_DISCARDED=&H4000
LMEM_FIXED=&H0
LMEM_INVALID_HANDLE=&H8000
LMEM_LOCKCOUNT=&HFF
LMEM_MODIFY=&H80
LMEM_MOVEABLE=&H2
LMEM_NOCOMPACT=&H10
LMEM_NODISCARD=&H20
LMEM_VALID_FLAGS=&HF72
LMEM_ZEROINIT=&H40
LNOTIFY_DISCARD=2
LNOTIFY_MOVE=1
LNOTIFY_OUTOFMEM=0
LOAD_DLL_DEBUG_EVENT=6
LOCALE_ICENTURY=&H24 'century format specifier
LOCALE_ICOUNTRY=&H5 'country code
LOCALE_ICURRDIGITS=&H19 '# local monetary digits
LOCALE_ICURRENCY=&H1B 'positive currency mode
LOCALE_IDATE=&H21 'short date format ordering
```

```
LOCALE_IDAYLZERO=&H26 'leading zeros in day field
LOCALE_IDEFAULTCODEPAGE=&HB 'default code page
LOCALE_IDEFAULTCOUNTRY=&HA 'default country code
LOCALE_IDEFAULTLANGUAGE=&H9 'default language id
LOCALE_IDIGITS=&H11 'number of fractional digits
LOCALE_IINTLCURRDIGITS=&H1A '# intl monetary digits
LOCALE_ILANGUAGE=&H1 'language id
LOCALE_ILDATE=&H22 'long date format ordering
LOCALE_ILZERO=&H12 'leading zeros for decimal
LOCALE_IMEASURE=&HD '0=metric, 1=US
LOCALE_IMONLZERO=&H27 'leading zeros in month field
LOCALE_INEGCURR=&H1C 'negative currency mode
LOCALE_INEGSEPBYSPACE=&H57 'mon sym sep by space from neg amt
LOCALE_INEGSIGNPOSN=&H53 'negative sign position
LOCALE_INEGSYMPRECEDES=&H56 'mon sym precedes neg amt
LOCALE_IPOSSEPBYSPACE=&H55 'mon sym sep by space from pos amt
LOCALE_IPOSSIGNPOSN=&H52 'positive sign position
LOCALE_IPOSSYMPRECEDES=&H54 'mon sym precedes pos amt
LOCALE_ITIME=&H23 'time format specifier
LOCALE_ITLZERO=&H25 'leading zeros in time field
LOCALE_NOUSEROVERRIDE=&H80000000  'do not use user overrides
LOCALE_S1159=&H28 'AM designator
LOCALE_S2359=&H29 'PM designator
LOCALE_SABBREVCTRYNAME=&H7 'abbreviated country name
LOCALE_SABBREVDAYNAME1=&H31 'abbreviated name for Monday
LOCALE_SABBREVDAYNAME2=&H32 'abbreviated name for Tuesday
LOCALE_SABBREVDAYNAME3=&H33 'abbreviated name for Wednesday
LOCALE_SABBREVDAYNAME4=&H34 'abbreviated name for Thursday
LOCALE_SABBREVDAYNAME5=&H35 'abbreviated name for Friday
LOCALE_SABBREVDAYNAME6=&H36 'abbreviated name for Saturday
LOCALE_SABBREVDAYNAME7=&H37 'abbreviated name for Sunday
LOCALE_SABBREVLANGNAME=&H3 'abbreviated language name
LOCALE_SABBREVMONTHNAME1=&H44 'abbreviated name for January
LOCALE_SABBREVMONTHNAME10=&H4D 'abbreviated name for October
LOCALE_SABBREVMONTHNAME11=&H4E 'abbreviated name for November
LOCALE_SABBREVMONTHNAME12=&H4F 'abbreviated name for December
LOCALE_SABBREVMONTHNAME13=&H100F
LOCALE_SABBREVMONTHNAME2=&H45 'abbreviated name for February
LOCALE_SABBREVMONTHNAME3=&H46 'abbreviated name for March
LOCALE_SABBREVMONTHNAME4=&H47 'abbreviated name for April
LOCALE_SABBREVMONTHNAME5=&H48 'abbreviated name for May
LOCALE_SABBREVMONTHNAME6=&H49 'abbreviated name for June
LOCALE_SABBREVMONTHNAME7=&H4A 'abbreviated name for July
LOCALE_SABBREVMONTHNAME8=&H4B 'abbreviated name for August
LOCALE_SABBREVMONTHNAME9=&H4C 'abbreviated name for September
LOCALE_SCOUNTRY=&H6 'localized name of country
LOCALE_SCURRENCY=&H14 'local monetary symbol
LOCALE_SDATE=&H1D 'date separator
```

```
LOCALE_SDAYNAME1=&H2A 'long name for Monday
LOCALE_SDAYNAME2=&H2B 'long name for Tuesday
LOCALE_SDAYNAME3=&H2C 'long name for Wednesday
LOCALE_SDAYNAME4=&H2D 'long name for Thursday
LOCALE_SDAYNAME5=&H2E 'long name for Friday
LOCALE_SDAYNAME6=&H2F 'long name for Saturday
LOCALE_SDAYNAME7=&H30 'long name for Sunday
LOCALE_SDECIMAL=&HE 'decimal separator
LOCALE_SENGCOUNTRY=&H1002 'English name of country
LOCALE_SENGLANGUAGE=&H1001 'English name of language
LOCALE_SGROUPING=&H10 'digit grouping
LOCALE_SINTLSYMBOL=&H15 'intl monetary symbol
LOCALE_SLANGUAGE=&H2 'localized name of language
LOCALE_SLIST=&HC 'list item separator
LOCALE_SLONGDATE=&H20 'long date format string
LOCALE_SMONDECIMALSEP=&H16 'monetary decimal separator
LOCALE_SMONGROUPING=&H18 'monetary grouping
LOCALE_SMONTHNAME1=&H38 'long name for January
LOCALE_SMONTHNAME10=&H41 'long name for October
LOCALE_SMONTHNAME11=&H42 'long name for November
LOCALE_SMONTHNAME12=&H43 'long name for December
LOCALE_SMONTHNAME2=&H39 'long name for February
LOCALE_SMONTHNAME3=&H3A 'long name for March
LOCALE_SMONTHNAME4=&H3B 'long name for April
LOCALE_SMONTHNAME5=&H3C 'long name for May
LOCALE_SMONTHNAME6=&H3D 'long name for June
LOCALE_SMONTHNAME7=&H3E 'long name for July
LOCALE_SMONTHNAME8=&H3F 'long name for August
LOCALE_SMONTHNAME9=&H40 'long name for September
LOCALE_SMONTHOUSANDSEP=&H17 'monetary thousand separator
LOCALE_SNATIVECTRYNAME=&H8 'native name of country
LOCALE_SNATIVEDIGITS=&H13 'native ascii 0-9
LOCALE_SNATIVELANGNAME=&H4 'native name of language
LOCALE_SNEGATIVESIGN=&H51 'negative sign
LOCALE_SPOSITIVESIGN=&H50 'positive sign
LOCALE_SSHORTDATE=&H1F 'short date format string
LOCALE_STHOUSAND=&HF 'thousand separator
LOCALE_STIME=&H1E 'time separator
LOCALE_STIMEFORMAT=&H1003 'time format string
LOCKFILE_EXCLUSIVE_LOCK=&H2
LOCKFILE_FAIL_IMMEDIATELY=&H1
LOGON32_LOGON_BATCH=4
LOGON32_LOGON_INTERACTIVE=2
LOGON32_LOGON_SERVICE=5
LOGON32_PROVIDER_DEFAULT=0
LOGON32_PROVIDER_WINNT35=1
LOGPIXELSX=88 'Logical pixels/inch in X
LOGPIXELSY=90 'Logical pixels/inch in Y
```

```
LPTR=(LMEM_FIXED+LMEM_ZEROINIT)
LPTx=&H80 'Set if ID is for LPT device
lst1=&H460
lst10=&H469
lst11=&H46A
lst12=&H46B
lst13=&H46C
lst14=&H46D
lst15=&H46E
lst16=&H46F
lst2=&H461
lst3=&H462
lst4=&H463
lst5=&H464
lst6=&H465
lst7=&H466
lst8=&H467
lst9=&H468
LTGRAY_BRUSH=1
LZERROR_BADINHANDLE=(-1)  'invalid input handle
LZERROR_BADOUTHANDLE=(-2) 'invalid output handle
LZERROR_BADVALUE=(-7) 'input parameter out of range
LZERROR_GLOBLOCK=(-6) 'bad Global handle
LZERROR_PUBLICLOC=(-5) 'insufficient memory for LZFile struct
LZERROR_READ=(-3) 'corrupt compressed file format
LZERROR_UNKNOWNALG=(-8) 'compression algorithm not recognized
LZERROR_WRITE=(-4) 'out of space for output file

M
MA_ACTIVATE=1
MA_ACTIVATEANDEAT=2
MA_NOACTIVATE=3
MA_NOACTIVATEANDEAT=4
MAC_CHARSET=77
MAILSLOT_NO_MESSAGE=(-1)
MAILSLOT_WAIT_FOREVER=(-1)
MAP_COMPOSITE=&H40 'convert to composite chars
MAP_FOLDCZONE=&H10 'fold compatibility zone chars
MAP_FOLDDIGITS=&H80 'all digits to ASCII 0-9
MAP_PRECOMPOSED=&H20 'convert to precomposed chars
MARKPARITY=3
MARSHAL_E_FIRST=&H80040120
MARSHAL_E_LAST=&H8004012F
MARSHAL_S_FIRST=&H40120
MARSHAL_S_LAST=&H4012F
MAX_DEFAULTCHAR=2
MAX_LANA=254  'lana's in range 0 to MAX_LANA
MAX_LEADBYTES=12  '5 ranges, 2 bytes ea., 0 term.
```

```
MAX_MONITORS=4
MAX_PATH=260
MAX_PRIORITY=99
MAXByte=&HFF
MAXCHAR=&H7F
MAXDWORD=&HFFFF
MAXERRORLENGTH=128  'max error text length (including NULL)
MAXIMUM_ALLOWED=&H2000000
MAXLONG=&H7FFFFFFF
MAXPNAMELEN=32  'max product name length (including NULL)
MAXSHORT=&H7FFF
MAXSTRETCHBLTMODE=4
MAXWORD=&HFFFF
MB_ABORTRETRYIGNORE=&H2&
MB_APPLMODAL=&H0&
MB_COMPOSITE=&H2 'use composite chars
MB_DEFAULT_DESKTOP_ONLY=&H20000
MB_DEFBUTTON1=&H0&
MB_DEFBUTTON2=&H100&
MB_DEFBUTTON3=&H200&
MB_DEFMASK=&HF00&
MB_ICONASTERISK=&H40&
MB_ICONEXCLAMATION=&H30&
MB_ICONHAND=&H10&
MB_ICONINFORMATION=MB_ICONASTERISK
MB_ICONMASK=&HF0&
MB_ICONQUESTION=&H20&
MB_ICONSTOP=MB_ICONHAND
MB_MISCMASK=&HC000&
MB_MODEMASK=&H3000&
MB_NOFOCUS=&H8000&
MB_OK=&H0&
MB_OKCANCEL=&H1&
MB_PRECOMPOSED=&H1 'use precomposed chars
MB_RETRYCANCEL=&H5&
MB_SETFOREGROUND=&H10000
MB_SYSTEMMODAL=&H1000&
MB_TASKMODAL=&H2000&
MB_TYPEMASK=&HF&
MB_USEGLYPHCHARS=&H4 'use glyph chars, not ctrl chars
MB_YESNO=&H4&
MB_YESNOCANCEL=&H3&
MCI_ALL_DEVICE_ID=-1 'Matches all MCI devices
MCI_ANIM_GETDEVCAPS_CAN_REVERSE=&H4001&
MCI_ANIM_GETDEVCAPS_CAN_STRETCH=&H4007&
MCI_ANIM_GETDEVCAPS_FAST_RATE=&H4002&
MCI_ANIM_GETDEVCAPS_MAX_WINDOWS=&H4008&
MCI_ANIM_GETDEVCAPS_NORMAL_RATE=&H4004&
```

```
MCI_ANIM_GETDEVCAPS_PALETTES=&H4006&
MCI_ANIM_GETDEVCAPS_SLOW_RATE=&H4003&
MCI_ANIM_INFO_TEXT=&H10000
MCI_ANIM_OPEN_NOSTATIC=&H40000
MCI_ANIM_OPEN_PARENT=&H20000
MCI_ANIM_OPEN_WS=&H10000
MCI_ANIM_PLAY_FAST=&H40000
MCI_ANIM_PLAY_REVERSE=&H20000
MCI_ANIM_PLAY_SCAN=&H100000
MCI_ANIM_PLAY_SLOW=&H80000
MCI_ANIM_PLAY_SPEED=&H10000
MCI_ANIM_PUT_DESTINATION=&H40000 'also  MCI_WHERE
MCI_ANIM_PUT_SOURCE=&H20000 'also  MCI_WHERE
MCI_ANIM_REALIZE_BKGD=&H20000
MCI_ANIM_REALIZE_NORM=&H10000
MCI_ANIM_RECT=&H10000
MCI_ANIM_STATUS_FORWARD=&H4002&
MCI_ANIM_STATUS_HPAL=&H4004&
MCI_ANIM_STATUS_HWND=&H4003&
MCI_ANIM_STATUS_SPEED=&H4001&
MCI_ANIM_STATUS_STRETCH=&H4005&
MCI_ANIM_STEP_FRAMES=&H20000
MCI_ANIM_STEP_REVERSE=&H10000
MCI_ANIM_UPDATE_HDC=&H20000
MCI_ANIM_WHERE_DESTINATION=&H40000
MCI_ANIM_WHERE_SOURCE=&H20000
MCI_ANIM_WINDOW_DEFAULT=&H0&
MCI_ANIM_WINDOW_DISABLE_STRETCH=&H200000
MCI_ANIM_WINDOW_ENABLE_STRETCH=&H100000
MCI_ANIM_WINDOW_HWND=&H10000
MCI_ANIM_WINDOW_STATE=&H40000
MCI_ANIM_WINDOW_TEXT=&H80000
MCI_BREAK=&H811
MCI_BREAK_HWND=&H200&
MCI_BREAK_KEY=&H100&
MCI_BREAK_OFF=&H400&
MCI_CD_OFFSET=1088
MCI_CLOSE=&H804
MCI_COPY=&H852
MCI_CUE=&H830
MCI_CUT=&H851
MCI_DELETE=&H856
MCI_DEVTYPE_ANIMATION=519
MCI_DEVTYPE_CD_AUDIO=516
MCI_DEVTYPE_DAT=517
MCI_DEVTYPE_DIGITAL_VIDEO=520
MCI_DEVTYPE_FIRST=MCI_DEVTYPE_VCR
MCI_DEVTYPE_FIRST_USER=&H1000
```

```
MCI_DEVTYPE_LAST=MCI_DEVTYPE_SEQUENCER
MCI_DEVTYPE_OTHER=521
MCI_DEVTYPE_OVERLAY=515
MCI_DEVTYPE_SCANNER=518
MCI_DEVTYPE_SEQUENCER=523
MCI_DEVTYPE_VCR=513
MCI_DEVTYPE_VIDEODISC=514
MCI_DEVTYPE_WAVEFORM_AUDIO=522
MCI_ESCAPE=&H805
MCI_FIRST=&H800
MCI_FORMAT_BYTES=8
MCI_FORMAT_FRAMES=3
MCI_FORMAT_HMS=1
MCI_FORMAT_MILLISECONDS=0
MCI_FORMAT_MSF=2
MCI_FORMAT_SAMPLES=9
MCI_FORMAT_SMPTE_24=4
MCI_FORMAT_SMPTE_25=5
MCI_FORMAT_SMPTE_30=6
MCI_FORMAT_SMPTE_30DROP=7
MCI_FORMAT_TMSF=10
MCI_FREEZE=&H844
MCI_FROM=&H4&
MCI_GETDEVCAPS=&H80B
MCI_GETDEVCAPS_CAN_EJECT=&H7&
MCI_GETDEVCAPS_CAN_PLAY=&H8&
MCI_GETDEVCAPS_CAN_RECORD=&H1&
MCI_GETDEVCAPS_CAN_SAVE=&H9&
MCI_GETDEVCAPS_COMPOUND_DEVICE=&H6&
MCI_GETDEVCAPS_DEVICE_TYPE=&H4&
MCI_GETDEVCAPS_HAS_AUDIO=&H2&
MCI_GETDEVCAPS_HAS_VIDEO=&H3&
MCI_GETDEVCAPS_ITEM=&H100&
MCI_GETDEVCAPS_USES_FILES=&H5&
MCI_INFO=&H80A
MCI_INFO_FILE=&H200&
MCI_INFO_PRODUCT=&H100&
MCI_LAST=&HFFF
MCI_LOAD=&H850
MCI_LOAD_FILE=&H100&
MCI_MODE_NOT_READY=(MCI_STRING_OFFSET+12)
MCI_MODE_OPEN=(MCI_STRING_OFFSET+18)
MCI_MODE_PAUSE=(MCI_STRING_OFFSET+17)
MCI_MODE_PLAY=(MCI_STRING_OFFSET+14)
MCI_MODE_RECORD=(MCI_STRING_OFFSET+15)
MCI_MODE_SEEK=(MCI_STRING_OFFSET+16)
MCI_MODE_STOP=(MCI_STRING_OFFSET+13)
MCI_NOTIFY=&H1&
```

```
MCI_NOTIFY_ABORTED=&H4
MCI_NOTIFY_FAILURE=&H8
MCI_NOTIFY_SUCCESSFUL=&H1
MCI_NOTIFY_SUPERSEDED=&H2
MCI_OPEN=&H803
MCI_OPEN_ALIAS=&H400&
MCI_OPEN_ELEMENT=&H200&
MCI_OPEN_ELEMENT_ID=&H800&
MCI_OPEN_SHAREABLE=&H100&
MCI_OPEN_TYPE=&H2000&
MCI_OPEN_TYPE_ID=&H1000&
MCI_OVLY_GETDEVCAPS_CAN_FREEZE=&H4002&
MCI_OVLY_GETDEVCAPS_CAN_STRETCH=&H4001&
MCI_OVLY_GETDEVCAPS_MAX_WINDOWS=&H4003&
MCI_OVLY_INFO_TEXT=&H10000
MCI_OVLY_OPEN_PARENT=&H20000
MCI_OVLY_OPEN_WS=&H10000
MCI_OVLY_PUT_DESTINATION=&H40000
MCI_OVLY_PUT_FRAME=&H80000
MCI_OVLY_PUT_SOURCE=&H20000
MCI_OVLY_PUT_VIDEO=&H100000
MCI_OVLY_RECT=&H10000
MCI_OVLY_STATUS_HWND=&H4001&
MCI_OVLY_STATUS_STRETCH=&H4002&
MCI_OVLY_WHERE_DESTINATION=&H40000
MCI_OVLY_WHERE_FRAME=&H80000
MCI_OVLY_WHERE_SOURCE=&H20000
MCI_OVLY_WHERE_VIDEO=&H100000
MCI_OVLY_WINDOW_DEFAULT=&H0&
MCI_OVLY_WINDOW_DISABLE_STRETCH=&H200000
MCI_OVLY_WINDOW_ENABLE_STRETCH=&H100000
MCI_OVLY_WINDOW_HWND=&H10000
MCI_OVLY_WINDOW_STATE=&H40000
MCI_OVLY_WINDOW_TEXT=&H80000
MCI_PASTE=&H853
MCI_PAUSE=&H809
MCI_PLAY=&H806
MCI_PUT=&H842
MCI_REALIZE=&H840
MCI_RECORD=&H80F
MCI_RECORD_INSERT=&H100&
MCI_RECORD_OVERWRITE=&H200&
MCI_RESUME=&H855
MCI_SAVE=&H813
MCI_SAVE_FILE=&H100&
MCI_SEEK=&H807
MCI_SEEK_TO_END=&H200&
MCI_SEEK_TO_START=&H100&
```

```
MCI_SEQ_DIV_PPQN=(0+MCI_SEQ_OFFSET)
MCI_SEQ_DIV_SMPTE_24=(1+MCI_SEQ_OFFSET)
MCI_SEQ_DIV_SMPTE_25=(2+MCI_SEQ_OFFSET)
MCI_SEQ_DIV_SMPTE_30=(4+MCI_SEQ_OFFSET)
MCI_SEQ_DIV_SMPTE_30DROP=(3+MCI_SEQ_OFFSET)
MCI_SEQ_FILE=&H4002
MCI_SEQ_FORMAT_SONGPTR=&H4001
MCI_SEQ_MAPPER=65535
MCI_SEQ_MIDI=&H4003
MCI_SEQ_NONE=65533
MCI_SEQ_OFFSET=1216
MCI_SEQ_SET_MASTER=&H80000
MCI_SEQ_SET_OFFSET=&H1000000
MCI_SEQ_SET_PORT=&H20000
MCI_SEQ_SET_SLAVE=&H40000
MCI_SEQ_SET_TEMPO=&H10000
MCI_SEQ_SMPTE=&H4004
MCI_SEQ_STATUS_DIVTYPE=&H400A&
MCI_SEQ_STATUS_MASTER=&H4008&
MCI_SEQ_STATUS_OFFSET=&H4009&
MCI_SEQ_STATUS_PORT=&H4003&
MCI_SEQ_STATUS_SLAVE=&H4007&
MCI_SEQ_STATUS_TEMPO=&H4002&
MCI_SET=&H80D
MCI_SET_AUDIO=&H800&
MCI_SET_AUDIO_ALL=&H4001&
MCI_SET_AUDIO_LEFT=&H4002&
MCI_SET_AUDIO_RIGHT=&H4003&
MCI_SET_DOOR_CLOSED=&H200&
MCI_SET_DOOR_OPEN=&H100&
MCI_SET_OFF=&H4000&
MCI_SET_ON=&H2000&
MCI_SET_TIME_FORMAT=&H400&
MCI_SET_VIDEO=&H1000&
MCI_SOUND=&H812
MCI_SOUND_NAME=&H100&
MCI_SPIN=&H80C
MCI_STATUS=&H814
MCI_STATUS_CURRENT_TRACK=&H8&
MCI_STATUS_ITEM=&H100&
MCI_STATUS_LENGTH=&H1&
MCI_STATUS_MEDIA_PRESENT=&H5&
MCI_STATUS_MODE=&H4&
MCI_STATUS_NUMBER_OF_TRACKS=&H3&
MCI_STATUS_POSITION=&H2&
MCI_STATUS_READY=&H7&
MCI_STATUS_START=&H200&
MCI_STATUS_TIME_FORMAT=&H6&
```

```
MCI_STEP=&H80E
MCI_STOP=&H808
MCI_STRING_OFFSET=512   'if this number is changed you MUST
MCI_SYSINFO=&H810
MCI_SYSINFO_INSTALLNAME=&H800&
MCI_SYSINFO_NAME=&H400&
MCI_SYSINFO_OPEN=&H200&
MCI_SYSINFO_QUANTITY=&H100&
MCI_TO=&H8&
MCI_TRACK=&H10&
MCI_UNFREEZE=&H845
MCI_UPDATE=&H854
MCI_USER_MESSAGES=(&H400+MCI_FIRST)
MCI_VD_ESCAPE_STRING=&H100&
MCI_VD_FORMAT_TRACK=&H4001
MCI_VD_GETDEVCAPS_CAN_REVERSE=&H4002&
MCI_VD_GETDEVCAPS_CAV=&H20000
MCI_VD_GETDEVCAPS_CLV=&H10000
MCI_VD_GETDEVCAPS_FAST_RATE=&H4003&
MCI_VD_GETDEVCAPS_NORMAL_RATE=&H4005&
MCI_VD_GETDEVCAPS_SLOW_RATE=&H4004&
MCI_VD_MEDIA_CAV=(MCI_VD_OFFSET+3)
MCI_VD_MEDIA_CLV=(MCI_VD_OFFSET+2)
MCI_VD_MEDIA_OTHER=(MCI_VD_OFFSET+4)
MCI_VD_MODE_PARK=(MCI_VD_OFFSET+1)
MCI_VD_OFFSET=1024
MCI_VD_PLAY_FAST=&H20000
MCI_VD_PLAY_REVERSE=&H10000
MCI_VD_PLAY_SCAN=&H80000
MCI_VD_PLAY_SLOW=&H100000
MCI_VD_PLAY_SPEED=&H40000
MCI_VD_SEEK_REVERSE=&H10000
MCI_VD_SPIN_DOWN=&H20000
MCI_VD_SPIN_UP=&H10000
MCI_VD_STATUS_DISC_SIZE=&H4006&
MCI_VD_STATUS_FORWARD=&H4003&
MCI_VD_STATUS_MEDIA_TYPE=&H4004&
MCI_VD_STATUS_SIDE=&H4005&
MCI_VD_STATUS_SPEED=&H4002&
MCI_VD_STEP_FRAMES=&H10000
MCI_VD_STEP_REVERSE=&H20000
MCI_WAIT=&H2&
MCI_WAVE_GETDEVCAPS_INPUTS=&H4001&
MCI_WAVE_GETDEVCAPS_OUTPUTS=&H4002&
MCI_WAVE_INPUT=&H400000
MCI_WAVE_MAPPER=(MCI_WAVE_OFFSET+1)
MCI_WAVE_OFFSET=1152
MCI_WAVE_OPEN_BUFFER=&H10000
```

```
MCI_WAVE_OUTPUT=&H800000
MCI_WAVE_PCM=(MCI_WAVE_OFFSET+0)
MCI_WAVE_SET_ANYINPUT=&H4000000
MCI_WAVE_SET_ANYOUTPUT=&H8000000
MCI_WAVE_SET_AVGBYTESPERSEC=&H80000
MCI_WAVE_SET_BITSPERSAMPLE=&H200000
MCI_WAVE_SET_BLOCKALIGN=&H100000
MCI_WAVE_SET_CHANNELS=&H20000
MCI_WAVE_SET_FORMATTAG=&H10000
MCI_WAVE_SET_SAMPLESPERSEC=&H40000
MCI_WAVE_STATUS_AVGBYTESPERSEC=&H4004&
MCI_WAVE_STATUS_BITSPERSAMPLE=&H4006&
MCI_WAVE_STATUS_BLOCKALIGN=&H4005&
MCI_WAVE_STATUS_CHANNELS=&H4002&
MCI_WAVE_STATUS_FORMATTAG=&H4001&
MCI_WAVE_STATUS_LEVEL=&H4007&
MCI_WAVE_STATUS_SAMPLESPERSEC=&H4003&
MCI_WHERE=&H843
MCI_WINDOW=&H841
MCIERR_BAD_CONSTANT=(MCIERR_BASE+34)
MCIERR_BAD_INTEGER=(MCIERR_BASE+14)
MCIERR_BAD_TIME_FORMAT=(MCIERR_BASE+37)
MCIERR_BASE=256
MCIERR_CANNOT_LOAD_DRIVER=(MCIERR_BASE+10)
MCIERR_CANNOT_USE_ALL=(MCIERR_BASE+23)
MCIERR_CREATEWINDOW=(MCIERR_BASE+91)
MCIERR_CUSTOM_DRIVER_BASE=(MCIERR_BASE+256)
MCIERR_DEVICE_LENGTH=(MCIERR_BASE+54)
MCIERR_DEVICE_LOCKED=(MCIERR_BASE+32)
MCIERR_DEVICE_NOT_INSTALLED=(MCIERR_BASE+50)
MCIERR_DEVICE_NOT_READY=(MCIERR_BASE+20)
MCIERR_DEVICE_OPEN=(MCIERR_BASE+9)
MCIERR_DEVICE_ORD_LENGTH=(MCIERR_BASE+55)
MCIERR_DEVICE_TYPE_REQUIRED=(MCIERR_BASE+31)
MCIERR_DRIVER=(MCIERR_BASE+22)
MCIERR_DRIVER_INTERNAL=(MCIERR_BASE+16)
MCIERR_DUPLICATE_ALIAS=(MCIERR_BASE+33)
MCIERR_DUPLICATE_FLAGS=(MCIERR_BASE+39)
MCIERR_EXTENSION_NOT_FOUND=(MCIERR_BASE+25)
MCIERR_EXTRA_CHARACTERS=(MCIERR_BASE+49)
MCIERR_FILE_NOT_FOUND=(MCIERR_BASE+19)
MCIERR_FILE_NOT_SAVED=(MCIERR_BASE+30)
MCIERR_FILE_READ=(MCIERR_BASE+92)
MCIERR_FILE_WRITE=(MCIERR_BASE+93)
MCIERR_FILENAME_REQUIRED=(MCIERR_BASE+48)
MCIERR_FLAGS_NOT_COMPATIBLE=(MCIERR_BASE+28)
MCIERR_GET_CD=(MCIERR_BASE+51)
MCIERR_HARDWARE=(MCIERR_BASE+6)
```

```
MCIERR_ILLEGAL_FOR_AUTO_OPEN=(MCIERR_BASE+47)
MCIERR_INTERNAL=(MCIERR_BASE+21)
MCIERR_INVALID_DEVICE_ID=(MCIERR_BASE+1)
MCIERR_INVALID_DEVICE_NAME=(MCIERR_BASE+7)
MCIERR_INVALID_FILE=(MCIERR_BASE+40)
MCIERR_MISSING_COMMAND_STRING=(MCIERR_BASE+11)
MCIERR_MISSING_DEVICE_NAME=(MCIERR_BASE+36)
MCIERR_MISSING_PARAMETER=(MCIERR_BASE+17)
MCIERR_MISSING_STRING_ARGUMENT=(MCIERR_BASE+13)
MCIERR_MULTIPLE=(MCIERR_BASE+24)
MCIERR_MUST_USE_SHAREABLE=(MCIERR_BASE+35)
MCIERR_NEW_REQUIRES_ALIAS=(MCIERR_BASE+43)
MCIERR_NO_CLOSING_QUOTE=(MCIERR_BASE+38)
MCIERR_NO_ELEMENT_ALLOWED=(MCIERR_BASE+45)
MCIERR_NO_INTEGER=(MCIERR_BASE+56)
MCIERR_NO_WINDOW=(MCIERR_BASE+90)
MCIERR_NONAPPLICABLE_FUNCTION=(MCIERR_BASE+46)
MCIERR_NOTIFY_ON_AUTO_OPEN=(MCIERR_BASE+44)
MCIERR_NULL_PARAMETER_BLOCK=(MCIERR_BASE+41)
MCIERR_OUT_OF_MEMORY=(MCIERR_BASE+8)
MCIERR_OUTOFRANGE=(MCIERR_BASE+26)
MCIERR_PARAM_OVERFLOW=(MCIERR_BASE+12)
MCIERR_PARSER_INTERNAL=(MCIERR_BASE+15)
MCIERR_SEQ_DIV_INCOMPATIBLE=(MCIERR_BASE+80)
MCIERR_SEQ_NOMIDIPRESENT=(MCIERR_BASE+87)
MCIERR_SEQ_PORT_INUSE=(MCIERR_BASE+81)
MCIERR_SEQ_PORT_MAPNODEVICE=(MCIERR_BASE+83)
MCIERR_SEQ_PORT_MISCERROR=(MCIERR_BASE+84)
MCIERR_SEQ_PORT_NONEXISTENT=(MCIERR_BASE+82)
MCIERR_SEQ_PORTUNSPECIFIED=(MCIERR_BASE+86)
MCIERR_SEQ_TIMER=(MCIERR_BASE+85)
MCIERR_SET_CD=(MCIERR_BASE+52)
MCIERR_SET_DRIVE=(MCIERR_BASE+53)
MCIERR_UNNAMED_RESOURCE=(MCIERR_BASE+42)
MCIERR_UNRECOGNIZED_COMMAND=(MCIERR_BASE+5)
MCIERR_UNRECOGNIZED_KEYWORD=(MCIERR_BASE+3)
MCIERR_UNSUPPORTED_FUNCTION=(MCIERR_BASE+18)
MCIERR_WAVE_INPUTSINUSE=(MCIERR_BASE+66)
MCIERR_WAVE_INPUTSUNSUITABLE=(MCIERR_BASE+72)
MCIERR_WAVE_INPUTUNSPECIFIED=(MCIERR_BASE+69)
MCIERR_WAVE_OUTPUTSINUSE=(MCIERR_BASE+64)
MCIERR_WAVE_OUTPUTSUNSUITABLE=(MCIERR_BASE+70)
MCIERR_WAVE_OUTPUTUNSPECIFIED=(MCIERR_BASE+68)
MCIERR_WAVE_SETINPUTINUSE=(MCIERR_BASE+67)
MCIERR_WAVE_SETINPUTUNSUITABLE=(MCIERR_BASE+73)
MCIERR_WAVE_SETOUTPUTINUSE=(MCIERR_BASE+65)
MCIERR_WAVE_SETOUTPUTUNSUITABLE=(MCIERR_BASE+71)
MDIS_ALLCHILDSTYLES=&H1
```

```
MDITILE_HORIZONTAL=&H1
MDITILE_SKIPDISABLED=&H2
MDITILE_VERTICAL=&H0
MDM_BLIND_DIAL=&H200
MDM_CCITT_OVERRIDE=&H40
MDM_CELLULAR=&H8
MDM_COMPRESSION=&H1
MDM_ERROR_CONTROL=&H2
MDM_FLOWCONTROL_HARD=&H10
MDM_FLOWCONTROL_SOFT=&H20
MDM_FORCED_EC=&H4
MDM_SPEED_ADJUST=&H80
MDM_TONE_DIAL=&H100
MDM_V23_OVERRIDE=&H400
MDMSPKR_CALLSETUP=&H3
MDMSPKR_DIAL=&H1
MDMSPKR_OFF=&H0
MDMSPKR_ON=&H2
MDMSPKRFLAG_CALLSETUP=&H8
MDMSPKRFLAG_DIAL=&H2
MDMSPKRFLAG_OFF=&H1
MDMSPKRFLAG_ON=&H4
MDMVOL_HIGH=&H2
MDMVOL_LOW=&H0
MDMVOL_MEDIUM=&H1
MDMVOLFLAG_HIGH=&H4
MDMVOLFLAG_LOW=&H1
MDMVOLFLAG_MEDIUM=&H2
MEM_E_INVALID_LINK=&H80080010
MEM_E_INVALID_ROOT=&H80080009
MEM_E_INVALID_SIZE=&H80080011
MENU_EVENT=&H8 'Event contains menu event record
MERGECOPY=&HC000CA '(DWORD) dest=(source AND pattern)
MERGEPAINT=&HBB0226 '(DWORD) dest=(NOT source) OR dest
META_ANIMATEPALETTE=&H436
META_ARC=&H817
META_BITBLT=&H922
META_CHORD=&H830
META_CREATEBRUSHINDIRECT=&H2FC
META_CREATEFONTINDIRECT=&H2FB
META_CREATEPALETTE=&HF7
META_CREATEPATTERNBRUSH=&H1F9
META_CREATEPENINDIRECT=&H2FA
META_CREATEREGION=&H6FF
META_DELETEOBJECT=&H1F0
META_DIBBITBLT=&H940
META_DIBCREATEPATTERNBRUSH=&H142
META_DIBSTRETCHBLT=&HB41
```

```
META_ELLIPSE=&H418
META_ESCAPE=&H626
META_EXCLUDECLIPRECT=&H415
META_EXTFLOODFILL=&H548
META_EXTTEXTOUT=&HA32
META_FILLREGION=&H228
META_FLOODFILL=&H419
META_FRAMEREGION=&H429
META_INTERSECTCLIPRECT=&H416
META_INVERTREGION=&H12A
META_LINETO=&H213
META_MOVETO=&H214
META_OFFSETCLIPRGN=&H220
META_OFFSETVIEWPORTORG=&H211
META_OFFSETWINDOWORG=&H20F
META_PAINTREGION=&H12B
META_PATBLT=&H61D
META_PIE=&H81A
META_POLYGON=&H324
META_POLYLINE=&H325
META_POLYPOLYGON=&H538
META_REALIZEPALETTE=&H35
META_RECTANGLE=&H41B
META_RESIZEPALETTE=&H139
META_RESTOREDC=&H127
META_ROUNDRECT=&H61C
META_SAVEDC=&H1E
META_SCALEVIEWPORTEXT=&H412
META_SCALEWINDOWEXT=&H410
META_SELECTCLIPREGION=&H12C
META_SELECTOBJECT=&H12D
META_SELECTPALETTE=&H234
META_SETBKCOLOR=&H201
META_SETBKMODE=&H102
META_SETDIBTODEV=&HD33
META_SETMAPMODE=&H103
META_SETMAPPERFLAGS=&H231
META_SETPALENTRIES=&H37
META_SETPIXEL=&H41F
META_SETPOLYFILLMODE=&H106
META_SETRELABS=&H105
META_SETROP2=&H104
META_SETSTRETCHBLTMODE=&H107
META_SETTEXTALIGN=&H12E
META_SETTEXTCHAREXTRA=&H108
META_SETTEXTCOLOR=&H209
META_SETTEXTJUSTIFICATION=&H20A
META_SETVIEWPORTEXT=&H20E
```

```
META_SETVIEWPORTORG=&H20D
META_SETWINDOWEXT=&H20C
META_SETWINDOWORG=&H20B
META_STRETCHBLT=&HB23
META_STRETCHDIB=&HF43
META_TEXTOUT=&H521
MEVT_F_CALLBACK=&H40000000
MEVT_F_LONG=&H80000000
MEVT_F_SHORT=&H0&
MF_APPEND=&H100&
MF_BITMAP=&H4&
MF_BYCOMMAND=&H0&
MF_BYPOSITION=&H400&
MF_CALLBACKS=&H8000000
MF_CHANGE=&H80&
MF_CHECKED=&H8&
MF_CONV=&H40000000
MF_DELETE=&H200&
MF_DISABLED=&H2&
MF_ENABLED=&H0&
MF_END=&H80
MF_ERRORS=&H10000000
MF_GRAYED=&H1&
MF_HELP=&H4000&
MF_HILITE=&H80&
MF_HSZ_INFO=&H1000000
MF_INSERT=&H0&
MF_LINKS=&H20000000
MF_MASK=&HFF000000
MF_MENUBARBREAK=&H20&
MF_MENUBREAK=&H40&
MF_MOUSESELECT=&H8000&
MF_OWNERDRAW=&H100&
MF_POPUP=&H10&
MF_POSTMSGS=&H4000000
MF_REMOVE=&H1000&
MF_SENDMSGS=&H2000000
MF_SEPARATOR=&H800&
MF_STRING=&H0&
MF_SYSMENU=&H2000&
MF_UNCHECKED=&H0&
MF_UNHILITE=&H0&
MF_USECHECKBITMAPS=&H200&
MFCOMMENT=15
MH_CLEANUP=4
MH_CREATE=1
MH_DELETE=3
MH_KEEP=2
```

```
MHDR_DONE=&H1 'done bit
MHDR_INQUEUE=&H4 'reserved for driver
MHDR_PREPARED=&H2 'set if header prepared
MHDR_VALID=&H7 'valid flags / ;Internal /
MIDI_CACHE_ALL=1
MIDI_CACHE_BESTFIT=2
MIDI_CACHE_QUERY=3
MIDI_CACHE_VALID=(MIDI_CACHE_ALL Or MIDI_CACHE_BESTFIT Or
                  MIDI_CACHE_QUERY Or MIDI_UNCACHE)
MIDI_IO_STATUS=&H20&
MIDI_MAPPER=-1&
MIDI_UNCACHE=4
MIDICAPS_CACHE=&H4
MIDICAPS_LRVOLUME=&H2 'separate left-right volume control
MIDICAPS_STREAM=&H8 'driver supports midiStreamOut directly
MIDICAPS_VOLUME=&H1 'supports volume control
MIDIERR_BASE=64
MIDIERR_INVALIDSETUP=(MIDIERR_BASE+5) 'invalid setup
MIDIERR_LASTERROR=(MIDIERR_BASE+5) 'last error in range
MIDIERR_NODEVICE=(MIDIERR_BASE+4) 'port not connected
MIDIERR_NOMAP=(MIDIERR_BASE+2) 'no current map
MIDIERR_NOTREADY=(MIDIERR_BASE+3) 'hardware is still busy
MIDIERR_STILLPLAYING=(MIDIERR_BASE+1) 'still playing
MIDIERR_UNPREPARED=(MIDIERR_BASE+0) 'header not prepared
MIDIMAPPER=(-1)   'Cannot be cast to DWORD as RC complains
MIDIPROP_GET=&H40000000
MIDIPROP_SET=&H80000000
MIDIPROP_TEMPO=&H2&
MIDIPROP_TIMEDIV=&H1&
MIDISTRM_ERROR=-2
MIM_CLOSE=MM_MIM_CLOSE
MIM_DATA=MM_MIM_DATA
MIM_ERROR=MM_MIM_ERROR
MIM_LONGDATA=MM_MIM_LONGDATA
MIM_LONGERROR=MM_MIM_LONGERROR
MIM_MOREDATA=MM_MIM_MOREDATA
MIM_OPEN=MM_MIM_OPEN
MIN_PRIORITY=1
MINCHAR=&H80
MINLONG=&H80000000
MINSHORT=&H8000
MIXER_GETCONTROLDETAILSF_LISTTEXT=&H1&
MIXER_GETCONTROLDETAILSF_QUERYMASK=&HF&
MIXER_GETCONTROLDETAILSF_VALUE=&H0&
MIXER_GETLINECONTROLSF_ALL=&H0&
MIXER_GETLINECONTROLSF_ONEBYID=&H1&
MIXER_GETLINECONTROLSF_ONEBYTYPE=&H2&
MIXER_GETLINECONTROLSF_QUERYMASK=&HF&
```

```
MIXER_GETLINEINFOF_COMPONENTTYPE=&H3&
MIXER_GETLINEINFOF_DESTINATION=&H0&
MIXER_GETLINEINFOF_LINEID=&H2&
MIXER_GETLINEINFOF_QUERYMASK=&HF&
MIXER_GETLINEINFOF_SOURCE=&H1&
MIXER_GETLINEINFOF_TARGETTYPE=&H4&
MIXER_LONG_NAME_CHARS=64
MIXER_OBJECTF_AUX=&H50000000
MIXER_OBJECTF_HANDLE=&H80000000
MIXER_OBJECTF_HMIDIIN=(MIXER_OBJECTF_HANDLE Or
                        MIXER_OBJECTF_MIDIIN)
MIXER_OBJECTF_HMIDIOUT=(MIXER_OBJECTF_HANDLE Or
                        MIXER_OBJECTF_MIDIOUT)
MIXER_OBJECTF_HMIXER=(MIXER_OBJECTF_HANDLE Or
                        MIXER_OBJECTF_MIXER)
MIXER_OBJECTF_HWAVEIN=(MIXER_OBJECTF_HANDLE Or
                        MIXER_OBJECTF_WAVEIN)
MIXER_OBJECTF_HWAVEOUT=(MIXER_OBJECTF_HANDLE Or
                        MIXER_OBJECTF_WAVEOUT)
MIXER_OBJECTF_MIDIIN=&H40000000
MIXER_OBJECTF_MIDIOUT=&H30000000
MIXER_OBJECTF_MIXER=&H0&
MIXER_OBJECTF_WAVEIN=&H20000000
MIXER_OBJECTF_WAVEOUT=&H10000000
MIXER_SETCONTROLDETAILSF_CUSTOM=&H1&
MIXER_SETCONTROLDETAILSF_QUERYMASK=&HF&
MIXER_SETCONTROLDETAILSF_VALUE=&H0&
MIXER_SHORT_NAME_CHARS=16
MIXERCONTROL_CONTROLF_DISABLED=&H80000000
MIXERCONTROL_CONTROLF_MULTIPLE=&H2&
MIXERCONTROL_CONTROLF_UNIFORM=&H1&
MIXERCONTROL_CONTROLTYPE_BASS=(MIXERCONTROL_CONTROLTYPE_FADER+2)
MIXERCONTROL_CONTROLTYPE_BOOLEAN=(MIXERCONTROL_CT_CLASS_SWITCH Or
MIXERCONTROL_CT_SC_SWITCH_BOOLEAN Or MIXERCONTROL_CT_UNITS_BOOLEAN)
MIXERCONTROL_CONTROLTYPE_BOOLEANMETER=(MIXERCONTROL_CT_CLASS_METER Or
MIXERCONTROL_CT_SC_METER_POLLED Or MIXERCONTROL_CT_UNITS_BOOLEAN)
MIXERCONTROL_CONTROLTYPE_BUTTON=(MIXERCONTROL_CT_CLASS_SWITCH Or
MIXERCONTROL_CT_SC_SWITCH_BUTTON Or MIXERCONTROL_CT_UNITS_BOOLEAN)
MIXERCONTROL_CONTROLTYPE_CUSTOM=(MIXERCONTROL_CT_CLASS_CUSTOM Or
MIXERCONTROL_CT_UNITS_CUSTOM)
MIXERCONTROL_CONTROLTYPE_DECIBELS=(MIXERCONTROL_CT_CLASS_NUMBER Or
MIXERCONTROL_CT_UNITS_DECIBELS)
MIXERCONTROL_CONTROLTYPE_EQUALIZER=(MIXERCONTROL_CONTROLTYPE_FADER+4)
MIXERCONTROL_CONTROLTYPE_FADER=(MIXERCONTROL_CT_CLASS_FADER Or
MIXERCONTROL_CT_UNITS_UNSIGNED)
MIXERCONTROL_CONTROLTYPE_LOUDNESS=(MIXERCONTROL_CONTROLTYPE_BOOLEAN+4)
MIXERCONTROL_CONTROLTYPE_MICROTIME=(MIXERCONTROL_CT_CLASS_TIME Or
MIXERCONTROL_CT_SC_TIME_MICROSECS Or MIXERCONTROL_CT_UNITS_UNSIGNED)
```

```
MIXERCONTROL_CONTROLTYPE_MILLITIME=(MIXERCONTROL_CT_CLASS_TIME Or
MIXERCONTROL_CT_SC_TIME_MILLISECS Or MIXERCONTROL_CT_UNITS_UNSIGNED)
MIXERCONTROL_CONTROLTYPE_MIXER=(MIXERCONTROL_CONTROLTYPE_MULTIPLESELECT+1)
MIXERCONTROL_CONTROLTYPE_MONO=(MIXERCONTROL_CONTROLTYPE_BOOLEAN+3)
MIXERCONTROL_CONTROLTYPE_MULTIPLESELECT=(MIXERCONTROL_CT_CLASS_LIST Or
MIXERCONTROL_CT_SC_LIST_MULTIPLE Or MIXERCONTROL_CT_UNITS_BOOLEAN)
MIXERCONTROL_CONTROLTYPE_MUTE=(MIXERCONTROL_CONTROLTYPE_BOOLEAN+2)
MIXERCONTROL_CONTROLTYPE_MUX=(MIXERCONTROL_CONTROLTYPE_SINGLESELECT+1)
MIXERCONTROL_CONTROLTYPE_ONOFF=(MIXERCONTROL_CONTROLTYPE_BOOLEAN+1)
MIXERCONTROL_CONTROLTYPE_PAN=(MIXERCONTROL_CONTROLTYPE_SLIDER+1)
MIXERCONTROL_CONTROLTYPE_PEAKMETER=(MIXERCONTROL_CONTROLTYPE_SIGNEDMETER+1)
MIXERCONTROL_CONTROLTYPE_PERCENT=(MIXERCONTROL_CT_CLASS_NUMBER Or
MIXERCONTROL_CT_UNITS_PERCENT)
MIXERCONTROL_CONTROLTYPE_QSOUNDPAN=(MIXERCONTROL_CONTROLTYPE_SLIDER+2)
MIXERCONTROL_CONTROLTYPE_SIGNED=(MIXERCONTROL_CT_CLASS_NUMBER Or
MIXERCONTROL_CT_UNITS_SIGNED)
MIXERCONTROL_CONTROLTYPE_SIGNEDMETER=(MIXERCONTROL_CT_CLASS_METER Or
MIXERCONTROL_CT_SC_METER_POLLED Or MIXERCONTROL_CT_UNITS_SIGNED)
MIXERCONTROL_CONTROLTYPE_SINGLESELECT=(MIXERCONTROL_CT_CLASS_LIST Or
MIXERCONTROL_CT_SC_LIST_SINGLE Or MIXERCONTROL_CT_UNITS_BOOLEAN)
MIXERCONTROL_CONTROLTYPE_SLIDER=(MIXERCONTROL_CT_CLASS_SLIDER Or
MIXERCONTROL_CT_UNITS_SIGNED)
MIXERCONTROL_CONTROLTYPE_STEREOENH=(MIXERCONTROL_CONTROLTYPE_BOOLEAN+5)
MIXERCONTROL_CONTROLTYPE_TREBLE=(MIXERCONTROL_CONTROLTYPE_FADER+3)
MIXERCONTROL_CONTROLTYPE_UNSIGNED=(MIXERCONTROL_CT_CLASS_NUMBER Or
MIXERCONTROL_CT_UNITS_UNSIGNED)
MIXERCONTROL_CONTROLTYPE_UNSIGNEDMETER=(MIXERCONTROL_CT_CLASS_METER Or
MIXERCONTROL_CT_SC_METER_POLLED Or MIXERCONTROL_CT_UNITS_UNSIGNED)
MIXERCONTROL_CONTROLTYPE_VOLUME=(MIXERCONTROL_CONTROLTYPE_FADER+1)
MIXERCONTROL_CT_CLASS_CUSTOM=&H0&
MIXERCONTROL_CT_CLASS_FADER=&H50000000
MIXERCONTROL_CT_CLASS_LIST=&H70000000
MIXERCONTROL_CT_CLASS_MASK=&HF0000000
MIXERCONTROL_CT_CLASS_METER=&H10000000
MIXERCONTROL_CT_CLASS_NUMBER=&H30000000
MIXERCONTROL_CT_CLASS_SLIDER=&H40000000
MIXERCONTROL_CT_CLASS_SWITCH=&H20000000
MIXERCONTROL_CT_CLASS_TIME=&H60000000
MIXERCONTROL_CT_SC_LIST_MULTIPLE=&H1000000
MIXERCONTROL_CT_SC_LIST_SINGLE=&H0&
MIXERCONTROL_CT_SC_METER_POLLED=&H0&
MIXERCONTROL_CT_SC_SWITCH_BOOLEAN=&H0&
MIXERCONTROL_CT_SC_SWITCH_BUTTON=&H1000000
MIXERCONTROL_CT_SC_TIME_MICROSECS=&H0&
MIXERCONTROL_CT_SC_TIME_MILLISECS=&H1000000
MIXERCONTROL_CT_SUBCLASS_MASK=&HF000000
MIXERCONTROL_CT_UNITS_BOOLEAN=&H10000
MIXERCONTROL_CT_UNITS_CUSTOM=&H0&
```

```
MIXERCONTROL_CT_UNITS_DECIBELS=&H40000 'in 10ths
MIXERCONTROL_CT_UNITS_MASK=&HFF0000
MIXERCONTROL_CT_UNITS_PERCENT=&H50000 'in 10ths
MIXERCONTROL_CT_UNITS_SIGNED=&H20000
MIXERCONTROL_CT_UNITS_UNSIGNED=&H30000
MIXERLINE_COMPONENTTYPE_DST_DIGITAL=(MIXERLINE_COMPONENTTYPE_DST_FIRST+1)
MIXERLINE_COMPONENTTYPE_DST_FIRST=&H0&
MIXERLINE_COMPONENTTYPE_DST_HEADPHONES=(MIXERLINE_COMPONENTTYPE_DST_FIRST+5)
MIXERLINE_COMPONENTTYPE_DST_LAST=(MIXERLINE_COMPONENTTYPE_DST_FIRST+8)
MIXERLINE_COMPONENTTYPE_DST_LINE=(MIXERLINE_COMPONENTTYPE_DST_FIRST+2)
MIXERLINE_COMPONENTTYPE_DST_MONITOR=(MIXERLINE_COMPONENTTYPE_DST_FIRST+3)
MIXERLINE_COMPONENTTYPE_DST_SPEAKERS=(MIXERLINE_COMPONENTTYPE_DST_FIRST+4)
MIXERLINE_COMPONENTTYPE_DST_TELEPHONE=(MIXERLINE_COMPONENTTYPE_DST_FIRST+6)
MIXERLINE_COMPONENTTYPE_DST_UNDEFINED=(MIXERLINE_COMPONENTTYPE_DST_FIRST+0)
MIXERLINE_COMPONENTTYPE_DST_VOICEIN=(MIXERLINE_COMPONENTTYPE_DST_FIRST+8)
MIXERLINE_COMPONENTTYPE_DST_WAVEIN=(MIXERLINE_COMPONENTTYPE_DST_FIRST+7)
MIXERLINE_COMPONENTTYPE_SRC_ANALOG=(MIXERLINE_COMPONENTTYPE_SRC_FIRST+10)
MIXERLINE_COMPONENTTYPE_SRC_AUXILIARY=(MIXERLINE_COMPONENTTYPE_SRC_FIRST+9)
MIXERLINE_COMPONENTTYPE_SRC_COMPACTDISC=(MIXERLINE_COMPONENTTYPE_SRC_
  FIRST+5)
MIXERLINE_COMPONENTTYPE_SRC_DIGITAL=(MIXERLINE_COMPONENTTYPE_SRC_FIRST+1)
MIXERLINE_COMPONENTTYPE_SRC_FIRST=&H1000&
MIXERLINE_COMPONENTTYPE_SRC_LAST=(MIXERLINE_COMPONENTTYPE_SRC_FIRST+10)
MIXERLINE_COMPONENTTYPE_SRC_LINE=(MIXERLINE_COMPONENTTYPE_SRC_FIRST+2)
MIXERLINE_COMPONENTTYPE_SRC_MICROPHONE=(MIXERLINE_COMPONENTTYPE_SRC_FIRST+3)
MIXERLINE_COMPONENTTYPE_SRC_PCSPEAKER=(MIXERLINE_COMPONENTTYPE_SRC_FIRST+7)
MIXERLINE_COMPONENTTYPE_SRC_SYNTHESIZER=(MIXERLINE_COMPONENTTYPE_SRC_
  FIRST+4)
MIXERLINE_COMPONENTTYPE_SRC_TELEPHONE=(MIXERLINE_COMPONENTTYPE_SRC_FIRST+6)
MIXERLINE_COMPONENTTYPE_SRC_UNDEFINED=(MIXERLINE_COMPONENTTYPE_SRC_FIRST+0)
MIXERLINE_COMPONENTTYPE_SRC_WAVEOUT=(MIXERLINE_COMPONENTTYPE_SRC_FIRST+8)
MIXERLINE_LINEF_ACTIVE=&H1&
MIXERLINE_LINEF_DISCONNECTED=&H8000&
MIXERLINE_LINEF_SOURCE=&H80000000
MIXERLINE_TARGETTYPE_AUX=5
MIXERLINE_TARGETTYPE_MIDIIN=4
MIXERLINE_TARGETTYPE_MIDIOUT=3
MIXERLINE_TARGETTYPE_UNDEFINED=0
MIXERLINE_TARGETTYPE_WAVEIN=2
MIXERLINE_TARGETTYPE_WAVEOUT=1
MIXERR_BASE=1024
MIXERR_INVALCONTROL=(MIXERR_BASE+1)
MIXERR_INVALLINE=(MIXERR_BASE+0)
MIXERR_INVALVALUE=(MIXERR_BASE+2)
MIXERR_LASTERROR=(MIXERR_BASE+2)
MK_CONTROL=&H8
MK_E_CANTOPENFILE=&H800401EA
MK_E_CONNECTMANUALLY=&H800401E0
```

```
MK_E_ENUMERATION_FAILED=&H800401EF
MK_E_EXCEEDEDDEADLINE=&H800401E1
MK_E_FIRST=&H800401E0
MK_E_INTERMEDIATEINTERFACENOTSUPPORTED=&H800401E7
MK_E_INVALIDEXTENSION=&H800401E6
MK_E_LAST=&H800401EF
MK_E_MUSTBOTHERUSER=&H800401EB
MK_E_NEEDGENERIC=&H800401E2
MK_E_NO_NORMALIZED=&H80080007
MK_E_NOINVERSE=&H800401EC
MK_E_NOOBJECT=&H800401E5
MK_E_NOPREFIX=&H800401EE
MK_E_NOSTORAGE=&H800401ED
MK_E_NOTBINDABLE=&H800401E8
MK_E_NOTBOUND=&H800401E9
MK_E_SYNTAX=&H800401E4
MK_E_UNAVAILABLE=&H800401E3
MK_LBUTTON=&H1
MK_MBUTTON=&H10
MK_RBUTTON=&H2
MK_S_FIRST=&H401E0
MK_S_HIM=&H401E5
MK_S_LAST=&H401EF
MK_S_ME=&H401E4
MK_S_MONIKERALREADYREGISTERED=&H401E7
MK_S_REDUCED_TO_SELF=&H401E2
MK_S_US=&H401E6
MK_SHIFT=&H4
MM_ADLIB=9   'Ad Lib-compatible synthesizer
MM_ANISOTROPIC=8
MM_HIENGLISH=5
MM_HIMETRIC=3
MM_ISOTROPIC=7
MM_JOY1BUTTONDOWN=&H3B5
MM_JOY1BUTTONUP=&H3B7
MM_JOY1MOVE=&H3A0   'joystick
MM_JOY1ZMOVE=&H3A2
MM_JOY2BUTTONDOWN=&H3B6
MM_JOY2BUTTONUP=&H3B8
MM_JOY2MOVE=&H3A1
MM_JOY2ZMOVE=&H3A3
MM_LOENGLISH=4
MM_LOMETRIC=2
MM_MAX=MM_ANISOTROPIC
MM_MAX_FIXEDSCALE=MM_TWIPS
MM_MCINOTIFY=&H3B9   'MCI
MM_MCISIGNAL=&H3CB
MM_MCISYSTEM_STRING=&H3CA
```

```
MM_MICROSOFT=1   'Microsoft Corp.
MM_MIDI_MAPPER=1   'MIDI Mapper
MM_MIM_CLOSE=&H3C2
MM_MIM_DATA=&H3C3
MM_MIM_ERROR=&H3C5
MM_MIM_LONGDATA=&H3C4
MM_MIM_LONGERROR=&H3C6
MM_MIM_MOREDATA=&H3CC   'MIM_DONE w/ pending events
MM_MIM_OPEN=&H3C1   'MIDI input
MM_MIN=MM_TEXT
MM_MOM_CLOSE=&H3C8
MM_MOM_DONE=&H3C9
MM_MOM_OPEN=&H3C7   'MIDI output
MM_MOM_POSITIONCB=&H3CA 'Callback for MEVT_POSITIONCB
MM_MPU401_MIDIIN=11   'MPU401-compatible MIDI input port
MM_MPU401_MIDIOUT=10   'MPU401-compatible MIDI output port
MM_PC_JOYSTICK=12   'Joystick adapter
MM_SNDBLST_MIDIIN=4   'Sound Blaster MIDI input port
MM_SNDBLST_MIDIOUT=3   'Sound Blaster MIDI output port
MM_SNDBLST_SYNTH=5   'Sound Blaster internal synthesizer
MM_SNDBLST_WAVEIN=7   'Sound Blaster waveform input
MM_SNDBLST_WAVEOUT=6   'Sound Blaster waveform output
MM_TEXT=1
MM_TWIPS=6
MM_WAVE_MAPPER=2   'Wave Mapper
MM_WIM_CLOSE=&H3BF
MM_WIM_DATA=&H3C0
MM_WIM_OPEN=&H3BE   'waveform input
MM_WOM_CLOSE=&H3BC
MM_WOM_DONE=&H3BD
MM_WOM_OPEN=&H3BB   'waveform output
MMIO_ALLOCBUF=&H10000 'mmioOpen() should allocate a buffer
MMIO_COMPAT=&H0 'compatibility mode
MMIO_CREATE=&H1000 'create new file (or truncate file)
MMIO_CREATELIST=&H40 'mmioCreateChunk(): make a RIFF chunk
MMIO_CREATERIFF=&H20 'mmioCreateChunk(): make a LIST chunk
MMIO_DEFAULTBUFFER=8192   'default buffer size
MMIO_DELETE=&H200 'create new file (or truncate file)
MMIO_DENYNONE=&H40 'deny nothing to other processes
MMIO_DENYREAD=&H30 'deny reading to other processes
MMIO_DENYWRITE=&H20 'deny writing to other processes
MMIO_DIRTY=&H10000000   'I/O buffer is dirty
MMIO_EMPTYBUF=&H10 'mmioFlush(): empty the I/O buffer
MMIO_EXCLUSIVE=&H10 'exclusive-access mode
MMIO_EXIST=&H4000 'checks for existence of file
MMIO_FHOPEN=&H10 'mmioClose(): keep file handle open
MMIO_FINDCHUNK=&H10 'mmioDescend(): find a chunk by ID
MMIO_FINDLIST=&H40 'mmioDescend(): find a RIFF chunk
```

```
MMIO_FINDPROC=&H40000 'mmioInstallIOProc(): find an MMIOProc
MMIO_FINDRIFF=&H20 'mmioDescend(): find a LIST chunk
MMIO_GETTEMP=&H20000 'mmioOpen() should retrieve temp name
MMIO_INSTALLPROC=&H10000 'mmioInstallIOProc(): install MMIOProc
MMIO_OPEN_VALID=&H3FFFF 'valid flags for mmioOpen / ;Internal /
MMIO_PARSE=&H100 'parse new file returning path
MMIO_PUBLICPROC=&H10000000  'mmioInstallIOProc: install Globally
MMIO_READ=&H0 'open file for reading only
MMIO_READWRITE=&H2 'open file for reading and writing
MMIO_REMOVEPROC=&H20000 'mmioInstallIOProc(): remove MMIOProc
MMIO_RWMODE=&H3 'mask to get bits used for opening
MMIO_SHAREMODE=&H70 'file sharing mode number
MMIO_TOUPPER=&H10 'mmioStringToFOURCC(): cvt. to u-case
MMIO_UNICODEPROC=&H1000000 'mmioInstallIOProc(): Unicode MMIOProc
MMIO_VALIDPROC=&H11070000  'valid for mmioInstallIOProc
MMIO_WRITE=&H1 'open file for writing only
MMIOERR_BASE=256
MMIOERR_CANNOTCLOSE=(MMIOERR_BASE+4)  'cannot close
MMIOERR_CANNOTEXPAND=(MMIOERR_BASE+8)  'cannot expand file
MMIOERR_CANNOTOPEN=(MMIOERR_BASE+3)  'cannot open
MMIOERR_CANNOTREAD=(MMIOERR_BASE+5)  'cannot read
MMIOERR_CANNOTSEEK=(MMIOERR_BASE+7)  'cannot seek
MMIOERR_CANNOTWRITE=(MMIOERR_BASE+6) 'cannot write
MMIOERR_CHUNKNOTFOUND=(MMIOERR_BASE+9)  'chunk not found
MMIOERR_FILENOTFOUND=(MMIOERR_BASE+1)  'file not found
MMIOERR_OUTOFMEMORY=(MMIOERR_BASE+2)  'out of memory
MMIOERR_UNBUFFERED=(MMIOERR_BASE+10) 'file is unbuffered
MMIOM_CLOSE=4  'close file
MMIOM_OPEN=3  'open file
MMIOM_READ=MMIO_READ  'read (must equal MMIO_READ!)
MMIOM_RENAME=6  'rename specified file
MMIOM_SEEK=2  'seek to a new position in file
MMIOM_USER=&H8000  'beginning of user-defined messages
MMIOM_WRITE=MMIO_WRITE  'write (must equal MMIO_WRITE!)
MMIOM_WRITEFLUSH=5  'write and flush
MMSYSERR_ALLOCATED=(MMSYSERR_BASE+4)  'device already allocated
MMSYSERR_BADDEVICEID=(MMSYSERR_BASE+2)  'device ID out of range
MMSYSERR_BADERRNUM=(MMSYSERR_BASE+9)  'error value out of range
MMSYSERR_BASE=0
MMSYSERR_ERROR=(MMSYSERR_BASE+1)  'unspecified error
MMSYSERR_HANDLEBUSY=(MMSYSERR_BASE+12) 'handle being used
MMSYSERR_INVALFLAG=(MMSYSERR_BASE+10) 'invalid flag passed
MMSYSERR_INVALHANDLE=(MMSYSERR_BASE+5)  'device handle invalid
MMSYSERR_INVALIDALIAS=(MMSYSERR_BASE+13) '"not found in WIN.INI
MMSYSERR_INVALPARAM=(MMSYSERR_BASE+11) 'invalid parameter
MMSYSERR_LASTERROR=(MMSYSERR_BASE+13) 'last error in range
MMSYSERR_NODRIVER=(MMSYSERR_BASE+6)  'no device driver present
MMSYSERR_NOERROR=0  'no error
```

```
MMSYSERR_NOMEM=(MMSYSERR_BASE+7)  'memory allocation error
MMSYSERR_NOTENABLED=(MMSYSERR_BASE+3)  'driver failed enable
MMSYSERR_NOTSUPPORTED=(MMSYSERR_BASE+8)  'function not supported
MOD_ALT=&H1
MOD_CONTROL=&H2
MOD_FMSYNTH=4  'FM internal synth
MOD_MAPPER=5  'MIDI mapper
MOD_MIDIPORT=1  'output port
MOD_SHIFT=&H4
MOD_SQSYNTH=3  'square wave internal synth
MOD_SYNTH=2  'generic internal synth
MOM_CLOSE=MM_MOM_CLOSE
MOM_DONE=MM_MOM_DONE
MOM_OPEN=MM_MOM_OPEN
MOM_POSITIONCB=MM_MOM_POSITIONCB
MONO_FONT=8
mouse_eventC=&H2 'Event contains mouse event record
MOUSE_MOVED=&H1
MOUSEEVENTF_ABSOLUTE=&H8000 'absolute move
MOUSEEVENTF_LEFTDOWN=&H2 'left button down
MOUSEEVENTF_LEFTUP=&H4 'left button up
MOUSEEVENTF_MIDDLEDOWN=&H20 'middle button down
MOUSEEVENTF_MIDDLEUP=&H40 'middle button up
MOUSEEVENTF_MOVE=&H1 'mouse move
MOUSEEVENTF_RIGHTDOWN=&H8 'right button down
MOUSEEVENTF_RIGHTUP=&H10 'right button up
MOUSETRAILS=39
MOVEFILE_COPY_ALLOWED=&H2
MOVEFILE_DELAY_UNTIL_REBOOT=&H4
MOVEFILE_REPLACE_EXISTING=&H1
MS_CTS_ON=&H10&
MS_DSR_ON=&H20&
MS_NBF="MNBF"
MS_RING_ON=&H40&
MS_RLSD_ON=&H80&
MSGF_DDEMGR=&H8001
MSGF_DIALOGBOX=0
MSGF_MAINLOOP=8
MSGF_MAX=8
MSGF_MENU=2
MSGF_MESSAGEBOX=1
MSGF_MOVE=3
MSGF_NEXTWINDOW=6
MSGF_SCROLLBAR=5
MSGF_SIZE=4
MSGF_USER=4096
MULTIFILEOPENORD=1537
MWT_IDENTITY=1
```

```
MWT_LEFTMULTIPLY=2
MWT_MAX=MWT_RIGHTMULTIPLY
MWT_MIN=MWT_IDENTITY
MWT_RIGHTMULTIPLY=3


N
NAME_FLAGS_MASK=&H87
NCBACTION=&H77   'NCB ACTION
NCBADDGRNAME=&H36   'NCB ADD GROUP NAME
NCBADDNAME=&H30   'NCB ADD NAME
NCBASTAT=&H33   'NCB ADAPTER STATUS
NCBCALL=&H10   'NCB CALL
NCBCANCEL=&H35   'NCB CANCEL
NCBCHAINSEND=&H17   'NCB CHAIN SEND
NCBCHAINSENDNA=&H72   'NCB CHAIN SEND NO ACK
NCBDELNAME=&H31   'NCB DELETE NAME
NCBDGRECV=&H21   'NCB RECEIVE DATAGRAM
NCBDGRECVBC=&H23   'NCB RECEIVE BROADCAST DATAGRAM
NCBDGSEND=&H20   'NCB SEND DATAGRAM
NCBDGSENDBC=&H22   'NCB SEND BROADCAST DATAGRAM
NCBENUM=&H37   'NCB ENUMERATE LANA NUMBERS
NCBFINDNAME=&H78   'NCB FIND NAME
NCBHANGUP=&H12   'NCB HANG UP
NCBLANSTALERT=&H73   'NCB LAN STATUS ALERT
NCBLISTEN=&H11   'NCB LISTEN
NCBNAMSZ=16   'absolute length of a net name
NCBRECV=&H15   'NCB RECEIVE
NCBRECVANY=&H16   'NCB RECEIVE ANY
NCBRESET=&H32   'NCB RESET
NCBSEND=&H14   'NCB SEND
NCBSENDNA=&H71   'NCB SEND NO ACK
NCBSSTAT=&H34   'NCB SESSION STATUS
NCBTRACE=&H79   'NCB TRACE
NCBUNLINK=&H70   'NCB UNLINK
NEWFRAME=1
NEWTRANSPARENT=3   'use with SetBkMode()
NEXTBAND=3
NI_CHANGECANDIDATELIST=&H13
NI_CLOSECANDIDATE=&H11
NI_COMPOSITIONSTR=&H15
NI_FINALIZECONVERSIONRESULT=&H14
NI_OPENCANDIDATE=&H10
NI_SELECTCANDIDATESTR=&H12
NI_SETCANDIDATE_PAGESIZE=&H17
NI_SETCANDIDATE_PAGESTART=&H16
NIF_ICON=&H2
NIF_MESSAGE=&H1
NIF_TIP=&H4
```

```
NIM_ADD=&H0
NIM_DELETE=&H2
NIM_MODIFY=&H1
NMPWAIT_NOWAIT=&H1
NMPWAIT_USE_DEFAULT_WAIT=&H0
NMPWAIT_WAIT_FOREVER=&HFFFF
NO_ERROR=0 'dderror
NO_PRIORITY=0
NO_PROPAGATE_INHERIT_ACE=&H4
NOERROR=0
NONZEROLHND=(LMEM_MOVEABLE)
NONZEROLPTR=(LMEM_FIXED)
NOPARITY=0
NORM_IGNORECASE=&H1 'ignore case
NORM_IGNORENONSPACE=&H2 'ignore nonspacing chars
NORM_IGNORESYMBOLS=&H4 'ignore symbols
NORMAL_PRIORITY_CLASS=&H20
NOTSRCCOPY=&H330008 '(DWORD) dest=(NOT source)
NOTSRCERASE=&H1100A6 '(DWORD) dest=(NOT src) AND (NOT dest)
NRC_ACTSES=&HF 'no deletions, name has active sessions
NRC_BADDR=&H7 'illegal buffer address
NRC_BRIDGE=&H23  'ncb_lana_num field invalid
NRC_BUFLEN=&H1 'illegal buffer length
NRC_CANCEL=&H26  'command not valid to cancel
NRC_CANOCCR=&H24  'command completed while cancel occurring
NRC_CMDCAN=&HB 'command cancelled
NRC_CMDTMO=&H5 'command timed out
NRC_DUPENV=&H30  'name defined by another local process
NRC_DUPNAME=&HD 'duplicate name
NRC_ENVNOTDEF=&H34  'environment undefined. RESET required
NRC_GOODRET=&H0 'good return
NRC_IFBUSY=&H21  'interface busy, IRET before retrying
NRC_ILLCMD=&H3 'illegal command
NRC_ILLNN=&H13  'illegal name number
NRC_INCOMP=&H6 'message incomplete, issue another command
NRC_INUSE=&H16  'name in use on remote adapter
NRC_INVADDRESS=&H39  'invalid NCB address or length > segment
NRC_INVDDID=&H3B  'invalid NCB DDID
NRC_LOCKFAIL=&H3C  'lock of user area failed
NRC_LOCTFUL=&H11  'local session table full
NRC_MAXAPPS=&H36  'max number of applications exceeded
NRC_NAMCONF=&H19  'name conflict detected
NRC_NAMERR=&H17  'name deleted
NRC_NAMTFUL=&HE 'name table full
NRC_NOCALL=&H14  'no callname
NRC_NORES=&H9 'no resource available
NRC_NORESOURCES=&H38  'requested resources are not available
NRC_NOSAPS=&H37  'no saps available for netbios
```

```
NRC_NOWILD=&H15   'cannot put  in NCB_NAME
NRC_OPENERR=&H3F   'NETBIOS not loaded
NRC_OSRESNOTAV=&H35   'required OS resources exhausted
NRC_PENDING=&HFF   'asynchronous command is not yet finished
NRC_REMTFUL=&H12   'remote session table full
NRC_SABORT=&H18   'session ended abnormally
NRC_SCLOSED=&HA 'session closed
NRC_SNUMOUT=&H8 'session number out of range
NRC_SYSTEM=&H40   'system error
NRC_TOOMANY=&H22   'too many commands outstanding, retry later
NTM_BOLD=&H20&
NTM_ITALIC=&H1&
NTM_REGULAR=&H40&
NULL_BRUSH=5
NULL_PEN=8
NULLREGION=1
NUMBRUSHES=16 'number of brushes the device has
NUMCOLORS=24 'number of colors the device supports
NUMFONTS=22 'number of fonts the device has
NUMLOCK_ON=&H20 'the numlock light is on.
NUMMARKERS=20 'number of markers the device has
NUMPENS=18 'number of pens the device has
NUMRESERVED=106 'number of reserved entries in palette

O
OBJ_BITMAP=7
OBJ_BRUSH=2
OBJ_DC=3
OBJ_ENHMETADC=12
OBJ_ENHMETAFILE=13
OBJ_EXTPEN=11
OBJ_FONT=6
OBJ_MEMDC=10
OBJ_METADC=4
OBJ_METAFILE=9
OBJ_PAL=5
OBJ_PEN=1
OBJ_REGION=8
OBJECT_INHERIT_ACE=&H1
OBM_BTNCORNERS=32758
OBM_BTSIZE=32761
OBM_CHECK=32760
OBM_CHECKBOXES=32759
OBM_CLOSE=32754
OBM_COMBO=32738
OBM_DNARROW=32752
OBM_DNARROWD=32742
OBM_DNARROWI=32736
```

```
OBM_LFARROW=32750
OBM_LFARROWD=32740
OBM_LFARROWI=32734
OBM_MNARROW=32739
OBM_OLD_CLOSE=32767
OBM_OLD_DNARROW=32764
OBM_OLD_LFARROW=32762
OBM_OLD_REDUCE=32757
OBM_OLD_RESTORE=32755
OBM_OLD_RGARROW=32763
OBM_OLD_UPARROW=32765
OBM_OLD_ZOOM=32756
OBM_REDUCE=32749
OBM_REDUCED=32746
OBM_RESTORE=32747
OBM_RESTORED=32744
OBM_RGARROW=32751
OBM_RGARROWD=32741
OBM_RGARROWI=32735
OBM_SIZE=32766
OBM_UPARROW=32753
OBM_UPARROWD=32743
OBM_UPARROWI=32737
OBM_ZOOM=32748
OBM_ZOOMD=32745
OCR_CROSS=32515
OCR_IBEAM=32513
OCR_ICOCUR=32647
OCR_ICON=32641
OCR_NO=32648 'not in win3.1
OCR_NORMAL=32512
OCR_SIZE=32640
OCR_SIZEALL=32646
OCR_SIZENESW=32643
OCR_SIZENS=32645
OCR_SIZENWSE=32642
OCR_SIZEWE=32644
OCR_UP=32516
OCR_WAIT=32514
ODA_DRAWENTIRE=&H1
ODA_FOCUS=&H4
ODA_SELECT=&H2
ODDPARITY=1
ODS_CHECKED=&H8
ODS_DISABLED=&H4
ODS_FOCUS=&H10
ODS_GRAYED=&H2
ODS_SELECTED=&H1
```

```
ODT_BUTTON=4
ODT_COMBOBOX=3
ODT_LISTBOX=2
ODT_MENU=1
OEM_CHARSET=255
OEM_FIXED_FONT=10
OF_CANCEL=&H800
OF_CREATE=&H1000
OF_DELETE=&H200
OF_EXIST=&H4000
OF_PARSE=&H100
OF_PROMPT=&H2000
OF_READ=&H0
OF_READWRITE=&H2
OF_REOPEN=&H8000
OF_SHARE_COMPAT=&H0
OF_SHARE_DENY_NONE=&H40
OF_SHARE_DENY_READ=&H30
OF_SHARE_DENY_WRITE=&H20
OF_SHARE_EXCLUSIVE=&H10
OF_VERIFY=&H400
OF_WRITE=&H1
OFN_ALLOWMULTISELECT=&H200
OFN_CREATEPROMPT=&H2000
OFN_ENABLEHOOK=&H20
OFN_ENABLETEMPLATE=&H40
OFN_ENABLETEMPLATEHANDLE=&H80
OFN_EXPLORER=&H80000 'new look commdlg
OFN_EXTENSIONDIFFERENT=&H400
OFN_FILEMUSTEXIST=&H1000
OFN_HIDEREADONLY=&H4
OFN_LONGNAMES=&H200000 'force long names for 3.x modules
OFN_NOCHANGEDIR=&H8
OFN_NODEREFERENCELINKS=&H100000
OFN_NOLONGNAMES=&H40000 'force no long names for 4.x modules
OFN_NONETWORKBUTTON=&H20000
OFN_NOREADONLYRETURN=&H8000
OFN_NOTESTFILECREATE=&H10000
OFN_NOVALIDATE=&H100
OFN_OVERWRITEPROMPT=&H2
OFN_PATHMUSTEXIST=&H800
OFN_READONLY=&H1
OFN_SHAREAWARE=&H4000
OFN_SHAREFALLTHROUGH=2
OFN_SHARENOWARN=1
OFN_SHAREWARN=0
OFN_SHOWHELP=&H10
OFS_MAXPATHNAME=128
```

```
OIC_BANG=32515
OIC_HAND=32513
OIC_NOTE=32516
OIC_QUES=32514
OIC_SAMPLE=32512
OLE_E_ADVF=&H80040001
OLE_E_ADVISENOTSUPPORTED=&H80040003
OLE_E_BLANK=&H80040007
OLE_E_CANT_BINDTOSOURCE=&H8004000A
OLE_E_CANT_GETMONIKER=&H80040009
OLE_E_CANTCONVERT=&H80040011
OLE_E_CLASSDIFF=&H80040008
OLE_E_ENUM_NOMORE=&H80040002
OLE_E_FIRST=&H80040000
OLE_E_INVALIDHWND=&H8004000F
OLE_E_INVALIDRECT=&H8004000D
OLE_E_LAST=&H800400FF
OLE_E_NOCACHE=&H80040006
OLE_E_NOCONNECTION=&H80040004
OLE_E_NOSTORAGE=&H80040012
OLE_E_NOT_INPLACEACTIVE=&H80040010
OLE_E_NOTRUNNING=&H80040005
OLE_E_OLEVERB=&H80040000
OLE_E_PROMPTSAVECANCELLED=&H8004000C
OLE_E_STATIC=&H8004000B
OLE_E_WRONGCOMPOBJ=&H8004000E
OLE_S_FIRST=&H40000
OLE_S_LAST=&H400FF
OLE_S_MAC_CLIPFORMAT=&H40002
OLE_S_STATIC=&H40001
OLE_S_USEREG=&H40000
OLEOBJ_E_FIRST=&H80040180
OLEOBJ_E_INVALIDVERB=&H80040181
OLEOBJ_E_LAST=&H8004018F
OLEOBJ_E_NOVERBS=&H80040180
OLEOBJ_S_CANNOT_DOVERB_NOW=&H40181
OLEOBJ_S_FIRST=&H40180
OLEOBJ_S_INVALIDHWND=&H40182
OLEOBJ_S_INVALIDVERB=&H40180
OLEOBJ_S_LAST=&H4018F
ONE5STOPBITS=1
ONESTOPBIT=0
OPAQUE=2
OPEN_ALWAYS=4
OPEN_EXISTING=3
OPENCHANNEL=4110
ORD_LANGDRIVER=1 'The ordinal number for the entry point of
OUT_CHARACTER_PRECIS=2
```

```
OUT_DEFAULT_PRECIS=0
OUT_DEVICE_PRECIS=5
OUT_OUTLINE_PRECIS=8
OUT_RASTER_PRECIS=6
OUT_STRING_PRECIS=1
OUT_STROKE_PRECIS=3
OUT_TT_ONLY_PRECIS=7
OUT_TT_PRECIS=4
OUTPUT_DEBUG_STRING_EVENT=8


P
PAN_ANY=0   'Any
PAN_ARMSTYLE_INDEX=6
PAN_BENT_ARMS_DOUBLE_SERIF=11   'Non-Straight Arms/Double-Serif
PAN_BENT_ARMS_HORZ=7   'Non-Straight Arms/Horizontal
PAN_BENT_ARMS_SINGLE_SERIF=10   'Non-Straight Arms/Single-Serif
PAN_BENT_ARMS_VERT=9   'Non-Straight Arms/Vertical
PAN_BENT_ARMS_WEDGE=8   'Non-Straight Arms/Wedge
PAN_CONTRAST_HIGH=8   'High
PAN_CONTRAST_INDEX=4
PAN_CONTRAST_LOW=4   'Low
PAN_CONTRAST_MEDIUM=6   'Medium
PAN_CONTRAST_MEDIUM_HIGH=7   'Medium High
PAN_CONTRAST_MEDIUM_LOW=5   'Medium Low
PAN_CONTRAST_NONE=2   'None
PAN_CONTRAST_VERY_HIGH=9   'Very High
PAN_CONTRAST_VERY_LOW=3   'Very Low
PAN_CULTURE_LATIN=0
PAN_FAMILY_DECORATIVE=4   'Decorative
PAN_FAMILY_PICTORIAL=5   'Pictorial
PAN_FAMILY_SCRIPT=3   'Script
PAN_FAMILY_TEXT_DISPLAY=2   'Text and Display
PAN_FAMILYTYPE_INDEX=0
PAN_LETT_NORMAL_BOXED=4   'Normal/Boxed
PAN_LETT_NORMAL_CONTACT=2   'Normal/Contact
PAN_LETT_NORMAL_FLATTENED=5   'Normal/Flattened
PAN_LETT_NORMAL_OFF_CENTER=7   'Normal/Off Center
PAN_LETT_NORMAL_ROUNDED=6   'Normal/Rounded
PAN_LETT_NORMAL_SQUARE=8   'Normal/Square
PAN_LETT_NORMAL_WEIGHTED=3   'Normal/Weighted
PAN_LETT_OBLIQUE_BOXED=11   'Oblique/Boxed
PAN_LETT_OBLIQUE_CONTACT=9   'Oblique/Contact
PAN_LETT_OBLIQUE_FLATTENED=12   'Oblique/Flattened
PAN_LETT_OBLIQUE_OFF_CENTER=14   'Oblique/Off Center
PAN_LETT_OBLIQUE_ROUNDED=13   'Oblique/Rounded
PAN_LETT_OBLIQUE_SQUARE=15   'Oblique/Square
PAN_LETT_OBLIQUE_WEIGHTED=10   'Oblique/Weighted
PAN_LETTERFORM_INDEX=7
```

```
PAN_MIDLINE_CONSTANT_POINTED=9   'Constant/Pointed
PAN_MIDLINE_CONSTANT_SERIFED=10  'Constant/Serifed
PAN_MIDLINE_CONSTANT_TRIMMED=8   'Constant/Trimmed
PAN_MIDLINE_HIGH_POINTED=6   'High/Pointed
PAN_MIDLINE_HIGH_SERIFED=7   'High/Serifed
PAN_MIDLINE_HIGH_TRIMMED=5   'High/Trimmed
PAN_MIDLINE_INDEX=8
PAN_MIDLINE_LOW_POINTED=12   'Low/Pointed
PAN_MIDLINE_LOW_SERIFED=13   'Low/Serifed
PAN_MIDLINE_LOW_TRIMMED=11   'Low/Trimmed
PAN_MIDLINE_STANDARD_POINTED=3   'Standard/Pointed
PAN_MIDLINE_STANDARD_SERIFED=4   'Standard/Serifed
PAN_MIDLINE_STANDARD_TRIMMED=2   'Standard/Trimmed
PAN_NO_FIT=1   'No Fit
PAN_PROP_CONDENSED=6   'Condensed
PAN_PROP_EVEN_WIDTH=4   'Even Width
PAN_PROP_EXPANDED=5   'Expanded
PAN_PROP_MODERN=3   'Modern
PAN_PROP_MONOSPACED=9   'Monospaced
PAN_PROP_OLD_STYLE=2   'Old Style
PAN_PROP_VERY_CONDENSED=8   'Very Condensed
PAN_PROP_VERY_EXPANDED=7   'Very Expanded
PAN_PROPORTION_INDEX=3
PAN_SERIF_BONE=8   'Bone
PAN_SERIF_COVE=2   'Cove
PAN_SERIF_EXAGGERATED=9   'Exaggerated
PAN_SERIF_FLARED=14   'Flared
PAN_SERIF_NORMAL_SANS=11   'Normal Sans
PAN_SERIF_OBTUSE_COVE=3   'Obtuse Cove
PAN_SERIF_OBTUSE_SANS=12   'Obtuse Sans
PAN_SERIF_OBTUSE_SQUARE_COVE=5   'Obtuse Square Cove
PAN_SERIF_PERP_SANS=13   'Prep Sans
PAN_SERIF_ROUNDED=15   'Rounded
PAN_SERIF_SQUARE=6   'Square
PAN_SERIF_SQUARE_COVE=4   'Square Cove
PAN_SERIF_THIN=7   'Thin
PAN_SERIF_TRIANGLE=10   'Triangle
PAN_SERIFSTYLE_INDEX=1
PAN_STRAIGHT_ARMS_DOUBLE_SERIF=6 'Straight Arms/Double-Serif
PAN_STRAIGHT_ARMS_HORZ=2   'Straight Arms/Horizontal
PAN_STRAIGHT_ARMS_SINGLE_SERIF=5 'Straight Arms/Single-Serif
PAN_STRAIGHT_ARMS_VERT=4   'Straight Arms/Vertical
PAN_STRAIGHT_ARMS_WEDGE=3   'Straight Arms/Wedge
PAN_STROKE_GRADUAL_DIAG=2   'Gradual/Diagonal
PAN_STROKE_GRADUAL_HORZ=5   'Gradual/Horizontal
PAN_STROKE_GRADUAL_TRAN=3   'Gradual/Transitional
PAN_STROKE_GRADUAL_VERT=4   'Gradual/Vertical
PAN_STROKE_INSTANT_VERT=8   'Instant/Vertical
```

```
PAN_STROKE_RAPID_HORZ=7    'Rapid/Horizontal
PAN_STROKE_RAPID_VERT=6    'Rapid/Vertical
PAN_STROKEVARIATION_INDEX=5
PAN_WEIGHT_BLACK=10   'Black
PAN_WEIGHT_BOLD=8    'Bold
PAN_WEIGHT_BOOK=5    'Book
PAN_WEIGHT_DEMI=7    'Demi
PAN_WEIGHT_HEAVY=9   'Heavy
PAN_WEIGHT_INDEX=2
PAN_WEIGHT_LIGHT=3    'Light
PAN_WEIGHT_MEDIUM=6    'Medium
PAN_WEIGHT_NORD=11    'Nord
PAN_WEIGHT_THIN=4    'Thin
PAN_WEIGHT_VERY_LIGHT=2    'Very Light
PAN_XHEIGHT_CONSTANT_LARGE=4    'Constant/Large
PAN_XHEIGHT_CONSTANT_SMALL=2    'Constant/Small
PAN_XHEIGHT_CONSTANT_STD=3    'Constant/Standard
PAN_XHEIGHT_DUCKING_LARGE=7    'Ducking/Large
PAN_XHEIGHT_DUCKING_SMALL=5    'Ducking/Small
PAN_XHEIGHT_DUCKING_STD=6    'Ducking/Standard
PAN_XHEIGHT_INDEX=9
PANOSE_COUNT=10
PARITY_EVEN=&H400&
PARITY_MARK=&H800&
PARITY_NONE=&H100&
PARITY_ODD=&H200&
PARITY_SPACE=&H1000&
PASSTHROUGH=19
PATCOPY=&HF00021 '(DWORD) dest=pattern
PATINVERT=&H5A0049 '(DWORD) dest=pattern XOR dest
PATPAINT=&HFB0A09 '(DWORD) dest=DPSnoo
PC_EXPLICIT=&H2   'palette index is explicit to device
PC_INTERIORS=128 'Can do interiors
PC_NOCOLLAPSE=&H4 'do not match color to system palette
PC_NONE=0   'Polygonals not supported
PC_POLYGON=1 'Can do polygons
PC_RECTANGLE=2 'Can do rectangles
PC_RESERVED=&H1   'palette index used for animation
PC_SCANLINE=8 'Can do scanlines
PC_STYLED=32 'Can do styled borders
PC_TRAPEZOID=4 'Can do trapezoids
PC_WIDE=16 'Can do wide borders
PC_WIDESTYLED=64 'Can do wide styled borders
PC_WINDPOLYGON=4 'Can do winding polygons
PCF_16BITMODE=&H200&
PCF_DTRDSR=&H1&
PCF_INTTIMEOUTS=&H80&
PCF_PARITY_CHECK=&H8&
```

```
PCF_RLSD=&H4&
PCF_RTSCTS=&H2&
PCF_SETXCHAR=&H20&
PCF_SPECIALCHARS=&H100&
PCF_TOTALTIMEOUTS=&H40&
PCF_XONXOFF=&H10&
PD_ALLPAGES=&H0
PD_COLLATE=&H10
PD_DISABLEPRINTTOFILE=&H80000
PD_ENABLEPRINTHOOK=&H1000
PD_ENABLEPRINTTEMPLATE=&H4000
PD_ENABLEPRINTTEMPLATEHANDLE=&H10000
PD_ENABLESETUPHOOK=&H2000
PD_ENABLESETUPTEMPLATE=&H8000
PD_ENABLESETUPTEMPLATEHANDLE=&H20000
PD_HIDEPRINTTOFILE=&H100000
PD_NONETWORKBUTTON=&H200000
PD_NOPAGENUMS=&H8
PD_NOSELECTION=&H4
PD_NOWARNING=&H80
PD_PAGENUMS=&H2
PD_PRINTSETUP=&H40
PD_PRINTTOFILE=&H20
PD_RETURNDC=&H100
PD_RETURNDEFAULT=&H400
PD_RETURNIC=&H200
PD_SELECTION=&H1
PD_SHOWHELP=&H800
PD_USEDEVMODECOPIES=&H40000
PD_USEDEVMODECOPIESANDCOLLATE=&H40000
PDERR_CREATEICFAILURE=&H100A
PDERR_DEFAULTDIFFERENT=&H100C
PDERR_DNDMMISMATCH=&H1009
PDERR_GETDEVMODEFAIL=&H1005
PDERR_INITFAILURE=&H1006
PDERR_LOADDRVFAILURE=&H1004
PDERR_NODEFAULTPRN=&H1008
PDERR_NODEVICES=&H1007
PDERR_PARSEFAILURE=&H1002
PDERR_PRINTERCODES=&H1000
PDERR_PRINTERNOTFOUND=&H100B
PDERR_RETDEFFAILURE=&H1003
PDERR_SETUPFAILURE=&H1001
PDEVICESIZE=26 'Size required for device descriptor
PERF_100NSEC_MULTI_TIMER=(PERF_SIZE_LARGE Or
                         PERF_TYPE_COUNTER Or
                         PERF_DELTA_COUNTER Or
                         PERF_COUNTER_RATE Or
```

```
                                        PERF_TIMER_100NS Or
                                        PERF_MULTI_COUNTER Or
                                        PERF_DISPLAY_PERCENT)
PERF_100NSEC_MULTI_TIMER_INV=(PERF_SIZE_LARGE Or
                                        PERF_TYPE_COUNTER Or
                                        PERF_DELTA_COUNTER Or
                                        PERF_COUNTER_RATE Or
                                        PERF_TIMER_100NS Or
                                        PERF_MULTI_COUNTER Or
                                        PERF_INVERSE_COUNTER Or
                                        PERF_DISPLAY_PERCENT)
PERF_100NSEC_TIMER=(PERF_SIZE_LARGE Or
                           PERF_TYPE_COUNTER Or
                           PERF_COUNTER_RATE Or
                           PERF_TIMER_100NS Or
                           PERF_DELTA_COUNTER Or
                           PERF_DISPLAY_PERCENT)
PERF_100NSEC_TIMER_INV=(PERF_SIZE_LARGE Or
                                   PERF_TYPE_COUNTER Or
                                   PERF_COUNTER_RATE Or
                                   PERF_TIMER_100NS Or
                                   PERF_DELTA_COUNTER Or
                                   PERF_INVERSE_COUNTER Or
                                   PERF_DISPLAY_PERCENT)
PERF_AVERAGE_BASE=(PERF_SIZE_DWORD Or
                           PERF_TYPE_COUNTER Or
                           PERF_COUNTER_BASE Or
                           PERF_DISPLAY_NOSHOW Or
                           &H2)
PERF_AVERAGE_BULK=(PERF_SIZE_LARGE Or
                           PERF_TYPE_COUNTER Or
                           PERF_COUNTER_FRACTION Or
                           PERF_DISPLAY_NOSHOW)
PERF_AVERAGE_TIMER=(PERF_SIZE_DWORD Or
                            PERF_TYPE_COUNTER Or
                            PERF_COUNTER_FRACTION Or
                            PERF_DISPLAY_SECONDS)
PERF_COUNTER_BASE=&H30000 'base value used in fractions
PERF_COUNTER_BULK_COUNT=(PERF_SIZE_LARGE Or
                                     PERF_TYPE_COUNTER Or
                                     PERF_COUNTER_RATE Or
                                     PERF_TIMER_TICK Or
                                     PERF_DELTA_COUNTER Or
                                     PERF_DISPLAY_PER_SEC)
PERF_COUNTER_COUNTER=(PERF_SIZE_DWORD Or
                                PERF_TYPE_COUNTER Or
                                PERF_COUNTER_RATE Or
                                PERF_TIMER_TICK Or
```

```
                              PERF_DELTA_COUNTER Or
                              PERF_DISPLAY_PER_SEC)
PERF_COUNTER_ELAPSED=&H40000 'subtract counter from current time
PERF_COUNTER_FRACTION=&H20000 'divide ctr / base
PERF_COUNTER_HISTOGRAM=&H60000 'Counter begins or ends a histogram
PERF_COUNTER_HISTOGRAM_TYPE=&H80000000  'Counter begins or ends a histogram
PERF_COUNTER_MULTI_BASE=(PERF_SIZE_LARGE Or
                              PERF_TYPE_COUNTER Or
                              PERF_COUNTER_BASE Or
                              PERF_MULTI_COUNTER Or
                              PERF_DISPLAY_NOSHOW)
PERF_COUNTER_MULTI_TIMER=(PERF_SIZE_LARGE Or
                              PERF_TYPE_COUNTER Or
                              PERF_COUNTER_RATE Or
                              PERF_DELTA_COUNTER Or
                              PERF_TIMER_TICK Or
                              PERF_MULTI_COUNTER Or
                              PERF_DISPLAY_PERCENT)
PERF_COUNTER_MULTI_TIMER_INV=(PERF_SIZE_LARGE Or
                              PERF_TYPE_COUNTER Or
                              PERF_COUNTER_RATE Or
                              PERF_DELTA_COUNTER Or
                              PERF_MULTI_COUNTER Or
                              PERF_TIMER_TICK Or
                              PERF_INVERSE_COUNTER Or
                              PERF_DISPLAY_PERCENT)
PERF_COUNTER_NODATA=(PERF_SIZE_ZERO Or
                         PERF_DISPLAY_NOSHOW)
PERF_COUNTER_QUEUELEN=&H50000 'Use Queuelen processing func.
PERF_COUNTER_QUEUELEN_TYPE=(PERF_SIZE_DWORD Or
                              PERF_TYPE_COUNTER Or
                              PERF_COUNTER_QUEUELEN Or
                              PERF_TIMER_TICK Or
                              PERF_DELTA_COUNTER Or
                              PERF_DISPLAY_NO_SUFFIX)
PERF_COUNTER_RATE=&H10000 'divide ctr / delta time
PERF_COUNTER_RAWCOUNT=(PERF_SIZE_DWORD Or
                         PERF_TYPE_NUMBER Or
                         PERF_NUMBER_DECIMAL Or
                         PERF_DISPLAY_NO_SUFFIX)
PERF_COUNTER_TEXT=(PERF_SIZE_VARIABLE_LEN Or
                     PERF_TYPE_TEXT Or
                     PERF_TEXT_UNICODE Or
                     PERF_DISPLAY_NO_SUFFIX)
PERF_COUNTER_TIMER=(PERF_SIZE_LARGE Or
                      PERF_TYPE_COUNTER Or
                      PERF_COUNTER_RATE Or
                      PERF_TIMER_TICK Or
```

```
                            PERF_DELTA_COUNTER Or
                            PERF_DISPLAY_PERCENT)
PERF_COUNTER_TIMER_INV=(PERF_SIZE_LARGE Or
                            PERF_TYPE_COUNTER Or
                            PERF_COUNTER_RATE Or
                            PERF_TIMER_TICK Or
                            PERF_DELTA_COUNTER Or
                            PERF_INVERSE_COUNTER Or
                            PERF_DISPLAY_PERCENT)
PERF_COUNTER_VALUE=&H0 'display counter value
PERF_DATA_REVISION=1
PERF_DATA_VERSION=1
PERF_DELTA_BASE=&H800000 'compute base diff as well
PERF_DELTA_COUNTER=&H400000 'compute difference first
PERF_DETAIL_ADVANCED=200
PERF_DETAIL_EXPERT=300
PERF_DETAIL_NOVICE=100
PERF_DETAIL_WIZARD=400
PERF_DISPLAY_NO_SUFFIX=&H0 'no suffix
PERF_DISPLAY_NOSHOW=&H40000000  'value is not displayed
PERF_DISPLAY_PER_SEC=&H10000000  '"/sec"
PERF_DISPLAY_PERCENT=&H20000000  '"%"
PERF_DISPLAY_SECONDS=&H30000000  '"secs"
PERF_ELAPSED_TIME=(PERF_SIZE_LARGE Or
                        PERF_TYPE_COUNTER Or
                        PERF_COUNTER_ELAPSED Or
                        PERF_OBJECT_TIMER Or
                        PERF_DISPLAY_SECONDS)
PERF_INVERSE_COUNTER=&H1000000 'show as 1.00-value (assumes:
PERF_MULTI_COUNTER=&H2000000 'sum of multiple instances
PERF_NO_INSTANCES=-1  'no instances
PERF_NO_UNIQUE_ID=-1
PERF_NUMBER_DEC_1000=&H20000 'display as a decimal/1000
PERF_NUMBER_DECIMAL=&H10000 'display as a decimal integer
PERF_NUMBER_HEX=&H0 'display as HEX value
PERF_OBJECT_TIMER=&H200000 'use the object timer freq
PERF_RAW_BASE=(PERF_SIZE_DWOR
D Or
 PERF_TYPE_COUNTER Or
 PERF_COUNTER_BASE Or
 PERF_DISPLAY_NOSHOW Or
 &H3) 'fOr
 compatibility with pre-beta versions
PERF_RAW_FRACTION=(PERF_SIZE_DWOR
D Or
 PERF_TYPE_COUNTER Or
 PERF_COUNTER_FRACTION Or
 PERF_DISPLAY_PERCENT)
```

```
PERF_SAMPLE_BASE=(PERF_SIZE_DWOR
D Or
 PERF_TYPE_COUNTER Or
 PERF_COUNTER_BASE Or
 PERF_DISPLAY_NOSHOW Or
 &H1) 'fOr
 compatibility with pre-beta versions
PERF_SAMPLE_COUNTER=(PERF_SIZE_DWOR
D Or
 PERF_TYPE_COUNTER Or
 PERF_COUNTER_RATE Or
 PERF_TIMER_TICK Or
 PERF_DELTA_COUNTER Or
 PERF_DISPLAY_NO_SUFFIX)
PERF_SAMPLE_FRACTION=(PERF_SIZE_DWOR
D Or
 PERF_TYPE_COUNTER Or
 PERF_COUNTER_FRACTION Or
 PERF_DELTA_COUNTER Or
 PERF_DELTA_BASE Or
 PERF_DISPLAY_PERCENT)
PERF_SIZE_DWORD=&H0
PERF_SIZE_LARGE=&H100
PERF_SIZE_VARIABLE_LEN=&H300 'length is in CounterLength
PERF_SIZE_ZERO=&H200 'for Zero Length fields
PERF_TEXT_ASCII=&H10000 'ASCII using the CodePage field
PERF_TEXT_UNICODE=&H0 'type of text in text field
PERF_TIMER_100NS=&H100000 'use 100 NS timer time base units
PERF_TIMER_TICK=&H0 'use system perf. freq for base
PERF_TYPE_COUNTER=&H400 'an increasing numeric value
PERF_TYPE_NUMBER=&H0 'a number (not a counter)
PERF_TYPE_TEXT=&H800 'a text field
PERF_TYPE_ZERO=&HC00 'displays a zero
PHYSICALHEIGHT=111 'Physical Height in device units
PHYSICALOFFSETX=112 'Physical Printable Area x margin
PHYSICALOFFSETY=113 'Physical Printable Area y margin
PHYSICALWIDTH=110 'Physical Width in device units
PIPE_ACCESS_DUPLEX=&H3
PIPE_ACCESS_INBOUND=&H1
PIPE_ACCESS_OUTBOUND=&H2
PIPE_CLIENT_END=&H0
PIPE_NOWAIT=&H1
PIPE_READMODE_BYTE=&H0
PIPE_READMODE_MESSAGE=&H2
PIPE_SERVER_END=&H1
PIPE_TYPE_BYTE=&H0
PIPE_TYPE_MESSAGE=&H4
PIPE_UNLIMITED_INSTANCES=255
```

```
PIPE_WAIT=&H0
PLANES=14 'Number of planes
PM_NOREMOVE=&H0
PM_NOYIELD=&H2
PM_REMOVE=&H1
PO_DELETE=&H13 'printer is being deleted
PO_PORTCHANGE=&H20 'port is being changed
PO_REN_PORT=&H34 'PO_RENAME and PO_PORTCHANGE at same time.
PO_RENAME=&H14 'printer is being renamed
POLYFILL_LAST=2
POLYGONALCAPS=32 'Polygonal capabilities
PORT_TYPE_NET_ATTACHED=&H8
PORT_TYPE_READ=&H2
PORT_TYPE_REDIRECTED=&H4
PORT_TYPE_WRITE=&H1
POSTSCRIPT_DATA=37
POSTSCRIPT_IGNORE=38
POSTSCRIPT_PASSTHROUGH=4115
PR_JOBSTATUS=&H0
PRINTDLGORD=1538
PRINTER_ACCESS_ADMINISTER=&H4
PRINTER_ACCESS_USE=&H8
PRINTER_ALL_ACCESS=(STANDARD_RIGHTS_REQUIRED Or
                    PRINTER_ACCESS_ADMINISTER Or
                    PRINTER_ACCESS_USE)
PRINTER_ATTRIBUTE_DEFAULT=&H4
PRINTER_ATTRIBUTE_DIRECT=&H2
PRINTER_ATTRIBUTE_ENABLE_BIDI=&H800
PRINTER_ATTRIBUTE_HIDDEN=&H20
PRINTER_ATTRIBUTE_LOCAL=&H40
PRINTER_ATTRIBUTE_NETWORK=&H10
PRINTER_ATTRIBUTE_QUEUED=&H1
PRINTER_ATTRIBUTE_SHARED=&H8
PRINTER_ATTRIBUTE_WORK_OFFLINE=&H400
PRINTER_CHANGE_ADD_FORM=&H10000
PRINTER_CHANGE_ADD_JOB=&H100
PRINTER_CHANGE_ADD_PORT=&H100000
PRINTER_CHANGE_ADD_PRINT_PROCESSOR=&H1000000
PRINTER_CHANGE_ADD_PRINTER=&H1
PRINTER_CHANGE_ADD_PRINTER_DRIVER=&H10000000
PRINTER_CHANGE_ALL=&H7777FFFF
PRINTER_CHANGE_CONFIGURE_PORT=&H200000
PRINTER_CHANGE_DELETE_FORM=&H40000
PRINTER_CHANGE_DELETE_JOB=&H400
PRINTER_CHANGE_DELETE_PORT=&H400000
PRINTER_CHANGE_DELETE_PRINT_PROCESSOR=&H4000000
PRINTER_CHANGE_DELETE_PRINTER=&H4
PRINTER_CHANGE_DELETE_PRINTER_DRIVER=&H40000000
```

```
PRINTER_CHANGE_FORM=&H70000
PRINTER_CHANGE_JOB=&HFF00
PRINTER_CHANGE_PORT=&H700000
PRINTER_CHANGE_PRINT_PROCESSOR=&H7000000
PRINTER_CHANGE_PRINTER=&HFF
PRINTER_CHANGE_PRINTER_DRIVER=&H70000000
PRINTER_CHANGE_SET_FORM=&H20000
PRINTER_CHANGE_SET_JOB=&H200
PRINTER_CHANGE_SET_PRINTER=&H2
PRINTER_CHANGE_TIMEOUT=&H80000000
PRINTER_CHANGE_WRITE_JOB=&H800
PRINTER_CONTROL_PAUSE=1
PRINTER_CONTROL_PURGE=3
PRINTER_CONTROL_RESUME=2
PRINTER_CONTROL_SET_STATUS=4
PRINTER_ENUM_CONNECTIONS=&H4
PRINTER_ENUM_CONTAINER=&H8000
PRINTER_ENUM_DEFAULT=&H1
PRINTER_ENUM_EXPAND=&H4000
PRINTER_ENUM_FAVORITE=&H4
PRINTER_ENUM_ICON1=&H10000
PRINTER_ENUM_ICON2=&H20000
PRINTER_ENUM_ICON3=&H40000
PRINTER_ENUM_ICON4=&H80000
PRINTER_ENUM_ICON5=&H100000
PRINTER_ENUM_ICON6=&H200000
PRINTER_ENUM_ICON7=&H400000
PRINTER_ENUM_ICON8=&H800000
PRINTER_ENUM_ICONMASK=&HFF0000
PRINTER_ENUM_LOCAL=&H2
PRINTER_ENUM_NAME=&H8
PRINTER_ENUM_NETWORK=&H40
PRINTER_ENUM_REMOTE=&H10
PRINTER_ENUM_SHARED=&H20
PRINTER_ERROR_INFORMATION=&H80000000
PRINTER_ERROR_JAM=&H2
PRINTER_ERROR_OUTOFPAPER=&H1
PRINTER_ERROR_OUTOFTONER=&H4
PRINTER_ERROR_SEVERE=&H20000000
PRINTER_ERROR_WARNING=&H40000000
PRINTER_EXECUTE=(STANDARD_RIGHTS_EXECUTE Or
                    PRINTER_ACCESS_USE)
PRINTER_FONTTYPE=&H4000
PRINTER_READ=(STANDARD_RIGHTS_READ Or PRINTER_ACCESS_USE)
PRINTER_STATUS_BUSY=&H200
PRINTER_STATUS_DOOR_OPEN=&H400000
PRINTER_STATUS_ERROR=&H2
PRINTER_STATUS_INITIALIZING=&H8000
```

```
PRINTER_STATUS_IO_ACTIVE=&H100
PRINTER_STATUS_MANUAL_FEED=&H20
PRINTER_STATUS_NO_TONER=&H40000
PRINTER_STATUS_NOT_AVAILABLE=&H1000
PRINTER_STATUS_OFFLINE=&H80
PRINTER_STATUS_OUT_OF_MEMORY=&H200000
PRINTER_STATUS_OUTPUT_BIN_FULL=&H800
PRINTER_STATUS_PAGE_PUNT=&H80000
PRINTER_STATUS_PAPER_JAM=&H8
PRINTER_STATUS_PAPER_OUT=&H10
PRINTER_STATUS_PAPER_PROBLEM=&H40
PRINTER_STATUS_PAUSED=&H1
PRINTER_STATUS_PENDING_DELETION=&H4
PRINTER_STATUS_PRINTING=&H400
PRINTER_STATUS_PROCESSING=&H4000
PRINTER_STATUS_TONER_LOW=&H20000
PRINTER_STATUS_USER_INTERVENTION=&H100000
PRINTER_STATUS_WAITING=&H2000
PRINTER_STATUS_WARMING_UP=&H10000
PRINTER_WRITE=(STANDARD_RIGHTS_WRITE Or PRINTER_ACCESS_USE)
PRIVILEGE_SET_ALL_NECESSARY=(1)
PRNSETUPDLGORD=1539
PROCESS_HEAP_ENTRY_BUSY=&H4
PROCESS_HEAP_ENTRY_DDESHARE=&H20
PROCESS_HEAP_ENTRY_MOVEABLE=&H10
PROCESS_HEAP_REGION=&H1
PROCESS_HEAP_UNCOMMITTED_RANGE=&H2
PROFILE_KERNEL=&H20000000
PROFILE_SERVER=&H40000000
PROFILE_USER=&H10000000
PROOF_QUALITY=2
PS_ALTERNATE=8
PS_COSMETIC=&H0
PS_DASH=1 '-------
PS_DASHDOT=3 '_._._._
PS_DASHDOTDOT=4 '_.._.._
PS_DOT=2 '.......
PS_ENDCAP_FLAT=&H200
PS_ENDCAP_MASK=&HF00
PS_ENDCAP_ROUND=&H0
PS_ENDCAP_SQUARE=&H100
PS_GEOMETRIC=&H10000
PS_INSIDEFRAME=6
PS_JOIN_BEVEL=&H1000
PS_JOIN_MASK=&HF000
PS_JOIN_MITER=&H2000
PS_JOIN_ROUND=&H0
PS_NULL=5
```

```
PS_SOLID=0
PS_STYLE_MASK=&HF
PS_TYPE_MASK=&HF0000
PS_USERSTYLE=7
PSD_DEFAULTMINMARGINS=&H0 'default (printer's)
PSD_DISABLEMARGINS=&H10
PSD_DISABLEORIENTATION=&H100
PSD_DISABLEPAGEPAINTING=&H80000
PSD_DISABLEPAPER=&H200
PSD_DISABLEPRINTER=&H20
PSD_ENABLEPAGEPAINTHOOK=&H40000
PSD_ENABLEPAGESETUPHOOK=&H2000 'must be same as PD_*
PSD_ENABLEPAGESETUPTEMPLATE=&H8000 'must be same as PD_*
PSD_ENABLEPAGESETUPTEMPLATEHANDLE=&H20000 'must be same as PD_*
PSD_INHUNDREDTHSOFMILLIMETERS=&H8 '3rd of 4 possible
PSD_INTHOUSANDTHSOFINCHES=&H4 '2nd of 4 possible
PSD_INWININIINTLMEASURE=&H0 '1st of 4 possible
PSD_MARGINS=&H2 'use caller's
PSD_MINMARGINS=&H1 'use caller's
PSD_NOWARNING=&H80 'must be same as PD_*
PSD_RETURNDEFAULT=&H400 'must be same as PD_*
PSD_SHOWHELP=&H800 'must be same as PD_*
psh1=&H400
psh10=&H409
psh11=&H40A
psh12=&H40B
psh13=&H40C
psh14=&H40D
psh15=&H40E
psh16=&H40F
psh2=&H401
psh3=&H402
psh4=&H403
psh5=&H404
psh6=&H405
psh7=&H406
psh8=&H407
psh9=&H408
pshHelp=psh15
PST_FAX=&H21&
PST_LAT=&H101&
PST_NETWORK_BRIDGE=&H100&
PST_PARALLELPORT=&H2&
PST_RS232=&H1&
PST_RS422=&H3&
PST_RS423=&H4&
PST_RS449=&H5&
PST_SCANNER=&H22&
```

```
PST_TCPIP_TELNET=&H102&
PST_UNSPECIFIED=&H0&
PST_X25=&H103&
PT_BEZIERTO=&H4
PT_CLOSEFIGURE=&H1
PT_LINETO=&H2
PT_MOVETO=&H6
PURGE_RXABORT=&H2 'Kill pending/current reads to comm port.
PURGE_RXCLEAR=&H8 'Kill typeahead buffer if there.
PURGE_TXABORT=&H1 'Kill pending/current writes to comm port.
PURGE_TXCLEAR=&H4 'Kill transmit queue if there.
PWR_CRITICALRESUME=3
PWR_FAIL=(-1)
PWR_OK=1
PWR_SUSPENDREQUEST=1
PWR_SUSPENDRESUME=2

Q
QID_SYNC=&HFFFF
QS_ALLEVENTS=(QS_INPUT Or QS_POSTMESSAGE Or
               QS_TIMER Or QS_PAINT Or QS_HOTKEY)
QS_ALLINPUT=(QS_SENDMESSAGE Or QS_PAINT Or QS_TIMER Or
              QS_POSTMESSAGE Or QS_MOUSEBUTTON Or
              QS_MOUSEMOVE Or QS_HOTKEY Or QS_KEY)
QS_HOTKEY=&H80
QS_INPUT=(QS_MOUSE Or QS_KEY)
QS_KEY=&H1
QS_MOUSE=(QS_MOUSEMOVE Or QS_MOUSEBUTTON)
QS_MOUSEBUTTON=&H4
QS_MOUSEMOVE=&H2
QS_PAINT=&H20
QS_POSTMESSAGE=&H8
QS_SENDMESSAGE=&H40
QS_TIMER=&H10
QUERYESCSUPPORT=8
QUERYROPSUPPORT=40   'use to determine ROP support

R
R2_BLACK=1 '0
R2_COPYPEN=13 'P
R2_LAST=16
R2_MASKNOTPEN=3   'DPna
R2_MASKPEN=9 'DPa
R2_MASKPENNOT=5   'PDna
R2_MERGENOTPEN=12 'DPno
R2_MERGEPEN=15 'DPo
R2_MERGEPENNOT=14 'PDno
R2_NOP=11 'D
R2_NOT=6 'Dn
```

```
R2_NOTCOPYPEN=4    'PN
R2_NOTMASKPEN=8    'DPan
R2_NOTMERGEPEN=2   'DPon
R2_NOTXORPEN=10    'DPxn
R2_WHITE=16 '1
R2_XORPEN=7 'DPx
rad1=&H420
rad10=&H429
rad11=&H42A
rad12=&H42B
rad13=&H42C
rad14=&H42D
rad15=&H42E
rad16=&H42F
rad2=&H421
rad3=&H422
rad4=&H423
rad5=&H424
rad6=&H425
rad7=&H426
rad8=&H427
rad9=&H428
RASTER_FONTTYPE=&H1
RASTERCAPS=38 'Bitblt capabilities
RC_BANDING=2 'Device requires banding support
RC_BIGFONT=&H400 'supports >64K fonts
RC_BITBLT=1 'Can do standard BLT.
RC_BITMAP64=8   'Device can support >64K bitmap
RC_DEVBITS=&H8000
RC_DI_BITMAP=&H80   'supports DIB to memory
RC_DIBTODEV=&H200   'supports DIBitsToDevice
RC_FLOODFILL=&H1000 'supports FloodFill
RC_GDI20_OUTPUT=&H10 'has 2.0 output calls
RC_GDI20_STATE=&H20
RC_NONE=0
RC_OP_DX_OUTPUT=&H4000
RC_PALETTE=&H100 'supports a palette
RC_SAVEBITMAP=&H40
RC_SCALING=4 'Device requires scaling support
RC_STRETCHBLT=&H800 'supports StretchBlt
RC_STRETCHDIB=&H2000 'supports StretchDIBits
rct1=&H438
rct2=&H439
rct3=&H43A
rct4=&H43B
RDH_RECTANGLES=1
RDW_ALLCHILDREN=&H80
RDW_ERASE=&H4
```

```
RDW_ERASENOW=&H200
RDW_FRAME=&H400
RDW_INTERNALPAINT=&H2
RDW_INVALIDATE=&H1
RDW_NOCHILDREN=&H40
RDW_NOERASE=&H20
RDW_NOFRAME=&H800
RDW_NOINTERNALPAINT=&H10
RDW_UPDATENOW=&H100
RDW_VALIDATE=&H8
READ_CONTROL=&H20000
READ_CONTROL=&H20000
READ_WRITE=2
READAPI=0 'Flags for _lopen
REALTIME_PRIORITY_CLASS=&H100
REFERENCE_BLACK_MAX=4000
REFERENCE_BLACK_MIN=0
REFERENCE_WHITE_MAX=10000
REFERENCE_WHITE_MIN=6000 'words
REG_BINARY=3 'Free form binary
REG_CREATED_NEW_KEY=&H1 'New Registry Key created
REG_DWORD=4 '32-bit number
REG_DWORD_BIG_ENDIAN=5 '32-bit number
REG_DWORD_LITTLE_ENDIAN=4 '32-bit number (same as REG_DWORD)
REG_EXPAND_SZ=2 'Unicode nul terminated string
REG_FULL_RESOURCE_DESCRIPTOR=9 'Resource list in hardware desc.
REG_LEGAL_CHANGE_FILTER=(REG_NOTIFY_CHANGE_NAME Or
REG_NOTIFY_CHANGE_ATTRIBUTES Or REG_NOTIFY_CHANGE_LAST_SET Or
REG_NOTIFY_CHANGE_SECURITY)
REG_LEGAL_OPTION=(REG_OPTION_RESERVED Or
                  REG_OPTION_NON_VOLATILE Or
                  REG_OPTION_VOLATILE Or
                  REG_OPTION_CREATE_LINK Or
                  REG_OPTION_BACKUP_RESTORE)
REG_LINK=6 'Symbolic Link (unicode)
REG_MULTI_SZ=7 'Multiple Unicode strings
REG_NONE=0 'No value type
REG_NOTIFY_CHANGE_ATTRIBUTES=&H2
REG_NOTIFY_CHANGE_LAST_SET=&H4 'Time stamp
REG_NOTIFY_CHANGE_NAME=&H1 'Create or delete (child)
REG_NOTIFY_CHANGE_SECURITY=&H8
REG_OPENED_EXISTING_KEY=&H2 'Existing Key opened
REG_OPTION_BACKUP_RESTORE=4 'open for backup or restore
REG_OPTION_CREATE_LINK=2 'Created key is a symbolic link
REG_OPTION_NON_VOLATILE=0 'Key is preserved when rebooted
REG_OPTION_RESERVED=0 'Parameter is reserved
REG_OPTION_VOLATILE=1 'Key is not preserved when rebooted
REG_REFRESH_HIVE=&H2 'Unwind changes to last flush
```

```
REG_RESOURCE_LIST=8 'Resource list in the resource map
REG_RESOURCE_REQUIREMENTS_LIST=10
REG_SZ=1 'Unicode nul terminated string
REG_WHOLE_HIVE_VOLATILE=&H1 'Restore whole hive volatile
REGDB_E_CLASSNOTREG=&H80040154
REGDB_E_FIRST=&H80040150
REGDB_E_IIDNOTREG=&H80040155
REGDB_E_INVALIDVALUE=&H80040153
REGDB_E_KEYMISSING=&H80040152
REGDB_E_LAST=&H8004015F
REGDB_E_READREGDB=&H80040150
REGDB_E_WRITEREGDB=&H80040151
REGDB_S_FIRST=&H40150
REGDB_S_LAST=&H4015F
REGISTERED=&H4
REGISTERING=&H0
REGULAR_FONTTYPE=&H400
RELATIVE=2
REPLACEDLGORD=1541
RESETDEV=7 'Reset device if possible
RESOURCE_CONNECTED=&H1
RESOURCE_PUBLICNET=&H2
RESOURCE_REMEMBERED=&H3
RESOURCEDISPLAYTYPE_DOMAIN=&H1
RESOURCEDISPLAYTYPE_FILE=&H4
RESOURCEDISPLAYTYPE_GENERIC=&H0
RESOURCEDISPLAYTYPE_GROUP=&H5
RESOURCEDISPLAYTYPE_SERVER=&H2
RESOURCEDISPLAYTYPE_SHARE=&H3
RESOURCETYPE_ANY=&H0
RESOURCETYPE_DISK=&H1
RESOURCETYPE_PRINT=&H2
RESOURCETYPE_UNKNOWN=&HFFFF
RESOURCEUSAGE_CONNECTABLE=&H1
RESOURCEUSAGE_CONTAINER=&H2
RESOURCEUSAGE_RESERVED=&H80000000
RESTORE_CTM=4100
RGB_GAMMA_MAX=65000
RGB_GAMMA_MIN=2500 'words
RGN_AND=1
RGN_COPY=5
RGN_DIFF=4
RGN_MAX=RGN_COPY
RGN_MIN=RGN_AND
RGN_OR=2
RGN_XOR=3
RIGHT_ALT_PRESSED=&H1 'the right alt key is pressed.
RIGHT_CTRL_PRESSED=&H4 'the right ctrl key is pressed.
```

```
RIGHTMOST_BUTTON_PRESSED=&H2
RIP_EVENT=9
RPC_E_ATTEMPTED_MULTITHREAD=&H80010102
RPC_E_CALL_CANCELED=&H80010002
RPC_E_CALL_REJECTED=&H80010001
RPC_E_CANTCALLOUT_AGAIN=&H80010011
RPC_E_CANTCALLOUT_INASYNCCALL=&H80010004
RPC_E_CANTCALLOUT_INEXTERNALCALL=&H80010005
RPC_E_CANTCALLOUT_ININPUTSYNCCALL=&H8001010D
RPC_E_CANTPOST_INSENDCALL=&H80010003
RPC_E_CANTTRANSMIT_CALL=&H8001000A
RPC_E_CHANGED_MODE=&H80010106
RPC_E_CLIENT_CANTMARSHAL_DATA=&H8001000B
RPC_E_CLIENT_CANTUNMARSHAL_DATA=&H8001000C
RPC_E_CLIENT_DIED=&H80010008
RPC_E_CONNECTION_TERMINATED=&H80010006
RPC_E_DISCONNECTED=&H80010108
RPC_E_FAULT=&H80010104
RPC_E_INVALID_CALLDATA=&H8001010C
RPC_E_INVALID_DATA=&H8001000F
RPC_E_INVALID_DATAPACKET=&H80010009
RPC_E_INVALID_PARAMETER=&H80010010
RPC_E_INVALIDMETHOD=&H80010107
RPC_E_NOT_REGISTERED=&H80010103
RPC_E_OUT_OF_RESOURCES=&H80010101
RPC_E_RETRY=&H80010109
RPC_E_SERVER_CANTMARSHAL_DATA=&H8001000D
RPC_E_SERVER_CANTUNMARSHAL_DATA=&H8001000E
RPC_E_SERVER_DIED=&H80010007
RPC_E_SERVER_DIED_DNE=&H80010012
RPC_E_SERVERCALL_REJECTED=&H8001010B
RPC_E_SERVERCALL_RETRYLATER=&H8001010A
RPC_E_SERVERFAULT=&H80010105
RPC_E_SYS_CALL_FAILED=&H80010100
RPC_E_THREAD_NOT_INIT=&H8001010F
RPC_E_UNEXPECTED=&H8001FFFF
RPC_E_WRONG_THREAD=&H8001010E
RPC_S_ADDRESS_ERROR=1768&
RPC_S_ALREADY_LISTENING=1713&
RPC_S_ALREADY_REGISTERED=1711&
RPC_S_BINDING_HAS_NO_AUTH=1746&
RPC_S_CALL_FAILED=1726&
RPC_S_CALL_FAILED_DNE=1727&
RPC_S_CALL_IN_PROGRESS=1791&
RPC_S_CANNOT_SUPPORT=1764&
RPC_S_CANT_CREATE_ENDPOINT=1720&
RPC_S_DUPLICATE_ENDPOINT=1740&
RPC_S_ENTRY_ALREADY_EXISTS=1760&
```

```
RPC_S_ENTRY_NOT_FOUND=1761&
RPC_S_FP_DIV_ZERO=1769&
RPC_S_FP_OVERFLOW=1771&
RPC_S_FP_UNDERFLOW=1770&
RPC_S_GROUP_MEMBER_NOT_FOUND=1898&
RPC_S_INCOMPLETE_NAME=1755&
RPC_S_INTERFACE_NOT_FOUND=1759&
RPC_S_INTERNAL_ERROR=1766&
RPC_S_INVALID_AUTH_IDENTITY=1749&
RPC_S_INVALID_BINDING=1702&
RPC_S_INVALID_BOUND=1734&
RPC_S_INVALID_ENDPOINT_FORMAT=1706&
RPC_S_INVALID_NAF_ID=1763&
RPC_S_INVALID_NAME_SYNTAX=1736&
RPC_S_INVALID_NET_ADDR=1707&
RPC_S_INVALID_NETWORK_OPTIONS=1724&
RPC_S_INVALID_OBJECT=1900&
RPC_S_INVALID_RPC_PROTSEQ=1704&
RPC_S_INVALID_STRING_BINDING=1700&
RPC_S_INVALID_STRING_UUID=1705&
RPC_S_INVALID_TAG=1733&
RPC_S_INVALID_TIMEOUT=1709&
RPC_S_INVALID_VERS_OPTION=1756&
RPC_S_MAX_CALLS_TOO_SMALL=1742&
RPC_S_NAME_SERVICE_UNAVAILABLE=1762&
RPC_S_NO_BINDINGS=1718&
RPC_S_NO_CALL_ACTIVE=1725&
RPC_S_NO_CONTEXT_AVAILABLE=1765&
RPC_S_NO_ENDPOINT_FOUND=1708&
RPC_S_NO_ENTRY_NAME=1735&
RPC_S_NO_MORE_BINDINGS=1806&
RPC_S_NO_MORE_MEMBERS=1757&
RPC_S_NO_PROTSEQS=1719&
RPC_S_NO_PROTSEQS_REGISTERED=1714&
RPC_S_NOT_ALL_OBJS_UNEXPORTED=1758&
RPC_S_NOT_LISTENING=1715&
RPC_S_NOTHING_TO_EXPORT=1754&
RPC_S_OBJECT_NOT_FOUND=1710&
RPC_S_OUT_OF_RESOURCES=1721&
RPC_S_PROCNUM_OUT_OF_RANGE=1745&
RPC_S_PROTOCOL_ERROR=1728&
RPC_S_PROTSEQ_NOT_FOUND=1744&
RPC_S_PROTSEQ_NOT_SUPPORTED=1703&
RPC_S_SERVER_TOO_BUSY=1723&
RPC_S_SERVER_UNAVAILABLE=1722&
RPC_S_STRING_TOO_LONG=1743&
RPC_S_TYPE_ALREADY_REGISTERED=1712&
RPC_S_UNKNOWN_AUTHN_LEVEL=1748&
```

```
RPC_S_UNKNOWN_AUTHN_SERVICE=1747&
RPC_S_UNKNOWN_AUTHN_TYPE=1741&
RPC_S_UNKNOWN_AUTHZ_SERVICE=1750&
RPC_S_UNKNOWN_IF=1717&
RPC_S_UNKNOWN_MGR_TYPE=1716&
RPC_S_UNSUPPORTED_NAME_SYNTAX=1737&
RPC_S_UNSUPPORTED_TRANS_SYN=1730&
RPC_S_UNSUPPORTED_TYPE=1732&
RPC_S_UUID_NO_ADDRESS=1739&
RPC_S_WRONG_KIND_OF_BINDING=1701&
RPC_S_ZERO_DIVIDE=1767&
RPC_X_BAD_STUB_DATA=1783&
RPC_X_BYTE_COUNT_TOO_SMALL=1782&
RPC_X_ENUM_VALUE_OUT_OF_RANGE=1781&
RPC_X_NO_MORE_ENTRIES=1772&
RPC_X_NULL_REF_POINTER=1780&
RPC_X_SS_CANNOT_GET_CALL_HANDLE=1779&
RPC_X_SS_CHAR_TRANS_OPEN_FAIL=1773&
RPC_X_SS_CHAR_TRANS_SHORT_FILE=1774&
RPC_X_SS_CONTEXT_DAMAGED=1777&
RPC_X_SS_HANDLES_MISMATCH=1778&
RPC_X_SS_IN_NULL_CONTEXT=1775&
RT_ACCELERATOR=9&
RT_BITMAP=2&
RT_CURSOR=1&
RT_DIALOG=5&
RT_FONT=8&
RT_FONTDIR=7&
RT_ICON=3&
RT_MENU=4&
RT_RCDATA=10&
RT_STRING=6&
RTS_CONTROL_DISABLE=&H0
RTS_CONTROL_ENABLE=&H1
RTS_CONTROL_HANDSHAKE=&H2
RTS_CONTROL_TOGGLE=&H3
RUSSIAN_CHARSET=204

S
S_ALLTHRESHOLD=2
S_FALSE=&H1
S_LEGATO=1
S_NORMAL=0
S_OK=&H0
S_PERIOD1024=1 'Freq=N/1024
S_PERIOD2048=2 'Freq=N/2048 low pitch, more coarse hiss
S_PERIOD512=0 'Freq=N/512 high pitch, less coarse hiss
S_PERIODVOICE=3  'Source is frequency from voice channel (3)
```

```
S_QUEUEEMPTY=0
S_SERBDNT=(-5) 'Invalid note
S_SERDCC=(-7) 'Invalid note count
S_SERDDR=(-14) 'Invalid duration
S_SERDFQ=(-13) 'Invalid frequency
S_SERDLN=(-6) 'Invalid note length
S_SERDMD=(-10) 'Invalid mode
S_SERDPT=(-12) 'Invalid pitch
S_SERDSH=(-11) 'Invalid shape
S_SERDSR=(-15) 'Invalid source
S_SERDST=(-16) 'Invalid state
S_SERDTP=(-8) 'Invalid tempo
S_SERDVL=(-9) 'Invalid volume
S_SERDVNA=(-1) 'Device not available
S_SERMACT=(-3) 'Music active
S_SEROFM=(-2) 'Out of memory
S_SERQFUL=(-4) 'Queue full
S_STACCATO=2
S_THRESHOLD=1
S_WHITE1024=5 'Freq=N/1024
S_WHITE2048=6 'Freq=N/2048 low pitch, more coarse hiss
S_WHITE512=4 'Freq=N/512 high pitch, less coarse hiss
S_WHITEVOICE=7 'Source is frequency from voice channel (3)
SAVE_CTM=4101
SB_BOTH=3
SB_BOTTOM=7
SB_CTL=2
SB_ENDSCROLL=8
SB_HORZ=0
SB_LEFT=6
SB_LINEDOWN=1
SB_LINELEFT=0
SB_LINERIGHT=1
SB_LINEUP=0
SB_PAGEDOWN=3
SB_PAGELEFT=2
SB_PAGERIGHT=3
SB_PAGEUP=2
SB_RIGHT=7
SB_THUMBPOSITION=4
SB_THUMBTRACK=5
SB_TOP=6
SB_VERT=1
SBM_ENABLE_ARROWS=&HE4 'not in win3.1
SBM_GETPOS=&HE1 'not in win3.1
SBM_GETRANGE=&HE3 'not in win3.1
SBM_SETPOS=&HE0 'not in win3.1
SBM_SETRANGE=&HE2 'not in win3.1
```

```
SBM_SETRANGEREDRAW=&HE6 'not in win3.1
SBS_BOTTOMALIGN=&H4&
SBS_HORZ=&H0&
SBS_LEFTALIGN=&H2&
SBS_RIGHTALIGN=&H4&
SBS_SIZEBOX=&H8&
SBS_SIZEBOXBOTTOMRIGHTALIGN=&H4&
SBS_SIZEBOXTOPLEFTALIGN=&H2&
SBS_TOPALIGN=&H2&
SBS_VERT=&H1&
SC_ARRANGE=&HF110
SC_CLOSE=&HF060
SC_GROUP_IDENTIFIER="+"
SC_HOTKEY=&HF150
SC_HSCROLL=&HF080
SC_ICON=SC_MINIMIZE
SC_KEYMENU=&HF100
SC_MANAGER_ALL_ACCESS=(STANDARD_RIGHTS_REQUIRED Or
                       SC_MANAGER_CONNECT Or
                       SC_MANAGER_CREATE_SERVICE Or
                       SC_MANAGER_ENUMERATE_SERVICE Or
                       SC_MANAGER_LOCK Or
                       SC_MANAGER_QUERY_LOCK_STATUS Or
                       SC_MANAGER_MODIFY_BOOT_CONFIG)
SC_MANAGER_CONNECT=&H1
SC_MANAGER_CREATE_SERVICE=&H2
SC_MANAGER_ENUMERATE_SERVICE=&H4
SC_MANAGER_LOCK=&H8
SC_MANAGER_MODIFY_BOOT_CONFIG=&H20
SC_MANAGER_QUERY_LOCK_STATUS=&H10
SC_MAXIMIZE=&HF030
SC_MINIMIZE=&HF020
SC_MOUSEMENU=&HF090
SC_MOVE=&HF010
SC_NEXTWINDOW=&HF040
SC_PREVWINDOW=&HF050
SC_RESTORE=&HF120
SC_SCREENSAVE=&HF140
SC_SIZE=&HF000
SC_TASKLIST=&HF130
SC_VSCROLL=&HF070
SC_ZOOM=SC_MAXIMIZE
SCALINGFACTORX=114 'Scaling factor x
SCALINGFACTORY=115 'Scaling factor y
scr1=&H490
scr2=&H491
scr3=&H492
scr4=&H493
```

```
scr5=&H494
scr6=&H495
scr7=&H496
scr8=&H497
SCREEN_FONTTYPE=&H2000
SCROLLLOCK_ON=&H40 'the scrolllock light is on.
SCS_32BIT_BINARY=0
SCS_CAP_COMPSTR=&H1
SCS_CAP_MAKEREAD=&H2
SCS_CHANGEATTR=(GCS_COMPREADATTR Or GCS_COMPATTR)
SCS_CHANGECLAUSE=(GCS_COMPREADCLAUSE Or GCS_COMPCLAUSE)
SCS_DOS_BINARY=1
SCS_OS216_BINARY=5
SCS_PIF_BINARY=3
SCS_POSIX_BINARY=4
SCS_SETSTR=(GCS_COMPREADSTR Or GCS_COMPSTR)
SCS_WOW_BINARY=2
SE_ASSIGNPRIMARYTOKEN_NAME="SeAssignPrimaryTokenPrivilege"
SE_AUDIT_NAME="SeAuditPrivilege"
SE_BACKUP_NAME="SeBackupPrivilege"
SE_CHANGE_NOTIFY_NAME="SeChangeNotifyPrivilege"
SE_CREATE_PAGEFILE_NAME="SeCreatePagefilePrivilege"
SE_CREATE_PERMANENT_NAME="SeCreatePermanentPrivilege"
SE_CREATE_TOKEN_NAME="SeCreateTokenPrivilege"
SE_DACL_DEFAULTED=&H8
SE_DACL_PRESENT=&H4
SE_DEBUG_NAME="SeDebugPrivilege"
SE_ERR_ACCESSDENIED=5 'access denied
SE_ERR_ASSOCINCOMPLETE=27
SE_ERR_DDEBUSY=30
SE_ERR_DDEFAIL=29
SE_ERR_DDETIMEOUT=28
SE_ERR_DLLNOTFOUND=32
SE_ERR_FNF=2 'file not found
SE_ERR_NOASSOC=31
SE_ERR_OOM=8 'out of memory
SE_ERR_PNF=3 'path not found
SE_ERR_SHARE=26
SE_GROUP_DEFAULTED=&H2
SE_GROUP_ENABLED=&H4
SE_GROUP_ENABLED_BY_DEFAULT=&H2
SE_GROUP_LOGON_ID=&HC0000000
SE_GROUP_MANDATORY=&H1
SE_GROUP_OWNER=&H8
SE_INC_BASE_PRIORITY_NAME="SeIncreaseBasePriorityPrivilege"
SE_INCREASE_QUOTA_NAME="SeIncreaseQuotaPrivilege"
SE_LOAD_DRIVER_NAME="SeLoadDriverPrivilege"
SE_LOCK_MEMORY_NAME="SeLockMemoryPrivilege"
```

```
SE_MACHINE_ACCOUNT_NAME="SeMachineAccountPrivilege"
SE_OWNER_DEFAULTED=&H1
SE_PRIVILEGE_ENABLED=&H2
SE_PRIVILEGE_ENABLED_BY_DEFAULT=&H1
SE_PRIVILEGE_USED_FOR_ACCESS=&H80000000
SE_PROF_SINGLE_PROCESS_NAME="SeProfileSingleProcessPrivilege"
SE_REMOTE_SHUTDOWN_NAME="SeRemoteShutdownPrivilege"
SE_RESTORE_NAME="SeRestorePrivilege"
SE_SACL_DEFAULTED=&H20
SE_SACL_PRESENT=&H10
SE_SECURITY_NAME="SeSecurityPrivilege"
SE_SELF_RELATIVE=&H8000
SE_SHUTDOWN_NAME="SeShutdownPrivilege"
SE_SYSTEM_ENVIRONMENT_NAME="SeSystemEnvironmentPrivilege"
SE_SYSTEM_PROFILE_NAME="SeSystemProfilePrivilege"
SE_SYSTEMTIME_NAME="SeSystemtimePrivilege"
SE_TAKE_OWNERSHIP_NAME="SeTakeOwnershipPrivilege"
SE_TCB_NAME="SeTcbPrivilege"
SE_UNSOLICITED_INPUT_NAME="SeUnsolicitedInputPrivilege"
SECTION_ALL_ACCESS=STANDARD_RIGHTS_REQUIRED Or
                   SECTION_QUERY Or SECTION_MAP_WRITE Or
                   SECTION_MAP_READ Or SECTION_MAP_EXECUTE Or
                   SECTION_EXTEND_SIZE
SECTION_EXTEND_SIZE=&H10
SECTION_MAP_EXECUTE=&H8
SECTION_MAP_READ=&H4
SECTION_MAP_WRITE=&H2
SECTION_QUERY=&H1
SECURITY_ANONYMOUS_LOGON_RID=&H7
SECURITY_BATCH_RID=&H3
SECURITY_BUILTIN_DOMAIN_RID=&H20
SECURITY_CONTEXT_TRACKING=&H40000
SECURITY_CREATOR_GROUP_RID=&H1
SECURITY_CREATOR_OWNER_RID=&H0
SECURITY_DESCRIPTOR_MIN_LENGTH=(20)
SECURITY_DESCRIPTOR_REVISION=(1)
SECURITY_DESCRIPTOR_REVISION1=(1)
SECURITY_DIALUP_RID=&H1
SECURITY_EFFECTIVE_ONLY=&H80000
SECURITY_INTERACTIVE_RID=&H4
SECURITY_LOCAL_RID=&H0
SECURITY_LOCAL_SYSTEM_RID=&H12
SECURITY_LOGON_IDS_RID=&H5
SECURITY_NETWORK_RID=&H2
SECURITY_NT_NON_UNIQUE=&H15
SECURITY_NULL_RID=&H0
SECURITY_SERVICE_RID=&H6
SECURITY_SQOS_PRESENT=&H100000
SECURITY_VALID_SQOS_FLAGS=&H1F0000
```

```
SECURITY_WORLD_RID=&H0
SecurityAnonymous=1
SecurityIdentification=2
SEE_MASK_CLASSKEY=&H3
SEE_MASK_CLASSNAME=&H1
SEE_MASK_CONNECTNETDRV=&H80
SEE_MASK_DOENVSUBST=&H200
SEE_MASK_FLAG_DDEWAIT=&H100
SEE_MASK_FLAG_NO_UI=&H400
SEE_MASK_HOTKEY=&H20
SEE_MASK_ICON=&H10
SEE_MASK_IDLIST=&H4
SEE_MASK_INVOKEIDLIST=&HC
SEE_MASK_NOCLOSEPROCESS=&H40
SEEK_CUR=1   'seek relative to current position
SEEK_END=2   'seek relative to end of file
SEEK_SET=0   'seek to an absolute position
SELECT_CAP_CONVERSION=&H1
SELECT_CAP_SENTENCE=&H2
SELECTDIB=41    'DIB.DRV select dib escape
SELECTPAPERSOURCE=18
SEM_FAILCRITICALERRORS=&H1
SEM_NOGPFAULTERRORBOX=&H2
SEM_NOOPENFILEERRORBOX=&H8000
SERVER_ACCESS_ADMINISTER=&H1
SERVER_ACCESS_ENUMERATE=&H2
SERVER_ALL_ACCESS=(STANDARD_RIGHTS_REQUIRED Or
                    SERVER_ACCESS_ADMINISTER Or
                    SERVER_ACCESS_ENUMERATE)
SERVER_EXECUTE=(STANDARD_RIGHTS_EXECUTE Or
                   SERVER_ACCESS_ENUMERATE)
SERVER_READ=(STANDARD_RIGHTS_READ Or SERVER_ACCESS_ENUMERATE)
SERVER_WRITE=(STANDARD_RIGHTS_WRITE Or
                SERVER_ACCESS_ADMINISTER Or
                SERVER_ACCESS_ENUMERATE)
SERVICE_ACCEPT_PAUSE_CONTINUE=&H2
SERVICE_ACCEPT_SHUTDOWN=&H4
SERVICE_ACCEPT_STOP=&H1
SERVICE_ACTIVE=&H1
SERVICE_ALL_ACCESS=(STANDARD_RIGHTS_REQUIRED Or
                    SERVICE_QUERY_CONFIG Or
                    SERVICE_CHANGE_CONFIG Or
                    SERVICE_QUERY_STATUS Or
                    SERVICE_ENUMERATE_DEPENDENTS Or
                    SERVICE_START Or SERVICE_STOP Or
                    SERVICE_PAUSE_CONTINUE Or
                    SERVICE_INTERROGATE Or
                    SERVICE_USER_DEFINED_CONTROL)
SERVICE_CHANGE_CONFIG=&H2
```

```
SERVICE_CONTINUE_PENDING=&H5
SERVICE_CONTROL_CONTINUE=&H3
SERVICE_CONTROL_INTERROGATE=&H4
SERVICE_CONTROL_PAUSE=&H2
SERVICE_CONTROL_SHUTDOWN=&H5
SERVICE_CONTROL_STOP=&H1
SERVICE_ENUMERATE_DEPENDENTS=&H8
SERVICE_INACTIVE=&H2
SERVICE_INTERROGATE=&H80
SERVICE_NO_CHANGE=&HFFFF
SERVICE_PAUSE_CONTINUE=&H40
SERVICE_PAUSE_PENDING=&H6
SERVICE_PAUSED=&H7
SERVICE_QUERY_CONFIG=&H1
SERVICE_QUERY_STATUS=&H4
SERVICE_RUNNING=&H4
SERVICE_START=&H10
SERVICE_START_PENDING=&H2
SERVICE_STATE_ALL=(SERVICE_ACTIVE Or SERVICE_INACTIVE)
SERVICE_STOP=&H20
SERVICE_STOP_PENDING=&H3
SERVICE_STOPPED=&H1
SERVICE_USER_DEFINED_CONTROL=&H100
SERVICES_ACTIVE_DATABASE="ServicesActive"
SERVICES_FAILED_DATABASE="ServicesFailed"
SESSION_ABORTED=&H6
SESSION_ESTABLISHED=&H3
SET_ARC_DIRECTION=4102
SET_BACKGROUND_COLOR=4103
SET_BOUNDS=4109
SET_CLIP_BOX=4108
SET_MIRROR_MODE=4110
SET_POLY_MODE=4104
SET_SCREEN_ANGLE=4105
SET_SPREAD=4106
SET_TAPE_DRIVE_INFORMATION=1
SET_TAPE_MEDIA_INFORMATION=0
SETABORTPROC=9
SETALLJUSTVALUES=771
SETBREAK=8   'Set the device break line
SETCHARSET=772
SETCOLORTABLE=4
SETCOPYCOUNT=17
SETDIBSCALING=32
SETDTR=5 'Set DTR high
SETKERNTRACK=770
SETLINECAP=21
SETLINEJOIN=22
```

```
SetMiterLimitC=23
SETRGBSTRING="commdlg_SetRGBColor"
SETRTS=3 'Set RTS high
SETXOFF=1  'Simulate XOFF received
SETXON=2 'Simulate XON received
SEVERITY_ERROR=1
SEVERITY_SUCCESS=0
SHAREVISTRING="commdlg_ShareViolation"
SHGFI_ATTRIBUTES=&H800 'get attributes
SHGFI_DISPLAYNAME=&H200 'get display name
SHGFI_EXETYPE=&H2000 'return exe type
SHGFI_ICON=&H100 'get icon
SHGFI_ICONLOCATION=&H1000  'get icon location
SHGFI_LARGEICON=&H0 'get large icon
SHGFI_LINKOVERLAY=&H8000 'put a link overlay on icon
SHGFI_OPENICON=&H2 'get open icon
SHGFI_PIDL=&H8 'pszPath is a pidl
SHGFI_SELECTED=&H10000 'show icon in selected state
SHGFI_SHELLICONSIZE=&H4 'get shell size icon
SHGFI_SMALLICON=&H1 'get small icon
SHGFI_SYSICONINDEX=&H4000  'get system icon index
SHGFI_TYPENAME=&H400 'get type name
SHGFI_USEFILEATTRIBUTES=&H10 'use passed dwFileAttribute
SHGNLI_PIDL=&H1 'pszLinkTo is a pidl
SHGNLI_PREFIXNAME=&H2 'Make name "Shortcut to xxx"
SHIFT_PRESSED=&H10 'the shift key is pressed.
SHIFTJIS_CHARSET=128
SHOW_FULLSCREEN=3
SHOW_ICONWINDOW=2
SHOW_OPENNOACTIVATE=4
SHOW_OPENWINDOW=1
SHUTDOWN_NORETRY=&H1
SID_MAX_SUB_AUTHORITIES=(15)
SID_RECOMMENDED_SUB_AUTHORITIES=(1)
SID_REVISION=(1) 'Current revision level
SidTypeAlias=4
SidTypeDeletedAccount=6
SidTypeDomain=3
SidTypeGroup=2
SidTypeInvalid=7
SidTypeUnknown=8
SidTypeUser=1
SidTypeWellKnownGroup=5
SIMPLEREGION=2
SIMULATED_FONTTYPE=&H8000
SIZE_MAXHIDE=4
SIZE_MAXIMIZED=2
SIZE_MAXSHOW=3
```

```
SIZE_MINIMIZED=1
SIZE_RESTORED=0
SIZEFULLSCREEN=SIZE_MAXIMIZED
SIZEICONIC=SIZE_MINIMIZED
SIZENORMAL=SIZE_RESTORED
SIZEPALETTE=104 'Number of entries in physical palette
SIZEZOOMHIDE=SIZE_MAXHIDE
SIZEZOOMSHOW=SIZE_MAXSHOW
SLE_ERROR=&H1
SLE_MINORERROR=&H2
SLE_WARNING=&H3
SM_CMETRICS=44
SM_CMOUSEBUTTONS=43
SM_CXBORDER=5
SM_CXCURSOR=13
SM_CXDLGFRAME=7
SM_CXDOUBLECLK=36
SM_CXFIXEDFRAME=SM_CXDLGFRAME
SM_CXFRAME=32
SM_CXFULLSCREEN=16
SM_CXHSCROLL=21
SM_CXHTHUMB=10
SM_CXICON=11
SM_CXICONSPACING=38
SM_CXMIN=28
SM_CXMINTRACK=34
SM_CXSCREEN=0
SM_CXSIZE=30
SM_CXSIZEFRAME=SM_CXFRAME
SM_CXVSCROLL=2
SM_CYBORDER=6
SM_CYCAPTION=4
SM_CYCURSOR=14
SM_CYDLGFRAME=8
SM_CYDOUBLECLK=37
SM_CYFIXEDFRAME=SM_CYDLGFRAME
SM_CYFRAME=33
SM_CYFULLSCREEN=17
SM_CYHSCROLL=3
SM_CYICON=12
SM_CYICONSPACING=39
SM_CYKANJIWINDOW=18
SM_CYMENU=15
SM_CYMIN=29
SM_CYMINTRACK=35
SM_CYSCREEN=1
SM_CYSIZE=31
```

```
SM_CYSIZEFRAME=SM_CYFRAME
SM_CYVSCROLL=20
SM_CYVTHUMB=9
SM_DBCSENABLED=42
SM_DEBUG=22
SM_MENUDROPALIGNMENT=40
SM_MOUSEPRESENT=19
SM_PENWINDOWS=41
SM_RESERVED1=24
SM_RESERVED2=25
SM_RESERVED3=26
SM_RESERVED4=27
SM_SWAPBUTTON=23
SMTO_ABORTIFHUNG=&H2
SMTO_BLOCK=&H1
SMTO_NORMAL=&H0
SND_ALIAS=&H10000 'name is a WIN.INI [sounds] entry
SND_ALIAS_ID=&H110000 'name is a WIN.INI [sounds] entry
SND_ALIAS_START=0  'must be > 4096
SND_APPLICATION=&H80 'look for application association
SND_ASYNC=&H1 'play asynchronously
SND_FILENAME=&H20000 'name is a file name
SND_LOOP=&H8 'loop the sound until next sndPlaySound
SND_MEMORY=&H4 'lpszSoundName points to a memory file
SND_NODEFAULT=&H2 'silence not default, if sound not found
SND_NOSTOP=&H10 'don't stop any currently playing sound
SND_NOWAIT=&H2000 'don't wait if the driver is busy
SND_PURGE=&H40 'purge non-static events for task
SND_RESERVED=&HFF000000 these flags are reserved
SND_RESOURCE=&H40004 'name is a resource name or atom
SND_SYNC=&H0 'play synchronously (default)
SND_TYPE_MASK=&H170007
SND_VALID=&H1F 'valid flags / ;Internal /
SND_VALIDFLAGS=&H17201F 'Set of valid flag bits.
SOFTKEYBOARD_TYPE_C1=&H2
SOFTKEYBOARD_TYPE_T1=&H1
SORT_CHINESE_BIG5=&H0 'Chinese BIG5 order
SORT_CHINESE_UNICODE=&H1 'Chinese Unicode order
SORT_DEFAULT=&H0 'sorting default
SORT_JAPANESE_UNICODE=&H1 'Japanese Unicode order
SORT_JAPANESE_XJIS=&H0 'Japanese0xJIS order
SORT_KOREAN_KSC=&H0 'Korean KSC order
SORT_KOREAN_UNICODE=&H1 'Korean Unicode order
SORT_STRINGSORT=&H1000 'use string sort method
SP_APPABORT=(-2)
SP_BAUD=&H2&
SP_DATABITS=&H4&
```

```
SP_ERROR=(-1)
SP_HANDSHAKING=&H10&
SP_NOTREPORTED=&H4000
SP_OUTOFDISK=(-4)
SP_OUTOFMEMORY=(-5)
SP_PARITY=&H1&
SP_PARITY_CHECK=&H20&
SP_RLSD=&H40&
SP_SERIALCOMM=&H1&
SP_STOPBITS=&H8&
SP_USERABORT=(-3)
SPACEPARITY=4
SPECIFIC_RIGHTS_ALL=&HFFFF
SPI_GETACCESSTIMEOUT=60
SPI_GETANIMATION=72
SPI_GETBEEP=1
SPI_GETBORDER=5
SPI_GETDEFAULTINPUTLANG=89
SPI_GETDRAGFULLWINDOWS=38
SPI_GETFASTTASKSWITCH=35
SPI_GETFILTERKEYS=50
SPI_GETFONTSMOOTHING=74
SPI_GETGRIDGRANULARITY=18
SPI_GETHIGHCONTRAST=66
SPI_GETICONMETRICS=45
SPI_GETICONTITLELOGFONT=31
SPI_GETICONTITLEWRAP=25
SPI_GETKEYBOARDDELAY=22
SPI_GETKEYBOARDPREF=68
SPI_GETKEYBOARDSPEED=10
SPI_GETLOWPOWERACTIVE=83
SPI_GETLOWPOWERTIMEOUT=79
SPI_GETMENUDROPALIGNMENT=27
SPI_GETMINIMIZEDMETRICS=43
SPI_GETMOUSE=3
SPI_GETMOUSEKEYS=54
SPI_GETMOUSETRAILS=94
SPI_GETNONCLIENTMETRICS=41
SPI_GETPOWEROFFACTIVE=84
SPI_GETPOWEROFFTIMEOUT=80
SPI_GETSCREENREADER=70
SPI_GETSCREENSAVEACTIVE=16
SPI_GETSCREENSAVETIMEOUT=14
SPI_GETSERIALKEYS=62
SPI_GETSHOWSOUNDS=56
SPI_GETSOUNDSENTRY=64
SPI_GETSTICKYKEYS=58
SPI_GETTOGGLEKEYS=52
```

```
SPI_GETWINDOWSEXTENSION=92
SPI_GETWORKAREA=48
SPI_ICONHORIZONTALSPACING=13
SPI_ICONVERTICALSPACING=24
SPI_LANGDRIVER=12
SPI_SCREENSAVERRUNNING=97
SPI_SETACCESSTIMEOUT=61
SPI_SETANIMATION=73
SPI_SETBEEP=2
SPI_SETBORDER=6
SPI_SETCURSORS=87
SPI_SETDEFAULTINPUTLANG=90
SPI_SETDESKPATTERN=21
SPI_SETDESKWALLPAPER=20
SPI_SETDOUBLECLICKTIME=32
SPI_SETDOUBLECLKHEIGHT=30
SPI_SETDOUBLECLKWIDTH=29
SPI_SETDRAGFULLWINDOWS=37
SPI_SETDRAGHEIGHT=77
SPI_SETDRAGWIDTH=76
SPI_SETFASTTASKSWITCH=36
SPI_SETFILTERKEYS=51
SPI_SETFONTSMOOTHING=75
SPI_SETGRIDGRANULARITY=19
SPI_SETHANDHELD=78
SPI_SETHIGHCONTRAST=67
SPI_SETICONMETRICS=46
SPI_SETICONS=88
SPI_SETICONTITLELOGFONT=34
SPI_SETICONTITLEWRAP=26
SPI_SETKEYBOARDDELAY=23
SPI_SETKEYBOARDPREF=69
SPI_SETKEYBOARDSPEED=11
SPI_SETLANGTOGGLE=91
SPI_SETLOWPOWERACTIVE=85
SPI_SETLOWPOWERTIMEOUT=81
SPI_SETMENUDROPALIGNMENT=28
SPI_SETMINIMIZEDMETRICS=44
SPI_SETMOUSE=4
SPI_SETMOUSEBUTTONSWAP=33
SPI_SETMOUSEKEYS=55
SPI_SETMOUSETRAILS=93
SPI_SETNONCLIENTMETRICS=42
SPI_SETPENWINDOWS=49
SPI_SETPOWEROFFACTIVE=86
SPI_SETPOWEROFFTIMEOUT=82
SPI_SETSCREENREADER=71
SPI_SETSCREENSAVEACTIVE=17
```

```
SPI_SETSCREENSAVETIMEOUT=15
SPI_SETSERIALKEYS=63
SPI_SETSHOWSOUNDS=57
SPI_SETSOUNDSENTRY=65
SPI_SETSTICKYKEYS=59
SPI_SETTOGGLEKEYS=53
SPI_SETWORKAREA=47
SPIF_SENDWININICHANGE=&H2
SPIF_UPDATEINIFILE=&H1
SRCAND=&H8800C6  '(DWORD) dest=source AND dest
SRCCOPY=&HCC0020 '(DWORD) dest=source
SRCERASE=&H440328 '(DWORD) dest=source AND (NOT dest )
SRCINVERT=&H660046 '(DWORD) dest=source XOR dest
SRCPAINT=&HEE0086 '(DWORD) dest=source OR dest
SS_BLACKFRAME=&H7&
SS_BLACKRECT=&H4&
SS_CENTER=&H1&
SS_GRAYFRAME=&H8&
SS_GRAYRECT=&H5&
SS_ICON=&H3&
SS_LEFT=&H0&
SS_LEFTNOWORDWRAP=&HC&
SS_NOPREFIX=&H80 'Don't do "&" character translation
SS_RIGHT=&H2&
SS_SIMPLE=&HB&
SS_USERITEM=&HA&
SS_WHITEFRAME=&H9&
SS_WHITERECT=&H6&
ST_ADVISE=&H2
ST_BEGINSWP=0
ST_BLOCKED=&H8
ST_BLOCKNEXT=&H80
ST_CLIENT=&H10
ST_CONNECTED=&H1
ST_ENDSWP=1
ST_INLIST=&H40
ST_ISLOCAL=&H4
ST_ISSELF=&H100
ST_TERMINATED=&H20
STANDARD_RIGHTS_ALL=&H1F0000
STANDARD_RIGHTS_EXECUTE=(READ_CONTROL)
STANDARD_RIGHTS_READ=(READ_CONTROL)
STANDARD_RIGHTS_READ=(READ_CONTROL)
STANDARD_RIGHTS_REQUIRED=&HF0000
STANDARD_RIGHTS_WRITE=(READ_CONTROL)
STANDARD_RIGHTS_WRITE=(READ_CONTROL)
StartDocC=10
STARTF_FORCEOFFFEEDBACK=&H80
```

```
STARTF_FORCEONFEEDBACK=&H40
STARTF_RUNFULLSCREEN=&H20 'ignored for non-x86 platforms
STARTF_USECOUNTCHARS=&H8
STARTF_USEFILLATTRIBUTE=&H10
STARTF_USEPOSITION=&H4
STARTF_USESHOWWINDOW=&H1
STARTF_USESIZE=&H2
STARTF_USESTDHANDLES=&H100
stc1=&H440
stc10=&H449
stc11=&H44A
stc12=&H44B
stc13=&H44C
stc14=&H44D
stc15=&H44E
stc16=&H44F
stc17=&H450
stc18=&H451
stc19=&H452
stc2=&H441
stc20=&H453
stc21=&H454
stc22=&H455
stc23=&H456
stc24=&H457
stc25=&H458
stc26=&H459
stc27=&H45A
stc28=&H45B
stc29=&H45C
stc3=&H442
stc30=&H45D
stc31=&H45E
stc32=&H45F
stc4=&H443
stc5=&H444
stc6=&H445
stc7=&H446
stc8=&H447
stc9=&H448
STD_ERROR_HANDLE=-12&
STD_INPUT_HANDLE=-10&
STD_OUTPUT_HANDLE=-11&
STG_E_ABNORMALAPIEXIT=&H800300FA
STG_E_ACCESSDENIED=&H80030005
STG_E_CANTSAVE=&H80030103
STG_E_DISKISWRITEPROTECTED=&H80030013
STG_E_EXTANTMARSHALLINGS=&H80030108
```

```
STG_E_FILEALREADYEXISTS=&H80030050
STG_E_FILENOTFOUND=&H80030002
STG_E_INSUFFICIENTMEMORY=&H80030008
STG_E_INUSE=&H80030100
STG_E_INVALIDFLAG=&H800300FF
STG_E_INVALIDFUNCTION=&H80030001
STG_E_INVALIDHANDLE=&H80030006
STG_E_INVALIDHEADER=&H800300FB
STG_E_INVALIDNAME=&H800300FC
STG_E_INVALIDPARAMETER=&H80030057
STG_E_INVALIDPOINTER=&H80030009
STG_E_LOCKVIOLATION=&H80030021
STG_E_MEDIUMFULL=&H80030070
STG_E_NOMOREFILES=&H80030012
STG_E_NOTCURRENT=&H80030101
STG_E_NOTFILEBASEDSTORAGE=&H80030107
STG_E_OLDDLL=&H80030105
STG_E_OLDFORMAT=&H80030104
STG_E_PATHNOTFOUND=&H80030003
STG_E_READFAULT=&H8003001E
STG_E_REVERTED=&H80030102
STG_E_SEEKERROR=&H80030019
STG_E_SHAREREQUIRED=&H80030106
STG_E_SHAREVIOLATION=&H80030020
STG_E_TOOMANYOPENFILES=&H80030004
STG_E_UNIMPLEMENTEDFUNCTION=&H800300FE
STG_E_UNKNOWN=&H800300FD
STG_E_WRITEFAULT=&H8003001D
STG_S_CONVERTED=&H30200
STM_GETICON=&H171
STM_MSGMAX=&H172
STM_SETICON=&H170
STOCK_LAST=16
STOPBITS_10=&H1&
STOPBITS_15=&H2&
STOPBITS_20=&H4&
STREAM_CONTAINS_SECURITY=&H2
STREAM_MODIFIED_WHEN_READ=&H1
STRETCH_ANDSCANS=1
STRETCH_DELETESCANS=3
STRETCH_HALFTONE=4
STRETCH_ORSCANS=2
StretchBltC=2048
STYLE_DESCRIPTION_SIZE=32
SUBLANG_CHINESE_HONGKONG=&H3  'Chinese (Hong Kong)
SUBLANG_CHINESE_SIMPLIFIED=&H2  'Chinese (PR China)
SUBLANG_CHINESE_SINGAPORE=&H4  'Chinese (Singapore)
SUBLANG_CHINESE_TRADITIONAL=&H1  'Chinese (Taiwan)
```

```
SUBLANG_DEFAULT=&H1 'user default
SUBLANG_DUTCH=&H1 'Dutch
SUBLANG_DUTCH_BELGIAN=&H2 'Dutch (Belgian)
SUBLANG_ENGLISH_AUS=&H3 'English (Australian)
SUBLANG_ENGLISH_CAN=&H4 'English (Canadian)
SUBLANG_ENGLISH_EIRE=&H6 'English (Irish)
SUBLANG_ENGLISH_NZ=&H5 'English (New Zealand)
SUBLANG_ENGLISH_UK=&H2 'English (UK)
SUBLANG_ENGLISH_US=&H1 'English (USA)
SUBLANG_FRENCH=&H1 'French
SUBLANG_FRENCH_BELGIAN=&H2  'French (Belgian)
SUBLANG_FRENCH_CANADIAN=&H3 'French (Canadian)
SUBLANG_FRENCH_SWISS=&H4 'French (Swiss)
SUBLANG_GERMAN=&H1 'German
SUBLANG_GERMAN_AUSTRIAN=&H3 'German (Austrian)
SUBLANG_GERMAN_SWISS=&H2 'German (Swiss)
SUBLANG_ITALIAN=&H1 'Italian
SUBLANG_ITALIAN_SWISS=&H2 'Italian (Swiss)
SUBLANG_NEUTRAL=&H0 'language neutral
SUBLANG_NORWEGIAN_BOKMAL=&H1 'Norwegian (Bokma
SUBLANG_NORWEGIAN_NYNORSK=&H2 'Norwegian (Nynorsk)
SUBLANG_PORTUGUESE=&H2 'Portuguese
SUBLANG_PORTUGUESE_BRAZILIAN=&H1 'Portuguese (Brazilian)
SUBLANG_SPANISH=&H1 'Spanish (Castilian)
SUBLANG_SPANISH_MEXICAN=&H2 'Spanish (Mexican)
SUBLANG_SPANISH_MODERN=&H3  'Spanish (Modern)
SUBLANG_SYS_DEFAULT=&H2 'system default
SUCCESSFUL_ACCESS_ACE_FLAG=&H40
SW_ERASE=&H4
SW_HIDE=0
SW_INVALIDATE=&H2
SW_MAX=10
SW_MAXIMIZE=3
SW_MINIMIZE=6
SW_NORMAL=1
SW_OTHERUNZOOM=4
SW_OTHERZOOM=2
SW_PARENTCLOSING=1
SW_PARENTOPENING=3
SW_RESTORE=9
SW_SCROLLCHILDREN=&H1
SW_SHOW=5
SW_SHOWDEFAULT=10
SW_SHOWMAXIMIZED=3
SW_SHOWMINIMIZED=2
SW_SHOWMINNOACTIVE=7
SW_SHOWNA=8
SW_SHOWNOACTIVATE=4
```

```
SW_SHOWNORMAL=1
SWP_DRAWFRAME=SWP_FRAMECHANGED
SWP_FRAMECHANGED=&H20 'The frame changed: send WM_NCCALCSIZE
SWP_HIDEWINDOW=&H80
SWP_NOACTIVATE=&H10
SWP_NOCOPYBITS=&H100
SWP_NOMOVE=&H2
SWP_NOOWNERZORDER=&H200 'Don't do owner Z ordering
SWP_NOREDRAW=&H8
SWP_NOREPOSITION=SWP_NOOWNERZORDER
SWP_NOSIZE=&H1
SWP_NOZORDER=&H4
SWP_SHOWWINDOW=&H40
SYMBOL_CHARSET=2
SYNCHRONIZE=&H100000
SYSPAL_ERROR=0
SYSPAL_NOSTATIC=2
SYSPAL_STATIC=1
SYSTEM_ALARM_ACE_TYPE=&H3
SYSTEM_AUDIT_ACE_TYPE=&H2
SYSTEM_FIXED_FONT=16
SYSTEM_FONT=13
SZDDE_ITEM_ITEMLIST="TopicItemList"
SZDDESYS_ITEM_FORMATS="Formats"
SZDDESYS_ITEM_HELP="Help"
SZDDESYS_ITEM_RTNMSG="ReturnMessage"
SZDDESYS_ITEM_STATUS="Status"
SZDDESYS_ITEM_SYSITEMS="SysItems"
SZDDESYS_ITEM_TOPICS="Topics"
SZDDESYS_TOPIC="System"

T
TA_BASELINE=24
TA_BOTTOM=8
TA_CENTER=6
TA_LEFT=0
TA_MASK=(TA_BASELINE+TA_CENTER+TA_UPDATECP)
TA_NOUPDATECP=0
TA_RIGHT=2
TA_TOP=0
TA_UPDATECP=1
TC_CP_STROKE=&H4 'Can do ClipPrecision STROKE
TC_CR_90=&H8 'Can do CharRotAbility 90
TC_CR_ANY=&H10 'Can do CharRotAbility ANY
TC_EA_DOUBLE=&H200 'Can do EmboldenAbility DOUBLE
TC_GP_TRAP=2
TC_HARDERR=1
TC_IA_ABLE=&H400 'Can do ItalisizeAbility  ABLE
```

```
TC_NORMAL=0
TC_OP_CHARACTER=&H1 'Can do OutputPrecision CHARACTER
TC_OP_STROKE=&H2 'Can do OutputPrecision STROKE
TC_RA_ABLE=&H2000  'Can do RasterFontAble ABLE
TC_RESERVED=&H8000
TC_SA_CONTIN=&H100 'Can do ScaleAbility CONTINUOUS
TC_SA_DOUBLE=&H40  'Can do ScaleAbility DOUBLE
TC_SA_INTEGER=&H80 'Can do ScaleAbility INTEGER
TC_SCROLLBLT=&H10000 'do text scroll with blt
TC_SF_X_YINDEP=&H20 'Can do ScaleFreedom X_YINDEPENDENT
TC_SIGNAL=3
TC_SO_ABLE=&H1000  'Can do StrikeOutAbility  ABLE
TC_UA_ABLE=&H800 'Can do UnderlineAbility  ABLE
TC_VA_ABLE=&H4000  'Can do VectorFontAble ABLE
TCI_SRCCHARSET=1
TCI_SRCCODEPAGE=2
TCI_SRCFONTSIG=3
TECHNOLOGY=2 'Device classification
TEXTCAPS=34 'Text capabilities
TF_FORCEDRIVE=&H80
THAI_CHARSET=222
THREAD_BASE_PRIORITY_IDLE=-15
THREAD_BASE_PRIORITY_LOWRT=15
THREAD_BASE_PRIORITY_MAX=2
THREAD_BASE_PRIORITY_MIN=-2
THREAD_PRIORITY_ABOVE_NORMAL=(THREAD_PRIORITY_HIGHEST-1)
THREAD_PRIORITY_BELOW_NORMAL=(THREAD_PRIORITY_LOWEST+1)
THREAD_PRIORITY_ERROR_RETURN=(MAXLONG)
THREAD_PRIORITY_HIGHEST=THREAD_BASE_PRIORITY_MAX
THREAD_PRIORITY_IDLE=THREAD_BASE_PRIORITY_IDLE
THREAD_PRIORITY_LOWEST=THREAD_BASE_PRIORITY_MIN
THREAD_PRIORITY_NORMAL=0
THREAD_PRIORITY_TIME_CRITICAL=THREAD_BASE_PRIORITY_LOWRT
TIME_BYTES=&H4 'current byte offset
TIME_FORCE24HOURFORMAT=&H8 'always use 24 hour format
TIME_MIDI=&H10 'MIDI time
TIME_MS=&H1 'time in Milliseconds
TIME_NOMINUTESORSECONDS=&H1 'do not use minutes or seconds
TIME_NOSECONDS=&H2 'do not use seconds
TIME_NOTIMEMARKER=&H4 'do not use time marker
TIME_ONESHOT=0  'program timer for single event
TIME_PERIODIC=1  'program for continuous periodic event
TIME_SAMPLES=&H2 'number of wave samples
TIME_SMPTE=&H8 'SMPTE time
TIMEOUT_ASYNC=&HFFFF
TIMERR_BASE=96 'was 128, changed to match Win 31 Sonic
TIMERR_NOCANDO=(TIMERR_BASE+1) 'request not completed
TIMERR_NOERROR=(0)  'no error
```

```
TIMERR_STRUCT=(TIMERR_BASE+33) 'time struct size
TLS_OUT_OF_INDEXES=&HFFFF
TMPF_DEVICE=&H8
TMPF_FIXED_PITCH=&H1
TMPF_TRUETYPE=&H4
TMPF_VECTOR=&H2
TokenDefaultDacl=6
TokenGroups=2
TokenImpersonationLevel=9
TokenOwner=4
TokenPrimaryGroup=5
TokenPrivileges=3
TokenSource=7
TokenStatistics=10
TokenType=8
TokenUser=1
TPM_CENTERALIGN=&H4&
TPM_LEFTALIGN=&H0&
TPM_LEFTBUTTON=&H0&
TPM_RIGHTALIGN=&H8&
TPM_RIGHTBUTTON=&H2&
TRANSFORM_CTM=4107
TRANSPARENT=1
TRUETYPE_FONTTYPE=&H4
TRUNCATE_EXISTING=5
TT_AVAILABLE=&H1
TT_ENABLED=&H2
TT_POLYGON_TYPE=24
TT_PRIM_LINE=1
TT_PRIM_QSPLINE=2
TURKISH_CHARSET=162
TWOSTOPBITS=2
TYPE_E_AMBIGUOUSNAME=&H8002802C
TYPE_E_BADMODULEKIND=&H800288BD
TYPE_E_BUFFERTOOSMALL=&H80028016
TYPE_E_CANTCREATETMPFILE=&H80028CA3
TYPE_E_CANTLOADLIBRARY=&H80029C4A
TYPE_E_CIRCULARTYPE=&H80029C84
TYPE_E_DLLFUNCTIONNOTFOUND=&H8002802F
TYPE_E_DUPLICATEID=&H800288C6
TYPE_E_ELEMENTNOTFOUND=&H8002802B
TYPE_E_INCONSISTENTPROPFUNCS=&H80029C83
TYPE_E_INVALIDID=&H800288CF
TYPE_E_INVALIDSTATE=&H80028029
TYPE_E_INVDATAREAD=&H80028018
TYPE_E_IOERROR=&H80028CA2
TYPE_E_LIBNOTREGISTERED=&H8002801D
TYPE_E_NAMECONFLICT=&H8002802D
```

```
TYPE_E_OUTOFBOUNDS=&H80028CA1
TYPE_E_QUALIFIEDNAMEDISALLOWED=&H80028028
TYPE_E_REGISTRYACCESS=&H8002801C
TYPE_E_SIZETOOBIG=&H800288C5
TYPE_E_TYPEMISMATCH=&H80028CA0
TYPE_E_UNDEFINEDTYPE=&H80028027
TYPE_E_UNKNOWNLCID=&H8002802E
TYPE_E_UNSUPFORMAT=&H80028019
TYPE_E_WRONGTYPEKIND=&H8002802A

U
UI_CAP_2700=&H1
UI_CAP_ROT90=&H2
UI_CAP_ROTANY=&H4
UNIQUE_NAME=&H0
UNLOAD_DLL_DEBUG_EVENT=7

V
VALID_INHERIT_FLAGS=&HF
VARIABLE_PITCH=2
VER_PLATFORM_WIN32_NT=2
VER_PLATFORM_WIN32_WINDOWS=1
VER_PLATFORM_WIN32s=0
VERTRES=10 'Vertical width in pixels
VERTSIZE=6 'Vertical size in millimeters
VFF_BUFFTOOSMALL=&H4
VFF_CURNEDEST=&H1
VFF_FILEINUSE=&H2
VFFF_ISSHAREDFILE=&H1
VFT_APP=&H1&
VFT_DLL=&H2&
VFT_DRV=&H3&
VFT_FONT=&H4&
VFT_STATIC_LIB=&H7&
VFT_UNKNOWN=&H0&
VFT_VXD=&H5&
VFT2_DRV_COMM=&HA&
VFT2_DRV_DISPLAY=&H4&
VFT2_DRV_INPUTMETHOD=&HB&
VFT2_DRV_INSTALLABLE=&H8&
VFT2_DRV_KEYBOARD=&H2&
VFT2_DRV_LANGUAGE=&H3&
VFT2_DRV_MOUSE=&H5&
VFT2_DRV_NETWORK=&H6&
VFT2_DRV_PRINTER=&H1&
VFT2_DRV_SOUND=&H9&
VFT2_DRV_SYSTEM=&H7&
VFT2_FONT_RASTER=&H1&
```

```
VFT2_FONT_TRUETYPE=&H3&
VFT2_FONT_VECTOR=&H2&
VFT2_UNKNOWN=&H0&
VIEW_E_DRAW=&H80040140
VIEW_E_FIRST=&H80040140
VIEW_E_LAST=&H8004014F
VIEW_S_ALREADY_FROZEN=&H40140
VIEW_S_FIRST=&H40140
VIEW_S_LAST=&H4014F
VIF_ACCESSVIOLATION=&H200&
VIF_BUFFTOOSMALL=&H40000
VIF_CANNOTCREATE=&H800&
VIF_CANNOTDELETE=&H1000&
VIF_CANNOTDELETECUR=&H4000&
VIF_CANNOTREADDST=&H20000
VIF_CANNOTREADSRC=&H10000
VIF_CANNOTRENAME=&H2000&
VIF_DIFFCODEPG=&H10&
VIF_DIFFLANG=&H8&
VIF_DIFFTYPE=&H20&
VIF_FILEINUSE=&H80&
VIF_MISMATCH=&H2&
VIF_OUTOFMEMORY=&H8000&
VIF_OUTOFSPACE=&H100&
VIF_SHARINGVIOLATION=&H400&
VIF_SRCOLD=&H4&
VIF_TEMPFILE=&H1&
VIF_WRITEPROT=&H40&
VIFF_DONTDELETEOLD=&H2
VIFF_FORCEINSTALL=&H1
VK_ADD=&H6B
VK_ATTN=&HF6
VK_BACK=&H8
VK_CANCEL=&H3
VK_CAPITAL=&H14
VK_CLEAR=&HC
VK_CONTROL=&H11
VK_CRSEL=&HF7
VK_DECIMAL=&H6E
VK_DELETE=&H2E
VK_DIVIDE=&H6F
VK_DOWN=&H28
VK_END=&H23
VK_EREOF=&HF9
VK_ESCAPE=&H1B
VK_EXECUTE=&H2B
VK_EXSEL=&HF8
VK_F1=&H70
```

```
VK_F10=&H79
VK_F11=&H7A
VK_F12=&H7B
VK_F13=&H7C
VK_F14=&H7D
VK_F15=&H7E
VK_F16=&H7F
VK_F17=&H80
VK_F18=&H81
VK_F19=&H82
VK_F2=&H71
VK_F20=&H83
VK_F21=&H84
VK_F22=&H85
VK_F23=&H86
VK_F24=&H87
VK_F3=&H72
VK_F4=&H73
VK_F5=&H74
VK_F6=&H75
VK_F7=&H76
VK_F8=&H77
VK_F9=&H78
VK_HELP=&H2F
VK_HOME=&H24
VK_INSERT=&H2D
VK_LBUTTON=&H1
VK_LCONTROL=&HA2
VK_LEFT=&H25
VK_LMENU=&HA4
VK_LSHIFT=&HA0
VK_MBUTTON=&H4 'NOT contiguous with L RBUTTON
VK_MENU=&H12
VK_MULTIPLY=&H6A
VK_NEXT=&H22
VK_NONAME=&HFC
VK_NUMLOCK=&H90
VK_NUMPAD0=&H60
VK_NUMPAD1=&H61
VK_NUMPAD2=&H62
VK_NUMPAD3=&H63
VK_NUMPAD4=&H64
VK_NUMPAD5=&H65
VK_NUMPAD6=&H66
VK_NUMPAD7=&H67
VK_NUMPAD8=&H68
VK_NUMPAD9=&H69
VK_OEM_CLEAR=&HFE
```

```
VK_PA1=&HFD
VK_PAUSE=&H13
VK_PLAY=&HFA
VK_PRINT=&H2A
VK_PRIOR=&H21
VK_PROCESSKEY=&HE5
VK_RBUTTON=&H2
VK_RCONTROL=&HA3
VK_RETURN=&HD
VK_RIGHT=&H27
VK_RMENU=&HA5
VK_RSHIFT=&HA1
VK_SCROLL=&H91
VK_SELECT=&H29
VK_SEPARATOR=&H6C
VK_SHIFT=&H10
VK_SNAPSHOT=&H2C
VK_SPACE=&H20
VK_SUBTRACT=&H6D
VK_TAB=&H9
VK_UP=&H26
VK_ZOOM=&HFB
VOS__BASE=&H0&
VOS__PM16=&H2&
VOS__PM32=&H3&
VOS__WINDOWS16=&H1&
VOS__WINDOWS32=&H4&
VOS_DOS=&H10000
VOS_DOS_WINDOWS16=&H10001
VOS_DOS_WINDOWS32=&H10004
VOS_NT=&H40000
VOS_NT_WINDOWS32=&H40004
VOS_OS216=&H20000
VOS_OS216_PM16=&H20002
VOS_OS232=&H30000
VOS_OS232_PM32=&H30003
VOS_UNKNOWN=&H0&
VS_FF_DEBUG=&H1&
VS_FF_INFOINFERRED=&H10&
VS_FF_PATCHED=&H4&
VS_FF_PRERELEASE=&H2&
VS_FF_PRIVATEBUILD=&H8&
VS_FF_SPECIALBUILD=&H20&
VS_FFI_FILEFLAGSMASK=&H3F&
VS_FFI_SIGNATURE=&HFEEF04BD
VS_FFI_STRUCVERSION=&H10000
VS_USER_DEFINED=100
VS_VERSION_INFO=1
```

```
VTA_BASELINE=TA_BASELINE
VTA_BOTTOM=TA_RIGHT
VTA_CENTER=TA_CENTER
VTA_LEFT=TA_BOTTOM
VTA_RIGHT=TA_TOP
VTA_TOP=TA_LEFT

W
WA_ACTIVE=1
WA_CLICKACTIVE=2
WA_INACTIVE=0
WAVE_ALLOWSYNC=&H2
WAVE_FORMAT_1M08=&H1  '11.025 kHz, Mono, 8-bit
WAVE_FORMAT_1M16=&H4  '11.025 kHz, Mono, 16-bit
WAVE_FORMAT_1S08=&H2  '11.025 kHz, Stereo, 8-bit
WAVE_FORMAT_1S16=&H8  '11.025 kHz, Stereo, 16-bit
WAVE_FORMAT_2M08=&H10 '22.05  kHz, Mono, 8-bit
WAVE_FORMAT_2M16=&H40 '22.05  kHz, Mono, 16-bit
WAVE_FORMAT_2S08=&H20 '22.05  kHz, Stereo, 8-bit
WAVE_FORMAT_2S16=&H80 '22.05  kHz, Stereo, 16-bit
WAVE_FORMAT_4M08=&H100 '44.1 kHz, Mono, 8-bit
WAVE_FORMAT_4M16=&H400 '44.1 kHz, Mono, 16-bit
WAVE_FORMAT_4S08=&H200 '44.1 kHz, Stereo, 8-bit
WAVE_FORMAT_4S16=&H800 '44.1 kHz, Stereo, 16-bit
WAVE_FORMAT_DIRECT=&H8
WAVE_FORMAT_DIRECT_QUERY=(WAVE_FORMAT_QUERY Or
                         WAVE_FORMAT_DIRECT)
WAVE_FORMAT_PCM=1   'Needed in resource files
WAVE_FORMAT_QUERY=&H1
WAVE_INVALIDFORMAT=&H0 'invalid format
WAVE_MAPPED=&H4
WAVE_MAPPER=-1&
WAVE_VALID=&H3 ';Internal
WAVECAPS_LRVOLUME=&H8 'separate left-right volume control
WAVECAPS_PITCH=&H1 'supports pitch control
WAVECAPS_PLAYBACKRATE=&H2 'supports playback rate control
WAVECAPS_SYNC=&H10
WAVECAPS_VOLUME=&H4 'supports volume control
WAVERR_BADFORMAT=(WAVERR_BASE+0) 'unsupported wave format
WAVERR_BASE=32
WAVERR_LASTERROR=(WAVERR_BASE+3) 'last error in range
WAVERR_STILLPLAYING=(WAVERR_BASE+1) 'still something playing
WAVERR_SYNC=(WAVERR_BASE+3) 'device is synchronous
WAVERR_UNPREPARED=(WAVERR_BASE+2) 'header not prepared
WB_ISDELIMITER=2
WB_LEFT=0
WB_RIGHT=1
WC_COMPOSITECHECK=&H200 'convert composite to precomposed
```

```
WC_DEFAULTCHAR=&H40 'replace w/ default char
WC_DEFAULTCHECK=&H100 'check for default char
WC_DIALOG=8002&
WC_DISCARDNS=&H10 'discard non-spacing chars
WC_SEPCHARS=&H20 'generate separate chars
WH_CALLWNDPROC=4
WH_CBT=5
WH_DEBUG=9
WH_FOREGROUNDIDLE=11
WH_GETMESSAGE=3
WH_HARDWARE=8
WH_JOURNALPLAYBACK=1
WH_JOURNALRECORD=0
WH_KEYBOARD=2
WH_MAX=11
WH_MIN=(-1)
WH_MOUSE=7
WH_MSGFILTER=(-1)
WH_SHELL=10
WH_SYSMSGFILTER=6
WHDR_BEGINLOOP=&H4 'loop start block
WHDR_DONE=&H1 'done bit
WHDR_ENDLOOP=&H8 'loop end block
WHDR_INQUEUE=&H10 'reserved for driver
WHDR_PREPARED=&H2 'set if this header has been prepared
WHDR_VALID=&H1F 'valid flags / ;Internal /
WHITE_BRUSH=0
WHITE_PEN=6
WHITENESS=&HFF0062 '(DWORD) dest=WHITE
WHITEONBLACK=2
WIM_CLOSE=MM_WIM_CLOSE
WIM_DATA=MM_WIM_DATA
WIM_OPEN=MM_WIM_OPEN
WINDING=2
WINDOW_BUFFER_SIZE_EVENT=&H4 'contains change event record
WINSTA_ACCESSCLIPBOARD=&H4&
WINSTA_ACCESSPUBLICATOMS=&H20&
WINSTA_CREATEDESKTOP=&H8&
WINSTA_ENUMDESKTOPS=&H1&
WINSTA_ENUMERATE=&H100&
WINSTA_EXITWINDOWS=&H40&
WINSTA_READATTRIBUTES=&H2&
WINSTA_READSCREEN=&H200&
WINSTA_WRITEATTRIBUTES=&H10&
WM_ACTIVATE=&H6
WM_ACTIVATEAPP=&H1C
WM_ASKCBFORMATNAME=&H30C
WM_CANCELJOURNAL=&H4B
```

```
WM_CANCELMODE=&H1F
WM_CHANGECBCHAIN=&H30D
WM_CHAR=&H102
WM_CHARTOITEM=&H2F
WM_CHILDACTIVATE=&H22
WM_CHOOSEFONT_GETLOGFONT=(WM_USER+1)
WM_CHOOSEFONT_SETFLAGS=(WM_USER+102)
WM_CHOOSEFONT_SETLOGFONT=(WM_USER+101)
WM_CLEAR=&H303
WM_CLOSE=&H10
WM_COMMAND=&H111
WM_COMMNOTIFY=&H44 'no longer supported
WM_COMPACTING=&H41
WM_COMPAREITEM=&H39
WM_CONVERTREQUESTEX=&H108
WM_COPY=&H301
WM_COPYDATA=&H4A
WM_CREATE=&H1
WM_CTLCOLORBTN=&H135
WM_CTLCOLORDLG=&H136
WM_CTLCOLOREDIT=&H133
WM_CTLCOLORLISTBOX=&H134
WM_CTLCOLORMSGBOX=&H132
WM_CTLCOLORSCROLLBAR=&H137
WM_CTLCOLORSTATIC=&H138
WM_CUT=&H300
WM_DDE_ACK=(WM_DDE_FIRST+4)
WM_DDE_ADVISE=(WM_DDE_FIRST+2)
WM_DDE_DATA=(WM_DDE_FIRST+5)
WM_DDE_EXECUTE=(WM_DDE_FIRST+8)
WM_DDE_FIRST=&H3E0
WM_DDE_INITIATE=(WM_DDE_FIRST)
WM_DDE_LAST=(WM_DDE_FIRST+8)
WM_DDE_POKE=(WM_DDE_FIRST+7)
WM_DDE_REQUEST=(WM_DDE_FIRST+6)
WM_DDE_TERMINATE=(WM_DDE_FIRST+1)
WM_DDE_UNADVISE=(WM_DDE_FIRST+3)
WM_DEADCHAR=&H103
WM_DELETEITEM=&H2D
WM_DESTROY=&H2
WM_DESTROYCLIPBOARD=&H307
WM_DEVMODECHANGE=&H1B
WM_DRAWCLIPBOARD=&H308
WM_DRAWITEM=&H2B
WM_DROPFILES=&H233
WM_ENABLE=&HA
WM_ENDSESSION=&H16
WM_ENTERIDLE=&H121
```

```
WM_ENTERMENULOOP=&H211
WM_ERASEBKGND=&H14
WM_EXITMENULOOP=&H212
WM_FONTCHANGE=&H1D
WM_GETDLGCODE=&H87
WM_GETFONT=&H31
WM_GETHOTKEY=&H33
WM_GETMINMAXINFO=&H24
WM_GETTEXT=&HD
WM_GETTEXTLENGTH=&HE
WM_HOTKEY=&H312
WM_HSCROLL=&H114
WM_HSCROLLCLIPBOARD=&H30E
WM_ICONERASEBKGND=&H27
WM_IME_CHAR=&H286
WM_IME_COMPOSITION=&H10F
WM_IME_COMPOSITIONFULL=&H284
WM_IME_CONTROL=&H283
WM_IME_ENDCOMPOSITION=&H10E
WM_IME_KEYDOWN=&H290
WM_IME_KEYLAST=&H10F
WM_IME_KEYUP=&H291
WM_IME_NOTIFY=&H282
WM_IME_SELECT=&H285
WM_IME_SETCONTEXT=&H281
WM_IME_STARTCOMPOSITION=&H10D
WM_INITDIALOG=&H110
WM_INITMENU=&H116
WM_INITMENUPOPUP=&H117
WM_KEYDOWN=&H100
WM_KEYFIRST=&H100
WM_KEYLAST=&H108
WM_KEYUP=&H101
WM_KILLFOCUS=&H8
WM_LBUTTONDBLCLK=&H203
WM_LBUTTONDOWN=&H201
WM_LBUTTONUP=&H202
WM_MBUTTONDBLCLK=&H209
WM_MBUTTONDOWN=&H207
WM_MBUTTONUP=&H208
WM_MDIACTIVATE=&H222
WM_MDICASCADE=&H227
WM_MDICREATE=&H220
WM_MDIDESTROY=&H221
WM_MDIGETACTIVE=&H229
WM_MDIICONARRANGE=&H228
WM_MDIMAXIMIZE=&H225
WM_MDINEXT=&H224
```

```
WM_MDIREFRESHMENU=&H234
WM_MDIRESTORE=&H223
WM_MDISETMENU=&H230
WM_MDITILE=&H226
WM_MEASUREITEM=&H2C
WM_MENUCHAR=&H120
WM_MENUSELECT=&H11F
WM_MOUSEACTIVATE=&H21
WM_MOUSEFIRST=&H200
WM_MOUSELAST=&H209
WM_MOUSEMOVE=&H200
WM_MOVE=&H3
WM_NCACTIVATE=&H86
WM_NCCALCSIZE=&H83
WM_NCCREATE=&H81
WM_NCDESTROY=&H82
WM_NCHITTEST=&H84
WM_NCLBUTTONDBLCLK=&HA3
WM_NCLBUTTONDOWN=&HA1
WM_NCLBUTTONUP=&HA2
WM_NCMBUTTONDBLCLK=&HA9
WM_NCMBUTTONDOWN=&HA7
WM_NCMBUTTONUP=&HA8
WM_NCMOUSEMOVE=&HA0
WM_NCPAINT=&H85
WM_NCRBUTTONDBLCLK=&HA6
WM_NCRBUTTONDOWN=&HA4
WM_NCRBUTTONUP=&HA5
WM_NEXTDLGCTL=&H28
WM_NULL=&H0
WM_OTHERWINDOWCREATED=&H42 'no longer supported
WM_OTHERWINDOWDESTROYED=&H43 'no longer supported
WM_PAINT=&HF
WM_PAINTCLIPBOARD=&H309
WM_PAINTICON=&H26
WM_PALETTECHANGED=&H311
WM_PALETTEISCHANGING=&H310
WM_PARENTNOTIFY=&H210
WM_PASTE=&H302
WM_PENWINFIRST=&H380
WM_PENWINLAST=&H38F
WM_POWER=&H48
WM_PSD_ENVSTAMPRECT=(WM_USER+5)
WM_PSD_FULLPAGERECT=(WM_USER+1)
WM_PSD_GREEKTEXTRECT=(WM_USER+4)
WM_PSD_MARGINRECT=(WM_USER+3)
WM_PSD_MINMARGINRECT=(WM_USER+2)
WM_PSD_PAGESETUPDLG=(WM_USER)
```

```
WM_PSD_YAFULLPAGERECT=(WM_USER+6)
WM_QUERYDRAGICON=&H37
WM_QUERYENDSESSION=&H11
WM_QUERYNEWPALETTE=&H30F
WM_QUERYOPEN=&H13
WM_QUEUESYNC=&H23
WM_QUIT=&H12
WM_RBUTTONDBLCLK=&H206
WM_RBUTTONDOWN=&H204
WM_RBUTTONUP=&H205
WM_RENDERALLFORMATS=&H306
WM_RENDERFORMAT=&H305
WM_SETCURSOR=&H20
WM_SETFOCUS=&H7
WM_SETFONT=&H30
WM_SETHOTKEY=&H32
WM_SETREDRAW=&HB
WM_SETTEXT=&HC
WM_SHOWWINDOW=&H18
WM_SIZE=&H5
WM_SIZECLIPBOARD=&H30B
WM_SPOOLERSTATUS=&H2A
WM_SYSCHAR=&H106
WM_SYSCOLORCHANGE=&H15
WM_SYSCOMMAND=&H112
WM_SYSDEADCHAR=&H107
WM_SYSKEYDOWN=&H104
WM_SYSKEYUP=&H105
WM_TIMECHANGE=&H1E
WM_TIMER=&H113
WM_UNDO=&H304
WM_USER=&H400
WM_VKEYTOITEM=&H2E
WM_VSCROLL=&H115
WM_VSCROLLCLIPBOARD=&H30A
WM_WINDOWPOSCHANGED=&H47
WM_WINDOWPOSCHANGING=&H46
WM_WININICHANGE=&H1A
WN_ACCESS_DENIED=ERROR_ACCESS_DENIED
WN_ALREADY_CONNECTED=ERROR_ALREADY_ASSIGNED
WN_BAD_HANDLE=ERROR_INVALID_HANDLE
WN_BAD_LOCALNAME=ERROR_BAD_DEVICE
WN_BAD_NETNAME=ERROR_BAD_NET_NAME
WN_BAD_PASSWORD=ERROR_INVALID_PASSWORD
WN_BAD_POINTER=ERROR_INVALID_ADDRESS
WN_BAD_PROFILE=ERROR_BAD_PROFILE
WN_BAD_PROVIDER=ERROR_BAD_PROVIDER
WN_BAD_USER=ERROR_BAD_USERNAME
```

```
WN_BAD_VALUE=ERROR_INVALID_PARAMETER
WN_CANNOT_OPEN_PROFILE=ERROR_CANNOT_OPEN_PROFILE
WN_CONNECTION_CLOSED=ERROR_CONNECTION_UNAVAIL
WN_DEVICE_ERROR=ERROR_GEN_FAILURE
WN_DEVICE_IN_USE=ERROR_DEVICE_IN_USE
WN_EXTENDED_ERROR=ERROR_EXTENDED_ERROR
WN_FUNCTION_BUSY=ERROR_BUSY
WN_MORE_DATA=ERROR_MORE_DATA
WN_NET_ERROR=ERROR_UNEXP_NET_ERR
WN_NO_ERROR=NO_ERROR
WN_NO_MORE_ENTRIES=ERROR_NO_MORE_ITEMS
WN_NO_NET_OR_BAD_PATH=ERROR_NO_NET_OR_BAD_PATH
WN_NO_NETWORK=ERROR_NO_NETWORK
WN_NOT_CONNECTED=ERROR_NOT_CONNECTED
WN_NOT_CONTAINER=ERROR_NOT_CONTAINER
WN_NOT_SUPPORTED=ERROR_NOT_SUPPORTED
WN_OPEN_FILES=ERROR_OPEN_FILES
WN_OUT_OF_MEMORY=ERROR_NOT_ENOUGH_MEMORY
WN_SUCCESS=NO_ERROR
WN_WINDOWS_ERROR=ERROR_UNEXP_NET_ERR
WOM_CLOSE=MM_WOM_CLOSE
WOM_DONE=MM_WOM_DONE
WOM_OPEN=MM_WOM_OPEN
WPF_RESTORETOMAXIMIZED=&H2
WPF_SETMINPOSITION=&H1
WRITE_DAC=&H40000
WRITE_OWNER=&H80000
WRITEAPI=1
WS_BORDER=&H800000
WS_CAPTION=&HC00000  'WS_BORDER Or WS_DLGFRAME
WS_CHILD=&H40000000
WS_CHILDWINDOW=(WS_CHILD)
WS_CLIPCHILDREN=&H2000000
WS_CLIPSIBLINGS=&H4000000
WS_DISABLED=&H8000000
WS_DLGFRAME=&H400000
WS_EX_ACCEPTFILES=&H10&
WS_EX_DLGMODALFRAME=&H1&
WS_EX_NOPARENTNOTIFY=&H4&
WS_EX_TOPMOST=&H8&
WS_EX_TRANSPARENT=&H20&
WS_GROUP=&H20000
WS_HSCROLL=&H100000
WS_ICONIC=WS_MINIMIZE
WS_MAXIMIZE=&H1000000
WS_MAXIMIZEBOX=&H10000
WS_MINIMIZE=&H20000000
WS_MINIMIZEBOX=&H20000
```

```
WS_OVERLAPPED=&H0&
WS_OVERLAPPEDWINDOW=(WS_OVERLAPPED Or WS_CAPTION Or
                    WS_SYSMENU Or WS_THICKFRAME Or
                    WS_MINIMIZEBOX Or WS_MAXIMIZEBOX)
WS_POPUP=&H80000000
WS_POPUPWINDOW=(WS_POPUP Or WS_BORDER Or WS_SYSMENU)
WS_SIZEBOX=WS_THICKFRAME
WS_SYSMENU=&H80000
WS_TABSTOP=&H10000
WS_THICKFRAME=&H40000
WS_TILED=WS_OVERLAPPED
WS_TILEDWINDOW=WS_OVERLAPPEDWINDOW
WS_VISIBLE=&H10000000
WS_VSCROLL=&H200000
WVR_ALIGNBOTTOM=&H40
WVR_ALIGNLEFT=&H20
WVR_ALIGNRIGHT=&H80
WVR_ALIGNTOP=&H10
WVR_HREDRAW=&H100
WVR_REDRAW=(WVR_HREDRAW Or WVR_VREDRAW)
WVR_VALIDRECTS=&H400
WVR_VREDRAW=&H200

X
XCLASS_BOOL=&H1000
XCLASS_DATA=&H2000
XCLASS_FLAGS=&H4000
XCLASS_MASK=&HFC00
XCLASS_NOTIFICATION=&H8000
XST_ADVACKRCVD=13
XST_ADVDATAACKRCVD=16
XST_ADVDATASENT=15
XST_ADVSENT=11
XST_CONNECTED=2
XST_DATARCVD=6
XST_EXECACKRCVD=10
XST_EXECSENT=9
XST_INCOMPLETE=1
XST_INIT1=3   'mid-initiation states
XST_INIT2=4
XST_NULL=0   'quiescent states
XST_POKEACKRCVD=8
XST_POKESENT=7
XST_REQSENT=5   'active conversation states
XST_UNADVACKRCVD=14
XST_UNADVSENT=12
XTYP_ADVDATA=(&H10 Or XCLASS_FLAGS)
XTYP_ADVREQ=(&H20 Or XCLASS_DATA Or XTYPF_NOBLOCK)
```

```
XTYP_ADVSTART=(&H30 Or XCLASS_BOOL)
XTYP_ADVSTOP=(&H40 Or XCLASS_NOTIFICATION)
XTYP_CONNECT=(&H60 Or XCLASS_BOOL Or XTYPF_NOBLOCK)
XTYP_CONNECT_CONFIRM=(&H70 Or XCLASS_NOTIFICATION Or XTYPF_NOBLOCK)
XTYP_DISCONNECT=(&HC0 Or XCLASS_NOTIFICATION Or XTYPF_NOBLOCK)
XTYP_ERROR=(&H0 Or XCLASS_NOTIFICATION Or XTYPF_NOBLOCK)
XTYP_EXECUTE=(&H50 Or XCLASS_FLAGS)
XTYP_MASK=&HF0
XTYP_MONITOR=(&HF0 Or XCLASS_NOTIFICATION Or XTYPF_NOBLOCK)
XTYP_POKE=(&H90 Or XCLASS_FLAGS)
XTYP_REGISTER=(&HA0 Or XCLASS_NOTIFICATION Or XTYPF_NOBLOCK)
XTYP_REQUEST=(&HB0 Or XCLASS_DATA)
XTYP_SHIFT=4  'shift to turn XTYP_ into an index
XTYP_UNREGISTER=(&HD0 Or XCLASS_NOTIFICATION Or XTYPF_NOBLOCK)
XTYP_WILDCONNECT=(&HE0 Or XCLASS_DATA Or XTYPF_NOBLOCK)
XTYP_XACT_COMPLETE=(&H80 Or XCLASS_NOTIFICATION)
XTYPF_ACKREQ=&H8 'DDE_FACKREQ
XTYPF_NOBLOCK=&H2 'CBR_BLOCK will not work
XTYPF_NODATA=&H4 'DDE_FDEFERUPD
```

Index